The Bill of Rights,
The Courts, and The Law

THE VIRGINIA FOUNDATION FOR THE HUMANITIES & PUBLIC POLICY

THE BILL OF Rights

THE Courts &THE Law

THE LANDMARK CASES CASES THAT HAVE SHAPED AMERICAN SOCIETY

With Essays and Case Commentary by

LYNDA BUTLER   A.E. DICK HOWARD   ROBERT M. O'NEIL
BARBARA PERRY   RODNEY A. SMOLLA   MELVIN UROFSKY
EDITED BY DAVID BEARINGER

THIRD EDITION

Principal underwriter The Crestar Foundation
with additional support from Branch, Cabell & Company and Hunton & Williams.

vfh

Published by the Virginia Foundation for the Humanities and
Public Policy.

Library of Congress Catalog Card Number
98-61851

ISBN 0-9668919-1-0

THIRD EDITION

Printed in the United States of America.

Designed by Josef Beery.
Cover Illustration by Michael J. Powers.

Contents

Preface

The Bill of Rights is, arguably, the single most important document in American history. Over more than two hundred years, and especially in the past several decades, it has provided a strong and remarkably durable framework in which the limits of government, the scope of individual liberty, and the nature of our democratic system have been defined. At the same time, the American Bill of Rights has exerted a powerful influence on the movement toward democracy and freedom worldwide, and through a series of landmark cases, beginning with *Brown v. Board of Education* in 1954, its provisions have been subject to almost continual reinterpretation by the U.S. Supreme Court.

In many instances these decisions have been deeply controversial, whether the issue is school prayer, affirmative action, property "takings", pornography and free expression, criminal due process, doctor-assisted suicide, or the right to choose (or aggressively protest) an abortion. While many of the Court's landmark cases have had a direct impact on the lives of individuals and communities, the rulings themselves and the complex judicial questions and precedents that shaped these decisions are sometimes inaccessible, even to well educated and informed observers.

This Third Edition of *The Bill of Rights, The Courts, and The Law* is published by the Virginia Foundation for the Humanities in an effort to increase public understanding of the Bill of Rights, the American judicial process, and the cases themselves. Our goal has been to present these cases and their underlying issues fairly, to allow readers to examine the various legal arguments with the help of expert commentary, and to create the best, most accessible introduction to the Bill of Rights available to a non-scholarly audience. Like its two predecessors, this edition is designed to be used in classrooms, in public forums and discussions, and by individual readers.

Strictly speaking, not all of the cases abridged and printed here relate just to the *historic* Bill of Rights, that is, to the first ten amendments to the Constitution ratified in 1791. In fact, a number of these cases are rooted almost entirely in the Fourteenth Amendment, Section 1, which contains the Equal Protection and Due Process clauses that have defined so much of modern Supreme Court jurisprudence. Likewise, Section X of this edition is devoted to the fascinating interplay between federal and state constitutional guarantees of free speech and equal protection. Thus, our concerns here go beyond the Bill of Rights alone, to include the wider spectrum of individual liberties guaranteed by the Constitution. We hope this book will foster a deeper appreciation of those liberties; that it will increase understanding of how the Supreme Court interprets the Bill of Rights through a process that is fluid and at times unpredictable; and that it will encourage audiences to read and discuss the specific cases, many of which remain extremely controversial, and many of which contain some of the best, most passionate arguments ever written.

The idea of rights is woven throughout Virginia's history: from George Mason's *Virginia Declaration of Rights* to *Jefferson's Virginia Statute for Religious Freedom*; from the lawsuit challenging segregated public education in Prince Edward County, which ultimately became part of the 1954 *Brown* decision, to recent Supreme Court cases dealing with affirmative action (*City of Richmond v. J.A. Croson Company*), free speech and state neutrality toward religion (*Rosenberger v. Rector & Visitors of the University of Virginia*), and equal protection for women in access to education (*United States v. Virginia—VMI*), all of which are included here.

As to the Bill of Rights itself, Virginians George Mason and Patrick Henry helped prepare the original 20-article draft of the document and influenced its several revisions, while James Madison and Thomas Jefferson corresponded at length on the particulars of its scope and phrasing. Of the twelve amendments finally submitted by Congress to the states, ten were adopted. But final ratification was not assured until the favorable vote in the Virginia Senate on December 15, 1791. The Bill's structure and language were inspired by the Virginia Declaration of Rights. Its roots were in the idea of a social contract, first articulated by John Locke and later espoused by Jefferson and Mason. Madison and Henry guided the Bill through the perils of revision and ratification. But the far more difficult—unending—work of interpretation, application, and definition remained. That work continues today.

Jefferson foresaw the "inconveniences" ahead. He also foresaw the importance of the "legal check" a Bill of Rights would place in the hands of the judiciary. While many of the cases included in this volume would have been beyond the reach of the eighteenth century imagination, the underlying issues are much the same as those the nation faced in 1791. We are still struggling to find the proper balance between the needs of government and the rights of the individual. We are still defining the meaning of a free press, of free speech, of "unreasonable" search and seizure, and the "free exercise" of religion. We are still re-shaping the boundaries between church and state, between the interests of society and the rights of suspected criminals, between the preferences of the majority and the autonomy of each individual.

It is this ongoing process in which the Framers invested their faith. They apparently knew well that each temporary resolution of these issues would be met with a new challenge.

David Bearinger
Editor

Acknowledgements

Work leading to the current publication actually began in 1986 with special funding from the National Endowment for the Humanities. This initial grant allowed the Virginia Foundation to publish a volume of twenty-five landmark Supreme Court cases, which was used as a discussion text in sixty public forums around Virginia. In this effort we were assisted by an Advisory Committee that included Henry Abraham, A.E. Dick Howard, David Little, Robert Nusbaum, Timothy O'Rourke, Josephine Pacheco, Robert Rutland and Edgar Toppin. Melvin Urofsky provided scholarly commentary on each of the cases, and the success of this publication encouraged us to create a second edition which was published in 1991, in observance of the Bicentennial of the Bill of Rights.

The 1991 volume included thirty-eight cases, in an expanded format, with case and section commentary written by Professors A. E. Dick Howard, Robert O'Neil, Josephine Pacheco, Rodney A. Smolla, and Melvin Urofsky. Henry Abraham and Richard Merrill provided advice and counsel in developing this second edition, which was made possible with funding from the Commission on the Bicentennial of the United States Constitution, the Virginia Commission on the Bicentennial of the United States Constitution, and The Crestar Foundation. Along with the 1991 publication, support from these organizations made possible a second series of fifty community forums. Subsequently, a grant from the Bill of Rights Education Collaborative and the Pew Charitable Trusts allowed the VFH to conduct a semester-long curriculum development institute for teachers on The Bill of Rights, using the 1991 book as a course text.

Without the intellectual and financial contributions of these early advisors and supporters, the present edition would not have been possible.

The Virginia Foundation for the Humanities extends its special thanks to The Crestar Foundation, the principal underwriter of this Third Edition, and to the investment firm of Branch, Cabell & Company and the law firm of Hunton & Williams, which also provided major financial support. We are grateful, as well, to the Virginia Law Foundation and the American Bar Association Division for Public Education, both of which have provided funding for a new series of public forums based on this publication.

We would also like to thank the scholars who have contributed their insights and expertise to this volume: Professors Lynda Butler, A. E. Dick Howard, Robert M. O'Neil, Barbara A. Perry, Rodney A. Smolla, and Melvin Urofsky. It is difficult to imagine a stronger, or more congenial group of advisors. Perhaps more than any other factor, the individual reputations of these scholars and their ability to make complex issues and cases accessible to the non-scholarly reader account for the success of this publication.

Among this distinguished group, we would like to recognize Mel Urofsky in particular. Mel has been central to all three editions of the book and its related programs. He was the first to commit his time and energy to the project; and his successful use of abridged Supreme Court cases in a Teachers' Institute funded by VFH in the early 1980s led us to the idea for the original edition.

Special thanks are also due to Josef Beery who designed the book; to Tamara McCandless who organized it; to Jessica Coe who provided background research; and to Randolph Church whose work on behalf of this publication came at a crucial stage.

Finally, we want to acknowledge and express our deepest thanks to Richard T. Wilson III. Dick's belief that this book would be produced never wavered, even when others' did; and his tireless efforts to make sure that belief would become reality taught all of us something very important about commitment and the meaning of the phrase "*Ideas Matter.*"

Introduction

MELVIN UROFSKY

Shortly after the Philadelphia convention had finished its work, James Madison sent a copy of the proposed Constitution of the United States to his friend and mentor, Thomas Jefferson, then American Minister to France. For the most part, Jefferson approved of the new plan for government, but he made a short list of items he did not like, and at the top of that list put "the omission of a bill of rights providing clearly and without the aid of sophisms" for the generally accepted civil rights he considered fundamental. "Let me add," he scribbled in closing, "that a bill of rights is what the people are entitled to against every government on earth general and particular, and what no just government should refuse, or rest on inference."

It is now more than two centuries since Jefferson penned those words, and yet they have a sense of contemporary urgency. With the collapse of the Soviet empire in eastern Europe, and the overthrow of dictatorial governments in Asia and Africa, countries all over the world are attempting to create governments and constitutions that will entitle their citizens to those rights that "no just government should refuse." In many instances the constitution-writers of eastern Europe, Africa and Asia look to the Constitution of the United States and to its Bill of Rights, which they see as a model to emulate and, which they hope, will protect their liberties as it has those of the citizens of this nation.

Yet if we look at our own history, Jefferson's views were not widely shared at the time. Alexander Hamilton and others—including Madison at first—believed a separate bill of rights unnecessary since, as Hamilton put it, the Constitution is itself a bill of rights. But enough people thought otherwise and wanted their rights spelled out in detail; as a result, several of the states ratified the Constitution with the understanding that a bill of rights would be added when the new Congress convened.

On May 25, 1789, Madison introduced a number of proposals to protect individual rights and then shepherded them through Congress, despite criticism from some that they covered too much, and from others that they covered too little. By September, both the House of Representatives and the Senate had concurred in twelve proposals and sent them on to the states, which ratified the first ten amendments to the Constitution on December 15, 1791. Commonly grouped as the Bill of Rights, they have formed the legal basis for individual American freedoms ever since.

The first eight amendments spell out specific rights. The Tenth Amendment preserves powers to the states, and the Ninth declares that the people retain rights other than those enumerated in the Constitution. Although, as we shall see in the following sections, the Supreme Court has on numerous occasions extended protection to rights not listed in the Constitution, it has rarely relied on this article, leading some scholars to label it "the forgotten amendment."

We can follow a fairly clear path of historical development when we examine the roots of the first eight amendments. Some derive from ancient English tradition and others are uniquely American. Trial by jury and the right against self-incrimination, for example, were part of English law before the colonization of the New World, but the guarantee of counsel is an Anglo-American invention. The idea of a free press is a peculiarly American notion, and even today few countries in the world afford their press as much protection from governmental interference as we do. Similarly, at a time when nearly every country in Europe had an established church, the United States opted for religious freedom and diversity, a policy first adopted by Virginia in the form of Jefferson's Statute for Religious Freedom (1786).

The Bill of Rights, for well over a century, applied only against the federal government. Jefferson, Madison and others of the Founding Fathers believed the greatest threat to individual liberty would come from strong, central authority, and they looked to the states to serve as protectors of the rights of their citizens. In fact, the first significant attack did come from Congress, when it passed the Alien and Sedition Laws in 1798. These statutes severely curtailed freedom of speech and of the press, and made criticism of the government punishable by fine and/or imprisonment. The Supreme Court never had a chance to review the constitutionality of these laws, since Jefferson, following his election to the presidency in 1800, saw to their repeal.

For well over a hundred years following that episode, the federal government (except during the Civil War) rarely interfered with personal rights, and as a result no judicial tradition of civil liberties developed. The Supreme Court heard very few cases involving the Bill of Rights in the nineteenth century. In *Barron v. Baltimore* (1833), it reaffirmed the intent of the Framers that the Bill of Rights applied only to the federal government and not against the states. The only significant freedom-of-religion case, *Reynolds v. United States* (1879), dealt with a statute outlawing polygamy in the territories, which some Mormons challenged as abridging the free practice of their faith. In the decision, Chief Justice Morison Waite drew an important distinction between belief and action, holding that the government could do nothing to restrain belief, but could put reasonable restrictions on action. This distinction would later play a significant role in developing first Amendment jurisprudence.

During the latter decades of the nineteenth century and the first three decades of the twentieth, conservative judges devoted much of their time to protecting property rights against what they saw as the depredations enacted by state legislatures in the name of progress and protecting laborers. This effort gave the courts a not totally undeserved reputation as protectors of the propertied classes against the common folk, and following the turmoil of the court-packing plan during the 1930s, the Court ignored property cases for the next half-century. In the last few years, however, property cases are once again in the Courts, and this edition has appropriately included a new section devoted to that issue.

But the bulk of the Court's work in terms of the Bill of Rights has been defining individual liberties. Modern civil liberties doctrine really begins with the restrictions on speech and press imposed by the Wilson Administration during World War I. Carried away by wartime patriotism and hysteria, the government viewed any criticism of its policy or of the American system as subversive, and prosecuted a number of individuals for their stated opposition to American involvement in the war. In the first significant free-speech case, *Schenck v. United States* (1919), the Court upheld the conviction of a Socialist leader for urging young men to resist the draft. In his opinion for the Court, Justice Oliver Wendell Holmes, Jr., set forth a "clear and present danger" test; that is, "whether the words used are used in such circumstances and are of such a nature as to create a clear and present danger that will bring about the substantive evils Congress has a right to prevent."

Many dedicated civil libertarians objected to this view, and within a short time Holmes, joined by Louis D. Brandeis, took a different position. They maintained that, while the government could restrain really dangerous speech, it should, even in wartime, protect free expression as much as possible, for even wrong-headed views play an important role in social discourse. They believed the free competition of ideas to be essential to American democracy, even if the ideas expressed prove troublesome and their expression irritating.

This idea of protecting individual rights—whether of speech, religion or those involving criminal prosecution—no matter how distasteful the idea or the person, is the bedrock of modern libertarian jurisprudence. Holmes caught this well when he declared that freedom of speech exists not for the speech we like, but for the ideas we detest. How a society protects the rights of its least-liked members, be they radicals or accused criminals, determines the rights of the rest of its citizens. This theme occurs again and again in the cases reprinted here.

The first eight amendments, the traditional "Bill of Rights," are not the only guarantors of our liberties. The Fourteenth Amendment, ratified in 1868, is one of the three Civil War era changes designed primarily to free the slaves and then protect their rights. The Thirteenth Amendment abolished slavery, and the fifteenth prohibited denial of the ballot on account of race. The three Civil War amendments are concerned primarily with what we call civil rights, the protection of groups from discrimination, as opposed to civil liberties, which is about the rights of individuals.

The Fourteenth Amendment includes two key phrases: "No State shall...deprive any person of life, liberty, or property, without due process of law; nor deny to any person within its jurisdiction the equal protection of the laws." There has been and continues to be a heated debate over the intention of the people who drafted the Fourteenth Amendment regarding the meaning of these phrases. The Equal Protection Clause had no precedents, and seems to have originated in the Joint Committee on Reconstruction. The Due Process Clause, of course, came from the fifth Amendment, and so we know that in at least a limited area the Amendment's authors intended to apply similar protections—or at least procedural ones—against both the federal and state governments.

But did they mean to extend, through this clause, all of those liberties embodied in the Bill of Rights, to "nationalize" their protections? Did the Fourteenth Amendment incorporate those first eight amendments and apply them against the states? Or did the Committee on Reconstruction have a far more limited interpretation in mind? One can, as in most historical debates, summon evidence on both sides of the argument, but on balance it would seem that the Committee intended to protect the "fundamental rights of free men," and by this they meant to overrule *Barron* and apply the Bill of Rights to the states.

By now the debate is somewhat academic, because the Supreme Court has, through the process of "incorporation," ruled that most of the first eight amendments apply to the states through the Due Process Clause of the Fourteenth Amendment. The incorporation process began slowly, in *Gitlow v. New York* (1925). Justice Brandeis had earlier argued that the "liberty" protected by the Fourteenth Amendment had to be more than mere property rights, and Justice Sanford adopted this view (although then only *in dictum*) in *Gitlow*. "We may and do assume that freedom of speech and of the press—which are protected by the first Amendment from abridgment by Congress—are among the fundamental rights and 'liberties' protected by the due process clause of the Fourteenth Amendment from impairment by the States."

Over the next dozen years the Court incorporated other guarantees: freedom of the press in *Near v. Minnesota* (1931); a fair trial and the right to counsel in the notorious Scottsboro case, *Powell v. Alabama* (1932); freedom of religion in *Hamilton v. Regents of the University of California* (1934); and assembly and petition in *De Jonge v. Oregon* (1937).

Then in *Palko v. Connecticut* (1937), Justice Benjamin N. Cardozo indicated that the Fourteenth Amendment did not incorporate all of the Bill of Rights, and he put forward instead the notion of "selective" incorporation. The Fourteenth Amendment embodied only those principles of justice "so rooted in the tradition and conscience of our people as to be ranked as fundamental." Ten years later, in *Adamson v. California*, Justice Black's minority opinion rejected the idea of "selective" incorporation and argued instead for total adoption of all the guarantees. Black's "total incorporation" never gained a majority on the Court. However, although the Court has *theoretically* held fast to the Cardozo approach, it has in *practice* found nearly every right protected in the first eight amendments to be "fundamental" and has incorporated them through the Fourteenth.

In this process of expanding the Bill of Rights, the Court has been criticized for allegedly exceeding its authority, for going beyond strict interpretation of the Constitution and for creating policy. That the Court has brought new meaning to the first eight amendments is undeniable; that it has done so legitimately remains a point of contention among some scholars.

From the beginning of the Republic there has been a sporadic debate over the proper method of interpreting the Constitution. In his first term as President, George Washington asked his two chief advisors for their views on the constitutionality of Congress chartering a bank. Thomas Jefferson said Congress lacked the power, and advocated a strict and narrow reading of the Constitution—the government can do only those things the Constitution says it can do, and nothing more. Alexander Hamilton argued for a broader and more flexible view—the government can do everything except what it is expressly forbidden to do. Nearly a quarter-century later, Chief Justice John Marshall adopted the Hamiltonian argument, and in *McCulloch v. Maryland* (1819) (and elsewhere) explained the necessity of broad interpretation in order to allow the Constitution to grow and meet the country's changing needs.

In the contemporary debate, the opposing sides align themselves around the question of original intent vs. interpretation. The advocates of original intent are the intellectual heirs of Jefferson's narrow literalism, and argue that courts have no right to "modernize" the Constitution; if changes are necessary, then only the people can alter the organic law through the amendment process. For the courts to do so gives the judiciary power out of all proportion to the other branches in the federal scheme, and makes a small group of appointed officials superior not only to the elected branches but to the people as well. Advocates of this position often point to the 1973 abortion decision, *Roe v. Wade* and its offspring, as an example, of how this power has, in their opinion, been misused.

This emphasis on original intent has been derided as "clause-bound literalism," by supporters of a more activist bench. If the Constitution were merely a statute, they argue, then a literal interpretation would be appropriate; when and if a statute becomes dysfunctional, it is a relatively easy task to change it. But a constitution is not a simple legislative enactment; it is the organic law of the land, and deals with fundamental issues of power and responsibility. To amend it for anything less than a major substantive change would belittle it and sap it of its authority.

Interpreting the Constitution, in this view, calls for an evaluation of the spirit and meaning behind the clause in question. It is generally agreed, for example, that Congress can regulate railroads and airlines under the Commerce Clause; but neither trains nor planes are mentioned in the Constitution, so to justify that power one has to interpret the meaning of interstate commerce, to extrapolate what the Framers would have intended had they known about modern forms of transportation. Similarly, the Fourth Amendment protects one's home against unwarranted intrusions; should this mean protection against electronic intrusion as well, even though wiretapping is obviously not mentioned in the Constitution? Interpretationists argue that we live in the twentieth century, not the eighteenth, and the only way the Constitution can continue to be the valid and vital organic law it has been for two centuries is to interpret it in the light of contemporary conditions. They hold up the desegregation and integration cases as one example of the Court looking beyond words to discern meaning, and ask whether it would have been possible to amend the Constitution to secure equal rights for black Americans.

This historical overview is necessary to understanding not only the cases that are included in the third edition of this collection, but also the broader context in which they have been decided. Whatever power the originalist argument may have, and however many adherents it may have on the bench, the fact of the matter is that the Bill of Rights is not a mere listing of rights that the Founding generation believed to be an important part of its British heritage. The United States at the end of the twentieth century is a rapidly changing nation—economically, socially, politically and demographically.

Confronted by new situations which they see as endangering their liberties, Americans do what they have always done—they go to court and ask for a judicial determination of whether their constitutional rights have been violated. This has been a hallmark of American liberty throughout this century, and gives every indication of continuing into the next. And by raising these questions, and bringing them before the courts, they also perpetuate a vital aspect of our liberties, the application of traditional protections to new situations.

A comparison of the cases in this collection to those of the first two editions is illuminating. The first edition (1987) had twenty-five cases in eight sections. The second edition

(1991) had thirty-nine cases in ten sections; of those thirty-nine, eighteen had also been included in the first edition. In this volume there are fifty-four cases, of which twenty-two are new, in ten sections, two of which—Property Rights and Federalism—are new.

What drives the changes in emphasis? There are several causes, not the least of which is technology. In Section II (Free Speech and Access to Information), the case of *Reno v. American Civil Liberties Union* (1997) grew out of the Internet, which did not even exist when the first edition of this casebook went to press. In Section VII (Due Process, Privacy and Personal Autonomy), the issue of right to die is a direct product of modern medicine's ability to keep people alive, and the issue of whether individuals have the right to end their lives.

Another cause is the growing sentiment for limiting the power of the federal government, and devolving more and more programs once run by Washington onto the states. A new Section IX on Federalism is illustrative of this trend; in the first case, *Garcia v. San Antonio Metropolitan Transit Authority* (1985) held in effect that states had little or no recourse to the courts if they believed the federal government overstepped its bounds, but must resort to the political process for adjustment. In the three cases decided since 1995, it is quite clear that the courts will serve, as Justice Frank Murphy once described it, as "the umpire of the federal system."

In a related vein, a number of years ago Justice William J. Brennan, Jr. urged civil liberties advocates to begin to look to state courts and constitutions rather than to the federal courts for protection of basic rights. Section X, which was added in the second edition, shows the prescience of Justice Brennan's suggestion, as well as the growing role of state courts in this area.

One should also note that the Court headed by Chief Justice William H. Rehnquist is the most conservative since the Taft Court of the 1920s. This accounts for a number of features in this edition. There are no new cases in the section on Rights of the Accused. Although the Court has not reversed the major doctrinal expansions of the Warren era, such as *Gideon* and *Miranda*, it has chosen not to enlarge them either, and in many cases has limited them by imposing "totality of the circumstances" interpretations which give greater credence to police judgment. Similarly the inclusion of a new Section VIII on Property Rights shows how concerned the current Court is with this issue, a development that few scholars could have anticipated a decade ago.

Yet just as the conservative Taft Court of the 1920s also took the first steps in expanding the application of the Bill of Rights to the states through the doctrine of incorporation, so the Rehnquist Court also defies easy categorization. While cutting back on earlier decisions regarding affirmative action, it is still fiercely opposed to any effort to legitimate racial discrimination through law or regulation. While supposedly abandoning the ideal of a high wall of separation between church and state, it has rebuffed congressional efforts to lower that wall further than the Court believes appropriate. Although a number of the justices have condemned the abortion ruling in *Roe v. Wade* and the Court has partially limited its application, a majority of justices has refused to discard *Roe*'s central tenet, that a woman has a constitutionally protected right to an abortion. While refusing to constitutionalize a right to assisted suicide, the Court has made the right to die a liberty interest protected under the Fourteenth Amendment, and has suggested that if the states prove too rigid on end-of-life choices, it may well revisit the issue of assisted suicide. Finally, in what is certainly a strong blow for women's equality, the Court forced the Virginia Military Institute to abandon its males-only admission policy.

While there is much that is new in the following cases, there is also much that will be familiar. Certain ideas and issues that have been integral parts of the Court's jurisprudence for decades appear repeatedly in the new cases as well—broad and narrow interpretation, original intent, incorporation, fundamental values, and the role of the judiciary. Some of the decisions may seem unwise, but then the Court has never claimed infallibility; and it has, when necessary, reversed itself. In discussing these cases and the role of the Court it is important to address the underlying meaning of the Bill of Rights—not only what it meant to Jefferson and Madison, but what it means today. Without that understanding by the people it has been designed to protect, the Bill of Rights would cease to be our bulwark of freedom and would be little more than a scrap of paper.

Melvin I. Urofsky
August 1998

The Bill of Rights

For the purposes of discussion, the editors of this volume are considering the Bill of Rights to be the first ten amendments to the Constitution adopted in 1791, plus Section 1 of the Fourteenth Amendment adopted in 1868. The Fourteenth Amendment, Section 1, applies the Bill of Rights to the laws of the States and contains the "Due Process" and "Equal Protection" clauses that have figured prominently in so much of American legal history since the nineteenth century. These two clauses have also been important factors in many of the cases reprinted here, and in the ensuing public discussion about them.

AMENDMENT I (1791)

Congress shall make no law respecting an establishment of religion, or prohibiting the free exercise thereof; or abridging the freedom of speech, or of the press; or the right of the people peaceably to assemble, and to petition the Government for a redress of grievances.

AMENDMENT II (1791)

A well regulated Militia, being necessary to the security of a free State, the right of the people to keep and bear Arms, shall not be infringed.

AMENDMENT III (1791)

No Soldier shall, in time of peace be quartered in any house, without the consent of the Owner, nor in time of war, but in a manner to be prescribed by law.

AMENDMENT IV (1791)

The right of the people to be secure in their persons, houses, papers, and effects, against unreasonable searches and seizures, shall not be violated, and no Warrants shall issue, but upon probable cause, supported by Oath or affirmation, and particularly describing the place to be searched, and the persons or things to be seized.

AMENDMENT V (1791)

No person shall be held to answer for a capital, or otherwise infamous crime, unless on a presentment or indictment of a Grand Jury, except in cases arising in the land or naval forces, or in the Militia, when in actual service in time of War or public danger; nor shall any person be subject for the same offence to be twice put in jeopardy of life or limb; nor shall be compelled in any criminal case to be a witness against himself, nor be deprived of life, liberty, or property, without due process of law; nor shall private property be taken for public use, without just compensation.

AMENDMENT VI (1791)

In all criminal prosecutions, the accused shall enjoy the right to a speedy and public trial, by an impartial jury of the State and district wherein the crime shall have been committed, which district shall have been previously ascertained by law, and to be informed of the nature and cause of the accusation; to be confronted with the witnesses against him; to have compulsory process for obtaining Witnesses in his favor, and to have the Assistance of Counsel for his defense.

AMENDMENT VII (1791)

In Suits at common law, where the value in controversy shall exceed twenty dollars, the right of trial by jury shall be preserved, and no fact tried by a jury, shall be otherwise re-examined in any Court of the United States, than according to the rules of the common law.

AMENDMENT VIII (1791)

Excessive bail shall not be required, nor excessive fines imposed, nor cruel and unusual punishment inflicted.

AMENDMENT IX (1791)

The enumeration in the Constitution, of certain rights, shall not be construed to deny or disparage others retained by the people.

AMENDMENT X (1791)

The powers not delegated to the United States by the Constitution, nor prohibited by it to the States, are reserved to the States respectively, or to the people.

AMENDMENT XIV (1868)

SECTION 1. All persons born or naturalized in the United States and subject to the jurisdiction thereof, are citizens of the United States and of the State wherein they reside. No State shall make or enforce any law which shall abridge the privileges or immunities of citizens of the United States; nor shall any State deprive any person of life, liberty, or property, without due process of law; nor deny to any person within its jurisdiction the equal protection of the laws.

I Evolving Concepts

Reynolds v. Sims (1964)

Shaw v. Reno (1993)

Bush v. Vera (1996)

Abrams v. Johnson (1997)

Grand Rapids School District v. Ball (1985)

Agostini v. Felton (1997)

I Evolving Concepts

MELVIN UROFSKY

The Constitution, both the original document and the subsequent amendments, is the organic law of the land, designed to serve the needs of the American people for more than a passing season. Unlike legislative statutes, which address particular issues in specific terms, the Constitution talks in generalities; it sets out ideas and powers and limits which must be translated to meet particular problems. This is especially true of the Bill of Rights which appears to be quite specific, but which can become quite confusing when applied to individual situations.

Ever since *Marbury v. Madison* (1803), the Supreme Court has been the chief interpreter of the Constitution, informing the other branches of the national government as well as the states what is constitutionally permissible, what is required, and what is forbidden. There is no question but the Court interprets and reinterprets the Constitution, and that over time one "right" view gives way to another. Precedents are modified, fine-tuned, and on occasion reversed. The useful life of even an important decision has been estimated to be about forty years; by then it will have been reversed, abandoned, or incorporated into a more encompassing doctrine.

What guides the justices in this process? It is not enough to suggest, as Herbert Wechsler did, that cases should be decided by principled rules of decision-making, so that the country may rely on consistency and judicial integrity. One must ask what general philosophy of decision-making informs those rules. It is this philosophy which determines whether a Court is activist or restrained, what constitutional values it elevates, and what values it relegates to a secondary position.

For the past two decades the debate has centered on whether the Court should adhere strictly to the original intent of the Framers, as determined by the Constitution's own words and contemporary documents such as *The Federalist* and Madison's notes of the Philadelphia convention, or whether the Court should be interpretationist. Advocates of this latter policy believe the Court, in order to keep the Constitution alive and current to today's needs, must look beyond the simple words and interpret the spirit which animates them.

Both views have strengths as well as weaknesses. Adherence to original intent provides a greater consistency over time, and downplays the individual biases of the judges as against the wishes of the Framers. On the other hand, what John Hart Ely has called "clause-bound literalism" imposes the dead hand of the past upon the present, and prevents the current generation from responding flexibly to new challenges and opportunities. If the Court cannot find approval for a new program in the original intent, the only solution left is to amend the Constitution, an awkward and lengthy process.

For all the lip-service paid to original intent, the Court has had to adopt an interpretationist approach, if for no other reason than issues such as minority-majority districting and public aid to private schools were never contemplated by the Framers. As Justice William O. Douglas once remarked in connection with a wire-tapping case, original intent provided no guide whatsoever: "What did the Framers know about telephones?" All one can do is interpret the original spirit of the Framers, and then apply it in the most neutral manner possible to current controversies.

The cases in this section illustrate the Court's coming to grips with two new issues, legislative redistricting and the support of public school teachers carrying out certain tasks in parochial schools. To the observer, the Court's opinion may seem erratic, even contradictory, and this would not be an unfair characterization. But it is important to see the Court as reflective of American society as a whole, confused and divided over new issues for which there is little prior experience as a guide.

The initial apportionment plan, *Reynolds v. Sims*, was an "easy" one insofar as the judges, once they had found the appropriate jurisprudential rule—one man, one vote—had no difficulty deciding that malapportioned legislatures diluted the voting effectiveness of large numbers of citizens. Similarly, the early majority-minority cases were also easy, since they were seen as a remedy for decades of racial discrimination at the polls. But as the issues grew more complex, the Court found it harder to articulate a specific rule, or even an appropriate standard of review.

The two school cases also show that not all judges are cut from the same cloth. Each one brings his or her life experiences and views to the judging process, so that with changes of the Court's personnel, a case decided in one decade may be revisited in another with completely opposite results. Fortunately, the respect for precedent keeps the Court from revising all of its earlier decisions because one or two seats change hands. Eventually, a rule will be worked out that will survive changes of personnel, but that too is an evolving process.

▶ Unlike a legislative statute, the Constitution does not address specific situations. What are the relative advantages and disadvantages of a Constitution framed in generalities?

▶ What should guide judges in their decision-making? To what extent should judicial decisions reflect current moral and political ideas?

▶ Is it really possible to know the original intent behind some of the Constitution's more obscure clauses?

▶ Do the people have any control over a Court that is too rigidly literalist on the one hand, or too actively interpretationist on the other?

> ▶ The Constitution is constant; should the Court be as well? Should the Court be free to change its mind? How free should it be?
>
> ▶ The Constitution divides responsibility between the states and the federal government, and in the latter, among the executive, legislative, and judicial branches. In these cases, do you think either the states or other branches of the federal government should have decided the basic questions?
>
> ▶ How should the Constitution be kept up-to-date?

Reynolds v. Sims   MELVIN UROFSKY

State legislatures had, until 1962, complete control over how they apportioned legislative seats. Some states used population as the main criterion so that each district had roughly the same number of people. Other states, however, deliberately malapportioned districts for political purposes: to exclude blacks; to limit the influence of urban areas; or to simply keep power in the hands of established groups.

Before 1962, the question of fairness in legislative districting formulae was considered nonjusticiable; that is, incapable of resolution by the judiciary. Proponents of this view claimed that the make-up of political districts, whether for congressional seats or for state assemblies, constituted a political question. In *Colegrove v. Green* (1946), Justice Felix Frankfurter, in dismissing a suit against an Illinois congressional districting law, had stated that the "petitioners ask of this Court what it is beyond its competence to grant....This controversy concerns matters that bring courts into immediate and active relations with party contests. From the determination of such issues this Court has traditionally remained aloof." Only seven justices heard that case, however, and only four concurred in the judgment. Four years later the Court still refused to enter the "political thicket," and dismissed a suit against the Georgia county unit system.

The first hint of a change came in *Gomillion v. Lightfoot* (1960), when the Court struck down a blatant gerrymandering scheme in Alabama designed solely to disenfranchise black voters in Tuskegee. (Gerrymandering is the drawing of boundary lines so as to exclude certain groups or dilute their voting power. In Tuskegee the lines had been drawn so as to exclude nearly every black neighborhood.) Two years later, in *Baker v. Carr*, the Court agreed that apportionment cases were, in fact, justiciable, and reserved for a future case a determination whether apportionment schemes which favored certain groups violated the Equal Protection Clause.

That opportunity came in *Reynolds v. Sims*, a case resulting from an Alabama apportionment plan which had not changed since 1900, although the population of the state had grown considerably since then, and the state's own constitution mandated reapportionment every ten years. The Court held that the Equal Protection

Clause required that seats in both houses of a state legislature be apportioned on the basis of population, so that one person's vote counted equally with another's.

The *Baker* case, with its announcement that courts could review apportionment plans, led many states to change their apportionment formulae voluntarily; elsewhere reformers launched dozens of suits in state and federal courts to force reapportionment. Not everyone, of course, favored the new "one person, one vote" rule of *Reynolds* but it did provide a clear standard for both courts and legislatures to follow. Entrenched interest groups fought a futile rear-guard battle, and in Congress Senator Everett Dirkson of Illinois tried to secure a constitutional amendment to overrule the Court. When that failed, thirty-two states petitioned Congress for a convention to deal with the apportionment issue, only two shy of the required number. The opposition soon faded, however, as legislatures elected under the new formula showed no inclination to return to the old system.

The Court still hears apportionment cases; some involve little more than fine-tuning or involve questions of what factors legislatures must take into account when drawing lines. But the most recent group of cases raises a more fundamental issue, namely whether some gerrymandering may be allowed in order to enhance the voting power of minorities. That issue is treated in the cases that follow.

▶ Should the Court have entered the "political thicket," or would it have been better to have left these so-called political questions alone?

▶ Looking back now, are there any reasons to have kept the old system? Was there any benefit to it? Did it in any way advance democratic government?

▶ Political questions are normally considered those which should be resolved by the people at the polls, rather than by the courts. What happens if the people cannot solve a political problem? The apportionment schemes of many states made it impossible for a majority to secure a change, since the plans either kept power in a minority's hands, or gave that minority a veto over any legislation it did not like. What solution would have been possible in such a situation?

▶ Several states argued that the federal constitution did not require equal apportionment among the states, and allowed the membership of the House and Senate to be determined on different bases; therefore, the states should be allowed to do the same. Does this argument make sense? Why or why not?

▶ Assuming "one person one vote" is the right rule, what should be done about minorities who become submerged? Can or should they have special representation? (See Justice Harlan's dissent and *Shaw v. Reno*.)

Reynolds v. Sims 377 U.S. 533 (1964)

Mr. Chief Justice WARREN delivered the opinion of the Court.

[Previous cases] clearly established that the fundamental principle of representative government in this country is one of equal representation for equal numbers of people, without regard to race, sex, economic status, or place of residence within a State. Our problem, then, is to ascertain, in the instant cases, whether there are any constitutionally cognizable principles which would justify departures from the basic standard of equality among voters in the apportionment of seats in state legislatures. A predominant consideration in determining whether a State's legislative apportionment scheme constitutes an invidious discrimination violative of rights asserted under the Equal Protection Clause is that the rights allegedly impaired are individual and personal in nature. Undoubtedly, the right of suffrage is a fundamental matter in a free and democratic society. Especially since the right to exercise the franchise in a free and unimpaired manner is preservative of other basic civil and political rights, any alleged infringement of the right of citizens to vote must be carefully and meticulously scrutinized....

Legislators represent people, not trees or acres. Legislators are elected by voters, not farms or cities or economic interests. As long as ours is a representative form of government, the right to elect legislators in a free and unimpaired fashion is a bedrock of our political system. It could hardly be gainsaid that a constitutional claim had been asserted by an allegation that certain otherwise qualified voters had been entirely prohibited from voting for members of their state legislature. And, if a State should provide that the votes of citizens in one part of the State should be given two times, or five times, or 10 times the weight of votes of citizens in another part of the State, it could hardly be contended that the right to vote of those residing in the disfavored areas had not been effectively diluted. Of course, the effect of state legislative districting schemes which give the same number of representatives to unequal numbers of constituents is identical. Weighing the votes of citizens differently, by any method or means, merely because of where they happen to reside, hardly seems justifiable....

Logically, in a society ostensibly grounded on representative government, it would seem reasonable that a majority of the people of a State could elect a majority of that State's legislators. To sanction minority control of state legislative bodies would appear to deny majority rights in a way that far surpasses any possible denial of minority rights that might otherwise be thought to result. And the concept of equal protection has been traditionally viewed as requiring the uniform treatment of persons standing in the same relation to the governmental action questioned or challenged. With respect to the allocation of legislative representation, all voters, as citizens of a State, stand in the same relation regardless of where they live. Any suggested criteria for the differentiation of citizens are insufficient to justify any discrimination, as to the weight of their votes, unless relevant to the permissible purposes of legislative apportionment. Since the achieving of fair and effective representation for all citizens is concededly the basic aim of legislative apportionment, we conclude that the Equal Protection Clause guarantees the opportunity for equal participation by all voters in the election of state legislators. Diluting the weight of votes because of place of residence impairs basic constitutional rights under the Fourteenth Amendment just as much as invidious discriminations based upon factors such as race or economic status. Our constitutional system amply provides for the protection of minorities by means other than giving them majority control of state legislators.

We are told that the matter of apportioning representation in a state legislature is a complex and many-faceted one. We are advised that States can rationally consider factors other than population. We are admonished not to restrict the power of the States to impose differing views as to political philosophy on their citizens. We are cautioned about the dangers of entering into political thickets and mathematical quagmires. Our answer is this: a denial of constitutionally protected rights demands judicial protection; our oath and our office require no less of us. To the extent that a citizen's right to vote is debased, he is that much less a citizen. The weight of a citizen's vote cannot be made to depend on where he lives. Population is, of necessity, the starting point for consideration and the controlling criterion for judgment, in legislative apportionment controversies. A citizen, a qualified voter, is no more nor no less so because he lives in the city or on the farm. This is the clear and strong command of our Constitution's Equal Protection Clause. This is an essential part of the concept of a government of laws and not men. This is at the heart of Lincoln's vision of "government of the people, by the people, for the people." We hold that, as a basic constitutional standard, the Equal Protection Clause requires that the seats in both houses of a bicameral state legislature must be apportioned on a population basis. Simply stated, an individual's right to vote for state legislators is unconstitutionally impaired when its weight is in a substantial fashion diluted when compared with votes of citizens living in other parts of the State....

We find the federal analogy inapposite and irrelevant to state legislative districting schemes. Attempted reliance on the federal analogy appears often to be little more than an after-the-fact rationalization offered in defense of maladjusted state apportionment arrangements. The system or representation in the two Houses of the Federal Congress is one conceived out of compromise and concession indispensable to the establishment of our federal republic and is based on the consideration that in establishing our type of federalism a group of formerly independent States bound themselves together under one national government. Political subdivisions of States—counties, cities, or whatever—never were and never have been considered as sovereign entities. Rather, they have been traditionally regarded as subordinate governmental instrumentalities created by the State....

The Equal Protection Clause requires that a State make an honest and good faith effort to construct districts, in both houses of its legislature, as nearly of equal population as is practicable. We realize that it is a practical impossibility to arrange legislative districts so that each one has an identical number of residents, or citizens, or voters. Mathematical exactness or precision is hardly a workable constitutional requirement. So long as the divergences from a strict population standard are based on legitimate considerations incident to the effectuation of a rational state policy, some deviations from the equal-population principle are constitutionally permissible, but neither history alone, nor economic or other sorts of group interests, are permissible factors in attempting to justify disparities from population-based representation. Citizens, not history or economic interests, cast votes. Considerations of area alone provide an insufficient justification for deviations from the equal-population principle. Again, people, not land or trees or pastures, vote. Modern developments and improvements in transportation and communications make rather hollow, in the mid-1960's, most claims for allowing such deviations in order to insure effective representation for sparsely settled areas and to prevent legislative districts from becoming so large that the availability of access of citizens to their representatives is impaired. A consideration that appears to be of more substance in justifying some deviations from population-based representation in state legislatures is that of insuring some voice to political subdivisions, as political subdivisions. In many States much of the legislature's activity involves the enactment of so-called local legislation, directed only to the concerns of particular political subdivisions. And a State may legitimately desire to construct districts along political subdivision lines to deter the possibilities of gerrymandering. But if, even as a result of a clearly rational state policy of according some legislative representation to political subdivisions, population is submerged as the controlling consideration, the right of all of the State's citizens to cast an effective and adequately weighted vote would be unconstitutionally impaired....

Mr. Justice HARLAN, dissenting.

The Court's constitutional discussion is remarkable for its failure to address itself at all to the Fourteenth Amendment as a whole or to the legislative history of the Amendment pertinent to the matter at hand. Stripped of aphorisms, the Court's argument boils down to the assertion that petitioners' right to vote has been invidiously "debased" or "diluted" by systems of apportionment which entitle them to vote for fewer legislators than other voters, an assertion which is tied to the Equal Protection Clause only by the constitutionally frail tautology that "equal" means "equal." The history of the adoption of the Fourteenth Amendment provides conclusive evidence that neither those who proposed nor those who ratified the Amendment believed that the Equal Protection Clause limited the power of the States to apportion their legislatures as they saw fit. Moreover, the history demonstrates that the intention to leave this power undisturbed was deliberate and was widely believed to be essential to the adoption of the Amendment....

Although the Court provides only generalities in elaboration of its main thesis, its opinion nevertheless fully demonstrates how far removed these problems are from fields of judicial competence. Recognizing that "indiscriminate districting" is an invitation to "partisan gerrymandering," the Court nevertheless excluded virtually every basis for the formation of electoral districts other than "indiscriminate districting." In one or another of today's opinions, the Court declares it unconstitutional for a State to give consideration to any of the following in establishing legislative districts: (1) history; (2) "economic or other sorts of group interests"; (3) area; (4) geographical considerations; (5) a desire "to insure effective representation for sparsely settled areas"; (6) "availability of access of citizens to their representatives"; (7) theories of bicameralism (except those approved by the Court); (8) occupation; (9) "an attempt to balance urban and rural power"; (10) the preference of a majority of voters in the State. So far as presently appears, the only factor which a State may consider, apart from numbers, is political subdivisions. But even "a clearly rational state policy" recognizing this factor is unconstitutional if "population is submerged as the controlling consideration." I know of no principle of logic or practical or theoretical politics, still less any constitutional principle, which establishes all or any of these exclusions. The Court says only that "legislators represent people, not trees or acres."

This may be conceded. But it is surely equally obvious, and, in the context of elections, more meaningful to note that people are not ciphers and that legislators can represent their electors only be speaking for their interest—economic, social, political— many of which do reflect the place where the electors live. The Court does not establish, or indeed even attempt to make a case for the proposition that conflicting interests within a State can only be adjusted by disregarding them when voters are grouped for purposes of representation....

[Mr. Justice STEWART, joined by Mr. Justice CLARK, dissented in the Colorado and New York cases, while concurring in the others. In Colorado, the people through a referendum had approved a system analogous to the federal model; the lower house was apportioned on the basis of population and the upper chamber reflected political subdivisions. New York had a rational system which also tried to assure minimal representation to all counties in the state senate, since the cities, especially New York, would otherwise outvote the balance of the state in all matters.]

Shaw v. Reno MELVIN UROFSKY

In the dozen or so years after *Brown v. Board of Education* (1954), African-Americans made significant strides in their fight to secure equal rights. The Court struck down one state segregation law after another, making it virtually impossible to use racial classification as a means of ruling citizens' lives. Congress in 1964 enacted the most sweeping civil rights legislation in the nation's history; the following year it passed the Voting Rights Act which nullified state efforts to bar blacks from exercising the franchise and sent in federal registrars and marshals to ensure that African-Americans would be able to register and vote.

But now a new question arose. In *Gomillion v. Lightfoot* (1960), the Court had ruled that states could not draw irregular districting lines so as to exclude black voters. But what if states drew perfectly regular lines with districts of roughly equal numbers, but because of population distribution, blacks were in a minority in each district? One could have a state in which blacks made up approximately one-fourth of the total population, but did not constitute a majority in any district. Did this mean that the black vote had been diluted? Did minorities who had been discriminated against in the past now deserve some form of compensatory or affirmative action?

In Section 5 of the Voting Rights Act, Congress provided that in so-called "covered jurisdictions," that is, states which had a past history of voting discrimination, district lines might be required to give minorities proportional representation in the total make-up of the state's congressional delegation. Thus a state with eight representatives in the House and a twenty-five percent black population might be required to draw district lines so as to create two so-called "majority-minority" districts in which African-Americans would constitute a majority of the electorate.

A number of such districts were drawn in the 1970s and 1980s, and in white voter challenges, the Court approved majority-minority districts as a means of redressing past grievances. Moreover, instead of adopting the strict scrutiny standard normally used in racial classification, it utilized a much lower standard, deferring to Congress's policy-making power under the Enforcement Clauses of the Fourteenth and Fifteenth Amendments.

(Strict scrutiny is the most stringent constitutional test the Court applies. When confronted with a challenge that a state has engaged in racial classification, the State must first prove that it had a compelling state interest in doing so. If it can surmount this difficult evidentiary hurdle, the State must then show that it had acted in the least restrictive manner possible to achieve its goal. There have been very few instances when states have been able to make these showings.)

In that same time, however, enormous population shifts were occurring throughout the country in general, and in the South in particular. The 1990 census required a number of southern states to redraw their congressional district lines, and state legislatures, following previous practice, drew majority-minority districts with Justice Department approval to prevent vote dilution among the black population.

The Court that had heard *Reynolds* might well have approved such districting, but by the early 1990s the personnel of the Court had changed dramatically. The Rehnquist Court has taken a much more rigorous approach to questions of racial classification. It has been as unyielding as its predecessors in cases of discrimination against African-Americans. But it has also striven to achieve a "race-blind" interpretation of the Constitution, one in which race cannot be a factor in governmental activity.

It is clear from the following cases that the Court has not yet struck the balance it is seeking between a race-blind Constitution and a policy that prevents vote dilution of a minority that has suffered from state-sponsored discrimination in the past. The Court is attempting to develop a doctrine that takes into account two facts that are often in conflict: a Constitution that requires all citizens be treated equally before the law and a society in which racial discrimination still exists.

In *Shaw v. Reno*, the Court ruled that white citizens in North Carolina who lived in majority-minority districts had a justiciable claim under the Equal Protection Clause, and that the Court would henceforth apply a strict scrutiny standard to these cases.

In the earlier redistricting cases, the Court had adopted a lower standard, deferring to Congressional authority under the Enforcement Clauses of the Fourteenth and Fifteenth Amendments to require such districts in order to comply with the Voting Rights Act. There is no question that Congress has enforcement power, but the Rehnquist Court is divided on the issue of whether compliance with the terms of the Voting Rights Act constitutes a compelling state interest. In these cases the challenged plans allegedly contained such heavy-handed racial gerrymandering that the Court felt no need to reach that question.

> ▶ Majority-minority districts raise the issue of whether minorities should be treated as groups. Should voting in the United States be concerned with the interests of groups, or should it be focused entirely on rights of the individual?

> ▶ If one group is entitled to proportional representation, may others make the same claim? In states with a large Latino population, for example, should there be majority-minority Latino districts to ensure the election of Latino candidates? Women make up fifty percent of the population; should—could—district lines be drawn so that one half of all elected representatives are women?

> ▶ Congress, in passing the Voting Rights Act of 1965, certainly found evidence of past discrimination against blacks. Many whites and blacks voting today were born not only after *Brown* (1954) but after the passage of the Voting Rights Act of 1965. How long should the pre-1965 conditions govern restrictions on covered jurisdictions?

> ▶ If "regular" lines dilute the voting power of blacks as a group, should gerrymandering provide the solution? Why or why not?

> ▶ Should the standard of strict scrutiny apply in claims of discrimination by members of the majority white population? Why or why not?

Shaw v. Reno 509 U.S. 630 (1993)

Justice O'CONNOR delivered the opinion of the Court.

This case involves two of the most complex and sensitive issues this Court has faced in recent years: the meaning of the constitutional "right" to vote, and the propriety of race-based state legislation designed to benefit members of historically disadvantaged racial minority groups. As a result of the 1990 census, North Carolina became entitled to a twelfth seat in the United States House of Representatives. The General Assembly enacted a reapportionment plan that included one majority-black congressional district. After the Attorney General of the United States objected to the plan pursuant to Section 5 of the Voting Rights Act, the General Assembly passed new legislation creating a second majority-black district. Appellants allege that the revised plan, which contains district boundary lines of dramatically irregular shape, constitutes an unconstitutional racial gerrymander. The question before us is whether appellants have stated a cognizable claim.

The voting age population of North Carolina is approximately 78% white, 20% black, and 1% Native American; the remaining 1% is predominantly Asian. The black population is relatively dispersed; blacks constitute a majority of the general population in only 5 of the State's 100 counties. The largest concentrations of black citizens live in the Coastal Plain, primarily in the northern part. The General Assembly's first redistricting plan contained one majority-black district centered in that area of the State. This district is somewhat a hook shaped. Centered in the northeast portion of the State, it moves southward until it tapers to a narrow band; then, with finger-like extensions, it reaches far into the southern-most part of the State near the South Carolina border. District 1 has been compared to a "Rorschach ink-blot test" and a "bug splattered on a windshield."

The second majority-black district, District 12, is even more unusually shaped. It is approximately 160 miles long and, for much of its length, no wider than the I-85 corridor. It winds in snake-like fashion through tobacco country, financial centers, and manufacturing areas "until it gobbles in enough enclaves of black neighborhoods." Of the 10 counties through which District 12 passes, five are cut into three different districts; even towns are divided. One state legislator has remarked that "if you drove down the interstate with both car doors open, you'd kill most of the people in the district."

An understanding of the appellants' claim is critical to our resolution of the case. In their complaint, appellants did not claim that the General Assembly's reapportionment plan unconstitutionally "diluted" white voting strength. They did not even claim to be white. Rather, they alleged that the deliberate segregation of voters into separate districts on the basis of race violated their constitutional right to participate in a "color-blind" electoral process. This Court never has held that race-conscious state decisionmaking is impermissible in all circumstances. What appellants object to is redistricting legislation that is so extremely irregular on its face that it rationally can be viewed only as an effort to segregate the races for purposes of voting, without regard for traditional districting principles and without sufficiently compelling justification. We conclude that appellants have stated a claim upon which relief can be granted under equal protection.

Appellants contend that redistricting legislation that is so bizarre on its face that it is "unexplainable on grounds other than race," demands the same close scrutiny that we give other state laws that classify citizens by race. Our voting rights precedents support that conclusion. Redistricting differs from other kinds of state decisionmaking in that the legislature always is aware of race when it draws district lines, just as it is aware of age, economic status, religious and political persuasion, and a variety of other demographic factors. That sort of race consciousness does not lead inevitably to impermissible race discrimination. When members of a racial group live together in one community, a reapportionment plan that concentrates members of the group in one district and excludes them from others may reflect wholly legitimate purposes. The district lines may be drawn, for example, to provide for compact districts of contiguous territory, or to maintain the integrity of political subdivisions. The difficulty of proof, of course, does not mean that a racial gerrymander, once established, should receive less scrutiny than other state legislation classifying citizens by race. Moreover, it seems clear to us that proof sometimes will not be difficult at all. In some exceptional cases, a reapportionment plan may be so highly irregular that, on its face, it rationally cannot be understood as anything other than an effort to segregate voters on the basis of race. *Gomillion* was such a case. So, too, would be a case in which a State concentrated a dispersed minority population in a single district by disregarding traditional districting principles such as compactness, contiguity, and respect for political subdivisions. We emphasize that these criteria are important not because they are constitutionally required—they are not—but because they are objective factors that may serve to defeat a claim that a district has been gerrymandered on racial lines.

Put differently, we believe that reapportionment is one area in which appearances do matter. A reapportionment plan that includes in one district individuals who belong to the same race, but who are otherwise widely separated by geographical and political boundaries, and who may have little in common with one another but the color of their skin, bears an uncomfortable resemblance to political apartheid. It reinforces the perception that members of the same racial group—regardless of their age, education, economic status, or the community in which the live—think alike, share the same political interests, and will prefer the same candidates at the polls. We have rejected such perceptions elsewhere as impermissible racial stereotypes. By perpetuating such notions, a racial gerrymander may exacerbate the very patterns of racial bloc voting that majority-minority districting is sometimes said to counteract. The message that such districting sends to elected representatives is equally pernicious. When a district obviously is created solely to effectuate the perceived common interests of one racial group, elected officials are more likely to believe that their primary obligation is to represent only the members of that group, rather than their constituency as a whole. This is altogether antithetical to our system of representative democracy. For these reasons, we conclude that a plaintiff challenging a reapportionment statute under equal protection may state a claim by alleging that the legislation, though race-neutral on its face, rationally cannot be understood as anything other than an effort to separate voters into different districts on the basis of race, and that the separation lacks sufficient justification....

The state appellees suggest that a covered jurisdiction may have a compelling interest in creating majority-minority districts in order to comply with the Voting Rights Act. The States certainly have a very strong interest in complying with federal antidiscrimination laws that are constitutionally valid as interpreted and as applied. But in the context of a Fourteenth Amendment challenge, courts must bear in mind the difference between what the law permits, and what it requires. For example, on remand North Carolina might claim that it adopted the revised plan in order to comply with the "nonretrogression" principle. Under that principle, a proposed voting change cannot be precleared if it will lead to "a retrogression in the position of racial minorities with respect to their effective exercise of the electoral franchise." In *Beer v. United States* (1976), we held that a reapportionment plan that created one majority-minority district where none existed before passed muster under section 5 because it improved the position of racial minorities. Although the Court concluded that the redistricting scheme at issue in *Beer* was nonretrogressive, it did not hold that the plan, for that reason, was immune from constitutional challenge. The Court expressly declined to reach that question. Thus, we do not read *Beer* or any of our other cases to give covered jurisdictions carte blanche to engage in racial gerrymandering in the name of nonretrogression. The state appellees alternatively argue that the General Assembly's plan advanced a compelling interest entirely distinct from the Voting Rights Act. We previously have recognized a significant state interest in eradicating the effects of past racial discrimination. But the State must have a "strong basis in evidence for concluding that remedial action is necessary."

Racial classifications of any sort pose the risk of lasting harm to our society. They reinforce the belief, held by too many for too much of our history, that individuals should be judged by the color of their skin. Racial classifications with respect to voting carry particular dangers. Racial gerrymandering, even for remedial purposes, may balkanize us into competing racial factions; it threatens to carry us further from the goal of a political system in which race no longer matters. It is for these reasons that race-based districting by our state legislatures demands close judicial scrutiny. We hold that appellants have stated a claim under equal protection by alleging that the North Carolina General Assembly adopted a reapportionment scheme so irrational on its face that it can be understood only as an effort to segregate voters into separate voting districts because of their race, and that the separation lacks sufficient justification.

Reversed and remanded.

Justice WHITE, with whom Justice BLACKMUN and Justice STEVENS join, dissenting.

The notion that North Carolina's plan, under which whites remain a voting majority in a disproportionate number of congressional districts, might have violated appellants' constitutional rights is both a fiction and a departure from settled equal protection principles. The grounds for my disagreement are simply stated: Appellants have not presented a cognizable claim, because they have not alleged a cognizable injury. To date, we have held that only two types of state voting practices could give rise to a constitutional claim. The first involves direct and outright deprivation of the right to vote, for example by means of a poll tax or literacy test. Plainly, this variety is not implicated by appellants' allegations. The second type of unconstitutional practice is that which "affects the political strength of various groups," in violation of the Equal Protection Clause. As for this latter category, we have insisted that members of the political or racial group demonstrate that the challenged action have the intent and effect of unduly diminishing their influence on the political process.

The majority imagines a heretofore unknown type of constitutional claim. The logic of its theory appears to be that race-conscious redistricting that "segregates" by drawing odd-shaped lines is qualitatively different from race-conscious redistricting that affects groups in some other way. The distinction is without foundation....As I understand the majority's theory, a redistricting plan that uses race to "segregate" voters by drawing "uncouth" lines is harmful in a way that a plan that uses race to distribute voters differently is not, for the former "bears an uncomfortable resemblance to political apartheid." The distinction is untenable. The other part of the majority's explanation of its holding is related to its simultaneous discomfort and fascination with irregularly shaped districts. Lack of compactness or contiguity, like uncouth district lines, certainly is a helpful indicator that some form of gerrymandering (racial or other) might have taken place. But while district irregularities may provide strong indicia of a potential gerrymander, they do no more than that. In particular, they have no bearing on whether the plan ultimately is found to violate the Constitution. Given two districts drawn on similar, race-based grounds, the one does not become more injurious than the other simply by virtue of being snake-like. By focusing on looks rather than impact, the majority in its approach will unnecessarily hinder to some extent a State's voluntary effort to ensure a modicum of minority representation where the minority population is geographically dispersed. When the creation of a majority-minority district does not unfairly minimize the voting power of any other group, the Constitution does not justify, much less mandate, such obstruction.

Justice SOUTER also dissented.

Bush v. Vera MELVIN UROFSKY

In the preceding case, the Court did not reach a decision on the merits of the equal protection claim, but merely stated that such a claim could exist. It remanded the case to the district court for adjudication on the merits. In the meantime, other opponents of majority-minority districting began to challenge the practice. Justice O'Connor's opinion in *Shaw* raised the question of whether a bizarrely shaped district was a necessary condition of unconstitutionality. In *Miller v. Johnson* (1995), the Court responded in the negative. Justice Kennedy, writing for the majority, noted that "The essence of the equal protection claim recognized in *Shaw* is that the State has used race as a basis for separating voters into districts. Just as the State may not, absent extraordinary justification, segregate citizens on the basis of race in its public parks, buses, golf courses, beaches, and schools, so...it may not separate its citizens into different voting districts on the basis of race." (The High Court remanded the case; see *Abrams v. Johnson* (below).

One year later the Court handed down two redistricting decisions on the same day. In *Shaw v. Hunt* (sometimes called Shaw II), Chief Justice Rehnquist reiterated the Shaw I ruling that strict scrutiny should be the standard in districting cases, and found that North Carolina lacked the required compelling interest to create the majority-minority districts.

Bush v. Vera presented many of the same issues, but this one grew out of a Texas redistricting plan. The divisions in the Court's thinking are evident from the fractured voting pattern. Justice O'Connor wrote a plurality opinion joined in whole only by Chief Justice Rehnquist and Justice Kennedy, and to iterate her belief that under certain conditions majority-minority could be justified she had to write a separate concurrence., which led Justice Kennedy to write his own concurrence, arguing that whether such districting would automatically trigger strict scrutiny was still an open question. Justices Thomas and Scalia concurred only in the result, believing that all racial-motivated districting required strict scrutiny. Justice Stevens dissented, joined by Justices Ginsburg and Breyer, while Justice Souter dissented on other grounds, joined also by Ginsburg and Breyer.

After this decision had been handed down, commentators agreed on little except that the Court had not articulated any clear standards by which to judge when majority-minority districting triggered strict scrutiny, when it might be justifiable, and what duties States owed to create such districts under the Voting Rights Act.

▶ Do gerrymandered districts—if they are based on worthwhile goals—serve the democratic process well? Why or why not?

▶ After reading the opinions in this case, can you find any clear policy line in the Court's reasoning? If so, what is it?

▶ We have here two conflicting constitutional values. On the one hand is the power of the Congress to carry out the mandate of the Fifteenth Amendment to ensure that the vote is not denied due to race, and Congress has interpreted that to mean dilution of voting effectiveness as well as the ability to cast a ballot. On the other is the Equal Protection Clause, which says no citizen shall be deprived of the equal protection of the laws. Who should make the decision on which of these values will prevail, the Court or Congress?

Bush v. Vera 116 S.Ct. 1941 (1996)

Justice O'CONNOR announced the judgment of the Court and delivered an opinion, in which The Chief Justice and Justice KENNEDY join.

This is the latest in a series of appeals involving racial gerrymandering challenges to state redistricting efforts in the wake of the 1990 census....The plaintiffs, six Texas voters, challenged the state redistricting plan, alleging that 24 of Texas' 30 congressional districts constitute racial gerrymanders in violation of the Fourteenth Amendment. The three-judge United States District Court for the Southern District of Texas held Districts 18, 29, and 30 unconstitutional. Finding that, under this Court's decisions in Shaw I and Miller, the district lines at issue are subject to strict scrutiny, and that they are not narrowly tailored to serve a compelling state interest, we affirm....

[In the first part of the plurality opinion, Justice O'Connor concluded that because the case centered around racial classification, then the traditional standard of strict scruinty would apply, although in earlier redistricting cases the Court had adopted a lower standard and deferred to Congressional findings.]

Having concluded that strict scrutiny applies, we must determine whether the racial classifications embodied in any of the three districts are narrowly tailored to further a compelling state interest. Appellants point to three compelling interests: the interest in avoiding liability under the "results" test of VRA [Voting Rights Act] Section (b), the interest in remedying past and present racial discrimination, and the "nonretrogression" principle of VRA Section 5 (for District 18 only). We consider them in turn....

A Section 2 district that is *reasonably* compact and regular, taking into account traditional districting principles such as maintaining communities of interest and traditional boundaries, may pass strict scrutiny without having to defeat rival compact districts designed by plaintiffs' experts in endless "beauty contests." The dissenters misread us when they make the leap from our disagreement about the facts of this case to the conclusion that we are creating a "stalemate" by requiring the States to "get things just right,"...or to draw "the precise compact district that a court would impose in a successful Section 2 challenge." Rather, we adhere to our longstanding recognition of the importance in our federal system of each State's sovereign interest in implementing its redistricting plan....The constitutional problem arises only from the subordination of those principles to race.

Strict scrutiny remains, nonetheless, strict. The State must have a "strong basis in evidence" for finding that the threshold conditions for Section 2 liability are present....And, as we have noted above, the district drawn in order to satisfy Section 2 must not subordinate traditional districting principles to race substantially more than is "reasonably necessary" to avoid Section 2 liability. Districts 18, 29, and 30 fail to meet these requirements....

We have, however, already found that all three districts are bizarrely shaped and far from compact, and that those characteristics are predominantly attributable to gerrymandering that was racially motivated and/or achieved by the use of race as a proxy. District 30, for example, reaches out to grab small and apparently isolated minority communities which, based on the evidence presented, could not possibly form part of a compact majority-minority district, and does so in order to make up for minority populations closer to its core that it shed in a further suspect use of race as a proxy to further neighboring incumbents' interests.

These characteristics defeat any claim that the districts are narrowly tailored to serve the State's interest in avoiding liability under Section 2, because Section 2 does not require a State to create, on predominantly racial lines, a district that is not "reasonably compact." ...If, because of the dispersion of the minority population, a reasonably compact majority-minority district cannot be created, Section 2 does not require a majority-minority district; if a reasonably compact district can be created, nothing in [the law] requires the race-based creation of a district that is far from compact.

Appellants argue that bizarre shaping and noncompactness do not raise narrow tailoring concerns. Appellants claim that under [our precedents] "shape is relevant only as evidence of an improper motive." The United States takes a more moderate position, accepting that in the context of narrow tailoring, "consideration must be given to the extent to which the districts drawn by a State substantially depart from its customary redistricting practices," but asserting that insofar as bizarreness and noncompactness are necessary to achieve the State's compelling interest in compliance with Section 2 "while simultaneously achieving other legitimate redistricting goals," such as incumbency protection, the narrowly tailoring requirement is satisfied....

These arguments cannot save the districts before us: district shape is not irrelevant to the narrow tailoring inquiry. Our [prior] discussion served only to emphasize that the ultimate constitutional values at stake involve the harms caused by the use of unjustified racial classifications, and that bizarreness is not necessary to trigger strict scrutiny. Significant deviations from traditional districting principles, such as the bizarre shape and noncompactness demonstrated by the districts here, cause constitutional harm insofar as they convey the message that political identity is, or should be, predominantly racial. For example, the bizarre shaping of Districts 18 and 29, cutting across pre-existing precinct lines and other natural or traditional divisions, is not merely evidentially significant; it is part of the constitutional problem insofar as it disrupts nonracial bases of political identity and thus intensifies the emphasis on race.

Nor is the United States' argument availing here. In determining that strict scrutiny applies here, we agreed with the District Court that in fact the bizarre shaping and noncompactness of these districts were predominantly attributable to racial, not political, manipulation. The United States' argument, and that of the dissent address the case of an otherwise compact majority-minority district that is misshapen by predominantly nonracial, political manipulation. We disagree with the factual premise of Justice STEVENS' dissent, that these districts were drawn using "racial considerations only in a way reasonably designed" to avoid a Section 2 violation. The districts before us exhibit a level of racial manipulation that exceeds what Section 2 could justify.

The United States and the State next contend that the district lines at issue are justified by the State's compelling interest in "ameliorating the effects of racially polarized voting attributable to past and present racial discrimination. In support of that contention, they cite Texas' long history of discrimination against minorities in electoral processes, stretching from the Reconstruction to modern times, including violations of the Constitution and of the VRA.

A State's interest in remedying discrimination is compelling when two conditions are satisfied. First, the discrimination that the State seeks to remedy must be specific, "identified discrimination"; second, the State "must have had a 'strong basis in evidence' to conclude that remedial action was necessary, 'before it embarks on an affirmative action program.' " Here, the only current problem that appellants cite as in need of remediation is alleged vote dilution as a consequence of racial bloc voting, the same concern that underlies their VRA Section 2 compliance defense, which we have assumed to be valid for purposes of this opinion. We have indicated that such problems will not justify race-based districting unless "the State employs sound districting principles, and...the affected racial group's residential patterns afford the opportunity of creating districts in which they will be in the majority." Once that standard is applied, our agreement with the District Court's finding that these districts are not narrowly tailored to comply with Section 2 forecloses this line of defense.

The final contention offered by the State and private appellants is that creation of District 18 (only) was justified by a compelling state interest in complying with VRA Section 5. We have made clear that Section 5 has a limited substantive goal: "to insure that no voting-procedure changes would be made that would lead to a retrogression in the position of racial minorities with respect to their effective exercise of the electoral franchise." Appellants contend that this "nonretrogression" principle is implicated because Harris County had, for two decades, contained a congressional district in which African-American voters had succeeded in selecting representatives of their choice, all of whom were African-Americans.

The problem with the State's argument is that it seeks to justify not maintenance, but substantial augmentation, of the African-American population percentage in District 18. At the previous redistricting, in 1980, District 18's population was 40.8% African-American. As a result of Hispanic population increases and African-American emigration from the district, its population had reached 35.1% African-American and 42.2% Hispanic at the time of the 1990 census. The State has shown no basis for concluding that the increase to a 50.9% African-American population in 1991 was necessary to insure nonretrogression. Nonretrogression is not a license for the State to do whatever it deems necessary to insure continued electoral success; it merely mandates that the minority's opportunity to elect representatives of its choice not be diminished, directly or indirectly, by the State's actions. Applying that principle, it is clear that District 18 is not narrowly tailored to the avoidance of Section 5 liability.

The judgment of the District Court is

Affirmed.

[Justice O'CONNOR concurred with the plurality opinion in order to note two points. First, compliance with Section 2 of the Voting Rights Act does constitute a compelling state interest, and second, that this test can co-exist in principle with the Court's ruling. In other words, minority-majority districts could be drawn in a way to satisfy both the Court's strict scrutiny standard as well as the results test of Section 2 of the VRA. She went on to agree with the dissenters that Section 2 constitutes a critical part of the nation's commitment to racial equality. Justice KENNEDY also concurred separately in which he noted that even with a compelling interest, the state would still have to tailor narrowly its solution to the problem of racial discrimination. Justice THOMAS, joined by Justice SCALIA, concurred in the result, but argued that whether or not strict scrutiny was the proper test was never a close question, insofar as any racial classification automatically triggers strict scrutiny.]

Justice STEVENS, with whom Justice GINSBURG and Justice BREYER join, dissenting.

Today, the Court strikes down three of Texas' majority-minority districts, concluding, *inter alia*, that their odd shapes reveal that the State impermissibly relied on predominantly racial reasons when it drew the districts as it did. For two reasons, I believe that the Court errs in striking down those districts.

First, I believe that the Court has misapplied its own tests for racial gerrymandering, both by applying strict scrutiny to all three of these districts, and then by concluding that none can meet that scrutiny. In asking whether strict scrutiny should apply, the Court improperly ignores the "complex interplay" of political and geographical considerations that went into the creation of Texas' new congressional districts, and focuses exclusively on the role that race played in the State's decisions to adjust the shape of its districts. A quick comparison of the unconstitutional majority-minority districts with three equally bizarre majority-Anglo districts, demonstrates that race was not necessarily the predominant factor contorting the district lines. I would follow the fair implications of the District Court's findings, and conclude that Texas' entire map is a political, not a racial, gerrymander.

Even if strict scrutiny applies, I would find these districts constitutional, for each considers race only to the extent necessary to comply with the State's responsibilities under the Voting Rights Act while achieving other race-neutral political and geographical requirements. The plurality's finding to the contrary unnecessarily restricts the ability of States to conform their behavior to the Voting Rights Act while simultaneously complying with other race-neutral goals.

Second, even if I concluded that these districts failed an appropriate application of this still-developing law to appropriately read facts, I would not uphold the District Court decision. The decisions issued today serve merely to reinforce my conviction that the Court has, with its "analytically distinct" jurisprudence of racial gerrymandering, struck out into a jurisprudential wilderness that lacks a definable constitutional core and threatens to create harms more significant than any suffered by the individual plaintiffs challenging these districts. Though we travel ever farther from it with each passing decision, I would return to the well-traveled path that we left in *Shaw I*.

Justice SOUTER, with whom Justice GINSBURG and Justice BREYER join, dissenting.

 When the Court devises a new cause of action to enforce a constitutional provision, it ought to identify an injury distinguishable from the consequences of concededly constitutional conduct, and it should describe the elements necessary and sufficient to make out such a claim. Nothing less can give notice to those whose conduct may give rise to liability or provide standards for courts charged with enforcing the Constitution. Those principles of justification, fair notice, and guidance, have never been satisfied in the instance of the action announced three Terms ago in *Shaw v. Reno*, (1993), when a majority of this Court decided that a State violates the Fourteenth Amendment's Equal Protection Clause by excessive consideration of race in drawing the boundaries of voting districts, even when the resulting plan does not dilute the voting strength of any voters and so would not otherwise give rise to liability under the Fourteenth or Fifteenth Amendments, or under the Voting Rights Act.

The result of this failure to provide a practical standard for distinguishing between the lawful and unlawful use of race has not only been inevitable confusion in state houses and courthouses, but a consequent shift in responsibility for setting district boundaries from the state legislatures, which are invested with front-line authority by Article I of the Constitution, to the courts, and truly to this Court, which is left to superintend the drawing of every legislative district in the land.

Today's opinions do little to solve *Shaw*'s puzzles or return districting responsibility to the States. To say this is not to denigrate the importance of Justice O'CONNOR's position in her separate opinion, that compliance with Section 2 of the Voting Rights Act is a compelling state interest; her statement takes a very significant step toward alleviating apprehension that *Shaw* is at odds with the Voting Rights Act. It is still true, however, that the combined plurality, minority, and Court opinions do not ultimately leave the law dealing with a *Shaw* claim appreciably clearer or more manageable than *Shaw I* itself did. And to the extent that some clarity follows from the knowledge that race may be considered when reasonably necessary to conform to the Voting Rights Act, today's opinions raise the specter that this ostensible progress may come with a heavy constitutional price. The price of *Shaw I*, indeed, may turn out to be the practical elimination of a State's discretion to apply traditional districting principles, widely accepted in States without racial districting issues as well as in States confronting them. As the flaws of *Shaw I* persist, and as the burdens placed on the States and the courts by *Shaw* litigation loom larger with the approach of a new census and a new round of redistricting, the Court has to recognize that *Shaw*'s problems result from a basic misconception about the relation between race and districting principles, a mistake that no amount of case-by-case tinkering can eliminate. There is, therefore, no reason for confidence that the Court will eventually bring much order out of the confusion created by *Shaw I*, and because it has not, in any case, done so yet, I respectfully dissent.

Abrams v. Johnson   MELVIN UROFSKY

On remand from the Supreme Court, the District Court in Georgia reconsidered the constitutionality of the 1990 Georgia congressional apportionment plan, a plan found wanting by the High Court in *Miller v. Johnson* (1995). After the legislature had failed to develop a scheme that met court approval, the district court fashioned its own plan, one that included only a single majority-minority district. This plan was attacked on the grounds that the court, while it had the power to draft a plan, had failed to follow the rules in such situations laid down by the Supreme Court in earlier cases. More important, it had failed to follow the clear mandate of the Georgia legislature that it wanted two black-majority districts.

In his dissent in *Bush v. Vera*, Justice Souter had warned that the Court's failure to provide clear guidelines on redistricting would lead to the courts arrogating unto themselves the power that properly belonged in the legislature. Despite the fact that the Rehnquist Court has repeatedly avowed the principle of judicial deference to legislative policy-making, in the case of majority-minority districting a majority of the justices have consistently denied the power of the Congress under the Enforcement Clauses of the Fourteenth Amendment to impose a plan it deems necessary to give minorities voting effectiveness. It has also denied to the states their usual leeway in drawing less than compact or contiguous district lines.

Although the Court has never said that majority-minority districts are *per se* unconstitutional, after *Abrams* it appears questionable whether it will be possible to create such districts except in large cities, where such districts could be created in any circumstance. Efforts to draw together minorities in rural areas into bizarrely shaped districts may no longer be permitted under the Court's strict scrutiny test.

▶ Would you be more comfortable with federal courts or state legislatures drawing congressional districts? Why?

▶ The Georgia legislature is overwhelmingly white. It appears from the evidence that it was willing to create two majority-minority seats. One of the districts, however, would have been a rather odd shape. Given that preference, why should the courts have the power to override the popular will?

▶ Is there any legitimate reason to gerrymander in order to augment minority voting power? Would the same reason apply to farmers, who are also a minority in most states?

▶ If districts are drawn in what appears to be a race-blind manner, and there-fore do not yield even one majority-minority district, would that violate the Voting Rights Act of 1965? Do you think that a redistricting plan with no majority-minority districts would or should be ruled unconstitutional by the Court?

Abrams v. Johnson 117 S.Ct. 1925 (1997)

Justice KENNEDY delivered the opinion of the Court.

The electoral district lines for Georgia's congressional delegation are before us a second time, appeal now being taken from the trial court's rulings and determinations after our remand in *Miller v. Johnson*, (1995). The three-judge panel of the United States District Court for the Southern District of Georgia was affirmed in *Miller* after it found the Eleventh Congressional District unconstitutional as then drawn. Race, we held, must not be a pre-dominant factor in drawing the district lines.

Given the contorted shape of the district and the undue predominance of race in draw-ing its lines, it was unlikely the district could be redrawn without changing most or all of Georgia's congressional districts, 11 in total number. The plan being challenged contained three majority-black districts, and after our remand the complaint was amended to chal-lenge another of these, the then Second District. The trial court found this district, too, was improperly drawn under the standards we confirmed in *Miller*.

For the task of drawing a new plan, the court deferred to Georgia's legislature, but the legislature could not reach agreement. The court then drew its own plan, and the 1996 gen-eral elections were held under it. The court's plan contained but one majority-black district. The absence of a second, if not a third, majority-black district has become the principal point of contention. Though the elections have been completed, the plan remains in effect until changed by a valid legislative act, and the appellants ask us to set it aside.

The private appellants are various voters, defendant-intervenors below, who contend that the interests of Georgia's black population were not adequately taken into account. The United States, also a defendant-intervenor, joins in the appeal. The state officials, defendants below, do not object to the plan and appeared before us as appellees to defend it. The other set of appellees are the private plaintiffs, who argued that racial gerrymandering under the previous plan violated their right to equal protection.

The private appellants attack the court's plan on five grounds. First, citing *Upham v. Seamon* (1982), they say the District Court erred in disregarding the State's legislative policy choices and in making more changes than necessary to cure constitutional defects in the previous plan. Second and third, they allege the plan violates Sections 2 and 5 of the Voting

Rights Act of 1965. Fourth, they argue the court's plan contains significant population deviations and so violates the constitutional one person, one vote requirement. Fifth, they claim
the District Court erred in not allowing private intervention on the question of the Second
District's unconstitutionality. The challenges are unavailing, and we affirm the judgment of
the District Court.

We first address appellants' argument that the court exceeded the remedial power
authorized by our decisions, particularly *Upham v. Seamon*, by failing to follow policies of
the state legislature. When faced with the necessity of drawing district lines by judicial
order, a court, as a general rule, should be guided by the legislative policies underlying the
existing plan, to the extent those policies do not lead to violations of the Constitution or
the Voting Rights Act. Much of the argument from the parties centers around what legislative redistricting principles the District Court should have acknowledged in drawing its
plan. The appellants say the relevant redistricting guideline should be the three majority-
black districts of the precleared plan at issue in *Miller v. Johnson*; and, if not, the two
majority-black districts in an earlier legislative effort. These contentions require us to
recite some of the background against which the Georgia Legislature—and later the trial
court—attempted to draw the districts.

*[The Court here summarized the history of the suit, and the inability of the Georgia
legislature to reach agreement on a redistricting plan that would have passed constitutional
muster, thus leading the District Court to develop its own plan, with only one majority-minority
district.]*

Given this background, appellants say, the District Court's plan violates our direction in
Upham v. Seamon to take account of legislative preferences. In *Upham*, the district court
considered a reapportionment plan passed by the Texas Legislature. The Attorney General
had objected under Section 5 of the Voting Rights Act to a specific part of the plan, namely
the lines drawn for two contiguous districts in south Texas. He had approved the other
25 districts. The trial court, required to draw new lines, redrew not just the two districts
found objectionable and their neighbors but also some unrelated districts in Dallas County,
hundreds of miles to the north. In the absence of a finding that the legislature's
reapportionment plan offended either the Constitution or the Voting Rights Act, we held, the
district court "was not free...to disregard the political program" of the state legislature.

The instant case presents a quite different situation from *Upham*, and for several
reasons. In the first place, the precleared plan is not owed *Upham* deference to the extent the
plan subordinated traditional districting principles to racial considerations. *Upham* called
on courts to correct—not follow—constitutional defects in districting plans. In *Miller*, we
found that when the Georgia Legislature yielded to the Justice Department's threats, it also
adopted the Justice Department's entirely race-focused approach to redistricting—the
max-black policy. Using the precleared plan as the basis for a remedy would validate the
very maneuvers that were a major cause of the unconstitutional districting.

Second, the constitutional violation here affects a large geographic area of the State; any
remedy of necessity must affect almost every district. Almost every major population center
in Georgia was split along racial lines. Under the circumstances, the district court was
justified in making substantial changes to the existing plan consistent with Georgia's tradi-

tional districting principles, and considering race as a factor but not allowing it to predominate. This approach conforms to the rule explained in *Upham*.

Appellants' most specific objection under *Upham* is that the court's plan does not contain two majority-black districts. In particular, they point to the State's original 1991 redistricting plan, denied preclearance, which contained two majority-black districts. As we have suggested above, however, the State was subjected to steady Justice Department pressure to create the maximum number of majority-black districts, and there is considerable evidence the State was predominantly driven by this consideration even in developing its 1991 plan....

There is strong support, then, for finding the second majority-black district in Georgia's 1991 uncleared plan resulted in substantial part from the Justice Department's policy of creating the maximum number of majority-black districts. It is not Justice Department interference *per se* that is the concern, but rather the fact that Justice Department pressure led the State to act based on an overriding concern with race. Given this background, it would have been most problematic for the trial court to insist on retaining a second majority-black district without regard to other, neutral districting factors. The trial court did not adopt this course. Instead, it gave careful consideration to creation of a second black district on grounds that a black voting population was one factor in drawing a district; and it concluded it could not draw the second majority-black district without allowing that one consideration to predominate over other traditional and neutral districting principles, principles which were a valid expression of legislative policy. There is ample basis in the record to support these conclusions. No other plan demonstrated a second majority-black district could be drawn while satisfying the constitutional requirement that race not predominate over traditional districting principles. The District Court said in its opinion that "if Georgia had a concentrated minority population large enough to create a second majority-minority district without subverting traditional districting principles, the Court would have included one since Georgia's legislature probably would have done so." The statements of several witnesses support the trial court's independent conclusion it was not possible to do so....

The court-ordered plan is not violative of Section 2 of the Voting Rights Act. We reject appellants' contrary position, which is premised on impermissible vote dilution in the court's failure to create a second majority-black district. Section 2 of the Voting Rights Act applies to any "voting qualification or prerequisite to voting or standard, practice, or procedure...imposed or applied by any State or political subdivision."

Our decision in *Thornburg v. Gingles* (1986), set out the basic framework for establishing a vote dilution claim against at-large, multimember districts; we have since extended the framework to single-member districts. Plaintiffs must show three threshold conditions: first, the minority group "is sufficiently large and geographically compact to constitute a majority in a single-member district"; second, the minority group is "politically cohesive"; and third, the majority "votes sufficiently as a bloc to enable it...to defeat the minority's preferred candidate." Once plaintiffs establish these conditions, the court considers whether, "on the totality of circumstances," minorities have been denied an "equal opportunity" to "participate in the political process and to elect representatives of their choice."

The trial court found that to create a second majority-black district in Georgia would require subordinating Georgia's traditional districting policies and allowing race to predominate. We considered the determination in our discussion above and concluded it was well founded. If race is the predominant motive in creating districts, strict scrutiny applies, and the districting plan must be narrowly tailored to serve a compelling governmental interest in order to survive. We have assumed, without deciding, that compliance with Section 2 can be a compelling state interest. Here, there was no "strong basis in evidence," to conclude that vote dilution, in violation of Section 2, would occur in consequence of the court's plan. In fact, none of the three Gingles factors, the threshold findings for a vote dilution claim, were established here....

The private appellants contend the District Court's plan also violates Section 5 of the Voting Rights Act. As we noted above, Section 5 requires covered jurisdictions to obtain either administrative preclearance by the Attorney General or approval from the United States District Court for the District of Columbia for any change in a "standard, practice, or procedure with respect to voting," and requires that the proposed change "not have the purpose and will not have the effect of denying or abridging the right to vote on account of race or color." We have explained that "the purpose of Section 5 has always been to insure that no voting-procedure changes would be made that would lead to a retrogression in the position of racial minorities with respect to their effective exercise of the electoral franchise."

The question arises whether a court decree is subject to Section 5. We have held that "a decree of the United States District Court is not within reach of Section 5 of the Voting Rights Act" such that it must be precleared. The exception applies to judicial plans, devised by the court itself, not to plans submitted to the court by the legislature of a covered jurisdiction in response to a determination of unconstitutionality. Here, the District Court made clear it had devised its own plan, a proposition not in dispute. In *McDaniel v. Sanchez* (1981), we emphasized language in a Senate Committee report saying that, although preclearance does not apply to court-devised plans, "'in fashioning the plan, the court should follow the appropriate Section 5 standards, including the body of administrative and judicial precedents developed in Section 5 cases.'" This is a reasonable standard, at the very least as an equitable factor to take into account, if not as a statutory mandate.

Appellants, however, have some difficulty fixing on a benchmark against which to measure any retrogression. Private appellants say the benchmark should be either the State's initial 1991 plan, containing two majority-black districts, or the State's "policy and goal of creating two majority black districts." The Justice Department, for its part, contends the proper benchmark is the 1992 precleared plan, altered to cure its constitutional defects.

Here, as we have noted above in our discussions of both Upham and Section 2, appellants have not demonstrated it was possible to create a second majority-black district within constitutional bounds. So, even were we to accept one of their proposed benchmarks, their desired remedy would be unconstitutional. As it happens, none of appellants' proposed benchmarks is appropriate....The appropriate benchmark is, in fact, what the District Court concluded it would be: the 1982 plan, in effect for a decade. Appellants have not shown that black voters in any particular district suffered a retrogression in their voting strength under the court plan measured against the 1982 plan. Absent such proof, there is no violation of Section 5. We reject appellants' assertion that, even using the 1982 plan as a benchmark, the court's plan is retrogressive. They claim that under the 1982 plan one of the ten districts (10%) was majority black, while under the District Court's plan one of eleven districts (9%) is majority black, and therefore blacks do not have the same electoral opportunities under the District Court's plan. Under that logic, each time a State with a majority-minority district was allowed to add one new district because of population growth, it would have to be majority-minority. This the Voting Rights Act does not require.

Finally, appellants contend the District Court's plan violates the constitutional guarantee of one person, one vote under Article I, Section 2. *[The Court rejected the argument that a minor diminution in the percentage of black voters in majority black districts constituted a deprivation of the one person, one vote rule.]*

The task of redistricting is best left to state legislatures, elected by the people and as capable as the courts, if not more so, in balancing the myriad factors and traditions in legitimate districting policies. Here, the legislative process was first distorted and then unable to reach a solution. The District Court was left to embark on a delicate task with limited legislative guidance. The court was careful to take into account traditional state districting factors, and it remained sensitive to the constitutional requirement of equal protection of the laws. The judgment of the District Court is affirmed.

It is so ordered.

Justice BREYER, with whom Justice STEVENS, Justice SOUTER, and Justice GINSBURG join, dissenting.

The basic legal issue before us now is whether the District Court should have retained (not one but) two majority-minority districts. The majority holds that the District Court could lawfully create a new districting plan that retained only one such district. But in my view that decision departs dramatically from the Georgia Legislature's preference for two such districts—a preference embodied in the legislature's earlier congressional district plans. A two-district plan is not unconstitutional. And the District Court here, like the District Court in *Upham v. Seamon* (1982), "was not free...to disregard the political program of the...Legislature." For that reason, and others, I dissent.

The majority fully understands the relevance, and the importance, here of this Court's Upham decision. In Upham the Court said: " Just as a federal district court...should follow the policies and preferences of the State, as expressed...in the reapportionment plans proposed by the state legislature, whenever adherence to state policy does not detract from the requirements of the Federal Constitution,...a district court should similarly honor state policies in the context of congressional reapportionment." The majority here, referring to this language, agrees: "A court, as a general rule, should be guided by the legislative policies underlying the existing plan, to the extent those policies do not lead to violations of the Constitution or the Voting Rights Act." It is therefore common ground among us that the District Court should have drawn boundaries so as to leave two majority-minority districts rather than one—unless there was no such state policy or preference; unless the creation of two such districts would have violated the Constitution or the Voting Rights Act of 1965; or unless doing so simply would have proved impractical in light of other important districting objectives. Unlike the majority, I cannot find present here any of these three countervailing justifications.

No one denies that, if one looks at the redistricting plans proposed by the Georgia Legislature, one will find in them expressions of state "policies and preferences" for two majority-minority districts....What the District Court and the majority deny is that the "preferences" expressed in these three redistricting plans reflect the Georgia Legislature's true preference. The District Court said that "Georgia's current plan was not the product of Georgia's legislative will," but rather "was tainted by unconstitutional DOJ [Department of Justice] interference" into the "process" that produced the plan. The majority repeats the District Court's comment about DOJ's "thorough 'subversion of the redistricting process' since the 1990 census," adds that the "State was predominantly driven" by "steady Justice Department pressure," and concludes: "Interference by the Justice Department...disturbed any sound basis to defer to the 1991 unprecleared plan."

I believe, however, that the majority's conclusion—its reason for refusing to recognize the Georgia Legislature's two-district preference—is wrong both as a matter of fact and as a matter of law. The conclusion is factually inadequate because the testimony cited to show unusual DOJ pressure in the 1991 redistricting process shows nothing unusual. It shows only that the Justice Department told Georgia that it must comply with the VRA, which statement Georgia legislators might have considered an exhortation to create more than one majority-minority district. Indeed, the record indicates that a number of Georgia legislators affirmatively wanted two majority-minority districts. It also shows that the 1991 two-district plan was the result of an "'understanding' between the leadership in the legislature and the black caucus."

The majority is legally wrong because this Court has said that a court should determine a State's redistricting preferences by looking to the "plans proposed by the state legislature," not by evaluating the various political pressures that might have led individual legislators to vote one way rather than another (or, for that matter, by reviewing after-the-fact testimony regarding legislative intent). District plans, like other legislative Acts, may reflect not only reasoned argument but also political pressures, brought to bear by many different individuals and groups using subtle or unsubtle suggestions, promises or threats, of votes, support, publicity, and even lawsuits.

How can a court say that a legislative Act is legitimate—that it reflects legislative preferences or policies—when those who reason or cajole (or threaten suit) are farmers, businessmen, or consumer groups, but that the same legislative Act becomes illegitimate—that it does not reflect "true" legislative policy or preference—simply because those who seek to persuade (or threaten suit) represent the Justice Department. One cannot say that the Department's power is any less legitimate than that exercised by the many other groups that seek to influence legislative decisions; and its employees' sworn duty to uphold the law would seem more suitably characterized as a reason for paying greater attention to its views rather than as a reason for heeding them less. Regardless, I am not aware of any legal principle that supports the kind of distinction (among legislative pressures) that the District Court made; and the District Court's necessary reliance upon such a distinction, by itself, should warrant vacating the District Court's decision.

Moreover, what reason is there to believe that Georgia's Legislature did not "really" want the two majority-minority districts that its earlier plans created? There is—as I indicated earlier—evidence that a number of legislators did want two majority-minority districts. And the legislature was aware of Georgia's long, well documented history of past discrimination in voting....

I do not necessarily agree or disagree with those other aspects of the majority's opinion that I have not mentioned. But I shall stop with the main point. The Court, perhaps by focusing upon what it considered to be unreasonably pervasive positive use of race as a redistricting factor, has created a legal doctrine that will unreasonably restrict legislators' use of race, even for the most benign, or antidiscriminatory purposes. And that doctrine will draw the Court too deeply into an area of legislative responsibility. For the reasons set forth here, and in previous dissenting opinions, I do not believe that the Constitution embodies the doctrine that the majority enunciates. And I believe that Upham requires us to vacate the District Court's judgment and remand the suit.

Grand Rapids School District v. Ball   MELVIN UROFSKY

For much of this country's history, lip service has been paid to the ideal of separation of church and state. In fact, there have been no established churches since the early nineteenth century, and neither the states nor the federal government give money to religious organizations for the purpose of spreading their gospel. At the same time, as Justice Douglas once noted, "We are a religious people who presuppose a Supreme Being." Our money carries the motto "In God We Trust," we call ourselves "One Nation under God," we allow tax exemptions for donations to religious groups, and provide a number of tax-supported services, such as police and fire protection, to churches,synagogues and mosques without imposing corresponding property taxes.

Ever since large numbers of Catholics migrated to the United States in the mid-nineteenth century and began establishing parochial schools, Catholic leaders have called for the state to help support those schools. They argue that these schools are providing services to children, and without parochial schools, the public school systems would have to shoulder the additional burden. Until the mid-1960s these calls were consistently rejected. The onset of the Great Society's massive aid-to-education programs, however, permitted federal money to go to underwrite secular programs that would benefit children in private schools, the majority of whom are in religious-sponsored institutions.

The Court established a three-prong test in *Lemon v. Kurzman* (1971) to determine when state aid to parochial schools would be permissible. First, does the legislation have a definite secular purpose ("purpose" test); second, is the law in its effect religiously neutral, doing nothing to either advance or suppress religion ("effects" test); and third, does the law involve the government too heavily in religious affairs ("entanglement" test).

Normally, the first prong of the test is easily met, since the legislation nearly always has a straightforward secular purpose, such as providing services for students in church schools similar to those available in public schools. It is on the second and third parts of the tests that the laws usually fail. By a strict construction, any federal aid will invariably advance religion. For example, say the state provides a parochial school with $100,000 a year for remedial reading instruction, an obviously secular activity. Yet reading is important, and if the state did not provide the funds, the school itself would have to do so. By giving the school the $100,000 the government has freed up that much money in the school's regular budget—funds that can now be used for religious activity. Similarly, the government is required to ensure that money it appropriates is legally and efficiently expended, which means that it must monitor the church school's books, and may require changes in accounting or disbursement procedures. This obviously requires involvement with religious affairs

For the accommodationists, the fact that the church school uses the $100,000 for religious purposes, or that the government monitors the books, is of negligible importance. They see the schools as performing two functions: teaching secular studies and inculcating religion. The two need not be kept fully separate in order to meet the spirit of the First Amendment; for the accomodationists, a violation would be, for example, a case in which the government directs what is taught in religious schools.

In this case, and a companion case, *Aguilar v. Felton*, the Court struck down programs in Detroit and New York that used Title I money to pay for public school teachers going into parochial schools and conducting remedial programs during regular school hours. The Court also invalidated a community program offering courses in these schools after regular hours.

These two cases mark a high water mark of strict separation, and also indicate that only a bare majority of the Court endorsed the ruling. By 1985 the pendulum had begun to swing away from separation toward accomodation, and those who supported the high wall of separation worried that one or two changes on the Court might well see the wall come tumbling down.

▶ There is no doubt that children benefitted from the programs the Court disqualified in this case. What is more important, benefit to children or a strict adherence to the idea of a wall of separation?

▶ Is there any validity to the "slippery slope" argument here? If the Court permits one kind of program of this kind to continue, is the door then opened to other similar programs?

▶ Public education, according to the Court, is not a fundamental right, but a privilege the state is not constitutionally required to provide. If a parent chooses to forego this privilege because he or she wants a different type of education for the child, is any "right" to aid retained?

> ▶ Assume that Mr. and Mrs. X are fervent Nazis, and want their children edu-
> cated in a school that teaches Nazi doctrine, as well as the required secular
> subjects. Is there any reason the state should provide aid to that school?
> Although Christian forbearance and Nazi intolerance are totally different,
> is the analytical argument any different for providing aid in either case? If
> parents choose to raise their children along specific religious lines, they
> have the right to do so, and the state may not interfere. What, if any, assis-
> tance should the state provide? What may it provide?

Grand Rapids School District v. Ball 473 U.S. 373 (1985)

Mr. Justice BRENNAN delivered the opinion of the Court.

The School District of Grand Rapids, Michigan, adopted two programs in which classes for nonpublic school students are financed by the public school system, taught by teachers hired by the public school system, and conducted in "leased" classrooms in the nonpublic schools. Most of the nonpublic schools involved in the programs are sectarian religious schools. This case raises the questions whether these programs impermissibly involve the government in the support of sectarian religious activities and thus violate the Establishment Clause of the First Amendment.

At issue in this case are the Community Education and Shared Time programs offered in the nonpublic schools of Grand Rapids, Michigan. These programs, first instituted in the 1976-1977 school year, provide classes to nonpublic school students at public expense in classrooms located in and leased from the local nonpublic schools.

The Shared Time teachers are full-time employees of the public schools, who often move from classroom to classroom during the course of the school day. The School District of Grand Rapids hires Shared Time teachers in accordance with its ordinary hiring proce-dures. The public school system apparently provides all of the supplies, materials, and equipment used in connection with Shared Time instruction.

The Community Education Program is offered throughout the Grand Rapids communi-ty in schools and on other sites, for children as well as adults. The classes at issue here are taught in the nonpublic elementary schools and commence at the conclusion of the regular school day. Among the courses offered are Arts and Crafts, Home Economics, Spanish, Gymnastics, Yearbook Production, Christmas Arts and Crafts, Drama, Newspaper, Humanities, Chess, Model Building, and Nature Appreciation....

Although petitioners label the Shared Time and Community Education students as "part-time public school students," the students attending Shared Time and Community Education courses in facilities leased from a nonpublic school are the same students who attend that particular school otherwise. There is no evidence that any public school student has ever attended a Shared Time or Community Education class in a nonpublic school. The District Court found that "though Defendants claim the Shared Time program is available to all students, the record is abundantly clear that only nonpublic school students wearing the cloak of a 'public school student' can enroll in it." The District Court noted that "whereas public school students are assembled at the public facility nearest to their residence, students in religious schools are assembled on the basis of religion without any consideration of residence of school district boundaries." Thus, "beneficiaries are wholly designated on the basis of religion," and these "public school" classes, in contrast to ordinary public school classes which are largely neighborhood-based are as segregated by religion as are the schools at which they are offered.

Forty of the forty-one schools at which the programs operate are sectarian in character. The schools of course vary from one another, but substantial evidence suggests that they share deep religious purposes. For instance, the Parent Handbook of one Catholic school states the goals of Catholic education as "a God oriented environment which *permeates* the total education program," "a Christian atmosphere which guides and encourages participation in the church's commitment to social justice," and "a continuous development of knowledge of the Catholic faith, its traditions, teachings and theology." A policy statement of the Christian schools similarly proclaims that "it is not sufficient that the teachings of Christianity be a separate subject in the curriculum, but *the Word of God must be an all-pervading force in the educational program*." These Christian schools require all parents seeking to enroll their children either to subscribe to a particular doctrinal statement or to agree to have their children taught according to the doctrinal statement. The District Court found that the schools are "pervasively sectarian," and concluded "without hesitation that the purposes of these schools is to advance their particular religions," and that "a substantial portion of their functions are subsumed in the religious mission."

Respondents are six taxpayers who filed suit against the School District of Grand Rapids and a number of state officials. They charged that the Shared Time and Community Education programs violated the Establishment Clause of the First Amendment of the Constitution, made applicable to the States through the Fourteenth Amendment. After an 8-day bench trial, the District Court entered a judgment on the merits on behalf of respondents and enjoined further operation of the programs.

Applying the familiar three-part purpose, effect, and entanglement test set out in *Lemon v. Kurtzman* (1971), the court held that, although the purpose of the programs was secular, their effect was "distinctly impermissible."...We granted *certiorari*, and now affirm.

The First Amendment's guarantee the "Congress shall make no law respecting an establishment of religion," as our cases demonstrate, is more than a pledge that no single religion will be designated as a state religion. It is also more than a mere injunction that governmental programs discriminating among religions are unconstitutional. The Establishment Clause instead primarily proscribes "sponsorship, financial support, and active involvement of the sovereign in religious activity." As Justice Black, writing for the Court in *Everson v. Board of Education*, stated: "Neither [a State nor the Federal Government] can pass laws which aid one religion, aid all religions, or prefer one religion over another....No tax in any amount, large or small, can be levied to support any religious activities or institutions, whatever they may be called, or whatever form they may adopt to teach or practice religion."

Since *Everson* made clear that the guarantees of the Establishment Clause apply to the States, we have often grappled with the problem of state aid to non-public, religious schools. In all of these cases, our goal has been to give meaning to the sparse language and broad purposes of the Clause, while not unduly infringing on the ability of the States to provide for the welfare of their people in accordance with their own particular circumstances. Providing for the education of schoolchildren is surely a praiseworthy purpose. But our cases have consistently recognized that even such a praiseworthy, secular purpose cannot validate government aid to parochial schools when the aid has the effect of promoting a single religion or religion generally or when the aid unduly entangles the government in matters religious. For just as religion throughout history has provided spiritual comfort, guidance, and inspiration to many, it can also serve powerfully to divide societies and to exclude those whose beliefs are not in accord with particular religions or sects that have from time to time achieved dominance. The solution to this problem adopted by the Framers and consistently recognized by this Court is jealously to guard the right of every individual to worship according to the dictates of conscience while requiring the government to maintain a course of neutrality among religions, and between religion and non-religion. Only in this way can we "make room for as wide a variety of beliefs and creeds as the spiritual needs of man deem necessary: and sponsor an attitude on the part of government that shows no partiality to any one group and lets each flourish according to the zeal of its adherents and the appeal of its dogma."

We have noted that the three-part test first articulated in *Lemon v. Kurtzman*, guides "the general nature of our inquiry in this area." These tests "must not be viewed as setting the precise limits to the necessary constitutional inquiry, but serve only as guidelines with which to identify instances in which the objectives of the Establishment Clause have been impaired." We have particularly relied on *Lemon* in every case involving the sensitive relationship between government and religion in the education of our children. The government's activities in this area can have a magnified impact on impressionable young minds, and the occasional rivalry of parallel public and private school systems offers an all-too-ready opportunity for divisive rifts along religious lines in the body politic. The *Lemon* test concentrates attention on the issues—purposes, effect, entanglement—that determine whether a particular state action is an improper "law respecting an establishment of religion." We therefore reaffirm that state action alleged to violate the Establishment Clause should be measured against the *Lemon* criteria.

As has often been true in school aid cases, there is no dispute as to the first test. Both the District Court and the Court of Appeals found that the purpose of the Community Education and Shared Time programs was "manifestly secular." We find no reason to disagree with this holding, and therefore go on to consider whether the primary or principal effect of the challenged programs is to advance or inhibit religion.

Our inquiry must begin with a consideration of the nature of the institutions in which the programs operate. Of the 41 private schools where these "part-time public schools" have operated, 40 are identifiably religious schools. The District Court found, however, that "based upon the massive testimony and exhibits, the conclusion is inescapable that the religious institutions receiving instructional services from the public schools are sectarian in the sense that a substantial portion of their functions are subsumed in the religious mission."

...Given that 40 of the 41 schools in this case are thus "pervasively sectarian," the challenged public-school programs operating in the religious schools may impermissibly advance religion in three different ways. First, the teachers participating in the programs may become involved in intentionally or inadvertently inculcating particular religious tenets or beliefs. Second, the programs may provide a crucial symbolic link between government and religion, thereby enlisting—at least in the eyes of impressionable youngsters—the powers of government to the support of the religious denomination operating the school. Third, the programs may have the effect of directly promoting religion by impermissibly providing a subsidy to the primary religious mission of the institutions affected.

Although Establishment Clause jurisprudence is characterized by few absolutes, the Clause does absolutely prohibit government-financed or government-sponsored indoctrination into the beliefs of a particular religious faith....Such indoctrination, if permitted to occur, would have devastating effects on the right of each individual voluntarily to determine what to believe (and what not to believe) free of any coercive pressures from the State, while at the same time tainting the resulting religious beliefs with a corrosive secularism.

In *Meek v. Pittenger* [1975], the Court invalidated a statute providing for the loan of state-paid professional staff—including teachers—to nonpublic schools to provide remedial and accelerated instruction, guidance counseling and testing, and other services on the premises of the nonpublic schools. Such a program, if not subjected to a "comprehensive, discriminating, and continuing state surveillance," would entail an unacceptable risk that the state-sponsored instructional personnel would "advance the religious mission of the church-related schools in which they serve." Even though the teachers were paid by the State, "the potential for impermissible fostering of religion under these circumstances, although somewhat reduced, is nonetheless present." The program in *Meek*, if not sufficiently monitored, would simply have entailed too great a risk of state-sponsored indoctrination.

The programs before us today share the defect that we identified in *Meek*. With respect to the Community Education Program, the District Court found that "virtually every Community Education course conducted on facilities leased from nonpublic schools has an instructor otherwise employed full time by the same nonpublic school." These instructors, many of whom no doubt teach in the religious schools precisely because they are adherents of the controlling denomination and want to serve their religious community zealously, are expected during the regular school day to inculcate their students with the tenets and beliefs of their particular religious faith. Yet the premise of the program is that those instructors can put aside their religious convictions and engage in entirely secular Community Education instruction as soon as the school day is over. Moreover, they are expected to do so before the same religious-school students and in the same religious-school classrooms that they employed to advance religious purposes during the "official" school day. Nonetheless, as petitioners themselves asserted, Community Education classes are not specifically monitored for religious content.

We do not question that the dedicated and professional religious school teachers employed by the Community Education program will attempt in good faith to perform their secular mission conscientiously. Nonetheless, there is a substantial risk that, overtly or subtly, the religious message they are expected to convey during the regular school day will infuse the supposedly secular classes they teach after school. The danger arises "not because the public employee [is] likely deliberately to subvert his task to the service of religion, but rather because the pressures of the environment might alter his behavior from its normal course."

The Shared Time program, though structured somewhat differently, nonetheless also poses a substantial risk of state-sponsored indoctrination. The most important difference between the programs is that most of the instructors in the Shared Time program are full-time teachers hired by the public schools....Nonetheless, as with the Community Education program, no attempt is made to monitor the Shared Time courses for religious content.

Thus, despite these differences between the two programs, our holding in *Meek* controls the inquiry with respect to Shared Time, as well as Community Education. Shared Time instructors are teaching academic subjects in religious schools in courses virtually indistinguishable from the other courses offered during the regular religious-school day. The teachers in this program, even more than their Community Education colleagues, are "performing important educational services in schools in which education is an integral part of the dominant sectarian mission and in which an atmosphere dedicated to the advancement of religious belief is constantly maintained."...

Our cases have recognized that the Establishment Clause guards against more than direct, state-funded efforts to indoctrinate youngsters in specific religious beliefs. Government promotes religion as effectively when it fosters a close identification of its powers and responsibilities with those of any—or all—religious denominations as when it attempts to inculcate specific religious doctrines. If this identification conveys a message of government endorsement or disapproval of religion, a core purpose of the Establishment Clause is violated....

It follows that an important concern of the effects test is whether the symbolic union of church and state effected by the challenged governmental action is sufficiently likely to be perceived by adherents of the controlling denominations as an endorsement, and by the nonadherents as a disapproval, of their individual religious choices. The inquiry into this kind of effect must be conducted with particular care when many of the citizens perceiving the governmental message are children in their formative years. The symbolism of a union between church and state is most likely to influence children of tender years, whose experience is limited and whose beliefs consequently are the function of environment as much as of free and voluntary choice....

In the programs challenged in this case, the religious school students spend their typical school day moving between religious-school and "public-school" classes. Both types of classes take place in the same religious-school building and both are largely composed of students who are adherents of the same denomination. In this environment, the student would be unlikely to discern the crucial difference between the religious-school classes and the "public-school" classes, even if the latter were successfully kept free of religious indoctrination....Consequently, even the student who notices the "public school" sign temporarily posted would have before him a powerful symbol of state endorsement and encouragement of the religious beliefs taught in the same class at some other time during the day....This effect—the symbolic union of government and religion in one sectarian enterprise—is an impermissible effect under the Establishment Clause.

The Court has never accepted the mere possibility of subsidization as sufficient to invalidate an aid program. On the other hand, this effect is not wholly unimportant for Establishment Clause purposes. If it were, the public schools could gradually take on themselves the entire responsibility for teaching secular subjects on religious school premises. The question in each case must be whether the effect of the proffered aid is "direct and substantial," or indirect and incidental. "The problem, like many problems in constitutional law, is one of degree."

We have noted in the past that the religious school has dual functions, providing its students with a secular education while it promotes a particular religious perspective....The programs challenged here, which provide teachers in addition to the instructional equipment and materials, have a similar—and forbidden—effect of advancing religion. This kind of direct aid to the educational function of the religious school is indistinguishable from the provision of a direct cash subsidy to the religious school that is most clearly prohibited under the Establishment Clause.

Petitioners claim that the aid here flows primarily to the students, not to the religious schools. Of course, all aid to religious schools ultimately "flows to" the students, and petitioners' argument if accepted would validate all forms of nonideological aid to religious schools, including those explicitly rejected in our prior cases....

Petitioners also argue that this "subsidy" effect is not significant in this case, because the Community Education and Share Time programs supplemented the curriculum with courses not previously offered in the religious schools and not required by school rule or state regulation. WE do not find that this feature of the program is controlling. First, there is not way of knowing whether the religious schools would have offered some or all of these courses if the public school system had not offered them first. The distinction between courses that "supplement" and those that "supplant" the regular curriculum is therefore not nearly as clear as petitioners allege. Second, although the precise courses offered in these programs may have been new to the participating religious schools, their general subject matter— reading, math, etc.—was surely a part of the curriculum in the past, and the concerns of the Establishment Clause may thus be triggered despite the "supplemental" nature of the courses. Third, and most important, petitioners' argument would permit the public schools gradually to take over the entire secular curriculum of the religious school, for the latter could surely discontinue existing courses so that they might be replaced a year or two later by a Community Education or Shared Time course with the same content. The average religious school student, for instance, now spends 10 percent of the school day in Shared time classes. But there is no principled basis on which this Court can impose a limit on the percentage of the religious-school day that can be subsidized by the public school. To let the genie out of the bottle in this case would be to permit ever larger segments of the religious school curriculum to be turned over to the public school system, thus violating the cardinal principle that the State may not in effect become the prime supported of the religious school system.

We conclude that the challenged programs have the effect of promoting religion in three ways. The state-paid instructors, influenced by the pervasively sectarian nature of the religious schools in which they work, may subtly or overtly indoctrinate the students in partic- ular religious tenets at public expense. The symbolic union of church and state inherent in the provision of secular, state-provided instruction in the religious school buildings threat- ens to convey a message of state support for religion to students and to the general public. Finally, the programs in effect subsidize the religious functions of the parochial school by taking over a substantial portion of their responsibility for teaching secular subjects. For these reasons, the conclusion is inescapable that the Community Education and Shared Time programs have the "primary or principal" effect of advancing religion, and therefore violate the dictates of the Establishment Clause of the First Amendment.

Nonpublic schools have played an important role in the development of American edu- cation, and we have long recognized that parents and their children have the right to choose between public schools and available sectarian alternatives. As The Chief Justice noted in *Lemon v. Kurtzman*, "nothing we have said can be construed to disparage the role of church-related elementary and secondary schools in our national life. Their contribution has been and is enormous." But the Establishment Clause "rests on the belief that a union of government and religion tends to destroy government and to degrade religion." Therefore, "the Constitution decrees that religion must be a private matter for the individ- ual, the family, and the institutions of private choice, and that while some involvement and entanglement are inevitable, lines must be drawn."

Chief Justice BURGER, concurring in the judgment in part and dissenting in part.

I agree with the Court that, under our decisions in *Lemon v. Kurtzman* (1971), and *Earley v. DiCenso* (1971), the Grand Rapids Community Education program violates the Establishment Clause. As to the Share Time programs, I dissent for the reasons stated in my dissenting opinion in *Aguilar v. Felton*.

Justice O'CONNOR, concurring in the judgment in part and dissenting in part.

For the reasons stated in my dissenting opinion in *Aguilar v. Felton*, I dissent from the Court's holding that the Grand Rapids Shared Time program impermissibly advances religion. Like the New York Title I program, the Grand Rapids Shared Time program employs full-time public school teachers who offer supplemental instruction to parochial school children on the premises of religious schools. Nothing in the record indicates that Shared-Time instructors have attempted to proselytize their students. I see no reason why public school teachers in Grand Rapids are any more likely than their counterparts in New York to disobey their instructions.

The Court relies on the District Court's finding that a "significant portion of the Shared Time instructors previously taught in nonpublic schools, and many of these had been assigned to the same nonpublic school where they were previously employed." In fact, only 13 Shared Time instructors have ever been employed by a parochial school, and only a frac- tion of those 13 now work in a parochial school where they were previously employed. The experience of these few teachers does not significantly increase the risk that the perceived or actual effect of the Shared Time program will be to inculcate religion at public expense. I would uphold the Shared Time program.

I agree with the Court, however, that the Community Education program violates the Establishment Clause. The record indicates that Community Education courses in the parochial schools are overwhelmingly taught by instructors who are current full-time employees of the parochial school. The teachers offer secular subjects to the same parochial school students who attend their regular parochial school classes. In addition, the supervisors of the Community education program in the parochial schools are by and large the principals of the very schools where the classes are offered. When full-time parochial school teachers receive public funds to each secular courses to their parochial school students under parochial school supervision, I agree that the program has the perceived and actual effect of advancing the religious aims of the church-related schools. This is particularly the case where, as here, religion pervades the curriculum and the teachers are accustomed to bring religion to play in everything they teach. I concur in the judgment of the Court and the Community Education program violates the Establishment Clause.

Justice WHITE, dissenting.

I have long disagreed with the Court's interpretation and application of the Establishment Clause in the context of state aid to private schools. I am firmly of the belief that the Court's decisions in these cases, like its decision in *Lemon* and *Nyquist*, are "not required by the First Amendment and [are] contrary to the long-range interests of the country." For those same reasons, I am satisfied that what the States have sought to do in these cases is well within their authority and is not forbidden by the Establishment Clause. Hence, I dissent and would reverse the judgment in each of these cases.

Justice REHNQUIST, dissenting.

In Grand Rapids, the Court relies heavily on the principles of *Everson v. McCollum*, but declines to discuss the faulty "wall" premise upon which those cases rest. In doing so the Court blinds itself to the first 150 years' history of the Establishment Clause.

The Court today attempts to give content to the "effects" prong of the *Lemon* test by holding that a "symbolic link between government and religion" creates an impermissible effect. But one wonders how the teaching of "Math Topics," "Spanish," and "Gymnastics," which is struck down today, creates a greater "symbolic link" than the municipal creche upheld in *Lynch v. Donnelly*, or the legislative chaplain upheld in *Marsh v. Chambers* (1983).

A most unfortunate result of Grand Rapids is that to support its holding the Court, despite its disclaimers, impugns the integrity of public school teachers. Contrary to the law and the teachers' promises, they are assumed to be eager inculcators of religious dogma requiring, in the Court's words, "ongoing supervision." Not one instance of attempted religious inculcation exists in the records of the school aid cases decided today, even though both the Grand Rapids and New York programs have been in operation for a number of years. I would reverse.

Agostini v. Felton   MELVIN UROFSKY

To many, the fear that a change in Court personnel would lead to the dismember-ment of the wall of separation seemed ill-founded in the late 1980s and early 1990s. In a variety of cases the Court stuck to the precedents it had developed, and went so far in some cases that Congress passed the Religious Freedom Restoration Act in 1991 to rectify what it thought were too rigid constructions by the Court.

But, at the same time, in a series of cases beginning in the late '80s, the Court did begin to chip away at the wall, and especially at the effects and entanglement tests of *Lemon v. Kurzman*. In *Witters v. Washington Department of Services for the Blind* (1986), the Court permitted a recipient of a grant from a public agency to use that money to attend a religious-sponsored college for the express aim of becoming a minister. In *Zobrest v. Catalina Foothills School District* (1993), it permitted public funds to be used to pay a sign-language interpreter in a religious school. By 1994 a majority of the justices had expressed their belief that the rule set down in *Ball* and *Aguilar* should be reconsidered and perhaps overruled.

That message was not lost on the original plaintiffs in *Aguilar*, who used a proce-dural device to get their argument back before the high court. Following the origi-nal ruling, the District Court had issued an injunction against further use of Title I funds in parochial schools. Claiming that a series of cases had effectively overruled the basis for that injunction (the original *Aguilar* decision), they appealed to the Court under Rule 60(b) of the Federal Rules of Civil Procedure, which provide for relief from an injunction when the legal basis for that order has changed.

The slim majority that had been unhappy with *Ball* and *Aguilar*, and in fact with the entire entanglements test of Lemon, quickly seized upon this opportunity, and specifically overruled the earlier decision.

We can consider this case part of an evolving concept because it remains unclear how far the Court is willing to go in reversing nearly three decades of First Amendment jurisprudence. If, as some accomodationists charged, the earlier Court had been too rigid in its application of the Establishment Clause, then *Agostini v. Felton* may be seen as a simple correction, a move back toward the middle of the spectrum and a truer reading of what the Framers had intended. If, on the other hand, this is merely one point on a pendulum swing that has just begun, then it is impossible to tell what the current majority will eventually determine as the limits of public aid to religious education. And, of course, as in many such issues, a change of one or two seats on the Supreme Court may alter that course significantly.

▶ The Court is surely right in its argument that trying to live by the Aguilar rule has been difficult for the LEA's (local education agencies). Is that by itself suf-ficient grounds to overturn a precedent less than a dozen years old?

▶ In reading these two cases, *Ball* and *Agostini*, which argument do you find more persuasive? Why?

▶ Repeating the question from the last case: Is there any validity to the "slippery slope" argument here? If the Court permits one program of this kind to continue, is the door then opened to other similar programs?

▶ Rule 60(b) is not an easy rule to invoke, since it rarely happens that a court will overrule itself in such a short time. Reading both the Court's opinion and the dissent, do you believe that the basis for *Aguilar* was in fact abandoned? Why?

▶ Do you see this case as a reasoned and neutral application of jurisprudence, reflecting Constitutional principles, or do you see it as judicial activism, triggered by a change in Court personnel?

Agostini v. Felton 117 S.Ct. 1997 (1997)

Justice O'CONNOR delivered the opinion of the Court.

In *Aguilar v. Felton* (1985), this Court held that the Establishment Clause of the First Amendment barred the city of New York from sending public school teachers into parochial schools to provide remedial education to disadvantaged children pursuant to a congressionally mandated program. On remand, the [district court] entered a permanent injunction reflecting our ruling. Twelve years later, petitioners—the parties bound by that injunction—seek relief from its operation. Petitioners maintain that *Aguilar* cannot be squared with our intervening Establishment Clause jurisprudence and ask that we explicitly recognize what our more recent cases already dictate: *Aguilar* is no longer good law. We agree with petitioners that *Aguilar* is not consistent with our subsequent Establishment Clause decisions and further conclude that, on the facts presented here, petitioners are entitled under Federal Rule of Civil Procedure 60(b)(5) to relief from the operation of the District Court's prospective injunction.

Title I of the Elementary and Secondary Education Act of 1965 channels federal funds, through the States, to "local educational agencies" (LEA's) to provide remedial education, guidance, and job counseling to students who are failing, or at risk of failing, the State's student performance standards. Title I funds must be made available to all eligible children, regardless of whether they attend public schools, and the services provided to children attending private schools must be "equitable in comparison to services and other benefits for public school children." An LEA providing services to children enrolled in private schools is subject to a number of constraints that are not imposed when it provides aid to public schools. Title I services may be provided only to those private school students eligible for aid, and cannot be used to provide services on a "school-wide" basis. In addition, the LEA must retain complete control over Title I funds; retain title to all materials used to provide Title I services; and provide those services through public employees or other persons independent of the private school and any religious institution. The Title I services themselves must be "secular, neutral, and nonideological," and must "supplement, and in no case supplant, the level of services" already provided by the private school....

In 1978, six federal taxpayers—respondents here—sued the Board in the District Court. The District Court granted summary judgment for the Board, but the Court of Appeals for the Second Circuit reversed. In a 5-4 decision, this Court affirmed on the ground that the Board's Title I program necessitated "an excessive entanglement of church and state in the administration of Title I benefits." On remand the District Court permanently enjoined the Board "from using public funds for any plan or program under Title I to the extent that it requires, authorizes or permits public school teachers and guidance counselors to provide teaching and counseling services on the premises of sectarian schools within New York City."

The Board reverted to its prior practice of providing instruction at public school sites, at leased sites, and in mobile instructional units (essentially vans converted into classrooms) parked near the sectarian school. The Board also offered computer-aided instruction, which could be provided "on premises" because it did not require public employees to be physically present on the premises of a religious school. It is not disputed that the additional costs of complying with *Aguilar*'s mandate are significant. Since the 1986-1987 school year, the Board has spent over $100 million providing computer-aided instruction, leasing sites and mobile instructional units, and transporting students to those sites. These "*Aguilar* costs" reduce the amount of Title I money an LEA has available for remedial education, and LEA's have had to cut back on the number of students who receive Title I benefits.

The question we must answer is a simple one: Are petitioners entitled to relief from the District Court's permanent injunction under Rule 60(b)? Rule 60(b)(5) states: "On motion and upon such terms as are just, the court may relieve a party...from a final judgment or order...when it is no longer equitable that the judgment should have prospective application." We have held that it is appropriate to grant a Rule 60(b)(5) motion when the party seeking relief from an injunction or consent decree can show "a significant change either in factual conditions or in law." Petitioners argue that there have been two significant legal developments since *Aguilar* was decided: In *Board of Education of Kiryas Joel v. Grumet* (1994); a majority of Justices have expressed their views that *Aguilar* should be reconsidered or overruled and *Aguilar* has in any event been undermined by subsequent Establishment Clause decisions, including *Witters v. Washington Department of Services for the Blind* (1986), *Zobrest v. Catalina Foothills School District* (1993), and *Rosenberger v. Rector and Visitors of the University of Virginia* (1995). The statements made by five Justices in *Kiryas Joel* do not, in themselves, furnish a basis for concluding that our Establishment Clause jurisprudence has changed. The question of *Aguilar*'s propriety was not before us there. Thus, petitioners' ability to satisfy the prerequisites of Rule 60(b)(5) hinges on whether our later Establishment Clause cases have so undermined *Aguilar* that it is no longer good law.

In order to evaluate whether *Aguilar* has been eroded by our subsequent Establishment Clause cases, it is necessary to understand the rationale upon which *Aguilar*, as well as its companion case, *School District of Grand Rapids v. Ball* (1985), rested....Distilled to essentials, the Court's conclusion that the Shared Time program in *Ball* had the impermissible effect of advancing religion rested on three assumptions: (i) any public employee who works on the premises of a religious school is presumed to inculcate religion in her work; (ii) the presence of public employees on private school premises creates a symbolic union between church and state; and (iii) any and all public aid that directly aids the educational function of religious schools impermissibly finances religious indoctrination, even if the aid reaches such schools as a consequence of private decisionmaking. Additionally, in Aguilar there was a fourth assumption: that New York City's Title I program necessitated an excessive government entanglement with religion because public employees who teach on the premises of religious schools must be closely monitored to ensure that they do not inculcate religion.

Our more recent cases have undermined the assumptions upon which *Ball* and *Aguilar* relied. To be sure, the general principles we use to evaluate whether government aid violates the Establishment Clause have not changed since *Aguilar* was decided. For example, we continue to ask whether the government acted with the purpose of advancing or inhibiting religion and to explore whether the aid has the "effect" of advancing or inhibiting religion. What has changed since we decided *Ball* and *Aguilar* is our understanding of the criteria used to assess whether aid to religion has an impermissible effect.

As we have repeatedly recognized, government inculcation of religious beliefs has the impermissible effect of advancing religion. Our cases subsequent to *Aguilar* have, however, modified in two significant respects the approach we use to assess indoctrination. First, we have abandoned the presumption that the placement of public employees on parochial school grounds inevitably results in the impermissible effect of state-sponsored indoctrination or constitutes a symbolic union between government and religion. *Zobrest* expressly rejected the notion—relied on in *Ball* and *Aguilar*—that, solely because of her presence on private school property, a public employee will be presumed to inculcate religion in the students. *Zobrest* also implicitly repudiated the assumption that the presence of a public employee on private school creates an impermissible "symbolic link" between government and religion....

Second, we have departed from the rule relied on in *Ball* that all government aid that directly aids the educational function of religious schools is invalid. In *Witters*, we held that the Establishment Clause did not bar a State from issuing a vocational tuition grant to a blind person who wished to use the grant to attend a Christian college and become a pastor, missionary, or youth director. We observed that the tuition grants were "made available generally without regard to the sectarian-nonsectarian nature of the institution benefitted" and that the grants were disbursed directly to students and thus that any money that ultimately went to religious institutions did so "only as a result of the genuinely independent and private choices" of individuals. The same logic applied in *Zobrest*.

Zobrest and *Witters* make clear that, under current law, the Shared Time program in *Ball* and New York City's Title I program in *Aguilar* will not, as a matter of law, be deemed to have the effect of advancing religion through indoctrination. First, there is no reason to presume that, simply because she enters a parochial school classroom, a full-time public employee such as a Title I teacher will depart from her assigned duties and instructions and embark on religious indoctrination, any more than there was a reason in *Zobrest* to think an interpreter would inculcate religion by altering her translation of classroom lectures. *Zobrest* also repudiates *Ball*'s assumption that the presence of Title I teachers in parochial school classrooms will...create the impression of a "symbolic union" between church and State. Justice Souter maintains that Title I continues to foster a "symbolic union" between the Board and sectarian schools because it mandates "the involvement of public teachers in the instruction provided within sectarian schools" and "fuses public and private faculties." Justice Souter does not disavow the notion that Title I services may be provided to sectarian school students in off-campus locations. We do not see any perceptible (let alone dispositive) difference in the degree of symbolic union between a student receiving remedial instruction in a classroom on his sectarian school's campus and one receiving instruction in a van parked just at the school's curbside....

Where aid is allocated on the basis of neutral, secular criteria that neither favor nor disfavor religion, and is made available to both religious and secular beneficiaries on a nondiscriminatory basis, the aid is less likely to have the effect of advancing religion. In *Ball* and *Aguilar*, the Court gave this consideration no weight. Before and since those decisions, we have sustained programs that provided aid to all eligible children regardless of where they attended school. Applying this reasoning to New York City's Title I program, it is clear that Title I services are allocated on the basis of criteria that neither favor nor disfavor religion. The services are available to all children who meet the Act's eligibility requirements, no matter what their religious beliefs or where they go to school. The Board's program does not, therefore, give aid recipients any incentive to modify their religious beliefs or practices in order to obtain those services.

We turn now to *Aguilar*'s conclusion that New York City's Title I program resulted in an excessive entanglement between church and state....After *Zobrest* we no longer presume that public employees will inculcate religion simply because they happen to be in a sectarian environment. Since we have abandoned the assumption that properly instructed public employees will fail to discharge their duties faithfully, we must also discard the assumption that pervasive monitoring of Title I teachers is required.

To summarize, New York City's Title I program does not run afoul of any of three primary criteria we currently use to evaluate whether government aid has the effect of advancing religion: it does not result in governmental indoctrination; define its recipients by reference to religion; or create an excessive entanglement. We therefore hold that a federally funded program providing supplemental, remedial instruction to disadvantaged children on a neutral basis is not invalid under the Establishment Clause when such instruction is given on the premises of sectarian schools by government employees pursuant to a program containing safeguards such as those present here. The same considerations that justify this holding require us to conclude that this carefully constrained program also cannot reasonably be viewed as an endorsement of religion. Accordingly, we must acknowledge that *Aguilar*, as well as the portion of *Ball* addressing Grand Rapids' Shared Time program, are no longer good law.

Stare decisis does not prevent us from overruling a previous decision where there has been a significant change in or subsequent development of our constitutional law. Our

Establishment Clause jurisprudence has changed significantly since we decided *Ball* and *Aguilar*, so our decision to overturn those cases rests on far more than "a present doctrinal disposition to come out differently from the Court of 1985." We therefore overrule *Ball* and *Aguilar* to the extent those decisions are inconsistent with our current understanding of the Establishment Clause. We are only left to decide whether this change in law entitles petitioners to relief under Rule 60(b)(5). We conclude that it does. We reverse the judgment of the Court of Appeals and remand to the District Court with instructions to vacate its 1985 order.

Justice SOUTER, with whom Justices STEVENS and GINSBURG join, and with whom Justice BREYER joins in part, dissenting.

I believe *Aguilar* was a correct and sensible decision, and my only reservation about its opinion is that the emphasis on the excessive entanglement produced by monitoring religious instructional content obscured those facts that independently called for the application of two central tenets of Establishment Clause jurisprudence. The State is forbidden to subsidize religion directly and is just as surely forbidden to act in any way that could reasonably be viewed as religious endorsement. The flat ban on subsidization antedates the Bill of Rights and has been an unwavering rule in Establishment Clause cases, qualified only by the conclusion that state exactions from college students are not the sort of public revenues subject to the ban. (*Rosenberger v. Rector.*) The rule expresses the hard lesson learned over and over again in the American past and in the experiences of the countries from which we have come, that religions supported by governments are compromised just as surely as the religious freedom of dissenters is burdened when the government supports religion. The ban against state endorsement of religion addresses the same historical lessons. Governmental approval of religion tends to reinforce the religious message (at least in the short run) and, by the same token, to carry a message of exclusion to those of less favored views. The human tendency, of course, is to forget the hard lessons, and to overlook the history of governmental partnership with religion when a cause is worthy, and bureaucrats have programs. That tendency to forget is the reason for having the Establishment Clause (along with the Constitution's other structural and libertarian guarantees), in the hope of stopping the corrosion before it starts.

These principles were violated by the programs at issue in *Aguilar* and *Ball*, as a consequence of several significant features common to both: each provided classes on the premises of the religious schools, covering a wide range of subjects including some at the core of primary and secondary education, like reading and mathematics; while their services were termed "supplemental," the programs and their instructors necessarily assumed responsibility for teaching subjects that the religious schools would otherwise have been obligated to provide; the public employees carrying out the programs had broad responsibilities involving the exercise of considerable discretion; while the programs offered aid to nonpublic school students generally (and Title I went to public school students as well), participation by religious school students in each program was extensive; and, finally, aid flowed directly to the schools in the form of classes and programs, as distinct from indirect aid that reaches schools only as a result of independent private choice....

The Court's holding that *Aguilar* and the portion of *Ball* addressing the Shared Time program are "no longer good law" rests on mistaken reading. *Zobrest* is no sanction for overruling *Aguilar* or any portion of Ball. In *Zobrest* the Court did indeed recognize that the Establishment Clause lays down no absolute bar to placing public employees in a sectarian school, but the rejection of such a per se rule was hinged expressly on the nature of the employee's job, sign-language interpretation (or signing) and the circumscribed role of the signer. The Court explained: "The task of a sign-language interpreter seems to us quite different from that of a teacher or guidance counselor....Nothing in this record suggests that a sign-language interpreter would do more than accurately interpret whatever material is presented to the class as a whole. In fact, ethical guidelines require interpreters to 'transmit everything that is said in exactly the same way it was intended.'" The signer could thus be seen as more like a hearing aid than a teacher, and the signing could not be understood as an opportunity to inject religious content in what was supposed to be secular instruction. *Zobrest* accordingly holds only that in these limited circumstances where a public employee simply translates for one student the material presented to the class for the benefit of all students, the employee's presence in the sectarian school does not violate the Establishment Clause. Nor did *Zobrest*, implicitly or otherwise, repudiate the view that the involvement of public teachers in the instruction provided within sectarian schools looks like a partnership or union and implies approval of the sectarian aim. On the subject of symbolic unions and the strength of their implications, the lesson of *Zobrest* is merely that less is less.

The Court next claims that *Ball* rested on the assumption that "any and all public aid that directly aids the educational function of religious schools impermissibly finances religious indoctrination, even if the aid reaches such schools as a consequence of private decision-making." This mischaracterizes *Ball*. *Ball* did not establish that "any and all" such aid to religious schools necessarily violates the Establishment Clause. It held that the Shared Time program subsidized the religious functions of the parochial schools by taking over a significant portion of their responsibility for teaching secular subjects. The Court noted that it had "never accepted the mere possibility of subsidization...as sufficient to invalidate an aid program," and instead enquired whether the effect of the proffered aid was "direct and substantial" (and, so, unconstitutional) or merely "indirect and incidental" (and, so, permissible) emphasizing that the question "is one of degree." Witters and Zobrest did nothing to repudiate the principle, emphasizing rather the limited nature of the aid at issue in each case as well as the fact that religious institutions did not receive it directly from the State....

Finally, instead of aid that comes to the religious school indirectly in the sense that its distribution results from private decision-making, a public educational agency distributes Title I aid in the form of programs and services directly to the religious schools. In *Zobrest* and *Witters*, it was fair to say that individual students were themselves applicants for individual benefits. But under Title I, a local educational agency may receive federal funding by proposing programs approved to serve individual students who meet the criteria of need, which it then uses to provide such programs at the religious schools; students eligible for such programs may not apply directly for Title I funds. In sum, nothing since *Ball* and *Aguilar* and before this case has eroded the distinction between "direct and substantial" and "indirect and incidental." That principled line is being breached only here and now.

And if a scheme of government aid results in support for religion in some substantial degree, or in endorsement of its value, the formal neutrality of the scheme does not render the Establishment Clause helpless or the holdings in *Aguilar* and *Ball* inapposite.

(Justice GINSBURG dissented, joined by Justices STEVENS, SOUTER, and BREYER. She objected on technical grounds to the Court's use of Rule 60(b), claiming that a new majoirity had distorted the intent of the rule and also ignored stare decisis *in order to reach a result it wanted, a result unsupported by cases following* Ball *and* Aguilar.*)*

II Free Speech and Access to Information

New York Times v. Sullivan (1964)

New York Times v. United States (Pentagon Papers) (1971)

Miller v. California (1973)

Board of Education v. Pico (1982)

Texas v. Johnson (1989)/ United States v. Eichman (1990)

Madsen v. Women's Health Center (1994)

Reno v. American Civil Liberties Union (1997)

II Free Speech and Access to Information

ROBERT M. O'NEIL

The speech and press clauses of our First Amendment contain the oldest and most durable guarantee of free expression to be found anywhere in the world. Despite persistent pressures—for example, to make flag burning a crime—these words have never been altered or amended. They stand today just as they were proposed in 1789 and ratified in 1791.

Yet the meaning of these guarantees has changed markedly over time. In terms of the "speech" and "press" to which the First Amendment refers, there have been dramatic changes. The Framers knew and practiced relatively simple forms of spoken and written expression. They could hardly have anticipated motion pictures, radio and television, telephone, cable and fax, much less the Internet. Somehow the basic terms "speech" and "press" have simply adapted over time to keep pace with, and eventually to embrace, these new technologies. Even so, the levels of protection applied to different media have varied markedly, with licensed broadcasting (most notably) remaining a "second class" citizen within the world of communications.

There have also been extensions of First Amendment protection beyond words in any form—especially to non-verbal or symbolic expression. While we can never be certain such an extension would meet with favor from the Framers, we may assume that a generation quite familiar with the Boston Tea Party and other acts of symbolic protest would not have wished to confine their charter of liberty to words spoken or written on paper. Even so, there are those who even today argue for a narrow reading of the First Amendment and of the key terms it contains.

First Amendment case law is surprisingly recent. Cases in this area did not reach the Supreme Court until the 1920s. Only in the middle of that decade did the Justices extend the federal speech and press guarantees to the states—though most of them had comparable safeguards in their own constitutions. The development of the law since that time has been surprisingly slow; few cases likely to be cited in current courses or casebooks preceded the 1960s, when the pace of the First Amendment litigation went into high gear.

The courts generally indulge a vital presumption that speech (or expressive activity) is protected unless it loses protection under one of the several recognized exceptions. Speech that incites, or creates an imminent danger of unlawful conduct, may be regulated. Obscenity lies beyond the reach of the First Amendment, as does child pornography. "Fighting words" that pose an imminent risk of violence may incur sanctions, even though speech is involved. Defaming a private person may give rise to civil damages, as least so long as there is some evidence of fault. Commercial speech enjoys some protection—though false and misleading advertising, or promotion of illegal products and services may not claim First Amendment benefit. These and a few other carefully defined categories are the only exceptions; despite persistent efforts to add other exceptions, the courts in this country have been quite vigilant.

The Supreme Court has recently become especially critical of restrictions imposed on speech because of its message or viewpoint—hate speech codes or laws, for example, or efforts to ban such protest activities as flag desecration. Even where the expression may not be fully protected—fighting words, for example—government may not pick and choose on the basis of messages it likes or dislikes. Thus the protection for expression as such now extends quite clearly to the protection of viewpoints and messages as well.

On the other hand, regulation that deals only with the time, place, and manner of expression—and is therefore content-neutral—stands on somewhat firmer ground. Courts have long deferred to such restrictions designed to maintain the flow of traffic, curb excessive noise levels at certain times and in certain places, and to guard against conflicts in the use of scarce facilities. Though the line between content-based and content-neutral regulation is not always perfectly clear, the distinction is basic to First Amendment law.

Hardly a Term of the Supreme Court passes without several major new free speech and press cases. Often those cases deal with media—whether news media, or novel technologies like the Internet. Yet there are also a number of traditional issues—protests and demonstrations, newspaper and magazine publications, and access to parks and other physical speaking facilities. The remarkable durability of the First Amendment through its first two centuries bodes extremely well for the next century and beyond.

▶ While it is clear that the First Amendment fully protects political speech, what about the arts and entertainment? Do such different forms of expression equally claim protection under a single constitutional provision?

▶ By what process have courts moved from written and spoken words as "speech" and "press" to such new technologies as broadcasting, fax, and cable, and now the Internet? Would it help expressly to add each new medium to the terms of the First Amendment?

▶ Restrictions on speech are sometimes criminal (punishment for inciting a breach of the peace) and at other times civil (suits for damages for libel). What are the differences, and how differently should the two types of proceedings be treated?

▶ Why is there such a deep abhorrence to a "prior restraint"—that is, a court order that prevents a person from speaking, writing, or publishing?

▶ Would the Framers have been comfortable with the recent extension of "speech" to encompass symbolic or non-verbal communication?

▶ When a given event involves a mixture of both speech and conduct, how should courts factor out the elements—or should they treat it as all one or all the other?

▶ Should there be a general presumption that speech is protected unless it falls within one of the clearly defined exceptions (like incitement or fighting words)? Is that helpful?

New York Times v. Sullivan   MELVIN UROFSKY

The First Amendment guarantee of a free press assumes that the fullest public discussion is vital to a self-governing society. But libelous statements, like obscenity, were long considered beyond the reach of the First Amendment's protection. Not only could individuals sue for libel damages, but the state's police powers could be employed to protect the reputation of its citizens. In England, libel originally consisted of any statement, true or not, that injured a person's reputation; in America, since the eighteenth century truth has been a defense against charges of libel. So if Ms. Y stated that "Mr. X has embezzled funds from the church," Mr. X could sue on the grounds that his character had been defamed. Ms. Y could only escape punishment if she could prove her allegations true; she could not claim that her charges enjoyed First Amendment protection.

In March 1960, in a full-page advertisement in the *New York Times* entitled "Heed Their Rising Voices," a civil rights committee charged the existence of "an unprecedented wave of terror" against blacks in Montgomery, Alabama. Sullivan, the Montgomery police commissioner, sued the *Times* and several black clergymen who had signed the ad. He objected to a number of statements, and especially the claim that "truckloads of police armed with shotguns and tear gas ringed the Alabama State College Campus" in Montgomery, and that Martin Luther King, Jr., had been assaulted and arrested seven times.

There were, indeed, some errors of fact in the text; Dr. King had been arrested four times, not seven. But under Alabama law Sullivan only had to prove that he had suffered injury to his reputation or that the libel had brought him into public contempt. He did not have to prove that he had suffered any real financial injury. An Alabama jury found against the *Times*, and awarded Sullivan $500,000, which the state's high court upheld. The Supreme Court unanimously reversed. In holding that newspapers could not be held liable for comment on public officials, the Court thus opened a new chapter in First Amendment jurisprudence.

The philosophical argument is one James Madison would have clearly understood, namely, that in public debate even false statements have value in helping determine the truth. Justice Brennan quoted John Stuart Mill to this effect, that a false statement brings about "the clearer perception and livelier impression of truth, produced by its collision with error." Such collision inevitably occurs when there exists "uninhibited, robust and wide-open" public debate.

Unlike the obscenity cases, where the Court unsuccessfully sought some objective criteria to guide its decisions, the principle in the *Times* case is straightforward though its application is not. Public persons, such as government officials, have no protection against statements made about their public conduct, with the exception of false statements made knowingly and with malice; it is unclear, however, where the Court has drawn lines that define this group.

- We can agree that a public official's *public* conduct, that is, how he or she discharges the duties of office, must be open to full public scrutiny. But how far should this searchlight extend into the official's private life? Should we allow the press to print or broadcast whatever it deems newsworthy?

- Can one make a meaningful distinction between a senator's or a governor's public and private life?

- Should statements on public *issues* be protected regardless of who makes the statement?

- Is there any reason for the public to know or care about a public official's private affairs? Should we care, for example, if a mayor beats his wife or a councilperson is a lesbian? Why?

- Some critics have charged that the *Times* decision has made the press less careful with its facts and more willing to engage in reckless and irresponsible journalism. Is this a valid criticism?

- Many say that the press is so powerful and affluent that the Court should not give it protection. Is this a compelling viewpoint?

- In terms of balance, which makes for a more robust public exchange of ideas, a press operating under the *Times* rule or one that is held strictly accountable by pre-*Times* libel laws? Why?

New York Times Company v. Sullivan 376 U.S. 254 (1964)

Mr. Justice BRENNAN delivered the opinion of the Court.

We are required in this case to determine for the first time the extent to which the constitutional protection for speech and press limit a State's power to award damages in a libel action brought by a public official against critics of his official conduct....

Under Alabama law, a publication is "libelous per se" if the words "tend to injure a person in his reputation" or to "bring him into public contempt"; the trial court stated that the standard was met if the words are such as to "injure him in his public office, or impute misconduct to him in his office, or want of official integrity, or want of fidelity to a public trust." The jury must find that the words were published "of and concerning" the plaintiff, but where the plaintiff is a public official his place in the governmental hierarchy is sufficient evidence to support a finding that his reputation has been affected by statements that reflect upon the agency of which he is in charge. Once "libel per se" has been established, the defendant has no defense as to stated facts unless he can persuade the jury that they were true in all their particulars. Unless he can discharge the burden of proving truth, general damages are presumed, and may be awarded without proof of pecuniary injury. The question before us is whether this rule of liability, as applied to an action brought by a public official against critics of his official conduct, abridges the freedom of speech and of the press....

Respondents and the Alabama courts rely heavily on statements of this Court to the effect that the Constitution does not protect libelous publications. Those statements do not foreclose our inquiry here. None of the cases sustained the use of libel laws to impose sanctions upon expression critical of the official conduct of public officials. Like insurrection, contempt, advocacy of unlawful acts, breach of the peace, obscenity, solicitation of illegal business, and the various other formulae for the repression of expression that have been challenged in this Court, libel can claim no talismanic immunity from constitutional limitations. It must be measured by standards that satisfy the First Amendment....

We consider this case against the background of a profound national commitment to the principle that debate on public issues should be uninhibited, robust, and wide-open, and that it may well include vehement, caustic, and sometimes unpleasantly sharp attacks on government and public officials. The present advertisement, as an expression of grievance and protest on one of the major public issues of our time, would seem clearly to qualify for the constitutional protection. The question is whether it forfeits that protection by the falsity of some of its factual statements and by its alleged defamation of respondent. Authoritative interpretations of the First Amendment guarantees have consistently refused to recognize an exception for any test of truth—whether administered by judges, juries, or administrative officials—and especially not one that puts the burden of proving truth on the speaker. "The constitutional protection does not turn upon the truth, popularity, or social utility of the ideas and beliefs which are offered." Erroneous statement is inevitable in free debate and must be protected if the freedoms of expression are to have the "breathing space" that they "need to survive." Injury to official reputation affords no more warrant for repressing speech that would otherwise be free than does factual error. Criticism of official conduct does not lose its constitutional protection merely because it is effective criticism and hence diminishes official reputations.

If neither factual error nor defamatory content suffices to remove the constitutional shield from criticism of official conduct, the combination of the two elements is no less inadequate. This is the lesson to be drawn from the great controversy over the Sedition Act of 1798, 1 Stat. 596, which first crystallized a national awareness of the central meaning of the First Amendment. Although the Sedition Act was never tested in this Court, the attack upon its validity has carried the day in the court of history. Fines levied in its prosecution were repaid by Act of Congress on the ground that it was unconstitutional. Jefferson, as President, pardoned those who had been convicted and sentenced under the Act and remitted their fines. These views reflect a broad consensus that the Act, because of the restraint it imposed upon criticism of government and public officials, was inconsistent with the First Amendment....

What a State may not constitutionally bring about by means of a criminal statute is likewise beyond the reach of its civil law of libel. The fear of damage awards under a rule such as that invoked by the Alabama courts here may be markedly more inhibiting than the fear of prosecution under a criminal statute. The judgment awarded in this case—without the need for any proof of actual pecuniary loss—was 100 times greater than that provided by the Sedition Act. And since there is no double jeopardy limitation applicable to civil lawsuits, this is not the only judgment that may be awarded against petitioners for the same publication. Whether or not a newspaper can survive a succession of such judgments, the pall of fear and timidity imposed upon those who would give voice to public criticism is an atmosphere in which the First Amendment freedoms cannot survive....

Reversed and remanded.

Mr. Justice BLACK, with whom Mr. Justice DOUGLAS joins (concurring).

...I base my vote to reverse on the belief that the First and Fourteenth Amendments not merely "delimit" a State's power to award damages to "public officials against critics of their official conduct" but completely prohibit a State from exercising such a power. "Malice," even as defined by the Court, is an elusive, abstract concept, hard to prove and hard to disprove. The requirement that malice be proved provides at best an evanescent protection for the right critically to discuss public affairs. Therefore, I vote to reverse exclusively on the ground that the defendants had an absolute, unconditional constitutional right to publish in the Times advertisement their criticisms of the Montgomery agencies and officials....

New York Times Co. v. United States (The Pentagon Papers Case)

MELVIN UROFSKY

In 1971, both the *New York Times* and the *Washington Post* secured copies of a secret Defense Department study about the origins and conduct of the war in Vietnam. The *Times* began publication of the "Pentagon Papers," as they came to be called, on June 13, and the *Post* began its serialization five days later. The government immediately tried to bar publication, and sought injunctions against the two papers in local federal district courts. In both suits, the district judges ruled that the government had failed to prove that its reasons for suppression outweighed the constitutional right to a free press and the *Near* rule against prior restraint.

On appeal, the Circuit Court for the District of Columbia upheld the lower court verdict, while the Second Circuit in New York granted an injunction. All this took place in just over a week. The Supreme Court granted *certiorari* on June 25, heard arguments the next day, and handed down its decision on the 30th. The Court issued a temporary stay while it heard the case, in effect halting publication. Four of the justices—Black, Douglas, Brennan, and Marshall—dissented from granting *certiorari*, believing the issues so clear that the Court should have issued a summary judgment against the government. The final decision was issued *per curiam*, "by the Court," because although a majority agreed that the government could not prevent publication, no five justices agreed in the reasoning behind that opinion.

Part of the government's problem derived from the fact that many of the documents had become widely available. Justice Douglas commented in a footnote: "There are numerous sets of this material in existence and they apparently are not under any controlled custody. Moreover, the President has sent a set to the Congress. We start then with a case where there already is rather wide distribution of the material that is destined for publicity, not secrecy. I have gone over the material listed in the *in camera* brief of the United States. It is all history, not future events. None of it is more recent than 1968."

In fact scholars in the field and foreign affairs specialists already knew about or had seen much of this material. The Nixon Administration, in its effort to halt publication, cited reasons of national security; but it also found publication embarrassing. Some of the documents undermined the credibility of administration arguments about its conduct of foreign policy.

The case does raise some troubling questions. The Court has repeatedly held that in cases of genuine danger to national security, the government might attempt to secure prior restraint. But in only one instance to date has a court in fact barred publication on the grounds of danger to national security. In *United States v. Progressive, Inc.* (1979), U.S. District Judge Robert W. Warren issued an order suppressing an article entitled "The H-Bomb Secret: How We Got It, Why We're Telling It." The following year, as a result of an agreement with *The Progressive*, the government abandoned the case before an appeal could be prosecuted because similar material had been published during the litigation.

▶ Should the government be able to bar publication of information dangerous to national security?

▶ If so, who should determine if in fact the material is potentially harmful—the President or the Court?

> ▶ In Great Britain, the Official Secrets Act lets the government identify nearly anything it wants as a secret, and thus prevent publication. Would a similar law be appropriate in the United States?
>
> ▶ The standard by which a government request for prior restraint is evaluated is "grave and irreparable danger." Is this a precise standard?
>
> ▶ Some of the justices complained about the haste in which the Court granted *certiorari*, heard arguments, and delivered its opinion. Were the best interests of the country and of the Court well served or hurt by this speed—or was the speed inevitable under the circumstances?

New York Times Co. v. United States (The Pentagon Papers Case) 403 U.S. 713 (1971)

PER CURIAM.

We granted *certiorari* in these cases in which the United States seeks to enjoin the New York Times and the Washington Post from publishing the contents of a classified study entitled "History of U. S. Decision-Making Process on Viet Nam Policy."

Any system of prior restraints of expression comes to this Court bearing a heavy presumption against its constitutional validity. The Government "thus carries a heavy burden of showing justification for the enforcement of such a restraint." The District Court in the New York Times case and the District Court and the Court of Appeals in the Washington Post case held that the Government had not met that burden. We agree.

The judgment of the Court of Appeals for the District of Columbia Circuit is therefore affirmed. The order of the Court of Appeals for the Second Circuit is reversed and the case is remanded with directions to enter a judgment affirming the judgment of the District Court. The stays entered June 25, 1971, by the Court are vacated. The mandates shall issue forthwith.

So ordered.

Mr. Justice BLACK, with whom Mr. Justice DOUGLAS joins, concurring.

I adhere to the view that the Government's case against the *Washington Post* should have been dismissed and the injunction against the *New York Times* should have been vacated without oral argument when the cases were first presented to this Court. I believe that every moment's continuance of the injunctions against these newspapers amounts to a flagrant, indefensible, and continuing violation of the First Amendment. Furthermore, after oral arguments, I agree completely with my Brothers Douglas and Brennan. In my view it is unfortunate that some of my Brethren are apparently willing to hold that the publication of news may sometimes be enjoined. Such a holding would make a shambles of the First Amendment. The press was protected by the First Amendment so that it could bare the secrets of government and inform the people. Only a free and unrestrained press can effectively expose deception in government. To find that the President has "inherent power" to halt the publication of news by resort to the courts would wipe out the First Amendment. The word "security" is a broad, vague generality whose contours should not be invoked to abrogate the fundamental law embodied in the First Amendment....

Mr. Justice DOUGLAS, with whom Mr. Justice BLACK joins, concurring.

The First Amendment leaves, in my view, no room for governmental restraint on the press. There is, moreover, no statute barring the publication by the press of the material which the *Times* and *Post* seek to use. {18 U.S.C. Sec. 793 (e), prohibiting "communication" of information relating to the national defense that could be used to the injury of the United States, does not apply to publication.} It is apparent that Congress was capable of and did distinguish between publishing and communication in the various sections of the Espionage Act.

So any power that the Government possesses must come from its "inherent power." The power to wage war is "the power to wage war successfully." But the war power stems from a declaration of war. The Constitution by Article 1, Sec. 8, gives Congress, not the President, power "to declare War." Nowhere are presidential wars authorized. We need not decide therefore what leveling effect the war power of Congress might have.

These disclosures may have a serious impact. But that is no basis for sanctioning a previous restraint on the press. The Government says that it has inherent powers to go into court and obtain an injunction to protect national security. [*Near v. Minnesota*] repudiated that expansive doctrine in no uncertain terms. The dominant purpose of the First Amendment was to prohibit the widespread practice of governmental suppression of embarrassing information. A debate of large proportions goes on in the Nation over our posture in Vietnam. Open debate and discussion of public issues are vital to our national health. The stays in these cases that have been in effect for more than a week constitute a flouting of the principles of the First Amendment.

Mr. Justice BRENNAN, concurring.

The error that has pervaded these cases from the outset was the granting of any injunctive relief whatsoever, interim or otherwise. The entire thrust of the Government's claim throughout these cases has been that publication of the material sought to be enjoined "could," or "might," or "may" prejudice the national interest in various ways. But the First Amendment tolerates absolutely no prior judicial restraints of the press predicated upon surmise or conjecture that untoward consequences may result. Our cases, it is true, have indicated that there is a single, extremely narrow class of cases in which the First Amendment's ban on prior judicial restraint may be overridden. Our cases have thus far indicated that such cases may arise only when the Nation "is at war," during which times "no one would question but that a government might prevent actual obstruction to its recruiting service or the publication of the sailing dates of transports or the number and location of troops." Even if the present world situation were assumed to be tantamount to a time of war, or if the power of presently available armaments would justify even in peacetime the suppression of information that would set in motion a nuclear holocaust, in neither of these actions has the Government presented or even alleged that publication of items from or based upon the material at issue would cause the happening of an event of that nature. "The chief purpose of the First Amendment's guarantee is to prevent previous restraints upon publication." Thus, only governmental allegation and proof that publication must inevitably, directly and immediately cause the occurrence of an event kindred to imperiling the safety of a transport already at sea can support even the issuance of an interim restraining order. Unless and until the Government has clearly made out its case, the First Amendment commands that no injunction may issue.

Mr. Justice STEWART, with whom Mr. Justice WHITE joins, concurring.

The only effective restraint upon executive policy and power in the areas of national defense and international affairs may lie in an enlightened citizenry. For this reason, it is perhaps here that a press that is alert, aware, and free most vitally serves the basic purpose of the First Amendment. Yet it is elementary that the successful conduct of international diplomacy and the maintenance of an effective national defense require both confidentiality and secrecy. I think there can be but one answer to this dilemma, if dilemma it be. The responsibility must be where the power is. The Executive must have the largely unshared duty to determine and preserve the degree of internal security necessary to exercise its power successfully. It is the constitutional duty of the Executive—as a matter of sovereign prerogative and not as a matter of law as the courts know law—through the promulgation and enforcement of executive regulations to protect the confidentiality necessary to carry out its responsibilities in the fields of international relations and national defense. This is not to say that Congress and the courts have no role to play. Undoubtedly Congress has the power to enact specific and appropriate criminal laws to protect government property and preserve government secrets....

But in the cases before us we are asked neither to construe specific regulations nor to apply specific laws. We are asked, instead, to perform a function that the Constitution gave to the Executive, not the Judiciary. We are asked, quite simply, to prevent the publication by two newspapers of material that the Executive Branch insists should not, in the national interest, be published. I am convinced that the Executive is correct with respect to some of the documents involved. But I cannot say that disclosure of any of them will surely result in direct, immediate, and irreparable damage to our Nation or its people. That being so, there can under the First Amendment be but one judicial resolution of the issues before us. I join the judgments of the Court.

Mr. Justice WHITE, with whom Mr. Justice STEWART joins, concurring.

I concur in today's judgments, but only because of the concededly extraordinary protection against prior restraints enjoyed by the press under our constitutional system. I do not say that in no circumstances would the First Amendment permit an injunction against publishing information about government plans or operations. Nor, after examining the materials the Government characterizes as the most sensitive and destructive, can I deny that revelation of these documents will do substantial damage to public interests. Indeed, I am confident that their disclosure will have that result. But I nevertheless agree that the United

States has not satisfied the very heavy burden which it must meet to warrant an injunction against publication in these cases, at least in the absence of express and appropriately limited congressional authorization for prior restraints in circumstances such as these.

The Government's position is simply stated: The responsibility of the Executive for the conduct of the foreign affairs and for the security of the Nation is so basic that the President is entitled to an injunction against publication of a newspaper story whenever he can convince a court that the information to be revealed threatens "grave and irreparable" injury to the public interest; and the injunction should issue whether or not the material to be published is classified, whether or not publication would be lawful under relevant criminal statutes enacted by Congress and regardless of the circumstances by which the newspaper came into possession of the information. At least in the absence of legislation by Congress, based on its own investigations and findings, I am quite unable to agree that the inherent powers of the Executive and the courts reach so far as to authorize remedies having such sweeping potential for inhibiting publications by the press. To sustain the Government in these cases would start the courts down a long and hazardous road that I am not willing to travel, at least without congressional guidance and direction....

Mr. Justice MARSHALL, concurring.

I believe the ultimate issue in this case is whether this Court or the Congress has the power to make law. In some situations it may be that under whatever inherent powers the Executive may have, there is a basis for the invocation of the equity jurisdiction of this Court as an aid to prevent the publication of material damaging to "national security," however that term may be defined. It would, however, be utterly inconsistent with the concept of separation of powers for this Court to use its power of contempt to prevent behavior that Congress has specifically declined to prohibit. There would be a similar damage to the basic concept of these co-equal branches of Government if when the executive had adequate authority granted by Congress to protect "national security" it can choose instead to invoke the contempt power of a court to enjoin the threatened conduct. In these cases we are not faced with a situation where Congress has failed to provide the Executive with broad power to protect the Nation from disclosure of damaging state secrets. It is plain that Congress has specifically refused to grant the authority the Government seeks from this Court. It is not for this Court to fling itself into every breach perceived by some Government official....

Mr. Justice HARLAN, with whom Chief Justice BURGER and Mr. Justice BLACKMUN join, dissenting.

I consider that the Court has been almost irresponsibly feverish in dealing with these cases.

Both the Court of Appeals for the Second Circuit and the Court of Appeals for the District of Columbia Circuit rendered judgment on June 23. The *New York Times'* petition for *certiorari*, its motion for accelerated consideration thereof, and its application for interim relief were filed in this Court on June 24, at about 11 a.m. The application of the United States for interim relief in the Post case was also filed here on June 24, at about 7:15 p.m. This Court's order setting a hearing before us on June 26 at 11 a.m., a course which I joined only to avoid the possibility of even more peremptory action by the Court, was issued less than

24 hours later. The record in the Post case was filed with the Clerk shortly before 1 p.m. on June 25; the record in the Times case did not arrive until 7 or 8 o'clock that same night. The briefs of the parties were received less than two hours before argument on June 26....

These are difficult questions of fact, of law, and of judgment; the potential consequences of erroneous decision are enormous. The time which has been available to us, to the lower courts, and to the parties has been wholly inadequate for giving these cases the kind of consideration they deserve. It is a reflection on the stability of the judicial process that these great issues—as important as any that have arisen during my time on the Court—should have been decided under the pressures engendered by the torrent of publicity that has attended these litigations from their inception.

Forced as I am to reach the merits of these cases, I dissent from the opinion and judgments of the Court. Within the severe limitations imposed by the time constraints under which I have been required to operate, I can only state my reasons in telescoped form. It is plain to me that the scope of the judicial function in passing upon the activities of the Executive Branch of the Government in the field of foreign affairs is very narrowly restricted. This view is, I think, dictated by the concept of separation of powers upon which our constitutional system rests. I agree that, in performance of its duty to protect the values of the First Amendment against political pressures, the judiciary must review the initial Executive determination to the point of satisfying itself that the subject matter of the dispute does lie within the proper compass of the President's foreign relations power. Constitutional considerations forbid "a complete abandonment of judicial control." Moreover, the judiciary may properly insist that the determination that disclosure of the subject matter would irreparably impair the national security be made by the head of the Executive Department concerned—here the Secretary of State or the Secretary of Defense—after actual personal consideration by that officer. But in my judgment the judiciary may not properly go beyond these two inquiries and redetermine for itself the probable impact of disclosure on the national security. "The very nature of executive decisions as to foreign policy is political, not judicial. Such decisions are wholly confided by our Constitution to the political departments. They are delicate, complex, and involve large elements of prophecy. They are and should be undertaken only by those directly responsible to the people whose welfare they advance or imperil. They are decisions of a kind for which the Judiciary has neither aptitude, facilities nor responsibility and which has long been held to belong in the domain of political power not subject to judicial intrusion or inquiry."...

Pending further hearings in each case conducted under the appropriate ground rules, I would continue the restraints on publication. I cannot believe that the doctrine prohibiting prior restraints reaches to the point of preventing courts from maintaining the status quo long enough to act responsibly in matters of such national importance as those involved here.

Mr. Justice BLACKMUN, dissenting.

I join Mr. Justice Harlan in his dissent. The First Amendment, after all, is only one part of an entire Constitution. First Amendment absolutism has never commanded a majority of this Court. What is needed here is a weighing, upon properly developed standards, of the broad right of the press to print and of the very narrow right of the Government to prevent. Such standards are not yet developed. The parties here are in disagreement as to what those standards should be. But even the newspapers concede that there are situations where restraint is in order and is constitutional. I therefore would remand these cases to be developed expeditiously, of course, but on a schedule permitting orderly presentation of evidence.

Miller v. California   MELVIN UROFSKY

This case constituted the Burger Court's first major decision on pornography. Miller had conducted a mass mailing campaign advertising illustrated books which he labeled "adult material." The brochures, according to the Court, "contained some descriptive printed material, [but] primarily they consist of pictures and drawings very explicitly depicting men and women in groups of two or more engaging in a variety of sexual activities with genitals often prominently displayed." California had arrested, tried and convicted Miller for the misdemeanor of "knowingly distributing obscene material."

The Court first took up obscenity as a constitutional question in *Roth v. United States* (1957); until then obscene material had been considered beyond the limits of First Amendment protection. Although *Roth* reasserted that obscenity is not "speech" and therefore not protected, the majority in that case also made clear that regulation of obscenity could raise First Amendment issues. In order to regulate obscenity, and do so without violating the First Amendment, the state would have to define precisely what it considered to be obscene material. Much of the litigation for the next fifteen years focused on this effort at definition. Rarely did the Court deal with the fundamental question of what important state interests justified efforts to restrain pornography.

Perhaps the justices avoided the question because they could not agree on a viable definition of obscenity. Justice Brennan, in his *Roth* opinion, stated this seemingly simple test of pornography: "whether to the average person, applying contemporary community standards, the dominant theme of the material taken as a whole appeals to prurient interest." Over the next few years the Court attempted to refine this definition with references to socially redeeming value or the lack thereof; the method and tone of distribution; the application of a national standard; and other considerations. Between 1957 and 1968, the Court heard thirteen obscenity cases which elicited *fifty-five* separate opinions. Justice Stewart in one case just threw up his hands at the problem of definition, and declared that in regard to hard-core pornography, all he could say was "I know it when I see it." The difficulty, of course, lies in the fact that all of the standards put forth by the Court are *subjective*, and as the humorist Tom Lehrer reminded us, "Obscenity is in the eye of the beholder."

Miller attempted to get the Court out of the literary and artistic criticism business, and to make obscenity primarily a question of fact to be tried, like all other questions of fact, by local juries. The test is an expansion of *Roth*, and whether it will work any better is difficult to tell, since the Court has avoided taking any similar cases on appeal since then.

> ▶ Aside from the protection of children, are there any justifiable reasons for a state to regulate pornography? Does the Constitution forbid consenting adults privately indulging in pornographic activities?
>
> ▶ Since definition is obviously critical in this area, who should determine what constitutes obscene material, the legislature, the courts, or civil juries?
>
> ▶ Is the so-called LAPS test set out in this case, (i.e., "whether the work, taken as a whole, lacks serious literary, artistic, political, or scientific value,") any more workable than Justice Brennan's "contemporary community standards" formula stated in *Roth*?
>
> ▶ Should the state be empowered to stop an adult person from voluntarily and knowingly going into a movie theater to watch a pornographic film, or renting an X-rated tape to watch at home, or purchasing a book or magazine with explicit sexual content to read at home?
>
> ▶ Civil libertarians worry that efforts to establish community criteria will adversely affect important new works of art, and recall that James Joyce's *Ulysses* was once banned as obscene. Does the community have the right to ban material it finds offensive? What, if any, limits should be imposed on this power? How might such power be abused?
>
> ▶ Is pornographic material harmful? To whom? How? Can this be proven?

Miller v. California 413 U.S. 15 (1973)

Mr. Chief Justice BURGER delivered the opinion of the Court.

This is one of a group of "obscenity-pornography" cases being reviewed by the Court in a re-examination of standards enunciated in earlier cases involving what Mr. Justice Harlan called "the intractable obscenity problem." This case involves the application of a State's criminal obscenity statute to a situation in which sexually explicit materials have been thrust by aggressive sales action upon unwilling recipients who had in no way indicated any desire to receive such materials. This Court has recognized that the States have a legitimate interest in prohibiting dissemination or exhibition of obscene material when the mode of dissemination carries with it a significant danger of offending the sensibilities of unwilling recipients or of exposure to juveniles. It is in this context that we are called on to define the standards which must be used to identify obscene material that a State may regulate.

Since the Court now undertakes to formulate standards more concrete than those in the past, it is useful for us to focus on two of the landmark cases in the somewhat tortured history of the Court's obscenity decisions. While *Roth* presumed "obscenity" to be "utterly without redeeming social value," *Memoirs v. Massachusetts* [1966] required that to prove obscenity it must be affirmatively established that the material is "utterly without redeeming social value." Thus, even as they repeated the words of *Roth*, the *Memoirs* plurality produced a drastically altered test that called on the prosecution to prove a negative, i.e., that the material was "utterly without redeeming social value"—a burden virtually impossible to discharge. Apart from the initial formulation in the *Roth* case, no majority of the Court has at any given time been able to agree on a standard to determine what constitutes obscene, pornographic material subject to regulation under the States' police power. The variety of views is not remarkable, for in the area of freedom of speech and press the courts must always remain sensitive to any infringement on genuinely serious literary, artistic, political, or scientific expression. This is an area in which there are few eternal verities....

This much has been categorically settled by the Court, that obscene material is unprotected by the First Amendment. We acknowledge, however, the inherent dangers of undertaking to regulate any form of expression. State statutes designed to regulate obscene materials must be carefully limited. As a result, we now confine the permissible scope of such regulation to works which depict or describe sexual conduct. That conduct must be specifically defined by the applicable state law, as written or authoritatively construed. A state offense must also be limited to works which, taken as a whole, appeal to the prurient interest in sex, which portray sexual conduct in a patently offensive way, and which, taken as a whole, do not have serious literary, artistic, political, or scientific value.

The basic guidelines for the trier of fact must be: (a) whether "the average person, applying contemporary community standards" would find that the work, taken as a whole, appeals to the prurient interest, (b) whether the work depicts or describes, in a patently offensive way, sexual conduct specifically defined by the applicable state law, and (c) whether the work, taken as a whole, lacks serious literary, artistic, political, or scientific value. We do not adopt as a constitutional standard the "utterly without redeeming social value" test; that concept has never commanded the adherence of more than three Justices at one time. If a state law that regulates obscene material is thus limited, as written or construed, First Amendment values are adequately protected by the ultimate power of appellate courts to conduct an independent review of constitutional claims when necessary.

We emphasize that it is not our function to propose regulatory schemes for the States. It is possible, however, to give a few plain examples of what a state statute could define for regulation under the second part (b) of the standard announced in this opinion: (a) Patently offensive representations or descriptions of ultimate sexual acts, normal or perverted, actual or simulated. (b) Patently offensive representations or descriptions of masturbation, excretory functions, and lewd exhibition of the genitals.

Sex and nudity may not be exploited without limit by films or pictures exhibited or sold in places of public accommodation any more than live sex and nudity can be exhibited or sold without limit in such public places. At a minimum, prurient, patently offensive depiction or description of sexual conduct must have serious literary, artistic, political, or scientific value to merit First Amendment protection. For example, medical books for the education of physicians and related personnel necessarily use graphic illustrations and descriptions of human anatomy. In resolving the inevitably sensitive questions of fact and law, we must continue to rely on the jury system, accompanied by the safeguards that judges, rules of evidence, presumption of innocence and other protective features provide, as we do with rape, murder and a host of other offenses against society and its individual members.

Mr. Justice Brennan, author of the opinions of the Court, or the plurality opinions, in [several cases] has abandoned his former position and now maintains that no formulation of this Court, the Congress, or the States can adequately distinguish obscene material unprotected by the First Amendment from protected expression. Paradoxically, he indicates that suppression of unprotected obscene material is permissible to avoid exposure to unconsenting adults, as in this case, and to juveniles, although he gives no indication of how the division between protected and nonprotected materials may be drawn with greater precision for these purposes than for regulation of commercial exposure to consenting adults only. Nor does he indicate where in the Constitution he finds the authority to distinguish between a willing "adult" one month past the state law age of majority and a willing "juvenile" one month younger.

Under the holdings announced today, no one will be subject to prosecution for the sale or exposure of obscene materials unless these materials depict or describe patently offensive "hard core" sexual conduct specifically defined by the regulating state law, as written or construed. We are satisfied that these specific prerequisites will provide fair notice to a dealer in such materials that his public and commercial activities may bring prosecution. If the inability to define regulated materials with ultimate, god-like precision altogether removes the power of the States or the Congress to regulate, then "hard core" pornography may be exposed without limit to the juvenile, the passerby, and the consenting adult alike, as, indeed, Mr. Justice Douglas contends. In this belief, however, he now stands alone. Today, for the first time since *Roth*, a majority of this Court has agreed on concrete guidelines to isolate "hard core" pornography from expression protected by the First Amendment....

Under a national Constitution, fundamental First Amendment limitations on the powers of the States do not vary from community to community, but this does not mean that there are, or should or can be, fixed, uniform national standards of precisely what appeals to the "prurient interest" or is "patently offensive." These are essentially questions of fact, and our nation is simply too big and too diverse for this Court to reasonably expect that such standards could be articulated for all 50 States in a single formulation, even assuming the prerequisite consensus exists. To require a State to structure obscenity proceedings around evidence of a national "community standard" would be an exercise in futility. Neither the State's alleged failure to offer evidence of "national standards," nor the trial court's charge that the jury consider state community standards, were constitutional errors in this case. It is neither realistic nor constitutionally sound to read the First Amendment as requiring that the people of Maine or Mississippi accept public depiction of conduct found tolerable in Las Vegas, or New York City. People in different States vary in their tastes and attitudes, and this diversity is not to be strangled by the absolutism of imposed uniformity. . . . .

In sum we (a) reaffirm the *Roth* holding that obscene material is not protected by the First Amendment; (b) hold that such material can be regulated by the States, subject to the specific safeguards enunciated above, without a showing that the material is "utterly without redeeming social value"; and (c) hold that obscenity is to be determined by applying "contemporary community standards," not "national standards."...

Vacated and remanded.

Mr. Justice DOUGLAS, dissenting.

To send men to jail for violating standards they cannot understand, construe, and apply is a monstrous thing to do in a Nation dedicated to fair trials and due process. We deal with highly emotional, not rational, questions. To many the Song of Solomon is obscene. I do not think we, the judges, were ever given the constitutional power to make definitions of obscenity. If it is to be defined, let the people debate and decide by a constitutional amendment what they want to ban as obscene and what standards they want the legislatures and the courts to apply. Whatever the choice, the courts will have some guidelines. Now we have none except our own predilections.

Mr. Justice BRENNAN, with whom Mr. Justice STEWART and Mr. Justice MARSHALL join, dissenting.

In my dissent [in *Paris Adult Theatre I v. Slaton*] I noted that I had no occasion to consider the extent of state power to regulate the distribution of sexually oriented material to juveniles or the offensive exposure of such material to unconsenting adults. I need not now decide whether a statute might be drawn to impose, within the requirements of the First Amendment, criminal penalties for the precise conduct at issue here. For it is clear that under my dissent in *Paris*, the statute here is unconstitutionally overbroad, and therefore invalid on its face....

Board of Education v. Pico   MELVIN UROFSKY

A conservative political group, Parents of New York United (PONYU), objected to certain books in the libraries of the Island Trees Union Free School District. They condemned the books as "improper for school students." The school board appointed a "Book Review Committee" of several parents and members of the school staff; after examining the books, the committee recommended that most be retained. The board rejected this report, and ordered all but one of the books removed. The board justified its actions by describing the books it had removed as "anti-American, anti-Christian, anti-Semitic, and just plain filthy." Five senior high school students and one junior high school student brought suit claiming that the board, by denying them access to the books, had denied them rights protected by the First Amendment. The Court, by a narrow margin, upheld their claim that the First Amendment gave them a "right" to receive information.

The cases immediately aroused national attention because the proscribed list included books by several of the country's outstanding authors, including Kurt Vonnegut, Desmond Morris, Langston Hughes, Richard Wright, and Bernard Malamud. The incident called up memories of Nazis burning books by Jews and others whose views went against the official policy. But in constitutional terms the issues—even if not easily resolvable—could at least be set forth clearly.

First, does the Constitution in general and the First Amendment in particular, mean different things in different environments? It is obvious, for example, that prisoners in jail do not enjoy the same rights as nonincarcerated citizens. Is a school such a special environment that some constitutional rights may be restricted, in view of the school's need to inculcate certain values and maintain order? In the landmark case of *Tinker v. Des Moines School District* (1969), the Court had acknowledged the schools' special needs, but at the same time ruled that these needs could not be invoked to unduly restrict students' rights, nor could certain political viewpoints be treated differently than others by school officials.

Second, it would appear that the right to express one's ideas freely is nullified if the would-be audience is precluded from hearing those ideas. Freedom of speech thus implies a reciprocal freedom to receive information. According to this view, if we allow a person to publish radical essays, we must allow people who desire to purchase and read them the opportunity to do so. But are the rights constitutionally equivalent? Case law holds that, with very few exceptions, a person may say anything. It does not hold that people have a right to hear everything. First Amendment case law is far from clear on whether one has a "right to receive information."

▶ How far should school authorities be allowed to go in controlling what students hear or read in school?

▶ Is there a difference between school officials controlling which books the library may purchase, and controlling which ones it may withdraw from the shelves?

▶ The Court could not reach a majority opinion; only Justice White's concurrence in the result allowed resolution. What should be the proper resolution?

▶ Both majority and minority opinions seem to agree that the state has a right, indeed a duty, to inculcate certain values in students. Is there a conflict between the state's interests in promulgating certain values and basic First Amendment concerns?

▶ Historically, one of the goals of education in a free society has been to help students develop a critical attitude, so that instead of passively accepting established ideas, they may freely question the official dogma. Is this a valid goal? If so, how can the Island Trees School Board's position be rationalized?

> ▶ Should school boards control curriculum and library contents? If not, who should?
>
> ▶ To what extent has television changed the standards of obscenity and vulgarity? Why object to books such as these when far worse language is frequently heard on television?

Board of Education v. Pico 102 S.Ct. 2799 (1982)

Justice BRENNAN announced the judgment of the Court, and delivered an opinion in which Justice MARSHALL and Justice STEVENS joined, and in which Justice BLACKMUN joined except for Part II-A-(1).

The principal question presented is whether the First Amendment imposes limitations upon the exercise by a local school board of its discretion to remove library books from high school and junior high school libraries.

I. Petitioners are the Board of Education of the Island Trees Union Free School District No. 26 in New York. Respondents are five high school students and one junior high school student. In September 1975, three Board members attended a conference sponsored by Parents of New York United (PONYU), a politically conservative organization of parents concerned about education legislation. At the conference these Board members obtained lists of books described by one member as "objectionable" and by another as "improper fare for school students." It was later determined that the High School library contained nine of the listed books, and that another listed book was in the Junior High school library.[1] In February 1976, the Board gave an "unofficial direction" that the listed books be removed from the library shelves and delivered to the Board's offices, so that Board members could read them. When this directive was carried out, it became publicized, and the Board issued a press release justifying its action. It characterized the removed books as "anti-American, anti-Christian, anti-Semitic, and just plain filthy," and concluded that "It is our duty, our moral obligation, to protect the children in our schools from this moral danger as surely as from physical and medical dangers." A short time later, the Board appointed a "Book Review Committee," consisting of several parents and members of the school staff to recommend whether the books should be retained. The Committee recommended that some (but not all) of the listed books be retained. The Board substantially rejected the Committee's report later that month, deciding that only one book, Slaughter House Five should be returned to the High School library without restriction. The Board gave no reasons for rejecting the recommendations of the Committee that it had appointed.

---

1. The nine books in the High School library were: *Slaughter House Five*, by Kurt Vonnegut, Jr.; *The Naked Ape*, by Desmond Morris; *Down These Mean Streets*, by Piri Thomas; *Best Short Stories of Negro Writers*, edited by Langston Hughes; *Go Ask Alice*, of anonymous authorship; *Laughing Boy*, by Oliver LaFarge; *Black Boy*, by Richard Wright; *A Hero Ain't Nothin' But A Sandwich*, by Alice Childress; and *Soul On Ice*, by Eldridge Cleaver. The book in the Junior High School library was *A Reader for Writers*, edited by Jerome Archer. Still another listed book, *The Fixer*, by Bernard Malamud, was found to be included in the curriculum of a twelfth grade literature course.

Respondents alleged that petitioners had "ordered the removal of the books from school libraries and proscribed their use in the curriculum because particular passages in the books offended their social, political and moral tastes and not because the books, taken as a whole, were lacking in educational value." Respondents claimed that the Board's actions denied them their rights under the First Amendment. The District Court granted summary judgment in favor of the petitioners. A three judge panel of the Court of Appeals for the Second Circuit reversed. Each judge on the panel wrote a separate opinion.

II. We emphasize at the outset the limited nature of the substantive question presented by the case before us. Our precedents have long recognized certain constitutional limits upon the power of the State to control even the curriculum and classroom....As this case is presented to us, it does not involve textbooks, or indeed any books that Island Trees students would be required to read. Respondents do not seek in this Court to impose limitations upon their school board's discretion to prescribe the curricula of the Island Trees schools. On the contrary, the only books at issue in this case are library books, books that by their nature are optional rather than required reading. Our adjudication of the present case thus does not intrude into the classroom, or into the compulsory courses taught there. Furthermore, even as to library books, the action before us does not involve the acquisition of books. Respondents have not sought to compel their school board to add to the school library shelves any books that students desire to read. Rather, the only action challenged in this case is the removal from the school libraries of books originally placed there by the school authorities, or without objection from them....

The issue before us in this case is a narrow one, both substantively and procedurally. It may best be restated as two distinct questions. First, Does the First Amendment impose any limitations upon the discretion of petitioners to remove library books from the Island Trees schools? Second, If so, do the affidavits and other evidentiary materials before the District Court, construed most favorably to respondents, raise a genuine issue of fact whether petitioners might have exceeded those limitations?...

A. (1) The Court has long recognized that local school boards have broad discretion in the management of school affairs. We have also acknowledged that public schools are vitally important as vehicles for "inculcating fundamental values necessary to the maintenance of a democratic political system." We are therefore in full agreement with petitioners that local school boards must be permitted "to establish and apply their curriculum in such a way as to transmit community values," and that "there is a legitimate and substantial community interest in promoting respect for authority and traditional values be they social, moral, or political." At the same time, however, we have necessarily recognized that the discretion of the States and local school boards in matters of education must be exercised in a manner that comports with the transcendent imperatives of the First Amendment. Students do not "shed their rights to freedom of speech or expression at the schoolhouse gate" and therefore local school boards must discharge their "important, delicate, and highly discretionary functions" within the limits and constraints of the First Amendment.

Of course, courts should not "intervene in the resolution of conflicts which arise in the daily operations of school systems" unless "basic constitutional values" are "directly and sharply implicated" in those conflicts. But we think that the First Amendment rights of students may be directly and sharply implicated by the removal of books from the shelves of a school library....We have held that in a variety of contexts "the Constitution protects the right to receive information and ideas." This right is an inherent corollary of the rights of free speech and press that are explicitly guaranteed by the Constitution, in two senses. First, the right to receive ideas follows ineluctably from the sender's First Amendment right to send them. More importantly, the right to receive ideas is a necessary predicate to the recipient's meaningful exercise of his own rights of speech, press, and political freedom. Students too are beneficiaries of this principle. In sum, just as access to ideas makes it possible for citizens generally to exercise their rights of free speech and press in a meaningful manner, such access prepares students for active and effective participation in the pluralistic, often contentious society in which they will soon be adult members. Of course all First Amendment rights accorded to students must be construed "in light of the special characteristics of the school environment." But the special characteristics of the school library make that environment especially appropriate for the recognition of the First Amendment rights of students....

(2) In rejecting petitioners' claim of absolute discretion to remove books from their school libraries, we do not deny that local school boards have a substantial legitimate role to play in the determination of school library content. We thus must turn to the question of the extent to which the First Amendment places limitations upon the discretion of petitioners to remove books from their libraries....

Petitioners rightly possess significant discretion to determine the content of their school libraries. But that discretion may not be exercised in a narrowly partisan or political manner. If a Democratic school board, motivated by party affiliation, ordered the removal of all books written by or in favor of Republicans, few would doubt that the order violated the constitutional rights of the students denied access to those books. The same conclusion would surely apply if an all-white school board, motivated by racial animus, decided to remove all books authored by blacks or advocating racial equality and integration. Our Constitution does not permit the official suppression of ideas. Thus whether petitioners' removal of books from their school libraries denied respondents their First Amendment rights depends upon the motivation behind petitioners' action. If petitioners intended by their removal decision to deny respondents access to ideas with which petitioners disagreed, and if this intent was the decisive factor in petitioners' decision, then petitioners have exercised their discretion in violation of the Constitution....

In brief, we hold that local school boards may not remove books from school library shelves simply because they dislike the ideas contained in those books and seek by their removal to "prescribe what shall be orthodox in politics, nationalism, religion, or other matters of opinion." Such purposes stand inescapably condemned by our precedents.

B. We now turn to the remaining question presented by this case: Do the evidentiary materials that were before the District Court, when construed most favorably to respondents, raise a genuine issue of material fact whether petitioners exceeded constitutional limitations in exercising their discretion to remove books from the school libraries? We conclude that the materials do raise such a question.

Before the District Court, respondents claimed that petitioners' decision to remove the books "was based upon their personal values, morals and tastes." Respondents also claimed that petitioners objected to the books in part because excerpts from them were "anti-American." The accuracy of these claims was partially conceded by petitioners, and petitioners' own affidavits lent further support to respondents' claim. In addition, the record developed in the District Court shows that when petitioners offered their first public explanation for the removal of the books, they relied in part on the assertion that the removed books were "anti-American," and "offensive to Americans in general." Furthermore, while the Book Review Committee appointed by petitioners was instructed to make its recommendations based upon criteria that appear on their face to be permissible—the books' "educational suitability," "good taste," "relevance," and "appropriateness to age and grade level"—the Committee's recommendations were essentially rejected by petitioners, without any statement of reasons for doing so. Finally, while petitioners originally defended their removal decision with the explanation that "these books contain obscenities, blasphemies, and perversion beyond description," one of the books, A Reader for Writers, was removed even though it contained no such language.

Standing alone, this evidence respecting the substantive motivations behind petitioners' removal decision would not be decisive. This would be a very different case if the record demonstrated that petitioners had employed established, regular, and facially unbiased procedures for the review of controversial materials. But the actual record in the case before us suggests the exact opposite. Petitioners' removal procedures were vigorously challenged below by respondents, and the evidence on this issue sheds further light on the issue of petitioners' motivations. Respondents alleged that in making their removal decision petitioners ignored "the advice of literary experts," the views of "librarians and teachers within the Island Trees Schools system," the advice of the superintendent of schools, and the guidance of "publications that rate books for junior and senior high school students." Respondents also claimed that petitioners' decision was based solely on the fact that the books were named on the PONYU list and that petitioners "did not undertake an independent review of other books in the school libraries." Evidence before the District Court lends support to these claims. In sum, respondents' allegations and some of the evidentiary materials presented below do not rule out the possibility that petitioners' removal procedures were highly irregular and *ad hoc*—the antithesis of those procedures that might tend to allay suspicions regarding petitioners' motivations.

Justice BLACKMUN, concurring in part and concurring in the judgement.

While I agree with much in today's plurality opinion, and while I accept the standard laid down by the plurality to guide proceedings on remand, I write separately because I have a somewhat different perspective on the nature of the First Amendment right involved.

I. To my mind, this case presents a particularly complex problem because it involves two competing principles of constitutional stature. On the one hand, its seems entirely appropriate that the State use "public schools to inculcate fundamental values necessary to the maintenance of a democratic political system." On the other hand, it is beyond dispute that schools and school boards must operate within the confines of the First Amendment. In combination with more generally applicable First Amendment rules, most particularly the central proscription of content-based regulations of speech, these cases yield a general principle: the State may not suppress exposure to ideas—for the sole purpose of suppressing exposure to those ideas—absent sufficiently compelling reasons. This principle necessarily applies in at least a limited way to public education. Surely this is true in an extreme case.

In my view, then, the principle involved here is both narrower and more basic than the "right to receive information" identified by the plurality. I do not suggest that the State has any affirmative obligation to provide students with information or ideas, something that may well be associated with a "right to receive." And I do not believe, as the plurality suggests, that the right at issue here is somehow associated with the peculiar nature of the school library; if schools may be used to inculcate ideas, surely libraries may play a role in that process. Instead, I suggest that certain forms of state discrimination between ideas are improper. In particular, our precedents command the conclusion that the State may not act to deny access to an idea simply because state officials disapprove of that idea for partisan or political reasons....

II. In my view, we strike a proper balance here by holding that school officials may not remove books for the purpose of restricting access to the political ideas or social perspectives discussed in them, when that action is motivated simply by the officials' disapproval of the ideas involved. The school board must "be able to show that its action was caused by something more than a mere desire to avoid the discomfort and unpleasantness that always accompany an unpopular viewpoint" and that the board had something in mind in addition to the suppression of partisan or political views it did not share. As I view it, this is a narrow principle. School officials must be able to choose one book over another, without outside interference, when the first book is deemed more relevant to the curriculum, or better written, or when one of a host of other politically neutral reasons is present....

A tension exists between the properly inculcative purposes of public education and any limitation on the school board's absolute discretion to choose academic materials. But that tension demonstrates only that the problem here is a difficult one, not that the problem should be resolved by choosing one principle over another. School officials may seek to instill certain values "by persuasion and example," or by choice of emphasis. That sort of positive educational action, however, is the converse of an intentional attempt to shield students from certain ideas that officials find politically distasteful. The principle involved here may be difficult to apply in an individual case. But on a record as sparse as the one before us, the plurality can hardly be faulted for failing to explore every possible ramification of those of us who originally felt that the case should not be taken," the case is here, and must be decided. Because I believe that the plurality has derived a standard similar to the one compelled by my analysis, I join all but Part IIA(1) of the plurality opinion.

[Justice WHITE concurred in the judgment, on the basis that the lower court had found facts to support its decision on narrow grounds. He believed the plurality opinion went further than necessary.]

Chief Justice BURGER, with whom Justices POWELL, REHNQUIST, and O'CONNOR join, dissenting.

In an attempt to deal with a problem in an area traditionally left to the states, a plurality of the Court, in a lavish expansion going beyond any prior holding under the First Amendment, expresses its view that a school board's decision concerning what books are to be in the school library is subject to federal court review. Were this to become the law, this Court would come perilously close to becoming a "super censor" of school board library decisions. Stripped to its essentials, the issue comes down to two important propositions: first, whether local schools are to be administered by elected schools boards, or by federal judges and teenage pupils; and second whether the values of morality, good taste, and relevance to education are valid reasons for school board decisions concerning the contents of a school library. In an attempt to place this case within the protection of the First Amendment, the plurality suggests a new "right" that, when shorn of the plurality's rhetoric, allows this Court to impose its own views about what books must be made available to students.

In this case, no restraints of any kind are placed on the students. They are free to read the books in question, which are available at public libraries and bookstores; they are free to discuss them in the classroom or elsewhere. Despite this, the plurality suggest that there is a new First Amendment "entitlement" to have access to particular books in a school library. This "right" purportedly follows "ineluctably" from the sender's First Amendment right to freedom of speech and as a "necessary predicate" to the recipient's meaningful exercise of his own rights of speech, press, and political freedom. No such right, however, has previously been recognized.

Whatever role the government might play as a conduit of information, schools in particular ought not be made a slavish courier of the material of third parties. If, as we have held, schools may legitimately be used as vehicles for "inculcating fundamental values necessary to the maintenance of a democratic political system," school authorities must have broad discretion to fulfill that obligation. How are "fundamental values" to be inculcated except by having school boards make content-based decisions about the appropriateness of retaining materials in the school library and curriculum? In order to fulfill its function, an elected school board must express its views on the subjects which are taught to its students. In doing so those elected officials express the views of their community; they may err, of course, and the voters may remove them. It is a startling erosion of the very idea of democratic government to have this Court arrogate to itself the power the plurality asserts today.

The plurality concludes that under the Constitution school boards cannot choose to retain or dispense with books if their discretion is exercised in a "narrowly partisan and political manner." The plurality concedes that permissible factors are whether books are "pervasively vulgar" or educationally unsuitable. "Educational suitability," however, is a standardless phrase. The plurality also tells us that a book may be removed from a school library if it is "pervasively vulgar." But why must the vulgarity by "pervasive" to be offensive? Vulgarity might be concentrated in a single poem or a single chapter or a single page, yet still be inappropriate. Or a school board might reasonably conclude that even "random" vulgarity is inappropriate for teenage school students....

Undoubtedly the validity of many book removals will ultimately turn on a judge's evaluation of the books. Discretion must be used, and the appropriate body to exercise that discretion is the local elected school board, not judges....

Justice POWELL, dissenting.

The plurality opinion today rejects a basic concept of public school education in our country: that the States and locally elected school boards should have the responsibility for determining the educational policy of the public schools. After today's decision any junior high school student, by instituting a suit against a school board or teacher, may invite a judge to overrule an educational decision by the official body designated by the people to operate the schools.

It is fair to say that no single agency of government at any level is closer to the people whom it serves than the typical school board. I therefore view today's decision with genuine dismay. Whatever the final outcome of this suit and suits like it, the resolution of educational policy decisions through litigation, and the exposure of school board members to liability for such decisions, can be expected to corrode the school board's authority and effectiveness. As is evident from the generality of the plurality's "standard" for judicial review, the decision as to the educational worth of a book is a highly subjective one. Judges rarely are as competent as school authorities to make this decision; nor are judges responsive to the parents and people of the school district....

A school board's attempt to instill in its students the ideas and values on which a democratic system depends is viewed as an impermissible suppression of other ideas and values on which other systems of government and other societies thrive. Books may not be removed because they are indecent; extol violence, intolerance and racism; or degrade the dignity of the individual. Human history, not the least of the twentieth century, records the power and political life of these very ideas. But they are not our ideas or values. Although I would leave this educational decision to the duly constituted board, I certainly would not require a school board to promote ideas and values repugnant to a democratic society or to teach such values to children. In different contexts and in different times, the destruction of written materials has been the symbol of despotism and intolerance. But the removal of nine vulgar or racist books from a high school library by a concerned local school board does not raise this specter. For me, today's decision symbolizes a debilitating encroachment upon the institutions of a free people.

Justice REHNQUIST, with whom Chief Justice BURGER and Justice POWELL join, dissenting.

The District Court was correct in granting summary judgment. I agree fully with the views expressed by The Chief Justice, and concur in his opinion. I disagree with Justice Brennan's opinion because it is largely hypothetical in character, failing to take account of the facts as admitted by the parties pursuant to local rules of the District Court, and because it is analytically unsound and internally inconsistent....

In the course of his discussion, Justice Brennan states: "The school board's discretion may not be exercised in a narrowly partisan or political manner. If a Democratic school board, motivated by party affiliation, ordered the removal of all books written by or in favor of Republicans, few would doubt that the order violated the constitutional rights of the students."

I can cheerfully concede all of this, but as in so many other cases the extreme examples are seldom the ones that arise in the real world of constitutional litigation. In this case the facts taken most favorably to respondents suggest that nothing of this sort happened. The nine books removed undoubtedly did contain "ideas," but it is apparent that eight of them contained demonstrable amounts of vulgarity and profanity, and the ninth contained nothing that could be considered partisan or political. Respondents admitted as much. Petitioners did not, for the reasons stated hereafter, run afoul of the First and Fourteenth Amendments by removing these particular books from the library in the manner in which they did. I would save for another day—feeling quite confident that that day will not arrive—the extreme examples posed in Justice Brennan's opinion.

B. Had petitioners been the members of a town council, I suppose all would agree that, absent a good deal more than is present in this record, they could not have prohibited the sale of these books by private booksellers within the municipality. But we have also recognized that the government may act in other capacities than as sovereign, and when it does the First Amendment may speak with a different voice. When it acts as an educator, at least at the elementary and secondary school level, the government is engaged in inculcating social values and knowledge in relatively impressionable young people. Obviously there are innumerable decisions to be made as to what courses should be taught, what books should be purchased, or what teachers should be employed. In every one of these areas the members of a school board will act on the basis of their own personal or moral values, will attempt to mirror those of the community, or will abdicate the making of such decisions to so-called "experts." In this connection I find myself entirely in agreement with the observation of a lower federal court that it is "permissible and appropriate for local boards to make educational decisions based upon their personal, social, political and moral views." In the very course of administering the many-faceted operations of a school district, the mere decision to purchase some books will necessarily preclude the possibility of purchasing others. The decision to teach a particular subject may preclude the possibility of teaching another subject. A decision to replace a teacher because of ineffectiveness may by implication be seen as a disparagement of the subject matter taught. In each of these instances, however, the book or the exposure to the subject matter may be acquired elsewhere. The managers of the school district are not proscribing it as to the citizenry in general, but are simply determining that it will not be included in the curriculum or school library. In short, actions by the government as educator do not raise the same First Amendment concerns as actions by the government as sovereign.

...II. It is the very existence of a right to receive information, in the junior high school and high school setting, which I find wholly unsupported by our past decisions and inconsistent with the necessarily selective process of elementary and secondary education.

A. The right described by Justice Brennan has never been recognized in the decisions of this Court and is not supported by their rationale. Our past decisions in this area have concerned freedom of speech and expression, not the right of access to particular ideas. Despite Justice Brennan's suggestion to the contrary, this Court has never held that the First

Amendment grants junior high school and high school students a right of access to certain information in school. It is true that the Court has recognized a limited version of that right in other settings, and Justice Brennan quotes language from several such decisions in order to demonstrate the viability of the right-to-receive doctrine. But not one of these cases concerned or even purported to discuss elementary or secondary educational institutions....

B. There are even greater reasons for rejecting Justice Brennan's analysis, however. Public schools fulfill the vital role of "inculcating fundamental values necessary to the maintenance of a democratic political system." The idea that such students have a right of access, in the school, to information other than that thought by their educators to be necessary is contrary to the very nature of an inculcative education. Education consists of the selective presentation and explanation of ideas. The effective acquisition of knowledge depends upon an orderly exposure to relevant information. Nowhere is this more true than in elementary and secondary schools, where, unlike the broad-ranging inquiry available to university students, the courses taught are those thought most relevant to the young students' individual development. Of necessity, elementary and secondary educators must separate the relevant from the irrelevant, the appropriate from the inappropriate. Determining what information not to present to the students is often as important as identifying relevant material. This winnowing process necessarily leaves much information to be discovered by students at another time or in another place, and is fundamentally inconsistent with any constitutionally required eclecticism in public education....

After all else is said, however, the most obvious reason that petitioners' removal of the books did not violate respondents' right to receive information is the ready availability of the books elsewhere. Students are not denied books by their removal from a school library. The books may be borrowed from a public library, read at a university library, purchased at a bookstore, or loaned by a friend. The government as educator does not seek to reach beyond the confines of the school. Indeed, following the removal from the school library of the books at issue in this case, the local public library put all nine books on display for public inspection. Their contents were fully accessible to any inquisitive student.

C. Justice Brennan's own discomfort with the idea that students have a right to receive information from their elementary or secondary schools is demonstrated by the artificial limitations which he places upon the right—limitations which are supported neither by logic nor authority and which are inconsistent with the right itself. The attempt to confine the right to the library is one such limitation. As a second limitation, Justice Brennan distinguishes the act of removing a previously acquired book from the act of refusing to acquire the book in the first place. If Justice Brennan truly has found a "right to receive ideas," however, this distinction between acquisition and removal makes little sense. The failure of a library to acquire a book denies access to its contents just as effectively as does the removal of the book from the library's shelf....

Justice Brennan's reliance on the "suppression of ideas" to justify his distinction between acquisition and removal of books has additional logical pitfalls. Presumably the distinction is based upon the greater visibility and the greater sense of conscious decision thought to be involved in the removal of a book, as opposed to that involved in the refusal to acquire a book. But if "suppression of ideas" is to be the talisman, one would think that a school board's public announcement of its refusal to acquire certain books would have every bit as much impact on public attention as would an equally publicized decision to remove the books. And yet only the latter action would violate the First Amendment under Justice Brennan's analysis.

The final limitation placed by Justice Brennan upon his newly discovered right is a motive requirement: the First Amendment is violated only "if petitioners intended by their removal decision to deny respondents access to ideas with which petitioners disagreed." But bad motives and good motives alike deny access to the books removed. If there truly is a constitutional right to receive information, it is difficult to see why the reason for the denial makes any difference. Of course Justice Brennan's view is that intent matters because the First Amendment does not tolerate an officially prescribed orthodoxy. But his reasoning mixes First Amendment apples and oranges. The right to receive information differs from the right to be free from an officially prescribed orthodoxy. Not every educational denial of access to information casts a pall of orthodoxy over the classroom....

Justice O'CONNOR, dissenting.

If the school board can set the curriculum, select teachers, and determine initially what books to purchase for the school library, it surely can decide which books to discontinue or remove from the school library so long as it does not also interfere with the right of students to read the material and to discuss it. As Justice Rehnquist persuasively argues, the plurality's analysis overlooks the fact that in this case the government is acting in its special role as educator. I do not personally agree with the board's action with respect to some of the books in question here, but it is not the function of the courts to make the decisions that have been properly relegated to the elected members of school boards. It is the school board that must determine educational suitability, and it has done so in this case. I therefore join The Chief Justice's dissent.

Texas v. Johnson / United States v. Eichman   ROBERT M. O'NEIL

The United States flag has throughout most of our history been a symbol of unique importance. We have revered it and protected it in many and various ways. We salute it and pledge allegiance to it at public ceremonies. We applaud its display at international gatherings. Police officers in some communities are required to wear a flag patch on their uniforms. When a flag has become old and tattered, we insist that it be retired or interred with dignity.

It is hardly surprising that many states made it a crime to desecrate the flag—an act which usually involves defacing, damaging or physically mistreating the flag in ways that show disrespect or contempt. These laws were frequently tested during the Vietnam war period—by people who burned the flag, or who stapled a flag patch to the seat of their pants, or who altered it (as by inserting a Vietcong flag in place of the stars.) The issue several times reached the Supreme Court. None of the convictions was ever upheld. The Justices once reversed a flag-burning conviction—

though only because the jury might have convicted a man on the basis of a speech he gave rather than because of his treatment of the flag. In every case the Court stopped just short of the ultimate question whether free expression included showing disrespect for the flag.

During World War II the Supreme Court had held that states could not require anyone to salute the flag against conscience or belief. The Justices noted our reverence for the flag, but insisted that government could not demand a uniform public show of allegiance; other ways should be found, they urged, to inculcate patriotism among citizens, even in time of war.

Thus the stage had been set for the Court to reach the ultimate question in a Texas case (*Texas v. Johnson*, 1989), where the state courts had already struck down the state's flag desecration law as a violation of free speech. A bare majority of the Justices held that states could not make peaceful protest a crime, even where its focus was the national flag. There was no danger to other persons or to property, and the government had not shown an act unrelated to speech which could be reached without encroaching on free expression.

Later that year Congress passed a slightly narrower law that made flag desecration a federal crime. President Bush signed the law with reluctance, believing that a constitutional amendment was necessary and preferable. The law asked the Supreme Court to accelerate review, which the Court did in the spring of 1990. The decision early in the summer, by the same margin as the Texas case the year before, reached the same conclusion. Once again lawmakers had tried to do what the First Amendment does not permit them to do—to make peaceful protest a crime because of the target or object of that protest.

Thus a constitutional amendment would be needed to reach flag desecration. Both houses of Congress soon considered a possible amendment, but neither recorded the two thirds majority required for approval. Thus the issue appeared to have died during the summer of 1990.

▶ The United States flag may be a symbol, but obviously a symbol unlike any other. Why do some lawmakers, veterans and others feel so strongly about protecting the flag from desecration?

▶ Why do some protesters see flag desecration as an effective means of protest? What kind of message are they seeking to send—and to whom?

▶ Suppose a person in the course of burning a flag sets a nearby house on fire? Is he immune from prosecution under these cases? Would it matter if the person living in the house was a government official whose views the protestor was attacking as he set fire to the flag?

> ▶ The flag burning cases finally reached the Supreme Court during a time of unusual international peace. Would it—or should it—have made any difference if the nation was at war?

> ▶ Could lawmakers punish certain public employees for defiling or desecrating the flag? How about school teachers? Police officers? The person whose job it is to raise the flag each morning over the state capitol, city hall or a county building?

> ▶ The Court has spoken in these cases about promoting patriotism and good citizenship in other ways. What are some of those ways that do not abridge free speech? Can school boards require students to study respect for the flag in their social studies courses?

Texas v. Johnson 491 U.S. 397 88-155 (1989)

Justice BRENNAN delivered the opinion of the Court.

After publicly burning an American flag as a means of political protest, Gregory Lee Johnson was convicted of desecrating a flag in violation of Texas law. This case presents the question whether his conviction is consistent with the First Amendment. We hold that it is not.

Johnson was convicted of flag desecration for burning the flag rather than for uttering insulting words. This fact somewhat complicates our consideration of his conviction under the First Amendment. We must first determine whether Johnson's burning of the flag constituted expressive conduct, permitting him to invoke the First Amendment in challenging his conviction. If his conduct was expressive, we next decide whether the State's regulation is related to the suppression of free expression. If the State's regulation is not related to expression, then the less stringent standard we announced in *United States v. O'Brien* for regulations of noncommunicative conduct controls. If it is, then we are outside of *O'Brien's* test, and we must ask whether this interest justifies Johnson's conviction under a more demanding standard. A third possibility is that the State's asserted interest is simply not implicated on these facts, and in that event the interest drops out of the picture.

The First Amendment literally forbids the abridgement only of "speech," but we have long recognized that its protection does not end at the spoken or written word. While we have rejected "the view that an apparently limitless variety of conduct can be labeled 'speech' whenever the person engaging in the conduct intends thereby to express an idea," we have acknowledged that conduct may be "sufficiently imbued with elements of communication to fall within the scope of the First and Fourteenth Amendments."

In deciding whether particular conduct possesses sufficient communicative elements to bring the First Amendment into play, we have asked whether "[a]n intent to convey a particularized message was present, and [whether] the likelihood was great that the message would be understood by those who viewed it." Hence, we have recognized the expressive nature of students' wearing of black armbands to protest American military involvement in Vietnam, *Tinker v. Des Moines Independent Community School Dist.*; of a sit-in by blacks in a "whites only" area to protest segregation, *Brown v. Louisiana*; of the wearing of American military uniforms in a dramatic presentation criticizing American involvement in Vietnam, Schacht v. United States; and of picketing about a wide variety of causes, see, *e.g., Food Employees v. Logan Valley Plaza, Inc.; United States v. Grace.*

Especially pertinent to this case are our decisions recognizing the communicative nature of conduct relating to flags. Attaching a peace sign to the flag, saluting the flag, and displaying a red flag, we have held, all may find shelter under the First Amendment. That we have had little difficulty identifying an expressive element in conduct relating to flags should not be surprising. The very purpose of a national flag is to serve as a symbol of our country; it is, one might say, "the one visible manifestation of two hundred years of nationhood." Thus, we have observed:

> [T]he flag salute is a form of utterance. Symbolism is a primitive but
> effective way of communicating ideas. The use of an emblem or flag to
> symbolize some system, idea, institution, or personality, is a short cut from
> mind to mind. Causes and nations, political parties, lodges and ecclesiastical
> groups seek to knit the loyalty of their followings to a flag or banner, a color
> or design.

Pregnant with expressive content, the flag as readily signifies this Nation as does the combination of letters found in "America."

We have not automatically concluded, however, that any action taken with respect to the flag is expressive. Instead, in characterizing such action for First Amendment purposes, we have considered the context in which it occurred. In [Spence v. Washington], for example, we emphasized that Spence's taping of a peace sign to his flag was "roughly simultaneous with and concededly triggered by the Cambodian incursion and the Kent State tragedy." The State of Washington had conceded, in fact, that Spence's conduct was a form of communication, and we stated that "the State's concession is inevitable on this record."

The State of Texas conceded for purposes of its oral argument in this case that Johnson's conduct was expressive conduct, and this concession seems to us as prudent as was Washington's in Spence. Johnson burned an American flag as part—indeed, as the culmination—of a political demonstration that coincided with the convening of the Republican Party and its renomination of Ronald Reagan for President. The expressive, overtly political nature of this conduct was both intentional and overwhelmingly apparent. At his trial, Johnson explained his reasons for burning the flag as follows: "The American Flag was burned as Ronald Reagan was being renominated as President. And a more powerful statement of symbolic speech, whether you agree with it or not, couldn't have been made at that time. It's quite a just position [juxtaposition]. We had new patriotism and no patriotism." In these circumstances, Johnson's burning of the flag was conduct "sufficiently imbued with elements of communication," to implicate the First Amendment.

The Government generally has a freer hand in restricting expressive conduct than it has in restricting the written or spoken word. It may not, however, proscribe particular conduct because it has expressive elements. "[W]hat might be termed the more generalized guarantee of freedom of expression makes the communicative nature of conduct an inadequate basis for singling out that conduct for proscription. A law directed at the communicative nature of conduct must, like a law *directed at* speech itself, be justified by the substantial showing of need that the First Amendment requires." It is, in short, not simply the verbal or nonverbal nature of the expression, but the governmental interest at stake, that helps to determine whether a restriction on that expression is valid.

Thus, although we have recognized that where "speech" and "nonspeech" elements are combined in the same course of conduct, a sufficiently important governmental interest in regulating the nonspeech element can justify incidental limitations on First Amendment freedoms," we have limited the applicability of *O'Brien*'s relatively lenient standard to those cases in which "the governmental interest is unrelated to the suppression of free expression." In stating, moreover, that *O'Brien*'s test "in the last analysis is little, if any, different from the standard applied to time, place, or manner restrictions," we have highlighted the requirement that the governmental interest in question be unconnected to expression in order to come under *O'Brien*'s less demanding rule.

In order to decide whether *O'Brien*'s test applies here, therefore, we must decide whether Texas has asserted an interest in support of Johnson's conviction that is unrelated to the suppression of expression. If we find that an interest asserted by the State is simply not implicated on the facts before us, we need not ask whether *O'Brien*'s test applies. The State offers two separate interests to justify this conviction: preventing breaches of the peace, and preserving the flag as a symbol of nationhood and national unity. We hold that the first interest is not implicated on this record and that the second is related to the suppression of expression.

Texas claims that its interest in preventing the breaches of the peace justifies Johnson's conviction for flag desecration. However, no disturbance of the peace actually occurred or threatened to occur because of Johnson's burning of the flag. Although the State stresses the disruptive behavior of the protestors during their march toward City Hall, it admits that "no actual breach of the peace occurred at the time of the flagburning or in response to the flagburning." The State's emphasis on the protestors' disorderly actions prior to arriving at City Hall is not only somewhat surprising given that no charges were brought on the basis of this conduct, but it also fails to show that a disturbance of the peace was a likely reaction to Johnson's conduct. The only evidence offered by the State at trial to show the reaction to Johnson's actions was the testimony of several persons who had been seriously offended by the flag-burning.

The State's position, therefore, amounts to a claim that an audience that takes serious offense at particular expression is necessarily likely to disturb the peace and that the expression may be prohibited on this basis. Our precedents do not countenance such a presumption. On the contrary, they recognize that a principal "function of free speech under our system of government is to invite dispute. It may indeed best serve its high purpose when it induces a condition of unrest, creates dissatisfaction with conditions as they are, or even stirs people to anger." It would be odd indeed to conclude *both* that "if it is the speaker's opinion that gives offense, that consequence is a reason for according it constitutional protection," *and* that the Government may ban the expression of certain disagreeable ideas on the unsupported presumption that their very disagreeableness will provoke violence.

Thus, we have not permitted the Government to assume that every expression of a provocative idea will incite a riot, but have instead required careful consideration of the actual circumstances surrounding such expression, asking whether the expression "is directed to inciting or producing imminent lawless action and is likely to incite or produce such action." To accept Texas' arguments that it need only demonstrate "the potential for the breach of the peace," and that every flag-burning necessarily possesses that potential, would be to eviscerate our holding in *Brandenburg* [*v. Ohio*]. This we decline to do.

Nor does Johnson's expressive conduct fall within that small class of "fighting words" that are "likely to provoke the average person to retaliation, and thereby cause a breach of the peace." No reasonable onlooker would have regarded Johnson's generalized expression of dissatisfaction with the policies of the Federal Government as a direct personal insult or an invitation to exchange fisticuffs.

We thus conclude that the State's interest in maintaining order is not implicated on these facts. The State need not worry that our holding will disable it from preserving the peace. We do not suggest that the First Amendment forbids a State to prevent "imminent lawless action." And, in fact, Texas already has a statute specifically prohibiting breaches of the peace, which tends to confirm that Texas need not punish this flag desecration in order to keep the peace.

The State also asserts an interest in preserving the flag as a symbol of nationhood and national unity. In *Spence*, we acknowledged that the Government's interest in preserving the flag's special symbolic value "is directly related to expression in the context of activity" such as affixing a peace symbol to a flag. We are equally persuaded that this interest is related to expression in the case of Johnson's burning of the flag. The State, apparently, is concerned that such conduct will lead people to believe either that the flag does not stand for nationhood and national unity, but instead reflects other, less positive concepts, or that the concepts reflected in the flag do not in fact exist, that is, we do not enjoy unity as a Nation. These concerns blossom only when a person's treatment of the flag communicates some message, and thus are related "to the suppression of free expression" within the meaning of *O'Brien*. We are thus outside of *O'Brien*'s test altogether.

It remains to consider whether the State's interest in preserving the flag as a symbol of nationhood and national unity justifies Johnson's conviction.

As in *Spence*, "[w]e are confronted with a case of prosecution for the expression of an idea through activity," and "[a]ccordingly, we must examine with particular care the interests advanced by [petitioner] to support its prosecution." Johnson was not, we add, prosecuted for the expression of just any idea; he was prosecuted for his expression of dissatisfaction with the policies of this country, expression situated at the core of our First Amendment values.

Moreover, Johnson was prosecuted because he knew that his politically charged expression would cause "serious offense." If he had burned the flag as a means of disposing of it because it was dirty or torn, he would not have been convicted of flag desecration under this Texas law: federal law designates burning as the preferred means of disposing of a flag "when it is in such condition that it is no longer a fitting emblem for display," and Texas has no quarrel with this means of disposal. The Texas law is thus not aimed at protecting the physical integrity of the flag in all circumstances, but is designed instead to protect it only against impairments that would cause serious offense to others. Texas concedes as much: "Section 42.09(b) reaches only those severe acts of physical abuse of the flag carried out in way likely to be offensive. The statute mandates intentional or knowing abuse, that is, the kind of mistreatment that is not innocent, but rather is intentionally designed to seriously offend other individuals."

If there is a bedrock principle underlying the First Amendment, it is that the Government may not prohibit the expression of an idea simply because society finds the idea itself offensive or disagreeable.

We have not recognized an exception to this principle even where our flag has been involved. In *Street v. New York*, (1969), we held that a State may not criminally punish a person for uttering words critical of the flag. Rejecting the argument that the conviction could be sustained on the ground that Street had "failed to show the respect for our national symbol which may properly be demanded of every citizen," we concluded that "the constitutionally guaranteed `freedom to be intellectually...diverse or even contrary,' and the `right to differ as to things that touch the heart of the existing order,' encompass the freedom to express publicly one's opinion about our flag, including those opinions which are defiant or contemptuous." Nor may the Government, we have held, compel conduct that would evince respect for the flag. "To sustain the compulsory flag salute we are required to say that a Bill of Rights which guards the individual's right to speak his own mind, left it open to public authorities to compel him to utter what is not in his mind."

It is not the State's ends, but its means, to which we object. It cannot be gainsaid that there is a special place reserved for the flag in this Nation, and thus we do not doubt that the Government has a legitimate interest in making efforts to "prescrv[e] the national flag as an unalloyed symbol for our country." We reject the suggestion, urged at oral argument by counsel for Johnson, that the Government lacks "any state interest whatsoever" in regulating the manner in which the flag may be displayed. Congress has, for example, enacted precatory regulations describing the proper treatment of the flag, and we cast no doubt on the legitimacy of its interest in making such recommendations. To say that the Government has an interest in encouraging proper treatment for the flag, however, is not to say that it may criminally punish a person for burning a flag as a means of political protest. "National unity as an end which officials may foster by persuasion and example is not in question. The problem is whether under our Constitution compulsion as here employed is a permissible means for its achievement."

We are fortified in today's conclusion by our conviction that forbidding criminal punishment for conduct such as Johnson's will not endanger the special role played by our flag or the feelings it inspires. To paraphrase Justice Holmes, we submit that nobody can suppose that this one gesture of an unknown man will change our Nation's attitude towards its flag. Indeed, Texas' argument that the burning of an American flag "is an act having a high likelihood to cause a breach of the peace," and its statute's implicit assumption that physical mistreatment of the flag will lead to "serious offense," tend to confirm that the flag's special role is not in danger; if it were, no one would riot or take offense because a flag had been burned.

We are tempted to say, in fact, that the flag's deservedly cherished place in our community will be strengthened, not weakened, by our holding today. Our decision is a reaffirmation of the principles of freedom and inclusiveness that the flag best reflects, and of the conviction that our toleration of criticism such as Johnson's is a sign and source of our strength. Indeed, one of the proudest images of our flag, the one immortalized in our own national anthem, is of the bombardment it survived at Fort McHenry. It is the Nation's resilience, not its rigidity, that Texas sees reflected in the flag—and it is that resilience that we reassert today.

The way to preserve the flag's special role is not to punish those who feel differently about these matters. It is to persuade them that they are wrong. "To courageous, self-reliant men, with confidence in the power of free and fearless reasoning applied through the processes or popular government, no danger flowing from speech can be deemed clear and present, unless the incidence of the evil apprehended is so imminent that it may befall before there is opportunity for full discussion. If there be time to expose through discussion the falsehood and fallacies, to avert the evil by the processes of education, the remedy to be applied is more speech, not enforced silence." And, precisely because it is our flag that is involved, one's response to the flag-burner may exploit the uniquely persuasive power of the flag itself. We can imagine no more appropriate response to burning a flag than waving one's own, no better way to counter a flag-burner's message than by saluting the flag that burns, no surer means of preserving the dignity even of the flag that burned than by—as one witness here did—according its remains a respectful burial. We do not consecrate the flag by punishing its desecration, for in doing so we dilute the freedom that this cherished emblem represents.

Johnson was convicted for engaging in expressive conduct. The State's interest in preventing breaches of the peace does not support his conviction because Johnson's conduct did not threaten to disturb the peace. Nor does the State's interest in preserving the flag as a symbol of nationhood and national unity justify his criminal conviction for engaging in political expression. The judgment of the Texas Court of Criminal Appeals is therefore

Affirmed.

Justice KENNEDY, concurring.

I write not to qualify the words Justice Brennan chooses so well, for he says with power all that is necessary to explain our ruling. I join his opinion without reservation, but with a keen sense that this case, like others before us from time to time, exacts its personal toll. This prompts me to add to our pages these few remarks.

The case before us illustrates better than most that the judicial power is often difficult in its exercise. We cannot here ask another branch to share responsibility, as when the argument is made that a statute is flawed or incomplete. For we are presented with a clear and simple statute to be judged against a pure command of the Constitution. The outcome can be laid at no door but ours.

The hard fact is that sometimes we must make decisions we do not like. We make them because they are right, right in the sense that the law and the Constitution, as we see them, compel the result. And so great is our commitment to the process that, except in the rare case, we do not pause to express distaste for the result, perhaps for fear of undermining a valued principle that dictates the decision. This is one of those rare cases.

Our colleagues in dissent advance powerful arguments why respondent may be convicted for his expression, reminding us that among those who will be dismayed by our holding will be some who have had the singular honor of carrying the flag in battle. And I agree that the flag holds a lonely place of honor in an age when absolutes are distrusted and simple truths are burdened by unneeded apologetics.

With all respect to those views, I do not believe the Constitution gives us the right to rule as the dissenting members of the Court urge, however painful this judgment is to announce. Though symbols often are what we ourselves make of them, the flag is constant in expressing beliefs Americans share, beliefs in law and peace and that freedom which sustains the human spirit. The case here today forces recognition of the costs to which those beliefs commit us. It is poignant but fundamental that the flag protects those who hold it in contempt.

For all the record shows, this respondent was not a philosopher and perhaps did not even possess the ability to comprehend how repellent his statements must be to the Republic itself. But whether or not he could appreciate the enormity of the offense he gave, the fact remains that his acts were speech, in both the technical and the fundamental meaning of the Constitution. So I agree with the Court that he must go free.

Chief Justice REHNQUIST, with whom Justice WHITE and Justice O'CONNOR join, dissenting.

In holding this Texas statute unconstitutional, the Court ignores Justice Holmes' familiar aphorism that "a page of history is worth a volume of logic." *New York Trust Co. v. Eisner*, (1921). For more than 200 years, the American flag has occupied a unique position as the symbol of our Nation, a uniqueness that justifies a governmental prohibition against flag burning in the way respondent Johnson did here.

The American flag, then, throughout more than 200 years of our history, has come to be the visible symbol embodying our Nation. It does not represent the views of any particular political party, and it does not represent any particular political philosophy. The flag is not simply another "idea" or "point of view" competing for recognition in the marketplace of ideas. Millions and millions of Americans regard it with an almost mystical reverence regardless of what sort of social, political, or philosophical beliefs they may have. I cannot agree that the First Amendment invalidates the Act of Congress, and the laws of 48 of the 50 States, which make criminal the public burning of the flag.

Here it may equally well be said that the public burning of the American flag by Johnson was no essential part of any exposition of ideas, and at the same time it had a tendency to incite a breach of the peace. Johnson was free to make any verbal denunciation of the flag that he wished; indeed, he was free to burn the flag in private. He could publicly burn other symbols of the Government or effigies of political leaders. He did lead a march through the streets of Dallas, and conducted a rally in front of the Dallas City Hall. He engaged in a "die-in" to protest nuclear weapons. He shouted out various slogans during the march including: "Reagan, Mondale, which will it be? Either one means World War III"; "Ronald Reagan, killer of the hour, Perfect example of U.S. power"; and "red, white and blue, we spit on you, you stand for plunder, you will go under." For none of these acts was he arrested or prosecuted; it was only when he proceeded to burn publicly an American flag stolen from its rightful owner that he violated the Texas statute.

The Court concludes its opinion with a regrettably patronizing civics lecture, presumably addressed to the Members of both Houses of Congress, the members of the 48 state legislatures that enacted prohibitions against flag burning, and the troops fighting under the flag in Vietnam who objected to its being burned: "The way to preserve the flag's special role is not to punish those who feel differently about these matters. It is to persuade them that they are wrong." The Court's role as the final expositor of the Constitution is well established, but its role as a platonic guardian admonishing those responsible to public opinion as if they were truant school children has no similar place in our system of government. The cry of "no taxation without representation" animated those who revolted against the English Crown to found our Nation—the idea that those who submitted to government should have some say as to what kind of laws would be passed. Surely one of the high purposes of a democratic society is to legislate against conduct that is regarded as evil and profoundly offensive to the majority of the people—whether it be murder, embezzlement, pollution, or flag burning.

Our Constitution wisely places limits on the powers of legislative majorities to act, but the declaration of such limits by this Court, "is, at all times, a question of much delicacy, which ought seldom, if ever, to be decided in the affirmative, in a doubtful case." *Fletcher v. Peck*, 6 Cranch 87, 128 (1810) (Marshall, C.J.) Uncritical extension of constitutional protection to the burning of the flag risks the frustration of the very purpose for which organized governments are instituted. The Court decides that the American flag is just another symbol, about which not only must opinions pro and con be tolerated, but for which the most minimal public respect may not be enjoined. The government may conscript men into the Armed Forces where they must fight and perhaps die for the flag, but the government may not prohibit the public burning of the banner under which they fight. I would uphold the Texas statute as applied in this case.

United States v. Eichman 496 U.S. 310 89-1433 (1990)

Justice BRENNAN delivered the opinion of the Court.

After our decision in *Johnson*, Congress passed the Flag Protection Act of 1989. The Act provides in relevant part:

> (a)(1) Whoever knowingly mutilates, defaces, physically defiles, burns, maintains on the floor or ground, or tramples upon any flag of the United States shall be fined under this title or imprisoned for not more than one year, or both.

> (2) This subsection does not prohibit any conduct consisting of the disposal of a flag when it has become worn or soiled.

(b) As used in this section, the term `flag of the United States' means any flag
of the United States, or any part thereof, made of any substance, of any size, in
a form that is commonly displayed.

The Government concedes in this case, as it must, that appellees' flag-burning constituted expressive conduct; but invites us to reconsider our rejection in *Johnson* of the claim that
flag-burning as a mode of expression, like obscenity or "fighting words," does not enjoy the
full protection of the First Amendment. This we decline to do. The only remaining question
is whether the Flag Protection Act is sufficiently distinct from the Texas statute that it may
constitutionally be applied to proscribe appellees' expressive conduct.

The Government contends that the Flag Protection Act is constitutional because, unlike
the statute addressed in *Johnson*, the Act does not target expressive conduct on the basis of
the content of its message. The Government asserts an interest in "protect[ing] the physical
integrity of the flag under all circumstances" in order to safeguard the flag's identity "`as
the unique and unalloyed symbol of the Nation.'" The Act proscribes conduct (other than
disposal that damages or mistreats the flag, without regard to the actor's motive, his intended message, or the likely effects of his conduct on onlookers. By contrast, the Texas statute
expressly prohibited only those acts of physical flag desecration "that the actor knows will
seriously offend" onlookers, and the former federal statute prohibited only those acts of
desecration that "cas[t] contempt upon" the flag.

Although the Flag Protection Act contains no explicit content-based limitation on the
scope of prohibited conduct, it is nevertheless clear that the Government's asserted *interest*
is "related `to the suppression of free expression,'" and concerned with the content of such
expression. The Government's interest in protecting the "physical integrity" of a privately
owned flag rests upon the perceived need to preserve the flag's status as a symbol of
our Nation and certain national ideals. But the mere destruction or disfigurement of a
particular physical manifestation of the symbol, without more, does not diminish or
otherwise affect the symbol itself in any way. For example, the secret destruction of a flag in
one's basement would not threaten the flag's recognized meaning. Rather, the Government's
desire to preserve the flag as a symbol for certain national ideals is implicated "only when
a person's treatment of the flag communicates [a] message" to others that is inconsistent
with those ideals.

Moreover, the precise language of the Act's prohibitions confirms Congress' interest in
the communicative impact of flag destruction. The Act criminalizes the conduct of anyone
who "knowingly mutilates, defaces, physically defiles, burns, maintains on the floor or
ground, or tramples upon any flag." Each of the specified terms—with the possible exception of "burns"—unmistakably connotes disrespectful treatment of the flag and suggests a
focus on those acts likely to damage the flag's symbolic value. And the explicit exemption
for disposal of "worn or soiled" flags protects certain acts traditionally associated with
patriotic respect for the flag.

As we explained in *Johnson*: "[I]f we were to hold that a State may forbid flag-burning
wherever it is likely to endanger the flag's symbolic role—as where, for example, a person
ceremoniously burns a dirty flag—we would be...permitting a State to `prescribe what
shall be orthodox' by saying that one may burn the flag to convey one's attitude toward it

and its referents only if one does not endanger the flag's representation of nationhood and national unity." Although Congress cast the Flag Protection Act in somewhat broader terms than the Texas statute at issue in Johnson, the Act still suffers from the same fundamental flaw: it suppresses expression out of concern for its likely communicative impact. Despite the Act's wider scope, its restriction on expression cannot be "'justified without reference to the content of the regulated speech.'" (State's interest in protecting flag's symbolic value is directly related to suppression of expression and thus *O'Brien* test is inapplicable even where statute declared "simply...that *nothing* may be affixed or superimposed on a United States flag). The Act therefore must be subjected to "the most exacting scrutiny," and for the reasons stated in *Johnson*, the Government's interest cannot justify its infringement on First Amendment rights. We decline the Government's invitation to reassess this conclusion in light of Congress' recent recognition of a purported "national consensus" favoring a prohibition on flag-burning. Even assuming such a consensus exists, any suggestion that the Government's interest in suppressing speech becomes more weighty as popular opposition to that speech grows is foreign to the First Amendment.

Madsen v. Women's Health Center   ROBERT M. O'NEIL

During the 1980s, protests against abortion clinics became increasingly strident and contentious. Various anti-abortion, or "right to life" groups, which had for years conveyed their views in less visible ways, now took to the streets. They organized a series of demonstrations that were designed to discourage patients or prospective patients from seeking medical services of the type such clinics offered. Initially directed only at the clinic facilities, such protests eventually targeted also the homes and families of physicians who performed abortions.

Over time, these demonstrations had the desired effect. It became more difficult for patients or others seeking information about abortions to run the gauntlet. Some substantial number of such patients either abandoned their quest, or sought the termination of pregnancy through other means. Meanwhile, physicians and other clinic staff members faced mounting obstacles in the pursuit of their practice. Noise levels could at times be intense. Some protest groups waved icons and symbols like bloody dolls in the faces of patients entering a clinic.

The protests occasionally turned violent; indeed, in several dramatic instances, anti-abortion crusaders inflicted physical harm and even death upon such professionals, solely because of their occupation. As one would expect, abortion clinics and those who staffed them turned increasingly to the courts for relief. They pointed out that their patients had, under *Roe v. Wade*, a clear constitutional right to seek such medical advice and service.

On the other hand, the protestors argued that they were engaged in the exercise of their First Amendment rights—that no matter how abhorrent or distasteful the message might be, the Bill of Rights protects all forms of peaceful demonstration. That a protest might be effective, and might deter some who observed it from pursuing even a constitutionally protected course of action—seeking an abortion, for example—did not deprive the demonstrators of their First Amendment rights.

The tension between these two values of so high a constitutional order was certain to reach the Supreme Court. It did so through a case that began in the coastal community of Melbourne, Florida. An anti-abortion group had announced their plans to demonstrate in front of an abortion clinic, as they had done in other nearby communities. The clinic managers obtained a state court order that barred the protestors from physically blocking or interfering with access to or egress from the clinic. Some months later, the clinic sought a broader injunction, claiming that the original decree did not adequately protect its patients and their right to seek medical care in that facility. The trial judge took further evidence, focused on the recent activities of the protestors, and expanded the original order. The new decree restrained activity of several types. It enjoined the protestors from entering a thirty-six foot "buffer zone" around the clinic, so that patients would be freer to come and go without interference. The order also barred demonstrators, during the clinic's business hours, from shouting or yelling or chanting "within earshot" of clinic patients, or displaying "images observable" by patients in the facility.

Two other features of the order were controversial. The trial judge told the demonstrators they must not, within three hundred feet of the entrance, physically approach any person who was seeking access to the clinic, unless the person "indicates a desire to communicate" by approaching a demonstrator. Finally, protestors were not to gather or picket or demonstrate, or use sound equipment, within three hundred feet of the homes of clinic staff members, or block their coming and going (or that of guests and others) on their walks or driveways.

The anti-abortion groups argued all these provisions deprived them of free speech, and were unnecessary to enable the clinic to serve its patients. The Florida Supreme Court upheld the injunction, recognizing that it did inhibit expression on the protestors' part, but finding the order no broader than necessary to meet the needs of the clinic and its patients. The Supreme Court agreed to review the case as a way of balancing these contending interests.

▶ How can courts draw the line between peaceful protest (which involves both speech and conduct) and violent demonstrations?

▶ Does the focus or target of a protest or demonstration affect the scope of protestors' free speech rights? What if the demonstrators are seeking to deter the exercise of someone else's constitutional rights or liberties?

▶ What difference, if any, should it make that the object or target of a demonstration is an abortion clinic? Is there a risk (as Justice Scalia warns in his opinion in this case) that cases dealing with anti-abortion protest will develop legal standards that may distort other branches of free speech law—say, political protests?

> ▶ Does it make a difference whether restrictions on protests and demonstrations are imposed by a court or by a legislative body? Which is likely to know the facts better? Which is likely to be more sensitive to free expression?
>
> ▶ Most "buffer zones" consist of a set number of feet from the clinic entrance. Could a court or a legislature impose a "floating" buffer that would vary in size according to changing conditions and needs?
>
> ▶ Does government have a valid interest in protecting the homes of clinic staff members from demonstrations and protests? How far does that interest extend, and to what types of expressive activity?

Judy Madsen, et al., Petitioners v. Women's Health Center, Inc., et al. 512 U.S. 753 (1994)

Chief Justice REHNQUIST delivered the opinion of the Court.

We begin with the 36-foot buffer zone. The state court prohibited petitioners from "congregating, picketing, patrolling, demonstrating or entering" any portion of the public right-of-way or private property within 36 feet of the property line of the clinic as a way of ensuring access to the clinic. This free-speech buffer zone requires that petitioners move to the other side of Dixie Way and away from the driveway of the clinic, where the state found they repeatedly had interfered with the free access of patients and staff....The buffer zone also applies to private property to the north and west of the clinic property....The 36-foot buffer zone protecting the entrances to the clinic and the parking lot is a means of protecting unfettered ingress to and egress from the clinic, and ensuring that petitioners do not block traffic on Dixie Way. The state court seems to have had few other options to protect access given the narrow confines around the clinic....The state court was convinced that allowing the petitioners to remain on the clinic's sidewalk and driveway was not a viable option in view of the failure of the first injunction to protect access. And allowing the petitioners to stand in the middle of Dixie Way would obviously block vehicular traffic....On balance, we hold that the 36-foot buffer zone around the clinic entrances and driveway burdens no more free speech than necessary to accomplish governmental interest at stake....The inclusion of private property on the back and side of the clinic in the 36-foot buffer zone raises different concerns....Patients and staff wishing to reach the clinic do not have to cross the private property abutting the clinic property on the north and west, and nothing in the record indicates that petitioners' activities on the private property have obstructed access to the clinic....We hold that on the record before us the 36-foot buffer zone as applied to the private property to the north and west of the clinic burdens more speech than necessary to protect access to the clinic.

In response to high noise levels outside the clinic, the state court restrained the petitioners from "singing, chanting, whistling, shouting, yelling, use of bullhorns, auto horns, sound amplification equipment or other sounds or images observable to or within earshot of the patients inside the [c]linic" during the hours of 7:30 a.m. through noon on Mondays through Saturdays. We must, of course, take account of the place to which the regulations apply in determining whether these restrictions burden more speech than necessary....Noise control is particularly important around hospitals and medical facilities during surgery and recovery periods, and in evaluating another injunction involving a medical facility, we stated:

> Hospitals, after all are not factories or mines or assembly plants. They are hospitals, where human ailments are treated, where patients and relatives alike are often under emotional strain and worry, where pleasing and comforting patients are principal facets of the day's activity, and where the patient and his family...need a restful, uncluttered, relaxing, and helpful atmosphere....

> We hold that the limited noise restrictions imposed by the state court order burden no more speech than necessary to ensure the health and well-being of the patients at the clinic. The First Amendment does not demand that patients at a medical facility undertake Herculean efforts to escape the cacophony of political protests....

The same, however, cannot be said for the "images observable" provision of the state court's order. This broad prohibition on all "images observable" burdens more speech than necessary to achieve the purpose of limiting threats to clinic patients or their families....The only plausible reason a patient would be bothered by "images observable" inside the clinic would be if the patient found the expression contained in such images disagreeable. But it is much easier for the clinic to pull its curtains than for a patient to stop up her ears, and no more is required to avoid seeing placards through the windows of the clinic. This provision of the injunction violates the First Amendment.

The state court ordered that petitioners refrain from physically approaching any person seeking services of the clinic "unless such person indicates a desire to communicate" in an area within 300 feet of the clinic. The state court was attempting to prevent clinic patients and staff from being "stalked" or "shadowed" by the petitioners as they approached the clinic....

But it is difficult, indeed, to justify a prohibition on all uninvited approaches of persons seeking the services of the clinic, regardless of how peaceful the contact may be, without burdening more speech than necessary to prevent intimidation and to ensure access to the clinic. Absent evidence that the protestors' speech is independently proscribable (i.e., "fighting words" or threats), or is so infused with violence as to be indistinguishable from a threat of physical harm,...this provision cannot stand. "As a general matter, we have indicated that in public debate our citizens must tolerate insulting, and even outrageous, speech in order to provide adequate breathing space to the freedoms protected by the First Amendment."...The "consent" requirement alone invalidates this provision; it burdens more speech than is necessary to prevent intimidation and to ensure access to the clinic.

The final substantive regulation challenged by petitioners relates to a prohibition against picketing, demonstrating, or using sound amplification equipment within 300 feet of the residences of clinic staff....The same analysis applies to the use of sound amplification equipment here as that discussed above: the government may simply demand that petitioners turn down the volume if the protests overwhelm the neighborhood....

The record before us does not contain sufficient justification for this broad a ban on picketing; it appears that a limitation on the time, duration of picketing, and number of pickets outside a smaller zone could have accomplished the desired result....

In sum, we uphold the noise restrictions and the 36-foot buffer zone around the clinic entrances and driveway because they burden no more speech than necessary to eliminate the unlawful conduct targeted by the state court's injunction. We strike down as unconstitutional the 36-foot buffer zone as applied to the private property to the north and west of the clinic, the "images observable" provision, the 300-foot no-approach zone around the clinic, and the 300-foot buffer zone around the residences, because these provisions sweep more broadly than necessary to accomplish the permissible goals of the injunction. Accordingly, the judgment of the Florida Supreme Court is

Affirmed in part, and reversed in part.

Justice SCALIA, with whom Justice KENNEDY and Justice THOMAS join, concurring in the judgment in part and dissenting in part.

The judgment in today's case has an appearance of moderation and Solomonic wisdom, upholding as it does some portions of the injunction while disallowing others. That appearance is deceptive. The entire injunction in this case departs so far from the established course of our jurisprudence that in any other context it would have been regarded as a candidate for summary reversal.

But the context here is abortion....Today the *ad hoc* nullification machine claims its latest, greatest, and most surprising victim: the First Amendment.

Because I believe that the judicial creation of a 36-foot zone in which only a particular group, which had broken no law, cannot exercise its rights of speech, assembly, and association, and the judicial enactment of a noise prohibition, applicable to that group and that group alone, are profoundly at odds with our First Amendment precedents and traditions, I dissent....

What we have decided here seems to be, and will be reported by the media as, an abortion case. But it will go down in the law books, it will be cited, as a free-speech injunction case—and the damage its novel principles produce will be considerable. The proposition that injunctions against speech are subject to a standard indistinguishable from (unless perhaps more lenient in its application than) the "intermediate scrutiny" standard we have used for "time, place, and manner" legislative restrictions; the notion that injunctions against speech need not be closely tied to any violation of law, but may simply implement sound social policy; and the practice of accepting trial-court conclusions permitting injunctions without considering whether those conclusions are supported by any findings of fact—these latest by-products of our abortion jurisprudence ought to give all friends of liberty great concern....

Reno v. American Civil Liberties Union   ROBERT M. O'NEIL

The idea of barring offensive material from new communications media has ancient roots. Throughout the twentieth century, courts have sustained such efforts, and in the process have denied new technologies the full protection of the First Amendment. So it was with motion pictures; starting in 1915, the Supreme Court relegated film to a lesser place in the universe of expression.

Radio and television fared even less well in the courts; on the premise that "scarcity" was a fact of life on the airwaves, broadcasters have always been treated like second class citizens when it comes to freedom of speech. Thus the FCC may bar the saying on the air of the "seven dirty words" and may require broadcasters to grant air time to a victim of a "personal attack"—even though such burdens could not possibly be imposed on the editor of a magazine or newspaper.

Even cable has never enjoyed full First Amendment protection; in the summer of 1997, the Supreme Court upheld Congress' mandate that cable systems carry all signals of local public and commercial stations.

Against this background, it was hardly surprising that the Internet also became a target of Congressional censorship. Early in 1996, Congress adopted the Communications Decency Act (CDA). Key provisions of that law made it a crime to post "indecent" or "patently offensive" material on the Internet within reach of minors. The Act provided for an early challenge on a "fast track," that began with three federal judges, and would lead then directly to the Supreme Court.

The CDA had followed a tortuous path through Congress. The Senate initially passed an even more restrictive version authored by retiring Senator James Exon. The House, at Speaker Newt Gingrich's urging, refused to concur, and adopted instead a bill that would call upon the Internet industry to regulate itself. But the momentum behind the Senate approach proved insuperable. The Exon language eventually prevailed in both houses, with the President's blessing.

CDA supporters argued that the courts had long upheld curbs on "indecent" material on radio and television, and that such material could do comparable harm to young people through the Internet. They also noted that "patently offensive" was an element in the test of obscenity—a field in which the courts had shown substantial solicitude for minors. So the First Amendment calculus seemed problematic, against the background of other new technologies.

The digital community was quick to take up the challenge. Two test cases were promptly filed. The one that was headed for the High Court, filed in Philadelphia, reflected the concerns of librarians, public interest groups, information resources and a host of other non-profit groups. These plaintiffs convinced the three district judges that the "indecency" curb could readily put them out of business—not because they were in the business of luring young people astray, but because of the broad and imprecise terms of the Communications Decency Act.

The plaintiffs also persuaded the trial court that none of the several defenses Congress had put in the law would really enable conscientious providers to be certain that possibly "indecent" material did not reach the eyes of minors.

The case was argued only about fourteen months after the passage of the law. Many organizations filed *amicus curiae* briefs on both sides, though predominantly in support of the plaintiff non-profit groups. Those briefs, like the briefs of the parties themselves, went well beyond the immediate issues surrounding the legality of the "indecency" clause, and asked the Court to recognize the very essence of the Internet as a novel and exciting medium of communication and information. To the delight of many observers, the Justices were quite ready for that challenge. They would see in cyberspace a medium quite different from any of the other communications technologies on which they had ruled rather grudgingly in the past.

▶ What are the practical differences between speech on the Internet and spoken or printed words, which might seem to warrant different treatment of content in cyberspace?

▶ How strong is the government interest in protecting minors from obscenity and similar material? How does the government protect minors without—as the Supreme Court warned in 1957 it must not do—"reducing the adult population to reading only what is fit for children"?

▶ How convincing was the claim that "indecency" should be valid as applied to the Internet because the Supreme Court had consistently upheld broadcast regulations like the "seven dirty words" rule? What differences between the Internet and broadcasting might bear on this issue?

▶ If Congress could not make it unlawful to post "indecent" material on the Internet, what other regulatory options might there be to protect minors from potentially harmful material?

▶ To what degree may states regulate the flow or posting of information on the Internet? Do states have more or less power here than they already have over content in magazines, newspapers, and other media?

▶ Should the treatment of other materials in cyberspace—obscenity and child pornography, for example—be different from the treatment of such unlawful categories of expression in print?

Janet Reno, Attorney General of the United States, et al., Appellants v. American Civil Liberties Union et al. 521 U.S. 844 (1997)

Justice STEVENS delivered the opinion of the Court.

...The Internet is an international network of interconnected computers....The Internet has experienced "extraordinary growth."...Individuals can obtain access to the Internet from many different sources, generally hosts themselves or entities with a host affiliation....

Anyone with access to the Internet may take advantage of a wide variety of communication and information retrieval methods. These methods are constantly evolving and difficult to categorize precisely. But, as presently constituted, those most relevant to this case are electronic mail ("e-mail"), automatic mailing list services ("mail exploders," sometimes referred to as "listservs"), "newsgroups," "chat rooms," and the "World Wide Web." All of these methods can be used to transmit text; most can transmit sound, pictures, and moving video images. Taken together, these tools constitute a unique medium—known to its users as "cyberspace"—located in no particular geographical location but available to anyone, anywhere in the world, with access to the Internet....

Sexually explicit material on the Internet includes text, pictures, and chat and "extends from the modestly titillating to the hardest-core."...Though such material is widely available, users seldom encounter such contact accidentally. "A document's title or a description of the document will usually appear before the document itself...and in many cases the user will receive detailed information about a site's content before he or she need take the step to access the document. Almost all sexually explicit images are preceded by warnings as to the content." For that reason, the "odds are slim" that a user would enter a sexually explicit site by accident.... "A child requires some sophistication and some ability to read to retrieve material and thereby to use the Internet unattended."...In *Ginsberg*, we upheld the constitutionality of a New York statute that prohibited selling to minors under 17 years of age material that was considered obscene as to them even if not obscene to adults....In *Pacifica*, we upheld a declaratory order of the Federal Communications Commission, holding that the broadcast of a recording of 12-minute monologue entitled "Filthy Words" that had previously been delivered to a live audience "could have been the subject of administrative sanctions."...

As with the New York statute at issue in *Ginsberg*, there are significant differences between the order upheld in *Pacifica* and the CDA. First, the order in *Pacifica*, issued by an agency that had been regulating radio stations for decades, targeted a specific broadcast that represented a rather dramatic departure from traditional program content in order to designate when—rather than whether—it would be permissible to air such a program in that particular medium. The CDA's broad categorical prohibitions are not limited to particular times and are not dependent on any evaluation by an agency familiar with the unique characteristics of the Internet. Second, unlike the CDA, the Commission's declaratory order was not punitive; we expressly refused to decide whether the indecent broadcast "would justify a criminal prosecution. *Id.*, at 750. Finally, the Commission's order applied to a medium which as a matter of history had "received the most limited First Amendment protection," *id.*, at 748, in large part because warnings could not adequately protect the listener from unexpected program content. The Internet, however, has no comparable history. Moreover, the District Court found that the risk of encountering indecent material by accident is remote because a series of affirmative steps is required to access specific material....

In *Southeastern Promotions, Ltd. v. Conrad*,...we observed that "[e]ach medium of expression...may present its own problems." Thus, some of our cases have recognized special justifications for regulation of the broadcast media that are not applicable to other speakers....In these cases, the Court relied on the history of extensive government regulation of the broadcast medium,...the scarcity of available frequencies at its inception,...and its "invasive" nature....Those factors are not present in cyberspace. Neither before nor after the enactment of the CDA have the vast democratic fora of the Internet been subject to the type of government supervision and regulation that has attended the broadcast industry. Moreover, the Internet is not as "invasive" as radio or television. The District Court specifically found that "[c]ommunications over the Internet do not 'invade' an individual's home or appear on one's computer screen unbidden. Users seldom encounter content 'by accident.'"...It also found that "[a]lmost all sexually explicit images are preceded by warnings as to the content," and cited testimony that "'odds are slim' that a user would come across a sexually explicit sight by accident."...

Finally, unlike the conditions that prevailed when Congress first authorized regulation of the broadcast spectrum, the Internet can hardly be considered a "scarce" expressive commodity. It provides relatively unlimited, low-cost capacity for communication of all kinds....This dynamic, multifaceted category of communication includes not only traditional print and news services, but also audio, video, and still images, as well as interactive, real-time dialogue. Through the use of chat rooms, any person with a phone line can become a town crier with a voice that resonates farther than it could from any soapbox. Through the use of Web pages, mail exploders, and newsgroups, the same individual can become a pamphleteer. As the District Court found, "the content on the Internet is as diverse as human thought."...We agree with its conclusion that our cases provide no basis for qualifying the level of First Amendment scrutiny that should be applied to this medium.

Regardless of whether the CDA is so vague that it violates the Fifth Amendment, the many ambiguities concerning the scope of its coverage render it problematic for purposes of the First Amendment. For instance, each of the two parts of the CDA uses a different linguistic form. The first uses the word "indecent,"...while the second speaks of material that "in context, depicts or describes, in terms patently offensive as measured by contemporary community standards, sexual or excretory activities or organs"....Given the absence of a definition of either term, this difference in language will provoke uncertainty among speakers about how the two standards relate to each other and just what they mean. Could a speaker confidently assume that a serious discussion about birth control practices, homosexuality,...or the consequences of prison rape would not violate the CDA? This uncertainty undermines the likelihood that the CDA has been carefully tailored to the congressional goal of protecting minors from potentially harmful materials. The vagueness of the CDA is a matter of special concern for two reasons. First, the CDA is a content-based regulation of speech. The vagueness of such a regulation raises special First Amendment concerns because of its obvious chilling effect on free speech....Second, the CDA is a criminal statute. In addition to the opprobrium and stigma of a criminal conviction, the CDA threatens violators with penalties including up to two years in prison for each act of violation. The severity of criminal sanctions may well cause speakers to remain silent rather than communicate even arguably unlawful words....

The Government argues that the statute is no more vague than the obscenity standard this Court established in *Miller v. California*....In contrast to *Miller* and our other previous cases, the CDA thus presents a greater threat of censoring speech that, in fact, falls outside the statute's scope. Given the vague contours of the coverage of the statute, it unquestionably silences some speakers whose messages would be entitled to constitutional protection. That danger provides further reason for insisting that the statute not be overly broad. The CDA's burden on protected speech cannot be justified if it could be avoided by a more carefully drafted statute.

We are persuaded that the CDA lacks the precision that the First Amendment requires when a statute regulates the content of speech. In order to deny minors access to potentially harmful speech, the CDA effectively suppresses a large amount of speech that adults have a constitutional right to receive and to address to one another. That burden on adult speech is unacceptable if less restrictive alternatives would be at least as effective in achieving the legitimate purpose that the statute was enacted to serve....In arguing that the CDA does not so diminish adult communication, the Government relies on the incorrect factual premise that prohibiting a transmission whenever it is known that one if its recipients is a minor would not interfere with adult-to-adult communication....

The District Court found that at the time of trial existing technology did not include any effective method for a sender to prevent minors from obtaining access to its communications on the Internet without also denying access to adults. The Court found no effective way to determine the age of a user who is accessing material through e-mail, mail exploders, newsgroups, or chat rooms....As a practical matter, the Court also found that it would be prohibitively expensive for noncommercial   as well as some commercial— speakers who have Web sites to verify that their users are adults....

The breadth of CDA's coverage is wholly unprecedented. Unlike the regulations upheld in *Ginsberg* and *Pacifica*, the scope of the CDA is not limited to commercial speech or commercial entities. Its open-ended prohibitions embrace all non-profit entities and individuals posting indecent messages or displaying them on their own computers in the presence of minors. The general, undefined terms "indecent" and "patently offensive" cover large amounts of nonpornographic material with serious educational or other value. Moreover, the "community standards" criterion as applied to the Internet means that any communication available to a nation-wide audience will be judged by the standards of the community most likely to be offended by the message. The regulated subject matter includes any of the seven "dirty words" used in the *Pacifica* monologue, the use of which the Government's expert acknowledged could constitute a felony....It may also extend to discussions about prison rape or safe sexual practices, artistic images that include nude subjects, and arguably the card catalogue of the Carnegie library....The breadth of this content-based restriction of speech imposes an especially heavy burden on the Government to explain why a less restrictive provision would not be as effective as the CDA. It has not done so....Particularly in the light of the absence of any detailed findings by the Congress, or even hearings addressing the special problems of the CDA, we are persuaded that the CDA is not narrowly tailored if that requirement has any meaning at all....

As a matter of constitutional tradition, in the absence of evidence to the contrary, we presume that the governmental regulation of the content of speech is more likely to interfere with the free exchange of ideas than to encourage it. The interest in encouraging freedom of expression in a democratic society outweighs any theoretical but unproven benefit of censorship....

Justice O'CONNOR, with whom The Chief Justice joins, concurring in the judgment in part and dissenting in part.

I write separately to explain why I view the Communications Decency Act of 1996 (CDA) as little more than an attempt by Congress to create "adult zones" on the Internet. Our precedent indicates that the creation of such zones can be constitutionally sound. Despite the soundness of its purpose, however, portions of the CDA are unconstitutional because they stray from the blueprint our prior cases have developed from constructing a "zoning law" that passes constitutional muster.

III Church and State

Engel v. Vitale (1962)

Edwards v. Aguillard (1987)

Department of Human Resources of Oregon v. Smith (1990)

Rosenberger v. Rector and Visitors of the University of Virginia (1995)

City of Boerne v. Flores (1997)

III Church and State

RODNEY A. SMOLLA

The Virginia Statute for Religious Freedom, drafted by Thomas Jefferson and shephereded through the Virginia Legislature in 1786 by James Madison, was the precursor of the First Amendment to the Bill of Rights, which proclaims in ringing terms that "Congress shall make no law respecting an establishment of religion, or prohibiting the free exercise thereof ..." Jefferson envisioned a "wall of separation" between Church and State. It has been left to later generations to litigate what exactly this concept of "wall of separation" should mean.

In interpreting the Free Exercise Clause, the Supreme Court has struggled with a number of interlocking issues. There is no dispute that the government may not dictate religious belief. But what happens when the government merely regulates conduct, not belief, yet the regulation of that *conduct* has the "real-world" affect of interfering with someone's religious practices? Here the Court's answers have not always been consistent. In an early decision, *Reynolds v. United States* (1878), the Court sustained a ban on polygamy in what was then the federal territory of Utah, even though the law interfered with a tenet of the Mormon religion, which at that time condoned polygamous marriages. In contrast, the Court in *Wisconsin v. Yoder* (1972) held that an Amish Mennonite group had a right under the First Amendment to refuse to send their children to accredited Wisconsin schools, thus excusing them for religious reasons from the state's compulsory education laws.

On the Establishment Clause side, the Court has also struggled. It is settled that the Establishment Clause means at least that neither a state nor the federal government can set up a church, pass laws that aid one religion, aid all religions, or prefer one religion over another. Taxes may not be levied to support religious activities or institutions. Beyond these basics, however, there is much dispute. Those who favor strict separation of Church and State would strike down virtually all entanglement between government and religion. Others, however, would permit many forms of state financial aid to religious enterprises, and in turn would give the government wide latitude to engage in religious rituals and display religious symbols.

▶ To what extent may governmental institutions engage in religious rituals? The Court has held that prayers may not be conducted in public school classrooms, or in graduation ceremonies. But the Court permitted a state legislature to open its sessions with a prayer. What might explain the different results?

▶ Many of our public rituals, from the Pledge of Allegiance to the Flag to the motto "In God We Trust" on coins and currency make open reference to God. Should the First Amendment be understood as making such references impermissible?

▶ The two great religion clauses, the Establishment Clause and the Free Exercise Clause, at times appear to be in conflict. In order to accommodate the free exercise of religion by citizens, for example, government may be tempted to give those citizens "a break" from the requirements of generally applicable laws. Thus a public school may wish to permit students to leave school to attend religious instruction, or to re-schedule an exam that falls on a religious holiday. Yet at some point, the government's "accommodation" of the free exercise of religion may be seen as an "establishment" of religion, because it is perceived as endorsing or promoting religious beliefs. In a conflict between the values of the Establishment Clause and the values of The Free Exercise Clause, which Clause should predominate?

▶ Justice William O. Douglas, writing the opinion for the Court in *Zorach v. Clauson* (1952), wrote the following famous sentence: "We are a religious people whose institutions presuppose a Supreme Being." What does this statement mean? Is it wrong or right?

Engel v. Vitale MELVIN UROFSKY

New York, like many states prior to 1962, opened its school day with a prayer, in this case a "non-sectarian" prayer composed by the Board of Regents. Other states and localities used other invocations, such as the Lord's Prayer, or borrowed from sectarian services. The decision in *Engel*, holding that such official prayers violated the First Amendment's Establishment Clause, created such a furor partly because people had become used to schools and other public functions beginning with a prayer. They assumed it was "the American way," and that the Court was now, as some critics charged, "taking God out of the schools." The uproar increased when, in *Abington School District v. Schempp* (1963), the Court also prohibited required reading of biblical verses and recitation of the Lord's Prayer.

It is difficult to take issue with Justice Black's analysis in this case. Is there anything that more directly resembles state control of religion than prescribing a specific prayer and then requiring people to say that prayer? Yet a quarter-century after the Court handed down this decision, there are still those who believe the Court decided the case wrongly and that the Constitution allows the state to mandate prayer in the schools. In order to get around the *Engel* decision a number of amendments to the Constitution have been proposed, but so far none has received congressional assent.

▶ Did the Court outlaw praying in school? What exactly did the Court prohibit?

▶ If prayer is, as some theologians suggest, a dialogue with God, how does mandated and prescribed prayer square with this notion of religion?

▶ Should children be allowed to pray whenever they want? Does Engel preclude them from doing so?

▶ Justice Douglas puts forward a literalist view of the First Amendment. The Court has never adopted this viewpoint, but is there anything logically wrong in his analysis?

▶ There are, as Justice Stewart notes in his dissent, many religious statements that are "official," such as the verse of the national anthem which he quotes. Does the fact that religious sentiment appears there and in other places, such as on coins, make those appearances "religious establishment?"

▶ Is the basic issue of this case religion *per se*, or the role of the state? Does it make a difference?

Engel v. Vitale 370 U.S. 424 (1962)

Mr. Justice BLACK delivered the opinion of the Court.

The respondent Board of Education of Union Free School District No. 9, New Hyde Park, New York, acting in its official capacity under state law, directed the School District's principal to cause the following prayer to be said aloud by each class in the presence of a teacher at the beginning of each school day:

> Almighty God, we acknowledge our dependence upon Thee, and we beg Thy blessings upon us, our parents, our teachers and our Country.

This daily procedure was adopted on the recommendation of the State Board of Regents, a governmental agency created by the State Constitution to which the New York Legislature has granted broad supervisory, executive, and legislative powers over the State's public school system. These state officials composed the prayer which they recommended and published as a part of their "Statement on Moral and Spiritual Training in the Schools," saying: "We believe that this Statement will be subscribed to by all men and women of good will, and we call upon all of them to aid in giving life to our program."...

We think that by using its public school system to encourage recitation of the regents' prayer, the State of New York has adopted a practice wholly inconsistent with the Establishment Clause. There can, of course, be no doubt that New York's program of daily classroom invocation of God's blessings as prescribed in the Regents' prayer is a religious activity. It is a solemn avowal of divine faith and supplication for the blessings of the Almighty. The nature of such a prayer has always been religious, none of the respondents has denied this and the trial court expressly so found....

The petitioners contend among other things that the state laws requiring or permitting use of the Regents' prayer must be struck down as a violation of the Establishment Clause because that prayer was composed by governmental officials as a part of a governmental program to further religious beliefs. For this reason, petitioners argue, the State's use of the Regents' prayer in its public school system breaches the constitutional wall of separation between Church and State. We agree with that contention since we think that the constitutional prohibition against laws respecting an establishment of religion must at least mean that in this country it is no part of the business of government to compose official prayers for any group of the American people to recite as a part of a religious program carried on by government.

It is a matter of history that this very practice of establishing governmentally composed prayers for religious services was one of the reasons which caused many of our early colonists to leave England and seek religious freedom in America. The Book of Common Prayer, which was created under governmental direction and which was approved by Acts of Parliament in 1548 and 1549, set out in minute detail the accepted form and content of prayer and other religious ceremonies to be used in the established, tax-supported Church of England....

It is an unfortunate fact of history that when some of the very groups which had most strenuously opposed the established Church of England found themselves sufficiently in control of colonial governments in this country to write their own prayers into law, they passed laws making their own religion the official religion of their respective colonies. Indeed, as late as the time of the Revolutionary War, there were established churches in at least eight of the thirteen former colonies and established religions in at least four of the other five. But the successful Revolution against English political domination was shortly followed by intense opposition to the practice of establishing religion by law. This opposition crystallized rapidly into an effective political force in Virginia where the minority religious groups such as Presbyterians, Lutherans, Quakers and Baptists had gained such strength that the adherents to the established Episcopal Church were actually a minority themselves. In 1785-1786, those opposed to the established Church, led by James Madison and Thomas Jefferson, who, though themselves not members of any of these dissenting religious groups, opposed all religious establishments by law on grounds of principle, obtained the enactment of the famous "Virginia Bill for Religious Liberty" by which all religious groups were placed on an equal footing so far as the State was concerned. Similar though less far-reaching legislation was being considered and passed in other States....

The First Amendment was added to the Constitution to stand as a guarantee that neither the power nor the prestige of the Federal Government would be used to control, support or influence the kinds of prayer the American people can say—that the people's religions must not be subjected to the pressures of government for change each time a new political administration is elected to office. Under that Amendment's prohibition against governmental establishment of religion, as reinforced by the provisions of the Fourteenth Amendment, government in this country, be it state or federal, is without power to prescribe by law any particular form of prayer which is to be used as an official prayer in carrying on any program of governmentally sponsored religious activity.

There can be no doubt that New York's state prayer program officially establishes the religious beliefs embodied in the Regents' prayer. The respondents' argument to the contrary, which is largely based upon the contention that the Regents' prayer is "nondenominational" and the fact that the program, as modified and approved by state courts, does not require all pupils to recite the prayer but permits those who wish to do so to remain silent or be excused from the room, ignores the essential nature of the program's constitutional defects. Neither the fact that the prayer may be denominationally neutral nor the fact that its observance on the part of the students is voluntary can serve to free it from the limitations of Establishment Clause, as it might from the Free Exercise Clause, of the First Amendment, both of which are operative against the States by virtue of the Fourteenth Amendment. Although these two clauses may in certain instances overlap, they forbid two quite different kinds of governmental encroachment upon religious freedom. The Establishment Clause, unlike the Free Exercise Clause, does not depend upon any showing of direct governmental compulsion and is violated by the enactment of laws which establish an official religion whether those laws operate directly to coerce nonobserving individuals or not. This is not to say, of course, that laws officially prescribing a particular form of religious worship do not involve coercion of such individuals. When the power, prestige and financial support of government is placed behind a particular religious belief, the indirect coercive pressure upon religious minorities to conform to the prevailing officially approved religion is plain. But the purposes underlying the Establishment Clause go much further than that. Its first and most immediate purpose rested on the belief that a union of government and religion tends to destroy government and to degrade religion. The history of governmentally established religion, both in England and in this country, showed that whenever government had allied itself with one particular form of religion, the inevitable result had been that it had incurred the hatred, disrespect and even contempt of those who held contrary beliefs. That same history showed that many people had lost their respect for any religion that had relied upon the support of government to spread its faith. The Establishment Clause thus stands as an expression of principle on the part of the Founders of our Constitution that religion is too personal, too sacred, too holy, to permit its "unhallowed perversion" by a civil magistrate. Another purpose of the Establishment Clause rested upon an awareness of the historical fact that governmentally established religions and religious persecutions go hand in hand. The Founders knew that only a few years after the Book of Common Prayer became the only accepted form of religious services in the established Church of England, an Act of Uniformity was passed to compel all Englishmen to attend those services and to make it a criminal offense to conduct or attend religious gatherings of any other kind—a law which was consistently flouted by dissenting religious groups in England and which contributed to widespread persecutions of people like John Bunyan who persisted in holding "unlawful [religious] meetings...to the great disturbance and distraction of the good subjects of this kingdom...." And they knew that similar persecutions had received the sanction of law in several of the colonies in this country soon after the establishment of official religions in those colonies. It was in large part to get completely away from this sort of systematic religious persecution that the Founders brought into being our Nation, our Constitution, and our Bill of Rights with its prohibition against any governmental establishment of religion. The New York laws officially prescribing the Regents' prayer are inconsistent both with the purposes of the Establishment Clause and with the Establishment Clause itself.

It has been argued that to apply the Constitution in such a way as to prohibit state laws respecting an establishment of religious services in public schools is to indicate a hostility toward religion or toward prayer. Nothing, of course, could be more wrong. The history of man is inseparable from the history of religion. And perhaps it is not too much to say that since the beginning of that history many people have devoutly believed that "More things are wrought by prayer than this world dreams of." It was doubtless largely due to men who believed this that there grew up a sentiment that caused men to leave the cross-currents of officially established state religions and religious persecution in Europe and come to this country filled with the hope that they could find a place in which they could pray when they pleased to the God of their faith in the language they chose. And there were men of this same faith in the power of prayer who led the fight for adoption of our Constitution and also for our Bill of Rights with the very guarantees of religious freedom that forbid the sort of governmental activity which New York has attempted here. These men knew that the First Amendment, which tried to put an end to governmental control of religion and of prayer, was not written to destroy either. They knew rather that it was written to quiet well-justified fears which nearly all of them felt arising out of an awareness that governments of the past had shackled men's tongues to make them speak only the religious thoughts that government wanted them to speak and to pray only to the God that government wanted them to pray to. It is neither sacrilegious nor antireligious to say that each separate government in this country should stay out of the business of writing or sanctioning official prayers and leave that purely religious function to the people themselves and to those the people choose to look to for religious guidance....

The judgement of the Court of Appeals of New York is reversed and the cause remanded for further proceedings not inconsistent with this opinion.

Reversed and remanded.

Mr. Justice DOUGLAS, concurring.

It is customary in deciding a constitutional question to treat it in its narrowest form. Yet at times the setting of the question gives it a form and content which no abstract treatment could give. The point for decision is whether the Government can constitutionally finance a religious exercise. Our system at the federal and state levels is presently honeycombed with such financing. Nevertheless, I think it is an unconstitutional under-taking whatever form it takes.

First, a word as to what this case does not involve.

Plainly, our Bill of Rights would not permit a State or the Federal Government to adopt an official prayer and penalize anyone who would not utter it. This, however, is not that case, for there is no element of compulsion or coercion in New York's regulation requiring that public schools be opened each day with the prayer....

As I read this regulation, a child is free to stand or not stand, to recite or not recite, with-out fear of reprisal or even comment by the teacher or any other school official.

In short, the only one who need utter the prayer is the teacher; and no teacher is com-plaining of it. Students can stand mute or even leave the classroom, if they desire....
The question presented by this case is therefore an extremely narrow one. It is whether New York oversteps the bounds when it finances a religious exercise.

What New York does on the opening of its public schools is what we do when we open court. Our Crier has from the beginning announced the convening of the Court and then added "God save the United States and this Honorable Court." That utterance is a supplica-tion, a prayer in which we, the judges, are free to join, but which we need not recite any more than the students need recite the New York prayer.

What New York does on the opening of its public schools is what each House of Congress does at the opening of each day's business. Yet for me the principal is the same, no matter how briefly the prayer is said, for in each of the instances given the person praying is a public official on the public payroll, performing a religious exercise in a governmental insti-tution. It is said that the element of coercion is inherent in the giving of this prayer. If that is true here, it is also true of the prayer with which this Court is convened, and of those that open the Congress. Few adults, let alone children, would leave our courtroom or the Senate or the House while those prayers are being given. Every such audience is in a sense a "cap-tive" audience....

Mr. Justice STEWART, dissenting.

A local school board in New York has provided that those pupils who wish to do so may join in a brief prayer at the beginning of each school day, acknowledging their dependence upon God and asking His blessing upon them and upon their parents, their teachers, and their country. The Court today decides that in permitting this brief non-denominational prayer the school board has violated the Constitution of the United States. I think this decision is wrong.

The Court does not hold, nor could it, that New York has interfered with the free exercise of anybody's religion. For the state courts have made clear that those who object to reciting the prayer must be entirely free of any compulsion to do so, including any "embarrassments and pressures." But the Court says that in permitting school children to say this simple prayer, the New York authorities have established "an official religion."

With all respect, I think the Court has misapplied a great constitutional principle. I cannot see how an "official religion" is established by letting those who want to say a prayer say it. On the contrary, I think that to deny the wish of these school children to join in reciting this prayer is to deny them the opportunity of sharing in the spiritual heritage of our Nation....

The Court today says that the state and federal governments are without constitutional power to prescribe any particular form of words to be recited by any group of the American people on any subject touching religion. One of the stanzas of "The Star-Spangled Banner," made our National Anthem by Act of Congress in 1931, contains these verses:

> Blest with victory and peace,
>> may the heav'n rescued land
> Praise the Pow'r that hath made
>> and preserved us a nation!

> Then conquer we must,
>> when our cause it is just,
> And this be our motto
> In God is our Trust.

In 1954 Congress added a phrase to the Pledge of Allegiance to the Flag so that it now contains the words "one Nation under God, indivisible, with liberty and justice for all." In 1952 Congress enacted legislation calling upon the President each year to proclaim a National Day of Prayer. Since 1865 the words "IN GOD WE TRUST" have been impressed on our coins.

Countless similar examples could be listed, but there is no need to belabor the obvious. It was all summed up by this Court just ten years ago in a single sentence: "We are a religious people whose institutions presuppose a Supreme Being."

I do not believe that this Court, or the Congress, or the President has by the actions and practices I have mentioned established an "official religion" in violation of the Constitution. And I do not believe the State of New York has done so in this case. What each has done has been to recognize and to follow the deeply entrenched and highly cherished spiritual traditions of our Nation—traditions which come down to us from those who almost two hundred years ago avowed their "firm Reliance on the Protection of divine Providence" when they proclaimed the freedom and independence of this brave new world.

I dissent.

Edwards v. Aguillard   RODNEY A. SMOLLA

One of the most famous trials of this century is the Scopes case, the so-called 1927 "Monkey Trial" in Dayton, Tennessee, in which a young school teacher named John Scopes was prosecuted for teaching Darwin's theory of evolution; that is, that man has evolved from a lower form of animal. Clarence Darrow defended Scopes, and knowing he would lose the trial, laid the ground for an appeal to the Supreme Court. The Tennessee high court, however, blocked the appeal by dismissing the conviction on a technicality. Tennessee, after the scorn heaped on it, did not prosecute anyone else under its anti-evolution law, nor did any of the other states with similar statutes. But neither did they repeal the laws.

Forty years later, in *Epperson v. Arkansas* (1968), a school teacher in Arkansas sought a declaratory judgment on the constitutionality of that state's anti-evolution law, which prohibited teachers in state schools from teaching "the theory or doctrine that mankind ascended or descended from a lower order of animals." She claimed that she could not teach her assigned biology course according to the syllabus without violating the law. The state's highest court avoided the issue, and refused to go on record as to what the law meant. The Supreme Court, however, ruled that the law attempted to impose religious beliefs, and therefore violated the First Amendment.

In 1987, the Supreme Court decided a "sequel" to *Epperson*, involving a Louisiana law entitled the "Balanced Treatment for Creation-Science and Evolution-Science in Public Instruction Act," popularly known as the "Creationism Act." The law prohibited the teaching of the theory of evolution in public schools unless accompanied by instruction in "creation science." No school was required to teach evolution or creation science, but if either one was taught, the other also had to be taught. The Creationism Act defined the two theories as "scientific evidences" for creation of evolution and "the inferences from those scientific evidences." The Act recited that its purpose was the protection of "academic freedom."

▶ Is creationism a science? Is the definition of what is or is not science a matter for legislatures to determine?

▶ Was the result in *Edwards* required by the result in *Epperson*, or are the two cases distinguishable?

▶ *Epperson* holds that a state law may not require the teaching of evolution, and *Edwards* holds that a law may not require "equal time" for evolution and creationism if either is taught. Would a state law that prohibited the teaching of creationism in public schools altogether be unconstitutional?

▶ What if there is no state law on the subject at all? After *Edwards*, could a public school biology teacher in a state where no such law existed teach creation science without violating the Establishment Clause? Does it make a difference whether he or she is motivated by a personal religious belief that a divine creator was responsible for creation?

Edwards v. Aguillard 482 U.S. 578 (1987)

Justice BRENNAN delivered the opinion of the Court.

The Creationism Act forbids the teaching of the theory of evolution in public schools unless accompanied by instruction in "creation science." No school is required to teach evolution or creation science. If either is taught, however, the other must also be taught. The theories of evolution and creation science are statutorily defined as "the scientific evidences for [creation or evolution] and inferences from those scientific evidences."

Appellees, who include parents of children attending Louisiana public schools, Louisiana teachers, and religious leaders, challenged the constitutionality of the Act in District court, seeking an injunction and declaratory relief. Appellants, Louisiana officials charged with implementing the Act, defended on the ground that the purpose of the Act is to protect a legitimate secular interest, namely, academic freedom....

The Establishment Clause forbids the enactment of any law "respecting an establishment of religion." The Court has applied a three-pronged test to determine whether legislation comports with the Establishment Clause. First, the legislature must have adopted the law with a secular purpose. Second, the statute's principal of primary effect must be one that neither advances nor prohibits religion. Third, the statute must not result in an excessive entanglement of government with religion. State action violates the Establishment Clause if it fails to satisfy any of these prongs....

The Court has been particularly vigilant in monitoring compliance with the Establishment Clause in elementary and secondary schools....Students in such institutions are impressionable and their attendance is involuntary....Furthermore, "[t]he public school is at once the symbol of our democracy and the most pervasive means for promoting our common destiny. In no activity of the State is it more vital to keep out divisive forces than in its schools....

Consequently, the Court has been required often to invalidate statutes which advance religion in public elementary and secondary schools....

Therefore, in employing the three-pronged *Lemon* test, we must do so mindful of the particular concerns that arise in the context of public elementary and secondary schools. We now turn to the evolution of the Act under the *Lemon* test.

..."The purpose prong of the *Lemon* test asks whether government's actual purpose is to endorse or disapprove of religion." A governmental intention to promote religion is clear when the State enacts a law to serve a religious purpose....If the law was enacted for the purpose of endorsing religion, "no consideration of the second or third criteria is necessary." In this case, the petitioners have identified no clear secular purpose for the Louisiana Act.

True, the Act's stated purpose is to protect academic freedom....However, even if "academic freedom" is read to mean "teaching all of the evidence" with respect to the origin of human beings, the Act does not further this purpose. The goal of providing a more comprehensive science curriculum is not furthered either by outlawing the teaching of evolution or by requiring the teaching of creation science.

While the Court is normally deferential to a State's articulation of a secular purpose, it is required that the statement of such purpose be sincere and not a sham....

It is clear from the legislative history that the purpose of the legislative sponsor, Senator Bill Keith, was to narrow the science curriculum. During the legislative hearings, Senator Keith stated: "My preference would be that neither [creationism nor evolution] be taught." ...It is clear that requiring schools to teach creation science with evolution does not advance academic freedom....As the president of the Louisianan Science Teachers Association testified, "[a]ny scientific concept that's based on established fact can be included in our curriculum already, and no legislation allowing this is necessary." The Act provides Louisiana schoolteachers with no new authority. Thus the stated purpose is not furthered by it.

If the Louisiana legislature's purpose was solely to maximize the comprehensiveness and effectiveness of science instruction, it would have encouraged the teaching of all scientific theories about the origins of humankind. But under the Act's requirements, teachers who were once free to teach any and all facets of this subject are now unable to do so. Moreover, the Act fails even to ensure that creation science will be taught, but instead requires the teaching of this theory only when the theory of evolution is taught....Thus the Act does not serve to protect academic freedom, but has the distinctly different purpose of discrediting "evolution by counterbalancing its teaching at every turn with teaching of creation science...."

...The preeminent purpose of the Louisiana legislature was clearly to advance the religious viewpoint that a supernatural being created humankind....Furthermore, it is not happenstance that the legislature required the teaching of a theory that coincided with this religious view. The legislative history documents that the Act's primary purpose was to change the science curriculum of public schools in order to provide persuasive advantage to a particular religious doctrine that rejects the factual basis of evolution in its entirety....

...The Creationism Act is designed *either* to promote the theory of creation science which embodies a particular religious tenet by requiring that creation science be taught whenever evolution is taught or to prohibit the teaching of a scientific theory disfavored by certain religious sects by forbidding the teaching of evolution when creation science is not also taught. The Establishment Clause, however, forbids *alike* the preference of a religious doctrine or the prohibition of theory which is deemed antagonistic to a particular dogma. Because the primary purpose of the Creationism Act is to advance a particular religious belief, the Act endorses religion in violation of the First Amendment.

We do not imply that a legislature could never require that scientific critiques of prevailing scientific theories be taught....Teaching a variety of scientific theories about the origins of humankind to schoolchildren might be validly done with the clear secular intent of enhancing the effectiveness of science instruction. But because the primary purpose of the Creationism Act is to endorse a particular religious doctrine, the Act furthers religion in violation of the Establishment Clause.

The judgment of the Court of Appeals therefore is

Affirmed.

Justice POWELL, with whom Justice O'CONNOR joins, concurring.

I write separately to note certain aspects of the legislative history, and to emphasize that nothing in the Court's opinion diminishes the traditionally broad discretion accorded state and local school officials in the selection of the public school curriculum.

...When, as here, "both courts below are unable to discern an arguably valid secular purpose, the Court normally should hesitate to find one." My examination of the language and the legislative history of the Balanced Treatment Act confirms that the intent of the Louisiana legislature was to promote a particular religious belief....

Here, it is clear that religious belief is the Balanced Treatment Act's "reason for existence." The tenets of creation-science parallel the Genesis story of creation, and this is a religious belief. "[N]o legislative recitation of a supposed secular purpose can blind us to that fact...."

The legislature acted with the unconstitutional purpose of structuring the public school curriculum to make it compatible with a particular religious belief: the "divine creation of man."

...Whatever the academic merit of particular subjects or theories, the Establishment Clause limits the discretion of state officials to pick and choose among them for the purpose of promoting a particular religious belief. The language of the statute and its legislative history convince me that the Louisiana legislature exercised its discretion for this purpose in the case.

A decision respecting the subject matter to be taught in public schools does not violate the Establishment Clause simply because the material to be taught "'happens to consider or harmonize with the tenets of some or all religions.'"

As matter of history, school children can and should properly be informed of all aspects of this Nation's religious heritage. I would see no constitutional problem if school children were taught the nature of the Founding Fathers' religious beliefs and how these beliefs affected the attitudes of the times and the structure of our government. Courses in comparative religion of course are customary and constitutionally appropriate. In fact, since religion permeates our history, a familiarity with the nature of religoius beliefs is necessary to understand many historical as well as contemporary events. In addition, it is worth noting that the Establishment Clause does not prohibit *per se* the educational use of religious documents in public school education....The Establishment Clause is properly understood to prohibit the use of the Bible and other religious documents in public school education only when the purpose of the use is to advance a particular religious belief.

Justice SCALIA, with whom The CHIEF JUSTICE joins, dissenting.

Even if I agreed with the questionable premise that legislation can be invalidated under the Establishment Clause on the basis of its motivation alone, without regard to its effects, I would still find no justification for today's decision. The Louisiana legislators who passed the "Balanced Treatment for Creation-Science and Evolution-Science Act," each of whom had sworn to support the Constitution, wree well aware of the potential Establishment Clause problems and considered that aspect of the legislation with great care. After seven hearings and several months of study, resulting in substantial revision of the original proposal, they approved the Act overwhelmingly and specifically articulated the secular purpose they meant it to serve. Although the record contains abundant evidence of the sincerity of that purpose (the only issue pertinent to this case), the Court today holds, essentially on the basis of "its visceral knowledge regarding what *must* have motivated the legislators," that the members of the Louisiana Legislature knowingly violated their oaths and then lied about it. I dissent....

We have relatively little information upon which to judge the motives of those who supported the Act. About the only direct evidence is the statute itself and transcripts of the seven committee hearings at which it was considered. Unfortunately, several of those hearings were sparsely attended, and the legislators who were present revealed little about their motives. We have no committee reports, no floor debates, no remarks inserted into the legislative history, no statement from the Governor, and no post-enactment statements or testimony from the bill's sponsor of any other legislators. Nevertheless, there is ample evidence that the majority is wrong in holding that the Balanced Treatment Act is without secular purpose....

Our task is not to judge the debate about teaching the origins of life, but to ascertain what the members of the Louisiana Legislature believed. The vast majority of them voted to approve a bill which explicitly stated a secular purpose; what is crucial is not their wisdom in believing that purpose would be achieved by the fill, but their *sincerity* in believing it would be.

...Striking down a law approved by the democratically elected representatives of the people is no minor matter. "The cardinal principle of statutory construction is to save and not to destroy. We have repeatedly held that as between two possible interpretations of a statute, by one of which it would be unconstitutional and by the other valid, our plain duty is to adopt that which will save the act." So, too, it seems to me, with discerning statutory purpose. Even if the legislative history were silent or ambiguous about the existence of a secular purpose— and here it is not—the statute should survive *Lemon*'s purpose test. But even more validation than mere legislative history is present here. The Louisiana Legislature explicitly set forth its secular purpose ("protecting academic freedom") in the very text of the Act.

The legislative history gives ample evidence of the sincerity of the Balanced Treatment Act's articulated purpose. Witness after witness urged the legislators to support the Act so that students would not be "indoctrinated" but would instead be free to decide for themselves, based upon a fair presentation of the scientific evidence, about the origin of life....

It is undoubtedly true that what prompted the Legislature to direct its attention to the misrepresentation of evolution in the schools (rather than the inaccurate presentation of other topics) was its awareness of the tension between evolution and the religious beliefs of many children. But even appellees concede that a valid secular purpose is not rendered impermissible simply because its pursuit is promoted by concern for religious sensitivities....

In sum, even if one concedes, for the sake of argument, that a majority of the Louisiana Legislature voted for the Balanced Treatment Act partly in order to foster (rather than merely eliminate discrimination against) Christian fundamentalist beliefs, our cases establish that that alone would not suffice to invalidate the Act, so long as there was a genuine secular purpose as well. We have, moreover, no adequate basis for disbelieving the secular purpose set forth in the Act itself, or for concluding that it is a sham enacted to conceal the legislators' violation of their oaths of office....

I have to this point assumed the validity of the *Lemon* "purpose" test....In the past we have attempted to justify our embarrassing Establishment Clause jurisprudence on the ground that it "sacrifices clarity and predictability for flexibility."...I think it is time that we sacrifice some "flexibility" for "clarity and predictability." Abandoning *Lemon*'s purpose test—a test which exacerbates the tension between the Free Exercise and Establishment

Clauses, has no basis in the language or history of the amendment, and, as today's decision shows, has wonderfully flexible consequences—would be a good place to start.

Department of Human Resources of Oregon v. Smith   RODNEY A. SMOLLA

The Religion Clauses clearly forbid direct governmental regulation of religious beliefs. Government may not compel affirmation of a belief in God, nor may it punish the expression of religious concerns it believes to be false, or impose special disabilities on persons solely because of their religious status or views.

This sort of direct attempt by government to regulate religious belief, however, is exceedingly rare, and most modern cases centering on the Free Exercise Clause do not involve direct attempts at regulation of belief or practice. Most contemporary conflicts over the free exercise of religion involve laws that regulate conduct in some general way—such as requiring induction into the armed services, or forbidding polygamous marriages, or compelling attendance at school, or forbidding possession of hallucinogenic drugs. When, if ever, should the Free Exercise Clause be interpreted as requiring the government to excuse an individual from the operation of a law of general applicability, so as to accommodate that individual's free exercise of religion?

In this case Alfred Smith and Galen Black were fired from their jobs because they ingested peyote for sacramental purposes at a ceremony of the Native American Church. An Oregon criminal law prohibited the possession of peyote. When Smith and Black applied for unemployment compensation, they were denied it. The Supreme Court had previously held, in a line of cases that began in *Sherbert v. Verner* (1963), that state unemployment insurance could not be conditioned on an individual's willingness to forgo conduct required by his religion, when that conduct was otherwise legal. Smith and Black argued that the same rule should apply to them, even though Oregon law made ingestion of peyote illegal, because that Oregon law itself was unconstitutional. They claimed a constitutional right to ingest small quantities of peyote as part of a religious sacrament.

> ▶ Did Oregon make a convincing case that its prohibition on the ingestion of even small quantities of peyote during religious rituals served a valid state interest? Was the interest purely symbolic? If so, should that be sufficient reason to sustain the law?
>
> ▶ During prohibition, an exception existed for the sacramental use of wine in religious services. After the *Smith* case, could a state prohibit the drinking of all alcohol, including wine in religious services?

Department of Human Resources of Oregon v. Smith 110 S.Ct. 1595 (1990)

Justice SCALIA delivered the opinion of the Court.

Oregon law prohibits the knowing or intentional possession of a "controlled substance" unless the substance has been prescribed by a medical practitioner. The law defines "controlled substance" as [including] the drug peyote, a hallucinogen derived from the plant *Lophophorawilliamsii lemaire.*

Respondents Alfred Smith and Galen Black were fired from their jobs with a private drug rehabilitation organization because they ingested peyote for sacramental purposes at a ceremony of the Native American Church, of which both are members. When respondents applied to petitioner Employment Division for unemployment compensation, they were determined to be ineligible for benefits because they had been discharged for work-related "misconduct."

[Respondents' claim for relief rests on] our decisions in *Sherbert v. Verner, Thomas v. Review Board, Indiana Employment Security Div.* (1981),...and *Hobbie v. Unemployment Appeals Commission of Florida*, in which we held that a State could not condition the availability of unemployment insurance on an individual's willingness to forgo conduct required by his religion....However, the conduct at issue in those cases was not prohibited by law.

The free exercise of religion means, first and foremost, the right to believe and profess whatever religious doctrine one desires. Thus, the First Amendment obviously excludes all "governmental regulation of religious *beliefs* as such."

But the "exercise of religion" often involves not only belief and profession but the performance of (or abstention from) physical acts: assembling with others for a worship service, participating in the sacramental use of bread and wine, proselytizing, abstaining from certain foods or certain modes of transportation. It would be true, we think (though no case of ours has involved the point), that a state would be "prohibiting the free exercise [of religion]" if it sought to ban such acts or abstentions only when they are engaged in for religious reasons, or only because of the religious belief that they display. It would doubtless be unconstitutional, for example, to ban the casting of statues that are to be used for worship purposes," or to prohibit bowing down before a golden calf.

We have never held that an individual's religious beliefs excuse him from compliance with an otherwise valid law prohibiting conduct that the State is free to regulate. On the contrary, the record of more than a century of our free exercise jurisprudence contradicts that proposition. As described succinctly by Justice Frankfurter in *Minersville School Dist. Bd. of Educ. V Gobitis*: "Conscientious scruples have not, in the course of the long struggle for religious toleration, relieved the individual from obedience to a general law not aimed at the promotion or restriction of religious beliefs. The mere possession of religious convictions which contradict the relevant concerns of a political society does not relieve the citizen from the discharge of political responsibilities." We first had occasion to assert that principle in *Reynolds v. United States*, where we rejected the claim that criminal laws against polygamy could not be constitutionally applied to those whose religion commanded the practice. "Laws," we said. " are made for the government of actions, and while they cannot interfere with mere religious belief and opinions, they may with practices....Can a man excuse his practices to the contrary because of his religious belief? To permit this would be to make the professed doctrines of religious belief superior to the law of the land, and in effect to permit every citizen to become a law unto himself."

Our most recent decision involving a neutral, generally applicable regulatory law that compelled activity forbidden by an individual's religion was *United States v. Lee*. There, an Amish employer, on behalf of himself and his employees, sought exemption from collection and payment of Social Security taxes on the ground that the Amish faith prohibited participation in governmental support programs. We rejected the claim that an exemption was constitutionally required. There would be no way, we observed, to distinguish the Amish believer's objection to Social Security taxes from the religious objections that others might have to the collection or use of other taxes....

Respondents argue that even though exemption from generally applicable criminal laws need not automatically be extended to religiously motivated actors, at least the claim for a religious exemption must be evaluated under the balancing test set forth in *Sherbert v. Verner*. Under the *Sherbert* test, governmental actions that substantially burden a religious practice must be justified by a compelling governmental interest....In recent years we have abstained from applying the *Sherbert* test (outside the unemployment compensation field) at all.

Even if we were inclined to breathe into *Sherbert* some life beyond the unemployment compensation field, we would not apply it to require exemptions from a generally applicable criminal law.

[It is not] possible to limit the impact of respondents' proposal by requiring a "compelling state interest" only when the conduct prohibited is "central" to the individual's religion. It is no more appropriate for judges to determine the "centrality" of religious beliefs before applying a "compelling interest" test in the free exercise field, than it would be for them to determine the "importance" of ideas before applying the "compelling interest" test in the free speech field....As we affirmed only last Term, "[i]t is not within the judicial ken to question the centrality of particular beliefs or practices to a faith, or the validity of particular litigants' interpretation of those creeds."

Because respondents' ingestion of peyote was prohibited under Oregon law, and because that prohibition is constitutional, Oregon may, consistent with the Free Exercise Clause, deny respondents unemployment compensation when their dismissal results from use of the drug. The decision of the Oregon Supreme Court is accordingly reversed.

Justice O'CONNOR, with whom Justice BRENNAN, Justice MARSHALL, and Justice BLACKMUN join, concurring in the judgments.

...Respondents invoke our traditional compelling interest test to argue that the Free Exercise Clause requires the State to grant them a limited exemption from its general criminal prohibition against the possession of peyote. The Court today, however, denies them even the opportunity to make that argument, concluding that "the sounder approach, and the approach in accord with the vast majority of our precedents, is to hold the [compelling interest] test inapplicable to" challenges to general criminal prohibitions.

In my view, however, the essence of a free exercise claim is relief from a burden imposed by government on religious practices or beliefs, whether the burden is imposed directly through laws that prohibit or compel specific religious practices, or indirectly through laws that, in effect, make abandonment of one's own religion or conformity to the religious beliefs of others the price of an equal place in the civil community....

A State that makes criminal an individual's religiously motivated conduct burdens that individual's free exercise of religion in the severest manner possible, for it "results in the choice to the individual of either abandoning his religious principle or facing criminal prosecution."

Given the range of conduct that a State might legitimately make criminal, we cannot assume, merely because a law carries criminal sanctions and is generally applicable, that the First Amendment *never* requires the State to grant a limited exemption for religiously motivated conduct.

Moreover, we have not "rejected" or "declined to apply" the compelling interest test in our recent cases. Recent cases have instead affirmed that test as a fundamental part of our First Amendment doctrine....

There is no dispute that Oregon's criminal prohibition of peyote places a severe burden on the ability of respondents to freely exercise their religion. Peyote is a sacrament of the Native American Church and is regarded as vital to respondents' ability to practice their religion....Under Oregon law, as construed by that State's highest court, members of the Native American Church must choose between carrying out the ritual embodying their religious beliefs and avoidance of criminal prosecution. That choice is, in my view, more than sufficient to trigger First Amendment scrutiny....

Thus, the critical question in this case is whether exempting respondents from the State's general criminal prohibition "will unduly interfere with fulfillment of the governmental interest."...

I believe that granting a selective exemption in this case would seriously impair Oregon's compelling interest in prohibiting possession of peyote by its citizens. Under such circumstances, the Free Exercise Clause does not require the State to accommodate respondents' religiously motivated conduct....

Justice BLACKMUN, with whom Justice BRENNAN and Justice MARSHALL join, dissenting.

In weighing respondents' clear interest in the free exercise of their religion against Oregon's asserted interest in enforcing its drug laws, it is important to articulate in precise terms the state interest involved. It is not the State's broad interest in fighting the critical "war on drugs" that must be weighed against respondents' claim, but the State's narrow interest in refusing to make an exception for the religious, ceremonial use of peyote....

The State's interest in enforcing its prohibition in order to be sufficiently compelling to outweigh a free exercise claim, cannot be merely abstract or symbolic. The State cannot plausibly assert that unbending application of a criminal prohibition is essential to fulfill any compelling interest, if it does not, in fact, attempt to enforce that prohibition....Oregon has never sought to prosecute respondents, and does not claim that ithas made significant enforcement efforts against other religious users of peyote. The State's asserted interest thus amounts only to the symbolic preservation of an unenforced prohibition. But a government interest in "symbolism, even symbolism for so worthy a cause as the abolition of unlawful drugs," cannot suffice to abrogate the constitutional rights of individuals.

Similarly, this Court's prior decisions have not allowed a government to rely on mere speculation about potential harms, but have demanded evidentiary support for a refusal to allow a religious exception....

The State of Oregon cannot, consistently with the Free Exercise Clause, deny respondents unemployment benefits.

I dissent.

Rosenberger v. Rector and Visitors of the University of Virginia
RODNEY A. SMOLLA

The First Amendment contains many guarantees, including protection of freedom of speech, the free exercise of religion, and the prohibition of any law "respecting an establishment" of religion. At times the values that animate these various guarantees appear to be in tension. Modern freedom of speech cases, for example, have entrenched the principle that the government may not discriminate on the basis of the content or viewpoint of speech. Modern Establishment Clause cases generally forbid the use of tax money to directly support religious enterprises. In the *Rosenberger* case these two values came into apparent conflict. At issue was whether the University of Virginia could use money generated from student activity fees to fund the printing costs of a religious magazine sponsored by a Christian student group on campus. The University funded a wide variety of other student groups and activities through such student fees, but refused to fund the religious magazine, citing the principle of separation of Church and State. The Christian student group claimed that this amounted to discrimination on the basis of its religious viewpoint, a violation of the Free Speech Clause.

> ▶ Are there times when it is necessary to "violate" the Free Speech Clause in order to comply with the Establishment Clause? When the two clauses come into conflict, which should control?
>
> ▶ The University regulation at issue did not discriminate against any particular religion, but rather against all religious expression. Why did the Court nonetheless treat this is a form of viewpoint-discrimination? Was the Court's reasoning sound?

▶ The Court in *Rosenberger* spent a great deal of time focusing on the precise details of the University of Virginia program. There was much discussion, for example, about the exact nature of the student fee program, and on the fact that the money was paid directly to the printer, not to the religious organization itself. This is characteristic of many contemporary cases decided under the Religion Clauses. The cases often seem to turn on fine nuances. Is it appropriate for the interpretation of such grand concepts as "freedom of religion" and "establishment of religion" to focus on what so often appear to be narrow "technicalities?" Or is such fine line-drawing inevitable in the application of constitutional guarantees to concrete, real-life controversies?

Rosenberger v. Rector and Visitors of the University of Virginia 115 S. Ct. 2510 (1995)

Justice KENNEDY delivered the opinion of the Court.

The University of Virginia, an instrumentality of the Commonwealth for which it is named and thus bound by the First and Fourteenth Amendments, authorizes the payment of outside contractors for the printing costs of a variety of student publications. It withheld any authorization for payments on behalf of petitioners for the sole reason that their student paper "primarily promotes or manifests a particular belief in or about a deity or an ultimate reality." That the paper did promote or manifest views within the defined exclusion seems plain enough. The challenge is to the University's regulation and its denial of authorization, the case raising issues under the Speech and Establishment Clauses of the First Amendment.

I

The public corporation we refer to as the "University" is denominated by state law as "the Rector and Visitors of the University of Virginia," and it is responsible for governing the school. Founded by Thomas Jefferson in 1819, and ranked by him, together with the authorship of the Declaration of Independence and of the Virginia Act for Religious Freedom, as one of his proudest achievements, the University is among the Nation's oldest and most respected seats of higher learning. It has more than 11,000 undergraduate students, and 6,000 graduate and professional students. An understanding of the case requires a somewhat detailed description of the program the University created to support extracurricular student activities on its campus.

Before a student group is eligible to submit bills from its outside contractors for payment by the fund described below, it must become a "Contracted Independent Organization" (CIO). CIO status is available to any group the majority of whose members are students, whose managing officers are fulltime students, and that complies with certain procedural requirements. A CIO must file its constitution with the University; must pledge not to discriminate in its membership; and must include in dealings with third parties and in all written materials a disclaimer, stating that the CIO is independent of the University and that the University is not responsible for the CIO. CIOs enjoy access to University facilities, including meeting rooms and computer terminals. A standard agreement signed between each CIO and the University provides that the benefits and opportunities afforded to CIOs "should not be misinterpreted as meaning that those organizations are part of or controlled by the University, that the University is responsible for the organizations' contracts or other acts or omissions, or that the University approves of the organizations' goals or activities."

All CIOs may exist and operate at the University, but some are also entitled to apply for funds from the Student Activities Fund (SAF). Established and governed by University Guidelines, the purpose of the SAF is to support a broad range of extracurricular student activities that "are related to the educational purpose of the University." The SAF is based on the University's "recognition that the availability of a wide range of opportunities" for its students "tends to enhance the University environment." The Guidelines require that it be administered "in a manner consistent with the educational purpose of the University as well as with state and federal law." The SAF receives its money from a mandatory fee of $14 per semester assessed to each fulltime student. The Student Council, elected by the students, has the initial authority to disburse the funds, but its actions are subject to review by a faculty body chaired by a designee of the Vice President for Student Affairs.

Some, but not all, CIOs may submit disbursement requests to the SAF. The Guidelines recognize 11 categories of student groups that may seek payment to thirdparty contractors because they "are related to the educational purpose of the University of Virginia." One of these is "student news, information, opinion, entertainment, or academic communications media groups." The Guidelines also specify, however, that the costs of certain activities of CIOs that are otherwise eligible for funding will not be reimbursed by the SAF. The student activities which are excluded from SAF support are religious activities, philanthropic contributions and activities, political activities, activities that would jeopardize the University's tax exempt status, those which involve payment of honoraria or similar fees, or social entertainment or related expenses. The prohibition on "political activities" is defined so that it is limited to electioneering and lobbying. The Guidelines provide that "these restrictions on funding political activities are not intended to preclude funding of any otherwise eligible student organization which...espouses particular positions or ideological viewpoints, including those that may be unpopular or are not generally accepted." A "religious activity," by contrast, is defined as any activity that "primarily promotes or manifests a particular belief in or about a deity or an ultimate reality."

The Guidelines prescribe these criteria for determining the amounts of thirdparty disbursements that will be allowed on behalf of each eligible student organization: the size of the group, its financial selfsufficiency, and the Universitywide benefit of its activities. If an organization seeks SAF support, it must submit its bills to the Student Council, which pays the organization's creditors upon determining that the expenses are appropriate. No direct payments are made to the student groups. During the 19901991 academic year, 343 student groups qualified as CIOs. One hundred thirtyfive of them applied for support from the SAF, and 118 received funding. Fifteen of the groups were funded as "student news, information, opinion, entertainment, or academic communications media groups."

Petitioners' organization, Wide Awake Productions (WAP), qualified as a CIO. Formed by petitioner Ronald Rosenberger and other undergraduates in 1990, WAP was established "to publish a magazine of philosophical and religious expression," "to facilitate discussion which fosters an atmosphere of sensitivity to and tolerance of Christian viewpoints," and "to provide a unifying focus for Christians of multicultural backgrounds." WAP publishes Wide Awake: A Christian Perspective at the University of Virginia. The paper's Christian viewpoint was evident from the first issue, in which its editors wrote that the journal "offers a Christian perspective on both personal and community issues, especially those relevant to college students at the University of Virginia." The editors committed the paper to a twofold mission: "to challenge Christians to live, in word and deed, according to the faith they proclaim and to encourage students to consider what a personal relationship with Jesus Christ means." The first issue had articles about racism, crisis pregnancy, stress, prayer, C.S. Lewis' ideas about evil and free will, and reviews of religious music. In the next two issues, Wide Awake featured stories about homosexuality, Christian missionary work, and eating disorders, as well as music reviews and interviews with University professors. Each page of Wide Awake, and the end of each article or review, is marked by a cross. The advertisements carried in Wide Awake also reveal the Christian perspective of the journal. For the most part, the advertisers are churches, centers for Christian study, or Christian bookstores. By June 1992, WAP had distributed about 5,000 copies of Wide Awake to University students, free of charge.

WAP had acquired CIO status soon after it was organized. This is an important consideration in this case, for had it been a "religious organization," WAP would not have been accorded CIO status. As defined by the Guidelines, a "religious organization" is "an organization whose purpose is to practice a devotion to an acknowledged ultimate reality or deity." At no stage in this controversy has the University contended that WAP is such an organization.

A few months after being given CIO status, WAP requested the SAF to pay its printer $5,862 for the costs of printing its newspaper. The Appropriations Committee of the Student Council denied WAP's request on the ground that Wide Awake was a "religious activity" within the meaning of the Guidelines, i.e., that the newspaper "promoted or manifested a particular belief in or about a deity or an ultimate reality." It made its determination after examining the first issue. WAP appealed the denial to the full Student Council, contending that WAP met all the applicable Guidelines and that denial of SAF support on the basis of the magazine's religious perspective violated the Constitution. The appeal was denied without further comment, and WAP appealed to the next level, the Student Activities Committee. In a letter signed by the Dean of Students, the committee sustained the denial of funding....

II

It is axiomatic that the government may not regulate speech based on its substantive content or the message it conveys. Other principles follow from this precept. In the realm of private speech or expression, government regulation may not favor one speaker over another. Discrimination against speech because of its message is presumed to be unconstitutional. These rules informed our determination that the government offends the First Amendment when it imposes financial burdens on certain speakers based on the content of their expression. When the government targets not subject matter but particular views taken by speakers on a subject, the violation of the First Amendment is all the more blatant. Viewpoint discrimination is thus an egregious form of content discrimination. The government must abstain from regulating speech when the specific motivating ideology or the opinion or perspective of the speaker is the rationale for the restriction....

The University does acknowledge (as it must in light of our precedents) that "ideologically driven attempts to suppress a particular point of view are presumptively unconstitutional in funding, as in other contexts," but insists that this case does not present that issue because the Guidelines draw lines based on content, not viewpoint. As we have noted, discrimination against one set of views or ideas is but a subset or particular instance of the more general phenomenon of content discrimination. And, it must be acknowledged, the distinction is not a precise one. It is, in a sense, something of an understatement to speak of religious thought and discussion as just a viewpoint, as distinct from a comprehensive body of thought. The nature of our origins and destiny and their dependence upon the existence of a divine being have been subjects of philosophic inquiry throughout human history. We conclude, nonetheless, that here, as in *Lamb's Chapel*, viewpoint discrimination is the proper way to interpret the University's objections to Wide Awake. By the very terms of the SAF prohibition, the University does not exclude religion as a subject matter but selects for disfavored treatment those student journalistic efforts with religious editorial viewpoints. Religion may be a vast area of inquiry, but it also provides, as it did here, a specific premise, a perspective, a standpoint from which a variety of subjects may be discussed and considered. The prohibited perspective, not the general subject matter, resulted in the refusal to make thirdparty payments, for the subjects discussed were otherwise within the approved category of publications....

The University tries to escape the consequences of our [prior precedents] by urging that this case involves the provision of funds rather than access to facilities. The University begins with the unremarkable proposition that the State must have substantial discretion in determining how to allocate scarce resources to accomplish its educational mission. Citing our decisions, the University argues that contentbased funding decisions are both inevitable and lawful....

It does not follow, however,...that viewpointbased restrictions are proper when the University does not itself speak or subsidize transmittal of a message it favors but instead expends funds to encourage a diversity of views from private speakers. A holding that the University may not discriminate based on the viewpoint of private persons whose speech it facilitates does not restrict the University's own speech, which is controlled by different principles...

Vital First Amendment speech principles are at stake here. The first danger to liberty lies in granting the State the power to examine publications to determine whether or not they are based on some ultimate idea and if so for the State to classify them. The second, and corollary, danger is to speech from the chilling of individual thought and expression. That danger is especially real in the University setting, where the State acts against a background and tradition of thought and experiment that is at the center of our intellectual and philosophic tradition....For the University, by regulation, to cast disapproval on particular viewpoints of its students risks the suppression of free speech and creative inquiry in one of the vital centers for the nation's intellectual life, its college and university campuses....

The prohibition on funding on behalf of publications that "primarily promote or manifest a particular belief in or about a deity or an ultimate reality," in its ordinary and commonsense meaning, has a vast potential reach. The term "promote" as used here would comprehend any writing advocating a philosophic position that rests upon a belief in a deity or ultimate reality. And the term "manifests" would bring within the scope of the prohibition any writing that is explicable as resting upon a premise which presupposes the existence of a deity or ultimate reality...

Based on the principles we have discussed, we hold that the regulation invoked to deny SAF support, both in its terms and in its application to these petitioners, is a denial of their right of free speech guaranteed by the First Amendment. It remains to be considered whether the violation following from the University's action is excused by the necessity of complying with the Constitution's prohibition against state establishment of religion. We turn to that question.

III

...A central lesson of our decisions is that a significant factor in upholding governmental programs in the face of Establishment Clause attack is their neutrality towards religion. We have decided a series of cases addressing the receipt of government benefits where religion or religious views are implicated in some degree...We have held that the guarantee of neutrality is respected, not offended, when the government, following neutral criteria and evenhanded policies, extends benefits to recipients whose ideologies and viewpoints, including religious ones, are broad and diverse. More than once have we rejected the position that the Establishment Clause even justifies, much less requires, a refusal to extend free speech rights to religious speakers who participate in broadreaching government programs neutral in design.

The governmental program here is neutral toward religion. There is no suggestion that the University created it to advance religion or adopted some ingenious device with the purpose of aiding a religious cause. The object of the SAF is to open a forum for speech and to support various student enterprises, including the publication of newspapers, in recognition of the diversity and creativity of student life. The University's SAF Guidelines have a separate classification for, and do not make thirdparty payments on behalf of, "religious organizations," which are those "whose purpose is to practice a devotion to an acknowledged ultimate reality or deity." The category of support here is for "student news, information, opinion, entertainment, or academic communications media groups," of which Wide Awake was 1 of 15 in the 1990 school year. WAP did not seek a subsidy because of its Christian editorial viewpoint; it sought funding as a student journal, which it was.

The neutrality of the program distinguishes the student fees from a tax levied for the direct support of a church or group of churches. A tax of that sort, of course, would run contrary to Establishment Clause concerns dating from the earliest days of the Republic. The apprehensions of our predecessors involved the levying of taxes upon the public for the sole and exclusive purpose of establishing and supporting specific sects. The exaction here, by contrast, is a student activity fee designed to reflect the reality that student life in its many dimensions includes the necessity of wideranging speech and inquiry and that student expression is an integral part of the University's educational mission. The fee is mandatory, and we do not have before us the question whether an objecting student has the First Amendment right to demand a pro rata return to the extent the fee is expended for speech to which he or she does not subscribe. We must treat it, then, as an exaction upon the students. But the $14 paid each semester by the students is not a general tax designed to raise revenue for the University. The SAF cannot be used for unlimited purposes, much less the illegitimate purpose of supporting one religion. Much like the arrangement in *Widmar*, the money goes to a special fund from which any group of students with CIO status can draw for purposes consistent with the University's educational mission; and to the extent the student is interested in speech, withdrawal is permitted to cover the whole spectrum of speech, whether it manifests a religious view, an antireligious view, or neither. Our decision, then, cannot be read as addressing an expenditure from a general tax fund. Here, the disbursements from the fund go to private contractors for the cost of printing that which is protected under the Speech Clause of the First Amendment. This is a far cry from a general public assessment designed and effected to provide financial support for a church....

It does not violate the Establishment Clause for a public university to grant access to its facilities on a religionneutral basis to a wide spectrum of student groups, including groups which use meeting rooms for sectarian activities, accompanied by some devotional exercises. This is so even where the upkeep, maintenance, and repair of the facilities attributed to those uses is paid from a student activities fund to which students are required to contribute. The government usually acts by spending money...

By paying outside printers, the University in fact attains a further degree of separation from the student publication, for it avoids the duties of supervision, escapes the costs of upkeep, repair, and replacement attributable to student use, and has a clear record of costs...

To obey the Establishment Clause, it was not necessary for the University to deny eligibility to student publications because of their viewpoint. The neutrality commanded of the State by the separate Clauses of the First Amendment was compromised by the University's course of action. The viewpoint discrimination inherent in the University's regulation required public officials to scan and interpret student publications to discern their underlying philosophic assumptions respecting religious theory and belief. That course of action was a denial of the right of free speech and would risk fostering a pervasive bias or hostility to religion, which could undermine the very neutrality the Establishment Clause requires. There is no Establishment Clause violation in the University's honoring its duties under the Free Speech Clause.

The judgment of the Court of Appeals must be, and is, reversed.

It is so ordered.

[Concurring opinions of Justices O'CONNOR and THOMAS have been omitted.]

Justice SOUTER, with whom Justice STEVENS, Justice GINSBURG and Justice BREYER join, dissenting.

The Court today, for the first time, approves direct funding of core religious activities by an arm of the State. It does so, however, only after erroneous treatment of some familiar principles of law implementing the First Amendment's Establishment and Speech Clauses, and by viewing the very funds in question as beyond the reach of the Establishment Clause's funding restrictions as such. Because there is no warrant for distinguishing among public funding sources for purposes of applying the First Amendment's prohibition of religious establishment, I would hold that the University's refusal to support petitioners' religious activities is compelled by the Establishment Clause. I would therefore affirm.

The central question in this case is whether a grant from the Student Activities Fund to pay Wide Awake's printing expenses would violate the Establishment Clause. Although the Court does not dwell on the details of Wide Awake's message, it recognizes something sufficiently religious in the publication to demand Establishment Clause scrutiny. Although the Court places great stress on the eligibility of secular as well as religious activities for grants from the Student Activities Fund, it recognizes that such evenhanded availability is not by itself enough to satisfy constitutional requirements for any aid scheme that results in a benefit to religion. Something more is necessary to justify any religious aid. Some members of the Court, at least, may think the funding permissible on a view that it is indirect, since the money goes to Wide Awake's printer, not through Wide Awake's own checking account. The Court's principal reliance, however, is on an argument that providing religion with economically valuable services is permissible on the theory that services are economically indistinguishable from religious access to governmental speech forums, which sometimes is permissible. But this reasoning would commit the Court to approving direct religious aid beyond anything justifiable for the sake of access to speaking forums. The Court implicitly recognizes this in its further attempt to circumvent the clear bar to direct governmental aid to religion. Different members of the Court seek to avoid this bar in different ways. The opinion of the Court makes the novel assumption that only direct aid financed with tax revenue is barred, and draws the erroneous conclusion that the involuntary Student Activities Fee is not a tax....

City of Boerne v. Flores   RODNEY A. SMOLLA

The Supreme Court's decision in the "peyote case," *Department of Human Resources of Oregon v. Smith*, was highly controversial. Congress reacted to the *Smith* decision by enacting a new federal law, called "The Religious Freedom Restoration Act." The law, popularly known by its acronym "RFRA," passed with overwhelming bipartisan support and signed by President Clinton, was quite extraordinary in its blunt rejection of the Supreme Court's *Smith* ruling. The law and its accompanying legislative history explicitly stated that the Supreme Court was wrong in *Smith*, and that the better view of the meaning of the free exercise of religion was that reflected in such prior decisions as *Sherbert v. Verner* and *Wisconsin v. Yoder*, cases that appeared to endorse the proposition that even when the government merely passes "neutral" and "generally applicable" laws, such laws may not be applied in a manner that "substantially burdens" the free exercise of religion, unless the government demonstrates that the law was narrowly tailored to effectuate a "compelling" governmental interest. RFRA was a sweeping law; it purported to bind all governmental action at all levels: federal, state, and local. The practical effect of RFRA was thus to "overrule" a decision of the United States Supreme Court, by creating a broad federal statute that guaranteed a level of religious freedom greater than that created by the First Amendment itself, as interpreted by the Supreme Court in *Smith*.

But what was the source of Congress's authority to pass RFRA? Congress ordinarily has no power to "overrule" the Supreme Court. Congress argued that it was not actually overruling the decision in *Smith*, but merely passing civil rights legislation—in this case civil rights legislation protecting religion. Congress has frequently passed civil rights laws in the past that created protections greater than those contained in the Constitution itself. Congress argued that it had the authority to pass such laws under the powers granted to it in Section 5 of the Fourteenth Amendment, which states: "Congress shall have the power to enforce, by appropriate legislation, the provisions of this article." In the *Flores* decision, the Supreme Court examined the question of whether Congress did indeed have the constitutional power to enact RFRA.

> ▶ The decision in *Flores* is really not a decision interpreting freedom of religion, but a decision concerning "federalism," and the proper division of lawmaking authority between the federal government and the states. Yet the decision had profound consequences for the free exercise of religion. In the aftermath of *Flores*, could an individual state, such as Virginia, pass its own state-version of the Religious Freedom Restoration Act? Would such a law be constitutional? Would it be a good idea?
>
> ▶ The "constitutional dialogue" represented by *Smith*, the enactment of RFRA, and the subsequent decision in *Flores* shows us how the political and judicial branches of government all participate in formulating "constitutional" public policy. What are the appropriate roles of the various branches? What is the appropriate division of authority between the federal government and the states?

▶ The issue posed by *Smith*, RFRA, and *Flores* is not unique to the religion clauses. In many areas of constitutional law, we are faced with the question of whether our concept of a "constitutional right" is limited to laws that *intentionally* burden freedom or equality, or should rather be more broadly construed, to include laws that have *as their practical impact* some form of discrimination. Put simply, when the government is accused of race discrimination, or abridgement of freedom of speech, or prohibiting the free exercise of religion, should it be necessary to prove that the government actually *intended* to violate these protections? Or should it be enough that in practice, the law at issue in some substantial way burdens one race at the expense of another, or interferes with freedom of speech, or the free exercise of religion?

City of Boerne v. Flores 117 S. Ct. 2157 (1997)

Justice KENNEDY delivered the opinion of the Court.

A decision by local zoning authorities to deny a church a building permit was challenged under the Religious Freedom Restoration Act of 1993 (RFRA). The case calls into question the authority of Congress to enact RFRA. We conclude the statute exceeds Congress' power.

I

Situated on a hill in the city of Boerne, Texas, some 28 miles northwest of San Antonio, is St. Peter Catholic Church. Built in 1923, the church's structure replicates the mission style of the region's earlier history. The church seats about 230 worshippers, a number too small for its growing parish. Some 40 to 60 parishioners cannot be accommodated at some Sunday masses. In order to meet the needs of the congregation the Archbishop of San Antonio gave permission to the parish to plan alterations to enlarge the building.

A few months later, the Boerne City Council passed an ordinance authorizing the city's Historic Landmark Commission to prepare a preservation plan with proposed historic landmarks and districts. Under the ordinance, the Commission must preapprove construction affecting historic landmarks or buildings in a historic district.

Soon afterwards, the Archbishop applied for a building permit so construction to enlarge the church could proceed. City authorities, relying on the ordinance and the designation of a historic district (which, they argued, included the church), denied the application. The Archbishop brought this suit challenging the permit denial in the United States District Court for the Western District of Texas.

The complaint contained various claims, but to this point the litigation has centered on RFRA and the question of its constitutionality. The Archbishop relied upon RFRA as one basis for relief from the refusal to issue the permit. The District Court concluded that by enacting RFRA Congress exceeded the scope of its enforcement power under Section 5 of the Fourteenth Amendment. The court certified its order for interlocutory appeal and the Fifth Circuit reversed, finding RFRA to be constitutional. We granted *certiorari* and now reverse.

II

Congress enacted RFRA in direct response to the Court's decision in *Employment Div., Dept. of Human Resources of Oregon v. Smith*. There we considered a Free Exercise Clause claim brought by members of the Native American Church who were denied unemployment benefits when they lost their jobs because they had used peyote. Their practice was to ingest peyote for sacramental purposes, and they challenged an Oregon statute of general applicability which made use of the drug criminal. In evaluating the claim, we declined to apply the balancing test set forth in *Sherbert v. Verner*, under which we would have asked whether Oregon's prohibition substantially burdened a religious practice and, if it did, whether the burden was justified by a compelling government interest. We stated: "[G]overnment's ability to enforce generally applicable prohibitions of socially harmful conduct...cannot depend on measuring the effects of a governmental action on a religious objector's spiritual development. To make an individual's obligation to obey such a law contingent upon the law's coincidence with his religious beliefs, except where the State's interest is 'compelling'...contradicts both constitutional tradition and common sense." The application of the *Sherbert* test, the *Smith* decision explained, would have produced an anomaly in the law, a constitutional right to ignore neutral laws of general applicability. The anomaly would have been accentuated, the Court reasoned, by the difficulty of determining whether a particular practice was central to an individual's religion. We explained, moreover, that it "is not within the judicial ken to question the centrality of particular beliefs or practices to a faith, or the validity of particular litigants' interpretations of those creeds."...

III

A. Under our Constitution, the Federal Government is one of enumerated powers. *McCulloch v. Maryland* (1819). The judicial authority to determine the constitutionality of laws, in cases and controversies, is based on the premise that the "powers of the legislature are defined and limited; and that those limits may not be mistaken, or forgotten, the constitution is written." (*Marbury v. Madison.*)

Congress relied on its Fourteenth Amendment enforcement power in enacting the most far reaching and substantial of RFRA's provisions, those which impose its requirements on the States. The Fourteenth Amendment provides, in relevant part: "Section 1....No State shall make or enforce any law which shall abridge the privileges or immunities of citizens of the United States; nor shall any State deprive any person of life, liberty, or property, without due process of law; nor deny to any person within its jurisdiction the equal protection of the laws....Section 5. The Congress shall have power to enforce, by appropriate legislation, the provisions of this article." The parties disagree over whether RFRA is a proper exercise of Congress' Section 5 power "to enforce" by "appropriate legislation" the constitutional guarantee that no State shall deprive any person of "life, liberty, or property, without due process of law" nor deny any person "equal protection of the laws."...

While the line between measures that remedy or prevent unconstitutional actions and measures that make a substantive change in the governing law is not easy to discern, and Congress must have wide latitude in determining where it lies, the distinction exists and must be observed. There must be a congruence and proportionality between the injury to be prevented or remedied and the means adopted to that end. Lacking such a connection, legislation may become substantive in operation and effect. History and our case law support drawing the distinction, one apparent from the text of the Amendment.

B. Regardless of the state of the legislative record, RFRA cannot be considered remedial, preventive legislation, if those terms are to have any meaning. RFRA is so out of proportion to a supposed remedial or preventive object that it cannot be understood as responsive to, or designed to prevent, unconstitutional behavior. It appears, instead, to attempt a substantive change in constitutional protections....

The stringent test RFRA demands of state laws reflects a lack of proportionality or congruence between the means adopted and the legitimate end to be achieved. If an objector can show a substantial burden on his free exercise, the State must demonstrate a compelling governmental interest and show that the law is the least restrictive means of furthering its interest. Claims that a law substantially burdens someone's exercise of religion will often be difficult to contest....Laws valid under *Smith* would fall under RFRA without regard to whether they had the object of stifling or punishing free exercise....

The substantial costs RFRA exacts, both in practical terms of imposing a heavy litigation burden on the States and in terms of curtailing their traditional general regulatory power, far exceed any pattern or practice of unconstitutional conduct under the Free Exercise Clause as interpreted in *Smith*. Simply put, RFRA is not designed to identify and counteract state laws likely to be unconstitutional because of their treatment of religion....

When Congress acts within its sphere of power and responsibilities, it has not just the right but the duty to make its own informed judgment on the meaning and force of the Constitution. This has been clear from the early days of the Republic....

Our national experience teaches that the Constitution is preserved best when each part of the government respects both the Constitution and the proper actions and determinations of the other branches. When the Court has interpreted the Constitution, it has acted within the province of the Judicial Branch, which embraces the duty to say what the law is. *Marbury v. Madison*. When the political branches of the Government act against the background of a judicial interpretation of the Constitution already issued, it must be understood that in later cases and controversies the Court will treat its precedents with the respect due them under settled principles, including *stare decisis*, and contrary expectations must be disappointed. RFRA was designed to control cases and controversies, such as the one before us; but as the provisions of the federal statute here invoked are beyond congressional authority, it is this Court's precedent, not RFRA, which must control....

The judgment of the Court of Appeals sustaining the Act's constitutionality is reversed.

[In a concurring opinion, Justice STEVENS argued that RFRA also violated the Establishment Clause, by granting special preferences to persons who seek exemption from governmental actions on religious grounds. In a concurring opinion, Justice SCALIA attacked the arguments of Justice O'CONNOR that Smith should be reconsidered and overruled.]

Justice O'CONNOR, with whom Justice BREYER joins except as to a portion of Part I, dissenting.

I dissent from the Court's disposition of this case. I agree with the Court that the issue before us is whether the Religious Freedom Restoration Act (RFRA) is a proper exercise of Congress' power to enforce Section 5 of the Fourteenth Amendment. But as a yardstick for measuring the constitutionality of RFRA, the Court uses its holding in *Employment Div., Dept. of Human Resources of Oregon v. Smith*, the decision that prompted Congress to enact RFRA as a means of more rigorously enforcing the Free Exercise Clause. I remain of the view that Smith was wrongly decided, and I would use this case to reexamine the Court's holding there. Therefore, I would direct the parties to brief the question whether *Smith* represents the correct understanding of the Free Exercise Clause and set the case for reargument. If the Court were to correct the misinterpretation of the Free Exercise Clause set forth in *Smith*, it would simultaneously put our First Amendment jurisprudence back on course and allay the legitimate concerns of a majority in Congress who believed that *Smith* improperly restricted religious liberty. We would then be in a position to review RFRA in light of a proper interpretation of the Free Exercise Clause....

[In dissenting opinions, Justice SOUTER and Justice BREYER agreed with Justice O'CONNOR that Smith *should be reconsidered.]*

IV Rights of the Accused: Police Procedure, Evidence, and Punishment

Gideon v. Wainwright (1963)

Miranda v. Arizona (1966)

Furman v. Georgia (1972)

Brewer v. Williams (1977)

New Jersey v. T.L.O. (1985)

Skinner v. Railway Labor Executives Association / National Treasury Employees v. Von Raab (1989)

IV Rights of the Accused: Police Procedure, Evidence, and Punishment

MELVIN UROFSKY

The Sixth Amendment provides that in "all criminal prosecutions, the accused shall enjoy the right...to have the Assistance of Counsel for his defense." It is thus a linch-pin, holding together the other rights granted to accused persons. Chief Justice Warren described the Sixth Amendment as protecting the Fifth.

The embodiment of this right in the Constitution marked a significant step beyond the older, and far more limited, British practice. English law permitted counsel for misdemeanors, but not in felony cases, although judges could permit defendants to have barristers argue points of law or help out in their defense in other ways. Not until the reform measures of 1836 did Parliament finally allow counsel in felony trials.

Twelve of the original thirteen states had abandoned the English rule by the time of the adoption of the Constitution. Section 35 of the Judiciary Act of 1789 formalized the American practice, but did so as a grant of privilege rather than as a recognition of right. If defendants chose to and had the resources, they could not be prevented from securing counsel; this did not mean that a court had to provide a lawyer if an indigent defendant wanted one.

The following year, however, in the Federal Crimes Act of 1790, Congress imposed a statutory duty on federal courts to assign counsel in capital cases—those in which the death penalty could be imposed as punishment. The Sixth Amendment, therefore, enunciated the general rule, and although no one supposed that it required counsel in non-capital cases, the practice developed in the nineteenth century of appointing lawyers for indigents in serious federal cases as well. In 1938, the Supreme Court in *Johnson v. Zerbst*, held that the Sixth Amendment required counsel in all federal criminal proceedings unless the defendant waived the right.

The Sixth Amendment originally applied only to the federal government, although a number of states included similar provisions in their own bills of rights.

Application varied from state to state, with some states limiting the right to capital cases and some extending it to felonies as well. The Court did not apply the right to the states until *Powell v. Alabama* (1932), the famous "Scottsboro Case." A nearly unanimous Court held that failure to make effective appointment of counsel in a capital case deprived defendants of their rights without due process of law.

The Court restricted this decision to capital cases, and Justice Sutherland did not base his ruling on the Sixth Amendment applied to the states through the Fourteenth, but rather on the Due Process Clause of the Fourteenth alone. Ten years later, in *Betts v. Brady*, the Court still refused to incorporate the Sixth Amendment guarantees, and held that counsel for indigent defendants, except in capital cases, was not a fundamental right crucial to a fair trial. But the justices did recognize that in some cases, where special circumstances existed, counsel might be necessary, and it endorsed a case-by-case enquiry to determine when such situations arose. *Gideon v. Wainwright*, the first case in this section, marks the end of one stage in the expansion of Sixth Amendment rights.

But *Gideon* is also the first step in another phase, making the right meaningful in all parts of the criminal justice process. To benefit from a right, one must know about it, and be able to use it at those crucial points where it provides the greatest protection. In *Crooker v. California* (1958), Justice Douglas entered a powerful dissent in a case involving the absence of a lawyer during interrogation of a suspect. "The mischief and abuse of the third degree," he wrote, "will be certain as long as an accused can be denied the right to counsel at this the most critical period of his ordeal. For what takes place in the secret confines of the police station may be more critical than what takes place at the trial."

Beginning with *Massiah v. United States* and *Escobedo v. Illinois* in 1964, the Court began expanding the meaning of "right to counsel." That same year, in *Malloy v. Hogan*, the Court made the Fifth Amendment guarantee against self-incrimination applicable to the states through the Fourteenth Amendment. In *Miranda v. Arizona*, the second case for discussion, these strands came together, and the case illustrates the interconnectedness of various constitutional rights.

Miranda and a number of other contemporary cases touched off a storm of debate, with critics accusing the Court of "coddling crooks" and favoring criminals at the expense of society. A third case in this group, *Brewer v. Williams*, although decided halfway through the Burger years, seems to many a worst-case example of this "coddling."

The remaining cases in this section—dealing with capital punishment (*Furman v. Georgia*), Search and Seizure (*New Jersey v. T.L.O.*), and drug testing (*National Treasury Employees v. Von Raab/ Skinner v. Railway Labor Executives Association*)—have been equally important and controversial. They illustrate the range and complexity of the issues dealt with by the Court in this sensitive area of defining and protecting the "rights of the accused."

▶ Is a right effective when it is enforced capriciously or inconsistently?

▶ Does rigorous enforcement of a right hamper the police? (Note Chief Justice Warren's reminder that the Federal Bureau of Investigation, the nation's most respected law enforcement agency, had abided by these rules for years, without losing its effectiveness.)

▶ The Sixth Amendment says "in all criminal proceedings." Should this mean only the trial stage, or does a "prosecution" stretch from accusation through appeal?

▶ If the police break their word, yet in doing so catch the criminal, should society be penalized? Or is society better off in the long run by having its constitutional rights preserved unimpaired?

▶ How can we be certain that the police will obey the rules, except by denying them the evidence illegally obtained?

▶ If the Courts have gone too far in enforcing the rights of the accused, where should the line be drawn?

Gideon v. Wainwright   MELVIN UROFSKY

In *Betts v. Brady* (1942), the Court held that the Fourteenth Amendment did not apply the Sixth Amendment's right to counsel to the states. The due process criterion, however, might require an attorney to be present in certain circumstances, such as cases involving, for example, highly technical legal questions or illiterate defendants; and these would be determined on a case-by-case basis. The next twenty years saw state and federal courts deluged with appeals by persons claiming special circumstances, and in the cases reaching the Supreme Court, the justices managed to find special circumstances in nearly every case they reviewed. They still held back, however, from reversing the *Betts* rule.

Clarence Earl Gideon did not claim special circumstances. The question of law was simple: Florida had charged and convicted him of breaking and entering a poolroom with intention to commit petit larceny. Gideon was neither illiterate nor mentally retarded nor a victim of racial prejudice; he just had no money for a lawyer and he wanted one to defend him in court. Once in prison, Gideon researched the issue, and then appealed to the Supreme Court *in forma pauperis.*

His request came at just the right time, when a majority of the Brethren believed *Betts* should be overturned. The Court also made its ruling retroactive, so that thousands of prisoners in Florida and other states who had been tried without counsel now either had to be retried or released. In Gideon's case, a retrial—this time with an attorney—led to his acquittal.

In *Argersinger v. Hamlin* (1972), the Court extended the right to counsel to misdemeanor cases in which conviction led to imprisonment.

> ▶ Prior to *Gideon*, the Supreme Court had not held right to counsel for a defendant in a non-capital case to be a "fundamental right." Is an attorney necessary in *all* cases—felony? misdemeanor? traffic? civil?
>
> ▶ Would the criminal justice system be more efficient if lawyers were excluded from trials for misdemeanor and other petty offenses? Would it be fair? Who draws the line?
>
> ▶ Would the same be true for other aspects of a trial? For example, is a jury necessary in all cases? Would it be just as fair, and more efficient, to have the judge hear the case and decide it on the merits, with jury trials reserved only for serious crimes?
>
> ▶ Relatively speaking, how important is efficiency in judicial proceedings?

Gideon v. Wainwright 372 U.S. 335. (1963)

Mr. Justice BLACK delivered the opinion of the Court.

Petitioner was charged in a Florida state court with having broken and entered a poolroom with intent to commit a misdemeanor. This offense is a felony under Florida law. Appearing in court without funds and without a lawyer, petitioner asked the court to appoint counsel for him, whereupon the following colloquy took place:

> The Court: Mr. Gideon, I am sorry, but I cannot appoint Counsel to represent you in this case. Under the laws of the State of Florida, the only time the Court can appoint Counsel to represent a Defendant is when that person is charged with a capital offense. I am sorry, but I will have to deny your request to appoint Counsel to defend you in this case.
>
> The Defendant: The United States Supreme Court says I am entitled to be represented by Counsel.

Put to trial before a jury, Gideon conducted his defense about as well as could be expected from a layman. He made an opening statement to the jury, cross-examined the State's witnesses, presented witnesses in his own defense, declined to testify himself, and made a short argument "emphasizing his innocence to the charge contained in the information filed in this case." The jury returned a verdict of guilty, and petitioner was sentenced to serve five years in the state prison. Later, petitioner filed in the Florida Supreme Court this *habeas corpus* petition attacking his conviction and sentence on the ground that the trial court's refusal to appoint counsel for him denied him rights "guaranteed by the Constitution and the Bill of Rights by the United States Government." Treating the petition for *habeas corpus* as properly before it, the State Supreme Court, "upon consideration thereof" but without an opinion, denied all relief. Since 1942, when Betts v. Brady was decided by a divided Court, the problem of a defendant's federal constitutional right to counsel in a state court has been a continuing source of controversy and litigation in both state and federal courts. To give this problem another review here, we granted *certiorari*. Since *Gideon* was proceeding *in forma pauperis*, we appointed counsel to represent him and requested both sides to discuss in their briefs and oral arguments the following: "Should this Court's holding in *Betts v. Brady* be reconsidered?" ...

The Sixth Amendment provides, "In all criminal prosecutions, the accused shall enjoy the right....to have the Assistance of Counsel for his defense." We have construed this to mean that in federal courts counsel must be provided for defendants unable to employ counsel unless the right is competently and intelligently waived. *Betts* argued that this right is extended to indigent defendants in state courts by the Fourteenth Amendment. In response the Court stated that, while the Sixth Amendment laid down "no rule for the conduct of the States, the question recurs whether the constraint laid by the Amendment upon the national courts expresses a rule so fundamental and essential to a fair trial, and so, to due process of law, that it is made obligatory upon the States by the Fourteenth Amendment." In order to decide whether the Sixth Amendment's guarantee of counsel is of this fundamental nature, the Court in *Betts* set out and considered "relevant data on the subject...afforded by consitutional and statutory provisions subsisting in the colonies and the States prior to the inclusion of the Bill of Rights in the national Constitution, and in the constitutional, legislative, and judicial history of the States to the present date." On the basis of this historical data the Court concluded that "appointment of counsel is not a fundamental right, essential to a fair trial." It was for this reason the *Betts* Court refused to accept the contention that the Sixth Amendment's guarantee of counsel for indigent federal defendants was extended to or, in the words of that Court, "made obligatory upon the States by the Fourteenth Amendment." Plainly, had the Court concluded that appointment of counsel for an indigent criminal defendant was "a fundamental right, essential to a fair trial," it would have held that the Fourteenth Amendment requires appointment of counsel in a state court, just as the Sixth Amendment requires in a federal court.

We think the Court in *Betts* had ample precedent for acknowledging that those guarantees of the Bill of Rights which are fundamental safeguards of liberty immune from federal abridgment are equally protected against state invasion by the Due Process Clause of the Fourteenth Amendment. This same principle was recognized, explained, and applied in *Powell v. Alabama*, a case upholding the right of counsel, where the Court held that despite sweeping language to the contrary in *Hurtado v. California* (1884), the Fourteenth Amendment "embraced" those "`fundamental principles of liberty and justice which lie at the base of all our civil and political institutions,'" even though they had been "specifically dealt with in another part of the federal Constitution."...

We accept *Betts v. Brady*'s assumption, based as it was on our prior cases, that a provision of the Bill of Rights which is "fundamental and essential to a fair trial" is made obligatory upon the States by the Fourteenth Amendment. We think the Court in *Betts* was wrong, however, in concluding that the Sixth Amendment's guarantee of counsel is not one of these fundamental rights. Ten years before *Betts v. Brady*, this Court, after full consideration of all the historical data examined in *Betts*, had unequivocally declared that "the right to the aid of counsel is of this fundamental character." *Powell v. Alabama* (1932). While the Court at the close of its Powell opinion did by its language, as this Court frequently does, limit its holding to the particular facts and circumstances of that case, its conclusions about the fundamental nature of the right to counsel are unmistakable. Several years later, in 1936, the Court reemphasized what it had said about the fundamental nature of the right to counsel in this language:

> We concluded that certain fundamental rights, safeguarded by the first eight amendments against federal action, were also safeguarded against state action by the due process of law clause of the Fourteenth Amendment, and among them the fundamental right of the accused to the aid of counsel in a criminal prosecution." *Grosjean v. American Press Co.* (1936).

And again in 1938 this Court said:

> The assistance of counsel is one of the safeguards of the Sixth Amendment deemed necessary to insure fundamental human rights of life and liberty....The Sixth Amendment stands as a constant admonition that if the constitutional safeguards it provides be lost, justice will not 'still be done.' *Johnson v. Zerbst* (1938).

In light of these and many other prior decisions of this Court, it is not surprising that the *Betts* Court, when faced with the contention that "one charged with crime, who is unable to obtain counsel, must be furnished counsel by the State," conceded that "expressions in the opinions of this court lend color to the argument...." The fact is that in deciding as it did— that "appointment of counsel is not a fundamental right, essential to a fair trial"—the Court in *Betts v. Brady* made an abrupt break with its own well-considered precedents. In returning to these old precedents, sounder we believe than the new, we but restore constitutional principles established to achieve a fair system of justice. Not only these precedents but also reason and reflection require us to recognize that in our adversary system of criminal justice, any person haled into court, who is too poor to hire a lawyer, cannot be assured a fair trial unless counsel is provided for him. This seems to us to be an obvious truth. Governments, both state and federal, quite properly spend vast sums of money to establish machinery to try defendants accused of crime. Lawyers to prosecute are everywhere deemed essential to protect the public's interest in an orderly society. Similarly, there are few defendants charged with crime, few indeed, who fail to hire the best lawyers they can get to prepare and present their defenses. That government hires lawyers to prosecute and defendants who have the money hire lawyers to defend are the strongest indications of the widespread belief that lawyers in criminal courts are necessities, not luxuries. The right of one charged with crime to counsel may not be deemed fundamental and essential to fair trials in some countries, but it is in ours. From the very beginning, our state and national constitutions and laws have laid great emphasis on procedural and substantive safeguards designed to assure fair trials before impartial tribunals in which every defendant stands equal before the law. This noble ideal cannot be realized if the poor man charged with crime has to face his accusers without a lawyer to assist him....

The Court in *Betts v. Brady* departed from the sound wisdom upon which the Court's holding in *Powell v. Alabama* rested. Florida, supported by two other States, has asked that *Betts v. Brady* be left intact. Twenty-two States, as friends of the Court, argue that *Betts* was "an anachronism when handed down" and that it should now be overruled. We agree.

The judgment is reversed and the case is remanded to the Supreme Court of Florida for further action not inconsistent with this opinion.

Miranda v. Arizona   MELVIN UROFSKY

In many, perhaps a majority of criminal investigations, when police confront a suspect, he or she will confess, and if this confession is given voluntarily, it will be admitted as evidence at the trial. Police practice, of course, strives to secure confessions, and while physical abuse in police investigations is now prohibited, a variety of psychological and emotional pressures can be brought to bear. For the poor, the illiterate, the homeless, the minority member, the uniformed police officer may often be an intimidating sight, a factor police use in their investigations.

Miranda had been arrested and taken to the police station under suspicion of kidnapping and rape. Two police officers questioned him without an attorney present, and at some point told him he did not have to talk, but that any statement he made could be used against him. After two hours, without any coercion or threats, Miranda confessed and signed a statement which later helped to convict him. (He had also been identified by a witness.)

The Fifth Amendment privilege against self-incrimination, like all rights, can be waived, provided it is waived voluntarily and knowingly. Beginning in the 1930s, the Supreme Court imposed restraints on what constituted a voluntary confession. Torture, beatings, interrogation to the point of exhaustion, solitary detainment and many similar practices had, unfortunately, been all too common in this country. But between the two extremes of police brutality and the criminal who cannot wait to confess, how can courts determine when a suspect has voluntarily confessed? The Miranda rules not only protect the accused, they also provide courts with a simple beginning test: if Miranda warnings are not given, any confession will be deemed involuntary.

The Miranda warnings are fairly simple. The police officer must inform the suspect that:

1. You have the right to remain silent.
2. Anything you do say may be used as evidence against you in a court of law.
3. You have the right to have an attorney present during questioning.
4. If you do not have the funds to secure an attorney, one will be provided for you.

The second part of Miranda is the right to counsel. *Gideon* extended the right to all trials, but the Court recognized that the most important time for a person to have legal advice is during the interrogatory stage at the police station, where the environment is intimidating and police, often without trying, can frighten a person into confession.

▶ For the first one hundred fifty years of this country's history under the Constitution and Bill of Rights, the Sixth Amendment had never been held to require a lawyer at a police station questioning. But if the *words* of the Sixth Amendment do not require a lawyer, does the *spirit* support the majority decision here?

▶ At what point is a lawyer necessary?

▶ If a person who can afford an attorney is allowed to have one present at the beginning of the process, is there any reason why a poor person should not also have access to counsel at that stage?

▶ Which groups in society benefit most from the *Miranda* ruling?

▶ Should the *Miranda* warnings be done away with entirely? Should some be kept and others eliminated? Or are they all equally necessary?

▶ Justice Harlan's dissent agrees with the majority that police coercion is bad, but believes that abuses can be controlled under the Due Process Clause. If police practices prove unfair or coercive, he says, they can be voided. Is there a standard that could be consistently applied to such practices?

Miranda v. Arizona 384 U.S. 436 (1966)

Mr. Chief Justice WARREN delivered the opinion of the Court.

The cases before us raise questions which go to the roots of our concepts of American criminal jurisprudence: the restraints society must observe consistent with the Federal Constitution in prosecuting individuals for crime. More specifically, we deal with the admissibility of statements obtained from an individual who is subjected to custodial police interrogation and the necessity for procedures which assure that the individual is accorded his privilege under the Fifth Amendment to the Constitution not to be compelled to incriminate himself.

We start here, as we did in *Escobedo*, with the premise that our holding is not an innovation in our jurisprudence, but is an application of principles long recognized and applied in other settings. We have undertaken a thorough re-examination of the *Escobedo* decision and the principles it announced, and we reaffirm it. That case was but an explication of basic rights that are enshrined in our Constitution—that "No person...shall be compelled in any criminal case to be a witness against himself," and that "the accused shall...have the Assistance of Counsel"—rights which were put in jeopardy in that case through official overbearing. These precious rights were fixed in our Constitution only after centuries of persecution and struggle. And in the words of Chief Justice Marshall, they were secured "for ages to come, and...designed to approach immortality as nearly as human institutions can approach it."

Our holding will be spelled out with some specificity in the pages which follow but briefly stated it is this: the prosecution may not use statements, whether exculpatory or inculpatory, stemming from custodial interrogation of the defendant unless it demonstrates the use of procedural safeguards effective to secure the privilege against self-incrimination. By custodial interrogation, we mean questioning initiated by law enforcement officers after a person has been taken into custody or otherwise deprived of his freedom of action in any significant way. As for the procedural safeguards to be employed, unless other fully effective means are devised to inform accused persons of their right of silence and to assure a continuous opportunity to exercise it, the following measures are required. Prior to any questioning, the person must be warned that he has a right to remain silent, that any statement he does make may be used as evidence against him, and that he has a right to the presence of an attorney, either retained or appointed. The defendant may waive effectuation of these rights, provided the waiver is made voluntarily, knowingly and intelligently. If, however, he indicates in any manner and at any stage of the process that he wishes to consult with an attorney before speaking there can be no questioning. Likewise, if the individual is alone and indicates in any manner that he does not wish to be interrogated, the police may not question him. The mere fact that he may have answered some questions or volunteered some statements on his own does not deprive him of the right to refrain from answering any further inquiries until he has consulted with an attorney and thereafter consents to be questioned.

The constitutional issue we decide in each of these cases is the admissibility of statements obtained from a defendant questioned while in custody or otherwise deprived of his freedom of action in any significant way. In each, the defendant was questioned by police officers, detectives, or a prosecuting attorney in a room in which he was cut off from the outside world. In none of these cases was the defendant given a full and effective warning of his rights at the outset of the interrogation process. In all the cases, the questioning elicited oral admissions, and in three of them, signed statements as well which were admitted at their trials. They all thus share salient features—incommunicado interrogation of individuals in a police-dominated atmosphere, resulting in self-incriminating statements without full warning of constitutional rights.

An understanding of the nature and setting of this in-custody interrogation is essential to our decisions today. The difficulty in depicting what transpires at such interrogations stems from the fact that in this country they have largely taken place incommunicado....

In these cases, we might not find the defendants' statements to have been involuntary in traditional terms. Our concern for adequate safeguards to protect precious Fifth Amendment rights is, of course, not lessened in the slightest. In each of the cases, the defendant was thrust into an unfamiliar atmosphere and run through menacing police interrogation procedures. The potentiality for compulsion is forcefully apparent, for example, in *Miranda*, where the indigent Mexican defendant was a seriously disturbed individual with pronounced sexual fantasies, and in Stewart, in which the defendant was an indigent Los Angeles Negro who had dropped out of school in the sixth grade. To be sure, the records do not evince overt physical coercion or patent psychological ploys. The fact remains that in none of these cases did the officers undertake to afford appropriate safeguards at the outset of the interrogation to insure that the statements were truly the product of free choice.

It is obvious that such an interrogation environment is created for no purpose other than to subjugate the individual to the will of his examiner. This atmosphere carries its own badge of intimidation. To be sure, this is not physical intimidation, but it is equally destructive of human dignity. The current practice of incommunicado interrogation is at odds with one of our Nation's most cherished principles—that the individual may not be compelled to incriminate himself. Unless adequate protective devices are employed to dispel the compulsion inherent in custodial surroundings, no statement obtained from the defendant can truly be the product of his free choice.

From the foregoing, we can readily perceive an intimate connection between the privilege against self-incrimination and police custodial questioning....An individual swept from familiar surrounding into police custody, surrounded by antagonistic forces, and subjected to the techniques of persuasion described above cannot be otherwise than under compulsion to speak. As a practical matter, the compulsion to speak in the isolated setting of the police station may well be greater than in courts or other official investigations, where there are often impartial observers to guard against intimidation or trickery....

Today, then, there can be no doubt that the Fifth Amendment privilege is available outside of criminal court proceedings and serves to protect persons in all settings in which their freedom of action is curtailed in any significant way from being compelled to incriminate themselves. We have concluded that without proper safeguards the process of in-custody interrogation of persons suspected or accused of crime contains inherently compelling pressures which work to undermine the individual's will to resist and to compel him to speak where he would not otherwise do so freely. In order to combat these pressures and to permit a full opportunity to exercise the privilege against self-incrimination, the accused must be adequately and effectively apprised of his rights and the exercise of those rights must be fully honored.

It is impossible for us to foresee the potential alternatives for protecting the privilege which might be devised by Congress or the States in the exercise of their creative rule-making capacities. Therefore we cannot say that the Constitution necessarily requires adherence to any particular solution for the inherent compulsions of the interrogation process as it is presently conducted. Our decision in no way creates a constitutional straitjacket which will handicap sound efforts at reform, nor is it intended to have this effect. We encourage Congress and the States to continue their laudable search for increasingly effective ways of protecting the rights of the individual while promoting efficient enforcement of our criminal laws. However, unless we are shown other procedures which are at least as effective in apprising accused persons of their right of silence and in assuring a continuous opportunity to exercise it, the following safeguards must be observed.

At the outset, if a person in custody is to be subjected to interrogation, he must first be informed in clear and unequivocal terms that he has the right to remain silent. For those unaware of the privilege, the warning is needed simply to make them aware of it—the threshold requirement for an intelligent decision as to its exercise. More important, such a warning is an absolute prerequisite in overcoming the inherent pressures of the interrogation atmosphere. It is not just the subnormal or woefully ignorant who succumb to an interrogator's imprecations, whether implied or expressly stated, that the interrogation will continue until a confession is obtained or that silence in the face of accusation is itself damning and will bode ill when presented to a jury. Further, the warning will show the individual that his interrogators are prepared to recognize his privilege should he choose to exercise it.

The Fifth Amendment privilege is so fundamental to our system of constitutional rule and the expedient of giving an adequate warning as to the availability of the privilege so simple, we will not pause to inquire in individual cases whether the defendant was aware of his rights without a warning being given. Assessments of the knowledge the defendant possessed, based on information as to his age, education, intelligence, or prior contact with authorities, can never be more than speculation; a warning is a clearcut fact. More important, whatever the background of the person interrogated, a warning at the time of the interrogation is indispensable to overcome its pressures and to insure that the individual knows he is free to exercise the privilege at that point in time.

The warning of the right to remain silent must be accompanied by the explanation that anything said can and will be used against the individual in court. This warning is needed in order to make him aware not only of the privilege, but also of the consequences of forgoing it. It is only through an awareness of these consequences that there can be any assurance of real understanding and intelligent exercise of the privilege. Moreover, this warning may serve to make the individual more acutely aware that he is faced with a phase of the adversary system—that he is not in the presence of persons acting solely in his interest.

The circumstances surrounding in-custody interrogation can operate very quickly to overbear the will of one merely made aware of this privilege by his interrogators. Therefore, the right to have counsel present at the interrogation is indispensable to the protection of the Fifth Amendment privilege under the system we delineate today. Our aim is to assure that the individual's right to choose between silence and speech remains unfettered throughout the interrogation process. A once-stated warning, delivered by those who will conduct the interrogation, cannot itself suffice to that end among those who most require knowledge of their rights. A mere warning given by the interrogators is not alone sufficient to accomplish that end. Prosecutors themselves claim that the admonishment of the right to remain silent without more "will benefit only the recidivist and the professional." Even preliminary advice given to the accused by his own attorney can be swiftly overcome by the secret interrogation process. Thus, the need for counsel to protect the Fifth Amendment privilege comprehends not merely a right to consult with counsel prior to questioning, but also to have counsel present during any questioning if the defendant so desires.

That presence of counsel at the interrogation may serve several significant subsidiary functions as well. If the accused decides to talk to his interrogators, the assistance of counsel can mitigate the dangers of untrustworthiness. With a lawyer present the likelihood that the police will practice coercion is reduced, and if coercion is nevertheless exercised the lawyer can testify to it in court. The presence of a lawyer can also help to guarantee that the accused gives a fully accurate statement to the police and that the statement is rightly reported by the prosecution at trial.

An individual need not make a pre-interrogation request for a lawyer. While such request affirmatively secures his right to have one, his failure to ask for a lawyer does not constitute a waiver. No effective waiver of the right to counsel during interrogation can be recognized unless specifically made after the warnings we here delineate have been given. The accused who does not know his rights and therefore does not make a request may be the person who most needs counsel....

Accordingly we hold that an individual held for interrogation must be clearly informed that he has the right to consult with a lawyer and to have the lawyer with him during interrogation under the system for protecting the privilege we delineate today. As with the warnings of the right to remain silent and that anything stated can be used in evidence against him, this warning is an absolute prerequisite to interrogation. No amount of circumstantial evidence that the person may have been aware of this right will suffice to stand in its stead. Only through such a warning is there ascertainable assurance that the accused was aware of this right.

If an individual indicates that he wishes the assistance of counsel before any interrogation occurs, the authorities cannot rationally ignore or deny his request on the basis that the individual does not have or cannot afford a retained attorney. The financial ability of the individual has no relationship to the scope of the rights involved here. The privilege against self-incrimination secured by the Constitution applies to all individuals. The need for counsel in order to protect the privilege exists for the indigent as well as the affluent. In fact, were we to limit these constitutional rights to those who can retain an attorney, our decisions today would be of little significance. The cases before us as well as the vast majority of confession cases with which we have dealt in the past involve those unable to retain counsel. While authorities are not required to relieve the accused of his poverty, they have the obligation not to take advantage of indigence in the administration of justice. Denial of counsel to the indigent at the time of interrogation while allowing an attorney to those who can afford one would be no more supportable by reason or logic than the similar situation at trial and on appeal....

In order fully to apprise a person interrogated of the extent of his rights under this system then, it is necessary to warn him not only that he has the right to consult with an attorney, but also that if he is indigent a lawyer will be appointed to represent him. Without this additional warning, the admonition of the right to consult with counsel would often be understood as meaning only that he can consult with a lawyer if he has one or has the funds to obtain one. The warning of a right to counsel would be hollow if not couched in terms that would convey to the indigent—the person most often subjected to interrogation—the knowledge that he too has a right to have counsel present. As with the warnings of the right to remain silent and of the general right to counsel, only by effective and express explanation to the indigent of this right can there be assurance that he was truly in a position to exercise it.

Once warnings have been given, the subsequent procedure is clear. If the individual indicates in any manner, at any time prior to or during questioning, that he wishes to remain silent, the interrogation must cease. At this point he has shown that he intends to exercise his Fifth Amendment privilege; any statements taken after the person invokes his privilege cannot be other than the product of compulsion, subtle or otherwise. Without the right to cut off questioning, the setting of in-custody interrogation operates on the individual to overcome free choice in producing a statement after the privilege has been once invoked. If the individual states that he wants an attorney, the interrogation must cease until an attorney is present. At that time, the individual must have an opportunity to confer with the attorney and to have him present during any subsequent questioning. If the individual cannot obtain an attorney and he indicates that he wants one before speaking to police, they must respect his decision to remain silent.

This does not mean, as some have suggested, that each police station must have a "station house lawyer" present at all times to advise prisoners. It does mean, however, that if police propose to interrogate a person they must make known to him that he is entitled to a lawyer and that if he cannot afford one, a lawyer will be provided for him prior to any interrogation. If authorities conclude that they will not provide counsel during a reasonable period of time in which investigation in the field is carried out, they may refrain from doing so without violating the person's Fifth Amendment privilege so long as they do not question him during that time.

If the interrogation continues without the presence of an attorney and a statement is taken, a heavy burden rests on the government to demonstrate that the defendant knowingly and intelligently waived his privilege against self-incrimination and his right to retained or appointed counsel. This Court has always set high standards of proof for the waiver of constitutional rights, and we reassert these standards as applied to in-custody interrogation. Since the State is responsible for establishing the isolated circumstances under which the interrogation takes place and has the only means of making available corroborated evidence of warning given during incommunicado interrogation, the burden is rightly on its shoulders....

In announcing these principles, we are not unmindful of the burdens which law enforcement officials must bear, often under trying circumstances. We also fully recognize the obligation of all citizens to aid in enforcing the criminal laws. This Court, while protecting individual rights, has always given ample latitude to law enforcement agencies in the legitimate exercise of their duties. The limits we have placed on the interrogation process should not constitute an undue interference with a proper system of law enforcement. As we have noted, our decision does not in any way preclude police from carrying out their traditional investigatory functions. Although confessions may play an important role in some convictions, the cases before us present graphic examples of the overstatement of the "need" for confessions. In each case authorities conducted interrogations ranging up to five days in duration despite the presence, through standard investigating practices, of considerable evidence against each defendant....

Over the years the Federal Bureau of Investigation has compiled an exemplary record of effective law enforcement while advising any suspect or arrested person, at the outset of an interview, that he is not required to make a statement, that any statement may be used against him in court, that the individual may obtain the services of an attorney of his own choice and, more recently, that he has a right to free counsel if he is unable to pay. A letter received from the Solicitor General in response to a question from the Bench makes it clear that the present pattern of warnings and respect for the rights of the individual followed as a practice by the FBI is consistent with the procedure which we delineate today.

The practice of the FBI can readily be emulated by state and local enforcement agencies. The argument that the FBI deals with different crimes than are dealt with by state authorities does not mitigate the significance of the FBI experience....

Mr. Justice CLARK, dissenting in Nos. 759, 760, and 761, and concurring in the result in No. 584.

It is with regret that I find it necessary to write in these cases. However, I am unable to join the majority because its opinion goes too far on too little, while my dissenting brethren do not go quite far enough. Nor can I join in the Court's criticism of the present practices of police and investigatory agencies as to custodial interrogation....The police agencies—all the way from municipal and state forces to the federal bureaus—are responsible for law enforcement and public safety in this country. I am proud of their efforts, which in my view are not fairly characterized by the Court's opinion....

Now, the Court fashions a constitutional rule that the police may engage in no custodial interrogation without additionally advising the accused that he has a right under the Fifth Amendment to the presence of counsel during interrogation and that, if he is without funds, counsel will be furnished him....Such a strict constitutional specific inserted at the nerve center of crime detection may well kill the patient. Since there is at this time a paucity of information and an almost total lack of empirical knowledge on the practical operation of requirements truly comparable to those announced by the majority, I would be more restrained lest we go too far too fast.

Mr. Justice HARLAN, with whom Mr. Justice STEWART and Mr. Justice WHITE join, dissenting.

I believe the decision for the Court represents poor constitutional law and entails harmful consequences for the country at large. How serious these consequences may prove to be only time can tell. But the basic flaws in the Court's justification seem to me readily apparent now once all sides of the problem are considered....

The thrust of the new rules is to negate all pressures, to reinforce the nervous or ignorant suspect, and ultimately to discourage any confession at all. The aim in short is toward "voluntariness" in a utopian sense, or to view it from a different angle, voluntariness with a vengeance.

To incorporate this notion into the Constitution requires a strained reading of history and precedent and a disregard of the very pragmatic concerns that alone may on occasion justify such strains. I believe that reasoned examination will show that the Due Process Clauses provide an adequate tool for coping with confessions and that, even if the Fifth Amendment privilege against self-incrimination be invoked, its precedents taken as a whole do not sustain the present rules. Viewed as a choice based on pure policy, these new rules prove to be a highly debatable, if not one-sided, appraisal of the competing interests, imposed over widespread objection, at the very time when judicial restraint is most called for by the circumstances....

I turn now to the Court's asserted reliance on the Fifth Amendment, an approach which I frankly regard as a trompe l'oeil. The Court's opinion in my view reveals no adequate basis for extending the Fifth Amendment's privilege against self-incrimination to the police station. Far more important, it fails to show that the Court's new rules are well supported, let alone compelled, by Fifth Amendment precedents. Instead, the new rules actually derive from quotation and analogy drawn from precedents under the Sixth Amendment, which should properly have no bearing on police interrogation.

The Court's opening contention, that the Fifth Amendment governs police station confessions, is perhaps not an impermissible extension of the law but it has little to commend itself in the present circumstances. Historically, privilege against self-incrimination did not bear at all on the use of extra-legal confessions, for which distinct standards evolved....Even those who would readily enlarge the privilege must concede some linguistic difficulties since the Fifth Amendment in terms proscribes only compelling any person "in any criminal case to be a witness against himself."

Though weighty, I do not say these points and similar ones are conclusive, for, as the Court reiterates, the privilege embodies basic principles always capable of expansion. Certainly the privilege does represent a protective concern for the accused and an emphasis upon accusatorial rather than inquisitorial values in law enforcement, although this is similarly true of other limitations such as the grand jury requirement and the reasonable doubt standard. Accusatorial values, however, have openly been absorbed into the due process standard governing confessions....Since extension of the general principle has already occurred, to insist that the privilege applies as such serves only to carry over inapposite historical details and engaging rhetoric and to obscure the policy choices to be made in regulating confessions.

Having decided that the Fifth Amendment privilege does apply in the police station, the Court reveals that the privilege imposes more exacting restrictions than does the Fourteenth Amendment's voluntariness test. It then emerges from a discussion of Escobedo that the Fifth Amendment requires for an admissible confession that it be given by one distinctly aware of his right not to speak and shielded from "the compelling atmosphere" of interrogation. From these key premises, the Court finally develops the safeguards of warning, counsel, and so forth. I do not believe these premises are sustained by precedents under the Fifth Amendment.

The more important premise is that pressure on the suspect must be eliminated though it be only the subtle influence of the atmosphere and surroundings. The Fifth Amendment, however, has never been thought to forbid all pressure to incriminate one's self in the situations covered by it....This is not to say that short of jail or torture any sanction is permissible in any case; policy and history alike may impose sharp limits. However, the Court's unspoken assumption that any pressure violates the privilege is not supported by the precedents and it has failed to show why the Fifth Amendment prohibits that relatively mild pressure the Due Process Clause permits.

The Court appears similarly wrong in thinking that precise knowledge of one's rights is a settled prerequisite under the Fifth Amendment to the loss of its protections....No Fifth Amendment precedent is cited for the Court's contrary view. There might of course be reasons apart from Fifth Amendment precedent for requiring warning or any other safeguard on questioning but that is a different matter entirely....

Examined as an expression of public policy, the Court's new regime proves so dubious that there can be no due compensation for its weakness in constitutional law....Precedent reveals that the Fourteenth Amendment in practice has been construed to strike a different balance, that the Fifth Amendment gives the Court little solid support in this context, and that the Sixth Amendment should have no bearing at all. Legal history has been stretched before to satisfy deep needs of society. In this instance, however, the Court has not and cannot make the powerful showing that its new rules are plainly desirable in the context of our society, something which is surely demanded before those rules are engrafted onto the Constitution and imposed on every State and country in the land.

Without at all subscribing to the generally black picture of police conduct painted by the Court, I think it must be frankly recognized at the outset that police questioning allowable under due process precedents may inherently entail some pressure on the suspect and may seek advantage in his ignorance or weaknesses....Until today, the role of the Constitution has been only to sift out undue pressure, not to assure spontaneous confessions.

The Court's new rules aim to offset these minor pressures and disadvantages intrinsic to any kind of police interrogation. The rules do not serve due process interests in preventing blatant coercion since, as I noted earlier, they do nothing to contain the policeman who is prepared to lie from the start. The rules work for reliability in confessions almost only in the Pickwickian sense that they can prevent some from being given at all....

Furman v. Georgia   MELVIN UROFSKY

The Court had been asked several times to review the constitutionality of the death penalty, but refused to do so until nearly a hundred cases flooded in on the appeals docket in 1971. It then took a handful of cases representative of the various claims. The *Furman* case is a good example of the Court slowly developing a new concept and attempting to reconcile contemporary moral ideas and constitutional principles.

It is important in this case to be clear on what the Court said and did not say. It did not say that the death penalty itself was unconstitutional, only that the provisions for imposing that penalty, as then provided for in law, were too vague and gave too much arbitrary discretion to the jury. The Court also did not, as in *Miranda*, lay out any specific remedy for this problem, but left it to the state legislatures to amend their laws. Every state which had the death penalty prior to *Furman* subsequently enacted a new capital punishment statute; these then became the subjects for a new round of court hearings.

The Court had obviously arrived at its decision in this case slowly and painfully. It handed down the decision *per curiam*, that is, "by the Court," since although a majority agreed on the result, they could not agree on the reasoning. At least two members of the Court believed that capital punishment violated the Eighth Amendment's ban on cruel or unusual punishment, but the majority refused to adopt this position.

Rather, because death is the ultimate punishment, a majority of the Court agreed that it had to be imposed, at least within the same state, in as non-arbitrary and fair a manner as possible. The pre-1972 laws, whatever their virtues, could not claim consistency. They left enormous discretion to judges and juries, who could, for whatever reason, choose to impose capital punishment or not. Very often, two defendants accused and convicted of the same crime received wildly disparate sentences; one going to prison for a term of years, and the other to the electric chair or gas chamber. Unfortunately, the only difference between the two usually seemed to be race, with black defendants receiving the death sentence in disproportionate numbers.

The Court won praise in a number of circles for deferring to the states for revised criteria. This, after all, is how a federal system is supposed to work, with a central Supreme Court establishing minimal constitutional criteria, and then leaving it to the states to work out the details. Unfortunately, the subsequent history of capital punishment litigation has led to more rather than less confusion.

On the positive side, all states now have some specific criteria to guide judges and juries in determining when and if the death penalty should be imposed; all states also provide for automatic review of any case in which capital punishment has been imposed. And it has become axiomatic that because the death penalty is irrevocable, each case must be examined carefully to ensure that justice has been done.[2]

On the negative side, the Court seems to have come around to some of the same problems it condemned only a few years earlier. By insisting that each case be individualized, it has opened up room for the same type of arbitrary discretion it condemns in *Furman*. Moreover, it has yet to face up to the problems of racial discrimination in the imposition of the death penalty—something the NAACP and other groups have complained about for years.

> ▶ The key question, according to some writers, is whether the death penalty should be considered "cruel and unusual" punishment in this day and age. Should it?
>
> ▶ To what sources may the Court look to determine the meaning of "cruel and unusual" punishment?

---

2. In Virginia, the relevant sections of the Code to guide juries are as follows:

Sec. 19.2-264.2. Conditions for imposition of death sentence.—In assessing the penalty of any person convicted of an offense for which the death penalty may be imposed, a sentence of death shall not be imposed unless the court or jury shall (1) after consideration of the past criminal record of convictions of the defendant, find that there is a probability that the defendant would commit criminal acts of violence that would constitute a continuing serious threat to society or that his conduct in committing the offense for which he stands charged was outrageously or wantonly vile, horrible or inhuman in that it involved torture, depravity of mind or an aggravated battery to the victim; and (2) recommend that the penalty be imposed.

▶ Many people complain about the inordinate delays attending a death sentence. People are tried and convicted of heinous crimes, sentenced to death, and years later are still alive as their lawyers find one way or another to "cheat the hangman." Is there anything in this case which works against justice being done? If so, what is it?

Furman v. Georgia 408 U.S. 238 (1972)

PER CURIAM

The Court holds that the imposition and carrying out of the death penalty in these cases constitutes cruel and unusual punishment in violation of the Eighth and Fourteenth Amendments. The judgment in each case is therefore reversed insofar as it leaves undisturbed the death sentence imposed, and the cases are remanded for further proceedings. *So ordered.*

Judgment in each case reversed in part and cases remanded.

Mr. Justice DOUGLAS, Mr. Justice BRENNAN, Mr. Justice STEWART, Mr. Justice WHITE, and Mr. Justice MARSHALL have filed separate opinions in support of the judgments.

Mr. Chief Justice BURGER, Mr. Justice BLACKMUN, Mr. Justice POWELL, and Mr. Justice REHNQUIST have filed separate dissenting opinions.

Sec. 19.2-264.4. Sentence proceeding.—A. Upon a finding that the defendant is guilty of an offense which may be punishable by death, a proceeding shall be held which shall be limited to a determination as to whether the defendant shall be sentenced to death of life imprisonment. In case of trial by jury, where a sentence of death is not recommended, the defendant shall be sentenced to imprisonment for life.

B. In cases of trial by jury, evidence may be presented as to any matter which the court deems relevant to sentence, except that reports under the provisions of Sec. 19.2-299, or under any rule of court, shall not be admitted into evidence.

Evidence which may be admissible, subject to the rules of evidence governing admissibility, may include the circumstances surrounding the offense, the history and background of the defendant, and any other facts in mitigation of the offense. Facts in mitigation may include, but shall not be limited to, the following: (i) The defendant has no significant history of prior criminal activity, or (ii) the capital felony was committed while the defendant was under the influence of extreme mental or emotional disturbance or (iii) the victim was a participant in the defendant's conduct or consented to the act, or (iv) at the time of the commission of the capital felony, the capacity of the defendant to appreciate the criminality of his conduct or to conform his conduct to the requirements of law was significantly impaired; or (v) the age of the defendant at the time of the commission of the capital offense.

C. The penalty of death shall not be imposed unless the Commonwealth shall prove beyond a reasonable doubt that there is a probability based upon evidence of the prior history of the defendant or of the circumstances surrounding the commission of the offense of which he is accused that he would commit criminal acts of violence that would constitute a continuing serious threat to society, or that his conduct in committing the offense was outrageously or wantonly vile, horrible or inhuman, in that it involved torture, depravity of mind or aggravated battery to the victim.

Mr. Justice DOUGLAS, concurring.

In these three cases the death penalty was imposed, one of them for murder, and two for rape. In each the determination of whether the penalty should be death or a lighter punishment was left by the State to the discretion of the judge or of the jury. In each of the three cases the trial was to a jury....

In this country there was almost from the beginning a "rebellion against the common-law rule imposing a mandatory death sentence on all convicted murderers." The first attempted remedy was to restrict the death penalty to defined offenses such as "premeditated" murder. But juries took "the law into their own hands" and refused to convict on the capital offense.

> In order to meet the problem of jury nullification, legislatures did not try, as
> before, to refine further the definition of capital homicides. Instead they
> adopted the method of forthrightly granting juries the discretion which they
> had been exercising in fact.

The Court [in *McGautha v. California* (1971)] concluded "In light of history, experience, and the present limitations of human knowledge, we find it quite impossible to say that committing to the untrammeled discretion of the jury the power to pronounce life or death in capital cases is offensive to anything in the Constitution."

The Court refused to find constitutional dimensions in the argument that those who exercise their discretion to send a person to death should be given standards by which that discretion should be exercised....We are now imprisoned in the *McGautha* holding. Indeed the seeds of the present cases are in *McGautha*. Juries (or judges, as the case may be) have practically untrammeled discretion to let an accused live or insist that he die....

A law that stated that anyone making more than $50,000 would be exempt from the death penalty would plainly fail, as would a law that in terms said that Blacks, those who never went beyond the fifth grade in school, or those who made less than $3,000 a year, or those who were unpopular or unstable should be the only people executed. A law which in the overall view reaches that result in practice has no more sanctity than a law which in terms provides the same.

Thus, these discretionary statutes are unconstitutional in their operation. They are pregnant with discrimination and discrimination is an ingredient not compatible with the idea of equal protection of the laws that is implicit in the ban on "cruel and unusual" punishments.

Any law which is nondiscriminatory on its face may be applied in such a way as to violate the Equal Protection Clause of the Fourteenth Amendment. Such conceivably might be the fate of a mandatory death penalty, where equal or lesser sentences were imposed on the elite, a harsher one on the minorities or members of the lower castes. Whether a mandatory death penalty would otherwise be constitutional is a question I do not reach.

I concur in the judgments of the Court.

Mr. Justice BRENNAN, concurring.

...At bottom, then, the Cruel and Unusual Punishments Clause prohibits the infliction of uncivilized and inhuman punishments. The State, even as it punishes, must treat its members with respect for their intrinsic worth as human beings. A punishment is "cruel and unusual," therefore, if it does not comport with human dignity.

This formulation, of course, does not of itself yield principles for assessing the constitutional validity of particular punishments. Nevertheless, even though "this Court has had little occasion to give precise content to the [Clause]," there are principles recognized in our cases and inherent in the clause sufficient to permit a judicial determination whether a challenged punishment comports with human dignity.

The primary principle is that a punishment must not be so severe as to be degrading to the dignity of human beings....

In determining whether a punishment comports with human dignity, we are aided also by a second principle inherent in the Clause—that the State must not arbitrarily inflict a severe punishment. This principle derives from the notion that the State does not respect human dignity when, without reason, it inflicts upon some people a severe punishment that it does not inflict upon others....

A third principle inherent in the Clause is that a severe punishment must not be unacceptable to contemporary society....

The final principle inherent in the Clause is that a severe punishment must not be excessive. A punishment is excessive under this principle if it is unnecessary: the infliction of a severe punishment by the State cannot comport with human dignity when it is nothing more than the pointless infliction of suffering. If there is a significantly less severe punishment adequate to achieve the purposes for which the punishment is inflicted, the punishment inflicted is unnecessary and therefore excessive....

When the punishment of death is inflicted in a trivial number of the cases in which it is legally available, the conclusion is virtually inescapable that it is being inflicted arbitrarily. Indeed, it smacks of little more than a lottery system. The States claim, however, that this rarity is evidence not of arbitrariness, but of informed selectivity: Death is inflicted, they say, only in "extreme" cases.

Informed selectivity, of course, is a value not to be denigrated. Yet presumably the State could make precisely the same claim if there were 10 executions per year, or five, or even if there were but one. That there may be as many as 50 per year does not strengthen the claim. When the rate of infliction is at this low level, it is highly implausible that only the worst criminals or the criminals who commit the worst crimes are selected for this punishment. No one has yet suggested a rational basis that could differentiate in those terms the few who die from the many who go to prison. Crimes and criminals simply do not admit of a distinction that can be drawn so finely as to explain, on that ground, the execution of such a tiny sample of those eligible. Certainly the laws that provide for this punishment do not attempt to draw that distinction; all cases to which the laws apply are necessarily "extreme." Nor is the distinction credible in fact. If, for example, petitioner Furman or his crime illustrate the "extreme," then nearly all murderers and their murders are also "extreme." Furthermore, our procedures in death cases, rather than resulting in the selection of "extreme" cases for this punishment, actually sanction an arbitrary selection. For this Court has held that juries may, as they do, make the decision whether to impose a death sentence wholly unguided by standards governing that decision. In other words, our procedures are not constructed to guard against the totally capricious selection of criminals for the punishment of death.

Although it is difficult to imagine what further facts would be necessary in order to prove that death is, as my Brother Stewart puts it, "wantonly and freakishly" inflicted, I need not conclude that arbitrary infliction is patently obvious. I am not considering this punishment by the isolated light of one principle. The probability or arbitrariness is sufficiently substantial that it can be relied upon, in combination with the other principles, in reaching a judgment on the constitutionality of this punishment....

Mr. Justice STEWART, concurring.

...Legislatures—state and federal—have sometimes specified that the penalty of death shall be the mandatory punishment for every person convicted of engaging in certain designated criminal conduct. Congress, for example, has provided that anyone convicted of acting as a spy for the enemy in time of war shall be put to death. The Rhode Island Legislature has ordained the death penalty for a life term prisoner who commits murder. Massachusetts has passed a law imposing the death penalty upon anyone convicted of murder in the commission of a forcible rape. An Ohio law imposes the mandatory penalty of death upon the assassin of the President of the United States or the Governor of the State.

If we were reviewing death sentences imposed under these or similar laws, we would be faced with the need to decide whether capital punishment is unconstitutional for all crimes and under all circumstances. We would need to decide whether a legislature—state or federal—could constitutionally determine that certain criminal conduct is so atrocious that society's interest in deterrence and retribution wholly outweighs any considerations of reform or rehabilitation of the perpetrator, and that, despite the inconclusive empirical evidence, only the automatic penalty of death will provide maximum deterrence.

On that score I would say only that I cannot agree that retribution is a constitutionally impermissible ingredient in the imposition of punishment. The instinct for retribution is part of the nature of man, and channeling that instinct in the administration of criminal justice serves an important purpose in promoting the stability of a society governed by law. When people begin to believe the organized society is unwilling or unable to impose upon criminal offenders the punishment they "deserve," then there are sown the seeds of anarchy—of self-help, vigilante justice, and lynch law.

The constitutionality of capital punishment in the abstract is not, however, before us in these cases. For the Georgia and Texas legislatures have not provided that the death penalty shall be imposed upon all those who are found guilty of forcible rape. And the Georgia Legislature has not ordained that death shall be the automatic punishment for murder. In a word, neither State has made a legislative determination that forcible rape and murder can be deterred only by imposing the penalty of death upon all who perpetrate those offenses. As Mr. Justice White so tellingly puts it, "legislative will is not frustrated if the penalty is never imposed."

Instead, the death sentences now before us are the product of a legal system that brings them, I believe, within the very core of the Eighth Amendment's guarantee against cruel and unusual punishments, a guarantee applicable against the States through the Fourteenth Amendment. In the first place, it is clear that these sentences are "cruel" in the sense that they excessively go beyond, not in degree but in kind, the punishments that the state legislatures have determined to be necessary. In the second place, it is equally clear that these sentences are "unusual" in the sense that the penalty of death is infrequently imposed for murder, and that its imposition for rape is extraordinarily rare. But I do not rest by conclusion upon these two propositions alone.

These death sentences are cruel and unusual in the same way that being struck by lightening is cruel and unusual. For, of all the people convicted of rapes and murders in 1967 and 1968, many just as reprehensible as these, the petitioners are among a capriciously selected random handful upon whom the sentence of death has in fact been imposed. My concurring Brothers have demonstrated that, if any basis can be discerned for the selection of these few to be sentenced to die, it is the constitutionally impermissible basis of race. But racial discrimination has not been proved, and I put it to one side. I simply conclude that the Eighth and Fourteenth Amendments cannot tolerate the infliction of a sentence of death under legal systems that permit this unique penalty to be so wantonly and so freakishly imposed.

For these reasons I concur in the judgments of the Court.

Mr. Justice WHITE, concurring.

The facial constitutionality of statutes requiring the imposition of the death penalty for first degree murder, for more narrowly defined categories of murder or for rape would present quite different issues under the Eighth Amendment than are posed by the cases before us. In joining the Court's judgment, therefore, I do not at all intimate that the death penalty is unconstitutional per se or that there is no system of capital punishment that would comport with the Eighth Amendment. That question, ably argued by several of my Brethren, is not presented by these cases and need not be decided.

The narrower question to which I address myself concerns the constitutionality of capital punishment statutes under which (1) the legislature authorizes the imposition of the death penalty for murder or rape; (2) the legislature does not itself mandate the penalty in any particular class or kind of case (that is, legislative will is not frustrated if the penalty is never imposed) but delegates to judges or juries the decisions as to those cases, if any, in which the penalty will be utilized; and (3) judges and juries have ordered the death penalty with such infrequency that the odds are now very much against imposition and execution of the penalty with respect to any convicted murderer or rapist. It is in this context that we must consider whether the execution of these petitioners violates the Eighth Amendment.

I begin with what I consider a near truism: that the death penalty could so seldom be imposed that it would cease to be a credible deterrent or measurably to contribute to any other end of punishment in the criminal justice system. It is perhaps true that no matter how infrequently those convicted of rape or murder are executed, the penalty so imposed is not disproportionate to the crime and those executed may deserve exactly what they received. It would also be clear that executed defendants are finally and completely incapacitated from again committing rape or murder or any other crime. But when imposition of the penalty reaches a

certain degree of infrequency, it would be very doubtful that any existing general need for retribution would be measurably satisfied. Nor could it be said with confidence that society's
need for specific deterrence justifies death for so few when for so many in like circumstances
life imprisonment or shorter prison terms are judged sufficient, or that community values are
measurably reenforced by authorizing a penalty so rarely invoked.

Most important, a major goal of the criminal law—to deter others by punishing the
convicted criminal—would not be substantially served where the penalty is so seldom
invoked that it ceases to be the credible threat essential to influence the conduct of others.
For present purposes I accept the morality and utility of punishing one person to influence
another. I accept also the effectiveness of punishment generally and need not reject the
death penalty as a more effective deterrent than a lesser punishment. But common sense
and experience tell us that seldom-enforced laws become ineffective measures for controlling human conduct and that the death penalty, unless imposed with sufficient frequency,
will make little contribution to deterring those crimes for which it may be exacted....

It is also my judgment that this point has been reached with respect to capital punishment as it is presently administered under the statutes involved in these cases. Concededly,
it is difficult to prove as a general proposition that capital punishment, however administered, more effectively serves the ends of the criminal law than does imprisonment. But
however that may be, I cannot avoid the conclusion that as the statutes before us are now
administered, the penalty is so infrequently imposed that the threat of execution is too
attenuated to be of substantial service to criminal justice.

I need not restate the facts and figures that appear in the opinion of my Brethren. Nor
can I "prove" my conclusion from these data. But like my Brethren, I must arrive at judgment; and I can do no more than state a conclusion based on 10 years of almost daily exposure to the facts and circumstances of hundreds and hundreds of federal and state criminal cases involving crimes for which death is the authorized penalty. That conclusion, as I
have said, is that the death penalty is exacted with great infrequency even for the most
atrocious crimes and that there is no meaningful basis for distinguishing the few cases in
which it is imposed from the many cases in which it is not. The short of it is that the policy
of vesting sentencing authority primarily in juries—a decision largely motivated by the
desire to mitigate the harshness of the law and to bring community judgment to bear on
the sentence as well as guilt or innocence—has so effectively achieved its aims that capital
punishment within the confines of the statutes now before us has for all practical purposes
run its course....

I concur in the judgments of the Court.

Mr. Justice MARSHALL, concurring.

...A punishment may be deemed cruel and unusual for any one of four distinct reasons.

First, there are certain punishments which inherently involve so much physical pain and
suffering that civilized people cannot tolerate them—*e.g.*, use of the rack, the thumbscrew, or
other modes of torture. Regardless of public sentiment with respect to imposition of one of
these punishments in a particular case or at any one moment in history, the Constitution prohibits it. These are punishments that have been barred since the adoption of the Bill of Rights.

Second, there are punishments which are unusual, signifying that they were previously unknown as penalties for a given offense....

Third, a penalty may be cruel and unusual because it is excessive and serves no valid legislative purpose. The decisions previously discussed are replete with assertions that one of the primary functions of the cruel and unusual punishments clause is to prevent excessive or unnecessary penalties....

Fourth, where a punishment is not excessive and serves a valid legislative purpose, it still may be invalid if popular sentiment abhors it....

There is but one conclusion that can be drawn from all of this—i.e., the death penalty is an excessive and unnecessary punishment which violates the Eighth Amendment. The statistical evidence is not convincing beyond all doubt, but, it is persuasive. It is not improper at this point to take judicial notice of the fact that for more than 200 years men have labored to demonstrate that capital punishment serves no purpose that life imprisonment could not serve equally as well. And they have done so with great success. Little if any evidence has been adduced to prove the contrary. The point has now been reached at which deference to the legislatures is tantamount to abdication of our judicial roles as factfinders, judges, and ultimate arbiters of the Constitution. We know that at some point the presumption of constitutionality accorded legislative acts gives way to a realistic assessment of those acts. This point comes when there is sufficient evidence available so that judges can determine not whether the legislature acted wisely, but whether it had any rational basis whatsoever for acting. We have this evidence before us now. There is no rational basis for concluding that capital punishment is not excessive. It therefore violates the Eighth Amendment.

In addition, even if capital punishment is not excessive, it nonetheless violates the Eighth Amendment because it is morally unacceptable to the people of the United States at this time in their history....

Mr. Chief Justice BURGER; with whom Mr. Justice BLACKMUN, Mr. Justice POWELL, and Mr. Justice REHNQUIST join, dissenting.

While I cannot endorse the process of decision-making that has yielded today's result and the restraints which that result imposes on legislative action, I am not altogether displeased that legislative bodies have been given the opportunity, and indeed unavoidable responsibility, to make a thorough re-evaluation of the entire subject of capital punishment. If today's opinions demonstrate nothing else, they starkly show that this is an area where legislatures can act far more effectively than courts.

The legislatures are free to eliminate capital punishment for specific crimes or to carve-out limited exceptions to a general abolition of the penalty, without adherence to the conceptual strictures of the Eighth Amendment. The legislatures can and should make an assessment of the deterrent influence of capital punishment, both generally and as affecting the commission of specific types of crimes. If legislatures come to doubt the efficacy of capital punishment, they can abolish it, either completely or on a selective basis. If new evidence persuades them that they have acted unwisely, they can reverse their field and reinstate the penalty to the extent it is thought warranted. An Eighth Amendment ruling by judges cannot be made with such flexibility or discriminating precision....

The five opinions in support of the judgment differ in many respects, but they share a willingness to make sweeping factual assertions, unsupported by empirical data, concerning the manner of imposition and effectiveness of capital punishment in this country. Legislatures will have the opportunity to make a more penetrating study of these claims with the familiar and effective tools available to them as they are not to us.

Brewer v. Williams   MELVIN UROFSKY

The facts of this case are set forth in detail in the majority opinion. It would seem from the evidence that even if Williams did not actually kill the girl, he did hide the body; his defense, in fact, was that another employee had murdered the girl, and Williams, fearful that his record would cause the blame to fall on him, had hidden the corpse. On retrial, the jury did not believe him and again found him guilty of murder. The Supreme Court upheld the second conviction on the grounds that the police, having already uncovered a great deal of evidence, would have "inevitably discovered" the rest, even without the confession.

The case recalls Justice Holmes's famous comment that freedom of speech is not for the speech we agree with, but for the speech we detest. Even if one is sure that Williams is the guilty party, it is also clear that the police broke their word to his attorneys. The Constitution, it must be remembered, protects not only innocent persons but the guilty as well. The more detestable the crime, the greater the temptation on the part of authorities to break the rules. As Justice Brandeis said, the government is the great teacher; if its representatives are lawless, we will copy them.

Yet there are always some exceptions to general rules. In this case, for example, the little girl might still have been alive at the time of the "interrogation"; shouldn't the police have acted to determine this possibility so that she might have been rescued before freezing to death? The Court has recognized exceptions to the *Miranda* rule; in a recent case the Court upheld interrogation of a robbery suspect to determine where he had thrown a pistol, since an innocent party might presumably have been hurt by it.

> ▶ Did the police act properly in this case?
>
> ▶ Once the police made those promises should they have kept their word?
>
> ▶ Does the conversation in the police car constitute interrogation?
>
> ▶ Should Williams's confession be treated as voluntary?
>
> ▶ Once a suspect is in custody, his or her freedom has been limited: the person cannot walk away, cannot stop the police from talking, cannot protect his privacy. Should special rules apply in custodial situations to ensure adherence to constitutional requirements?

Brewer v. Williams 430 U.S. 387 (1977)

Mr. Justice STEWART delivered the opinion of the Court.

On the afternoon of December 24, 1968, a 10-year-old girl named Pamela Powers went with her family to the YMCA in Des Moines, Iowa, to watch a wrestling tournament in which her brother was participating. When she failed to return from a trip to the washroom, a search for her began. The search was unsuccessful.

Robert Williams who had recently escaped from a mental hospital, was a resident of the YMCA. Soon after the girl's disappearance Williams was seen in the YMCA lobby carrying some clothing and a large bundle wrapped in a blanket. He obtained help from a 14-year-old boy in opening the street door of the YMCA and the door to his automobile parked outside. When Williams placed the bundle in the front seat of his car the boy "saw two legs in it and they were skinny and white." Before anyone could see what was in the bundle Williams drove away. His abandoned car was found the following day in Davenport, Iowa, roughly 160 miles east of Des Moines. A warrant was then issued in Des Moines for his arrest on a charge of abduction.

On the morning of December 26, a Des Moines lawyer named Henry McKnight went to the Des Moines police station and informed the officers present that he had just received a long distance call from Williams, and that he had advised Williams to turn himself in to the Davenport police. Williams did surrender that morning to the police in Davenport, and they booked him on the charge specified in the arrest warrant and gave him the warnings required by *Miranda v. Arizona*. The Davenport police then telephoned their counterparts in Des Moines to inform them that Williams had surrendered. McKnight, the lawyer, was still at the Des Moines police headquarters, and Williams conversed with McKnight on the telephone. In the presence of the Des Moines chief of police and a police detective named Leaming, McKnight advised Williams that Des Moines police officers would be driving to Davenport to pick him up, that the officers would not interrogate him or mistreat him, and that Williams was not to talk to the officers about Pamela Powers until after consulting with McKnight upon his return to Des Moines. As a result of these conversations, it was agreed between McKnight and the Des Moines police officials that Detective Leaming and a fellow officer would drive to Davenport to pick up Williams, that they would bring him directly back to Des Moines, and that they would not question him during the trip.

In the meantime Williams was arraigned before a judge in Davenport on the outstanding arrest warrant. The judge advised him of his Miranda rights and committed him to jail. Before leaving the courtroom, Williams conferred with a lawyer named Kelly, who advised him not to make any statements until consulting with McKnight back in Des Moines.

Detective Leaming and his fellow officer arrived in Davenport about noon to pick up Williams and return him to Des Moines. Soon after their arrival they met with Williams and Kelly, who, they understood, was acting as Williams' lawyer. Detective Leaming repeated the Miranda warnings, and told Williams:

> We both know that you're being represented here by Mr. Kelly and you're being
> represented by Mr. McKnight in Des Moines, and...I want you to remember
> this because we'll be visiting between here and Des Moines.

Williams then conferred again with Kelly alone, and after this conference Kelly reiterated to Detective Leaming that Williams was not to be questioned about the disappearance of Pamela Powers until after he had consulted with McKnight back in Des Moines. When Leaming expressed some reservations, Kelly firmly stated that the agreement with McKnight was to be carried out—that there was to be no interrogation of Williams during the automobile journey to Des Moines. Kelly was denied permission to ride in the police car back to Des Moines with Williams and the two officers.

The two detectives, with Williams in their charge, then set out on the 160-mile drive. At no time during the trip did Williams express a willingness to be interrogated in the absence of an attorney. Instead, he stated several times that "when I get to Des Moines and see Mr. McKnight, I am going to tell you the whole story." Detective Leaming knew that Williams was a former mental patient, and knew also that he was deeply religious.

The detective and his prisoner soon embarked on a wide-ranging conversation covering a variety of topics, including the subject of religion. Then, not long after leaving Davenport and reaching the interstate highway, Detective Leaming delivered what has been referred to in the briefs and oral arguments as the "Christian burial speech." Addressing Williams as "Reverend," the detective said:

> I want to give you something to think about while we're traveling down the road....Number one, I want you to observe the weather conditions, it's raining, it's sleeting, it's freezing, driving is very treacherous, visibility is poor, it's going to be dark early this evening. They are predicting several inches of snow for tonight, and I feel that you yourself are the only person that knows where this little girl's body is, that you yourself have only been there once, and if you get a snow on top of it you yourself may be unable to find it. And, since we will be going right past the area on the way to Des Moines, I feel that we could stop and locate the body, that the parents of this little girl should be entitled to a Christian burial for the little girl who was snatched away from them on Christmas Eve and murdered. And I feel we should stop and locate it on the way in rather than waiting until morning and trying to come back out after a snow storm and possibly not being able to find it at all.

Williams asked Detective Leaming why he thought their route to Des Moines would be taking them past the girl's body, and Leaming responded that he knew the body was in the area of Mitchellville—a town they would be passing on the way to Des Moines. Leaming then stated: "I do not want you to answer me. I don't want to discuss it any further. Just think about it as we're riding down the road."

As the car approached Grinnell, a town approximately 100 miles west of Davenport, Williams asked whether the police had found the victim's shoes. When Detective Leaming replied that he was unsure, Williams directed the officers to a service station where he said he had left the shoes; a search for them proved unsuccessful. As they continued towards Des Moines, Williams asked whether the police had found the blanket, and directed the officers to a rest area where he said he had disposed of the blanket. Nothing was found. The car continued towards Des Moines, and as it approached Mitchellville, Williams said that he would show the officers where the body was. He then directed the police to the body of Pamela Powers.

Williams was indicted for first-degree murder. Before trial, his counsel moved to suppress all evidence relating to or resulting from any statements Williams had made during the automobile ride from Davenport to Des Moines. After an evidentiary hearing the trial judge denied the motion. He found that "an agreement was made between defense and counsel and the police officials to the effect that the Defendant was not to be questioned on the return trip to Des Moines," and that the evidence in question had been elicited from Williams during "a critical stage in the proceedings requiring the presence of counsel on his request." The judge ruled, however, that Williams had "waived his right to have an attorney present during the giving of such information."

The evidence in question was introduced over counsel's continuing objection at the subsequent trial. The jury found Williams guilty of murder....

It is clear that Williams was deprived of a constitutional right—the right to the assistance of counsel.

This right, guaranteed by the Sixth and Fourteenth Amendments, is indispensable to the fair administration of our adversary system of criminal justice. Its vital need at the pretrial stage has perhaps nowhere been more succinctly explained than in Mr. Justice Sutherland's memorable words for the Court 44 years ago in *Powell v. Alabama* [1933].

> During perhaps the most critical period of the proceedings against these defendants, that is to say, from the time of their arraignment until the beginning of their trial, when consultation, thoroughgoing investigation and preparation were vitally important, the defendants did not have the aid of counsel in any real sense, although they were as much entitled to such aid during that period as at the trial itself.

There has occasionally been a difference of opinion within the Court as to the peripheral scope of this constitutional right. But its basic contours, which are identical in state and federal contexts, are too well established to require extensive elaboration here. Whatever else it may mean, the right to counsel granted by the Sixth and Fourteenth Amendments means at least that a person is entitled to the help of a lawyer at or after the time that judicial proceedings have been initiated against him—"whether by way of formal charge, preliminary hearing, indictment, information, or arraignment."

There can be no doubt in the present case that judicial proceedings had been initiated against Williams before the start of the automobile ride from Davenport to Des Moines. A warrant had been issued for his arrest, he had been arraigned on that warrant before a judge in a Davenport courtroom, and he had been committed by the court to confinement in jail. The State does not contend otherwise.

There can be no serious doubt, either, that Detective Leaming deliberately and designedly set out to elicit information from Williams just as surely as—and perhaps more effectively than—if he had formally interrogated him. Detective Leaming was fully aware before departing for Des Moines that Williams was being represented in Davenport by Kelly and in Des Moines by McKnight. Yet he purposely sought during Williams' isolation from his lawyers to obtain as much incriminating information as possible. Indeed, Detective Leaming conceded as much when he testified at Williams' trial:

> Q. In fact, Captain, whether he was a mental patient or not, you were trying to get all the information you could before he got to his lawyer, weren't you?
>
> A. I was sure hoping to find out where that little girl was, yes, sir.

The state courts clearly proceeded upon the hypothesis that Detective Leaming's "Christian burial speech" had been tantamount to interrogation. Both courts recognized that Williams had been entitled to the assistance of counsel at the time he made the incriminating statements. Yet no such constitutional protection would have come into play if there had been no interrogation....

Rather, the clear rule of *Massiah* is that once adversary proceedings have commenced against an individual, he has a right to legal representation when the government interrogates him. It thus requires no wooden or technical application of the *Massiah* doctrine to conclude that Williams was entitled to the assistance of counsel guaranteed to him by the Sixth and Fourteenth Amendments.

The Iowa courts recognized that Williams had been denied the constitutional right to the assistance of counsel. They held, however, that he had waived that right during the course of the automobile trip from Davenport to Des Moines. The state trial court explained its determination of waiver as follows:

> The time element involved on the trip, the general circumstances of it, and more importantly the absence on the Defendant's part of any assertion of his right or desire not to give information absent the presence of his attorney, are the main foundations for the Court's conclusion that he voluntarily waived such right.

In its lengthy opinion affirming this determination the Iowa Supreme Court applied "the totality-of-circumstances test for a showing of waiver of constitutionally-protected rights in the absence of an express waiver," and concluded that "evidence of the time element involved on the trip, the general circumstances of it, and the absence of any request or expressed desire for the aid of counsel before or at the time of giving information, were sufficient to sustain a conclusion that defendant did waive his constitutional rights as alleged."

It is true that Williams had been informed of and appeared to understand his right to counsel. But waiver requires not merely comprehension but relinquishment, and Williams' consistent reliance upon the advice of counsel in dealing with the authorities refutes any suggestion that he waived that right. He consulted McKnight by long distance telephone before turning himself in. He spoke with McKnight by telephone again shortly after being booked. After he was arraigned, Williams sought out and obtained legal advice from Kelly. Williams again consulted with Kelly after Detective Leaming and his fellow officer arrived in Davenport. Throughout, Williams was advised not to make any statements before seeing McKnight in Des Moines, and was assured that the police had agreed not to question him. His statements while in the car that he would tell the whole story after seeing McKnight in

Des Moines were the clearest expressions by Williams himself that he desired the presence of an attorney before any interrogation took place. But even before making these statements, Williams had effectively asserted his right to counsel by having secured attorneys at both ends of the automobile trip, both of whom, acting as his agents, had made clear to the police that no interrogation was to occur during the journey. Williams knew of that agreement and, particularly in view of his consistent reliance on counsel, there is no basis for concluding that he disavowed it.

Despite Williams' express and implicit assertions of his right to counsel, Detective Leaming proceeded to elicit incriminating statements from Williams. Leaming did not preface this effort by telling Williams that he had a right to the presence of a lawyer, and made no effort at all to ascertain whether Williams wished to relinquish that right. The circumstances of record in this case thus provide no reasonable basis for finding that Williams waived his right to the assistance of counsel.

The Court of Appeals did not hold, nor do we, that under the circumstances of this case Williams could not, without notice to counsel, have waived his rights under the Sixth and Fourteenth Amendments. It only held, as do we, that he did not....

Mr. Justice MARSHALL, concurring.

I concur wholeheartedly in my Brother Stewart's opinion for the Court, but add these words in light of the dissenting opinions filed today. The dissenters have, I believe, lost sight of the fundamental constitutional backbone of our criminal law. They seem to think that Detective Leaming's actions were perfectly proper, indeed laudable, examples of "good police work." In my view, good police work is something far different from catching the criminal at any price. It is equally important that the police, as guardians of the law, fulfill their responsibility to obey its commands scrupulously....

Leaming knowingly isolated Williams from the protection of his lawyers and during that period he intentionally "persuaded" him to give incriminating evidence. It is this intentional police misconduct—not good police practice—that the Court rightly condemns. The heinous nature of the crime is no excuse, as the dissenters would have it, for condoning knowing and intentional police transgression of the constitutional rights of a defendant. If Williams is to go free—and given the ingenuity of Iowa prosecutors on retrial or in a civil commitment proceeding, I doubt very much that there is any chance a dangerous criminal will be loosed on the streets, the bloodcurdling cries of the dissents notwithstanding—it will hardly be because he deserves it. It will be because Detective Leaming, knowing full well that he risked reversal of Williams' conviction, intentionally denied Williams the right of every American under the Sixth Amendment to have the protective shield of a lawyer between himself and the awesome power of the State.

Mr. Justice POWELL, concurring.

As the dissenting opinion of The Chief Justice sharply illustrates, resolution of the issues in this case turns primarily on one's perception of the facts. There is little difference of opinion, among the several courts and numerous judges who have reviewed the case, as to the relevant constitutional principles: (i) Williams had the right to assistance of counsel; (ii) once that right attached (it is conceded that it had in this case), the State could not properly interrogate Williams in the absence of counsel unless he voluntarily and knowingly waived the right; and (iii) the burden was on the State to show that Williams in fact had waived the right before the police interrogated him.

The critical factual issue is whether there had been a voluntary waiver, and this turns in large part upon whether there was interrogation....

It is settled law that an inferred waiver of a constitutional right is disfavored. I find no basis in the record of this case—or in the dissenting opinions—for disagreeing with the conclusion of the District Court that "the State has produced no affirmative evidence whatsoever to support its claim of waiver."

The dissenting opinion of The Chief Justice states that the Court's holding today "conclusively presumes a suspect is legally incompetent to change his mind and tell the truth until an attorney is present." I find no justification for this view. On the contrary, the opinion of the Court is explicitly clear that the right to assistance of counsel may be waived, after it has attached, without notice to or consultation with counsel. We would have such a case here if petitioner had proved that the police officers refrained from coercion and interrogation, as they had agreed, and that Williams freely on his own initiative had confessed the crime.

Mr. Justice STEVENS, concurring.

Nothing that we write, no matter how well reasoned or forcefully expressed can bring back the victim of this tragedy or undo the consequences of the official neglect which led to the respondent's escape from a state mental institution. The emotional aspects of the case make it difficult to decide dispassionately, but do not qualify our obligation to apply the law with an eye to the future as well as with concern for the result in the particular case before us.

Underlying the surface issues in this case is the question, whether a fugitive from justice can rely on his lawyer's advice given in connection with a decision to surrender voluntarily. The defendant placed his trust in an experienced Iowa trial lawyer who in turn trusted the Iowa law enforcement authorities to honor a commitment made during negotiations which led to the apprehension of a potentially dangerous person. Under any analysis, this was a critical stage of the proceeding in which the participation of an independent professional was of vital importance to the accused and to society. At this stage—as in countless others in which the law profoundly affects the life of the individual—the lawyer is the essential medium through which the demands and commitments of the sovereign are communicated to the citizen. If, in the long run, we are seriously concerned about the individual's effective representation by counsel, the State cannot be permitted to dishonor its promise to this lawyer.

Mr. Chief Justice BURGER, dissenting.

The result in this case ought to be intolerable in any society which purports to call itself an organized society. It continues the Court—by the narrowest margin—on the much-criticized course of punishing the public for the mistakes and misdeeds of law enforcement officers, instead of punishing the officer directly, if in fact he is guilty of wrongdoing. It mechanically and blindly keeps reliable evidence from juries whether the claimed constitutional violation involves gross police misconduct or honest human error.

Williams is guilty of the savage murder of a small child; no member of the Court contends he is not. While in custody, and after no fewer than five warnings of his rights to silence and to counsel, he led police to the concealed body of his victim. The Court concedes Williams was not threatened or coerced and that he spoke and acted voluntarily and with full awareness of his constitutional rights. In the face of all this, the Court now holds that because Williams was prompted by the detective's statement—not interrogation but a statement—the jury must not be told how the police found the body.

Under well-settled precedents which the Court freely acknowledges, it is very clear that Williams had made a valid waiver of his Fifth Amendment right to silence and his Sixth Amendment right to counsel when he led police to the child's body. Indeed, even under the Court's analysis I do not understand how a contrary conclusion is possible.

The Court purports to apply as the appropriate constitutional waiver standard the familiar "intentional relinquishment or abandonment of a known right of privilege" test. The Court assumes, without deciding, that Williams' conduct and statements were voluntary. It concedes, as it must, that Williams had been informed of and fully understood his constitutional rights and the consequences of their waiver. Then, having either assumed or found every element necessary to make out a valid waiver under its own test, the Court reaches the astonishing conclusion that no valid waiver has been demonstrated....

The evidence is uncontradicted that Williams had abundant knowledge of his right to have counsel present and of his right to silence. Since the Court does not question his mental competence, it boggles the mind to suggest that Williams could not understand that leading police to the child's body would have other than the most serious consequences. All of the elements necessary to make out a valid waiver are shown by the record and acknowledged by the Court; we thus are left to guess how the Court reached its holding....

Mr. Justice WHITE, with whom Mr. Justice BLACKMUN and Mr. Justice REHNQUIST join, dissenting.

The strictest test of waiver which might be applied to this case is that quoted by the majority. In order to show that a right has been waived under this test, the State must prove "an intentional relinquishment or abandonment of a known right or privilege." The majority creates no new rule preventing an accused who has retained a lawyer from waiving his right to the lawyer's presence during questioning. The majority simply finds that no waiver was proved in this case. I disagree. That respondent knew of his right not to say anything to the officers without advice and presence of counsel is established on this record to a moral certainty. He was advised of the right by three officials of the State—telling at least one that he understood the right—and by two lawyers. Finally, he further demonstrated his knowledge of the right by informing the police that he would tell them the story in the presence of McKnight when they arrived in Des Moines. The issue in this case, then, is whether respondent relinquished that right intentionally.

Respondent relinquished his right not to talk to the police about his crime when the car approached the place where he had hidden the victim's clothes. Men usually intend to do what they do and there is nothing in the record to support the proposition that respondent's decision to talk was anything but an exercise of his own free will. Apparently, without any prodding from the officers, respondent—who had earlier said that he would tell the whole story when he arrived in Des Moines—spontaneously changed his mind about the timing of his disclosures when the car approached the places where he had hidden the evidence. However, even if his statements were influenced by Detective Leaming's above-quoted statement, respondent's decision to talk in the absence of counsel can hardly be viewed as the product of an overborne will. The statement by Leaming was not coercive; it was accompanied by a request that respondent not respond to it; and it was delivered hours before respondent decided to make any statement. Respondent's waiver was thus knowing and intentional.

The majority's contrary conclusion seems to rest on the fact that respondent "asserted" his right to counsel by retaining and consulting with one lawyer and by consulting with another. How this supports the conclusion that respondent's later relinquishment of his right not to talk in the absence of counsel was unintentional is a mystery. The fact that respondent consulted with counsel on the question whether he should talk to the police in counsel's absence makes his latter decision to talk in counsel's absence better informed and, if anything, more intelligent.

The majority recognizes that even after this "assertion" of his right to counsel, it would have found that respondent waived his right not to talk in counsel's absence if his waiver had been express—i.e., if the officers had asked him in the car whether he would be willing to answer questions in counsel's absence and if he had answered "yes." But waiver is not a formalistic concept. Waiver is shown whenever the facts establish that an accused knew of a right and intended to relinquish it. Such waiver, even if not express, was plainly shown here. The only other conceivable basis for the majority's holding is the implicit suggestion, that the right involved in *Massiah v. United States*, as distinguished from the right involved in *Miranda v. Arizona*, is a right not to be asked any questions in counsel's absence rather than a right not to answer any questions in counsel's absence, and that the right not to be asked questions must be waived before the questions are asked. Such wafer-thin distinctions cannot determine whether a guilty murderer should go free. The only conceivable purpose for the presence of counsel during questioning is to protect an accused from making incriminating answers. Questions, unanswered, have no significance at all. Absent coercion—no matter how the right involved is defined—an accused is amply protected by a rule requiring waiver before or simultaneously with the giving by him of an answer or the making by him of a statement....

Mr. Justice BLACKMUN, with whom Mr. Justice WHITE and Mr. Justice REHNQUIST join, dissenting.

First, the police did not deliberately seek to isolate Williams from his lawyers so as to deprive him of the assistance of counsel. The isolation in this case was a necessary incident of transporting Williams to the county where the crime was committed.

Second, Leaming's purpose was not solely to obtain incriminating evidence. The victim had been missing for only two days, the police could not be certain that she was dead. Leaming, of course, in accord with his duty, was "hoping to find out where that little girl was," but such motivation does not equate with an intention to evade the Sixth Amendment.

Moreover, the Court seems to me to place an undue emphasis, and aspersion on what it and the lower courts have chosen to call the "Christian burial speech," and on Williams' "deeply religious" conviction.

Third, not every attempt to elicit information should be regarded as "tantamount to interrogation." I am not persuaded that Leaming's observations and comments, made as the police car traversed the snowy and slippery miles between Davenport and Des Moines that winter afternoon, were an interrogation, direct or subtle, of Williams.

In summary, it seems to me that the Court is holding that Massiah is violated whenever police engage in any conduct, in the absence of counsel, with the subjective desire to obtain information from a suspect after arraignment. Such a rule is far too broad.

New Jersey v. T.L.O. ROBERT M. O'NEIL

The rights of high school students come before the Supreme Court from time to time, and the results are not easy to predict. Almost a half century ago, the Court held that students could not be forced to salute the flag against their beliefs. In 1969, the Justices held that schools could not forbid students from wearing black armbands in peaceful protest of the Vietnam War. Students do not, said the Court, have to "check their rights at the schoolhouse gate."

Several years later the Court also applied basic guarantees of due process to the dismissal of students for violating school disciplinary rules. But the justices have also given schools much latitude in administering corporal punishment and in restricting the content of school newspapers.

In this case the issue was one of a school's right to search students' belongings. The student in question had been caught smoking in the girls' bathroom. An assistant vice principal called her in, and demanded that she open her purse. In the purse he saw not only cigarettes, but also cigarette rolling papers commonly used with marijuana. He then searched the purse thoroughly, and found some marijuana, a pipe, plastic bags, money and a list of students who owed her for marijuana.

When the state brought delinquency charges against her, the student claimed her rights of privacy had been violated by the search of the purse. The Court acknowledged that we do have some constitutional right to privacy—but held that schools do not need search warrants before searching a student or her belongings. The validity of a particular search then depends on its reasonableness—a standard which the majority found had been satisfied in this case.

> ▶ The Court felt here that seeing the cigarette papers gave the school official a reasonable basis to rummage through the purse. What evidence or information would create enough suspicion about a student to justify a complete search of her purse or backpack?

▶ Suppose the official had seen only an overdue library book when the purse was opened. Or a fake ID card. Would either of these justify a full search of the purse?

▶ Students also may keep personal materials in desks or lockers. Since these are school property, would the standard for a search be different? Higher? Or Lower?

▶ There was apparently no rule or regulation of the New Jersey School district that allowed such a search. What kind of rule could be written that would be consistent with the decision giving school officials the latitude they are allowed but also protected students' privacy?

▶ The accusation of delinquency can carry substantial effects, even though it is not a criminal charge. How much due process should a student receive when such a charge is filed?

▶ Suppose the smoking had occurred off the school campus? Would school officials still be justified in acting as they did?

New Jersey v. T.L.O. 83 U.S. 712 (1985)

Justice WHITE delivered the opinion of the Court.

We granted *certiorari* in this case to examine the appropriateness of the exclusionary rule as a remedy for searches carried out in violation of the Fourth Amendment by public school authorities. Our consideration of the proper application of the Fourth Amendment to the public schools, however, has led us to conclude that the search that gave rise to the case now before us did not violate the Fourth Amendment. Accordingly, we here address only the questions of the proper standard for assessing the legality of searches conducted by public school officials and the application of that standard to the facts of this case.

In determining whether the search at issue in this case violated the Fourth Amendment we are faced initially with the question whether that Amendment's prohibition on unreasonable searches and seizures applies to searches conducted by public school officials. We hold that it does.

It is now beyond dispute that "the Federal Constitution, by virtue of the Fourteenth Amendment, prohibits unreasonable searches and seizures by state officers." Equally indisputable is the proposition that the Fourteenth Amendment protects the rights of students against encroachment by public school officials:

> The Fourteenth Amendment, as now applied to the States, protects the citizen against the State itself and all of its creatures—Boards of Education not excepted. These have, of course, delicate, and highly discretionary functions, but none that they may not perform within the limits of the Bill of Rights.

That they are educating the young for citizenship is reason for scrupulous protection of Constitutional freedoms of the individual, if we are not to strangle the free mind at its source and teach youth to discount important principles of our government as mere platitudes. *West Virginia State Bd. of Ed. v. Barnette* (1943).

These two propositions—that the Fourth Amendment applies to the States through the Fourteenth Amendment, and that the actions of public school officials are subject to the limits placed on state action by the Fourteenth Amendment—might appear sufficient to answer the suggestion that the Fourth Amendment does not proscribe unreasonable searches by school officials. On reargument, however, the State of New Jersey has argued that the history of the Fourth Amendment indicates that the Amendment was intended to regulate only searches and seizures carried out by law enforcement officers; accordingly, although public school officials are concededly state agents for purposes of the Fourteenth Amendment, the Fourth Amendment creates no rights enforceable against them.

To hold that the Fourth Amendment applies to searches conducted by school authorities is only to begin the inquiry into the standards governing such searches. Although the underlying command of the Fourth Amendment is always that searches and seizures be reasonable, what is reasonable depends on the context within which a search takes place. The determination of the standard of reasonableness governing any specific class of searches requires "balancing the need to search against the invasion which the search entails." On one side of the balance are arrayed the individual's legitimate expectations of privacy and personal security; on the other, the government's need for effective methods to deal with breaches of public order.

We have recognized that even a limited search of the person is a substantial invasion of privacy. We have also recognized that searches of closed items of personal luggage are intrusions on protected privacy interests, for "the Fourth Amendment provides protection to the owner of every container that conceals its contents from plain view." A search of a child's person or of a closed purse or other bag carried on her person, no less than a similar search carried out on an adult, is undoubtedly a severe violation of subjective expectations of privacy.

Of course, the Fourth Amendment does not protect subjective expectations of privacy that are unreasonable or otherwise "illegitimate." To receive the protection of the Fourth Amendment, an expectation of privacy must be one that society is "prepared to recognize as legitimate." The State of New Jersey has argued that because of the pervasive supervision to which children in the schools are necessarily subject, a child has virtually no legitimate expectation of privacy in articles of personal property "unnecessarily" carried into a school. This argument has two factual premises: (1) the fundamental incompatibility of expectations of privacy with the maintenance of a sound educational environment: and (2) the minimal interest of the child in bringing any items of personal property into the school. Both premises are severely flawed.

Although this Court may take notice of the difficulty of maintaining discipline in the public schools today, the situation is not so dire that students in the schools may claim no legitimate expectations of privacy. We have recently recognized that the need to maintain order in a prison is such that prisoners retain no legitimate expectations of privacy in their cells, but it goes almost without saying that "[t]he prisoner and the schoolchild stand in wholly different circumstances, separated by the harsh facts of criminal conviction and incarceration." We are not yet ready to hold that the schools and the prisons need be equated for purposes of the Fourth Amendment.

Nor does the State's suggestion that children have no legitimate need to bring personal property into the schools seem well anchored in reality. Students at a minimum must bring to school not only the supplies needed for their studies, but also keys, money, and the necessaries of personal hygiene and grooming. In addition, students may carry on their persons or in purses or wallets such nondisruptive yet highly personal items as photographs, letters, and diaries. Finally, students may have perfectly legitimate reasons to carry with them articles of property needed in connection with extracurricular or recreational activities. In short, schoolchildren may find it necessary to carry with them a variety of legitimate, non-contraband items, and there is no reason to conclude that they have necessarily waived all rights to privacy in such items merely by bringing them onto school grounds.

Against the child's interest in privacy must be set the substantial interest of teachers and administrators in maintaining discipline in the classroom and on school grounds. Maintaining order in the classroom has never been easy, but in recent years, school disorder has often taken particularly ugly forms: drug use and violent crime in the schools have become major social problems. Even in schools that have been spared the most severe disciplinary problems, the preservation of order and a proper educational environment requires close supervision of schoolchildren, as well as the enforcement of rules against conduct that would be perfectly permissible if undertaken by an adult. "Events calling for discipline are frequent occurrences and sometimes require immediate, effective action." Accordingly, we have recognized that maintaining security and order in the schools requires a certain degree of flexibility in school disciplinary procedures, and we have respected the value of preserving the informality of the student-teacher relationship.

How, then, should we strike the balance between the schoolchild's legitimate expectations of privacy and the school's equally legitimate need to maintain an environment in which learning can take place? It is evident that the school setting requires some easing of the restrictions to which searches by public authorities are ordinarily subject. The warrant requirement, in particular, is unsuited to the school environment: requiring a teacher to obtain a warrant before searching a child suspected of an infraction of school rules (or of the criminal law) would unduly interfere with the maintenance of the swift and informal disciplinary procedures needed in the schools. Just as we have in other cases dispensed with the warrant requirement when "the burden of obtaining a warrant is likely to frustrate the governmental purpose behind the search," we hold today that school officials need not obtain a warrant before searching a student who is under their authority.

The school setting also requires some modification of the level of suspicion of illicit activity needed to justify a search. Ordinarily, a search—even one that may permissibly be carried out without a warrant—must be based upon "probable cause" to believe that a violation of the law has occurred. However, "probable cause" is not an irreducible requirement of a valid search. The fundamental command of the Fourth Amendment is that searches and seizures be reasonable, and although "both the concept of probable cause and the requirement of a warrant bear on the reasonableness of a search,...in certain limited circumstances neither is required." Thus, we have in a number of cases recognized the legality of searches and seizures based on suspicions that, although "reasonable," do not rise to the level of probable cause. Where a careful balancing of governmental and private interests suggests that the public interest is best served by a Fourth Amendment standard of reasonableness that stops short of probable cause, we have not hesitated to adopt such a standard.

We join the majority of courts that have examined this issue in concluding that the accommodation of the privacy interests of schoolchildren with the substantial need of teachers and administrators for freedom to maintain order in the schools does not require strict adherence to the requirement that searches be based on probable cause to believe that the subject of the search has violated or is violating the law. Rather, the legality of a search of a student should depend simply on the reasonableness, under all the circumstances, of the search. Determining the reasonableness of any search involves a twofold inquiry: first, one must consider "whether the...action was justified at its inception;" second, one must determine whether the search as actually conducted "was reasonable related in scope to the circumstances which justified the interference in the first place." Under ordinary circumstances, a search of a student by a teacher or other school official will be "justified at its inception" when there are reasonable grounds for suspecting that the search will turn up evidence that the student has violated or is violating either the law or the rules of the school. Such a search will be permissible in its scope when the measures adopted are reasonably related to the objectives of the search and not excessively intrusive in light of the age and sex of the student and the nature of the infraction.

This standard will, we trust, neither unduly burden the efforts of school authorities to maintain order in their schools nor authorize unrestrained intrusions upon the privacy of schoolchildren. By focusing attention on the question of reasonableness, the standard will spare teachers and school administrators the necessity of schooling themselves in the niceties of probable cause and permit them to regulate their conduct according to the dictates of reason and common sense. At the same time, the reasonableness standard should ensure that the interests of students will be invaded no more than is necessary to achieve the legitimate end of preserving order in the schools.

There remains the question of the legality of the search in this case. We recognize that the "reasonable grounds" standard applied by the New Jersey Supreme Court in its consideration of this question is not substantially different from the standard that we have adopted today. Nonetheless, we believe that the New Jersey court's application of that standard to strike down the search of T.L.O.'s purse reflects a somewhat crabbed notion of reasonableness. Our review of the facts surrounding the search leads us to conclude that the search was in no sense unreasonable for Fourth Amendment purposes.

Justice BRENNAN, with whom Justice MARSHALL joins, concurring in part and dissenting in part.

I agree that schoolteachers or principals, when not acting as agents of law enforcement authorities, generally may conduct a search of their students' belongings without first obtaining a warrant. To agree with the Court on this point is to say that school searches may justifiably be held to that extent to constitute an exception to the Fourth Amendment's warrant requirement. Such an exception, however, is not to be justified, as the Court apparently holds, by assessing net social value through application of an unguided "balancing test" in which "the individual's legitimate expectations of privacy and personal security" are weighted against "the government's need for effective methods to deal with breaches of public order." The Warrant Clause is something more than an exhortation to this Court to maximize social welfare as *we* see fit. It requires that the authorities must obtain a warrant before conducting a full-scale search. The undifferentiated governmental interest in law enforcement is insufficient to justify an exception to the warrant requirement. Rather, some *special* governmental interest beyond the need merely to apprehend lawbreakers is necessary to justify a categorical exception to the warrant requirement. For the most part, special governmental needs sufficient to override the warrant requirement flow from "exigency"—that is, from the press of time that makes obtaining a warrant either impossible or hopelessly infeasible. Only after finding an extraordinary governmental interest of this kind have we—or ought we—engage in a balancing test to determine if a warrant should nonetheless be required.

To require a showing of some extraordinary governmental interest before dispensing with the warrant requirement is not to undervalue society's need to apprehend violators of the criminal law. To be sure, forcing law enforcement personnel to obtain a warrant before engaging in a search will predictably deter the police from conducting some searches that they would otherwise like to conduct. But this is not an unintended *result* of the Fourth Amendment's protection of privacy; rather, it is the very *purpose* for which the Amendment was thought necessary. Only where the governmental interests at stake exceed those implicated in any ordinary law enforcement context—that is, only where there is some extraordinary governmental interest involved—is it legitimate to engage in a balancing test to determine whether a warrant is indeed necessary.

In this case, such extraordinary governmental interests do exist and are sufficient to justify an exception to the warrant requirement. Students are necessarily confined for most of the school day in close proximity to each other and to the school staff. I agree with the Court that we can take judicial notice of the serious problems of drugs and violence that plague our schools. As Justice Blackmun notes, teachers must not merely "maintain an environment conducive to learning" among children who "are inclined to test the outer boundaries of acceptable conduct, "but must also 'protect the very safety of students and school personnel.'" A teacher or principal could neither carry out essential teaching functions nor adequately protect student's safety if required to wait for a warrant before conducting a necessary search.

Skinner v. Railway Labor Executives Association/
National Treasury Employees v. Von Raab   ROBERT M. O'NEIL

Testing drivers for alcohol content has been a major weapon of law enforcement for some time. While recognizing that such tests do invade the privacy of the driver, the Supreme Court has allowed testing when, for example, there is reasonable cause in a driver's behavior to suspect that he or she is under the influence or alcohol or drugs. In such cases the Supreme Court has balanced the undoubted privacy interest of the individual against compelling safety interests of society.

The use of wide-scale drug tests among persons holding sensitive jobs is a more recent development—a product not only of increasing concern about drug use and its contribution to specific accidents, but also of more reliable and readily usable testing procedures. The constitutionality of these new procedures was bound to reach the Supreme Court, as it did in a pair of cases decided in the spring of 1989.

One case involved people who worked directly for the government—employees of the Customs Service who were up for promotion or transfer to positions that involved drug enforcement or the use of firearms. The other case involved federal rules applied to certain railroad employees—people who technically work for a private employer, but are subject to national transportation and safety standards.

In upholding the drug testing laws in both cases, the majority of the Justices relied not only on earlier cases involving driver blood tests, but also on the special and growing concern about safety in the two sectors that generated the regulations being reviewed. But the Court did insist that, in the case of the customs service employees being promoted or transferred, the net be tight enough to reach only employees who were likely to have access to sensitive material.

> ▶ The regulations were drawn to cover only certain sensitive jobs within the two sectors. Are there some activities so sensitive that all employees could be required to take drug tests?
>
> ▶ The timing and frequency of the testing were not an issue before the Court in these cases. How often could such tests be given—monthly? weekly? daily?
>
> ▶ Need tests of this sort be announced, or could they be conducted on a random or spot basis? Or would that depend on the sensitivity of the agency or the position?
>
> ▶ What effects might follow from such tests? Suppose the results were used not only to bar a person from initial employment or promotion, but were used as the basis for criminal charges as well?
>
> ▶ Suppose in practice the tests were seldom given to white employees, but overwhelmingly to minority employees or applicants? Would the Supreme Court take a different view of such a pattern of administration?

Skinner v. Railway Labor Executives Association 87-1555 (1989)

Justice KENNEDY delivered the opinion of the Court.

The Federal Railroad Safety Act of 1970 authorizes the Secretary of Transportation to "prescribe, as necessary, appropriate rules, regulation, orders, and standards for all areas of railroad safety." Finding that alcohol and drug abuse by railroad employees poses a serious threat to safety, the Federal Railroad Administration (FRA) has promulgated regulations that mandate blood and urine tests of employees who are involved in certain train accidents. The FRA also has adopted regulations that do not require, but do authorize, railroads to administer breath and urine tests to employees who violate certain safety rules. The question presented by this case is whether these regulations violate the Fourth Amendment.

The Fourth Amendment provides that "[t]he right of the people to be secure in their persons, houses, papers, and effects, against unreasonable searches and seizures, shall not be violated...." The Amendment guarantees the privacy, dignity, and security of persons against certain arbitrary and invasive acts by officers of the Government or those acting at their direction. Before we consider whether the tests in question are reasonable under the Fourth Amendment, we must inquire whether the tests are attributable to the Government or its agents, and whether they amount to searches or seizures. We turn to those matters.

Although the Fourth Amendment does not apply to a search and seizure, even an arbitrary one, effected by a private party on his own initiative, the Amendment protects against such intrusions if the private party acted as an instrument or agent of the Government. A railroad that complies with the provisions of Subpart C of the regulations does so by compulsion of sovereign authority, and the lawfulness of its acts is controlled by the Fourth Amendment. Petitioners contend, however, that the Fourth Amendment is not implicated by Subpart D of the regulation, as nothing in Subpart D compels any testing by private railroads.

We are unwilling to conclude, in the context of this facial challenge, that breath and urine tests required by private railroads in reliance on Subpart D will not implicate the Fourth Amendment. Whether a private party should be deemed an agent or instrument of the Government for Fourth Amendment purposes necessarily turns on the degree of the Government's participation in the private party's activities, a question that can only be resolved "in light of all the circumstances." The fact that the Government has not compelled a private party to perform a search does not, by itself, establish that the search is a private one. Here, specific features of the regulations combine to convince us that the Government did more than adopt a passive position toward the underlying private conduct.

The regulations, including those in Subpart D, preempt state laws, rules, or regulations covering the same subject matter, and are intended to supersede "any provision of a collective bargaining agreement, or arbitration award construing such an agreement. They also confer upon the FRA the right to receive certain biological samples and test results procured by railroads pursuant to Subpart D. In addition, a railroad may not divest itself of, or otherwise compromise by contract, the authority conferred by Subpart D. As the Agency explained, such "authority...is conferred for the purpose of promoting the public safety, and a railroad may not shackle itself in a way inconsistent with its duty to promote the public safety." Nor is a covered employee free to decline his employer's request to submit to breath or urine tests under the conditions set forth in Subpart D. An employee who refuses to submit to the tests must be withdrawn from covered service.

In light of these provisions, we are unwilling to accept petitioners' submission that tests conducted by private railroads in reliance on Subpart D will be primarily the result of private initiative. The Government has removed all legal barriers to the testing authorized by Subpart D, and indeed has made plain not only its strong preference for testing, but also its desire to share the fruits of such intrusions. In addition, it has mandated that the railroads not bargain away the authority to perform tests granted by Subpart D. These are clear indices of the Government's encouragement, endorsement, and participation, and suffice to implicate the Fourth Amendment.

Our precedents teach that where, as here, the Government seeks to obtain physical evidence from a person, the Fourth Amendment may be relevant at several levels. The initial detention necessary to procure the evidence may be a seizure of the person, if the detention amounts to a meaningful interference with his freedom of movement. Obtaining and examining the evidence may also be a search, if doing so infringes an expectation of privacy that society is prepared to recognize as reasonable.

We have long recognized that a "compelled instrusio[n] into the body for blood to be analyzed for alcohol content" must be deemed a Fourth Amendment search. In light of our society's concern for the security of one's person, it is obvious that this physical intrusion, penetrating beneath the skin, infringes an expectation of privacy that society is prepared to recognize as reasonable. The ensuing chemical analysis of the sample to obtain physiological data is a further invasion of the tested employee's privacy interests. Much the same is true of the breath-testing procedures required under Subpart D of the regulations. Subjecting a person to a breathalyzer test we considered in *Schmerber*, should also be deemed a search.

Unlike the blood-testing procedure at issue in *Schmerber*, the procedures prescribed by the FRA regulations for collecting and testing urine samples do not entail a surgical intrusion into the body. It is not disputed, however, that chemical analysis of urine, like that of blood, can reveal a host of private medical facts about an employee, including whether she is epileptic, pregnant, or diabetic. Nor can it be disputed that the process of collecting the sample to be tested, which may in some cases involve visual or aural monitoring of the act of urination, itself implicated privacy interests. As the Court of Appeals for the Fifth Circuit has stated:

> There are few activities in our society more personal or private that the
> passing of urine. Most people describe it by euphemisms if they talk about it
> at all. It is a function traditionally performed without public observation;
> indeed, its performance in public is generally prohibited by law as well as
> social custom. *National Treasury Employees Union v. Von Raab*.

Because it is clear that the collection and testing of urine intrudes upon expectations of privacy that society has long recognized as reasonable, the Federal Courts of Appeals have concluded unanimously, and we agree, that these intrusions must be deemed searches under the Fourth Amendment.

In view of our conclusion that the collection and subsequent analysis of the requisite biological samples must be deemed Fourth Amendment searches, we need not characterize the employer's antecedent interference with the employee's freedom of movement as an independent Fourth Amendment seizure. As our precedents indicate, not every governmental interference with an individual's freedom of movement raises such constitutional concerns that there is a seizure of the person. For present purposes, it suffices to note that any limitation on an employee's freedom of movement that is necessary to obtain the blood, urine, or breath samples contemplated by the regulations must be considered in assessing the intrusiveness of the searches effected by the Government's testing program.

To hold that the Fourth Amendment is applicable to the drug and alcohol testing prescribed by the FRA regulations is only to begin the inquiry into the standards governing such intrusions. For the Fourth Amendment does not proscribe all searches and seizures, but only those that are unreasonable. What is reasonable, of course, "depends on all the circumstances surrounding the search or seizure and the nature of the search or seizure itself." Thus, the permissibility of a particular practice "is judged by balancing its intrusion on the individual's Fourth Amendment interests against its promotion of legitimate governmental interest." In most criminal cases, we strike this balance in favor of the procedures described by the Warrant Clause of the Fourth Amendment.

The Government's need to rely on private railroads to set the testing process in motion also indicates that insistence on a warrant requirement would impede the achievement of the Government's objective. Railroad supervisors, like school officials, see *New Jersey v. T.L.O.*, and hospital administrators, are not in the business of investigating violations of the criminal laws or enforcing administrative codes, and otherwise have little occasion to become familiar with the intricacies of the Court's Fourth Amendment jurisprudence. Imposing unwieldy warrant procedures...upon supervisors, who would otherwise have no reason to be familiar with such procedures, is simply unreasonable.

In sum, imposing a warrant requirement in the present context would add little to the assurances of certainty and regularity already afforded by the regulations, while significantly hindering, and in many cases frustrating, the objectives of the Government's testing program. We do not believe that a warrant is essential to render the intrusions here at issue reasonable under the Fourth Amendment.

Our cases indicate that even a search that may be performed without a warrant must be based, as a general matter, on probable cause to believe that the person to be searched has violated the law. When the balance of interests precludes insistence on a showing of probable cause, we have usually required "some quantum of individualized suspicion" before concluding that a search is reasonable. We made it clear, however, that a showing of individualized suspicion is not a constitutional floor, below which a search must be presumed unreasonable. In limited circumstances, where the privacy interests implicated by the search are minimal, and where an important governmental interest furthered by the intrusion would be placed in jeopardy by a requirement of individualized suspicion, a search may be reasonable despite the absence of such suspicion. We believe this is true of the intrusions in question here.

By and large, intrusions on privacy under the FRA regulations are limited. To the extent transportation and like restrictions are necessary to procure the requisite blood, breath, and urine samples for testing, this interference alone is minimal given the employment context in which it takes place. Ordinarily, an employee consents to significant restrictions in his freedom of movement where necessary for his employment, and few are free to come and go as they please during working hours. Any additional interference with a railroad employee's freedom of movement that occurs in the time it takes to procure a blood, breath, or urine sample for testing cannot, by itself, be said to infringe significant privacy interests.

Our decision in *Schmerber v. California*, (1966), indicates that the same is true of the blood tests required by the FRA regulations. In that case, we held that a State could direct that a blood sample be withdrawn from a motorist suspected of driving while intoxicated, despite his refusal to consent to the intrusion. We noted that the test was performed in a reasonable manner, as the motorist's "blood was taken by a physician in a hospital environment according to accepted medical practices." We said also that the intrusion occasioned by a blood test is not significant, since such "tests are a commonplace in these days of periodic physical examinations and experience with them teaches that the quantity of blood extracted is minimal, and that for most people the procedure involves virtually no risk, trauma, or pain." *Schmerber* thus confirmed "society's judgment that blood tests do not constitute an unduly extensive imposition on an individual's privacy and bodily integrity."

The breath tests authorized by Subpart D of the regulations are even less intrusive that the blood tests prescribed by Subpart C. Unlike blood tests, breath tests do not require piercing the skin and may be conducted safely outside a hospital environment and with a minimum of inconvenience or embarrassment. Further, breath tests reveal the level of alcohol in the employee's bloodstream and nothing more. Like the blood-testing procedures mandated by Subpart C, which can be used only to ascertain the presence of alcohol or controlled substances in the bloodstream, breath tests reveal no other facts in which the employee has a substantial privacy interest. In all the circumstances, we cannot conclude that the administration of a breath test implicates significant privacy concerns.

A more difficult question is presented by urine tests. Like breath tests, urine tests are not invasive of the body and, under the regulations, may not be used as an occasion for inquiring into private facts unrelated to alcohol or drug use. We recognize, however, that the procedures for collecting the necessary samples, which require employees to perform an excretory function traditionally shielded by great privacy, raise concerns not implicated by blood or breath tests. While we would not characterize these additional privacy concerns as minimal in most contexts, we note that the regulations endeavor to reduce the intrusiveness of the collection process. The regulations do not require that samples be furnished under the direct observation of a monitor, despite the desirability of such a procedure to ensure the integrity of the sample. The sample is also collected in a medical environment, by personnel unrelated to the railroad employer, and is thus not unlike similar procedures encountered often in the context of a regular physical examination.

More importantly, the expectations of privacy of covered employees are diminished by reason of their participation in an industry that is regulated pervasively to ensure safety, a goal dependent, in substantial part, on the health and fitness of covered employees. This relation between safety and employee fitness was recognized by Congress when it enacted the Hours of Service Act in 1907, and also when it authorized the Secretary to "test...railroad facilities, equipment, rolling stock, operations, *or persons*, as he deems necessary to carry out the provisions" of the Federal Railroad Safety Act of 1970. It has also been recognized by state governments, and has long been reflected in industry practice, as evidenced by the industry's promulgation and enforcement of Rule G. Indeed, the Agency found, and the Court of Appeals acknowledged, that "most railroads require periodic physical examinations for train and engine employees and certain other employees."

We do not suggest, of course, that the interest in bodily security enjoyed by those employed in a regulated industry must always be considered minimal. Here, however, the covered employees have long been a principal focus of regulatory concern. As the dissenting judge below noted, "[t]he reason is obvious. An idle locomotive, sitting in the roundhouse, is harmless. It becomes lethal when operated negligently by persons who are under the influence of alcohol or drugs." Though some of the privacy interests implicated by the toxicological testing at issue reasonably might be viewed as significant in other contexts, logic and history show that a diminished expectation of privacy attaches to information relating to the physical condition of covered employees and to this reasonable means of procuring such information. We conclude, therefore, that the testing procedures contemplated by Subparts C and D pose only limited threats to the justifiable expectations of privacy of covered employees.

By contrast, the government interest in testing without a showing of individualized suspicion is compelling. Employees subject to the tests discharge duties fraught with such risks of injury to others that even a momentary lapse of attention can have disastrous consequences. Much like persons who have routine access to dangerous nuclear power facilities, employees who are subject to testing under the FRA regulations can cause great human loss before any signs of impairment become noticeable to supervisors or others. An impaired employee, the Agency found, will seldom display any outward "signs detectable by the lay person or, in many cases, even the physician." This view finds ample support in the railroad industry's experience with Rule G, and in the judgment of the courts that have examined analogous testing schemes. Indeed, while respondents posit that impaired employees might be detected without alcohol or drug testing, the premise of respondents' lawsuit is that even the occurrence of a major calamity will not give rise to a suspicion of impairment with respect to any particular employee.

A requirement of particularized suspicion of drug or alcohol use would seriously impede an employer's ability to obtain this information, despite its obvious importance. Experience confirms the Agency's judgment that the scene of a serious rail accident is chaotic. Investigators who arrive at the scene shortly after a major accident has occurred may find it difficult to determine which members of a train crew contributed to its occurrence. Obtaining evidence that might give rise to the suspicion that a particular employee is impaired, a difficult endeavor in the best of circumstances, is most impracticable in the aftermath of a serious accident. While events following the rule violations that activate the testing authority of Subpart D may be less chaotic, objective indicia of impairment are absent in these instances as well. Indeed, any attempt to gather evidence relating to the possible impairment of particular employees likely would result in the loss or deterioration of the evidence furnished by the tests. It would be unrealistic, and inimical to the Government's goal of ensuring safety in rail transportation, to require a showing a individualized suspicion in these circumstances.

We conclude that the compelling government interests served by the FRA's regulations would be significantly hindered if railroads were required to point to specific facts giving rise to a reasonable suspicion of impairment before testing a given employee. In view of our conclusion that, on the present record, the toxicological testing contemplated by the regulations is not an undue infringement on the justifiable expectations of privacy of covered employees, the Government's compelling interests outweigh privacy concerns.

The possession of unlawful drugs is a criminal offense that the Government may punish, but it is a separate and far more dangerous wrong to perform certain sensitive tasks while under the influence of those substances. Performing those tasks while impaired by alcohol is, of course, equally dangerous, though consumption of alcohol is legal in most other contexts. The Government may take all necessary and reasonable regulatory steps to prevent or deter that hazardous conduct, and since the gravamen of the evil is performing certain functions while concealing the substance in the body, it may be necessary, as in the case before us, to examine the body or its fluids to accomplish the regulatory purpose. The necessity to perform that regulatory function with respect to railroad employees engaged in safety-sensitive tasks, and the reasonableness of the system for doing so, have been established in this case.

Justice MARSHALL, with whom Justice BRENNAN joins, dissenting.

The issue in this case is not whether declaring war on illegal drugs is good public policy. The importance of ridding our society of such drugs is, by now, apparent to all. Rather, the issue here is whether the Government's deployment in that war of a particularly draconian weapon—the compulsory collection and chemical testing of railroad workers' blood and urine—comports with the Fourth Amendment. Precisely because the need for action against the drug scourge is manifest, the need for vigilance against unconstitutional excess is great. History teaches that grave threats to liberty often come in times of urgency, when constitutional rights seem too extravagant to endure. The World War II relocation-camp cases, and the Red Scare and McCarthy-Era internal subversion cases, are only the most extreme reminders that when we allow fundamental freedoms to be sacrificed in the name of real or perceived exigency, we invariably come to regret it.

In permitting the Government to force entire railroad crews to submit to invasive blood and urine tests, even when it lacks any evidence of drug or alcohol use or other wrongdoing, the majority today joins those shortsighted courts which have allowed basic constitutional rights to fall prey to momentary emergencies. The majority holds that the need of the Federal Railroad Administration (FRA) to deter and diagnose train accidents outweighs any "minimal" intrusions on personal dignity and privacy posed by mass toxicological testing of persons who have given no indication whatsoever of impairment. In reaching this result, the majority ignores the text and doctrinal history of the Fourth Amendment, which require that highly intrusive searches of this type be based on probable cause, not on the evanescent cost-benefit calculations of agencies or judges. But the majority errs even under its own utilitarian standards, trivializing the raw intrusiveness of, and overlooking serious conceptual and operational flaws in, the FRA's testing program. These flaws cast grave doubts on whether that program, though born of good intentions, will do more than ineffectually symbolize the Government's opposition to drug use.

The majority purports to limit its decision to postaccident testing of workers in "safety-sensitive" jobs, much as it limits its holding in the companion case to testing of transferees to jobs involving drug interdiction or the use of firearms. But the damage done to the Fourth Amendment is not so easily cabined. The majority's acceptance of dragnet blood and urine testing ensures that the first, and worst, casualty of the war on drugs will be the precious liberties of our citizens. I therefore dissent.

Until recently, an unbroken line of cases had recognized probable cause as an indispensable prerequisite for a full-scale search, regardless whether such a search was conducted pursuant to a warrant or under one of the recognized exceptions to the warrant requirement. Only where the Government action in question had a "substantially less intrusive" impact on privacy, and thus clearly fell short of a full-scale search, did we relax the probable cause standard. Even in this class of cases, we almost always required the Government to show some individualized suspicion to justify the search. The few searches which we upheld in the absence of individualized justification were routinized, fleeting, and nonintrusive encounters conducted pursuant to regulatory programs which entailed no contact with the person.

National Treasury Employees v. Von Raab 86-1879 (1989)

Justice KENNEDY delivered the opinion of the Court.

We granted *certiorari* to decide whether it violates the Fourth Amendment for the United States Customs Service to require a urinalysis test from employees who seek transfer or promotion to certain positions.

It is clear that the Customs Service's drug testing program is not designed to serve the ordinary needs of law enforcement. Test results may not be used in a criminal prosecution of the employee without the employee's consent. The purposes of the program are to deter drug use among those eligible for promotion to sensitive positions within the Service and to prevent the promotion of drug users to those positions. These substantial interests, no less than the Government's concern for safe rail transportation at issue in *Railway Labor Executives*, present a special need that may justify departure from the ordinary warrant and probable cause requirements.

Petitioners do not contend that a warrant is required by the balance of privacy and governmental interests in this context, nor could any such contention withstand scrutiny. We have recognized before that requiring the Government to procure a warrant for every work-related intrusion "would conflict with 'the common-sense realization that government offices could not function if every employment decision became a constitutional matter.'" Even if Customs Service employees are more likely to be familiar with the procedures required to obtain a warrant than most other Government workers, requiring a warrant in this context would serve only to divert valuable agency resources from the Service's primary mission. The Customs Service has been entrusted with pressing responsibilities, and its mission would be compromised if it were required to seek search warrants in connection with routine, yet sensitive, employment decisions.

Furthermore, a warrant would provide little or nothing in the way of additional protection of personal privacy. A warrant serves primarily to advise the citizen that an intrusion is authorized by law and limited in its permissible scope and to interpose a neutral magistrate between the citizen and the law enforcement officer "engaged in the often competitive enterprise of ferreting out crime." But in the present context, "the circumstances justifying toxicological testing and the permissible limits of such intrusions are defined narrowly and specifically..., and doubtless are well known to covered employees." Under the Customs program, every employee who seeks a transfer to a covered position knows that he must take a drug test, and is likewise aware of the procedures the Service must follow in administering the test. A covered employee is simply not subject "to the discretion of the official in the field." The process becomes automatic when the employee elects to apply for, and thereafter pursue, a covered position. Because the Service does not make a discretionary determination to search based on a judgment that certain conditions are present, there are simply "no special facts for a neutral magistrate to evaluate."

Even where it is reasonable to dispense with the warrant requirement in the particular circumstances, a search ordinarily must be based on probable cause. Our cases teach, however, that the probable-cause standard "'is peculiarly related to criminal investigations.'" In particular, the traditional probable-cause standard may be unhelpful in analyzing the reasonableness of routine administrative functions, especially where the Government seeks to *prevent* the development of hazardous conditions or to detect violations that rarely generate articulable grounds for searching any particular place or person. Our precedents have settled that, in certain limited circumstances, the Government's need to discover such latent or hidden conditions, or to prevent their development, is sufficiently compelling to justify the intrusion on privacy entailed by conducting such searches without any measure of individualized suspicion. We think the Government's need to conduct the suspicionless searches required by the Customs program outweighs the privacy interests of employees engaged directly in drug interdiction, and of those who otherwise are required to carry firearms.

The Customs Service is our Nation's first line of defense against one of the greatest problems affecting the health and welfare of our population. We have adverted before to "the veritable national crisis in law enforcement caused by smuggling of illicit narcotics." Our cases also reflect the traffickers' seemingly inexhaustible repertoire of deceptive practices and elaborate schemes for importing narcotics. The record in this case confirms that, through the adroit selection of source locations, smuggling routes, and increasingly elaborate methods of concealment, drug traffickers have managed to bring into this country increasingly large quantities of illegal drugs. The record also indicates, and it is well known, that drug smugglers do not hesitate to use violence to protect their lucrative trade and avoid apprehension.

Many of the Service's employees are often exposed to this criminal element and to the controlled substances they seek to smuggle into the country. The physical safety of these employees may be threatened, and many may be tempted not only by bribes from the traffickers with whom they deal, but also by their own access to vast sources of valuable contraband seized and controlled by the Service. The Commissioner indicated below that "Customs [o]fficers have been shot, stabbed, run over, dragged by automobiles, and assaulted with blunt objects while performing their duties." At least nine officers have died in the line of duty since 1974. He also noted that Customs officers have been the targets of bribery by drug smugglers on numerous occasions, and several have been removed from the Service for accepting bribes and other integrity violations.

It is readily apparent that the Government has a compelling interest in ensuring that front-line interdiction personnel are physically fit, and have unimpeachable integrity and judgment. Indeed, the Government's interest here is at least as important as its interest in searching travelers entering the country. We have long held that travelers seeking to enter the country may be stopped and required to submit to a routine search without probable cause, or even founded suspicion, "because of national self protection reasonably requiring one entering the country to identify himself as entitled to come in, and his belongings as effects which may be lawfully brought in." This national interest in self protection could be irreparably damaged if those charged with safeguarding it were, because of their own drug use, unsympathetic to their mission of interdicting narcotics. A drug user's indifference to the Service's basic mission or, even worse, his active complicity with the malefactors, can facilitate importation of sizable drug shipments or block apprehension of dangerous criminals. The public interest demands effective measures to bar drug users from positions directly involving the interdiction of illegal drugs.

The public interest likewise demands effective measures to prevent the promotion of drug users to positions that require the incumbent to carry a firearm, even if the incumbent is not engaged directly in the interdiction of drugs. Customs employees who may use deadly force plainly "discharge duties fraught with such risks of injury to others that even a momentary lapse of attention can have disastrous consequences." We agree with the Government that the public should not bear the risk that employees who may suffer from impaired perception and judgment will be promoted to positions where they may need to employ deadly force. Indeed, ensuring against the creation of this dangerous risk will itself further Fourth Amendment values, as the use of deadly force may violate the Fourth Amendment in certain circumstances.

Against these valid public interests we must weigh the interference with individual liberty that results from requiring these classes of employees to undergo a urine test. The interference with individual privacy that results from the collection of a urine sample for subsequent chemical analysis could be substantial in some circumstances. We have recognized, however, that the "operational realities of the workplace" may render entirely reasonable certain work-related intrusions by supervisors and co-workers that might be viewed as unreasonable in other contexts. While these operational realities will rarely affect an employee's expectations of privacy with respect to searches of his person, or of personal effects that the employee may bring to the workplace, it is plain that certain forms of public employment may diminish privacy expectations even with respect to such personal searches. Employees of the United States Mint, for example, should expect to be subject to certain routine personal searches when they leave the workplace every day. Similarly, those who join our military or intelligence services may not only be required to give what in other contexts might be viewed as extraordinary assurances of trustworthiness and probity, but also may expect intrusive inquiries into their physical fitness for those special positions.

We think Customs employees who are directly involved in the interdiction of illegal drugs or who are required to carry firearms in the line of duty likewise have a diminished expectation of privacy in respect to the intrusions occasioned by a urine test. Unlike most private citizens or government employees in general, employees involved in drug interdiction reasonably should expect effective inquiry into their fitness and probity. Much the same is true of employees who are required to carry firearms. Because successful performance of their duties depends uniquely on their judgment and dexterity, these employees cannot reasonable expect to keep from the Service personal information that bears directly on their fitness. While reasonable tests designed to elicit this information doubtless infringe some privacy expectations, we do not believe these expectations outweigh the Government's compelling interests in safety and in the integrity of our borders.

V Racial Discrimination and Preference

Brown v. Board of Education of Topeka (1954)

South Carolina v. Katzenbach (1966)

Swann v. Charlotte-Mecklenburg Board of Education (1971)

Regents of the University of California v. Bakke (1978)

City of Richmond v. J.A. Croson Company (1989)

V Racial Discrimination and Preference

MELVIN UROFSKY

The Constitution begins with a grandiloquent Preamble: "We the People of the United States, in Order to form a more perfect Union, establish Justice, insure domestic Tranquility, provide for the common defense, promote the general Welfare, and secure the Blessings of Liberty to ourselves and our Posterity, do ordain and establish this Constitution for the United States of America." "We the People," however, were not *all* the people, and the Union was far from perfect. The Constitution acknowledged and made legal the institution of slavery. It would take a bloody Civil War to expurgate that evil, but even a century after that war, the nation would continue to find the promise of "a more perfect Union" elusive. The question of race has been a central theme of our cultural history, and a central preoccupation of our constitutional experience.

Contemporary constitutional principles governing race discrimination remain dominated by the Supreme Court's landmark 1954 school desegregation decision, *Brown v. Board of Education*. In the eyes of many, *Brown* is the single most important Supreme Court case in American history, for in it the Court finally set the nation on the path toward genuine racial justice, proclaiming the elemental moral and legal point that invidious laws forcing the races to remain separate stigmatize the minority race, and are *inherently* unequal.

There is little disagreement in America today that *Brown* was correctly decided. The centuries of discrimination that African-Americans and other minority groups have suffered was wrong, and it was imperative that the wrong be righted. But there is enormous disagreement over what "righting the wrong" should mean. Today public debate focuses on the appropriate reach of such remedial laws as the Voting Rights Act, or the concept of "affirmative action." To some these laws are necessary correctives still needed to offset the lingering effects of many years of past discrimination. To others there is something inherently wrong in *any* race-conscious government activity, and programs such as affirmative action merely substitute one form of racism for another. Today this debate is particularly acute in the arena of university admissions, where many universities engage in some degree of race-consciousness to diversify their student bodies. In recent years the Supreme Court has shown an increasing hostility toward affirmative action programs, but it has not ruled such programs entirely unconstitutional.

▶ Why has racial harmony been so difficult to achieve in America? Is the American national experience unique in this regard, or is ethnic and racial strife endemic to the human experience? How can laws best eliminate, or at least reduce, racial tension?

▶ Should the purpose of the Constitution's guarantee of equal protection of the laws be to simply eliminate discrimination? Or should it go beyond that purpose, attempting to actually achieve meaningful *integration*, a genuinely shared social and cultural experience?

▶ What are the moral and legal arguments for and against "affirmative action?" In an ideal world, perhaps all race-consciousness would be gone. Perhaps we would pay no more attention to the color of a person's skin than we do to the color of a person's eyes—race would become something of only trivial, passing, cosmetic importance. But do we live in such a world today? What—if anything—do the "realities" of our world teach us about the desirability or non-desirability of retaining affirmative action programs?

Brown v. Board of Education of Topeka MELVIN UROFSKY

Few cases in American Constitutional history have had the impact of the school desegregation case; however far this country has come in treating its black citizens as equal members of society, and however far it still has to go, a turning point came in May 1954. Yet *Brown*, which held that segregation in public schools on the basis of race violated the Constitution, was not cut from whole cloth; one can trace its roots quite precisely.

Following the Civil War, Congress attempted to utilize the Thirteenth and Fourteenth Amendments to protect the newly freed slaves and ensure them equal treatment by society. But in the *Civil Rights Cases* (1883), the Supreme Court ruled that the Reconstruction amendments did not give Congress the power to meddle in social relationships. At that same time, the southern states had begun segregating blacks in schools, on trains, and in other public places. The Court gave its approval to segregation in *Plessy v. Ferguson* (1896), and held that the Equal Protection Clause did not prohibit racial separation, provided blacks had access to equal facilities and services. The "separate but equal" doctrine, upheld in *Plessy*, thus became the cornerstone of the elaborate segregationist structure the southern and border states developed in the early twentieth century.

The NAACP, organized in 1910, soon after began its long legal campaign against racial discrimination in general and segregation in particular. At first, the NAACP concentrated on proving that facilities provided for blacks failed to measure up to those available for whites. In *Missouri ex. rel. Gaines v. Canada* (1938), a black applicant had been refused admission to the University of Missouri Law School solely because of his race. Since the state had no black law school, it offered to pay his tuition to an out-of-state school. Chief Justice Hughes vetoed the proposal; Missouri either had to build an in-state law school for blacks, or admit Gaines to the white school. In *Sweatt v. Painter* (1950), the Court ordered blacks admitted to the University of Texas Law School, on evidence that the black law school did not measure up in quality to that in Austin.

By 1953, when the NAACP challenged school segregation in a half-dozen states, its lawyers stood ready to challenge not only the inequality of segregated schools, but the constitutionality of segregation itself. The Court, after initial arguments, rescheduled the case and asked counsel for both sides to discuss whether the *Plessy* doctrine should be overturned.

The finale came in May 1954, when the Court ruled that segregation by race violated the Fourteenth Amendment's Equal Protection Clause; in a companion case, *Bolling v. Sharpe*, it held segregation in the District of Columbia unconstitutional under the Fifth Amendment. Over the next thirty years, the Court built upon the *Brown* decision to eradicate the vestiges of constitutional support for racial classification.

▶ Much of the criticism of the *Brown* decision has centered on the Court's alleged failure to understand the original intent of the Fourteenth Amendment, which supposedly only dealt with legal and not civil rights. Legal rights are those, such as suffrage, which are spelled out in law. Civil rights are those which deal with how one is treated by society. Is it possible to separate one from the other?

▶ The *Plessy* decision reflected the prevailing social thought of the time; *Brown* mirrored a new attitude toward race. Can both be right?

▶ The Court, in one ruling, struck a death blow at the laws of over a dozen states, and drastically affected the lives of their citizens. Although the Court's power is rarely used so dramatically, should an unelected body have that power?

▶ Is there any other way blacks could have won equal rights in this country other than going through the courts?

Brown v. Board of Education of Topeka 349 U.S. 294 (1954)

Mr. Chief Justice WARREN delivered the opinion of the Court.

These cases come to us from the States of Kansas, South Carolina, Virginia, and Delaware. They are premised on different facts and different local conditions, but a common legal question justifies their consideration together in this consolidated opinion.

In each of the cases, minors of the Negro race, through their legal representatives, seek the aid of the courts in obtaining admission to the public schools of their community on a nonsegregated basis. In each instance, they have been denied admission to schools attended by white children under laws requiring or permitting segregation according to race. This segregation was alleged to deprive the plaintiffs of the equal protection of the laws under the Fourteenth Amendment. In each of the cases other than the Delaware case, a three-judge federal district court denied relief to the plaintiffs on the so-called "separate but equal" doctrine announced by this Court in *Plessy v. Ferguson*, [1896]. Under that doctrine, equality of treatment is accorded when the races are provided substantially equal facilities, even though these facilities be separate. In the Delaware case, the Supreme Court of Delaware adhered to that doctrine, but ordered that the plaintiffs be admitted to the white schools because of their superiority to the Negro schools.

The plaintiffs contend that segregated public schools are not "equal" and cannot be made "equal," and that hence they are deprived of the equal protection of the laws. Because of the obvious importance of the question presented, the Court took jurisdiction. Argument was heard in the 1952 Term, and reargument was heard this Term on certain questions propounded by the Court.

Reargument was largely devoted to the circumstances surrounding the adoption of the Fourteenth Amendment in 1868. It covered exhaustively consideration of the Amendment in Congress, ratification by the states, then existing practices in racial segregation, and the views of proponents and opponents of the Amendment. This discussion and our own investigation convince us that, although these sources cast some light, it is not enough to resolve the problem with which we are faced. At best, they are inconclusive. The most avid proponents of the post-War amendments undoubtedly intended them to remove all legal distinctions among "all persons born or naturalized in the United States." Their opponents, just as certainly, were antagonistic to both the letter and the spirit of the Amendments and wished them to have the most limited effect. What others in Congress and the state legislatures had in mind cannot be determined with any degree of certainty.

An additional reason for the inconclusive nature of the Amendment's history, with respect to segregated schools, is the status of public education at that time. In the South, the movement toward free common schools, supported by general taxation, had not yet taken hold. Education of white children was largely in the hands of private groups. Education of Negroes was almost nonexistent, and practically all of the race were illiterate. In fact, any education of Negroes was forbidden by law in some states. Today, in contrast, many Negroes have achieved outstanding success in the arts and sciences as well as in the business and professional world. It is true that public school education at the time of the Amendment had advanced further in the North, but the effect of the Amendment on Northern States was generally ignored in the congressional debates. Even in the North, the conditions of public education did not approximate those existing today. The curriculum was usually rudimentary; ungraded schools were common in rural areas; the school term was but three months a year in many states; and compulsory school attendance was virtually unknown. As a consequence, it is not surprising that there should be so little in the history of the Fourteenth Amendment relating to its intended effect on public education.

In the first cases in this Court construing the Fourteenth Amendment, decided shortly after its adoption, the Court interpreted it as proscribing all state-imposed discriminations against the Negro race. The doctrine of "separate but equal" did not make its appearance in this Court until 1896 in the case of *Plessy v. Ferguson, supra,* involving not education but transportation. American courts have since labored with the doctrine for over half a century. In this court, there have been six cases involving the "separate but equal" doctrine in the field of public education....In none of these cases was it necessary to re-examine the doctrine to grant relief to the Negro plaintiff. And in *Sweatt v. Painter,* [1950], the Court expressly reserved decision on the question whether *Plessy v. Ferguson* should be held inapplicable to public education.

In the instant cases, that question is directly presented. Here, unlike *Sweatt v. Painter,* there are findings below that the Negro and white schools involved have been equalized, or are being equalized, with respect to buildings, curricula, qualifications and salaries of teachers, and other "tangible" factors. Our decision, therefore, cannot turn on merely a comparison of these tangible factors in the Negro and white schools involved in each of the cases. We must look instead to the effect of segregation itself on public education.

In approaching this problem, we cannot turn the clock back to 1868 when the Amendment was adopted, or even to 1896 when *Plessy v. Ferguson* was written. We must consider public education in the light of its full development and its present place in American life throughout the Nation. Only in this way can it be determined if segregation in public schools deprives these plaintiffs of the equal protection of the laws.

Today, education is perhaps the most important function of state and local governments. Compulsory school attendance laws and the great expenditures for education both demonstrate our recognition of the importance of education to our democratic society. It is required in the performance of our most basic public responsibilities, even service in the armed forces. It is the very foundation of good citizenship. Today it is a principal instrument in awakening the child to cultural values, in preparing him for later professional training, and in helping him to adjust normally to his environment. In these days, it is doubtful that any child may reasonably be expected to succeed in life if he is denied the opportunity of an education. Such an opportunity, where the state has undertaken to provide it, is a right which must be made available to all on equal terms.

We come then to the question presented: Does segregation of children in public schools solely on the basis of race, even though the physical facilities and other "tangible" factors may be equal, deprive the children of the minority groups of equal educational opportunities? We believe that it does.

In *Sweatt v. Painter,* in finding that a segregated law school for Negroes could not provide them equal educational opportunities, this Court relied in large part on "those qualities which are incapable of objective measurement but which make for greatness in a law school." In *McLaurin v. Oklahoma State Regents,* [1950], the Court, in requiring that a Negro admitted to a white graduate school be treated like all other students, again resorted to intangible considerations: "...his ability to study, to engage in discussions and exchange views with other students, and, in general, to learn his profession." Such considerations apply with added force to children in grade and high schools. To separate them from others of similar age and qualifications solely because of their race generates a feeling of inferiority as to their status in the community that may affect their hearts and minds in a way unlikely ever to be undone. The effect of this separation on their educational opportunities was well stated by a finding in the Kansas case by a court which nevertheless felt compelled to rule against the Negro plaintiff:

> Segregation of white and colored children in public schools has a detrimental effect upon the colored children. The impact is greater when it has the sanction of the law; for the policy of separating the races is usually interpreted as denoting the inferiority of the negro group. A sense of inferiority affects the motivation of a child to learn. Segregation with the sanction of law, therefore, has a tendency to [retard] the educational and mental development of Negro children and to deprive them of some of the benefits they would receive in a racial[ly] integrated school system.

Whatever may have been the extent of psychological knowledge at the time of *Plessy v. Ferguson*, this finding is amply supported by modern authority. Any language in *Plessy v. Ferguson* contrary to this finding is rejected.

We conclude that in the field of public education the doctrine of "separate but equal" has no place. Separate educational facilities are inherently unequal. Therefore, we hold that the plaintiffs and others similarly situated for whom the actions have been brought are, by reason of the segregation complained of, deprived of the equal protection of the laws guaranteed by the Fourteenth Amendment. This disposition makes unnecessary any discussion whether such segregation also violates the Due Process Clause of the Fourteenth Amendment.

Because these are class actions, because of the wide applicability of this decision, and because of the great variety of local conditions, the formulation of decrees in these cases presents problems of considerable complexity. On reargument, the consideration of appropriate relief was necessarily subordinated to the primary question—the constitutionality of segregation in public education. We have now announced that such segregation is a denial of the equal protection of the laws. In order that we may have the full assistance of the parties in formulating decrees, the cases will be restored to the docket, and the parties are requested to present further argument on Questions 4 and 5 previously propounded by the Court for the reargument this Term. The Attorney General of the United States is again invited to participate. The Attorneys General of the states requiring or permitting segregation in public education will also be permitted to appear as *amici curiae* upon request to do so by September 15, 1954, and submission of briefs by October 1, 1954.

It is so ordered.

South Carolina v. Katzenbach MELVIN UROFSKY

Following the Civil War, all of the Reconstruction amendments dealing with voting rights of black citizens had clauses granting Congress enforcement powers, but Congress rarely used them. In the wake of John Kennedy's assassination, the commitment of Lyndon Johnson to civil rights, and the growing pressure of the civil rights movement, however, Congress finally began to exercise its authority over the opposition of southern states to full voting rights for blacks.

In 1965 Congress enacted the Voting Rights Act to remove major impediments to voting by black citizens, primarily in the southern states. The Act relied for its authority on the enforcement clause of the Fifteenth Amendment. South Carolina challenged the law on the grounds that Congress had misinterpreted the provision, and that it had no independent legislative power, but could only initiate law suits to secure equal voting rights.

In private, the members of the Court welcomed the various civil rights and voting acts. In the decade following *Brown*, Congress had passed three civil rights acts. But President Eisenhower showed little interest in lending the prestige of the Executive to the battle until provoked by the Little Rock school crisis. This had left the Court, the "least dangerous branch," the one with neither the power of the sword nor of the purse, to carry the burden in the struggle for racial equality. Still although the courts can "declare" rights, only the legislative and executive branches can enforce them.

This may explain in part the sweeping language the Chief Justice employed in this case. That language expounded a very broad interpretation of congressional power. Carried to its logical extreme, the argument gave congress a discretionary power over the most minute aspects of state activity.

> ▶ We have often asked in these cases whether the Court has assumed an active role that more properly belongs to the legislatures. In this case Congress did act. Was its action proper?
>
> ▶ What happens to federalist principles here? What powers are left to the states after this decision?
>
> ▶ Would racial relations have been different if Congress had tried to use its powers more effectively a hundred years earlier?

South Carolina v. Katzenbach 383 U.S. 307 (1966)

Mr. Chief Justice WARREN delivered the opinion of the Court.

The Voting Rights Act [of 1965] was designed by Congress to banish the blight of racial discrimination in voting, which has infected the electoral process in parts of our country for nearly a century. The Act creates stringent new remedies for voting discrimination where it persists on a pervasive scale, and in addition the statute strengthens existing remedies for pockets of voting discrimination elsewhere in the country. Congress assumed the power to prescribe these remedies from Sec. 2 of the Fifteenth Amendment, which authorizes the National Legislature to effectuate by "appropriate" measures the constitutional prohibition against racial discrimination in voting. We hold that the sections of the Act which are properly before us are an appropriate means for carrying out Congress' constitutional responsibilities and are consonant with all other provisions of the Constitution. We therefore deny South Carolina's request that enforcement of these sections of the Act be enjoined.

I. The constitutional propriety of the Voting Rights Act of 1965 must be judged with reference to the historical experience which it reflects. Before enacting the measure, Congress explored with great care the problem of racial discrimination in voting....

Two points emerge vividly from the voluminous legislative history of the Act contained in the committee hearings and floor debates. First: Congress felt itself confronted by an insidious and pervasive evil which had been perpetuated in certain parts of our country through unremitting and ingenious defiance of the Constitution. Second: Congress concluded that the unsuccessful remedies which it had prescribed in the past would have to be replaced by sterner and more elaborate measures in order to satisfy the clear commands of the Fifteenth Amendment....

According to the evidence in recent Justice Department voting suits, [discriminatory application of voting tests] is now the principal method used to bar Negroes from the polls. Discriminatory administration of voting qualifications has been found in all eight Alabama cases, in all nine Louisiana cases, and in all nine Mississippi cases which have gone to final judgment. Moreover, in almost all of these cases, the courts have held that the discrimination was pursuant to a widespread "pattern or practice." White applicants for registration have often been excused altogether from the literacy and understanding tests or have been given easy versions, have received extensive help from voting officials, and have been registered despite serious errors in their answers. Negroes, on the other hand, have typically been required to pass difficult versions of all the tests, without any outside assistance and without the slightest error. The good-morals requirement is so vague and subjective that it has constituted an open invitation to abuse at the hands of voting officials. Negroes obliged to obtain vouchers from registered voters have found it virtually impossible to comply in areas where almost no Negroes are on the rolls.

In recent years, Congress has repeatedly tried to cope with the problem by facilitating case-by-case litigation against voting discrimination....

Despite the earnest efforts of the Justice Department and of many federal judges, these new laws have done little to cure the problem of voting discrimination....Voting suits are unusually onerous to prepare, sometimes requiring as many as 6,000 man-hours spent combing through registration records in preparation for trial. Litigation has been exceedingly slow, in part because of the ample opportunities for delay afforded voting officials and others involved in the proceedings. Even when favorable decisions have finally been obtained, some of the States affected have merely switched to discriminatory devices not covered by the federal decrees or have enacted difficult new tests designed to prolong the existing disparity between white and Negro registration. Alternatively, certain local officials have defied and evaded court orders or have simply closed their registration offices to freeze the voting rolls. The provision of the 1960 law authorizing registration by federal officers has had little impact on local maladministration because of its procedural complexities....

II. The Voting Rights Act of 1965 reflects Congress' firm intention to rid the country of racial discrimination in voting. The heart of the Act is a complex scheme of stringent reme dies aimed at areas where voting discrimination has been most flagrant. The first of the remedies, contained in Sec. 4 (a), is the suspension of literacy tests and similar voting qualifications for a period of five years from the last occurrence of substantial voting discrimination. Section 5 prescribes a second remedy, the suspension of all new voting regulations pending review by federal authorities to determine whether their use would perpetuate voting discrimination. The third remedy, covered in Secs. 6(b), 7, 9, and 13(a), is the assignment of federal examiners on certification by the Attorney General to list qualified applicants who are thereafter entitled to vote in all elections....

III. These provisions of the Voting Rights Act of 1965 are challenged on the fundamental ground that they exceed the powers of Congress and encroach on an area reserved to the States by the Constitution. South Carolina and certain of the *amici curiae* also attack specific sections of the Act for more particular reasons. They argue that the coverage formula prescribed in Sec. 4(a)-(d) violates the principle of the equality of States, denies due process by employing an invalid presumption and by barring judicial review of administrative findings, constitutes a forbidden bill of attainder, and impairs the separation of powers by adjudicating guilt through legislation. They claim that the review of new voting rules required in Sec. 5 infringes Article III by directing the District Court to issue advisory opinions. They contend that the assignment of federal examiners authorized in Sec. 6(b) abridges due process by precluding judicial review of administrative findings and impairs the separation of powers by giving the Attorney General judicial functions; also that the challenge procedure prescribed in Sec. 9 denies due process on account of its speed. Finally, South Carolina and certain of the *amici curiae* maintain that Secs. 4(a) and 5, buttressed by Sec. 14(b) of the Act, abridge due process by limiting litigation to a distant forum.

Some of these contentions may be dismissed at the outset. The word "person" in the context of the Due Process Clause of the Fifth Amendment cannot, by any reasonable mode of interpretation, be expanded to encompass the States of the Union, and to our knowledge this has never been done by any court. Likewise, courts have consistently regarded the Bill of Attainder Clause of Article I and the principle of the separation of powers only as protections for individual persons and private groups, those who are peculiarly vulnerable to nonjudicial determinations of guilt. Nor does a State have standing as the parent of its citizens to invoke these constitutional provisions against the Federal Government, the ultimate (patriae) of every American citizen. The objections to the Act which are raised under these provisions may therefore be considered only as additional aspects of the basic question presented by the case: Has Congress exercised its powers under the Fifteenth Amendment in an appropriate manner with relation to the States?

The ground rules for resolving this question are clear. The language and purpose of the Fifteenth Amendment, the prior decisions construing its several provisions, and the general doctrines of constitutional interpretation, all point to one fundamental principle. As against the reserved powers of the States, Congress may use any rational means to effectuate the constitutional prohibition of racial discrimination in voting.

Section 1 of the Fifteenth Amendment declares that "the right of citizens of the United States to vote shall not be denied or abridged by the United States or by any State on account of race, color, or previous condition of servitude." This declaration has always been treated as self-executing and has repeatedly been construed, without further legislative specification, to invalidate state voting qualifications or procedures which are discriminatory on their face or in practice. These decisions have been rendered with full respect for the general rule that States "have broad powers to determine the conditions under which the right of suffrage may be exercised." The gist of the matter is that the Fifteenth Amendment supersedes contrary exertions of state power. "When a State exercises power wholly within the domain of state interest, it is insulated from federal judicial review. But such insulation is not carried over when state power is used as an instrument for circumventing a federally protected right."

South Carolina contends that the cases cited above are precedents only for the authority of the judiciary to strike down state statutes and procedures—that to allow an exercise of this authority by Congress would be to rob the courts of their rightful constitutional role. On the contrary, Sec. 2 of the Fifteenth Amendment expressly declares that "Congress shall have power to enforce this article by appropriate legislation." By adding this authorization, the Framers indicated that Congress was to be chiefly responsible for implementing the rights created in Sec. 1. "It is the power of Congress which has been enlarged. Congress is authorized to enforce the prohibitions by appropriate legislation. Some legislation is contemplated to make the amendments fully effective." Accordingly, in addition to the courts, Congress has full remedial powers to effectuate the constitutional prohibition against racial discrimination in voting....

The basic test to be applied in a case involving Sec. 2 of the Fifteenth Amendment is the same as in all cases concerning the express powers of Congress with relation to the reserved powers of the States. Chief Justice Marshall laid down the classic formulation, 50 years before the Fifteenth Amendment was ratified:

Let the end be legitimate, let it be within the scope of the constitution, and all means which are appropriate, which are plainly adapted to that end, which are not prohibited, but consist with the letter and spirit of the constitution, are constitutional.

The Court has subsequently echoed his language in describing each of the Civil War Amendments....

We therefore reject South Carolina's argument that Congress may appropriately do no more than to forbid violations of the Fifteenth Amendment in general terms—that the task of fashioning specific remedies or of applying them to particular localities must necessarily be left entirely to the courts. Congress is not circumscribed by any such artificial rules under Sec. 2 of the Fifteenth Amendment. In the oft-repeated words of Chief Justice Marshall, referring to another specific legislative authorization in the Constitution, "This power, like all others vested in Congress, is complete in itself, may be exercised to its utmost extent, and acknowledges no limitations, other than are prescribed in the constitution."

IV. Congress exercised its authority under the Fifteenth Amendment in an inventive manner when it enacted the Voting Rights Act of 1965. First: The measure prescribes remedies for voting discrimination which go into effect without any need for prior adjudication. This was clearly a legitimate response to the problem, for which there is ample precedent under other constitutional provisions. Congress had found that case-by-case litigation was inadequate to combat widespread and persistent discrimination in voting, because of the inordinate amount of time and energy required to overcome the obstructionist tactics invariably encountered in these lawsuits. After enduring nearly a century of systematic resistance to the Fifteenth Amendment, Congress might well decide to shift the advantage of time and inertia from the perpetrators of the evil to its victims. The question remains, of course, whether the specific remedies prescribed in the Act were an appropriate means of combatting the evil, and to this question we shall presently address ourselves.

Second: The Act intentionally confines these remedies to a small number of States and political subdivisions which in most instances were familiar to Congress by name. This, too, was a permissible method of dealing with the problem. Congress had learned that substantial voting discrimination presently occurs in certain sections of the country, and it knew no way of accurately forecasting whether the evil might spread elsewhere in the future. In acceptable legislative fashion, Congress chose to limit its attention to the geographic areas where immediate action seemed necessary. The doctrine of the equality of States, invoked by South Carolina, does not bar this approach, for that doctrine applies only to the terms upon which States are admitted to the Union, and not to the remedies for local evils which have subsequently appeared....[The Court then examined, and upheld, the particular sections of the Act.]

Mr. Justice BLACK, concurring and dissenting.

I agree with substantially all of the Court's opinion sustaining the power of Congress under Sec. 2 of the Fifteenth Amendment to suspend state literacy tests and similar voting qualifications and to authorize the Attorney General to secure the appointment of federal examiners to register qualified voters in various sections of the country. Section 1 of the Fifteenth Amendment provides that "the right of citizens of the United States to vote shall not be denied or abridged by the United States or by any State on account of race, color, or previous condition of servitude." In addition to this unequivocal command to the States and the Federal Government that no citizen shall have his right to vote denied or abridged because of race or color, Sec. 2 of the Amendment unmistakably gives Congress specific power to go further and pass appropriate legislation to protect this right to vote against any method of abridgement no matter how subtle....

Though I agree with most of the Court's conclusions, I dissent from its holding that every part of Sec. 5 of the Act is constitutional. Section 4(a), to which Sec. 5 is linked, suspends for five years all literacy tests and similar devices in those States coming within the formula of Sec. 4(b). Section 5 goes on to provide that a State covered by Sec. 4(b) can in no way amend its constitution or laws relating to voting without first trying to persuade the Attorney General of the United States or the Federal District Court for the District of Columbia that the new proposed laws do not have the purpose and will not have the effect of denying the right to vote to citizens on account of their race or color. I think this section is unconstitutional on at least two grounds.

(a) The Constitution gives federal courts jurisdiction over cases and controversies only. If it can be said that any case or controversy arises under this section which gives the District Court for the District of Columbia jurisdiction to approve or reject state laws or constitutional amendments, then the case or controversy must be between a State and the United States Government. But it is hard for me to believe that a justiciable controversy can arise in the constitutional sense from a desire by the United States Government or some of its officials to determine in advance what legislative provisions a State may enact or what constitutional amendments it may adopt. If this dispute between the Federal Government and the States amounts to a case or controversy it is a far cry from the traditional constitutional notion of a case or controversy as a dispute over the meaning of enforceable laws or the manner in which they are applied. An if by this section Congress has created a case or controversy, and I do not believe it has, then it seems to me that the most appropriate judicial forum for settling these important questions is this Court acting under its original Art. III, Sec. 2, jurisdiction to try cases in which a State is a party. At least a trial in this Court would treat the States with the dignity to which they should be entitled as constituent members of our Federal Union....

(b) My second and more basic objection to Sec. 5 is that Congress has here exercised its power under Sec. 2 of the Fifteenth Amendment through the adoption of means that conflict with the most basic principles of the Constitution. As the Court says, the limitations of the power granted under Sec. 2 are the same as the limitations imposed on the exercise of any of the powers expressly granted Congress by the Constitution. The classic formulation of these constitutional limitations was stated by Chief Justice Marshall when he said "Let the end be legitimate, let it be within the scope of the constitution, and all means which are appropriate, which are plainly adapted to that end, *which are not prohibited, but consist with the letter and spirit of the constitution,* are constitutional." (Emphasis added.) Section 5, by providing that some of the States cannot pass state laws or adopt state constitutional amendments without first being compelled to beg federal authorities to approve their policies, so distorts our constitutional structure of government as to render any distinction drawn in the Constitution between state and federal power almost meaningless....

Swann v. Charlotte-Mecklenburg Board of Education   MELVIN UROFKSY

This case was the first major race case decided by the Burger Court, and its decision reaffirmed the judiciary's commitment to equal treatment of all Americans, regardless of race. It also took a major step toward involving the courts in the day-to-day affairs of local public schools.

The case arose from a desegregation suit in the Charlotte, North Carolina metropolitan area, in which nearly thirty percent of the students were black. In 1969, after several years of operating under a court-approved desegregation plan, about half of the black students attended previously all-white schools; the other half went to all-black schools. The District Court found this pace of desegregation too slow, and ordered local school authorities to prepare a more effective plan. The school board turned in several proposals, all of which the District Court rejected; the court then appointed its own expert to prepare a plan. This proposal called for pairing schools in the white sections of the district with inner city black schools, with the busing of some elementary school students in both directions. The Court of Appeals overturned the plan, since it found that busing and the pairing of schools would "place an unreasonable burden on the board and the system's pupils."

In one of the last major decisions under Chief Justice Earl Warren, *Green v. County School Board* (1968), the Court made known its displeasure at the slow pace of integration. In the second *Brown* case (1955), the Court ordered segregated schools to desegregate "with all deliberate speed." It had hoped this formula of encouragement rather than confrontation would lead to cooperation by Southern school and governmental officials; instead, school systems often emphasized the *deliberate* rather than the *speed*. Fifteen years after *Brown*, only a tiny fraction of southern black students attended integrated schools. The South had hoped that the appointment of conservative justices would lead to a reversal of the Warren Court's doctrines; Swann not only confirmed those doctrines, but approved of busing as a legitimate means to speed up the process.

Following *Swann*, Congress found dozens of proposals to curb busing, and in 1974 the Education Amendments established a "priority of remedies" to be used by federal courts to promote desegregation. It also barred any order that would require transportation of a student to "a school other than the school closest or next closest to his place of residence." However, the same act included an important qualification stating that none of its provisions were intended "to modify or diminish the authority of the courts of the United States to enforce fully the Fifth and Fourteenth Amendments." As a result, when courts found that only busing would effectively desegregate schools, they had no problem utilizing that remedy despite the 1974 act.

▶ Are there other remedies to segregation, besides busing, that are preferable and more effective?

▶ *Swann* can be understood as furthering the shift in the Court's outlook from simply opposing segregation to actively requiring integration. Does the Equal Protection Clause justify this? Is there a difference between "desegregation" and "integration?"

▶ If the Court can order positive steps, then it and lower courts can also monitor those steps, and indeed order changes. Is it a good idea for courts to be involved in such matters, say, as running the Boston schools? Who else can do it? Who should?

Swann v. Charlotte-Mecklenburg Board of Education 402 U.S. 1 (1971)

Mr. Chief Justice BURGER delivered the opinion of the Court.

The problems encountered by the lower courts make plain that we should now try to amplify guidelines, however incomplete and imperfect, for the assistance of school authorities and courts. Elimination of dual school systems has been rendered more difficult by changes since 1954 in the structure and patterns of communities, the growth of student population, movement of families, and other changes, some of which had marked impact on school planning, sometimes neutralizing or negating remedial action before it was fully implemented. Rural areas accustomed for half a century to the consolidated school systems implemented by bus transportation could make adjustments more readily than metropolitan areas. The objective today remains to eliminate from the public schools all vestiges of state-imposed segregation. If school authorities fail in their affirmative obligations under *Brown* and later holdings, judicial authority may be invoked. Once a right and a violation have been shown, the scope of a district court's equitable powers to remedy past wrongs is broad. The task is to correct, by a balancing of the individual and collective interests, the condition that offends the Constitution. But it is important to remember that judicial powers may be exercised only on the basis of a constitutional violation.

School authorities are traditionally charged with broad power to formulate and implement educational policy and might well conclude, for example, that in order to prepare students to live in a pluralistic society each school should have a prescribed ratio of Negro to white students reflecting the proportion for the district as a whole. To do this as an educational policy is of a constitutional violation, however, that would not be within the authority of a federal court....

(1) Racial Balances or Racial Quotas. We do not reach in this case the question whether a showing that school segregation is a consequence of other types of state action, without any discriminatory action by the school authorities, is a consitutional violation requiring remedial action by a school desegregation decree. Our aim in these cases is to see that school authorities exclude no people of a racial minority from any school, directly or indirectly, on account of race; it does not and cannot embrace all the problems of racial prejudice, even when those problems contribute to disproportionate racial concentrations in some schools. In this case it is urged that the District Court has imposed a racial balance requirement of 71%-29% on individual schools. The District Court opinion contains intimations that the "norm" is a fixed mathematical racial balance reflecting the pupil constituency of the system. If we were to read the holding of the District Court to require, as a matter of substantive constitutional right, any particular degree of racial balance or mixing, that approach would be disapproved and we would be obliged to reverse. The constitutional command to desegregate schools does not mean that every school in every community must always reflect the racial composition of the school system as a whole. But the use made of mathematical ratios was no more than a starting point in the process of shaping a remedy, rather than an inflexible requirement. As we said in *Green*, a school authority's remedial plan or a district court's remedial decree is to be judged by its effectiveness. Awareness of the racial composition of the whole school system is likely to be a useful starting point in shaping a remedy to correct past constitutional violations. In sum, the very limited use made of mathematical ratios was within the equitable remedial discretion of the District Court.

(2) One-Race Schools. The record in this case reveals the familiar phenomenon that in metropolitan areas minority groups are often found concentrated in one part of the city. In some circumstances certain schools may remain all or largely of one race until new schools can be provided or neighborhood patterns change. Schools all or predominantly of one race in a district of mixed population will require close scrutiny to determine that school assign-

ments are not part of state-enforced segregation. In light of the above, it should be clear that the existence of some small number of one-race, or virtually one-race, schools within a district is not in and of itself the mark of a system which still practices segregation by law. But the court should scrutinize such schools, and the burden upon the school authorities will be to satisfy the court that their racial composition is not the result of present or past discriminatory action on their part....

(3) Remedial Altering of Attendance Zones. The maps submitted in these cases graphically demonstrate that one of the principal tools employed by school planners and by courts to break up the dual school system has been a frank—and sometimes drastic—gerrymandering of school districts and attendance zones. An additional step was pairing, "clustering," or "grouping" of schools with attendance assignments made deliberately to accomplish the transfer of Negro students out of formerly segregated Negro schools and transfer of white students to formerly all-Negro schools. More often than not, these zones are neither compact nor contiguous; indeed they may be on opposite ends of the city. As an interim corrective measure, this cannot be said to be beyond the broad remedial powers of a court.

Absent a constitutional violation there would be no basis for judicially ordering assignment of students on a racial basis. All things being equal, with no history of discrimination, it might well be desirable to assign pupils to schools nearest their homes. But all things are not equal in a system that has been deliberately constructed and maintained to enforce racial segregation. The remedy for such segregation may be administratively awkward, inconvenient, and even bizarre in some situations and may impose burdens on some; but all awkwardness and inconvenience cannot be avoided in the interim period when remedial adjustments are being made to eliminate the dual school systems. No fixed or even substantially fixed guidelines can be established as to how far a court can go, but it must be recognized that there are limits. The objective is to dismantle the dual school system. "Racially neutral" assignment plans may fail to counteract the continuing effects of past school segregation resulting from discriminatory location of school sites or distortion of school size in order to achieve or maintain an artificial racial separation. When school authorities present a district court with a "loaded game board," affirmative action in the form of remedial altering of attendance zones is proper to achieve truly nondiscriminatory assignments. We hold that the pairing and grouping of non-contiguous school zones is a permissible tool and such action is to be considered in light of the objectives sought....

(4) Transportation of Students. No rigid guidelines are possible about the scope of permissible transportation of students as an implement of a remedial decree. Bus transportation has been an integral part of the public education system for years. Eighteen million of the Nation's public school children, approximately 39%, were transported to their schools by bus in 1969-1970 in all parts of the country. The importance of bus transportation as a normal and accepted tool of educational policy is readily discernible. The decree provided that the trips for elementary school pupils average about seven miles and the District Court found that they would take "not over 35 minutes at the most." This system compares favorably with the transportation plan previously operated in Charlotte under which each day 23,600 students on all grade levels were transported an average of 15 miles one way for an

average trip requiring over an hour. In these circumstances, we find no basis for holding that the local school authorities may not be required to employ bus transportation as one tool of school desegregation. Desegregation plans cannot be limited to the walk-in school. An objection to transportation of students may have validity when the time or distance of travel is so great as to risk either the health of the children or significantly impinge on the educational process. District courts must weigh the soundness of any transportation plan in light of what is said in subdivisions (1), (2), and (3) above. The reconciliation of competing values in a desegregation case is, of course, a difficult task with many sensitive facets but fundamentally no more so than remedial measures courts of equity have traditionally employed....

At some point, these school authorities and others like them should have achieved full compliance with this Court's decision in *Brown I*. The systems will then be "unitary" in the sense required by our decisions in *Green* and *Alexander*. It does not follow that the communities served by such systems will remain demographically stable, for in a growing, mobile society, few will do so. Neither school authorities nor district courts are constitutionally required to make year-by-year adjustments of the racial composition of student bodies once the affirmative duty to desegregate has been accomplished and racial discrimination through official action is eliminated from the system. This does not mean that federal courts are without power to deal with future problems; but in the absence of a showing that either the school authorities or some other agency of the State has deliberately attempted to fix or alter demographic patterns to affect the racial composition of the schools, further intervention by a district court should not be necessary.

Regents of the University of California v. Bakke MELVIN UROFSKY

This case is a logical extension of the ideas implicit in *Swann*, namely, that true equality requires more than the elimination of the outward signs of racial discrimination; it requires positive steps toward achieving a society free from the legacies of racial discrimination. The decades of past discrimination, however, left terrible marks, including the *de facto* exclusion of blacks from better jobs, better schools, better housing and, practically, from some of the professions. The argument for so-called "affirmative action" ran along this line: In order to overcome the residue of oppression, blacks would need an extra helping hand for a while; they should therefore be accorded not just equal treatment, but also some preferential treatment. This could take the form of setting aside for them certain percentages of better jobs, college and university admissions, etc.

The *Bakke* case arose from a preferential admissions program at the University of California Davis Medical School. Out of 100 positions in each year's entering class, the school reserved sixteen specifically for minority candidates. In effect, Davis ran two admissions programs: one to sift "regular" applicants, and choose eighty-four admissions out of a candidate pool of close to 3,000 persons; another special admissions program, that accepted students with lower grade point averages and MCAT scores if they were minority members. Allen Bakke applied in both 1973 and 1974 and failed to win admission, even though his grade and MCAT scores were higher than those of students accepted under the minority program.

After a third rejection, Bakke sued in state court claiming he had been denied his rights under the Equal Protection Clause, and that the special admissions program violated both the California constitution and Title VI of the 1964 Civil Rights Act. The state trial court found that the Davis special program operated as an unconstitutional racial quota system, and the California Supreme Court, without passing on state constitutional or federal statutory questions, ruled that the University had thus violated the Fourteenth Amendment's Equal Protection Clause. The University, against the advice of many civil rights and civil liberties organizations, then petitioned the United States Supreme Court for a *writ of certiorari*.

The Court's opinion offered something for everyone, but fully satisfied no one. Four members of the Court believed that Bakke had been discriminated against in light of the mandate of Title VI of the 1964 Civil Rights Act and that he must thus be admitted; race could not be a factor in admissions policies. Four members believed race could be a factor; that while it was regrettable that some majority members would suffer, society could impose this penalty on a few to make up for past transgressions against many. Justice Powell's opinion which he based on constitutional (Fourteenth Amendment) rather than on statutory grounds, held race could be taken into account as one of several factors (four members of the Court agreed with him), and that Bakke had been discriminated against and should be admitted (in which the first group of four members agreed). But the Solomonic decision did not answer the larger question regarding the circumstances under which affirmative action programs are constitutionally permissible.

▶ Is "affirmative action" a fair way to compensate minorities for past discrimination? Is there a better way to do it?

▶ Should the Court be involved in suits of this type? If a state is trying to help a minority, should the Court simply allow it to do so?

▶ Some critics argue that "affirmative action" is merely another word for quotas, which nearly all civil rights groups oppose. Is this a fair criticism?

▶ Courts talk about "goals" and "quotas." Is there a difference?

▶ What, if anything, does the Equal Protection Clause require of any plan to help disadvantaged minorities?

▶ Is there a point at which "affirmative action" turns into "reverse discrimination"—the latter theoretically barred by both statute and the Constitution?

Regents of the University of California v. Bakke 438 U.S. 265 (1978)

Mr. Justice POWELL announced the judgment of the Court.

This case presents a challenge to the special admissions program of the petitioner, the Medical School of the University of California at Davis, which is designed to assure the admission of a specified number of students from certain minority groups. The Supreme Court of California held the special admissions program unlawful, enjoined petitioner from considering the race of any applicant, and ordered Bakke's admission. For the reasons stated in the following opinion, I believe that so much of the judgment of the California court as holds petitioner's special admissions program unlawful and directs that respondent be admitted to the Medical School must be affirmed. For the reasons expressed in a separate opinion, my Brother The Chief Justice, Mr. Justice Stewart, Mr. Justice Rehnquist, and Mr. Justice Stevens concur in this judgment. I also conclude for the reasons stated in the following opinion that the portion of the court's judgment enjoining petitioner from according any consideration to race in its admissions process must be reversed. For reasons expressed in separate opinions, my Brothers Mr. Justice Brennan, Mr. Justice White, Mr. Justice Marshall, and Mr. Justice Blackmun concur in this judgment.

Affirmed in part and reversed in part....

Because the special admissions program involved a racial classification, the supreme court [of California] held itself bound to apply strict scrutiny. It then turned to the goals the University presented as justifying the special program. Although the court agreed that the goals of integrating the medical profession and increasing the number of physicians willing to serve members of minority groups were compelling state interests, it concluded that the special admissions program was not the least intrusive means of achieving those goals. Without passing on the state constitutional or the federal statutory grounds cited in the trial court's judgment, the California court held that the Equal Protection Clause required that "no applicant may be rejected because of his race, in favor of another who is less qualified, as measured by standards applied without regard to race."...

[Sections I and II have been omitted.]

III. A. The parties disagree as to the level of judicial scrutiny to be applied to the special admissions program. En route to this crucial battle over the scope of judicial review, the parties fight a sharp preliminary action over the proper characterization of the special admissions program. Petitioner prefers to view it as establishing a "goal" of minority representation in the medical school. Respondent, echoing the courts below, labels it a racial quota. This semantic distinction is beside the point: the special admissions program is undeniably a classification based on race and ethnic background. To the extent that there existed a pool of at least minimally qualified minority applicants to fill the 16 special admissions seats, white applicants could compete only for 84 seats in the entering class, rather than the 100 open to minority applicants. Whether this limitation is described as a quota or a goal, it is a line drawn on the basis of race and ethnic status.

The guarantees of the 14th Amendment extend to persons. Its language is explicit. The guarantee of equal protection cannot mean one thing when applied to one individual and something else when applied to a person of another color. If both are not accorded the same protection, then it is not equal. Nevertheless, petitioner argues that the court below erred in applying strict scrutiny because white males are not a "discrete and insular minority" requiring extraordinary protection from the majoritarian political process. This rationale, however, has never been invoked in our decisions as a prerequisite to subjecting racial or ethnic distinctions to strict scrutiny. Nor has this Court held that discreteness and insularity constitute necessary preconditions to holding that a particular classification is invidious....Racial and ethnic classifications, however, are subject to stringent examination without regard to these additional characteristics. We declared as much in the first cases explicitly to recognize racial distinctions as suspect. Racial and ethnic distinctions of any sort are inherently suspect and thus call for the most exacting judicial examination.

B....Over the past 30 years, this Court has embarked upon the crucial mission of interpreting the Equal Protection Clause with the view of assuring to all persons "the protection of equal laws," in a Nation confronting a legacy of slavery and racial discrimination. Because the landmark decisions in this area arose in response to the continued exclusion of Negroes from the mainstream of American society, they could be characterized as involving discrimination by the "majority" white race against the Negro minority. But they need not be read as depending upon that characterization for their results. It suffices to say that "over the years, this Court consistently repudiated `distinctions between citizens solely because of their ancestry' as being `odious to a free people whose institutions are founded upon the doctrine of equality.'" Petitioner urges us to adopt for the first time a more restrictive view of the Equal Protection Clause and hold that discrimination against members of the white "majority" cannot be suspect if its purpose can be characterized as "benign." The clock of our liberties, however, cannot be turned back to 1868. It is far too late to argue that the guarantee of equal protection to all persons permits the recognition of special wards entitled to a degree of protection greater than that accorded others. "The 14th Amendment is not directed solely against discrimination due to a `two-class theory'—that is, based upon differences between `white' and Negro."

Once the artificial line of a "two-class theory" of the 14th Amendment is put aside, the difficulties entailed in varying the level of judicial review according to a perceived "preferred" status of a particular racial or ethnic minority are intractable. The concepts of "majority" and "minority" necessarily reflect temporary arrangements and political judgments. As observed above, the white "majority" itself is composed of various minority groups, most of which can lay claim to a history of prior discrimination at the hands of the state and private individuals. Not all of these groups can receive preferential treatment and corresponding judicial tolerance of distinctions drawn in terms of race and nationality, for then the only "majority" left would be a new minority of White Anglo-Saxon Protestants. There is no principled basis for deciding which groups would merit "heightened judicial solicitude" and which would not. Courts would be asked to evaluate the extent of the prejudice and consequent harm suffered by various minority groups. Those whose societal injury is thought to exceed some arbitrary level of tolerability then would be entitled to preferential classifications at the expense of individuals belonging to other groups. Those classifications would be free from exacting judicial scrutiny. As these preferences began to have their desired effect, and the consequences of past discrimination were undone, new judicial rankings would be necessary. The kind of variable sociological and political analy-

sis necessary to produce such rankings simply does not lie within the judicial competence—even if they otherwise were politically feasible and socially desireable.

Moreover, there are serious problems of justice connected with the idea of preference
itself. First, it may not always be clear that a so-called preference is in fact benign. Courts
may be asked to validate burdens imposed upon individual members of particular groups
in order to advance the group's general interest. Nothing in the Constitution supports the
notion that individuals may be asked to suffer otherwise impermissible burdens in order to
enhance the societal standing of their ethnic groups. Second, preferential programs may
only reinforce common stereotypes holding that certain groups are unable to achieve success without special protection based on a factor having no relationship to individual
worth. Third, there is a measure of inequity in forcing innocent persons in respondent's
position to bear the burdens of redressing grievances not of their making. By hitching the
meaning of the Equal Protection Clause to these transitory considerations, we would be
holding, as a constitutional principle, that judicial scrutiny of classifications touching on
racial and ethnic background may vary with the ebb and flow of political forces. Disparate
constitutional tolerance of such classifications well may serve to exacerbate racial and ethnic antagonisms rather than alleviate them. Also, the mutability of a constitutional principle, based upon shifting political and social judgments, undermines the chances for consistent application of the Constitution from one generation to the next, a critical feature of its
coherent interpretation....

If it is the individual who is entitled to judicial protection against classifications based
upon his racial or ethnic background because such distinctions impinge upon personal
rights, rather than the individual only because of his membership in a particular group,
then constitutional standards may be applied consistently. Political judgments regarding the
necessity for the particular classification may be weighed in the constitutional balance but
the standard of justification will remain constant. This is as it should be, since those political judgments are the product of rough compromise struck by contending groups within
the democratic process. When they touch upon an individual's race or ethnic background,
he is entitled to a judicial determination that the burden he is asked to bear on that basis is
precisely tailored to serve a compelling governmental interest....

IV. We have held that in "order to justify the use of a suspect classification, a State must
show that its purpose or interest is both constitutionally permissible and substantial, and
that its use of the classification is `necessary to the accomplishment' of its purpose or the
safeguarding of its interest." The special admissions program purports to serve the purposes of: (i) "reducing the historic deficit of traditionally disfavored minorities in medical
schools and the medical profession;" (ii) countering the effects of societal discrimination;
(iii) increasing the number of physicians who will practice in communities currently
underserved; and (iv) obtaining the educational benefits that flow from an ethnically
diverse student body. It is necessary to decide which, if any, of these purposes is substantial
enough to support the use of a suspect classification.

A. If petitioner's purpose is to assure within its student body some specified percentage
of a particular group merely because of its race or ethnic origin, such a preferential purpose
must be rejected not as insubstantial but as facially invalid. Preferring members of any one

group for no reason other than race or ethnic origin is discrimination for its own sake. This the Constitution forbids.

B. The State certainly has a legitimate and substantial interest in ameliorating, or eliminating where feasible, the disabling effects of identified discrimination. The school desegregation cases attest to the importance of this state goal, which is far more focused than the remedying of the effects of "societal discrimination," an amorphous concept of injury that may be ageless in its reach into the past. We have never approved a classification that aids persons perceived as members of relatively victimized groups at the expense of other innocent individuals in the absence of judicial, legislative, or administrative findings of constitutional or statutory violations....Without such findings of constitutional or statutory violations, it cannot be said that the government has any greater interest in helping one individual than in refraining from harming another. Thus, the government has no compelling justification for inflicting such harm.

Petitioner does not purport to have made, and is in no position to make, such findings. Its broad mission is education, not the formulation of any legislative policy or the adjudication of particular claims of illegality...

C. Petitioner identifies, as another purpose of its program, improving the delivery of health care services to communities currently underserved. It may be assumed that in some situations a State's interest in facilitating the health care of its citizens is sufficiently compelling to support the use of suspect classification. But there is virtually no evidence in the record indicating that petitioner's special admissions program is either needed or geared to promote that goal. Petitioner simply has not carried its burden of demonstrating that it must prefer members of particular ethnic groups over all other individuals in order to promote better health care delivery to deprived citizens. Indeed, petitioner has not shown that its preferential classification is likely to have any significant effect on the problem.

D. The fourth goal asserted by petitioner is the attainment of a diverse student body. This clearly is a constitutionally permissible goal for an institution of higher education. Academic freedom, though not a specifically enumerated constitutional right, long has been viewed as a special concern of the First Amendment. The freedom of a university to make its own judgments as to education includes the selection of its student body. Thus, in arguing that its universities must be accorded the right to select those students who will contribute the most to the "robust exchange of ideas," petitioner invokes a countervailing constitutional interest, that of the First Amendment. In this light, petitioner must be viewed as seeking to achieve a goal that is of paramount importance in the fulfillment of its mission. It may be argued that there is greater force to these views at the undergraduate level than in a medical school where the training is centered primarily on professional competency. But even at the graduate level, our tradition and experience lend support to the view that the contribution of diversity is substantial. Physicians serve a heterogeneous population. An otherwise qualified medical student with a particular background— whether it be ethnic, geographic, culturally advantaged or disadvantaged—may bring to a professional school of medicine experiences, outlooks and ideas that enrich the training of its student body and better equip its graduates to render with understanding their vital service to humanity.

Ethnic diversity, however, is only one element in a range of factors a university properly may consider in attaining the goal of a heterogeneous student body. Although a university must have wide discretion in making the sensitive judgments as to who should be admitted, constitutional limitations protecting individual rights may not be disregarded. Respondent urges—and the courts below have held—that petitioner's dual admissions program is a racial classification that impermissibly infringes his rights under the 14th Amendment. As the interest of diversity is compelling in the context of a university's admissions program, the question remains whether the program's racial classification is necessary to promote this interest.

V. A. It may be assumed that the reservation of a specified number of seats in each class for individuals from the preferred ethnic groups would contribute to the attainment of considerable ethnic diversity in the student body. But petitioner's argument that this is the only effective means of serving the interest of diversity is seriously flawed....

The experience of other university admissions programs, which take race into account in achieving the educational diversity valued by the First Amendment, demonstrates that the assignment of a fixed number of places to a minority group is not a necessary means toward that end....In such an admissions program, race or ethnic background may be deemed a "plus" in a particular applicant's file, yet it does not insulate the individual from comparison with all other candidates for the available seats. The file of a particular black applicant may be examined for his potential contribution to diversity without the factor of race being decisive when compared, for example, with that of an applicant identified as an Italian-American if the latter is thought to exhibit qualities more likely to promote beneficial educational pluralism. Such qualities could include exceptional personal talents, unique work or service experience, leadership potential, maturity, demonstrated compassion, a history of overcoming disadvantage, ability to communicate with the poor, or other qualifications deemed important. In short, an admissions program operated in this way is flexible enough to consider all pertinent elements of diversity in light of the particular qualifications of each applicant, and to place them on the same footing for consideration, although not necessarily according them the same weight. Indeed, the weight attributed to a particular quality may vary from year to year depending upon the "mix" both of the student body and the applicants for the incoming class.

B. In summary, it is evident that the Davis special admissions program involves the use of an explicit racial classification never before countenanced by this Court. It tells applicants who are not Negro, Asian, or "Chicano" that they are totally excluded from a specific percentage of the seats in an entering class. No matter how strong their qualifications, quantitative and extracurricular, including their own potential for contribution to educational diversity, they are never afforded the chance to compete with applicants from the preferred groups for the special admission seats. At the same time, the preferred applicants have the opportunity to compete for every seat in the class. The fatal flaw in petitioner's program is its disregard of individual rights as guaranteed by the 14th Amendment. Such rights are not absolute. But when a State's distribution of benefits or imposition of burdens hinges on the color of a person's skin or ancestry, that individual is entitled to a demonstration that the challenged classification is necessary to promote a substantial state interest. Petitioner has failed to carry this burden. For this reason, that portion of the California court's judgment holding petitioner's special admissions programs invalid under the 14th Amendment must be affirmed.

C. In enjoining petitioner from ever considering the race of any applicant, however, the courts below failed to recognize that the State has a substantial interest that legitimately may be served by a properly devised admissions program involving the competitive consideration of race and ethnic origin. For this reason, so much of the California court's judgment as enjoins petitioner from any consideration of the race of any applicant must be reversed.

VI. With respect to respondent's entitlement to an injunction directing his admission to the Medical School, petitioner has conceded that it could not carry its burden of proving that, but for the existence of its unlawful special admissions program, respondent still would not have been admitted. Hence, respondent is entitled to the injunction, and that portion of the judgment must be affirmed.

Mr. Justice BRENNAN, Mr. Justice WHITE, Mr. Justice MARSHALL, and Mr. Justice BLACK-MUN, concurring in the judgment in part and dissenting.

The Court today affirms the constitutional power of Federal and State Government to act affirmatively to achieve equal opportunity for all. The difficulty of the issue presented has resulted in many opinions, no single one speaking for the Court. But this should not and must not mask the central meaning of today's opinions: Government may take race into account when it acts not to demean or insult any racial groups, but to remedy disadvantages cast on minorities by past racial prejudice, at least when appropriate findings have been made by judicial, legislative, or administrative bodies with competence to act in this area....

We agree with Mr. Justice Powell that, as applied to the case before us, Title VI goes no further in prohibiting the use of race than the Equal Protection Clause of the 14th Amendment itself. We also agree that the effect of the California Supreme Court's decision would be to prohibit the University from establishing in the future affirmative action programs that take race into account. Since we conclude that the affirmative admissions program at the Davis Medical School is constitutional, we would reverse the judgment below in all respects. Mr. Justice Powell agrees that some uses of race in university admissions are permissible and, therefore, he joins with us to make five votes to reverse the judgment below insofar as it prohibits the University from establishing race-conscious programs in the future....

[Sections I and II have been omitted.]

III. A. Our cases have always implied that an "overriding statutory purpose" could be found that would justify racial classifications. We conclude, therefore, that racial classifications are not per se invalid under the 14th Amendment. Accordingly, we turn to the problem of articulating what our role should be in reviewing state action that expressly classifies by race....

Unquestionably we have held that a government practice or statute which restricts "fundamental rights" or which contains "suspect classifications" is to be subjected to "strict scrutiny." But no fundamental right is involved here. Nor do whites as a class have any of the "traditional indicia of suspectness: the class is not saddled with such disabilities, or subjected to such a history of purposeful unequal treatment, or relegated to such a position of political powerlessness as to command extraordinary protection from the majoritarian political process." Moreover, if the University's representations are credited, this is not a case where racial classifications are "irrelevant and therefore prohibited." Nor has anyone suggested that the University's purposes contravene the cardinal principle that racial classifications that stigmatize—because they are drawn on the presumption that one race is inferior to another or because they put the weight of government behind racial hatred and separatism—are invalid without more...

First, race, like "gender-based classifications too often has been inexcusably utilized to stereotype and stigmatize politically powerless segments of society." While a carefully tailored statute designed to remedy past discrimination could avoid these vices, we nonetheless have recognized that the line between honest and thoughtful appraisal of the effects of past discrimination and paternalistic stereotyping is not so clear and that a statute based on the latter is patently capable of stigmatizing all women with a badge of inferiority. State programs designed ostensibly to ameliorate the effects of past racial discrimination obviously create the same hazard of stigma, since they may promote racial separatism and reinforce the views of those who believe that members of racial minorities are inherently incapable of succeeding on their own.

Second, race, like gender and illegitimacy, is an immutable characteristic which its possessors are powerless to escape or set aside. While a classification is not per se invalid because it divides classes on the basis of an immutable characteristic, it is nevertheless true that such divisions are contrary to our deep belief that "legal burdens should bear some relationship to individual responsibility or wrongdoing" and that advancement sanctioned, sponsored, or approved by the State should ideally be based on individual merit or achievement, or at least on factors within the control of an individual. Because this principle is so deeply rooted it might be supposed that it would be considered in the legislative process and weighed against the benefits of programs preferring individuals because of their race. But this is not necessarily so: The "natural consequence of our governing processes may well be that the most `discrete and insular' of whites will be called upon to bear the immediate, direct costs of benign discrimination." Moreover, it is clear from our cases that there are limits beyond which majorities may not go when they classify on the basis of immutable characteristics. Thus, even if the concern for individualism is weighed by the political process, that weighing cannot waive the personal rights of individuals under the 14th Amendment....

IV. Davis' articulate purpose of remedying the effects of past societal discrimination is, under our cases, sufficiently important to justify the use of race-conscious admissions programs where there is a sound basis for concluding that minority underrepresentation is substantial and chronic, and that the handicap of past discrimination is impeding access of minorities to the medical school.

B. Properly construed, therefore, our prior cases unequivocally show that a state government may adopt race-conscious programs if the purpose of such programs is to remove the disparate racial impact its actions might otherwise have and if there is reason to believe that the disparate impact is itself the product of past discrimination, whether its own or that of society at large. There is no question that Davis' program is valid under this test. Certainly, Davis had a sound basis for believing that the problem of underrepresentation of minorities was substantial and chronic and that the problem was attributable to handicaps imposed on minority applicants by past and present racial discrimination. Until at least 1973, the practice of medicine in this country was, in fact, if not in law, largely the prerogative of whites. In 1950, for example, while Negroes comprised 10% of the total population, Negro physicians constituted only 2.2% of the total number of physicians. By 1970, the gap between the proportion of Negroes in medicine and their proportion in the population had widened: The number of Negroes employed in medicine remained frozen at 2.2% while the Negro population had increased to 11.1%. The number of Negro admittees to predominantly white medical schools, moreover, had declined in absolute numbers during the years 1955 to 1964. Moreover, Davis had very good reason to believe that the national pattern of underrepresentation of minorities in medicine would be perpetuated if it retained a single admissions standard. For example, the entering classes in 1968 and 1969, the years in which such a standard was used, included only one Chicano and two Negroes out of 100 admittees. Nor is there any relief from this pattern of underrepresentation in the statistics for the regular admissions program in later years.

Davis clearly could conclude that the serious and persistent underrepresentation of minorities in medicine depicted by these statistics is the result of handicaps under which minority applicants labor as a consequence of a background of deliberate, purposeful discrimination against minorities in education and in society generally, as well as in the medical profession...

C. The second prong of our test—whether the Davis program stigmatizes any discrete group or individual and whether race is reasonably used in light of the program's objectives—is clearly satisfied by the Davis program. It is not even claimed that Davis' program in any way operates to stigmatize or single out any discrete and insular, or even any identifiable, nonminority group. Nor will harm comparable to that imposed upon racial minorities by exclusion or separation on grounds of race be the likely result of the program. It does not, for example, establish an exclusive preserve for minority students apart from and exclusive of whites. Rather, its purpose is to overcome the effects of segregation by bringing the races together. True, whites are excluded from participation in the special admissions program, but this fact only operates to reduce the number of whites to be admitted in the regular admissions program in order to permit admission of a reasonable percentage—less than their proportion of the California population—of otherwise underrepresented qualified minority applicants....

E. Finally, Davis' special admissions program cannot be said to violate the Constitution simply because it has set aside a predetermined number of places for qualified minority applicants rather than using minority status as a positive factor to be considered in evaluating the applications of disadvantaged racial minorities, a determination of the degree of preference to be given is unavoidable, and any given preference that results in the exclusion of a white candidate is not more or less constitutionally acceptable than a program such as that at Davis. Furthermore, the extent of the preference inevitably depends on how many minority applicants the particular school is seeking to admit in any particular year so long as the number of qualified minority applicants exceeds that number. There is no sensible, and certainly no constitutional, distinction between, for example, adding a set number of points to the admissions rating of disadvantaged minority applicants as an expression of the preference with the expectation that this will result in the admission of an approximately determined number of qualified minority applicants and setting a fixed number of places for such applicants as was done here....

[Mr. Justice BLACKMUN and Mr. Justice MARSHALL entered separate opinions concurring in part and dissenting in part.]

Mr. Justice STEVENS, with whom The Chief Justice, Mr. Justice STEWART, and Mr. Justice REHNQUIST join, concurring in the judgment in part and dissenting in part.

It is always important at the outset to focus precisely on the controversy before the Court. It is particularly important to do so in this case because correct identification of the issues will determine whether it is necessary or appropriate to express any opinion about the legal status of any admissions program other than petitioner's. This is not a class action. Bakke challenged petitioner's special admissions program, claiming that it denied him a place in the medical school because of his race in violation of the Federal and California Constitutions and of Title VI of the Civil Rights Act of 1964. The California Supreme Court upheld his challenge and ordered him admitted. If the state court was correct in its view that the University's special program was illegal, and that Bakke was therefore unlawfully excluded from the medical school because of his race, we should affirm its judgment, regardless of our views about the legality of admissions programs that are not now before the Court. It is perfectly clear that the question whether race can ever be used as a factor in an admissions decision is not an issue in this case, and that discussion of that issue is inappropriate.

In this case, we are presented with a constitutional question of undoubted and unusual importance. Since, however, a dispositive statutory claim was raised at the very inception of this case, it is our plain duty to confront it. The University excluded Bakke from participation in its program of medical education because of his race. The University also acknowledges that it was, and still is, receiving federal financial assistance. The plain language of Title VI therefore requires affirmance of the judgment below. A different result cannot be justified unless that language misstates the actual intent of the Congress that enacted the statute or the statute is not enforceable in a private action. Neither conclusion is warranted. Petitioner contends that exclusion of applicants on the basis of race does not violate Title VI if the exclusion carries with it no racial stigma. No such qualification or limitation of the categorical prohibition of "exclusion" is justified by the statute or its history. It seems clear that the proponents of Title VI assumed that the Constitution itself required a colorblind standard on the part of government, but that does not mean that the legislation only codifies an existing constitutional prohibition. The statutory prohibition against discrimination in federally funded projects contained in 601 is more than a simple paraphrasing of what the Fifth or 14th Amendment would require. The Act's proponents plainly considered Title VI consistent with their view of the Constitution and they sought to provide an affective weapon to implement that view. Title VI has independent force, with language and emphasis in addition to that found in the Constitution. As with other provisions of the Civil Rights Act, Congress' expression of its policy to end racial discrimination may independently proscribe conduct that the Constitution does not. However, we need not decide the congruence—or lack of congruence—of the controlling statute and the Constitution since the meaning of the Title VI ban on exclusion is crystal clear: Race cannot be the basis of excluding anyone from participation in a federally funded program....

City of Richmond v. J.A. Croson Company   MELVIN UROFKSY

One of the major issues in the debate over civil rights has been the problem of affirmative action, of how much preference, if any, society should provide groups that have historically been the victims of discrimination in order to help them compete in the future on an equal basis. Both Congress and the Executive have adopted affirmative action programs in different contexts, and in many instances these have become the models for state and local affirmative action efforts.

The Supreme Court in several cases beginning with *Bakke* had upheld the idea of affirmative action, although in certain instances it had ruled the particular program impermissible under the Equal Protection Clause. In a major decision in 1981, it had affirmed a congressional set-aside program in which a certain percentage of contracts in a federally-financed program had to be reserved for minority contractors, which Congress defined with some specificity (*Fullilove v. Klutznick*).

The city council of Richmond, Virginia, in establishing a set-aside program for its expenditures, adopted the same definition of minorities as the one Congress had used. The J.A. Croson Company bid on a contract to replace toilet fixtures in the city jail, and then began searching for a minority contractor to supply some of the equipment. At first it could find no one interested, and when it did find a firm, the resulting costs pushed the total price above the contract limit. Croson asked the city to revise the contract, or excuse it from the set-aside; the city refused, and Croson sued.

A majority of the Court, for a variety of reasons, found the Richmond program unconstitutional. Justice O'Connor's majority opinion held that the city had failed to establish a compelling governmental interest, and that it had not narrowly tailored its plan to meet specific goals. She also drew a distinction between the powers granted to Congress under the Fourteenth Amendment, and those that could be exercised by the states, indicating that state and local governments had far less leeway than Congress in attempting to remediate social problems. O'Connor then indicated the criteria she believed would be appropriate in measuring the validity of a local program.

The immediate reaction to the decision was consternation on the part of many cities and states which had set-aside programs, and an increase in litigation by majority contractors challenging these programs. There is a difference of opinion whether the Court's criteria merely require better justification and drafting of set-aside programs, or whether the whole idea of affirmative action plans of any sort may now be constitutionally suspect.

> ▶ Does Justice O'Connor's decision forbid all local set-aside programs, or does she indicate that some programs may be permissible? If so, what criteria does she establish?
>
> ▶ Do you agree with the distinction she draws between the powers of Congress under the Fourteenth Amendment and those of the states? Can you conceive of a plan where Congress might delegate some of that authority?

City of Richmond v. J.A. Croson Company 109 S.CT. 706 (1989)

Justice O'CONNOR announced the judgment of the Court in which the Chief Justice and Justices WHITE, STEVENS, SCALIA, and KENNEDY joined in parts; Justices BRENNAN, MARSHALL, and BLACKMUN dissented.

In this case, we confront once again the tension between the Fourteenth Amendment's guarantee of equal treatment to all citizens, and the use of race-based measures to ameliorate the effects of past discrimination on the opportunities enjoyed by members of minority groups in our society. In *Fullilove v. Klutznick* (1980), we held that a congressional program requiring that 10% of certain federal construction grants be awarded to minority contractors did not violate the equal protection principles embodied in the Due Process Clause of the Fifth Amendment. Relying largely on our decision in *Fullilove*, some lower federal courts have applied a similar standard of review in assessing the constitutionality of state and local minority set-aside provisions under the Equal Protection Clause of the Fourteenth Amendment. Since our decision two Terms ago in *Wygant v. Jackson Board of Education* (1986), the lower federal courts have attempted to apply its standards in evaluating the constitutionality of state and local programs which allocate a portion of public contracting opportunities exclusively to minority-owned businesses. We noted probable jurisdiction in this case to consider the applicability of our decision in *Wygant* to a minority set-aside program adopted by the city of Richmond, Virginia.

On April 11, 1983, the Richmond City Council adopted the Minority Business Utilization Plan (the Plan). The Plan required prime contractors to whom the city awarded construction contracts to subcontract at least 30% of the dollar amount of the contract to one or more Minority Business Enterprises (MBEs). The 30% set-aside did not apply to city contracts awarded to minority-owned prime contractors.

The Plan defined an MBE as "[a] business at least fifty-one (51) percent of which is owned and controlled...by minority group members." "Minority group members" were defined as "[c]itizens of the United States who are Blacks, Spanish-speaking, Orientals, Indians, Eskimos, or Aleuts." There was not geographic limit to the Plan; an otherwise qualified MBE from anywhere in the United States could avail itself of the 30% set-aside. The Plan declared that it was "remedial" in nature, and enacted "for the purpose of promot-

ing wider participation by minority business enterprises in the construction of public projects." The Plan expired on June 30, 1988, and was in effect for approximately five years.

The Plan authorized the Director of the Department of General Services to promulgate
rules which "shall allow waivers in those individual situations where a contractor can prove
to the satisfaction of the director that the requirements herein cannot be achieved." To this
end, the Director promulgated Contract Clauses, Minority Business Utilization Plan....

Opponents of the ordinance questioned both its wisdom and its legality. They argued
that a disparity between minorities in the population of Richmond and the number of
prime contracts awarded to MBEs had little probative value in establishing discrimination
in the construction industry. Representatives of various contractors' associations questioned whether there were enough MBEs in the Richmond area to satisfy the 30% set-aside
requirement. Mr. Murphy noted that only 4.7% of all construction firms in the United States
were minority owned and that 41% of these were located in California, New York, Illinois,
Florida, and Hawaii. He predicted that the ordinance would thus lead to a windfall for the
few minority firms in Richmond.

The parties and their supporting *amici* fight an initial battle over the scope of the city's
power to adopt legislation designed to address the effects of past discrimination. Relying on
our decision in *Wygant*, appellee argues that the city must limit any race-based remedial
efforts to eradicating the effects of its own prior discrimination. This is essentially the position taken by the Court of Appeals below. Appellant argues that our decision in *Fullilove* is
controlling, and that as a result the city of Richmond enjoys sweeping legislative power to
define and attack the effects of prior discrimination in its local construction industry. We
find that neither of these two rather stark alternatives can withstand analysis.

In *Fullilove*, we upheld the minority set-aside contained in the Public Works Employment
Act of 1977 against a challenge based on the equal protection component of the Due Process
Clause. The Act authorized a four billion dollar appropriation for federal grants to state and
local governments for use in public works projects. The primary purpose of the Act was to
give the national economy a quick boost in a recessionary period; funds had to be committed
to state or local grantees by September 30, 1977. The Act also contained the following requirement: "Except to the extent the Secretary determines otherwise, no grant shall be made
under this Act...unless the applicant gives satisfactory assurance to the Secretary that at least
10 per centum of the amount of each grant shall be expended for minority business enterprises." MBEs were defined as businesses effectively controlled by "citizens of the United
States who are Negroes, Spanish-speaking, Orientals, Indians, Eskimos, and Aleuts."

The principal opinion in *Fullilove*, written by Chief Justice Burger, did not employ "strict
scrutiny" or any other traditional standard of equal protection review. The Chief Justice
noted at the outset that although racial classifications call for close examination, the Court
was at the same time, "bound to approach [its] task with appropriate deference to the
Congress, a co-equal branch charged by the Constitution with the power to 'provide for
the...general Welfare of the United States' and 'to enforce by appropriate legislation,' the
equal protection guarantees of the Fourteenth Amendment."

Appellant and its supporting *amici* rely heavily on *Fullilove* for the proposition that a city
council, like Congress, need not make specific findings of discrimination to engage in race-

conscious relief. Thus, appellant argues "[i]t would be a perversion of federalism to hold that the federal government has a compelling interest in remedying the effects of racial discrimination in its own public works program, but a city government does not."

What appellant ignores is that Congress, unlike any State or political subdivision, has a specific constitutional mandate to enforce the dictates of the Fourteenth Amendment. The power to "enforce" may at times also include the power to define situations which *Congress* determines threatened principles of equality and to adopt prophylactic rules to deal with those situations. The Civil War Amendments themselves worked a dramatic change in the balance between congressional and state power over matters of race. Speaking of the Thirteenth and Fourteenth Amendments in *Ex Parte Virginia* (1880), the Court stated: "They were intended to be, what they really are, limitations of the powers of the States and enlargements of the power of Congress."

That Congress may identify and redress the effects of society-wide discrimination does not mean that, *a fortiori*, the States and their political subdivisions are free to decide that such remedies are appropriate. Section 1, of the Fourteenth Amendment is an explicit *constraint* on state power, and the States must undertake any remedial efforts in accordance with that provision. To hold otherwise would be to cede control over the content of the Equal Protection Clause to the 50 state legislatures and their myriad political subdivisions. The mere recitation of a benign or compensatory purpose for the use of a racial classification would essentially entitle the States to exercise the full power of Congress under Section 5 of the Fourteenth Amendment and insulate any racial classification from judicial scrutiny under Section 1. We believe that such a result would be contrary to the intentions of the Framers of the Fourteenth Amendment, who desired to place clear limits on the States' use of race as a criterion for legislative action, and to have the federal courts enforce those limitations.

The Equal Protection Clause of the Fourteenth Amendment provides that "[N]o state shall...deny to *any person* within its jurisdiction the equal protection of laws" (emphasis added). As this Court has noted in the past, the "rights created by the first section of the Fourteenth Amendment are, by its terms, guaranteed to the individual. The rights established are personal rights." The Richmond Plan denies certain citizens the opportunity to compete for a fixed percentage of public contracts bases solely upon their race. To whatever racial group these citizens belong, their "personal rights" to be treated with equal dignity and respect are implicated by a rigid rule erecting race as the sole criterion in an aspect of public decisionmaking.

Appellant argues that it is attempting to remedy various forms of past discrimination that are alleged to be responsible for the small number of minority businesses in the local contracting industry. Among these the city cites the exclusion of blacks from skilled construction trade unions and training programs. This past discrimination has prevented them "from following the traditional path from laborer to entrepreneur." The city also lists a host of nonracial factors which would seem to face a member of any racial group attempting to establish a new business enterprise, such as deficiencies in working capital, inability to meet bonding requirements, unfamiliarity with bidding procedures, and disability caused by an inadequate track record.

While there is no doubt that the sorry history of both private and public discrimination in this country has contributed to a lack of opportunities for black entrepreneurs, this observation, standing alone, cannot justify a rigid racial quota in the awarding of public contracts in Richmond, Virginia. Like the claim that discrimination in primary and secondary schooling justifies a rigid racial preference in medical school admissions, an amorphous claim that there has been past discrimination in a particular industry cannot justify the use of an unyielding racial quota.

It is sheer speculation how many minority firms there would be in Richmond absent past societal discrimination, just as it was sheer speculation how many minority medical students would have been admitted to the medical school at Davis absent past discrimination in educational opportunities. Defining these sorts of injuries as "identified discrimination" would give local governments license to create a patchwork of racial preferences based on statistical generalizations about any particular field of endeavor.

Reliance on the disparity between the number of prime contracts awarded to minority firms and the minority population of the city of Richmond is similarly misplaced. There is no doubt that "[w]here gross statistical disparities can be shown, they alone in a proper case may constitute prima facie proof of a pattern or practice of discrimination" under Title VII. But it is equally clear that "[w]hen special qualifications are required to fill particular jobs, comparisons to the general population (rather than to the smaller group of individuals who possess the necessary qualifications) may have little probative value."

In the employment context, we have recognized that for certain entry level positions requiring minimal training, statistical comparisons of the racial composition of an employer's workforce to the racial composition of the relevant population may be probative of a pattern of discrimination. But where special qualifications are necessary, the relevant statistical pool for purposes of demonstrating discriminatory exclusion must be the number of minorities qualified to undertake the particular task.

In this case, the city does not even know how many MBEs in the relevant market are qualified to undertake prime or subcontracting work in public construction projects. Nor does the city know what percentage of total city construction dollars minority firms now receive as subcontractors on prime contracts let by the city.

To a large extent, the set-aside of subcontracting dollars seems to rest on the unsupported assumption that white prime contractors simply will not hire minority firms. Indeed, there is evidence in this record that overall minority participation in city contracts in Richmond is seven to eight percent, and that minority contractor participation in Community Block Development Grant construction projects is 17% to 22%. Without any information on minority participation in subcontracting, it is quite simply impossible to evaluate overall minority representation in the city's construction expenditures....

In sum, none of the evidence presented by the city points to any identified discrimination in the Richmond construction industry. We, therefore, hold that the city has failed to demonstrate a compelling interest in apportioning public contracting opportunities on the basis of race. To accept Richmond's claim that past societal discrimination alone can serve as the basis for rigid racial preferences would be to open the door to competing claims for "remedial relief" for every disadvantaged group. The dream of a Nation of equal citizens in a society where race is irrelevant to personal opportunity and achievement would be lost in a mosaic of shifting preferences based on inherently unmeasurable claims of past wrongs. "Courts would be asked to evaluate the extent of the prejudice and consequent harm suffered by various minority groups. Those whose societal injury is thought to exceed some arbitrary level of tolerablity then would be entitled to preferential classifications...." We think such a result would be contrary to both the letter and spirit of a constitutional provision whose central command is equality.

The foregoing analysis applies only to the inclusion of blacks within the Richmond set-aside program. There is *absolutely no evidence* of past discrimination against Spanish-speaking, Oriental, Indian, Eskimo, or Aleut persons in any aspect of the Richmond construction industry. The District Court took judicial notice of the fact that the vast majority of "minority" persons in Richmond were black. It may well be that Richmond has never has an Aleut or Eskimo citizen. The random inclusion of racial groups that, as a practical matter, may never have suffered from discrimination in the construction industry in Richmond, suggests that perhaps the city's purpose was not in fact to remedy past discrimination.

Because the city of Richmond has failed to identify the need for remedial action in the awarding of its public construction contracts, its treatment of its citizens on a racial basis violates the dictates of the Equal Protection Clause. Accordingly, the judgment of the Court of Appeals for the Fourth Circuit is

Affirmed.

VI Equal Protection: Gender and Sexual Preference

Frontiero v. Richardson (1973)

Rostker v. Goldberg (1981)

Mississippi University for Women v. Hogan (1982)

Romer v. Evans (1996)

United States v. Virginia (VMI) (1996)

VI Equal Protection: Gender and Sexual Preference

BARBARA A. PERRY

The constitutional basis for gender and sexual preference cases is the Equal Protection Clause of the Fourteenth Amendment. The clause was virtually a dead letter until the Warren Court resuscitated it in racial discrimination cases of the 1950s. If the framers of the 14th Amendment intended the Equal Protection Clause to guarantee some level of equality (even if narrowly conceived by them in the 1860s), then the interpretation of equal protection was going to entail interpretation of *classifications*. When laws classified people and singled them out for different treatment based on that classification, the question arose whether a group so classified was receiving equal treatment under the law.

Consequently, the courts developed tests and standards by which to measure these classifications in order to determine if a group was not receiving equal protection. Conservative courts, which placed a premium on deference to legislatures in the 19th century and the first half of the 20th century, developed a very minimal standard for judging equal protection. They would ask: "Can the classifications in a challenged law be upheld on the basis of implied or stated legislative goals?"

Posing that question, courts applied the *"rational-relation"* test between legislative ends and classifications resulting in the unequal treatment of different groups of people. Even a *loose fit* between legislative ends and means was enough for courts to defer to legislatures in the pre-Warren Court era. One of the most infamous illustrations of the application of the "old" equal protection's "rational-relation" test is *Buck v. Bell* (1927), which upheld a Virginia statute allowing sterilization of people then classified as mental defectives who were confined to state institutions.

After 1937 the Court became far more willing to protect civil rights and liberties rather than the economic rights of business. Thus, the Warren and Burger Courts still applied the "rational-relation" test, but confined its use to legislative classifications in the sphere of economic regulation. In other words, the Court deferred to legislative attempts to regulate business. The Supreme Court's metamorphosis in the 1930s provided the genesis of the "new" interpretation of equal protection. In his now famous Footnote 4 of the 1938 case *U.S. v. Carolene Products Co.*, Justice Harlan Stone commented about the need for special protection for "discrete and insular" minorities. Any classification involving them would thereafter trigger *"strict scrutiny"* of legislation that affected such minorities.

During the Warren era in the 1950s, the Supreme Court began to impose strict scrutiny on laws burdening suspect classes (discrete and insular minorities) and on fundamental rights (those allowing free and open access to the political process) to protect civil rights and liberties. The Court had applied strict scrutiny even before the 1950s. In the 1944 Japanese internment case, the Court declared: "All legal restrictions which curtail the civil rights of a single racial group are immediately suspect." Nevertheless, the Court upheld the internment based on the wartime emergency. As applied by the Warren Court and thereafter, the strict judicial scrutiny test, unlike the rational-relation test, usually does not defer to the legislative process. Under strict scrutiny, the Court assumes the legislature has acted unconstitutionally until it can prove that its action is justified by a *compelling state interest.* There must be an *exact fit* between classifications and goals. Hence, the Warren Court exercised a two-tiered approach to equal protection. The first tier triggered strict scrutiny; the second level activated the rational-relation test.

The Supreme Court under Chief Justice Warren Burger (1969-86) seemed to have difficulty deciding on the definition of suspect classifications. So in a sense, it split the difference and created a middle tier of review. This *"intermediate scrutiny"* requires that the government demonstrate that its interests are important, if not compelling. The middle tier of review calls for a *close fit* between legislative classifications and goals. It is into this middle level of review that the Court eventually placed gender classifications. Thus far, neither gender nor sexual preference categories have earned the Court's highest level of review—strict scrutiny.

- There is no indication that the Framers of the Fourteenth Amendment meant to include women within the boundaries of the Equal Protection Clause. Should the Court have extended its meaning, making the Constitution flexible in response to the times, or should the justices go no further than their understanding of the Framers' original intent?

- Is it the Court's job to keep the Constitution "current," or should that only be accomplished through the amendment process?

- Some commentators have suggested that "equality" is an "empty idea" that is logically unsupportable, and therefore the Court should abandon the Equal Protection Clause except in instances of gross racial prejudice. In response, defenders of equality note its moral utility, and claim that a society which discriminates against any group is an unfair society. How far should the Court go in extending the umbrella of equal protection? Besides race, what should be a suspect category: Gender? Age? Sexual preference? Poverty? Disability?

- Is there any evidence to indicate that the United States places too much emphasis on equality to the detriment of individual liberty? Has equal protection jurisprudence created a culture of victimization in the United States?

Frontiero v. Richardson   MELVIN UROFSKY

The Court on several occasions has been asked to include gender as a suspect classification, beginning in 1971 with *Reed v. Reed*, a case that challenged a state law giving preference to men over women as administrators of estates. The Court unanimously struck down that statute, but did so on a simple rational basis test, the same kind of test applied to economic and regulatory legislation. Although the Court refused to extend to gender the same status as race in equal protection analysis, it became clear in subsequent cases that in fact the justices were examining gender classification with greater scrutiny than is normally applied in the minimal "reasonable relationship" test.

Frontiero challenged a federal law that allowed male members of the armed services to claim an automatic dependency allowance for their wives, regardless of whether the wives worked or how much the husbands contributed to their support. Under the same law a woman in the armed services, in order to secure the dependency allowance for her spouse, had to prove that she contributed over one-half of his support. While the justices agreed that the law violated the Equal Protection Clause, Justice Brennan could only get three of his colleagues to support his position that gender should be a suspect classification. Justices Powell, Burger and Blackmun concurred in the result, but on a rational test basis.

In subsequent cases, the Court has adopted what some scholars have called "intermediate scrutiny," a test that requires more evidence from the government for the need of gender classification, but not as much as in racial classifications.

- Should gender be a suspect category; that is, should any law that classifies men and women differently be treated as presumptively unconstitutional?

- Are the Court's holdings in the following cases consistent with the letter and/or spirit of the Equal Protection Clause?

- *Craig v. Boren* (1976), striking down an Oklahoma law prohibiting sale of "non-intoxicating" 3.2% beer to males under 21 and females under 18.

- *Michael M. v. Superior Court* (1981), upholding a California "statutory rape" law punishing the male, but not the female partner in intercourse when the female is under 18 and not the male's wife.

- *Johnson v. Transportation Agency, Santa Clara County* (1987), upholding an affirmative action program for women.

- *New York State Club Association v. New York City* (1988), upholding a city ordinance banning gender discrimination in clubs with more than 400 members or that did significant business with non-members or that served meals on a regular basis.

Frontiero v. Richardson   411 U.S. 677 (1973)

Mr. Justice BRENNAN announced the judgment of the Court in an opinion in which Mr. Justice DOUGLAS, Mr. Justice WHITE, and Mr. Justice MARSHALL join.

The question before us concerns the right of a female member of the uniformed service to claim her spouse as a "dependent" for the purposes of obtaining increased quarters allowances and medical and dental benefits on an equal footing with male members. Under the statutes, a serviceman may claim his wife as a "dependent" without regard to whether she is in fact dependent upon him for any part of her support but a servicewoman may not claim her husband as a "dependent" unless he is in fact dependent upon her for over one-half of his support....

At the outset, appellants contend that classifications based upon sex, like classifications based upon race, alienage, and national origin, are inherently suspect and must therefore be subjected to close judicial scrutiny. We agree....

There can be no doubt that our Nation has had a long and unfortunate history of sex discrimination. Traditionally, such discrimination was rationalized by an attitude of "romantic paternalism" which, in practical effect put women, not on a pedestal, but in a cage. As a result of notions such as these, our statute books gradually became laden with gross, stereo-typed distinctions between the sexes and, indeed, throughout much of the 19th century the position of women in our society was, in many respects, comparable to that of blacks under the pre-Civil War slave codes. Neither slaves nor women could hold office, serve on juries, or bring suit in their own names, and married women traditionally were denied the legal capacity to hold or convey property or to serve as legal guardians of their own children. And although blacks were guaranteed the right to vote in 1870, women were denied even that right until adoption of the 19th Amendment half a century later.

It is true, of course, that the position of women in America has improved markedly in recent decades. Nevertheless, it can hardly be doubted that, in part because of the high visibility of the sex characteristic, women still face pervasive, although at times more subtle, discrimination in our educational institutions, in the job market and, perhaps most conspicuously, in the political arena. Moreover, since sex, like race and national origin, is an immutable characteristic determined solely by the accident of birth, the imposition of special disabilities upon the members of a particular sex because of their sex would seem to violate "the basic concept of our system that legal burdens should bear some relationship to individual responsibility." And what differentiates sex from such nonsuspect statuses as intelligence or physical disability, and aligns it with the recognized suspect criteria, is that the sex characteristic frequently bears no relation to ability to perform or contribute to society. As a result, statutory distinctions between the sexes often have the effect of invidiously relegating the entire class of females to inferior legal status without regard to the actual capabilities of its individual members....We can only conclude that classifications based upon sex, like classifications based upon race, alienage, or national origin, are inherently suspect, and must therefore be subjected to strict judicial scrutiny. Applying the analysis mandated by that stricter standard of review, it is clear that the statutory scheme now before us is constitutionally invalid.

The Government concedes that the differential treatment accorded men and women under these statutes serves no purpose other than mere "administrative convenience." It maintains that, as an empirical matter, wives in our society frequently are dependent upon their husbands, while husbands rarely are dependent upon their wives. Thus, the Government argues that Congress might reasonably have concluded that it would be both cheaper and easier simply conclusively to presume that wives of male members are financially dependent upon their husbands, while burdening female members with the task of establishing dependency in fact. The Government offers no concrete evidence, however, tending to support its view that such differential treatment in fact saves the Government any money. In order to satisfy the demands of strict judicial scrutiny, the Government must demonstrate, for example, that it is actually cheaper to grant increased benefits with respect to all male members, than it is to determine which male members are in fact entitled to such benefits and to grant increased benefits only to those members whose wives actually meet the dependency requirement. In any case, our prior decisions make clear that, although efficacious administration of governmental programs is not without some importance, "the Constitution recognizes higher values than speed and efficiency." When we enter the realm of "strict judicial scrutiny," there can be no doubt that "administrative convenience" is not a shibboleth. On the contrary, any statutory scheme which draws a sharp line between the sexes, solely for the purpose of achieving administrative convenience, necessarily commands "dissimilar treatment for men and women who are similarly situated," and therefore involves the "very kind of arbitrary legislative choice forbidden by the Constitution.

Reversed.

Mr. Justice STEWART concurs in the judgment, agreeing that the statutes before us work an invidious discrimination in violation of the Constitution.

Mr. Justice POWELL, with whom Chief Justice BURGER and Mr. Justice BLACKMUN join, concurring in the judgment.

It is unnecessary for the Court in this case to characterize sex as a suspect classification, with all of the far-reaching implications of such a holding. Reed, which abundantly supports our decision today, did not add sex to the narrowly limited group of classifications which are inherently suspect. In my view, we can and should decide this case on the authority of Reed and reserve for the future any expansion of its rationale.

There is another, and I find compelling, reason for deferring a general categorizing of sex classifications as invoking the strictest test of judicial scrutiny. The Equal Rights Amendment, which if adopted will resolve the substance of this precise question, has been approved by the Congress. By acting prematurely and unnecessarily, as I view it, the Court has assumed a decisional responsibility at the very time when state legislatures, functioning within the traditional democratic process, are debating the proposed Amendment. It seems to me that this reaching out to preempt by judicial action a major political decision which is currently in process of resolution does not reflect appropriate respect for duly prescribed legislative process....

[Justice REHNQUIST dissented, citing the opinion of District Court Judge Rives, who doubted that the statute had a sex classification, and even if it did, it made no difference, since gender did not constitute a "suspect" classification.]

Rostker v. Goldberg MELVIN UROFSKY

In 1980 President Carter, in the light of a deteriorating international scene, asked Congress to reinstitute mandatory draft registration. Congress did so, but did not agree to the President's request that women as well as men should have to register, since it was firmly established policy that women would not be sent into combat. The all-male draft had never been challenged before, but two factors made a challenge to the 1980 law all but inevitable. First, women had become a significant part of the American military, and second, the women's movement has "raised the consciousness" of both men and women over institutionalized gender discrimination.

The Court, speaking through the Chief Justice, conceded that the law distinguished between men and women, but found the necessary justification in the fact that the Constitution had given Congress specific authority to provide for the national defense and to raise armies, and that it had chosen to do so with a policy that excluded women from combat—a policy whose wisdom the Court, without going into the matter, believed justifiable under Congress's broad discretion in this area.

Justice White dissented primarily on grounds of statutory interpretation, reading the legislative history in a manner different from that of the Chief Justice. Justice Marshall attacked the policy on Equal Protection grounds, but he too seemed more concerned with the legislative history than a straight-out equal protection analysis. Justice Brennan joined both dissents.

> ▶ Should the establishment and support of the armed forces be totally within congressional purview, or should it be subject to judicial review as are other laws?
>
> ▶ Can the decision to exclude women from combat, which is at the heart of the majority's reasoning, be justified under the Equal Protection Clause?
>
> ▶ If the exclusion is accepted, should other gender classifications affecting the military, such as the distinction in dependent pay in the *Frontiero* case, also be exempt from judicial scrutiny?
>
> ▶ Compare the analysis in this case to that in *Mississippi University for Women v. Hogan*; which is more persuasive?

Bernard Rostker v. Robert L. Goldberg 453 U.S. 57 (1981)

Justice REHNQUIST delivered the opinion of the Court; Justices BRENNAN, WHITE, and MARSHALL dissented.

The question presented is whether the Military Selective Service Act violates the Fifth Amendment to the United States Constitution in authorizing the President to require the registration of males and not females.

Congress is given the power under the Constitution "To raise and support Armies," "To provide and maintain a Navy," and "To make Rules for the Government and Regulation of the land naval Forces." Pursuant to this grant of authority Congress has enacted the Military Selective Service Act of 1976 (the MSSA or the Act). Section 3 of the Act empowers the President, by proclamation, to require the registration of "every male citizen" and male resident aliens between the ages of 18 and 26. The purpose of this registration is to facilitate any eventual conscription. The MSSA registration provision serves no other purpose beyond providing a pool for subsequent induction.

Registration for the draft had been discontinued in 1975. In early 1980, President Carter determined that it was necessary to reactivate the draft registration process. The immediate impetus for this decision was the Soviet armed invasion of Afghanistan. According to the administration's witnesses before the Senate Armed Services Committee, the resulting crisis in Southwestern Asia convinced the President that the "time has come" to use his present authority to require registration...as a necessary step to preserving or enhancing our national security interests."...The President also recommended that Congress take action to amend the MSSA to permit the registration and conscription of women as well as men.

Congress agreed that it was necessary to reactivate the registration process, and allocated funds for that purpose in a Joint Resolution. Although Congress considered the question at great length, it declined to amend the MSSA to permit the registration of women.

On July 2, 1980, the President, by Proclamation, ordered the registration of specified groups of young men pursuant to the authority by Section 3 of the Act. Registration was to commence on July 21, 1980.

Whenever called upon to judge the constitutionality of an Act of Congress—"the gravest and most delicate duty that this Court is called upon to perform,"—the Court accords "great weight to the decisions of Congress." The Congress is a coequal branch of government whose Members take the same oath we do to uphold the Constitution of the United States. As Justice Frankfurter noted, we must have "due regard to the fact that this Court is not exercising a primary judgment but is sitting in judgment upon those who also have taken the oath to observe the Constitution and who have the responsibility for carrying on government." The customary deference accorded the judgments of Congress is certainly appropriate when, as here, Congress specifically considered the question of the Act's constitutionality.

Not only is the scope of Congress' constitutional power in this area broad, but the lack of competence on the part of the courts is marked....

None of this is to say that Congress is free to disregard the Constitution when it acts in the area of military affairs. In that area, as any other, Congress remains subject to the limitations of the Due Process Clause, but the tests and limitations to be applied may differ because of the military context. We of course do not abdicate our ultimate responsibility to decide the constitutional question, but simply recognize that the Constitution itself requires such deference to congressional choice. In deciding the question before us we must be particularly careful not to substitute our judgment of what is desirable for that of Congress, or our own evaluation of evidence for a reasonable evaluation by the Legislative Branch.

No one could deny that under the test of *Craig v. Boren*, the Government's interest in raising and supporting armies is an "important governmental interest." Congress and its Committees carefully considered and debated two alternative means of furthering that interest: the first was to register only males for potential conscription, and the other was to register both sexes. Congress chose the former alternative. When that decision is challenged on equal protection grounds, the question a court must decide is not which alternative it would have chosen, had it been the primary decision maker, but whether that chosen by Congress denies equal protection of the laws.

This case is quite different from several of the gender-based discrimination cases we have considered in that, despite appellees' assertions, Congress did not act "unthinkingly" or "reflexively and not for any considered reason." The question of registering women for the draft not only received considerable national attention and was the subject of wide-ranging public debate, but also was extensively considered by Congress in hearings, floor debate, and in committee. Hearings held by both Houses of Congress in response to the President's request for authorization to register women adduced extensive testimony and evidence concerning the issue. These hearings built on other hearings held the previous year addressed to the same question.

The foregoing clearly establishes that the decision to exempt women from registration was not the "'accidental by-product of a traditional way of thinking about females.'" The issue was considered at great length, and Congress clearly expressed its purpose and intent....

Congress determined that any future draft, which would be facilitated by the registration scheme, would be characterized by a need for combat troops. The Senate Report explained, in a specific finding later adopted by both Houses, that "[i]f mobilization were to be ordered in a wartime scenario, the primary manpower need would be for combat replacements." Congress' determination that the need would be for combat troops if a draft took place was sufficiently supported by testimony adduced at the hearings so that the courts are not free to make their own judgment on the question. The purpose of registration, therefore, was to prepare for a draft of *combat* troops.

Women as a group, however, unlike men as a group, are not eligible for combat. The restrictions on the participation of women in combat in the Navy and Air Force are statutory. Under 10 U.S.C. Section 6015, "women may not be assigned to duty on vessels or in aircraft that are engaged in combat missions," and under 10 U.S.C. Section 8549 female members of the Air Force "may not be assigned to duty in aircraft engaged in combat missions." The Army and Marine Corps preclude the use of women in combat as a matter of established policy. Congress specifically recognized and endorsed the exclusion of women from combat in exempting women from registration. In the words of the Senate Report:

> The principle that women should not intentionally and routinely engage in
> combat is fundamental, and enjoys wide support among our people. It is uni-
> versally supported by military leaders who have testified before the

Committee....Current law and policy exclude women from being assigned to combat in our military forces, and the Committee reaffirms this policy.

The existence of the combat restrictions clearly indicates the basis for Congress' decision to exempt women from registration. The purpose of registration was to prepare for a draft of combat troops. Since women are excluded from combat, Congress concluded that they would not be needed in the event of a draft, and therefore decided not to register them. Again turning to the Senate Report:

In the Committee's view, the starting point for any discussion of the appropriateness of registering women for the draft is the question of the proper role of women in combat....The policy precluding the use of women in combat is, in the Committee's view, the most important reason, for not including women in a registration system.

The District Court stressed that the military need for women was irrelevant to the issue of their registration. As that court put it: "Congress could not constitutionally require registration under the MSSA of only black citizens or only white citizens, or single our any political or religious group simply because those groups contain sufficient persons to fill the needs of the Selective Service System." This reasoning is beside the point. The reason women are exempt from registration is not because military needs can be met by drafting men. This is not a case of Congress arbitrarily choosing to burden one of two similarly situated groups, such as would be the case with an all-black or all-white, or an all-Catholic or all-Lutheran, or an all-Republican or all-Democratic registration. Men and women, because of the combat restrictions on women, are simply not similarly situated for purposes of a draft or registration for a draft.

Congress' decision to authorize the registration of only men, therefore, does not violate the Due Process Clause. The exemption of women from registration is not only sufficiently but also closely related to Congress' purpose in authorizing registration. The fact that Congress and the Executive have decided that women should not serve in combat fully justifies Congress in not authorizing their registration, since the purpose of registration is to develop a pool of potential combat troops. As was the case in *Schlesinger v. Ballard, supra*, "the gender classification is not invidious, but rather realistically reflects the fact that the sexes are not similarly situated" in this case. The Constitution requires that Congress treat similarly situated persons similarly, not that it engage in gestures of superficial equality....

Mississippi University for Women v. Hogan   MELVIN UROFSKY

Mississippi University for Women had traditionally been an all-women's school, and had continued that policy when it established a nursing program, although it allowed men to take some classes. Joe Hogan wanted to enroll in the program, since it would have been more convenient for him to attend MUW than another state nursing school much farther from his home, but he was turned down on the sole grounds of gender. He sued, and Justice O'Connor applied what amounted almost to strict scrutiny in holding the all-women school unsupportable under the Equal Protection Clause.

In her analysis, Justice O'Connor rejected all the arguments put forward by the state and by *amici* in support of single-sex schools, arguments which Justice Powell found convincing.

> ▶ If one applies Justice O'Connor's analysis in this case of gender classification to the facts in *Rostker v. Goldberg*, what results would the Court have reached?
>
> ▶ Which analysis do you find more persuasive, that of the majority or Justice Powell's dissent? Why?

Mississippi University for Women v. Hogan 458 U.S. 718 (1982)

Justice O'CONNOR delivered the opinion of the Court; the CHIEF JUSTICE and Justices BLACKMUN, POWELL, and REHNQUIST dissented.

This case presents the narrow issue of whether a state statute that excludes males from enrolling in a state-supported professional nursing school violates the Equal Protection Clause of the Fourteenth Amendment.

The facts are not in dispute. In 1884, the Mississippi Legislature created the Mississippi Industrial Institute and College for the Education of White Girls of the State of Mississippi, now the oldest state-supported all-female college in the United States. The school, known today as Mississippi University for Women (MUW), has from its inception limited its enrollment to women.

In 1971, MUW established a School of Nursing, initially offering a 2-year associate degree. Three years later, the school instituted a 4-year baccalaureate program in nursing and today also offers a graduate program. The School of Nursing has its own faculty and administrative officers and establishes its own criteria for admission.

Respondent, Joe Hogan, is a registered nurse but does not hold a baccalaureate degree in nursing. Since 1974, he has worked as a nursing supervisor in a medical center in Columbus, the city in which MUW is located. In 1979, Hogan applied for admission to the MUW School of Nursing's baccalaureate program. Although he was otherwise qualified, he was denied admission to the School of Nursing solely because of his sex. School officials informed him that he could audit the courses in which he was interested, but could not enroll for credit.

Hogan filed an action in the United States District Court for the Northern District of Mississippi, claiming the single-sex admissions policy of MUW's School of Nursing violated the Equal Protection Clause of the Fourteenth Amendment....

We begin our analysis aided by several firmly established principles. Because the challenged policy expressly discriminates among applicants on the basis of gender, it is subject to scrutiny under the Equal Protection Clause of the Fourteenth Amendment. That this statutory policy discriminates against males rather than against females does not exempt it from scrutiny or reduce the standard of review. Our decisions also establish that the party seeking to uphold a statute that classifies individuals on the basis of their gender must carry the burden of showing an "exceedingly persuasive justification" for the classification. The burden is met only by showing at least that the classification serves "important governmental objectives and that the discriminatory means employed" are "substantially related to the achievement of those objectives."

Although the test for determining the validity of a gender-based classification is straightforward, it must be applied free of fixed notions concerning the roles and abilities of males and females. Care must be taken in ascertaining whether the statutory objective itself reflects archaic and stereotypic notions. Thus, if the statutory objective is to exclude or "protect" members of one gender because they are presumed to suffer from an inherent handicap or to be innately inferior, the objective itself is illegitimate.

If the State's objective is legitimate and important, we next determine whether the requisite direct, substantial relationship between objective and means is present. The purpose of requiring that close relationship is to assure that the validity of a classification is determined through reasoned analysis rather than through the mechanical application of traditional, often inaccurate, assumptions about the proper roles of men and women. The need for the requirement is amply revealed by reference to the broad range of statutes already invalidated by this Court, statutes that relied upon the simplistic, outdated assumption that gender could be used as a "proxy for other, more germane basis of classification," to establish a link between objective and classification.

Applying this framework, we now analyze the arguments advanced by the State to justify its refusal to allow males to enroll for credit in MUW's School of Nursing.

The State's primary justification for maintaining the single-sex admissions policy of MUW's School of Nursing is that it compensates for discrimination against women and, therefore, constitutes educational affirmative action. As applied to the School of Nursing, we find the State's argument unpersuasive.

In limited circumstances, a gender-based classification favoring one sex can be justified if it intentionally and directly assists members of the sex that is disproportionately burdened. However, we consistently have emphasized that "the mere recitation of a benign, compensatory purpose is not an automatic shield which protects against any inquiry into the actual purposes underlying a statutory scheme...."

Mississippi has made no showing that women lacked opportunities to obtain training in the field of nursing or to attain positions of leadership in that field when the MUW School of Nursing opened its door or that women currently are deprived of such opportunities. In fact, in 1970, the year before the School of Nursing's first class enrolled, women earned 94 percent of the nursing baccalaureate degrees conferred in Mississippi and 98.6 percent of the degrees earned nation-wide. As one would expect, the labor force reflects the same predominance of women in nursing. When MUW's School of Nursing began operation, nearly 98 percent of all employed registered nurses were female.

Rather than compensate for discriminatory barriers faced by women, MUW's policy of excluding males from admission to the School of Nursing tends to perpetuate the stereotyped view of nursing as an exclusively woman's job. By assuring that Mississippi allots more openings in its state-supported nursing schools to women than it does to men, MUW's admissions policy lends credibility to the old view that women, not men, should become nurses, and makes the assumption that nursing is a field for women a self-fulfilling prophecy. Thus, we conclude that, although the State recited a "benign, compensatory purpose," it failed to establish that the alleged objective is the actual purpose underlying the discriminatory classification.

The policy is invalid also because it fails the second part of the equal protection test, for the State has made no showing that the gender-based classification is substantially and directly related to its proposed compensatory objective. To the contrary, MUW's policy of permitting men to attend classes as auditors fatally undermines its claim that women, at least those in the School of Nursing, are adversely affected by the presence of men.

MUW permits men who audit to participate fully in classes. Additionally, both men and women take part in continuing education courses offered by the School of Nursing, in which regular nursing students also can enroll. The uncontroverted record reveals that admitting men to nursing classes does not affect teaching style, that the presence of men in the classroom would not affect the performance of the female nursing students, and that men in coeducational nursing schools do not dominate the classroom. In sum the record in this case is flatly inconsistent with the claim that excluding men from the School of Nursing is necessary to reach any of MUW's educational goals.

Thus, considering both the asserted interest and the relationship between the interest and the methods used by the State, we conclude that the State has fallen far short of establishing the "exceedingly persuasive justification" needed to sustain the gender-based classification. Accordingly, we hold that MUW's policy of denying males the right to enroll for credit in its School of Nursing violates the Equal Protection Clause of the Fourteenth Amendment....

Because we concluded that the State's policy of excluding males from MUW's School of Nursing violates the Equal Protection Clause of the Fourteenth Amendment, we affirm the judgment of the Court of Appeals.

It is so ordered.

Justice POWELL, with whom Justice REHNQUIST joins, dissenting.

The Court's opinion bows deeply to conformity. Left without honor—indeed, held unconstitutional—is an element of diversity that has characterized much of American education and enriched much of American life. The Court in effect holds today that no State now may provide even a single institution of higher learning open only to women students. It gives no heed to the efforts of the State of Mississippi to provide abundant opportunities for young men and young women to attend coeducational institutions, and none to the preferences of the more than 40,000 young women who over the years have evidenced their approval of an all-women's college by choosing Mississippi University for Women (MUW) over seven coeducational universities within the State. The Court decides today that the Equal Protection Clause makes it unlawful for the State to provide women with a traditionally popular and respected choice of educational environment. It does so in a case instituted by one man, who represents no class, and whose primary concern is personal convenience.

It is undisputed that women enjoy complete equality of opportunity in Mississippi's public system of higher education. Of the State's 8 universities and 16 junior colleges, all except MUW are coeducational. At least two other Mississippi universities would have provided respondent with the nursing curriculum that he wishes to pursue. No other male has joined in his complaint. The only groups with any personal acquaintance with MUW to file *amicus* briefs are female students and alumnae of MUW. And they have emphatically rejected respondent's arguments, urging that the State of Mississippi be allowed to continue offering the choice from which they have benefitted.

Nor is respondent significantly disadvantaged by MUW's all-female tradition. His constitutional complaint is based upon a single asserted harm: that he must *travel* to attend the state-supported nursing schools that concededly are available to him. The Court characterizes this injury as one of "inconvenience." This description is fair and accurate, though somewhat embarrassed by the fact that there is, of course, no constitutional right to attend a state-supported university in one's home town. Thus the Court, to redress respondent's injury of inconvenience, must rest its invalidation of MUW's single-sex program on a mode of "sexual stereotype" reasoning that has no application whatever to the respondent or the "wrong" of which he complains. At best this is anomalous. And ultimately the anomaly reveals legal error—that of applying a heightened equal protection standard, developed in cases of genuine sexual stereotyping, to a narrowly utilized state classification that provides an *additional* choice for women. Moreover, I believe that Mississippi's educational system should be upheld in the case even if this inappropriate method of analysis is applied.

Coeducation, historically, is a novel educational theory. From grade school through high school, college, and graduate and professional training, much of the Nation's population during much of our history has been educated in sexually segregated classrooms. At the college level, for instance, until recently some of the most prestigious colleges and universities—including most of the Ivy League—had long histories of single-sex education. As Harvard, Yale, and Princeton remained all-male colleges well into the second half of this century, the "Seven Sister" institutions established a parallel standard of excellence for women's colleges. Mount Holyoke, Smith, and Wellesley recently have made considered decisions to remain essentially single-sex institutions. Barnard retains its independence from Columbia, its traditional coordinate institution. Harvard and Radcliffe maintained separate admissions policies as recently at 1975.

The sexual segregation of students has been a reflection of, rather than an imposition upon, the preference of those subject to the policy. It cannot be disputed, for example, that the highly qualified women attending the leading women's colleges could have earned admission to virtually any college of their choice. Women attending such colleges have chosen to be there, usually expressing a preference for the special benefits of single-sex institutions. Similar decisions were made by the colleges that elected to remain open to women only.

The arguable benefits of single-sex colleges also continue to recognized by students of higher education. The Carnegie Commission on Higher Education has reported that it "favor[s] the continuation of colleges for women. They provide an element of diversity...and [an environment in which women] generally...speak up more in their classes,...hold more positions of leadership on campus,...and...have more role models and mentors among women teachers and administrators." A 10-year empirical study by the Cooperative Institutional Research Program of the American Council of Education and the University of California, Los Angeles, also has affirmed the distinctive benefits of single-sex colleges and universities....

Despite the continuing expressions that single-sex institutions may offer singular advantages to their students, there is no doubt that coeducational institutions are far more numerous. But their numerical predominance does not establish—in any sense properly cognizable by a court—that individual preferences for single-sex education are misguided or illegitimate, or that a State may not provide its citizens with a choice.

The issue in this case is whether a State transgresses the Constitution when—within the context of a public system that offers a diverse range of campuses, curricula, and educational alternatives—it seeks to accommodate the legitimate personal preferences of those desiring the advantages of an all-women's college. In my view, the Court errs seriously by assuming—without argument or discussion—that the equal protection standard generally applicable to sex discrimination is appropriate here. That standard was designed to free women from "archaic and overbroad generalizations...." In no previous case have we applied it to invalidate state efforts to *expand* women's choices. Nor are there prior sex discrimination decisions by this Court in which a male plaintiff, as in this case, had the choice of an equal benefit....

By applying heightened equal protection analysis to this case, the Court frustrates the liberating spirit of the Equal Protection Clause. It prohibits the States from providing women with an opportunity to choose the type of university they prefer. And yet it is these women whom the Court regards as the *victims* of an illegal, stereotyped perception of the role of women in our society. The Court reasons this way in a case in which no woman has complained, and the only complainant is a man who advances no claims on behalf of anyone else. His claim, it should be recalled, is not that he is being denied a substantive educational opportunity, or even the right to attend an all-male or a coeducational college. It is only that the colleges open to him are located at inconvenient distances.

The Court views this case as presenting a serious equal protection claim of sex discrimination. I do not, and I would sustain Mississippi's right to continue MUW on a rational-basis analysis. But I need not apply this "lowest tier" of scrutiny. I can accept for present purposes the standard applied by the Court: that there is a gender-based distinction that must serve an important governmental objective by means that are substantially related to its achievement. The record in this case reflects that MUW has a historic position in the State's educational system dating back to 1884. More than 2,000 women presently evidence their preference to MUW by having enrolled there. The choice is one that discriminated invidiously against no one. And the State's purpose in preserving that choice is legitimate and substantial. Generations of our finest minds, both among educators and students, have believed that single-sex, college-level institutions afford distinctive benefits. There are many persons, of course, who have different views. But simply because there are these differences is no reason—certainly none of constitutional dimension—to conclude that no substantial state interest is served when such a choice is made available....

A distinctive feature of America's tradition has been respect for diversity. This has been characteristic of the peoples from numerous lands who have built our country. It is the essence of our democratic system. At stake in this case as I see it is the preservation of a small aspect of this diversity. But that aspect is by no means insignificant, given our heritage of available choice between single-sex and coeducational institutions of higher learning. The Court answers that there is discrimination—not just that which may be tolerable, as for example between those candidates for admission able to contribute most to an educational institution and those able to contribute less—but discrimination of constitutional dimension. But, having found "discrimination," the Court finds it difficult to identify the victims. It hardly can claim that women are discriminated against. A constitutional case is held to exist solely because one man found it inconvenient to travel to any of the other institutions made available to him by the State of Mississippi. In essence he insists that he has a right to attend a college in his home community. This simply is not a sex discrimination case. The Equal Protection Clause was never intended to be applied to this kind of case.

[Chief Justice BURGER and Justice BLACKMUN dissented separately.]

Romer v. Evans BARBARA PERRY

Several cities in Colorado passed laws banning discrimination based on sexual orientation in housing, employment, education, public accommodations, health and welfare services, and other transactions and activities. Subsequently, voters in Colorado adopted by a statewide referendum "Amendment 2" to the state's constitution, which precluded all legislative, executive, or judicial action at any level of state or local government intended to protect the status of persons based on their "homosexual, lesbian or bisexual orientation, conduct, practices or relationships." Aggrieved homosexuals and municipalities challenged the amendment in state court. The Colorado Supreme Court eventually declared that Amendment 2 was subject to strict scrutiny under the Equal Protection Clause of the Fourteenth Amendment because it infringed on the fundamental right of gays and lesbians to participate in the political process. It returned the case to the state trial court for a decision on the merits of the case. The trial court ruled that Amendment 2 failed to satisfy the requirements of strict scrutiny.

Colorado appealed to the U.S. Supreme Court, which held that Amendment 2 did indeed violate the Equal Protection Clause of the Fourteenth Amendment. Justice Kennedy's majority opinion argued that no state may "deem a class of persons a stranger to its laws." Writing for his fellow dissenters (Chief Justice William Rehnquist and Justice Clarence Thomas), Justice Antonin Scalia angrily attacked Justice Kennedy for "imposing upon all Americans the resolution favored by the elite class from which the members of this institution are selected." Scalia asserted that if states could pass anti-sodomy laws (which the Court had upheld in 1986), they could surely bar special legal protection of homosexuals.

> ▶ What are the strengths and weaknesses of Justice Kennedy's reasoning that Colorado's Amendment 2 blocked homosexuals' access to the political process?
>
> ▶ Do you agree or disagree with Justice Scalia's conclusion to his dissent, in which he accuses the majority of "an act not of judicial judgment but of political will?" What does his statement say about the role of the Court?
>
> ▶ Does the Equal Protection Clause allow *any* classifications in the law based on sexual preference? For example, do you believe a "Don't Ask, Don't Tell" policy toward gays in the military is constitutional?

Romer v. Evans 64 LW 4353 (1996)

Justice KENNEDY delivered the opinion of the Court.

One century ago, the first Justice Harlan admonished this Court that the Constitution "neither knows nor tolerates classes among citizens." *Plessy v. Ferguson* (1896) (dissenting opinion) Unheeded then, those words now are understood to state a commitment to the law's neutrality where the rights of persons are at stake. The Equal Protection Clause enforces this principle and today requires us to hold invalid a provision of Colorado's Constitution.

The enactment challenged in this case is an amendment to the Constitution of the State of Colorado, adopted in a 1992 statewide referendum. The parties and the state courts refer to it as "Amendment 2," its designation when submitted to the voters. The impetus for the amendment and the contentious campaign that preceded its adoption came in large part from ordinances that had been passed in various Colorado municipalities....What gave rise to the statewide controversy was the protection the ordinances afforded to persons discriminated against by reason of their sexual orientation. Amendment 2 repeals these ordinances to the extent they prohibit discrimination on the basis of "homosexual, lesbian or bisexual orientation, conduct, practices or relationships." Colo. Const., Art. II, Section 30b.

Yet Amendment 2, in explicit terms, does more than repeal or rescind these provisions. It prohibits all legislative, executive or judicial action at any level of state or local government designed to protect the named class, a class we shall refer to as homosexual persons or gays and lesbians....The State's principal argument in defense of Amendment 2 is that it puts gays and lesbians in the same position as all other persons. So, the State says, the measure does no more than deny homosexuals special rights. This reading of the amendment's language is implausible. We rely not upon our own interpretation of the amendment but upon the authoritative construction of Colorado's Supreme Court. The state court, deeming it unnecessary to determine the full extent of the amendment's reach, found it invalid even on a modest reading of its implications....

Sweeping and comprehensive is the change in legal status effected by this law. So much is evident from the ordinances that the Colorado Supreme Court declared would be void by operation of Amendment 2. Homosexuals, by state decree, are put in a solitary class with respect to transactions and relations in both the private and governmental spheres. The amendment withdraws from homosexuals, but no others, specific legal protection from the injuries caused by discrimination, and it forbids reinstatement of these laws and policies....

Amendment 2 bars homosexuals from securing protection against the injuries that these public accommodations laws address. That in itself is a severe consequence, but there is more. Amendment 2, in addition, nullifies specific legal protections for this targeted class in all transactions in housing, sale of real estate, insurance, health and welfare services, private education, and employment....The repeal of these measures and the prohibition against their future reenactment demonstrates that Amendment 2 has the same force and effect in Colorado's governmental sector as it does elsewhere and that it applies to policies as well as ordinary legislation.

Amendment 2's reach may not be limited to specific laws passed for the benefit of gays and lesbians. It is a fair, if not necessary, inference from the broad language of the amendment that it deprives gays and lesbians even of the protection of general laws and policies that prohibit arbitrary discrimination in governmental and private settings....If this consequence follows from Amendment 2, as its broad language suggests, it would compound the constitutional difficulties the law creates. The state court did not decide whether the amendment has this effect, however, and neither need we....In any event, even if, as we doubt, homosexuals could find some safe harbor in laws of general application, we cannot accept the view that Amendment 2's prohibition on specific legal protections does no more than deprive homosexuals of special rights. To the contrary, the amendment imposes a special disability upon those persons alone. Homosexuals are forbidden the safeguards that others enjoy or may seek without constraint. They can obtain specific protection against discrimination only by enlisting the citizenry of Colorado to amend the state constitution or perhaps, on the State's view, by trying to pass helpful laws of general applicability. This is so no matter how local or discrete the harm, no matter how public and widespread the injury. We find nothing special in the protections Amendment 2 withholds. These are protections taken for granted by most people either because they already have them or do not need them; these are protections against exclusion from an almost limitless number of transactions and endeavors that constitute ordinary civic life in a free society.

The Fourteenth Amendment's promise that no person shall be denied the equal protection of the laws must coexist with the practical necessity that most legislation classifies for one purpose or another, with resulting disadvantage to various groups or persons....We have attempted to reconcile the principle with the reality by stating that, if a law neither burdens a fundamental right nor targets a suspect class, we will uphold the legislative classification so long as it bears a rational relation to some legitimate end....

Amendment 2 fails, indeed defies, even this conventional inquiry. First, the amendment has the peculiar property of imposing a broad and undifferentiated disability on a single named group, an exceptional and, as we shall explain, invalid form of legislation. Second, its sheer breadth is so discontinuous with the reasons offered for it that the amendment seems inexplicable by anything but animus toward the class that it affects; it lacks a rational relationship to legitimate state interests.

Taking the first point, even in the ordinary equal protection case calling for the most deferential of standards, we insist on knowing the relation between the classification adopted and the object to be attained. The search for the link between classification and objective gives substance to the Equal Protection Clause; it provides guidance and discipline for the legislature, which is entitled to know what sorts of laws it can pass; and it marks the limits of our own authority. In the ordinary case, a law will be sustained if it can be said to advance a legitimate government interest, even if the law seems unwise or works to the disadvantage of a particular group, or if the rationale for it seems tenuous....

Amendment 2 confounds this normal process of judicial review. It is at once too narrow and too broad. It identifies persons by a single trait and then denies them protection across the board. The resulting disqualification of a class of persons from the right to seek specific protection from the law is unprecedented in our jurisprudence. The absence of precedent for Amendment 2 is itself instructive; "[d]iscriminations of an unusual character especially suggest careful consideration to determine whether they are obnoxious to the constitutional provision."

....It is not within our constitutional tradition to enact laws of this sort. Central both to the idea of the rule of law and to our own Constitution's guarantee of equal protection is the principle that government and each of its parts remain open on impartial terms to all who seek its assistance. "Equal protection of the laws is not achieved through indiscriminate imposition of inequalities."...Respect for this principle explains why laws singling out a certain class of citizens for disfavored legal status or general hardships are rare. A law declaring that in general it shall be more difficult for one group of citizens than for all others to seek aid from the government is itself a denial of equal protection of the laws in the most literal sense. "The guaranty of 'equal protection of the laws is a pledge of the protection of equal laws.'"...

A second and related point is that laws of the kind now before us raise the inevitable inference that the disadvantage imposed is born of animosity toward the class of persons affected. "[I]f the constitutional conception of `equal protection of the laws' means anything, it must at the very least mean that a bare...desire to harm a politically unpopular group cannot constitute a legitimate governmental interest."...Even laws enacted for broad and ambitious purposes often can be explained by reference to legitimate public policies which justify the incidental disadvantages they impose on certain persons. Amendment 2, however, in making a general announcement that gays and lesbians shall not have any particular protections from the law, inflicts on them immediate, continuing, and real injuries that outrun and belie any legitimate justifications that may be claimed for it. We conclude that, in addition to the far reaching deficiencies of Amendment 2 that we have noted, the principles it offends, in another sense, are conventional and venerable; a law must bear a rational relationship to a legitimate governmental purpose, ...and Amendment 2 does not.

The primary rationale the State offers for Amendment 2 is respect for other citizens' freedom of association, and in particular the liberties of landlords or employers who have personal or religious objections to homosexuality. Colorado also cites its interest in conserving resources to fight discrimination against other groups. The breadth of the Amendment is so far removed from these particular justifications that we find it impossible to credit them. We cannot say that Amendment 2 is directed to any identifiable legitimate purpose or discrete objective. It is a status based enactment divorced from any factual context from which we could discern a relationship to legitimate state interests; it is a classification of persons undertaken for its own sake, something the Equal Protection Clause does not permit. "[C]lass legislation...[is] obnoxious to the prohibitions of the Fourteenth Amendment...."

We must conclude that Amendment 2 classifies homosexuals not to further a proper legislative end but to make them unequal to everyone else. This Colorado cannot do. A State cannot so deem a class of persons a stranger to its laws. Amendment 2 violates the Equal Protection Clause, and the judgment of the Supreme Court of Colorado is affirmed.

Justice SCALIA, whom Chief Justice REHNQUIST and Justice THOMAS join, dissenting.

The Court has mistaken a *Kulturkampf* for a fit of spite. The constitutional amendment before us here is not the manifestation of a "bare...desire to harm" homosexuals, ante, but is rather a modest attempt by seemingly tolerant Coloradans to preserve traditional sexual mores against the efforts of a politically powerful minority to revise those mores through use of the laws....

In holding that homosexuality cannot be singled out for disfavorable treatment, the Court contradicts a decision, unchallenged here, pronounced only 10 years ago, see *Bowers v. Hardwick*, 478 U.S. 186 (1986), and places the prestige of this institution behind the proposition that opposition to homosexuality is as reprehensible as racial or religious bias. Whether it is or not is precisely the cultural debate that gave rise to the Colorado constitutional amendment (and to the preferential laws against which the amendment was directed). Since the Constitution of the United States says nothing about this subject, it is left to be resolved by normal democratic means, including the democratic adoption of provisions in state constitutions. This Court has no business imposing upon all Americans the resolution favored by the elite class from which the Members of this institution are selected, pronouncing that "animosity" toward homosexuality, is evil. I vigorously dissent....

Despite all of its hand wringing about the potential effect of Amendment 2 on general antidiscrimination laws, the Court's opinion ultimately does not dispute all this, but assumes it to be true. The only denial of equal treatment it contends homosexuals have suffered is this: They may not obtain preferential treatment without amending the state constitution. That is to say, the principle underlying the Court's opinion is that one who is accorded equal treatment under the laws, but cannot as readily as others obtain preferential treatment under the laws, has been denied equal protection of the laws. If merely stating this alleged "equal protection" violation does not suffice to refute it, our constitutional jurisprudence has achieved terminal silliness.

The central thesis of the Court's reasoning is that any group is denied equal protection when, to obtain advantage (or, presumably, to avoid disadvantage), it must have recourse to a more general and hence more difficult level of political decisionmaking than others. The world has never heard of such a principle, which is why the Court's opinion is so long on emotive utterance and so short on relevant legal citation. And it seems to me most unlikely that any multilevel democracy can function under such a principle....

I turn next to whether there was a legitimate rational basis for the substance of the constitutional amendmentfor the prohibition of special protection for homosexuals. It is unsurprising that the Court avoids discussion of this question, since the answer is so obviously yes. The case most relevant to the issue before us today is not even mentioned in the Court's opinion: In *Bowers v. Hardwick*, 478 U.S. 186 (1986), we held that the Constitution does not prohibit what virtually all States had done from the founding of the Republic until very recent yearsmaking homosexual conduct a crime. That holding is unassailable, except by those who think that the Constitution changes to suit current fashions....If it is constitutionally permissible for a State to make homosexual conduct criminal, surely it is constitutionally permissible for a State to enact other laws merely disfavoring homosexual conduct....

The foregoing suffices to establish what the Court's failure to cite any case remotely in point would lead one to suspect: No principle set forth in the Constitution, nor even any imagined by this Court in the past 200 years, prohibits what Colorado has done here. But the case for Colorado is much stronger than that. What it has done is not only unprohibited, but eminently reasonable, with close, congressionally approved precedent in earlier constitutional practice....The Court's opinion contains grim, disapproving hints that Coloradans have been guilty of "animus" or "animosity" toward homosexuality, as though that has been established as Unamerican. Of course it is our moral heritage that one should not hate any human being or class of human beings. But I had thought that one could consider certain conduct reprehensible—murder, for example, or polygamy, or cruelty to animals—and could exhibit even "animus" toward such conduct. Surely that is the only sort of "animus" at issue here: moral disapproval of homosexual conduct, the same sort of moral disapproval that produced the centuries old criminal laws that we held constitutional in Bowers....

That is where Amendment 2 came in. It sought to counter both the geographic concentration and the disproportionate political power of homosexuals by (1) resolving the controversy at the statewide level, and (2) making the election a single issue contest for both sides. It put directly, to all the citizens of the State, the question: Should homosexuality be given special protection? They answered no. The Court today asserts that this most democratic of procedures is unconstitutional. Lacking any cases to establish that facially absurd proposition, it simply asserts that it must be unconstitutional, because it has never happened before....

...The Court today, announcing that Amendment 2 "defies...conventional [constitutional] inquiry,"...and "confounds [the] normal process of judicial review," employs a constitutional theory heretofore unknown to frustrate Colorado's reasonable effort to preserve traditional American moral values. The Court's stern disapproval of "animosity" towards homosexuality might be compared with what an earlier Court (including the revered Justices Harlan and Bradley) said in *Murphy v. Ramsey*, 114 U.S. 15 (1885), rejecting a constitutional challenge to a United States statute that denied the franchise in federal territories to those who engaged in polygamous cohabitation....

I would not myself indulge in such official praise for heterosexual monogamy, because I think it no business of the courts (as opposed to the political branches) to take sides in this culture war....

When the Court takes sides in the culture wars, it tends to be with the knights rather than the villains—and more specifically with the Templars, reflecting the views and values of the lawyer class from which the Court's Members are drawn. How that class feels about homosexuality will be evident to anyone who wishes to interview job applicants at virtually any of the Nation's law schools. The interviewer may refuse to offer a job because the applicant is a Republican; because he is an adulterer; because he went to the wrong prep school or belongs to the wrong country club; because he eats snails; because he is a womanizer; because she wears real animal fur; or even because he hates the Chicago Cubs. But if the interviewer should wish not to be an associate or partner of an applicant because he disapproves of the applicant's homosexuality, then he will have violated the pledge which the Association of American Law Schools requires all its member schools to exact from job interviewers: "assurance of the employer's willingness" to hire homosexuals....This law school view of what "prejudices" must be stamped out may be contrasted with the more plebeian attitudes that apparently still prevail in the United States Congress, which has been unresponsive to repeated attempts to extend to homosexuals the protections of federal civil rights laws....

Today's opinion has no foundation in American constitutional law, and barely pretends to. The people of Colorado have adopted an entirely reasonable provision which does not even disfavor homosexuals in any substantive sense, but merely denies them preferential treatment. Amendment 2 is designed to prevent piecemeal deterioration of the sexual morality favored by a majority of Coloradans, and is not only an appropriate means to that legitimate end, but a means that Americans have employed before. Striking it down is an act, not of judicial judgment, but of political will. I dissent.

United States v. Virginia (VMI) BARBARA PERRY

In the 1990s, the battle over single-gender institutions shifted to two state-supported, all-male military academies—the Citadel in South Carolina and the Virginia Military Institute (VMI). The latter, founded in 1839 and long revered by many in Virginia for the bravery of its cadets during the Civil War, was subjected to a law suit in 1990 when the United States Justice Department responded to the complaint of a female high school student who wanted to attend VMI. The Justice Department argued that women were being denied equal protection of the state's laws in violation of the Fourteenth Amendment because they could not attend the publicly funded military academy. The case came before U.S. District Court Judge Jackson Kiser, who ruled in favor of VMI, concluding that the presence of women would fundamentally change the atmosphere at the school and likely require the abolition of the institute's famed "adversative" method of training (in which first-year students are labeled "rats," and treated as such by upperclassmen). The Justice Department appealed the decision to the Fourth Circuit Court of Appeals, which found VMI in violation of the Fourteenth Amendment's Equal Protection Clause, and offered the school three options:(1) admit women; (2) establish an equivalent all-female program; or (3) transform the state-supported institute into a private school. In 1993, the U.S. Supreme Court let stand the Fourth Circuit's decision; and the state of Virginia chose the second option by establishing the Virginia Women's Institute for Leadership (VWIL) at nearby Mary Baldwin College.

In 1996 the Supreme Court ruled 7:1, in an opinion written by Justice Ruth Bader Ginsburg, that the 157-year-old VMI's all male status, inasmuch as it was supported by state funding, violated the Equal Protection Clause. In addition, the Court found that the women's quasi-military leadership program at Mary Baldwin was in no way equivalent to the VMI experience. The lone dissenter was Justice Antonin Scalia, who argued that the Court's ruling would jeopardize even private single-gender institutions. (Justice Thomas recused himself because his son attended VMI.) While the Citadel promptly made plans to admit women, VMI's decision to do so was not immediate. Its Board considered making the institute private, but eventually bowed to the Court's ruling after a narrow vote within the Board to keep VMI a state institution. It actively recruited females for the fall of 1997 and enrolled more than 30 young women in the class of 2001.

▶ Justice Ginsburg states in her majority opinion that "inherent differences" between men and women "remain cause for celebration." Why can't they be celebrated at a state-funded, single-sex military academy? Should co-ed military academies and the armed forces take biological differences into account when setting physical standards for men and women?

▶ Does the Court's reasoning in *VMI* extend to single-gender programs in public elementary and secondary schools? What about private single-gender colleges?

▶ As in his *Romer* dissent, Justice Scalia again accuses the Court's majority of writing the "current preferences of the society (and in some cases only the counter-majoritarian preferences of the society's law-trained elite) into our basic law." What does he mean?

United States v. Virginia (VMI) 64 LW 4581 (1996)

Justice GINSBURG delivered the opinion of the Court.

Virginia's institutions of higher learning include an incomparable military college, Virginia Military Institute (VMI). The United States maintains that the Constitution's equal protection guarantee precludes Virginia from reserving exclusively to men the unique educational opportunities VMI affords. We agree.

Founded in 1839, VMI is today the sole single sex school among Virginia's 15 public institutions of higher learning. VMI's distinctive mission is to produce "citizen soldiers," men prepared for leadership in civilian life and in military service. VMI pursues this mission through pervasive training of a kind not available anywhere else in Virginia. Assigning prime place to character development, VMI uses an "adversative method" modeled on English public schools and once characteristic of military instruction. VMI constantly endeavors to instill physical and mental discipline in its cadets and impart to them a strong moral code. The school's graduates leave VMI with heightened comprehension of their capacity to deal with duress and stress, and a large sense of accomplishment for completing the hazardous course.

VMI has notably succeeded in its mission to produce leaders; among its alumni are military generals, Members of Congress, and business executives. The school's alumni overwhelmingly perceive that their VMI training helped them to realize their personal goals. VMI's endowment reflects the loyalty of its graduates; VMI has the largest per student endowment of all undergraduate institutions in the Nation.

Neither the goal of producing citizen soldiers nor VMI's implementing methodology is inherently unsuitable to women. And the school's impressive record in producing leaders has made admission desirable to some women. Nevertheless, Virginia has elected to preserve exclusively for men the advantages and opportunities a VMI education affords.

From its establishment in 1839 as one of the Nation's first state military colleges,...VMI has remained financially supported by Virginia and "subject to the control of the [Virginia] General Assembly,"....VMI today enrolls about 1,300 men as cadets. Its academic offerings in the liberal arts, sciences, and engineering are also available at other public colleges and universities in Virginia. But VMI's mission is special: "'to produce educated and honorable men, prepared for the varied work of civil life, imbued with love of learning, confident in the functions and attitudes of leadership, possessing a high sense of public service, advocates of the American democracy and free enterprise system, and ready as citizen soldiers to defend their country in time of national peril.'"...

The cross petitions in this case present two ultimate issues. First, does Virginia's exclusion of women from the educational opportunities provided by VMI for military training and civilian leadership development deny to women "capable of all of the individual activities required of VMI cadets,"...the equal protection of the laws guaranteed by the Fourteenth Amendment? Second, if VMI's "unique" situation,...-as Virginia's sole single sex public institution of higher education offend the Constitution's equal protection principle, what is the remedial requirement?

We note, once again, the core instruction of this Court's pathmarking decisions in *J. E. B. v. Alabama ex rel. T. B.*...(1994), and *Mississippi Univ. for Women*, ...: Parties who seek to defend gender based government action must demonstrate an "exceedingly persuasive justification" for that action....

Without equating gender classifications, for all purposes, to classifications based on race or national origin, the Court, in post-*Reed* decisions, has carefully inspected official action that closes a door or denies opportunity to women (or to men)....To summarize the Court's current directions for cases of official classification based on gender: Focusing on the differential treatment or denial of opportunity for which relief is sought, the reviewing court must determine whether the proffered justification is "exceedingly persuasive." The burden of justification is demanding and it rests entirely on the State. See *Mississippi Univ. for Women*. The State must show "at least that the [challenged] classification serves 'important governmental objectives and that the discriminatory means employed' are 'substantially related to the achievement of those objectives.' "...The justification must be genuine, not hypothesized or invented *post hoc* in response to litigation....

The heightened review standard our precedent establishes does not make sex a proscribed classification. Supposed "inherent differences" are no longer accepted as a ground for race or national origin classifications....Physical differences between men and women, however, are enduring.... "Inherent differences" between men and women, we have come to appreciate, remain cause for celebration, but not for denigration of the members of either sex or for artificial constraints on an individual's opportunity. Sex classifications may be used to compensate women "for particular economic disabilities [they have] suffered,"...to "promot[e] equal employment opportunity,"...to advance full development of the talent and capacities of our Nation's people. But such classifications may not be used, as they once were,...to create or perpetuate the legal, social, and economic inferiority of women.

Measuring the record in this case against the review standard just described, we conclude that Virginia has shown no "exceedingly persuasive justification" for excluding all women from the citizen soldier training afforded by VMI. We therefore affirm the Fourth Circuit's initial judgment, which held that Virginia had violated the Fourteenth Amendment's Equal Protection Clause. Because the remedy proffered by Virginia, the Mary Baldwin VWIL program, does not cure the constitutional violation, i.e., it does not provide equal opportunity, we reverse the Fourth Circuit's final judgment in this case.

The Fourth Circuit initially held that Virginia had advanced no state policy by which it could justify, under equal protection principles, its determination "to afford VMI's unique type of program to men and not to women." Virginia challenges that "liability" ruling and asserts two justifications in defense of VMI's exclusion of women. First, the Commonwealth contends, "single sex education provides important educational benefits,"...and the option of single sex education contributes to "diversity in educational approaches." Second, the Commonwealth argues, "the unique VMI method of character development and leadership training," the school's adversative approach, would have to be modified were VMI to admit women. We consider these two justifications in turn.

Single sex education affords pedagogical benefits to at least some students, Virginia emphasizes, and that reality is uncontested in this litigation. Similarly, it is not disputed that diversity among public educational institutions can serve the public good. But Virginia has not shown that VMI was established, or has been maintained, with a view to diversifying, by its categorical exclusion of women, educational opportunities within the State. In cases of this genre, our precedent instructs that "benign" justifications proffered in defense of categorical exclusions will not be accepted automatically; a tenable justification must describe actual state purposes, not rationalizations for actions in fact differently grounded....

In sum, we find no persuasive evidence in this record that VMI's male only admission policy "is in furtherance of a state policy of 'diversity.'" No such policy, the Fourth Circuit observed, can be discerned from the movement of all other public colleges and universities in Virginia away from single sex education....A purpose genuinely to advance an array of educational options, as the Court of Appeals recognized, is not served by VMI's historic and constant plan to "affor[d] a unique educational benefit only to males." However "liberally" this plan serves the State's sons, it makes no provision whatever for her daughters. That is not equal protection.

Virginia next argues that VMI's adversative method of training provides educational benefits that cannot be made available, unmodified, to women. Alterations to accommodate women would necessarily be "radical," so "drastic," Virginia asserts, as to transform, indeed "destroy," VMI's program....

It is also undisputed, however, that "the VMI methodology could be used to educate women." The District Court even allowed that some women may prefer it to the methodology a women's college might pursue. "[S]ome women, at least, would want to attend [VMI] if they had the opportunity," the District Court recognized, and "some women," the expert testimony established, "are capable of all of the individual activities required of VMI cadets." The parties, furthermore, agree that "some women can meet the physical standards [VMI] now impose[s] on men." In sum, as the Court of Appeals stated, "neither the goal of producing citizen soldiers," VMI's *raison d'être*, "nor VMI's implementing methodology is inherently unsuitable to women."...

The United States does not challenge any expert witness estimation on average capacities or preferences of men and women. Instead, the United States emphasizes that time and again since this Court's turning point decision in *Reed v. Reed*, 404 U.S. 71 (1971), we have cautioned reviewing courts to take a "hard look" at generalizations or "tendencies" of the kind pressed by Virginia, and relied upon by the District Court. See O'Connor, Portia's Progress, 66 *N.Y.U.L. Rev.* 1546, 1551 (1991). State actors controlling gates to opportunity, we have instructed, may not exclude qualified individuals based on "fixed notions concerning the roles and abilities of males and females." *Mississippi Univ. for Women*, 458 U.S., at 725....

It may be assumed, for purposes of this decision, that most women would not choose VMI's adversative method....[I]t is also probable that "many men would not want to be educated in such an environment."...Education, to be sure, is not a "one size fits all" business. The issue, however, is not whether "women—or men—should be forced to attend VMI"; rather, the question is whether the State can constitutionally deny to women who have the will and capacity, the training and attendant opportunities that VMI uniquely affords....

Women's successful entry into the federal military academies, and their participation in the Nation's military forces, indicate that Virginia's fears for the future of VMI may not be solidly grounded. The State's justification for excluding all women from "citizen soldier" training for which some are qualified, in any event, cannot rank as "exceedingly persuasive," as we have explained and applied that standard....

In the second phase of the litigation, Virginia presented its remedial plan—maintain VMI as a male only college and create VWIL as a separate program for women....A remedial decree, this Court has said, must closely fit the constitutional violation; it must be shaped to place persons unconstitutionally denied an opportunity or advantage in "the position they would have occupied in the absence of [discrimination]."...Virginia chose not to eliminate, but to leave untouched, VMI's exclusionary policy. For women only, however, Virginia proposed a separate program, different in kind from VMI and unequal in tangible and intangible facilities....

VWIL affords women no opportunity to experience the rigorous military training for which VMI is famed....Instead, the VWIL program "deemphasize[s]" military education, and uses a "cooperative method" of education "which reinforces self esteem."...Virginia maintains that these methodological differences are "justified pedagogically," based on "important differences between men and women in learning and developmental needs," "psychological and sociological differences" Virginia describes as "real" and "not stereotypes."... As earlier stated, generalizations about "the way women are," estimates of what is appropriate for most women, no longer justify denying opportunity to women whose talent and capacity place them outside the average description. Notably, Virginia never asserted that VMI's method of education suits most men. It is also revealing that Virginia accounted for its failure to make the VWIL experience "the entirely militaristic experience of VMI" on the ground that VWIL "is planned for women who do not necessarily expect to pursue military careers." By that reasoning, VMI's "entirely militaristic" program would be inappropriate for men in general or as a group, for "[o]nly about 15% of VMI cadets enter career military service."...In myriad respects other than military training, VWIL does not qualify as VMI's equal. VWIL's student body, faculty, course offerings, and facilities hardly match VMI's. Nor can the VWIL graduate anticipate the benefits associated with VMI's 157year history, the school's prestige, and its influential alumni network....

Virginia, in sum, while maintaining VMI for men only, has failed to provide any "comparable single gender women's institution." Instead, the Commonwealth has created a VWIL program fairly appraised as a "pale shadow" of VMI in terms of the range of curricular choices and faculty stature, funding, prestige, alumni support and influence....Virginia's remedy does not match the constitutional violation; the State has shown no "exceedingly persuasive justification" for withholding from women qualified for the experience premier training of the kind VMI affords....

Women seeking and fit for a VMI quality education cannot be offered anything less, under the State's obligation to afford them genuinely equal protection....There is no reason to believe that the admission of women capable of all the activities required of VMI cadets would destroy the Institute rather than enhance its capacity to serve the "more perfect Union."

Justice SCALIA dissenting.

Today the Court shuts down an institution that has served the people of the Commonwealth of Virginia with pride and distinction for over a century and a half. To achieve that desired result, it rejects (contrary to our established practice) the factual findings of two courts below, sweeps aside the precedents of the Court, and ignores the history of our people. As to fact: it explicitly rejects the finding that there exist "gender-based developmental differences" supporting Virginia's restriction of the "adversative" method to only a men's institution, and the finding that the all-male composition of the Virginia Military Institute (VMI) is essential to that institution's character. As to precedent: it drastically revises our established standards for reviewing sex-based classifications. And as to history: it counts for nothing the long tradition, enduring down to the present, of men's military colleges supported by both States and the Federal Government.

Much of the Court's opinion is devoted to deprecating the closed mindedness of our forebears with regard to women's education, and even with regard to the treatment of women in areas that have nothing to do with education. Closed minded they were as every age is, including our own, with regard to matters it cannot guess, because it simply does not consider them debatable. The virtue of a democratic system with a First Amendment is that it readily enables the people, over time, to be persuaded that what they took for granted is not so, and to change their laws accordingly. That system is destroyed if the smug assurances of each age are removed from the democratic process and written into the Constitution. So to counterbalance the Court's criticism of our ancestors, let me say a word in their praise: they left us free to change. The same cannot be said of this most illiberal Court, which has embarked on a course of inscribing one after another of the current preferences of the society (and in some cases only the counter majoritarian preferences of the society's law trained elite) into our Basic Law. Today it enshrines the notion that no substantial educational value is to be served by an all men's military academy so that the decision by the people of Virginia to maintain such an institution denies equal protection to women who cannot attend that institution but can attend others. Since it is entirely clear that the Constitution of the United Statesthe old onetakes no sides in this educational debate, I dissent.

I shall devote most of my analysis to evaluating the Court's opinion on the basis of our current equal protection jurisprudence, which regards this Court as free to evaluate everything under the sun by applying one of three tests: "rational basis" scrutiny, intermediate scrutiny, or strict scrutiny. These tests are no more scientific than their names suggest, and a further element of randomness is added by the fact that it is largely up to us which test will be applied in each case....

I have no problem with a system of abstract tests such as rational basis, intermediate, and strict scrutiny (though I think we can do better than applying strict scrutiny and intermediate scrutiny whenever we feel like it). Such formulas are essential to evaluating whether the new restrictions that a changing society constantly imposes upon private conduct comport with that "equal protection" our society has always accorded in the past. But in my view the function of this Court is to preserve our society's values regarding (among other things) equal protection, not to revise them; to prevent backsliding from the degree of restriction the Constitution imposed upon democratic government, not to prescribe, on our own authority, progressively higher degrees. For that reason it is my view that, whatever abstract tests we may choose to devise, they cannot supersedeand indeed ought to be crafted so as to reflectthose constant and unbroken national traditions that embody the people's understanding of ambiguous constitutional texts. More specifically, it is my view that "when a practice not expressly prohibited by the text of the Bill of Rights bears the endorsement of a long tradition of open, widespread, and unchallenged use that dates back to the beginning of the Republic, we have no proper basis for striking it down."

The all male constitution of VMI comes squarely within such a governing tradition....In other words, the tradition of having government funded military schools for men is as well rooted in the traditions of this country as the tradition of sending only men into military combat. The people may decide to change the one tradition, like the other, through democratic processes; but the assertion that either tradition has been unconstitutional through the centuries is not law, but politics smuggled into law. And the same applies, more broadly, to single sex education in general, which, as I shall discuss, is threatened by today's decision with the cut off of all state and federal support....

Today, however, change is forced upon Virginia, and reversion to single sex education is prohibited nationwide, not by democratic processes but by order of this Court. Even while bemoaning the sorry, bygone days of "fixed notions" concerning women's education,...the Court favors current notions so fixedly that it is willing to write them into the Constitution of the United States by application of custom built "tests." This is not the interpretation of a Constitution, but the creation of one....

As is frequently true, the Court's decision today will have consequences that extend far beyond the parties to the case. What I take to be the Court's unease with these consequences, and its resulting unwillingness to acknowledge them, cannot alter the reality.

Under the constitutional principles announced and applied today, single sex public education is unconstitutional. By going through the motions of applying a balancing test asking whether the State has adduced an "exceedingly persuasive justification" for its sex based classificationthe Court creates the illusion that government officials in some future case will have a clear shot at justifying some sort of single sex public education....

The Supreme Court of the United States does not sit to announce "unique" dispositions. Its principal function is to establish precedent that is, to set forth principles of law that every court in America must follow. As we said only this Term, we expect both ourselves and lower courts to adhere to the "rationale upon which the Court based the results of its earlier decisions."...

And the rationale of today's decision is sweeping: for sex based classifications, a redefinition of intermediate scrutiny that makes it indistinguishable from strict scrutiny. Indeed, the Court indicates that if any program restricted to one sex is "uniqu[e]," it must be opened to members of the opposite sex "who have the will and capacity" to participate in it. I suggest that the single sex program that will not be capable of being characterized as "unique" is not only unique but nonexistent.

In any event, regardless of whether the Court's rationale leaves some small amount of room for lawyers to argue, it ensures that single sex public education is functionally dead. The costs of litigating the constitutionality of a single sex education program, and the risks of ultimately losing that litigation, are simply too high to be embraced by public officials....Should the courts happen to interpret that vacuous phrase as establishing a standard that is not utterly impossible of achievement, there is considerable risk that whether the standard has been met will not be determined on the basis of the record evidenceindeed, that will necessarily be the approach of any court that seeks to walk the path the Court has trod today. No state official in his right mind will buy such a high cost, high risk lawsuit by commencing a single sex program. The enemies of single sex education have won; by persuading only seven Justices (five would have been enough) that their view of the world is enshrined in the Constitution, they have effectively imposed that view on all 50 States.

VII Due Process, Privacy, and Personal Autonomy

Griswold v. Connecticut (1965)

Roe v. Wade (1973)

Bowers v. Hardwick (1986)

Cruzan v. Director, Missouri Department of Health (1990)

Planned Parenthood of Southeastern Pennsylvania v. Casey (1992)

Washington v. Glucksberg / Vacco v. Quill (1997)

VII Due Process, Privacy, and Personal Autonomy

MELVIN UROFSKY

The Ninth Amendment to the Constitution declares that "The enumeration in the Constitution, of certain rights, shall not be construed to deny or disparage others retained by the people." What the Framers intended by these words is unclear, and the Ninth has never been a major source of constitutional jurisprudence. One thing is clear, though: there are rights beyond those listed in the first eight amendments. The Supreme Court in the early part of the twentieth century found that the Due Process Clauses of the Fifth and Fourteenth Amendments protected certain nonenumerated rights, primarily those attached to property and contract, but also some involved with individual liberties.

Due process has two meanings. First, it refers to the fairness of procedures the government must follow when dealing with its citizens, in both civil and criminal matters; procedural due process constitutes the rules of the game. But the Court also found a second meaning, and determined that there is a substantive aspect to due process which includes those rights considered essential to life, liberty and the pursuit of happiness. The conservative justices who sat on the Court from the 1880s to the 1930s used this substantive due process to erect barriers against state reform programs. Laws regulating wages, hours and working conditions, they declared, violated due process by impinging on the protected property rights of employers. Yet in other cases, they also found that due process involved individual rights, such as marriage, travel, and directing the education of children. Following the New Deal, the property-oriented notion of substantive due process went into decline, avoided by courts and stigmatized as reactionary by scholars and the public alike. This also eclipsed, at least temporarily, the use of due process to protect other forms of individual liberty.

One must understand the bad reputation substantive due process had in order to appreciate what the Court did in *Griswold v. Connecticut*. The type of right claimed, privacy in the marital chamber, is nowhere mentioned in the Constitution. One might, as Justice Goldberg did, rely on the Ninth Amendment, but little precedent supported that approach. The obvious answer lay in due process, with its substantive rights of life and liberty. But the Court, still keenly aware of the opprobrium surrounding the due process doctrine, hesitated to go in that direction; so in one of the most creative decisions in the Court's history, Justice Douglas identified "penumbras" and "emanations" to do the job.

Although the Court initially avoided tying rights of privacy and bodily autonomy to substantive due process, as Justice Harlan immediately suggested, that approach proved workable and gained credibility over time. The justices began to frame their opinions in terms of liberty interests which they located in the broader area of substantive due process. The generation of justices who succeeded the New Deal appointees had no personal feud with due process, and it quickly became a useful instrument in their jurisprudence.

All of the justices in the *Griswold* majority, it should be noted, found that some "fundamental values" do deserve special constitutional protection. The questions in all these cases are: how does the Court determine what those fundamental values are, and how does it determine where they should be placed in the hierarchy of constitutionally protected rights? In less than ten years, the Court moved from finding that a right to privacy existed to the position that this right, coupled with the notion of personal autonomy, included a woman's right to an abortion. Later, the Court, by only a bare majority, found that privacy did not include homosexual rights to sex. It subsequently found that a right to die existed, although qualified by legitimate state interests, but the Court unanimously found that this right did not include a right to physician-assisted suicide.

Substantive due process went into decline because of the sense that courts used the doctrine in an arbitrary manner to strike down legislation they did not like. Modern critics are raising a similar cry, and charge that the courts are using the doctrine to impose their sense of individual liberty on the states without regard either to the original intent of the Constitution or the will of the people. These cases illustrate quite sharply the issue of interpretation vs. strict construction, and the many questions to which this issue gives rise.

▶ If the Constitution and contemporary documents, such as the *Federalist*, do not mention a particular right does that mean that the right does not exist?

▶ Does the Ninth Amendment apply only to rights recognized in 1791? How do we know whether or not a particular right existed then?

▶ Is the Court the only mechanism we have to keep the Constitution abreast of the times? What others are there? How efficient are they in operation?

▶ In these cases, the justices are dealing with difficult issues for which they could find little guidance in the sources. Are these "principled" decisions; that is, do they try to identify the spirit of the Constitution and then apply it to a new problem in a logical and honest manner? In these cases the Court often refers to privacy. Is privacy the correct term, or do the justices mean autonomous behavior? Is there a difference? If so, how should this difference be reflected in law?

Griswold v. Connecticut   MELVIN UROFSKY

This case has been referred to as "a living landmark," and is one of the most influential decisions handed down by recent courts.

The case arose out of Connecticut's laws against providing either information about birth control or contraceptive materials. The executive director of the Planned Parenthood League of Connecticut and the league's medical director at its New Haven Center were prosecuted under these laws for giving information, instruction and medical advice to married persons on how to avoid conception.

The issue had come before the Court earlier in *Poe v. Ullman* (1961), but the Court at that time had refused to deal with the merits of the issue, and had dismissed the case for lack of justiciability. Justice Harlan, however, had filed an eloquent dissenting opinion, in which he had raised the issue of whether privacy could be protected under the Constitution.

Until *Griswold*, the Court had never faced this issue directly. There had been a number of cases in which the Court had implied that the Constitution protected certain activities of a private nature; but that is a long way from proclaiming a constitutionally protected general right of privacy.

There had been some writings on privacy, and it is generally conceded that the modern doctrine of legally protected privacy began with an article written by Louis D. Brandeis and Samuel D. Warren in 1891. Later on, after he joined the Supreme Court, Mr. Justice Brandeis on several occasions referred to a right to be let alone as that right most prized by civilized persons.

But the Constitution never specifically mentions privacy, and the majority opinion by Justice Douglas, as well as the concurring opinions, find this right as existing by implication rather than by explicit protection. This "interpretationist" approach to the Constitution sees the need to extrapolate the broad intent of the Framers, and then apply that intent to modern circumstances. The dissenting justices reflect the "literalist" belief that only those rights specifically mentioned in the document can be enforced against the federal or state governments.

In one sense, the majority "got it right" in terms of public opinion. In 1987, President Reagan named Robert Bork to succeed Lewis F. Powell, Jr. on the Court. Bork had been a strong critic of the *Griswold* opinion, and had often stated that he did not believe the Constitution included a right to privacy. The opponents to Bork's nomination used this to defeat him, when it became clear that a majority of the American people believed that a right of privacy not only existed, but had constitutional sanction.

> ◗ Which approach, the literalist or the interpretationist, is more compelling in this case?
>
> ◗ Should the Court limit itself to a literal exposition, or should it seek to cast eighteenth century ideas into twentieth century modes?

- Is a right to privacy important enough to warrant constitutional status?

- How far should the right to privacy doctrine be extended?

- *Griswold* continues to exert a powerful influence, because aside from the legal questions, many people believe that, as Justice Douglas argued, the marital chamber should be beyond the reach of the state. Starting with that assumption, how far can the arguments for limitations on state authority reasonably be carried?

- Is it desirable for the state to be involved in any intrusions on private affairs? Can one draw a simple and well-defined line regarding privacy? Who should draw it?

- Should questions of morality be the state's concern, and if so, to what extent?

Griswold v. Connecticut 381 U.S. 479 (1965)

Mr. Justice DOUGLAS delivered the opinion of the Court.

We do not sit as a super-legislature to determine the wisdom, need, and propriety of laws that touch economic problems, business affairs, or social conditions. This law, however, operates directly on an intimate relation of husband and wife and their physician's role in one aspect of that relation.

The association of people is not mentioned in the Constitution nor in the Bill of Rights. The right to educate a child in a school of the parents' choice—whether public or private or parochial—is also not mentioned. Nor is the right to study any particular subject or any foreign language. Yet the First Amendment has been construed to include certain of those rights. The right to educate one's children as one chooses is made applicable to the States. The same dignity is given the right to study the German language in a private school. In other words, the State may not, consistently with the spirit of the First Amendment, contract the spectrum of available knowledge. The right of freedom of speech and press includes not only the right to utter or to print, but the right to distribute, the right to receive, the right to read and freedom of inquiry, freedom of thought, and freedom to teach—indeed the freedom of the entire university community. Without those peripheral rights the specific rights would be less secure....In other words, the First Amendment has a penumbra where privacy is protected from governmental intrusion....

Specific guarantees in the Bill of Rights have penumbras, formed by emanations from those guarantees that help give them life and substance....Various guarantees create zones of privacy. The right of association contained in the penumbra of the First Amendment is one, as we have seen. The Third Amendment in its prohibition against the quartering of soldiers "in any house" in time of peace without the consent of the owner is another facet of that privacy. The Fourth Amendment explicitly affirms the "right of the people to be secure in their persons, houses, papers, and effects against unreasonable searches and seizures." The Fifth Amendment in its Self-Incrimination Clause enables the citizen to create a zone of privacy which government may not force him to surrender to his detriment. The Ninth Amendment provides: "The enumeration in the Constitution, of certain rights, shall not be construed to deny or disparage others retained by the people." The Fourth and Fifth Amendments were described in *Boyd v. United States* [1886], as protection against all governmental invasions "of the sanctity of a man's home and the privacies of life." We recently referred to the Fourth Amendment as creating a "right to privacy, no less important than any other right carefully and particularly reserved to the people." We have had many controversies over these penumbral rights of "privacy and repose." These cases bear witness that the right of privacy which presses for recognition here is a legitimate one.

The present case, then, concerns a relationship lying within the zone of privacy created by several fundamental constitutional guarantees. And it concerns a law which, in forbidding the use of contraceptives rather than regulating their manufacture or sale, seeks to achieve its goals by means having a maximum destructive impact upon that relationship. Such a law cannot stand in light of the familiar principle, so often applied by this Court, that a "governmental purpose to control or prevent activities constitutionally subject to state regulation may not be achieved by means which sweep unnecessarily broadly and thereby invade the area of protected freedoms." Would we allow the police to search the sacred precincts of marital bedrooms for telltale signs of the use of contraceptives? The very idea is repulsive to the notions of privacy surrounding the marriage relationship.

We deal with a right of privacy older than the Bill of Rights—older than our political parties, older than our school system. Marriage is a coming together for better or for worse, hopefully enduring, and intimate to the degree of being sacred. The association promotes a way of life, not causes; a harmony in living, not political faiths; a bilateral loyalty, not commercial or social projects. Yet it is an association for as noble a purpose as any involved in our prior decisions.

Reversed.

Mr. Justice GOLDBERG, whom Chief Justice WARREN and Mr. Justice BRENNAN join, concurring.

Although I have not accepted the view that "due process" as used in the 14th Amendment incorporates all of the first eight Amendments, I do agree that the concept of liberty protects those personal rights that are fundamental, and is not confined to the specific terms of the Bill of Rights. My conclusion that the concept of liberty is not so restricted and that it embraces the right of marital privacy though that right is not mentioned explicitly in the Constitution is supported both by numerous decisions of this Court, referred to in the Court's opinion, and by the language and history of the Ninth Amendment. I add these words to emphasize the relevance of that Amendment to the Court's holding. The language and history of the Ninth Amendment reveal that the Framers of the Constitution believed that there are additional fundamental rights, protected from governmental infringement, which exist alongside those fundamental rights specifically mentioned in the first eight constitutional amendments.

The Ninth Amendment reads, "The enumeration in the Constitution, of certain rights, shall not be construed to deny or disparage others retained by the people." The amendment is almost entirely the work of James Madison. It was proffered to quiet expressed fears that a bill of specifically enumerated rights could not be sufficiently broad to cover all essential rights and that the specific mention of certain rights would be interpreted as a denial that others were protected. While this Court has had little occasion to interpret the Ninth Amendment, "it cannot be presumed that any clause in the constitution is intended to be without effect." The Ninth Amendment to the Constitution may be regarded by some as a recent discovery, but since 1791 it has been a basic part of the Constitution which we are sworn to uphold. To hold that a right so basic and fundamental and so deep-rooted in our society as the right of privacy in marriage may be infringed because that right is not guaranteed in so many words by the first eight amendments to the Constitution is to ignore the Ninth Amendment and to give it no effect whatsoever....

A dissenting opinion suggests that my interpretation of the Ninth Amendment somehow "broadens the powers of this Court." I believe that misses the import of what I am saying. I do not mean to imply that the Ninth Amendment is applied against the States by the 14th. Nor do I mean to state that the Ninth Amendment constitutes an independent source of rights protected from infringement by either the States or Federal Government. Rather, the Ninth Amendment shows a belief of the Constitution's authors that fundamental rights exist that are not expressly enumerated in the first eight amendments and an intent that the list of rights included there not be exhaustive. This Court has held that the Fifth and 14th Amendments protect certain fundamental personal liberties. The Ninth Amendment simply shows the intent of the Constitution's authors that other fundamental personal rights should not be denied such protection or disparaged in any other way simply because they are not specifically listed in the first eight constitutional amendments. I do not see how this broadens the authority of the Court; rather it serves to support what this Court has been doing in protecting fundamental rights. Nor am I turning somersaults with history in arguing that the Ninth Amendment is relevant in a case dealing with a State's infringement of a fundamental right. While the Ninth Amendment—and indeed the entire Bill of Rights— originally concerned restrictions upon federal power, the subsequently enacted 14th Amendment prohibits the States as well from abridging fundamental personal liberties. And, the Ninth Amendment, in indicating that not all such liberties are specifically mentioned in the first eight amendments, is surely relevant in showing the existence of other fundamental personal rights, now protected from state, as well as federal, infringement....

Mr. Justice HARLAN, concurring in the judgement.

[Although he agreed with the results of the decision, Justice Harlan did not agree with the reasoning of either the majority opinion or Justice Goldberg's reliance on the Ninth Amendment. He preferred to rely on the Due Process Clause of the Fourteenth Amendment, which prohibits the states from denying any person life, liberty or property without due process of law. Due process can either be procedural, *which deals with the rules of the legal process, or* substantive, *which implies that certain unspecified rights exist within the general definition of due process.*

In the 1920s and 1930s, conservatives on the Court had used the doctrine of substantive due process to attach a variety of economic reforms. Following the Court crisis of the New Deal, the idea of substantive due process had fallen into disfavor. Justice Douglas created the idea of penumbras and emanations from the Bill of Rights in order to avoid the far easier argument that privacy was one of those right subsumed under due process. For a similar reason, Justice Goldberg utilized the Ninth Amendment.

Justice Harlan, on the other hand, believed privacy to be a fundamental right which constitutes the core of due process. He had said so in his dissent in Poe v. Ullman, *and in his concurrence he reiterated that argument, and in fact quoted at length from his earlier dissent. Harlan's concept of a new substantive due process, even though offered in concurrence, proved to be a more flexible doctrine than Douglas's penumbras, and it became the basis of subsequent Court decisions on privacy and other rights. See, for example,* Roe v. Wade.*]*

Mr. Justice WHITE, concurring in the judgment.

This is not the first time this Court has had occasion to articulate that the liberty entitled to protection under the 14th Amendment includes the right "to marry, establish a home and bring up children" and "the liberty to direct the upbringing and education of children" and that these are among "the basic civil rights of man." These decisions affirm that there is a "realm of family life which the state cannot enter" without substantial justification. Surely the right invoked in this case, to be free of regulation of the intimacies of the marriage relationship, "comes to this Court with momentum for respect lacking when appeal is made to liberties which derive merely from shifting economic arrangements." The Connecticut law deals rather substantially with this relationship. A statute with these effects bears a substantial burden of justification when attacked under the 14th Amendment....But such statutes, if reasonably necessary for the effectuation of a legitimate and substantial state interest, and not arbitrary or capricious in application, are not invalid under the Due Process Clause.

The State claims but one justification for its anti-use statute. There is no serious contention that Connecticut thinks the use of artificial or external methods of contraception immoral or unwise in itself, or that the anti-use statute is founded upon any policy of promoting population expansion. Rather, the statute is said to serve the State's policy against all forms of promiscuous or illicit sexual relationships, be they premarital or extramarital, concededly a permissible and legitimate legislative goal. Without taking issue with the premise that the fear of conception operates as a deterrent to such relationships in addition to the criminal proscriptions Connecticut has against such conduct, I wholly fail to see how the ban on the use of contraceptives by married couples in any way reinforces the State's ban on illicit sexual relationships. It is purely fanciful to believe that the broad proscription on use facilitates discovery of use by persons engaging in a prohibited relationship or for some other reason makes such use more unlikely and thus can be supported by any sort of administrative consideration. Perhaps the theory is that the flat ban on use prevents married people from possessing contraceptives and without the ready availability of such devices for use in the marital relationship, there will be no or less temptation to use them in extramarital ones. This reasoning rests on the premise that married people will comply with the anti-use ban in regard to their marital relationship, notwithstanding total nonenforcement in this context and apparent nonenforcibility, but will not comply with criminal statutes prohibiting extramarital affairs and the anti-use statute in respect to illicit sexual relationships, a premise whose validity has not been demonstrated and whose intrinsic validity is not very evident. At most the broad ban is of marginal utility to the declared objective. A statute limiting its prohibition on use to persons engaging in the prohibited relationship would serve the end posited by Connecticut in the same way, and with the same effectiveness, or ineffectiveness, as the broad anti-use statute under attack in this case. I find nothing in this record justifying the sweeping scope of this statute, with its telling effect on the freedoms of married persons, and therefore conclude that it deprives such persons of liberty without due process of law.

Mr. Justice BLACK, with whom Mr. Justice STEWART joins, dissenting.

The law is every bit as offensive to me as it is to my Brethren who, reciting reasons why it is offensive to them, hold it unconstitutional. But I cannot subscribe to their conclusion that the evil qualities they see in the law make it unconstitutional. The Court talks about a constitutional "right of privacy" as though there is some constitutional provision forbidding any law ever to be passed which might abridge the "privacy" of individuals. But there is not. There are, of course, guarantees in certain specific constitutional provisions which are designed in part to protect privacy at certain times and places with respect to certain activities.... "Privacy" is a broad, abstract and ambiguous concept which can easily be shrunken in meaning but which can also easily be interpreted as a constitutional ban against many things other than searches and seizures. I get nowhere in this case by talk about a constitutional "right of privacy" as an emanation from one or more constitutional provisions. I like my privacy as well as the next one, but I am nevertheless compelled to admit that government has a right to invade it unless prohibited by some specific constitutional provision....

This brings me to the arguments made by my Brothers Harlan, White and Goldberg. I discuss the due process and Ninth Amendment arguments together because on analysis they turn out to be the same thing—merely using different words to claim the power to invalidate any legislative act which the judges find irrational, unreasonable or offensive. If the due process formulas based on "natural justice" are to prevail, they require judges to determine what is or is not constitutional on the basis of their own appraisal of what laws are unwise or unnecessary. The power to make such decisions is of course that of a legislative body. I do not believe that we are granted power to measure constitutionality by our belief that the legislation is arbitrary, capricious or unreasonable, or accomplishes no justifiable purpose, or is offensive to our own notions of "civilized standards of conduct."

My Brother Goldberg has adopted the recent discovery that the Ninth Amendment as well as the Due Process Clause can be used by this Court as authority to strike down all state legislation which this Court thinks violates "fundamental principles of liberty and justice," or is contrary to the "traditions and collective conscience of our people." He also states, without proof satisfactory to me, that in making decisions on this basis judges will not consider "their personal and private notions." One may ask how they can avoid considering them....

I realize that many good and able men have eloquently spoken and written, sometimes in rhapsodical strains, about the duty of this Court to keep the Constitution in tune with the times. I reject that philosophy. The Constitution makers knew the need for change and provided for it. Amendments suggested by the people's elected representatives can be submitted to the people or their selected agent for ratification. The Due Process Clause with an "arbitrary and capricious" or "shocking to the conscience" formula was liberally used by this Court to strike down economic legislation in the early decades of this century, threatening, many people thought, the tranquility and stability of the Nation. That formula, based on subjective considerations of "natural justice," is no less dangerous when used to enforce this Court's views about personal rights than those about economic rights. I had thought that we had laid that formula, as a means for striking down state legislation, to rest....The late Judge Learned Hand, after emphasizing his view that judges should not use the due process formula suggested in the concurring opinions today or any other formula like it to invalidate legislation offensive to their "personal preferences," made the statement, with which I fully agree, that: "For myself it would be most irksome to be ruled by a bevy of Platonic Guardians, even if I knew how to choose them, which I assuredly do not." So far as I am concerned, Connecticut's law as applied here is not forbidden by any provision of the Federal Constitution as the Constitution was written, and I would therefore affirm.

Mr. Justice STEWART, whom Mr. Justice BLACK joins, dissenting.

I think this is an uncommonly silly law. But we are not asked in this case to say whether we think this law is unwise, or even asinine. We are asked to hold that it violates the Constitution. And that I cannot do. In the course of its opinion the Court refers to no less than six Amendments to the Constitution but does not say which of these Amendments, if any, it thinks is infringed by this Connecticut law. We are told that the Due Process Clause of the 14th Amendment is not, as such, the "guide" in this case. With that much I agree. There is no claim that this law is unconstitutionally vague or that the appellants were denied any of the elements of procedural due process at their trial. And the day has long passed since the Due Process Clause was regarded as a proper instrument for determining "the wisdom, need, and propriety" of state laws....

As to the First, Third, Fourth, and Fifth Amendments, I can find nothing in any of them to invalidate this Connecticut law, even assuming that all those Amendments are fully applicable against the States. To say that the Ninth Amendment has anything to do with this case is to turn somersaults with history. The Ninth Amendment, like its companion the Tenth, was simply to make clear that the adoption of the Bill of Rights did not alter the plan that the Federal Government was to be a government of express and limited powers. What provision of the Constitution, then, does make this state law invalid? The Court says it is the right of privacy "created by several fundamental constitutional guarantees." With all deference, I can find no such general right of privacy in the Bill of Rights, in any other part of the Constitution, or in any case ever before decided before this Court. At the oral argument we were told that the Connecticut law does not "conform to current community standards." But it is not the function of this Court to decide cases on the basis of community standards. If, as I should surely hope, the law before us does not reflect the standards of the people of

Connecticut, they can freely exercise their true Ninth and Tenth Amendment rights to persuade their elected representatives to repeal it. That is the constitutional way to take this law off the books.

Roe v. Wade MELVIN UROFSKY

Few cases in modern history, with the possible exception of *Brown v. Board of Education* (1954), have excited as much public controversy as *Roe v. Wade*. Moreover, while the essential rightness of the desegregation decision won fairly rapid public approval (even if not total acceptance in practice), a substantial number of people continue to believe that the Court was judicially, morally and politically wrong in the abortion decisions.

To understand the importance of this case, as well as the reaction it triggered, one must look at it in the context of both the civil rights and the women's movements. The effort by African-Americans to secure full legal equality under the Equal Protection Clause led other minorities to seek similar protection. While technically not a minority, women have historically been treated as inferior to men, and starting in the 1960s began pressing for equal treatment politically, economically, socially and legally. Women also wanted greater personal autonomy, especially control over their own bodies. It is in this context that the challenge to state abortion restrictions arose.

Most states in the early 1970s had statutes similar to the Texas law challenged in this case, which made it a crime to procure an abortion except "by medical advice for the purpose of saving the life of the mother." A pregnant single woman ("Jane Roe") and a licensed physician challenged the law. In a companion case, *Doe v. Bolton*, the Court also struck down a Georgia abortion statute that supposedly had a more "modern cast."

> ▶ Did the Court create a new right in this case, or did it merely recognize a new interpretation of other rights?
>
> ▶ Abortion did not become illegal until the middle of the nineteenth century, and at that time anti-abortion statutes usually resulted not from a morality crusade, but from efforts by doctors to professionalize their vocation and to do away with midwives. If abortion was not illegal in 1791, is it a legitimate Ninth Amendment right?
>
> ▶ To what extent should the Court take an activist role in the process of deciding complex and momentous social questions?
>
> ▶ What moral prinicples should the Court look to in deciding cases such as this?

Roe v. Wade 410 U.S. 113 (1973)

Mr. Justice BLACKMUN delivered the opinion of the Court....

We forthwith acknowledge our awareness of the sensitive and emotional nature of the abortion controversy, of the vigorous opposing views, even among physicians, and of the deep and seemingly absolute convictions that the subject inspires. One's philosophy, one's experience, one's exposure to the raw edges of human existence, one's religious training, one's attitudes toward life and family and their values, and the moral standards one establishes and seeks to observe, are all likely to influence and to color one's thinking and conclusions about abortion. In addition, population growth, pollution, poverty, and racial overtones tend to complicate and not to simplify the problem. Our task, of course, is to resolve the issue by constitutional measurement, free of emotion and of predilection. We seek earnestly to do this, and, because we do, we have inquired into, and in this opinion place some emphasis upon, medical and medical-legal history and what that history reveals abut man's attitudes toward the abortion procedure over the centuries....

The principal thrust of appellant's attack on the Texas statutes is that they improperly invade a right, said to be possessed by the pregnant woman, to choose to terminate her pregnancy....

The Constitution does not explicitly mention any right of privacy. However, the Court has recognized that a right of personal privacy, or a guarantee of certain areas or zones of privacy, does exist under the Constitution. In varying contexts, the Court or individual Justices have, indeed, found at least the roots of that right in the First Amendment, in the Fourth and Fifth Amendments; in the penumbras of the Bill of Rights; in the Ninth Amendment; or in the concept of liberty guaranteed by the first section of the 14th Amendment. These decisions make it clear that only personal rights that can be deemed "fundamental" or "implicit in the concept of ordered liberty" are included in this guarantee of personal privacy. They also make it clear that the right has some extension to activities relating to marriage, procreation, contraception, family relationships, and child rearing and education.

This right of privacy, whether it be founded in the 14th Amendment's concept of personal liberty and restrictions upon state action, as we feel it is, or, as the District Court determined, in the Ninth Amendment's reservation of rights to the people, is broad enough to encompass a woman's decision whether or not to terminate her pregnancy. The detriment that the State would impose upon the pregnant woman by denying this choice altogether is apparent. Specific and direct harm medically diagnosable even in early pregnancy may be involved. Maternity, or additional offspring, may force upon the woman a distressful life and future. Psychological harm may be imminent. Mental and physical health may be taxed by child care. There is also the distress, for all concerned, associated with the unwanted child, and there is a problem of bringing a child into a family already unable, psychologically and otherwise, to care for it. In others cases, as in this one, the additional difficulties and continuing stigma of unwed motherhood may be involved. All these are factors the woman and her responsible physician necessarily will consider in consultation.

On the basis of elements such as these, appellants and some *amici* argue that the woman's right is absolute and that she is entitled to terminate her pregnancy at whatever time, in whatever way, and for whatever reason she alone chooses. With this we do not agree. The Court's decision recognizing a right of privacy also acknowledge that some state regulation in areas protected by that right is appropriate. A state may properly assert important interests in safeguarding health, in maintaining medical standards, and in protecting potential life. At some point in pregnancy, these respective interests become sufficiently compelling to sustain regulation of the factors that govern the abortion decision. The privacy right involved, therefore, cannot be said to be absolute. In fact, it is not clear to us that the claim asserted by some *amici* that one has an unlimited right to do with one's body as one pleases bears a close relationship to the right of privacy previously articulated in the Court's decisions. The Court has refused to recognize an unlimited right of this kind in the past. We, therefore, conclude that the right of personal privacy includes the abortion decision, but that this right is not unqualified and must be considered against important state interests in regulation.

A. The appellee and certain *amici* argue that the fetus is a "person" within the language and meaning of the 14th Amendment. In support of this, they outline at length and in detail the well-known facts of fetal development. If this suggestion of personhood is established, the appellant's case, of course, collapses, for the fetus' right to life is then guaranteed specifically by the Amendment. On the other hand, the appellee conceded that no case could be cited that holds that a fetus is a person within the meaning of the 14th Amendment....

B. The pregnant woman cannot be isolated in her privacy. She carries an embryo and, later, a fetus, if one accepts the medical definitions of the developing young in the human uterus. The situation therefore is inherently different from marital intimacy, or bedroom possession of obscene material, or marriage, or procreation, or education, with which these others cases were concerned. It is reasonable and appropriate for a State to decide that at some point in time another interest, that of health of the mother or that of potential human life, becomes significantly involved. The woman's privacy is no longer sole and any right of privacy she possesses must be measured accordingly.

Texas argues that, apart from the 14th Amendment, life begins at conception and is present throughout pregnancy, and that, therefore, the State has a compelling interest in protecting that life from and after conception. We need not resolve the difficult question of when life begins. When those trained in the respective disciplines of medicine, philosophy, and theology are unable to arrive at any consensus, the judiciary, at this point in the development of man's knowledge, is not in a position to speculate as to the answer. It should be sufficient to note briefly the wide divergence of thinking on this most sensitive and difficult question. There has always been strong support for the view that life does not begin until live birth. This was the belief of the Stoics. It appears to be the predominant, though not the unanimous, attitude of the Jewish faith. It may be taken to represent also the position of a large segment of the Protestant community. The common law found greater significance in quickening. Physicians and their scientific colleagues have regarded that event with less interest and have tended to focus either upon conception, upon live birth, or upon the interim point at which the fetus becomes "viable," that is, potentially able to live outside the mother's womb, albeit with artificial aid. Viability is usually placed at about seven months (28 weeks) but may occur earlier, even at 24 weeks. The Aristotelian theory of "mediate animation," that held sway throughout the Middle Ages and the Renaissance in Europe, continued to be official Roman Catholic dogma until the 19th century, despite opposition to this "ensoulment" theory from those in the church who would recognize the existence of life from the moment of conception. The latter is now, of course, the official belief of the Catholic Church. This is a view strongly held by many non-Catholics as well, and by many physicians. Substantial problems for precise definition of this view are posed, however, by new embryological data that purport to indicate that conception is a "process" over time, rather than an event, and by new medical techniques such as menstrual extraction, the "morning-after" pill, implantation of embryos, artificial insemination, and even artificial wombs. In areas other than criminal abortion, the law has been reluctant to endorse any theory that life, as we recognize it, begins before live birth or to accord legal rights to the unborn except in narrowly defined situations and except when the rights are contingent upon live birth....In short, the unborn have never been recognized in the law as persons in the whole sense.

In view of all this, we do not agree that, by adopting one theory of life, Texas may override the rights of the pregnant woman that are at stake. We repeat, however, that the State does have an important and legitimate interest in preserving and protecting the health of the pregnant woman, whether she be a resident of the State or a nonresident who seeks medical consultation and treatment there, and that it has still another important and legitimate interest in protecting the potentiality of human life. These interests are separate and distinct. Each grows in substantiality as the woman approaches term and, at a point during pregnancy, each becomes "compelling."

With respect to the State's important and legitimate interest in the health of the mother, the "compelling" point, in the light of present medical knowledge, is at approximately the end of the first trimester. This is so because of the now established medical fact that until the end of the first trimester mortality in abortion is less than mortality in normal childbirth. It follows that, from and after this point, a State may regulate the abortion procedure to the extent that the regulation reasonably relates to the preservation and protection of maternal health. Examples of permissible state regulation in this area are requirements as to the qualifications of the person who is to perform the abortion; as to the licensure of that person; as to the facility in which the procedure is to be performed, that is, whether it must be a hospital or may be a clinic or some other place of less-than-hospital status; as to the licensing of the facility; and the like. This means, on the other hand, that for the period of pregnancy prior to this "compelling" point, the attending physician, in consultation with his patient, is free to determine, without regulation by the State, that, in his medical judgment, the patient's pregnancy should be terminated. If that decision is reached, the judgment may be effectuated by an abortion free of interference by the State.

With respect to the State's important and legitimate interest in potential life, the "compelling" point is at viability. This is so because the fetus then presumably has the capability of meaningful life outside the mother's womb. State regulation protective of fetal life after viability thus has both logical and biological justifications. If the State is interested in protecting fetal life after viability, it may go so far as to proscribe abortion during that period, except when it is necessary to preserve the life or health of the mother.

Measured against these standards, the Texas law sweeps too broadly. The statute makes no distinction between abortions performed early in pregnancy and those performed later, and it limits to a single reason, "saving" the mother's life, the legal justification for the procedure. The statute, therefore, cannot survive the constitutional attack made upon it here....

This holding, we feel, is consistent with the relative weights of the respective interests involved, with the lessons and examples of medical and legal history, with the lenity of the common law, and with the demands of the profound problems of the present day. The decision leaves the State free to place increasing restrictions on abortion as the period of pregnancy lengthens, so long as those restrictions are tailored to the recognized state interests. The decision vindicates the right of the physician to administer medical treatment according to his professional judgement up to the points where important state interests provide compelling justifications for intervention. Up to those points, the abortion decision in all its aspects is inherently, and primarily, a medical decision, and basic responsibility for it must rest with the physician. If an individual practitioner abuses the privilege of exercising proper medical judgment, the usual remedies, judicial and intraprofessional, are available....

It is so ordered.

Mr. Justice STEWART, concurring.

In 1963, this Court purported to sound the death knell for the doctrine of substantive due process. Barely two years later, [in *Griswold*], the Court held a Connecticut birth control law unconstitutional. In view of what had been so recently said in *Skrupa*, the Court's opinion in *Griswold* understandably did its best to avoid reliance on the Due Process Clause. Yet, the Connecticut law did not violate any specific provision of the Constitution. So it was clear to me then, and it is equally clear to me now, that the *Griswold* decision can be rationally understood only as a holding that the Connecticut statute substantively invaded the "liberty" that is protected by the Due Process Clause of the 14th Amendment. As so understood *Griswold* stands as one in a long line of pre-*Skrupa* cases decided under the doctrine of substantive due process, and I now accept it as such. The "liberty" protected by the Due Process Clause of the 14th Amendment covers more than those freedoms explicitly named in the Bill of Rights. Several decisions of this Court make clear that freedom of personal choice in matters of marriage and family life is one of the liberties protected by the Due Process Clause of the 14th Amendment....As recently as last Term, in *Eisenstadt v. Baird*, we recognized "the right of the individual, married or single, to be free from unwarranted governmental intrusion into matters so fundamentally affecting a person as the decision whether to bear or beget a child." That right necessarily includes the right of a woman to decide whether or not to terminate her pregnancy....

Mr. Justice DOUGLAS, concurring.

The Ninth Amendment obviously does not create federally enforceable rights. It merely says, "The enumeration in the Constitution, of certain rights, shall not be construed to deny or disparage others retained by the people." But a catalogue of these rights includes customary, traditional, and time-honored rights, amenities, privileges, and immunities that come within the sweep of "the Blessings of Liberty" mentioned in the preamble to the

Constitution. Many of them in my view come within the meaning of the term "liberty" as used in the 14th Amendment.

First is the autonomous control over the development and expression of one's intellect, interests, tastes, and personality. These are rights protected by the First Amendment and in my view they are absolute, permitting of no exception....

Second is freedom of choice in the basic decisions of one's life respecting marriage, divorce, procreation, contraception, and the education and upbringing of children. These "fundamental" rights, unlike those protected by the First Amendment, are subject to some control by the police power....

Third is the freedom to care for one's health and person, freedom from bodily restraint or compulsion, freedom to walk, stroll, or loaf. These rights, though fundamental, are likewise subject to regulation on a showing of "compelling state interest."...

A woman is free to make the basic decision whether to bear an unwanted child. Childbirth may deprive a woman of her preferred life style and force upon her a radically different and undesired future. Such reasoning is, however, only the beginning of the problem. The State has interests to protect. While childbirth endangers the lives of some women, voluntary abortion at any time and place regardless of medical standards would impinge on a rightful concern of society. The women's health is part of that concern; as is the life of the fetus after quickening. These concerns justify the State in treating the procedure as a medical one....

Mr. Justice WHITE, with whom Mr. Justice REHNQUIST joins, dissenting.

At the heart of the controversy in these cases are those recurring pregnancies that pose no danger whatsoever to the life or health of the mother but are nevertheless unwanted for any one or more of a variety of reasons—convenience, family planning, economics, dislike of children, the embarrassment of illegitimacy, etc. The common claim before us is that for any one of such reasons, or for no reason at all, and without asserting or claiming any threat to life or health, any woman is entitled to an abortion at her request if she is able to find a medical advisor willing to undertake the procedure. The Court for the most part sustains this position: During the period prior to the time the fetus becomes viable, the Constitution of the United States values the convenience, whim or caprice of the putative mother more than the life or potential life of the fetus; the Constitution, therefore, guarantees the right to an abortion as against any state law or policy seeking to protect the fetus from an abortion not prompted by more compelling reasons of the mother.

With all due respect, I dissent. I find nothing in the language or history of the Constitution to support the Court's judgment. The Court simply fashions and announces a new constitutional right for pregnant mothers and, with scarcely any reason or authority for its action, invests that right with sufficient substance to override most existing state abortion statutes. The upshot is that the people and the legislatures of the 50 States are constitutionally disentitled to weigh the relative importance of the continued existence and development of the fetus on the one hand against a spectrum of possible impacts on the mother on the other hand. As an exercise of raw judicial power, the court perhaps has authority to do what it does today; but in my view its judgment is an improvident and extravagant exercise of the power of judicial review that the Constitution extends to this Court....

Mr. Justice REHNQUIST, dissenting.

I have difficulty in concluding that the right of "privacy" is involved in this case. Texas bars the performance of a medical abortion by a licensed physician on a plaintiff such as Roe. A transaction resulting in an operation such as this is not "private" in the ordinary usage of that word....If the Court means by the term "privacy" no more than that the claim of a person to be free from unwanted state regulation of consensual transactions may be a form of "liberty" protected by the 14th Amendment, there is no doubt that similar claims have been upheld in our earlier decisions on the basis of that liberty. I agree that "liberty" embraces more than the rights found in the Bill of Rights. But that liberty is not guaranteed absolutely against deprivation, but only against deprivation without due process of law. The test traditionally applied in the area of social and economic legislation is whether or not a law such as that challenged has a rational relation to a valid state objective. The Due Process Clause of the 14th Amendment undoubtedly does place a limit, albeit a broad one, on legislative power to enact laws such as this. If the Texas statute were to prohibit an abortion even where the mother's life is in jeopardy, I have little doubt that such a statute would lack a rational relation to a valid state objective under the test stated. But the Court's sweeping invalidation of any restrictions on abortion during the first trimester is impossible to justify under that standard, and the conscious weighing of competing factors which the Court's opinion apparently substitutes for the established test is far more appropriate to a legislative judgment than to a judicial one....

Bowers v. Hardwick   MELVIN UROFSKY

Many states have laws regulating sexual conduct, some of which date back to colonial times. For the most part, when the activity is confined to consenting adults, the state avoids involvement, and these laws are rarely enforced. There are some who claim that the only reason many of them are still on the statute books is that no legislator wishes to take the lead in eliminating them, lest he or she be labeled an advocate of the conduct in question. Even in this case, when police inadvertently entered a bedroom and caught the defendant in the act, the state did not prosecute. In effect, the respondent was seeking a declaratory judgment that such laws were unconstitutional because they violated his right of privacy and that of other practicing homosexuals. If nothing else, *Bowers* is an indication of how society has changed. Until recently this type of case would never have been brought to court.

Given the fact that laws regulating sexual conduct are rarely enforced, the Court could have dismissed the suit since it did not constitute a valid "case or controversy" as required by the Constitution. But the Court wanted to send a message, both to the public and to the lower courts; namely, that the right to privacy first adumbrated in *Griswold* is not absolute, and that the Constitution cannot be used to support all actions merely on the basis of a claim of privacy.

The Court also recognized that, unlike marital privacy, homosexual sodomy had little public support. The Chief Justice noted that condemnation of homosexual practices "is firmly rooted in Judeo-Christian moral and ethical standards." Justice

White candidly admitted that "The Court is most vulnerable when it deals with judge-made constitutional law having little or no cognizable roots in the language or design of the Constitution."

Note, however, that four members of the Court were willing to extend the right of privacy to cover consensual acts between adults. Justice Powell originally believed that the right of privacy might be extended to homosexuals, but then changed his mind, and it was his vote that made the majority. Several years later, after he had left the bench, Powell stated that he had made a mistake in changing his vote, and that he should have stayed with what turned out to be the minority opinion. Had he done so, there might well have been a public outcry as loud if not as intensive as the one that greeted *Roe v. Wade*.

▶ Should sexual activity be regulated by the state? If so, to what extent?

▶ Is the statute in question enforceable?

▶ The Georgia code defined sodomy as "any sexual act involving the sex organs of one person and the mouth or anus of another." Some states have laws regarding coital positions. Should the state care about sexual activity between consenting adults? Why?

▶ Practically speaking, how should privacy be defined? Does the idea itself exclude any type of third-party or state interference?

▶ The idea that only "fundamental rights" deserve constitutional protection arguably makes sense; and the majority in this case dismisses the "right" to engage in consensual sodomy as not being fundamental. But what about the minority's view that it is not just the act that is in question, but the larger issue of permissible lifestyles and personal preferences?

▶ The Court here seems to say that no special privileges ought to be given to homosexuals, while in *Romer v. Evans* (1996), decided nearly a decade later, the Court indicates that gays and lesbians cannot be denied any rights. Could the reasoning in *Romer* apply equally well to the facts in *Bowers v. Hardwick?*

Bowers v. Hardwick 478 U.S. 186 (1986)

Mr. Justice WHITE delivered the opinion of the Court.

In August 1982, respondent was charged with violating the Georgia statute criminalizing sodomy by committing that act with another adult male in the bedroom of respondent's home. After a preliminary hearing, the District Attorney decided not to present the matter to the grand jury unless further evidence developed.

Respondent then brought suit in the Federal District Court, challenging the constitutionality of the statute insofar as it criminalized consensual sodomy. He asserted that he was a practicing homosexual, that the Georgia sodomy statute, as administered by the defendants, placed him in imminent danger of arrest, and that the statute for several reasons violates the Federal Constitution.

A divided panel of the Court of Appeals for the Eleventh Circuit went on to hold that the Georgia statute violated respondent's fundamental rights because his homosexual activity is a private and intimate association that is beyond the reach of state regulation by reason of the Ninth Amendment and the Due Process Clause of the Fourteenth Amendment. The case was remanded for trial, at which, to prevail, the State would have to prove that the statute is supported by a compelling interest and is the most narrowly drawn means of achieving that end.

Because other Courts of Appeals have arrived at judgments contrary to that of the Eleventh Circuit in this case, we granted the State's petition for *certiorari* questioning the holding that its sodomy statute violates the fundamental rights of homosexuals. We agree with the state that the Court of Appeals erred, and hence reverse its judgment.

This case does not require a judgment on whether laws against sodomy between consenting adults in general, or between homosexuals in particular, are wise or desirable. It raises no question about the right or propriety of state legislative decisions to repeal their laws that criminalize homosexual sodomy, or of state court decisions invalidating those laws on state constitutional grounds. The issue presented is whether the Federal Constitution confers a fundamental right upon homosexuals to engage in sodomy and hence invalidates the laws of the many States that still make such conduct illegal and have done so for a very long time. The case also calls for some judgment about the limits of the Court's role in carrying out its constitutional mandate....

We think it evident that none of the rights announced in [our earlier cases dealing with privacy] bears any resemblance to the claimed constitutional right of homosexuals to engage in acts of sodomy that is asserted in this case. No connection between family, marriage, or procreation on the one hand and homosexual activity on the other has been demonstrated, either by the Court of Appeals or by respondent. Moreover, any claim that these cases nevertheless stand for the proposition that any kind of private sexual conduct between consenting adults is constitutionally insulated from state proscription is unsupportable. Indeed, the Court's opinion in Carey twice asserted that the privacy right, which the Griswold line of cases found to be one of the protections provided by the Due Process Clause, did not reach so far.

Precedent aside, however, respondent would have us announce, as the Court of Appeals did, a fundamental right to engage in homosexual sodomy. This we are quite unwilling to do. It is true that despite the language of the Due Process Clauses of the Fifth and Fourteenth Amendments, which appears to focus only on the processes by which life, liberty, or property is taken, the cases are legion in which those Clauses have been interpreted to have substantive content, subsuming rights that to a great extent are immune from federal or state regulation or proscription. Among such cases are those recognizing rights that have little or no textual support in the constitutional language.

Striving to assure itself and the public that announcing rights not readily identifiable in the Constitution's text involves much more than the imposition of the Justices' own choice of values on the States and the Federal Government, the Court has sought to identify the nature of the rights qualifying for heightened judicial protection. In *Palko v. Connecticut* (1937), it was said that this category includes those fundamental liberties that are "implicit in the concept of ordered liberty," such that "neither liberty nor justice would exist if [they] were sacrificed." A different description of fundamental liberties appeared in *Moore v. East Cleveland* (1977), where they are characterized as those liberties that are "deeply rooted in this Nation's history and tradition."

It is obvious to us that neither of these formulations would extend a fundamental right to homosexuals to engage in acts of consensual sodomy. Proscriptions against that conduct have ancient roots. Sodomy was a criminal offense at common law and was forbidden by the laws of the original thirteen States when they ratified the Bill of Rights. In 1868, when the Fourteenth Amendment was ratified, all but 5 of the 37 States in the Union had criminal sodomy laws. In fact, until 1961, all 50 States outlawed sodomy, and today, 24 States and the District of Columbia continue to provide criminal penalties for sodomy performed in private and between consenting adults. Against this background, to claim that a right to engage in such conduct is "deeply rooted in this Nation's history and tradition" or "implicit in the concept of ordered liberty" is, at best, facetious.

Nor are we inclined to take a more expansive view of our authority to discover new fundamental rights embedded in the Due Process Clause. The Court is most vulnerable and comes nearest to illegitimacy when it deals with judge-made constitutional law having little or no cognizable roots in the language or design of the Constitution. That this is so was painfully demonstrated by the face-off between the Executive and the Court in the 1930's, which resulted in the repudiation of much of the substantive gloss that the Court had placed on the Due Process Clause of the Fifth and Fourteenth Amendments. There should be, therefore, great resistance to expand the substantive reach of those Clauses, particularly if it requires redefining the category of rights deemed to be fundamental. Otherwise, the Judiciary necessarily takes to itself further authority to govern the country without express constitutional authority. The claimed right pressed on us today falls far short of overcoming this resistance....

Even if the conduct at issue here is not a fundamental right, respondent asserts that there must be a rational basis for the law and that there is none in this case other than the presumed belief of a majority of the electorate in Georgia that homosexual sodomy is immoral and unacceptable. This is said to be an inadequate rationale to support the law. The law, however, is constantly based on notions of morality, and if all laws representing essentially moral choices are to be invalidated under the Due Process Clause, the courts will be very busy indeed. Even respondent makes no such claim, but insists that majority sentiments about the morality of homosexuality should be declared inadequate. We do not agree, and are unpersuaded that the sodomy laws of some 25 States should be invalidated on this basis.

Chief Justice BURGER, concurring.

I join the Court's opinion, but I write separately to underscore my view that in constitutional terms there is no such thing as a fundamental right to commit homosexual sodomy.

As the Court notes, the proscriptions against sodomy have very "ancient roots." Decisions of individuals relating to homosexual conduct have been subject to state intervention throughout the history of Western Civilization. Condemnation of those practices is firmly rooted in Judeao-Christian moral and ethical standards....To hold that the act of homosexual sodomy is somehow protected as a fundamental right would be to cast aside millennia of moral teaching.

This is essentially not a question of personal "preferences" but rather that of the legislative authority of the State. I find nothing in the Constitution depriving a State of the power to enact the statute challenged here.

Mr. Justice POWELL, concurring.

I join the opinion of the Court. I agree with the Court that there is no fundamental right— i.e, no substantive right under the Due Process Clause—such as that claimed by respondent, and found to exist by the Court of Appeals. This is not to suggest, however, that respondent may not be protected by the Eighth Amendment of the Constitution. The Georgia statute at issue in this case authorizes a court to imprison a person for up to 20 years for a single private, consensual act of sodomy. In my view, a prison sentence for such conduct—certainly a sentence of long duration—would create a serious Eighth Amendment issue. Under the Georgia statute a single act of sodomy, even in the private setting of a home, is a felony comparable in terms of the possible sentence imposed to serious felonies such as aggravated battery, first degree arson, and robbery.

In this case, however, respondent has not been tried, much less convicted and sentenced. Moreover, respondent has not raised the Eighth Amendment issue below. For these reasons this constitutional argument is not before us.

Mr. Justice BLACKMUN, with whom Justices BRENNAN, MARSHALL, and STEVENS join, dissenting.

This case is no more about "a fundamental right to engage in homosexual sodomy," as the Court purports to declare, than *Stanley v. Georgia* (1969), was about a fundamental right to watch obscene movies, or *Katz v. United States* (1967), was about a fundamental right to place interstate bets from a telephone booth. Rather, this case is about "the most comprehensive of rights and the right most valued by civilized men," namely "the right to be let alone."...

In its haste to reverse the Court of Appeals and hold that the Constitution does not "confer a fundamental right upon homosexuals to engage in sodomy," the Court relegates the actual statute being challenged to a footnote and ignores the procedural posture of the case before it. A fair reading of the statute and of the complaint clearly reveals that the majority has distorted the question this case presents.

First, the Court's almost obsessive focus on homosexual activity is particularly hard to justify in light of the broad language Georgia has used. Unlike the Court, the Georgia

Legislature has not proceeded on the assumption that homosexuals are so different from other citizens that their lives may be controlled in a way that would not be tolerated if it limited the choices of those other citizens. Rather, Georgia has provided that "[a] person commits the offense of sodomy when he performs or submits to any sexual act involving the sex organs of one person and the mouth or anus of another." The sex or status of the persons who engage in the act is irrelevant as a matter of state law. In fact, to the extent I can discern a legislative purpose for Georgia's 1968 enactment, that purpose seems to have been to broaden the coverage of the law to reach heterosexual as well as homosexual activity. Michael Hardwick's standing may rest in significant part on Georgia's apparent willingness to enforce against homosexuals a law it seems not to have any desire to enforce against heterosexuals. But his claim that [the Georgia law] involves an unconstitutional intrusion into his privacy and his right of intimate association does not depend in any way on his sexual orientation....

In construing the right to privacy, the Court has proceeded along two somewhat distinct, albeit complementary, lines. First, it has recognized a privacy interest with reference to certain decisions that are properly for the individual to make. Second, it has recognized a privacy interest with reference to certain places without regard for the particular activities in which the individuals who occupy them are engaged. The case before us implicates both the decisional and the spatial aspects of the right to privacy.

The Court concludes today that none of our prior cases dealing with various decisions that individuals are entitled to make free of governmental interference "bears any resemblance to the claimed constitutional right of homosexuals to engage in acts of sodomy that is asserted in this case." While it is true that these cases may be characterized by their connection to protection of the family, the Court's conclusion that they extend no further than this boundary ignores the warning against "closing our eyes to the basic reasons why certain rights associated with the family have been accorded shelter under the Fourteenth Amendment's Due Process Clause." We protect those rights not because they contribute, in some direct and material way, to the general public welfare, but because they form so central a part of an individual's life. "The concept of privacy embodies the 'moral fact that a person belongs to himself and not others nor to society as a whole.'" And so we protect the decision whether to marry precisely because marriage "is an association that promotes a way of life, not causes; a harmony in living, not political faiths; a bilateral loyalty, not commercial or social projects." We protect the decision whether to have a child because parenthood alters so dramatically an individual's self-definition, not because of demographic considerations or the Bible's command to be fruitful and multiply. And we protect the family because it contributes so powerfully to the happiness of individuals, not because of a preference for stereotypical households....

Only the most willful blindness could obscure the fact that sexual intimacy is "a sensitive, key relationship of human existence, central to family life, community welfare, and the development of human personality." The fact that individuals define themselves in a significant way through their intimate sexual relationships with others suggests, in a Nation as diverse as ours, that there may be many "right" ways of conducting those relationships, and that much of the richness of a relationship will come from the freedom an individual has to choose the form and nature of these intensely personal bonds.

In a variety of circumstances we have recognized that a necessary corollary of giving individuals freedom to choose how to conduct their lives is acceptance of the fact that different individuals will make different choices. For example, in holding that the clearly important state interest in public education should give way to a competing claim by the Amish to the effect that extended formal schooling threatened their way of life, the Court declared: "There can be no assumption that today's majority is `right' and the Amish and others like them are `wrong.' A way of life that is odd or even erratic but interferes with no rights or interests of others is not to be condemned because it is different." The Court claims that its decision today merely refuses to recognize a fundamental right to engage in homosexual sodomy; what the Court really has refused to recognize is the fundamental interest all individuals have in controlling the nature of their intimate associations with others.

The behavior for which Hardwick faces prosecution occurred in his own home, a place to which the Fourth Amendment attaches special significance. The Court's treatment of this aspect of the case is symptomatic of its overall refusal to consider the broad principles that have informed our treatment of privacy in specific cases. Just as the right to privacy is more than the mere aggregation of a number of entitlements to engage in specific behavior, so too, protecting the physical integrity of the home is more than merely a means of protecting specific activities that often take place there....

It took but three years for the Court to see the error in its analysis in *Minersville School District v. Gobitis* (1940), and to recognize that the threat to national cohesion posed by a refusal to salute the flag was vastly outweighed by the threat to those same values posed by compelling such a salute. See *West Virginia Board of Education v. Barnette* (1943). I can only hope that here, too, the Court soon will reconsider its analysis and conclude that depriving individuals of the right to choose for themselves how to conduct their intimate relationships poses a far greater threat to the values most deeply rooted in our Nation's history than tolerance of nonconformity could ever do. Because I think the Court today betrays those values, I dissent.

Mr. Justice STEVENS, with whom Justices BRENNAN and MARSHALL join, dissenting.

Like the statute that is challenged in this case, the rationale of the Court's opinion applies equally to the prohibited conduct regardless of whether the parties who engage in it are married or unmarried, or are of the same or different sexes. Sodomy was condemned as an odious and sinful type of behavior during the formative period of the common law. That condemnation was equally damning for heterosexual and homosexual sodomy. Moreover, it provided no special exemption for married couples. The license to cohabit and to produce legitimate offspring simply did not include any permission to engage in sexual conduct that was considered a "crime against nature."

The history of the Georgia statute before us clearly reveals this traditional prohibition of heterosexual, as well as homosexual, sodomy. Indeed, at one point in the 20th century, Georgia's law was construed to permit certain sexual conduct between homosexual women even though such conduct was prohibited between heterosexuals. The history of the statutes cited by the majority as proof for the proposition that sodomy is not constitutionally protected, similarly reveals a prohibition on heterosexual, as well as homosexual, sodomy.

Because the Georgia statute expresses the traditional view that sodomy is an immoral kind of conduct regardless of the identity of the persons who engage in it, I believe that a proper analysis of its constitutionality requires consideration of two questions: First, may a State totally prohibit the described conduct by means of a neutral law applying without exception to all persons subject to its jurisdiction? If not, may the State save the statute by announcing that it will only enforce the law against homosexuals? The two questions merit separate discussion.

Our prior cases make two propositions abundantly clear. First, the fact that the governing majority in a State has traditionally viewed a particular practice as immoral is not a sufficient reason for upholding a law prohibiting the practice; neither history nor tradition could save a law prohibiting miscegenation from constitutional attack. Second, individual decisions by married persons, concerning the intimacies of their physical relationship, even when not intended to produce offspring, are a form of "liberty" protected by the Due Process Clause of the Fourteenth Amendment. Moreover, this protection extends to intimate choices by unmarried as well as married persons.

In consideration of claims of this kind, the Court has emphasized the individual interest in privacy, but its decisions have actually been animated by an even more fundamental concern....

Society has every right to encourage its individual members to follow particular traditions in expressing affection for one another and in gratifying their personal desires. It, of course, may prohibit an individual from imposing his will on another to satisfy his own selfish interests. It also may prevent an individual from interfering with, or violating, a legally sanctioned and protected relationship, such as marriage. And it may explain the relative advantages and disadvantages of different forms of intimate expression. But when individual married couples are isolated from observation by others, the way in which they voluntarily choose to conduct their intimate relations is a matter for them—not the State—to decide. The essential "liberty" that animated the development of the law surely embraces the right to engage in nonreproductive, sexual conduct that others may consider offensive or immoral....

If the Georgia statute cannot be enforced as it is written—if the conduct it seeks to prohibit is a protected form of liberty for the vast majority of Georgia's citizens—the State must assume the burden of justifying a selective application of its law. Either the persons to whom Georgia seeks to apply its statute do not have the same interest in "liberty" that others have, or there must be a reason why the State may be permitted to apply a generally applicable law to certain persons that it does not apply to others.

The first possibility is plainly unacceptable. Although the meaning of the principle that "all men are created equal" is not always clear, it surely must mean that every free citizen has the same interest in "liberty" that he members of the majority share. From the standpoint of the individual, the homosexual and the heterosexual have the same interest in deciding how he will live his own life, and more narrowly, how he will conduct himself in his personal and voluntary association with his companions. State intrusion into the private conduct of either is equally burdensome.

The second possibility is similarly unacceptable. A policy of selective application must be supported by a neutral and legitimate interest—something more substantial than a habitual dislike for, or ignorance about, the disfavored group. Neither the State nor the Court has identified any such interest in this case. The Court has posited as a justification for the Georgia statute "the presumed belief of a majority of the electorate in Georgia that homosexual sodomy is immoral and unacceptable." But the Georgia electorate has expressed no such belief—instead, its representatives enacted a law that presumably reflects the belief that all sodomy is immoral and unacceptable. Unless the Court is prepared to conclude that such a law is constitutional, it may not rely on the work product of the Georgia Legislature to support its holding. For the Georgia statute does not single out homosexuals as a separate class meriting special disfavored treatment.

Nor, indeed, does the Georgia prosecutor even believe that all homosexuals who violate this statute should be punished. This conclusion is evident from the fact that the respondent in this very case has formally acknowledged in his complaint and in court that he has engaged, and intends to continue to engage, in the prohibited conduct, yet the State has elected not to process criminal charges against him. As Justice Powell points out, moreover, Georgia's prohibition on private, consensual sodomy has not been enforced for decades. The record of nonenforcement, in this case and in the last several decades, belies the Attorney General's representations about the importance of the State's selective application of its generally applicable law.

Both the Georgia statute and the Georgia prosecutor thus completely fail to provide the Court with any support for the conclusion that homosexual sodomy, simpliciter, is considered unacceptable conduct in that State, and that the burden of justifying a selective application of the generally applicable law has been met....

I respectfully dissent.

Cruzan v. Director, Missouri Department of Health   MELVIN UROFSKY

Current discussions about abortion center on the "right to life," referring, of course, to the right of the fetus to come to term and continue life outside the mother's womb. Is there also a "right to die?" Does the concept of privacy extend to the right to refuse or terminate medical intervention designed to prolong life? If one seeks to decide a right on the basis of its existence at the time of the framing of the Constitution and the Bill of Rights, then plainly there would be no case. The argument over the right to die is strictly modern, arising from the current ability of physicians to keep a person alive, often without much regard for the quality of that life. State courts wrestled with the problem in the fifteen years following *In re Quinlan*, the 1976 landmark decision of the New Jersey Supreme Court. That court allowed the removal of a respirator from a comatose patient, in accordance with the wishes of the patient's family. The court said that she had a constitutional right of privacy that permitted her to end her life. Since she was comatose, the family could make the decision for her.

The New Jersey decision relied on two legal traditions. The older one involved a common law right against unwanted touching, which had been interpreted over the years to mean that patients had a right not to receive treatment or medicine even when it would be in their best interests. The other strand was the newer constitutional right to privacy, first adumbrated by the U.S. Supreme Court in *Griswold v. Connecticut* (1965).

Between 1976 and 1989, state courts developed a fairly well-articulated body of case law that allowed a competent patient to refuse treatment, even if such refusal would lead to death; gave family or court-appointed guardians the power to act in the best interests of comatose patients, even including the cessation of life-sustaining treatment; and permitted the development of so-called "living wills" that allowed men and women to anticipate health crises and inform their medical and legal representatives what steps they wished taken, and what procedures should not be imposed. In 1989 the first "right-to-die" case reached the United States Supreme Court.

Nancy Beth Cruzan had been in "a persistent vegetative state" for seven years following an automobile accident, and received nutrition and water through a tube surgically implanted in her abdomen. All physicians agreed that she could never recover, but with the assistance of the tube she might survive as long as thirty years. When her family gave up hope that Nancy would recover, they asked that the feeding tube be withdrawn and that she be allowed to die. But their daughter had not provided a living will, and Missouri was one of three states that required a high evidentiary level to prove what the wishes of a comatose patient might be. As a result, the Missouri Supreme Court refused to allow the withdrawal of nourishment, claiming that the state's interest in the preservation of life was greater than the alleged right to privacy.

Chief Justice Rehnquist, in delivering the opinion of the Court, acknowledged that a limited "right to die" existed, a right based both in common law and constitutional origins. But the majority sustained the decision of the Missouri court, holding that a state, which had a general interest in the protection and preservation of life, could place reasonable limits upon that right, including requiring a level of evidence sufficient to prove that termination of treatment did, in fact, carry out the patient's wishes. Since Missouri recognized a living will as meeting this test, in the view of the majority, the state had not placed an undue burden on its citizens seeking to exercise their rights.

Following the Supreme Court decision, a friend of Nancy Cruzan came forward to say that she had heard Nancy once say that she never wanted to live as a vegetable. The local magistrate deemed this sufficient to meet the state's evidentiary requirement, and the attorney-general, having won his point on the state's right to establish criteria, did not challenge the judge's finding. The feeding tube was withdrawn, and Nancy Cruzan died.

- Without a formal statement (such as a Living Will), should the state accept any other evidence of a patient's wishes?

- Should the quality of life be a significant factor in deciding whether to use extraordinary means to keep a person alive?

- Is there a difference between refusing to allow the insertion of a feeding tube or respirator and removing such a device once it is in place?

- Is the maintenance of life a primary function of government? If so, when should the courts approve the termination of life? When a person is in a "persistent vegetative state"? When a person has committed a terrible crime? Never?

- Who decides when life has no meaning, when life to all intents and purposes has come to an end?

Cruzan v. Director, Missouri Department of Health 497 U.S. 261 (1990)

Chief Justice REHNQUIST delivered the opinion of the Court.

The common-law doctrine of informed consent is viewed as generally encompassing the right of a competent individual to refuse medical treatment. Beyond that, these decisions demonstrate both similarity and diversity in their approach to decision of what all agree is a perplexing question with unusually strong moral and ethical overtones. State courts have available to them for decision a number of sources—state constitutions, statutes, and common law—which are not available to us. In this Court, the question is simply and starkly whether the United States Constitution prohibits Missouri from choosing the rule of decision which it did. This is the first case in which we have been squarely presented with the issue of whether the United States Constitution grants what is in common parlance referred to as a "right to die"...It is the [better] part of wisdom not to attempt, by any general statement, to cover every possible phase of the subject.

The Fourteenth Amendment provides that no State shall "deprive any person of life, liberty, or property, without due process of law." The principle that a competent person has a constitutionally protected liberty interest in refusing unwanted medical treatment may be inferred from our prior decisions.

Just this Term, in the course of holding that a State's procedures for administering antipsychotic medication to prisoners were sufficient to satisfy due process concerns, we recognized that prisoners possess "a significant liberty interest in avoiding the unwanted administration of antipsychotic drugs under the Due Process Clause of the Fourteenth Amendment." Still other cases support the recognition of a general liberty interest in refusing medical treatment. But determining that a person has a "liberty interest" under the Due Process Clause does not end the inquiry; "whether respondent's constitutional rights have been violated must be determined by balancing his liberty interests against the relevant state interests."

Petitioners insist that under the general holdings of our cases, the forced administration of life-sustaining medical treatment, even of artificially-delivered food and water essential to life, would implicate a competent person's liberty interest. Although we think the logic of the cases discussed above would embrace such a liberty interest, the dramatic consequences involved in refusal of such treatment would inform the inquiry as to whether the deprivation of that interest is constitutionally permissible. But for purposes of this case, we assume that the United States Constitution would grant a competent person a constitutionally protected right to refuse lifesaving hydration and nutrition.

Petitioners go on to assert that an incompetent person should possess the same right in this respect as is possessed by a competent person.

The difficulty with petitioners' claim is that in a sense it begs the question: an incompetent person is not able to make an informed and voluntary choice to exercise a hypothetical right to refuse treatment or any other rights. Such a "right" must be exercised for her, if at all, by some sort of surrogate.

Here, Missouri has in effect recognized that under certain circumstances a surrogate may act for the patient in electing to have hydration and nutrition withdrawn in such a way as to cause death, but it has established a procedural safeguard to assure that the action of the surrogate conforms as best it may to the wishes expressed by the patient when competent. Missouri requires evidence of the incompetent's wishes as to the withdrawal of treatment to be proved by clear and convincing evidence. The question, then, is whether the United States Constitution forbids the establishment of this procedural requirement by the State. We hold that it does not.

Whether or not Missouri's clear and convincing evidence requirement comports with the United States Constitution depends in part on what interests the State may properly seek to protect in this situation. Missouri relies on its interest in the protection and preservation of human life, and there can be no gainsaying this interest. The choice between life and death is a deeply personal decision of obvious and overwhelming finality. We believe Missouri may legitimately seek to safeguard the personal element of this choice through the imposition of heightened evidentiary requirements. It cannot be disputed that the Due Process Clause protects an interest in life as well as an interest in refusing life-sustaining medical treatment. Not all incompetent patients will have loved ones available to serve as surrogate decisionmakers. And even where family members are present, "[t]here will, of course, be some unfortunate situations in which family members will not act to protect a patient." A State is entitled to guard against potential abuses in such situations. Similarly, a State is entitled to consider that a judicial proceeding to make a determination regarding an incompetent's wishes may very well not be an adversarial one, with the added guarantee of accurate factfinding that the adversary process brings with it. Finally, we think a State may properly decline to make judgments about the "quality" of life that a particular individual may enjoy, and simply assert an unqualified interest in the preservation of human life to be weighed against the constitutionally protected interests of the individual.

In our view, Missouri has permissibly sought to advance these interests through the adoption of a "clear and convincing" standard of proof to govern such proceedings. The more stringent the burden of proof a party must bear, the more that party bears the risk of an erroneous decision. We believe that Missouri may permissibly place an increased risk of an erroneous decision on those seeking to terminate an incompetent individual's life-sustaining treatment. An erroneous decision not to terminate results in a maintenance of the status quo; the possibility of subsequent developments such as advancements in medical science, the discovery of new evidence regarding the patient's intent, changes in the law, or simply the unexpected death of the patient despite the administration of life-sustaining treatment, at least create the potential that a wrong decision will eventually be corrected or its impact mitigated. An erroneous decision to withdraw life-sustaining treatment, however, is not susceptible of correction.

It is also worth noting that most, if not all, States simply forbid oral testimony entirely in determining the wishes of parties in transactions which, while important, simply do not have the consequences that a decision to terminate a person's life does. At common law and by statute in most States, the parole evidence rule prevents the variations of the terms of a written contract by oral testimony. There is no doubt that statutes requiring wills to be in writing, and statutes of frauds which require that a contract to make a will be in writing, on occasion frustrate the effectuation of the intent of a particular decedent, just as Missouri's requirement of proof in this case may have frustrated the effectuation of the not-fully-expressed desires of Nancy Cruzan. But the Constitution does not require general rules to work faultlessly; no general rule can.

In sum, we conclude that a State may apply a clear and convincing evidence standard in proceedings where a guardian seeks to discontinue nutrition and hydration of a person diagnosed to be in a persistent vegetative state. We note that many courts which have adopted some sort of substituted judgment procedure in situations like this, whether they limit consideration of evidence to the prior expressed wishes of the incompetent individual, or whether they allow more general proof of what the individual's decision would have been, require a clear and convincing standard of proof for such evidence.

The Supreme Court of Missouri held that in this case the testimony adduced at trial did not amount to clear and convincing proof of the patient's desire to have hydration and nutrition withdrawn. In so doing, it reversed a decision of the Missouri trial court which had found that the evidence "suggest[ed]" Nancy Cruzan would not have desired to continue such measures, but which had not adopted the standard of "clear and convincing evidence" enunciated by the Supreme Court. The testimony adduced at trial consisted primarily of Nancy Cruzan's statements made to a housemate about a year before her accident that she would not want to live should she face life as a "vegetable" and other observations to the same effect. The observations did not deal in terms with withdrawal of medical treatment or of hydration and nutrition. We cannot say that the Supreme Court of Missouri committed constitutional error in reaching the conclusion that it did.

Petitioners alternatively contend that Missouri must accept the "substituted judgment" of close family members even in the absence of substantial proof that their views reflect the views of the patient. In *Michael H.*, we upheld the constitutionality of California's favored treatment of traditional family relationships; such a holding may not be turned around into a constitutional requirement that a State must recognize the primacy of those relationships in a situation like this....Petitioners would seek to turn a decision which allowed a State to rely on family decisionmaking into a constitutional requirement that the State recognize such decisionmaking. But constitutional law does not work that way.

No doubt is engendered by anything in this record but that Nancy Cruzan's mother and father are loving and caring parents. If the State were required by the United States Constitution to repose a right of "substituted judgment" with anyone, the Cruzans would surely qualify. But we do not think the Due Process Clause requires the State to repose judgment on these matters with anyone but the patient herself. Close family members may have a strong feeling—a feeling not at all ignoble or unworthy, but not entirely disinterested, either—that they do not wish to witness the continuation of the life of a loved one which they regard as hopeless, meaningless, and even degrading. But there is no automatic assurance that the view of close family members will necessarily be the same as the patient's would have been had she been confronted with the prospect of her situation while competent. All of the reasons previously discussed for allowing Missouri to require clear and convincing evidence of the patient's wishes lead us to conclude that the State may choose to defer only to those wishes, rather than confide the decision to close family members.

The judgment of the Supreme Court of Missouri is

Affirmed.

Justice O'CONNOR, concurring.

As the Court notes, the liberty interest in refusing medical treatment flows from decisions involving the State's invasions into the body. Because our notions of liberty are inextricably entwined with our idea of physical freedom and self-determination, the Court has often deemed state incursions into the body repugnant to the interests protected by the Due Process Clause.

The State's imposition of medical treatment on an unwilling competent adult necessarily involves some form of restraint and intrusion. A seriously ill or dying patient whose wishes are not honored may feel a captive of the machinery required for life-sustaining measures or other medical interventions. Such forced treatment may burden that individual's liberty interests as much as any state coercion.

Whether or not the techniques used to pass food and water into the patient's alimentary tract are termed "medical treatment," it is clear they all involve some degree of intrusion and restraint. Requiring a competent adult to endure such procedures against her will burdens the patient's liberty, dignity, and freedom to determine the course of her own treatment. Accordingly, the liberty guaranteed by the Due Process Clause must protect, if it protects anything, an individual's deeply personal decision to reject medical treatment, including the artificial delivery of food and water.

I also write separately to emphasize that the Court does not today decide the issue whether a State must also give effect to the decisions of a surrogate decisionmaker. In my view, such a duty may well be constitutionally required to protect the patient's liberty interest in refusing medical treatment. Few individuals provide explicit oral or written instructions regarding their intent to refuse medical treatment should they become incompetent. States which decline to consider any evidence other than such instructions may frequently fail to honor a patient's appointment of a proxy to make health care decisions on her behalf.

Delegating the authority to make medical decisions to a family member or friend is becoming a common method of planning for the future. Several States have recognized the practical wisdom of such a procedure by enacting durable power of attorney statues that specifically authorize an individual to appoint a surrogate to make medical treatment decisions.

Other States allow an individual to designate a proxy to carry out the intent of a living will. These procedures for surrogate decisionmaking, which appear to be rapidly gaining in acceptance, may be a valuable additional safeguard of the patient's interest in directing his medical care.

Today's decision, holding only that the Constitution permits a State to require clear and convincing evidence of Nancy Cruzan's desire to have artificial hydration and nutrition withdrawn, does not preclude a future determination that the Constitution requires the States to implement the decisions of a patient's duly appointed surrogate. Nor does it prevent States from developing other approaches for protecting an incompetent individual's liberty interest in refusing medical treatment. No national consensus has yet emerged on the best solution for this difficult and sensitive problem. Today we decide only that one State's practice does not violate the Constitution; the more challenging task of crafting appropriate procedures for safe-guarding incompetents' liberty interests is entrusted to the "laboratory" of the States.

Justice SCALIA, concurring.

The various opinions in this case portray quite clearly the difficult, indeed agonizing, questions that are presented by the constantly increasing power of science to keep the human body alive for longer than any reasonable person would want to inhabit it. The States have begun to grapple with these problems through legislation. I am concerned, from the tenor of today's opinions, that we are poised to confuse that enterprise as successfully as we have confused the enterprise of legislating concerning abortion—requiring it to be conducted against a background of federal constitutional imperatives that are unknown because they are being newly crafted from Term to Term. That would be a great misfortune.

While I agree with the Court's analysis today, and therefore join in its opinion, I would have preferred that we announce, clearly and promptly, that the federal courts have no business in this field; that American law has always accorded the State the power to prevent, by force if necessary, suicide—including suicide by refusing to take appropriate measures necessary to preserve one's life; that the point at which life becomes "worthless," and the point at which the means necessary to preserve it become "extraordinary" or "inappropriate," are neither set forth in the Constitution nor known to the nine Justices of this Court any better than they are known to nine people picked at random from the Kansas City telephone directory; and hence, that even when it is demonstrated by clear and convincing evidence that a patient no longer wishes certain measures to be taken to preserve her life, it is up to the citizens of Missouri to decide, through their elected representatives, whether that wish will be honored. It is quite impossible (because the Constitution says nothing about the matter) that those citizens will decide upon a line less lawful than the one we would choose; and it is unlikely (because we know no more about "life-and-death" than they do) that they will decide upon a line less reasonable....

What I have said above is not meant to suggest that I would think it desirable, if we were sure that Nancy Cruzan wanted to die, to keep her alive by the means at issue here. I assert only that the Constitution has nothing to say about the subject. To raise up a constitutional right here we would have to create out of nothing (for it exists neither in text nor tradition) some constitutional principle whereby, although the State may insist that an individual come in out of the cold and eat food, it may not insist that he take medicine; and although it may pump his stomach empty of poison he has ingested, it may not fill his stomach with food he has failed to ingest. Are there, then, no reasonable and humane limits that ought not to be exceeded in requiring an individual to preserve his own life? There obviously are, but they are not set forth in the Due Process Clause. What assures us that those limits will not be exceeded is the same constitutional guarantee that is the source of most of our protection—what protects us, for example, from being assessed a tax of 100% of our income above the subsistence level, from being forbidden to drive cars, or from being required to send our children to school for 10 hours a day, none of which horribles is categorically prohibited by the Constitution. Our salvation is the Equal Protection Clause, which requires the democratic majority to accept for themselves and their loved ones what they impose on you and me. This Court need not, and has no authority to, inject into every field of human activity where irrationality and oppression may theoretically occur, and if it tries to do so it will destroy itself.

Justice BRENNAN, with whom Justice MARSHALL and Justice BLACKMUN join, dissenting.

Today the Court, while tentatively accepting that there is some degree of constitutionally protected liberty interest in avoiding unwanted medical treatment, including life-sustaining medical treatment such as artificial nutrition and hydration, affirms the decision of the Missouri Supreme Court. The majority opinion, as I read it, would affirm that decision on the ground that a State may require "clear and convincing" evidence of Nancy Cruzan's prior decision to forgo life-sustaining treatment under circumstances such as hers in order to ensure that her actual wishes are honored. Because I believe that Nancy Cruzan has a fundamental right to be free of unwanted artificial nutrition and hydration, which right is not outweighed by any interests of the State, and because I find that the improperly biased procedural obstacles imposed by the Missouri Supreme Court impermissibly burden that right, I respectfully dissent. Nancy Cruzan is entitled to choose to die with dignity.

The question before this Court is a relatively narrow one: whether the Due Process Clause allows Missouri to require a now-incompetent patient in an irreversible persistent vegetative state to remain on life-support absent rigorously clear and convincing evidence that avoiding the treatment represents the patient's prior, express choice. If a fundamental right is at issue, Missouri's rule of decision must be scrutinized under the standards this Court has always applied in such circumstances. Fundamental rights "are protected not only against heavy-handed frontal attack, but also from being stifled by more subtle governmental interference."

The starting point for our legal analysis must be whether a competent person has a constitutional right to avoid unwanted medical care. Earlier this Term, this Court held that the Due Process Clause of the Fourteenth Amendment confers a significant liberty interest in avoiding unwanted medical treatment. Today, the Court concedes that our prior decisions "support the recognition of a general liberty interest in refusing medical treatment." The Court, however, avoids discussing either the measure of that liberty interest or its application by assuming, for purposes of this case only, that a competent person has a constitutionally protected liberty interest in being free of unwanted artificial nutrition and hydration. Justice O'Connor's opinion is less parsimonious. She openly affirms that "the Court has often deemed state incursions into the body repugnant to the interests protected by the Due Process Clause," that there is a liberty interest in avoiding unwanted medical treatment and that it encompasses the right to be free of "artificially delivered food and water."

But if a competent person has a liberty interest to be free of unwanted medical treatment, as both the majority and Justice O'Connor concede, it must be fundamental.

The right to be free from medical attention without consent, to determine what shall be done with one's own body, *is* deeply rooted in this Nation's traditions, as the majority acknowledges. This right has long been "firmly entrenched in American tort law" and is securely grounded in the earliest common law. Freedom from unwanted medical attention is unquestionably among those principles "so rooted in the traditions and conscience of our people as to be ranked as fundamental."

That there may be serious consequences involved in refusal of the medical treatment at issue here does not vitiate the right under our common law tradition of medical self-determination. It is "a well-established rule of general law...that it is the patient, not the physician, who ultimately decides if treatment—any treatment—is to be given at all....The rule has never been qualified in its application by either the nature or purpose of the treatment, or the gravity of the consequences of acceding to or foregoing it." The fact that Nancy Cruzan is now incompetent [does not] deprive her of her fundamental rights.

The right to be free from unwanted medical attention is a right to evaluate the potential benefit of treatment and its possible consequences according to one's own values and to make a personal decision whether to subject oneself to the intrusion. For a patient like Nancy Cruzan, the sole benefit of medical treatment is being kept metabolically alive. Neither artificial nutrition nor any other form of medical treatment available today can cure or in any way ameliorate her condition.

There are also affirmative reasons why someone like Nancy might choose to forgo artificial nutrition and hydration under these circumstances. Dying is personal. And it is profound. For many, the thought of an ignoble end, steeped in decay, is abhorrent. A quiet, proud death, bodily integrity intact, is a matter of extreme consequence.

Although the right to be free of unwanted medical intervention, like other constitutionally protected interests, may not be absolute, no State interest could outweigh the rights of an individual in Nancy Cruzan's position. Whatever a State's possible interests in mandating life-support treatment under other circumstances, there is no good to be obtained here by Missouri's insistence that Nancy Cruzan remain on life-support systems if it is indeed her wish not to do so. Missouri does not claim, nor could it, that society as a whole will be benefitted by Nancy's receiving medical treatment. Thus, the State's general interest in life must accede to Nancy Cruzan's particularized and intense interest in self-determination in her choice of medical treatment. There is simply nothing legitimately within the State's purview to be gained by superseding her decision.

This is not to say that the State has no legitimate interests to assert here. As the majority recognizes, Missouri has a *parens patriae* interest in providing Nancy Cruzan, now incompetent, with as accurate as possible a determination of how she would exercise her rights under these circumstances. Second, if and when it is determined that Nancy Cruzan would want to continue treatment, the State may legitimately assert an interest in providing that treatment. But until Nancy's wishes have been determined, the only state interest that may be asserted is an interest in safeguarding the accuracy of that determination.

Accuracy, therefore, must be our touchstone. Missouri may constitutionally impose only those procedural requirements that serve to enhance the accuracy of a determination of Nancy Cruzan's wishes or are at least consistent with an accurate determination. The Missouri "safeguard" that the Court upholds today does not meet that standard. The determination needed in this context is whether the incompetent person would choose to live in a persistent vegetative state on life-support or to avoid this medical treatment. Missouri's rule of decision imposes a markedly asymmetrical evidentiary burden. Only evidence of specific statements of treatment choice made by the patient when competent is admissible to support a finding that the patient, now in a persistent vegetative state, would wish to avoid further medical treatment. Moreover, this evidence must be clear and convincing. No proof is required to support a finding that the incompetent person would wish to continue treatment.

In a hearing to determine the treatment preferences of an incompetent person, a court is not limited to adjusting burdens of proof as its only means of protecting against a possible imbalance. Indeed, any concern that those who come forward will present a one-sided view would be better addressed by appointing a guardian *ad litem*, who could use the State's powers of discovery to gather and present evidence regarding the patient's wishes. A guardian *ad litem*'s task is to uncover any conflicts of interest and ensure that each party likely to have relevant evidence is consulted and brought forward—for example, other members of the family, friends, clergy, and doctors. Missouri's heightened evidentiary standard attempts to achieve balance by discounting evidence; the guardian *ad litem* technique achieves balance by probing for additional evidence. Where, as here, the family members, friends, doctors and guardian *ad litem* agree, it is not because the process has failed, as the majority suggests. It is because there is no genuine dispute as to Nancy's preference.

The majority next argues that where, as here, important individual rights are at stake, a clear and convincing evidence standard has long been held to be an appropriate means of enhancing accuracy, citing decisions concerning what process an individual is due before he can be deprived of a liberty interest. In those cases, however, this Court imposed a clear and convincing standard as a constitutional minimum on the basis of its evaluation that one side's interests clearly outweighed the second side's interests and therefore the second side should bear the risk of error. In the cases cited by the majority, the imbalance imposed by a heightened evidentiary standard was not only acceptable but required because the standard was deployed to protect an individual's exercise of a fundamental right, as the majority admits. In contrast, the Missouri court imposed a clear and convincing standard as an obstacle to the exercise of a fundamental right.

The majority claims that the allocation of the risk of error is justified because it is more important not to terminate life-support for someone who would wish it continued than to honor the wishes of someone who would not. An erroneous decision to terminate life-support is irrevocable, says the majority, while an erroneous decision not to terminate "results in a maintenance of the status quo." But, from the point of view of the patient, an erroneous decision in either direction is irrevocable. An erroneous decision to terminate artificial nutrition and hydration, to be sure, will lead to failure of that last remnant of physiological life, the brain stem, and result in complete brain death. An erroneous decision not to terminate life-support, however, robs a patient of the very qualities protected by the right to avoid unwanted medical treatment. His own degraded existence is perpetuated; his family's suffering is protracted; the memory he leaves behind becomes more and more distorted.

Even more than its heightened evidentiary standard, the Missouri court's categorical exclusion of relevant evidence dispenses with any semblance of accurate factfinding. The court adverted to no evidence supporting its decision, but held that no clear and convincing, inherently reliable evidence had been presented to show that Nancy would want to avoid further treatment. In doing so, the court failed to consider statements Nancy had made to family members and a close friend. The court also failed to consider testimony from Nancy's mother and sister that they were certain that Nancy would want to discontinue artificial nutrition and hydration, even after the court found that Nancy's family was loving and without malignant motive. The court also failed to consider the conclusions of the guardian *ad litem*, appointed by the trial court, that there was clear and convincing evidence that Nancy would want to discontinue medical treatment and that this was in her best interests. The court did not specifically define what kind of evidence it would consider clear and convincing, but its general discussion suggests that only a living will or equivalently formal directive from the patient when competent would meet this standard.

When Missouri enacted a living statute, it specifically provided that the absence of a living will does not warrant a presumption that a patient wishes continued medical treatment. Thus, apparently not even Missouri's own legislature believes that a person who does not execute a living will fails to do so because he wishes continuous medical treatment under all circumstances.

The testimony of close friends and family members, on the other hand, may often be the best evidence available of what the patient's choice would be. It is they with whom the patient most likely will have discussed such questions and they who know the patient best.

The Missouri court's disdain for Nancy's statements in serious conversations not long before her accident, for the opinions of Nancy's family and friends as to her values, beliefs and certain choice, and even for the opinion of an outside objective factfinder appointed by the State evinces a disdain for Nancy Cruzan's own right to choose. The rules by which an incompetent person's wishes are determined must represent every effort to determine those wishes. The rule that the Missouri court adopted and that this Court upholds, however, skews the result away from a determination that as accurately as possible reflects the individual's own preferences and beliefs. It is a rule that transforms human beings into passive subjects of medical technology.

I cannot agree with the majority that where it is not possible to determine what choice an incompetent patient would make, a State's role as *parens patriae* permits the State automatically to make that choice itself. A State's legitimate interest in safeguarding a patient's choice cannot be furthered by simply appropriating it.

The majority justifies its position by arguing that, while close family members may have a strong feeling about the question, "there is no automatic assurance that the view of close family members will necessarily be the same as the patient's would have been had she been confronted with the prospect of her situation while competent." I cannot quarrel with this observation. But it leads only to another question: Is there any reason to suppose that a State is more likely to make the choice that the patient would have made than someone who knew the patient intimately? To ask this is to answer it.

A State's inability to discern an incompetent patient's choice still need not mean that a State is rendered powerless to protect that choice. But I would find that the Due Process Clause prohibits a State from doing more than that. A State may ensure that the person who makes the decision on the patient's behalf is the one whom the patient himself would have selected to make that choice for him. And a State may exclude from consideration anyone having improper motives. But a State generally must either repose the choice with the person whom the patient himself would most likely have chosen as proxy or leave the decision to the patient's family.

The new medical technology can reclaim those who would have been irretrievably lost a few decades ago and restore them to active lives. For Nancy Cruzan, it failed, and for others with wasting incurable disease it may be doomed to failure. In these unfortunate situations, the bodies and preferences and memories of the victims do not escheat to the State; nor does our Constitution permit the State or any other government to commandeer them. No singularity of feeling exists upon which such a government might confidently rely as *parens patriae*. Yet Missouri and this Court have displaced Nancy's own assessment of the processes associated with dying. They have discarded evidence of her will, ignored her values, and deprived her of the right to a decision as closely approximating her own choice as humanly possible. They have done so disingenuously in her name, and openly in Missouri's own. That Missouri and this Court may truly be motivated only by concern for incompetent patients makes no matter. As one of our most prominent jurists warned us decades ago: "Experience should teach us to be most on our guard to protect liberty when the government's purposes are beneficent....The greatest dangers to liberty lurk in insidious encroachment by men of zeal, well meaning but without understanding."

I respectfully dissent.

Justice STEVENS, dissenting.

[The Court] permits the State's abstract, undifferentiated interest in the preservation of life to overwhelm the best interests of Nancy Beth Cruzan, interests which would, according to an undisputed finding, be served by allowing her guardians to exercise her constitutional right to discontinue medical treatment. Ironically, the Court reaches this conclusion despite endorsing three significant propositions which should save it from any such dilemma. First, a competent individual's decision to refuse life-sustaining medical procedures is an aspect of liberty protected by the Due Process Clause of the Fourteenth Amendment. Second, upon a proper evidentiary showing, a qualified guardian may make that decision on behalf of an incompetent ward. Third, in answering the important question presented by this tragic case, it is wise "not to attempt by any general statement, to cover every possible phase of the subject." Together, these considerations suggest that Nancy Cruzan's liberty to be free from medical treatment must be understood in light of the facts and circumstances particular to her.

I would so hold: in my view, the Constitution requires the State to care for Nancy Cruzan's life in a way that gives appropriate respect to her own best interests.

This case is the first in which we consider whether, and how, the Constitution protects the liberty of seriously ill patients to be free from life-sustaining medical treatment. So put, the question is both general and profound. We need not, however, resolve the question in the abstract. Our responsibility as judges both enables and compels us to treat the problem as it is illuminated by the facts of the controversy before us.

The most important of those facts are these: "clear and convincing evidence" established that Nancy Cruzan is "oblivious to her environment except for reflexive responses to sound and perhaps to painful stimuli"; that "she has no cognitive or reflexive ability to swallow food or water"; that "she will never recover" these abilities; and that her "cerebral cortical atrophy is irreversible, permanent, progressive and ongoing." Recovery and consciousness are impossible; the highest cognitive brain function that can be hoped for is a grimace in "recognition of ordinarily painful stimuli." or an "apparent response to sound." Missouri's regulation is an unreasonable intrusion upon traditionally private matters encompassed within the liberty protected by the Due Process Clause.

The portion of this Court's opinion that considers the merits of this case is similarly unsatisfactory. It, too, fails to respect the best interests of the patient. It, too, relies on what is tantamount to a waiver rationale: the dying patient's best interests are put to one side and the entire inquiry is focused on her prior expressions of intent. An innocent person's constitutional right to be free from unwanted medical treatment is thereby categorically limited to those patients who had the foresight to make an unambiguous statement of their wishes while competent. The Court's decision affords no protection to children, to young people who are victims of unexpected accidents or illnesses, or to the countless thousands of elderly persons who either fail to decide, or fail to explain, how they want to be treated if they should experience a similar fate. Because Nancy Beth Cruzan did not have the foresight to preserve her constitutional right in a living will, or some comparable "clear and convincing" alternative, her right is gone forever and her fate is in the hands of the state legislature.

It is perhaps predictable that courts might undervalue the liberty at stake here. Because death is so profoundly personal, public reflection upon it is unusual. As this sad case shows, however, such reflection must become more common if we are to deal responsibly with the modern circumstances of death. Medical advances have altered the physiological conditions of death in ways that may be alarming: highly invasive treatment may perpetuate human existence through a merger of body and machine that some might reasonably regard as an insult to life rather than as its continuation. This Court has long recognized that the liberty to make the decisions and choices constitutive of private life is so fundamental to our "concept of ordered liberty," that those choices must occasionally be afforded more direct protection.

Respect for these choices has guided our recognition of rights pertaining to bodily integrity. The constitutional decisions identifying those rights, like the common-law tradition upon which they built, are mindful that the "makers of our Constitution...recognized the significance of man's spiritual nature." It may truly be said that "our notions of liberty are inextricably entwined with our idea of physical freedom and self determination." Thus we have construed the Due Process Clause to preclude physically invasive recoveries of evidence not only because such procedures are "brutal" but also because they are "offensive to human dignity."

It is against this background of decisional law, and the constitutional tradition which it illuminates, that the right to be free from unwanted life-sustaining medical treatment must be understood. Choices about death touch the core of liberty. Our duty, and the concomitant freedom, to come to terms with the conditions of our own mortality are undoubtedly "so rooted in the traditions and conscience of our people as to be ranked as fundamental," and indeed are essential incidents of the unalienable rights to life and liberty endowed us by our Creator.

The more precise constitutional significance of death is difficult to describe; not much may be said with confidence about death unless it is said from faith, and that alone is reason enough to protect the freedom to conform choices about death to individual conscience. We may also, however, justly assume that death is not life's simple opposite, or its necessary terminus, but rather its completion. Our ethical tradition has long regarded an appreciation of mortality as essential to understanding life's significance.

These considerations cast into stark relief the injustice, and unconstitutionality, of Missouri's treatment of Nancy Beth Cruzan. Nancy Cruzan's death, when it comes, will inevitably be the consequence of her tragic accident. But Nancy Cruzan's interest in life, no less than that of any other person, includes an interest in how she will be thought of after her death by those whose opinions mattered to her. There can be no doubt that her life made her dear to her family, and to others. How she dies will affect how that life is remembered. The trial court's order authorizing Nancy's parents to cease their daughter's treatment would have permitted the family that cares for Nancy to bring to a close her tragedy and her death. Missouri's objection to that order subordinates Nancy's body, her family, and the lasting significance of her life to the State's own interests. The decision we review thereby interferes with constitutional interests of the highest order.

To be constitutionally permissible, Missouri's intrusion upon these fundamental liberties must, at a minimum, bear a reasonable relationship to a legitimate state end. Missouri asserts that its policy is related to a state interest in the protection of life. In my view, however, it is an effort to define life, rather than to protect it, that is the heart of Missouri's policy. Missouri insists, without regard to Nancy Cruzan's own interests, upon equating her life with the biological persistence of her bodily functions. Nancy Cruzan, it must be remembered, is not now simply incompetent. She is in a persistent vegetative state, and has been so for seven years.

It seems to me that the Court errs insofar as it characterizes this case as involving "judgments about the 'quality' of life that a particular individual may enjoy." Nancy Cruzan is obviously "*alive*" in a physiological sense. But for patients like Nancy Cruzan, who have no consciousness and no chance of recovery, there is a serious question as to whether the mere persistence of their bodies is "*life*" as that word is commonly understood, or as it is used in both the Constitution and the Declaration of Independence. The State's unflagging determination to perpetuate Nancy Cruzan's physical existence is comprehensible only as an effort to define life's meaning, not as an attempt to preserve its sanctity.

This much should be clear from the oddity of Missouri's definition alone. Life, particularly human life, is not commonly thought of as a merely physiological condition or function. Its sanctity is often thought to derive from the impossibility of any such reduction. When people speak of life, they often mean to describe the experiences that comprise a person's history, as when it is said that somebody "led a good life." They may also mean to refer to the practical manifestation of the human spirit, a meaning captured by the familiar observation that somebody "added life" to an assembly. If there is a shared thread among the various opinions on this subject, it may be that life is an activity which is at once the matrix for and an integration of a person's interests. In any event, absent some theological abstraction, the idea of life is not conceived separately from the idea of a living person. Yet, it is by precisely such a separation that Missouri asserts an interest in Nancy Cruzan's life in opposition to Nancy Cruzan's own interests. The resulting definition is uncommon indeed.

My disagreement with the Court is unrelated to its endorsement of the clear and convincing standard of proof for cases of this kind. Indeed, I agree that the controlling facts must be established with unmistakable clarity. The critical question, however, is not how to prove the controlling facts but rather what proven facts should be controlling. In my view, the constitutional answer is clear: the best interests of the individual, especially when buttressed by the interests of all related third parties, must prevail over any general state policy that simply ignores those interests.

However commendable may be the State's interest in human life, it cannot pursue that interest by appropriating Nancy Cruzan's life as a symbol for its own purposes. Lives do not exist in abstraction from persons, and to pretend otherwise is not to honor but to desecrate the State's responsibility for protecting life. A State that seeks to demonstrate its commitment to life may do so by aiding those who are actively struggling for life and health. In this endeavor, unfortunately, no State can lack for opportunities: there can be no need to make an example of tragic cases like that of Nancy Cruzan.

I respectfully dissent.

Editor's Note:
Following the U.S. Supreme Court decision, Nancy Cruzan's case was returned to the Missouri courts. There it was finally resolved in a ruling announced on December 14, 1990, when Jasper County Probate Judge Charles Teel

ordered the Missouri Rehabilitation Center in Mount Vernon to accede to the Cruzan family's wishes and to remove the feeding tube, allowing Ms. Cruzan to die. Her physician, who had testified three years earlier that he opposed removal of the feeding tube, reversed his position saying in court that he now believed it to be in Cruzan's best interest to end her "living hell." At the same time, three former co-workers testified in November 1990 that Nancy Cruzan had told them she would not want to be kept alive by medical machinery if she became incapacitated. The Supreme Court had ruled that Missouri could require "clear and convincing" proof that Cruzan would want to die, and had returned the case to Teel to decide if such proof existed. Judge Teel found the evidence he needed: the feeding tube was removed, and Nancy Cruzan died twelve days later on December 29.   DB

Planned Parenthood of Southeastern Pennsylvania v. Casey
MELVIN UROFSKY

In the 1980 presidential campaign, Ronald Reagan promised that, if elected, he would appoint judges to the federal courts who would overturn *Roe v. Wade*. As president, Reagan did his best to carry out his campaign pledge, and the Justice Department questionnaire to prospective judicial appointees included questions on their views about abortion. Yet although Reagan and his successor George Bush named conservatives to the Court, the anticipated majority to overturn *Roe* never materialized. In a succession of cases, the Supreme Court chipped away at the absolutist position of *Roe*, at its trimester scheme, and at the restrictions it placed on states to keep them from interfering with a women's choice whether to abort or carry a fetus to term. In related cases the high court upheld congressional and state legislative decisions not to fund abortion procedures, as well as an executive ban forbidding doctors in clinics receiving federal funds from even telling their patients that abortion was an option.

In the 1989 case of *Webster v. Reproductive Health Service*, opponents of abortion believed that *Roe* would soon be overturned. Four members of the Court indicated that they considered *Roe* wrongly decided; all they needed was one more vote, and the most liberal members of the Court, William Brennan, Thurgood Marshall, and Harry Blackmun, would not remain on the bench much longer. Following that decision Pennsylvania, which had one of the most abortion-restrictive laws of any state, passed new measures specifically designed to create a test case in which the justices could directly confront the question of whether to overrule *Roe*.

Yet to everyone's surprise, the center of the Court—Sandra Day O'Connor, Anthony Kennedy and David Souter—all of whom had been appointed during the Reagan-Bush years and all of whom had earlier expressed dissatisfaction with *Roe*, decided to uphold its basic tenets. While striking down some of Pennsylvania's restrictions and upholding others, the plurality nonetheless reaffirmed a woman's right to choose. Joined by Justices Stevens and Blackmun, the Court once again turned back the attack on *Roe*.

What is somewhat surprising in the opinions are Justice O'Connor's frank assertion that the Court must be interpretationist and Justice Blackmun's acknowledgment that personnel changes on the Court might yet lead to a major jurisprudential reversal. O'Connor had not been considered an interpretationist before, but in the decade that she had been on the Court, she had been moving away from a strict conservative viewpoint (epitomized by Justice Scalia) toward a middle position, a position where she often found herself in the company of Justices Souter and Kennedy. The two Clinton appointees, Ruth Bader Ginsberg and David Breyer, also appear to be centrist, and commentators now note that for the first time since the days of Holmes and Brandeis, there is no identifiable liberal wing of the Supreme Court.

▶ Which is the more convincing argument, Justice O'Connor's that the weight of precedent should be honored because many people have come to rely upon it, or the Chief Justice's claim that a decision, if wrong, should be overturned?

▶ Justice O'Connor says the constitutional test is whether a state restriction imposes an "undue burden" on a woman seeking to exercise her choice. What in your opinion would constitute an "undue burden?"

▶ Justice Scalia believes that a simple rational basis test would suffice in determining the constitutionality of abortion-restrictive laws. That is the test that is normally used when rights are not involved. Would it be possible to strike down any abortion restriction under that test?

▶ The Chief Justice makes the argument, as he has done in many other cases (see, for example, his opinion in *Washington v. Glucksberg*), that in order to determine the scope of a liberty interest included in the Constitution, one has to look at whether that liberty interest existed, and in what form, at the time either of the adoption of the Constitution or of the Amendment involved. Under this theory, is there any way other than amendment to bring the Constitution up to date? If so, how?

Planned Parenthood of Southeastern Pennsylvania v. Casey
505 U.S. 833 (1992)

Justice O'CONNOR, Justice KENNEDY, and Justice SOUTER announced the judgment of the Court

Liberty finds no refuge in a jurisprudence of doubt. Yet 19 years after our holding that the Constitution protects a woman's right to terminate her pregnancy in its early stages, *Roe v. Wade* (1973), that definition of liberty is still questioned. Joining the respondents as *amicus curiae*, the United States, as it has done in five other cases in the last decade, again asks us to overrule *Roe*.

At issue in these cases are five provisions of the Pennsylvania Abortion Control Act of 1982, as amended in 1988 and 1989. The Act requires that a woman seeking an abortion give her informed consent prior to the abortion procedure, and specifies that she be provided with certain information at least 24 hours before the abortion is performed. Section 3205. For a minor to obtain an abortion, the Act requires the informed consent of one of her parents, but provides for a judicial bypass option if the minor does not wish to or cannot obtain a parent's consent. Section 3206. Another provision of the Act requires that, unless certain exceptions apply, a married woman seeking an abortion must sign a statement indicating that she has notified her husband of her intended abortion. Section 3209. The Act exempts compliance with these three requirements in the event of a "medical emergency," which is defined in Section 3203 of the Act. In addition to the above provisions regulating the performance of abortions, the Act imposes certain reporting requirements on facilities that provide abortion services.

After considering the fundamental constitutional questions resolved by *Roe*, principles of institutional integrity, and the rule of *stare decisis*, we are led to conclude this: the essential holding of *Roe v. Wade* should be retained and once again reaffirmed.

It must be stated at the outset and with clarity that *Roe*'s essential holding, the holding we reaffirm, has three parts. First is a recognition of the right of the woman to choose to have an abortion before viability and to obtain it without undue interference from the State. Before viability, the State's interests are not strong enough to support a prohibition of abortion or the imposition of a substantial obstacle to the woman's effective right to elect the procedure. Second is a confirmation of the State's power to restrict abortions after fetal viability, if the law contains exceptions for pregnancies which endanger the woman's life or health. And third is the principle that the State has legitimate interests from the outset of the pregnancy in protecting the health of the woman and the life of the fetus that may become a child. These principles do not contradict one another; and we adhere to each.

....Neither the Bill of Rights nor the specific practices of States at the time of the adoption of the Fourteenth Amendment marks the outer limits of the substantive sphere of liberty which the Fourteenth Amendment protects....

The inescapable fact is that adjudication of substantive due process claims may call upon the Court in interpreting the Constitution to exercise that same capacity which by tradition courts always have exercised: reasoned judgment. Its boundaries are not susceptible of expression as a simple rule. That does not mean we are free to invalidate state policy choices with which we disagree; yet neither does it permit us to shrink from the duties of our office....Men and women of good conscience can disagree, and we suppose some always shall disagree, about the profound moral and spiritual implications of terminating a pregnancy, even in its earliest stage. Some of us as individuals find abortion offensive to our most basic principles of morality, but that cannot control our decision. Our obligation is to define the liberty of all, not to mandate our own moral code. The underlying constitutional issue is whether the State can resolve these philosophic questions in such a definitive way that a woman lacks all choice in the matter, except perhaps in those rare circumstances in which the pregnancy is itself a danger to her own life or health, or is the result of rape or incest....

Our law affords constitutional protection to personal decisions relating to marriage, procreation, contraception, family relationships, child rearing, and education. Our cases recognize "the right of the individual, married or single, to be free from unwarranted governmental intrusion into matters so fundamentally affecting a person as the decision whether to bear or beget a child. Our precedents "have respected the private realm of family life which the state cannot enter." These matters, involving the most intimate and personal choices a person may make in a lifetime, choices central to personal dignity and autonomy, are central to the liberty protected by the Fourteenth Amendment. At the heart of liberty is the right to define one's own concept of existence, of meaning, of the universe, and of the mystery of human life. Beliefs about these matters could not define the attributes of personhood were they formed under compulsion of the State.

These considerations begin our analysis of the woman's interest in terminating her pregnancy but cannot end it, for this reason: though the abortion decision may originate within the zone of conscience and belief, it is more than a philosophic exercise. Abortion is a unique act. It is an act fraught with consequences for others: for the woman who must live with the implications of her decision; for the persons who perform and assist in the procedure; for the spouse, family, and society which must confront the knowledge that these procedures exist, procedures some deem nothing short of an act of violence against innocent human life; and, depending on one's beliefs, for the life or potential life that is aborted. Though abortion is conduct, it does not follow that the State is entitled to proscribe it in all instances. That is because the liberty of the woman is at stake in a sense unique to the human condition and so unique to the law. The mother who carries a child to full term is subject to anxieties, to physical constraints, to pain that only she must bear. That these sacrifices have from the beginning of the human race been endured by woman with a pride that ennobles her in the eyes of others and gives to the infant a bond of love cannot alone be grounds for the State to insist she make the sacrifice. Her suffering is too intimate and personal for the State to insist, without more, upon its own vision of the woman's role, however dominant that vision has been in the course of our history and our culture. The destiny of the woman must be shaped to a large extent on her own conception of her spiritual impera tives and her place in society.

It should be recognized, moreover, that in some critical respects the abortion decision is of the same character as the decision to use contraception, to which *Griswold v. Connecticut*, *Eisenstadt v. Baird*, and *Carey v. Population Services International* afford constitutional protection. We have no doubt as to the correctness of those decisions. They support the reasoning in *Roe* relating to the woman's liberty because they involve personal decisions concerning not only the meaning of procreation but also human responsibility and respect for it....

While we appreciate the weight of the arguments made on behalf of the State in the cases before us, arguments which in their ultimate formulation conclude that *Roe* should be overruled, the reservations any of us may have in reaffirming the central holding of *Roe* are outweighed by the explication of individual liberty we have given combined with the force of *stare decisis*. We turn now to that doctrine....A decision to overrule *Roe*'s essential holding under the existing circumstances would address error, if error there was, at the cost of both profound and unnecessary damage to the Court's legitimacy, and to the Nation's commitment to the rule of law. It is therefore imperative to adhere to the essence of *Roe*'s original decision, and we do so today.

....Much criticism has been directed at *Roe*, a criticism that always inheres when the Court draws a specific rule from what in the Constitution is but a general standard. We conclude, however, that the urgent claims of the woman to retain the ultimate control over her destiny and her body, claims implicit in the meaning of liberty, require us to perform that function. Liberty must not be extinguished for want of a line that is clear. And it falls to us to give some real substance to the woman's liberty to determine whether to carry her pregnancy to full term.

We conclude the line should be drawn at viability, so that before that time the woman has a right to choose to terminate her pregnancy. We adhere to this principle for two reasons.

First...*stare decisis*....

The second reason is that the concept of viability is the time at which there is a realistic possibility of maintaining and nourishing a life outside the womb, so that the independent existence of the second life can in reason and all fairness be the object of state protection that now overrides the rights of the woman....The viability line also has, as a practical matter, an element of fairness. In some broad sense it might be said that a woman who fails to act before viability has consented to the State's intervention on behalf of the developing child.

The woman's right to terminate her pregnancy before viability is the most central principle of *Roe v. Wade*. It is a rule of law and a component of liberty we cannot renounce.

On the other side of the equation is the interest of the State in the protection of potential life....The weight to be given this state interest, not the strength of the woman's interest, was the difficult question faced in *Roe*. We do not need to say whether each of us, had we been Members of the Court when the valuation of the state interest came before it as an original matter, would have concluded, as the *Roe* Court did, that its weight is insufficient to justify a ban on abortions prior to viability even when it is subject to certain exceptions. The ...immediate question is not the soundness of *Roe*'s resolution of the issue, but the precedential force that must be accorded to its holding. And we have concluded that the essential holding of *Roe* should be reaffirmed.

Yet it must be remembered that *Roe v. Wade* speaks with clarity in establishing not only the woman's liberty but also the State's "important and legitimate interest in potential life." That portion of the decision in *Roe* has been given too little acknowledgment and implementation by the Court in its subsequent cases. Those cases decided that any regulation touching upon the abortion decision must survive strict scrutiny, to be sustained only if drawn in narrow terms to further a compelling state interest. Not all of the cases decided under that formulation can be reconciled with the holding in *Roe* itself that the State has legitimate interests in the health of the woman and in protecting the potential life within her. In resolving this tension, we choose to rely upon *Roe*, as against the later cases....

The trimester framework no doubt was erected to ensure that the woman's right to choose not become so subordinate to the State's interest in promoting fetal life that her choice exists in theory but not in fact. We do not agree, however, that the trimester approach is necessary to accomplish this objective. A framework of this rigidity was unnecessary and in its later interpretation sometimes contradicted the State's permissible exercise of its powers.

Though the woman has a right to choose to terminate or continue her pregnancy before viability, it does not at all follow that the State is prohibited from taking steps to ensure that this choice is thoughtful and informed. Even in the earliest stages of pregnancy, the State may enact rules and regulations designed to encourage her to know that there are philosophic and social arguments of great weight that can be brought to bear in favor of continuing the pregnancy to full term and that there are procedures and institutions to allow adoption of unwanted children as well as a certain degree of state assistance if the mother chooses to raise the child herself....

We reject the trimester framework, which we do not consider to be part of the essential holding of *Roe*....Measures aimed at ensuring that a woman's choice contemplates the consequences for the fetus do not necessarily interfere with the right recognized in *Roe*, although those measures have been found to be inconsistent with the rigid trimester framework announced in that case....The trimester framework suffers from these basic flaws: in its formulation it misconceives the nature of the pregnant woman's interest; and in practice it undervalues the State's interest in potential life, as recognized in *Roe*.

....The Court's experience applying the trimester framework has led to the striking down of some abortion regulations which in no real sense deprived women of the ultimate decision. Those decisions went too far because the right recognized by *Roe* is a right "to be free from unwarranted governmental intrusion into matters so fundamentally affecting a person as the decision whether to bear or beget a child." Not all governmental intrusion is of necessity unwarranted; and that brings us to the other basic flaw in the trimester framework: even in *Roe*'s terms, in practice it undervalues the State's interest in the potential life within the woman....

The very notion that the State has a substantial interest in potential life leads to the conclusion that not all regulations must be deemed unwarranted. Not all burdens on the right to decide whether to terminate a pregnancy will be undue. In our view, the undue burden standard is the appropriate means of reconciling the State's interest with the woman's constitutionally protected liberty.

The concept of an undue burden has been utilized by the Court as well as individual Members of the Court, including two of us, in ways that could be considered inconsistent....A finding of an undue burden is a shorthand for the conclusion that a state regulation has the purpose or effect of placing a substantial obstacle in the path of a woman seeking an abortion of a nonviable fetus. A statute with this purpose is invalid because the means chosen by the State to further the interest in potential life must be calculated to inform the woman's free choice, not hinder it. And a statute which, while furthering the interest in potential life or some other valid state interest, has the effect of placing a substantial obstacle in the path of a woman's choice cannot be considered a permissible means of serving its legitimate ends....In our considered judgment, an undue burden is an unconstitutional burden....A law designed to further the State's interest in fetal life which imposes an undue burden on the woman's decision before fetal viability is unconstitutional.

Some guiding principles should emerge. What is at stake is the woman's right to make the ultimate decision, not a right to be insulated from all others in doing so. Regulations which do no more than create a structural mechanism by which the State, or the parent or guardian of a minor, may express profound respect for the life of the unborn are permitted, if they are not a substantial obstacle to the woman's exercise of the right to choose. Unless it has that effect on her right of choice, a state measure designed to persuade her to choose childbirth over abortion will be upheld if reasonably related to that goal. Regulations designed to foster the health of a woman seeking an abortion are valid if they do not constitute an undue burden.

There was a time, not so long ago, when a different understanding of the family and of the Constitution prevailed. In *Bradwell v. State* (1873), three Members of this Court reaffirmed the common-law principle that "a woman had no legal existence separate from her husband ... " Only one generation has passed since this Court observed that "woman is still regarded as the center of home and family life," with attendant "special responsibilities" that precluded full and independent legal status under the Constitution. These views, of course, are no longer consistent with our understanding of the family, the individual, or the Constitution.

[In her discussion of the spousal notification requirement, Justice O'Connor noted that in stable and happy marriages, women would of course discuss a question as serious as abortion with their husbands. But the fact of the matter was that one reason some women sought an abortion was because they did not enjoy a good marriage, and feared their husbands.]

....For the great many women who are victims of abuse inflicted by their husbands, or whose children are the victims of such abuse, a spousal notice requirement enables the husband to wield an effective veto over his wife's decision. Whether the prospect of notification itself deters such women from seeking abortions, or whether the husband, through physical force or psychological pressure or economic coercion, prevents his wife from obtaining an abortion until it is too late, the notice requirement will often be tantamount to the veto found unconstitutional in *Danforth*. The women most affected by this law—those who most reasonably fear the consequences of notifying their husbands that they are pregnant—are in the gravest danger.

The husband's interest in the life of the child his wife is carrying does not permit the State to empower him with this troubling degree of authority over his wife....A State may not give to a man the kind of dominion over his wife that parents exercise over their children. Women do not lose their constitutionally protected liberty when they marry....

We next consider the parental consent provision. Except in a medical emergency, an unemancipated young woman under 18 may not obtain an abortion unless she and one of her parents (or guardian) provides informed consent. If neither a parent nor a guardian provides consent, a court may authorize the performance of an abortion upon a determination that the young woman is mature and capable of giving informed consent and has in fact given her informed consent, or that an abortion would be in her best interests.

We have been over most of this ground before. Our cases establish, and we reaffirm today, that a State may require a minor seeking an abortion to obtain the consent of a parent or guardian, provided that there is an adequate judicial bypass procedure....

Our Constitution is a covenant running from the first generation of Americans to us and then to future generations. It is a coherent succession. Each generation must learn anew that the Constitution's written terms embody ideas and aspirations that must survive more ages than one. We accept our responsibility not to retreat from interpreting the full meaning of the covenant in light of all of our precedents. We invoke it once again to define the freedom guaranteed by the Constitution's own promise, the promise of liberty.

[Justice STEVENS concurred with the plurality, but like Justice BLACKMUN, would have struck down all of the law's provisions.]

Justice BLACKMUN, concurring in part, concurring in the judgment in part, and dissenting in part.

Three years ago, in *Webster v. Reproductive Health Services* (1989), four Members of this Court appeared poised to "cas[t] into darkness the hopes and visions of every woman in this country" who had come to believe that the Constitution guaranteed her the right to reproductive choice. All that remained between the promise of *Roe* and the darkness of the plurality was a single, flickering flame. Decisions since Webster gave little reason to hope that this flame would cast much light. But now, just when so many expected the darkness to fall, the flame has grown bright.

I do not underestimate the significance of today's joint opinion. Yet I remain steadfast in my belief that the right to reproductive choice is entitled to the full protection afforded by this Court before Webster. And I fear for the darkness as four Justices anxiously await the single vote necessary to extinguish the light.

Make no mistake, the joint opinion of Justices O'Connor, Kennedy, and Souter is an act of personal courage and constitutional principle....What has happened today should serve as a model for future Justices and a warning to all who have tried to turn this Court into yet another political branch.

In striking down the Pennsylvania statute's spousal notification requirement, the Court has established a framework for evaluating abortion regulations that responds to the social context of women facing issues of reproductive choice....And in applying its test, the Court remains sensitive to the unique role of women in the decisionmaking process....

While I believe that the joint opinion errs in failing to invalidate the other regulations, I am pleased that the joint opinion has not ruled out the possibility that these regulations may be shown to impose an unconstitutional burden. The joint opinion makes clear that its specific holdings are based on the insufficiency of the record before it. I am confident that in the future evidence will be produced to show that "in a large fraction of the cases in which [these regulations are] relevant, [they] will operate as a substantial obstacle to a woman's choice to undergo an abortion."...

In one sense, the Court's approach is worlds apart from that of The Chief Justice and Justice Scalia. And yet, in another sense, the distance between the two approaches is short- the distance is but a single vote.

I am 83 years old. I cannot remain on this Court forever, and when I do step down, the confirmation process for my successor well may focus on the issue before us today. That, I regret, may be exactly where the choice between the two worlds will be made.

Chief Justice REHNQUIST, with whom Justice WHITE, Justice SCALIA, and Justice THOMAS join, concurring in the judgment in part and dissenting in part.

The joint opinion, following its newly minted variation on *stare decisis*, retains the outer shell of *Roe v. Wade*, but beats a wholesale retreat from the substance of that case. We believe that *Roe* was wrongly decided, and that it can and should be overruled consistently with our traditional approach to *stare decisis* in constitutional cases. We would adopt the approach of the plurality in *Webster v. Reproductive Health Services* (1989), and uphold the challenged provisions of the Pennsylvania statute in their entirety.

In *Roe v. Wade*, the Court recognized a "guarantee of personal privacy" which "is broad enough to encompass a woman's decision whether or not to terminate her pregnancy." We are now of the view that, in terming this right fundamental, the Court in *Roe* read the earlier opinions upon which it based its decision much too broadly. Unlike marriage, procreation, and contraception, abortion "involves the purposeful termination of a potential life." *Harris v. McRae* (1980). The abortion decision must therefore "be recognized as *sui generis*, different in kind from the others that the Court has protected under the rubric of personal or family privacy and autonomy." One cannot ignore the fact that a woman is not isolated in her pregnancy, and that the decision to abort necessarily involves the destruction of a fetus....

Nor do the historical traditions of the American people support the view that the right to terminate one's pregnancy is "fundamental." The common law which we inherited from England made abortion after "quickening" an offense. At the time of the adoption of the Fourteenth Amendment, statutory prohibitions or restrictions on abortion were commonplace; in 1868, at least 28 of the then 37 States and 8 Territories had statutes banning or limiting abortion. By the turn of the century virtually every State had a law prohibiting or restricting abortion on its books. By the middle of the present century, a liberalization trend had set in. But 21 of the restrictive abortion laws in effect in 1868 were still in effect in 1973 when *Roe* was decided, and an overwhelming majority of the States prohibited abortion unless necessary to preserve the life or health of the mother. On this record, it can scarcely be said that any deeply rooted tradition of relatively unrestricted abortion in our history supported the classification of the right to abortion as "fundamental" under the Due Process Clause of the Fourteenth Amendment....

In the end...the joint opinion's argument is based solely on generalized assertions about the national psyche, on a belief that the people of this country have grown accustomed to the *Roe* decision over the last 19 years and have "ordered their thinking and living around" it. As an initial matter, one might inquire how the joint opinion can view the "central holding" of *Roe* as so deeply rooted in our constitutional culture, when it so casually uproots and disposes of that same decision's trimester framework. Furthermore, at various points in the past, the same could have been said about this Court's erroneous decisions that the Constitution allowed "separate but equal" treatment of minorities, see *Plessy v. Ferguson* (1896), or that "liberty" under the Due Process Clause protected "freedom of contract," see *Lochner v. New York* (1905). The "separate but equal" doctrine lasted 58 years after *Plessy*, and *Lochner*'s protection of contractual freedom lasted 32 years. However, the simple fact that a generation or more had grown used to these major decisions did not prevent the Court from correcting its errors in those cases, nor should it prevent us from correctly interpreting the Constitution here.

We therefore would hold that each of the challenged provisions of the Pennsylvania statute is consistent with the Constitution. It bears emphasis that our conclusion in this regard does not carry with it any necessary approval of these regulations. Our task is, as always, to decide only whether the challenged provisions of a law comport with the United States Constitution. If, as we believe, these do, their wisdom as a matter of public policy is for the people of Pennsylvania to decide.

Justice SCALIA, with whom The CHIEF JUSTICE, Justice WHITE, and Justice THOMAS join, concurring in the judgment in part and dissenting in part.

The States may, if they wish, permit abortion on demand, but the Constitution does not require them to do so. The permissibility of abortion, and the limitations upon it, are to be resolved like most important questions in our democracy: by citizens trying to persuade one another and then voting....

The issue in these cases is not whether the power of a woman to abort her unborn child is a "liberty" in the absolute sense; or even whether it is a liberty of great importance to many women. Of course it is both. The issue is whether it is a liberty protected by the Constitution of the United States. I am sure it is not. I reach that conclusion not because of anything so exalted as my views concerning the "concept of existence, of meaning, of the universe, and of the mystery of human life." Rather, I reach it for the same reason I reach the conclusion that bigamy is not constitutionally protected—because of two simple facts: (1) the Constitution says absolutely nothing about it, and (2) the longstanding traditions of American society have permitted it to be legally proscribed....

Applying the rational basis test, I would uphold the Pennsylvania statute in its entirety....

Washington v. Glucksberg / Vacco v. Quill   MELVIN UROFSKY

Following the decision in *Cruzan*, the interest in patient rights and in the so-called right to die expanded. Congress enacted legislation requiring all hospitals to inform their patients that, among their other rights, they could refuse treatment, even if that meant they would die from underlying illnesses. The country also witnessed the growth of what had hitherto been relatively unknown organizations, such as the Hemlock Society, that took the logic of *Quinlan* and *Cruzan* further, and demanded that people be allowed to commit suicide when they suffered from debilitating illnesses, and even that doctors be permitted to assist in these suicides. The issue grabbed national headlines thanks to the activities of Dr. Jack Kevorkian, who helped dozens of terminally ill patients commit suicide. Despite strenuous efforts by Wayne County, Washington, officials to prosecute Kevorkian either for murder or for violating the state's law against assisting suicides, no jury would convict. The jurors, like many Americans, saw Kevorkian as helping people in great pain end their suffering; others, however, condemned him as a murderer.

The fact of the matter is that for decades doctors have been helping elderly and terminally ill patients end their lives. In some instances it requires no more than telling them not to take their medication, or to stop going to treatments such as dialysis; in some cases doctors have given patients prescriptions for medication that, taken in sufficient quantity, would lead to death. Dr. Timothy Quill, the plaintiff in the New York case, had stunned the country by "coming out of the closet," as it were, and publicly acknowledging that he had given a patient a prescription for an overdose, and that this was common practice, an allegation soon confirmed by other doctors, especially those treating AIDS patients.

To test laws against assisted suicide, doctors, terminally ill patients, and organizations such as Compassion in Dying, launched suits against laws in Washington and New York. In the Washington case, they argued that a liberty interest under the Fourteenth Amendment gave people the right to end their lives, and that in exercising that right, they should not be prohibited from receiving the assistance of doctors. In New York the suit relied on an equal protection argument. If patients who were terminally ill could turn off their life support systems, then they were in effect committing suicide; therefore a law against suicide, and against physician assistance, denied them equal protection of the laws.

The Supreme Court unanimously rejected both arguments, but a close reading of the two cases indicates that the Court did not say that states were forbidden from passing laws that would allow physician-assisted suicide. Indeed, in the numerous concurrence filed with these two opinions, other members of the Court not only stated explicitly that individual states could take this route, but that under circumstances other than the facts presented in this case, they might be willing to reconsider the ruling.

The State of Oregon, following a referendum, had passed a law that, although it included a number of safeguards, explicitly allowed doctors to aid their patients in committing suicide. A court challenge had held up implementation of that law, but with the decisions in these two cases the lower courts dismissed the challenges. Numerous groups and thousands of individuals are waiting to see how the Oregon experiment works.

▶ In your opinion, is there any difference between a patient refusing to continue on life support apparatus and a terminally-ill person not on life support taking an overdose of prescription drugs? What is that difference?

▶ Compare the reasoning of Justice O'Connor in the *Casey* case above with that of Chief Justice Rehnquist in these two cases. Which do you think is the better reasoning for constitutional adjudication of alleged rights? Why?

▶ One of the great concerns of people opposed to assisted suicide is that it will lead to euthanasia, in which the sick and the elderly would be put to death against their will. What sort of safeguards might be built into a law to prevent such abuses?

▶ The American Medical Association as well as local medical societies have opposed laws permitting doctors to assist in suicide, arguing that their role is to save life, not end it. Yet doctors have for decades acted compassionately in helping people to end their suffering. Is there any reason why doctors should not be legally empowered to do openly what they have done covertly in the past?

Washington v. Glucksburg 117 S.Ct. 2257 (1997)

Chief Justice REHNQUIST delivered the opinion of the Court.

The question presented in this case is whether Washington's prohibition against "causing" or "aiding" a suicide offends the Fourteenth Amendment to the United States Constitution. We hold that it does not.

It has always been a crime to assist a suicide in the State of Washington. In 1854, Washington's first Territorial Legislature outlawed "assisting another in the commission of self-murder." Today, Washington law provides: "A person is guilty of promoting a suicide attempt when he knowingly causes or aids another person to attempt suicide."

Petitioners in this case are...doctors [who] occasionally treat terminally ill, suffering patients, and declare that they would assist these patients in ending their lives if not for Washington's assisted-suicide ban. In January 1994, respondents, along with three gravely ill, pseudonymous plaintiffs who have since died and Compassion in Dying, a nonprofit organization that counsels people considering physician-assisted suicide, sued in the United States District Court, seeking a declaration that the Washington law is, on its face, unconstitutional.

...The District Court agreed, and concluded that Washington's assisted-suicide ban is unconstitutional because it "places an undue burden on the exercise of [that] constitutionally protected liberty interest." [The Court of Appeals affirmed] We reverse.

We begin, as we do in all due-process cases, by examining our Nation's history, legal traditions, and practices....In almost every State—indeed, in almost every western democracy—it is a crime to assist a suicide. The States' assisted-suicide bans are not innovations. Rather, they are longstanding expressions of the States' commitment to the protection and preservation of all human life....Indeed, opposition to and condemnation of suicide—and, therefore, of assisting suicide—are consistent and enduring themes of our philosophical, legal, and cultural heritages.

More specifically, for over 700 years, the Anglo-American common-law tradition has punished or otherwise disapproved of both suicide and assisting suicide.

For the most part, the early American colonies adopted the common-law approach. For example, the legislators of the Providence Plantations, which would later become Rhode Island, declared, in 1647, that "self-murder is by all agreed to be the most unnatural, and it is by this present Assembly declared, to be that, wherein he that doth it, kills himself out of a premeditated hatred against his own life or other humor:...his goods and chattels are the king's custom, but not his debts nor lands; but in case he be an infant, a lunatic, mad or distracted man, he forfeits nothing."...

Over time, however, the American colonies abolished these harsh common-law penalties....That suicide remained a grievous, though nonfelonious, wrong is confirmed by the fact that colonial and early state legislatures and courts did not retreat from prohibiting assisting suicide....The earliest American statute explicitly to outlaw assisting suicide was enacted in New York in 1828.

Though deeply rooted, the States' assisted-suicide bans have in recent years been reexamined and, generally, reaffirmed. Because of advances in medicine and technology, Americans today are increasingly likely to die in institutions, from chronic illnesses. Public concern and democratic action are therefore sharply focused on how best to protect dignity and independence at the end of life, with the result that there have been many significant changes in state laws and in the attitudes these laws reflect. Many States, for example, now permit "living wills," surrogate health-care decisionmaking, and the withdrawal or refusal of life-sustaining medical treatment. At the same time, however, voters and legislators continue for the most part to reaffirm their States' prohibitions on assisting suicide.

The Due Process Clause guarantees more than fair process, and the "liberty" it protects includes more than the absence of physical restraint. In a long line of cases, we have held that, in addition to the specific freedoms protected by the Bill of Rights, the "liberty" specially protected by the Due Process Clause includes the rights to marry, to have children, to direct the education and upbringing of one's children, to marital privacy, to use contraception, to bodily integrity, and to abortion. We have also assumed, and strongly suggested, that the Due Process Clause protects the traditional right to refuse unwanted lifesaving medical treatment.

But we "have always been reluctant to expand the concept of substantive due process because guideposts for responsible decisionmaking in this unchartered area are scarce and open-ended." By extending constitutional protection to an asserted right or liberty interest, we, to a great extent, place the matter outside the arena of public debate and legislative action. We must therefore "exercise the utmost care whenever we are asked to break new ground in this field," lest the liberty protected by the Due Process Clause be subtly transformed into the policy preferences of the members of this Court.

The history of the law's treatment of assisted suicide in this country has been and continues to be one of the rejection of nearly all efforts to permit it. That being the case, our decisions lead us to conclude that the asserted "right" to assistance in committing suicide is not a fundamental liberty interest protected by the Due Process Clause.

The Constitution also requires, however, that Washington's assisted-suicide ban be rationally related to legitimate government interests. This requirement is unquestionably met here. As the court below recognized, Washington's assisted-suicide ban implicates a number of state interests.

First, Washington has an "unqualified interest in the preservation of human life." The State's prohibition on assisted suicide, like all homicide laws, both reflects and advances its commitment to this interest....

Respondents admit that "the State has a real interest in preserving the lives of those who can still contribute to society and enjoy life." The Court of Appeals also recognized Washington's interest in protecting life, but held that the "weight" of this interest depends on the "medical condition and the wishes of the person whose life is at stake." Washington, however, has rejected this sliding-scale approach and, through its assisted-suicide ban, insists that all persons' lives, from beginning to end, regardless of physical or mental condition, are under the full protection of the law. As we have previously affirmed, the States "may properly decline to make judgments about the 'quality' of life that a particular individual may enjoy." This remains true, as Cruzan makes clear, even for those who are near death.

The State also has an interest in protecting the integrity and ethics of the medical profession. In contrast to the Court of Appeals' conclusion that "the integrity of the medical profession would not be threatened in any way by [physician-assisted suicide]," the American Medical Association, like many other medical and physicians' groups, has concluded that "physician-assisted suicide is fundamentally incompatible with the physician's role as healer."

Next, the State has an interest in protecting vulnerable groups—including the poor, the elderly, and disabled persons—from abuse, neglect, and mistakes. The Court of Appeals dismissed the State's concern that disadvantaged persons might be pressured into physician-assisted suicide as "ludicrous on its face." We have recognized, however, the real risk of subtle coercion and undue influence in end-of-life situations.

The State's interest here goes beyond protecting the vulnerable from coercion; it extends to protecting disabled and terminally ill people from prejudice, negative and inaccurate stereotypes, and "societal indifference." The State's assisted-suicide ban reflects and reinforces its policy that the lives of terminally ill, disabled, and elderly people must be no less valued than the lives of the young and healthy, and that a seriously disabled person's suicidal impulses should be interpreted and treated the same way as anyone else's.

Finally, the State may fear that permitting assisted suicide will start it down the path to voluntary and perhaps even involuntary euthanasia. The Court of Appeals struck down Washington's assisted-suicide ban only "as applied to competent, terminally ill adults who wish to hasten their deaths by obtaining medication prescribed by their doctors." Washington insists, however, that the impact of the court's decision will not and cannot be so limited. If suicide is protected as a matter of constitutional right, it is argued, "every man and woman in the United States must enjoy it."

We need not weigh exactly the relative strengths of these various interests. They are unquestionably important and legitimate, and Washington's ban on assisted suicide is at least reasonably related to their promotion and protection. We therefore hold that Wash. Rev.Code Section 9A.36.060(1) (1994) does not violate the Fourteenth Amendment, either on its face or "as applied to competent, terminally ill adults who wish to hasten their deaths by obtaining medication prescribed by their doctors."

Throughout the Nation, Americans are engaged in an earnest and profound debate about the morality, legality, and practicality of physician-assisted suicide. Our holding permits this debate to continue, as it should in a democratic society. The decision of the en banc Court of Appeals is reversed, and the case is remanded for further proceedings consistent with this opinion.

It is so ordered.

Vacco v. Quill 117 S.Ct. 2293 (1997)

Chief Justice REHNQUIST delivered the opinion of the Court.

In New York, as in most States, it is a crime to aid another to commit or attempt suicide, but patients may refuse even lifesaving medical treatment. The question presented by this case is whether New York's prohibition on assisting suicide therefore violates the Equal Protection Clause of the Fourteenth Amendment. We hold that it does not.

Petitioners are various New York public officials. Respondents Timothy E. Quill, Samuel C. Klagsbrun, and Howard A. Grossman are physicians who practice in New York. They assert that although it would be "consistent with the standards of [their] medical practices" to prescribe lethal medication for "mentally competent, terminally ill patients" who are suffering great pain and desire a doctor's help in taking their own lives, they are deterred from doing so by New York's ban on assisting suicide. Respondents, and three gravely ill patients who have since died, sued the State's Attorney General in the United States District Court. They urged that because New York permits a competent person to refuse life-sustaining medical treatment, and because the refusal of such treatment is "essentially the same thing" as physician-assisted suicide, New York's assisted-suicide ban violates the Equal Protection Clause.

The District Court disagreed: "It is hardly unreasonable or irrational for the State to recognize a difference between allowing nature to take its course, even in the most severe situations, and intentionally using an artificial death-producing device." The court noted New York's "obvious legitimate interests in preserving life, and in protecting vulnerable persons," and concluded that "under the United States Constitution and the federal system it establishes, the resolution of this issue is left to the normal democratic processes within the State."

The Court of Appeals for the Second Circuit reversed. The court determined that, despite the assisted-suicide ban's apparent general applicability, "New York law does not treat equally all competent persons who are in the final stages of fatal illness and wish to hasten their deaths," because "those in the final stages of terminal illness who are on life-support systems are allowed to hasten their deaths by directing the removal of such systems; but those who are similarly situated, except for the previous attachment of life-sustaining equipment, are not allowed to hasten death by self-administering prescribed drugs." In the court's view, "the ending of life by [the withdrawal of life-support systems] is nothing more nor less than assisted suicide." The Court of Appeals then examined whether this supposed unequal treatment was rationally related to any legitimate state interests, and concluded that "to the extent that New York's statutes prohibit a physician from prescribing medications to be self-administered by a mentally competent, terminally-ill person in the final stages of his terminal illness, they are not rationally related to any legitimate state interest." We granted *certiorari,* and now reverse.

The Equal Protection Clause commands that no State shall "deny to any person within its jurisdiction the equal protection of the laws." This provision creates no substantive rights. Instead, it embodies a general rule that States must treat like cases alike but may treat unlike cases accordingly. If a legislative classification or distinction "neither burdens a fundamental right nor targets a suspect class, we will uphold it so long as it bears a rational relation to some legitimate end."

New York's statutes outlawing assisting suicide affect and address matters of profound significance to all New Yorkers alike. They neither infringe fundamental rights nor involve suspect classifications....These laws are therefore entitled to a "strong presumption of validity."

On their faces, neither New York's ban on assisting suicide nor its statutes permitting patients to refuse medical treatment treat anyone differently than anyone else or draw any distinctions between persons. Everyone, regardless of physical condition, is entitled, if competent, to refuse unwanted lifesaving medical treatment; no one is permitted to assist a suicide. Generally speaking, laws that apply evenhandedly to all "unquestionably comply" with the Equal Protection Clause.

The Court of Appeals, however, concluded that some terminally ill people—those who are on life-support systems—are treated differently than those who are not, in that the former may "hasten death" by ending treatment, but the latter may not "hasten death" through physician-assisted suicide. This conclusion depends on the submission that ending or refusing lifesaving medical treatment "is nothing more nor less than assisted suicide." Unlike the Court of Appeals, we think the distinction between assisting suicide and withdrawing life-sustaining treatment, a distinction widely recognized and endorsed in the medical profession and in our legal traditions, is both important and logical; it is certainly rational.

The distinction comports with fundamental legal principles of causation and intent. First, when a patient refuses life-sustaining medical treatment, he dies from an underlying fatal disease or pathology; but if a patient ingests lethal medication prescribed by a physician, he is killed by that medication.

Furthermore, a physician who withdraws, or honors a patient's refusal to begin, life-sustaining medical treatment purposefully intends, or may so intend, only to respect his patient's wishes and "to cease doing useless and futile or degrading things to the patient when the patient no longer stands to benefit from them." The same is true when a doctor provides aggressive palliative care; in some cases, painkilling drugs may hasten a patient's death, but the physician's purpose and intent is, or may be, only to ease his patient's pain. A doctor who assists a suicide, however, "must, necessarily and indubitably, intend primarily that the patient be made dead." Similarly, a patient who commits suicide with a doctor's aid necessarily has the specific intent to end his or her own life, while a patient who refuses treatment might not.

The law has long used actors' intent or purpose to distinguish between two acts that may have the same result. Put differently, the law distinguishes actions taken "because of" a given end from actions taken "in spite of" their unintended but foreseen consequences.

Given these general principles, it is not surprising that many courts, including New York courts, have carefully distinguished refusing life-sustaining treatment from suicide. In fact, the first state-court decision explicitly to authorize withdrawing lifesaving treatment noted the "real distinction between the self-infliction of deadly harm and a self-determination against artificial life support." And recently, the Michigan Supreme Court also rejected the argument that the distinction "between acts that artificially sustain life and acts that artificially curtail life" is merely a "distinction without constitutional significance—a meaningless exercise in semantic gymnastics," insisting that "the *Cruzan* majority disagreed and so do we.

Similarly, the overwhelming majority of state legislatures have drawn a clear line between assisting suicide and withdrawing or permitting the refusal of unwanted lifesaving medical treatment by prohibiting the former and permitting the latter. And "nearly all states expressly disapprove of suicide and assisted suicide either in statutes dealing with durable powers of attorney in health-care situations, or in 'living will' statutes." Thus, even as the States move to protect and promote patients' dignity at the end of life, they remain opposed to physician-assisted suicide.

New York is a case in point. The State enacted its current assisted-suicide statutes in 1965. Since then, New York has acted several times to protect patients' common-law right to refuse treatment. In so doing, however, the State has neither endorsed a general right to "hasten death" nor approved physician-assisted suicide. Quite the opposite: The State has reaffirmed the line between "killing" and "letting die." More recently, the New York State Task Force on Life and the Law studied assisted suicide and euthanasia and, in 1994, unanimously recommended against legalization. In the Task Force's view, "allowing decisions to forego life-sustaining treatment and allowing assisted suicide or euthanasia have radically different consequences and meanings for public policy."

This Court has also recognized, at least implicitly, the distinction between letting a patient die and making that patient die. In *Cruzan* we concluded that "the principle that a competent person has a constitutionally protected liberty interest in refusing unwanted medical treatment may be inferred from our prior decisions," and we assumed the existence of such a right for purposes of that case. But our assumption of a right to refuse treatment was grounded not, as the Court of Appeals supposed, on the proposition that patients have a general and abstract "right to hasten death," but on well established, traditional rights to bodily integrity and freedom from unwanted touching. In fact, we observed that "the majority of States in this country have laws imposing criminal penalties on one who assists another to commit suicide." *Cruzan* therefore provides no support for the notion that refusing life-sustaining medical treatment is "nothing more nor less than suicide.

For all these reasons, we disagree with respondents' claim that the distinction between refusing lifesaving medical treatment and assisted suicide is "arbitrary" and "irrational." Granted, in some cases, the line between the two may not be clear, but certainty is not required, even were it possible. Logic and contemporary practice support New York's judgment that the two acts are different, and New York may therefore, consistent with the Constitution, treat them differently. By permitting everyone to refuse unwanted medical treatment while prohibiting anyone from assisting a suicide, New York law follows a longstanding and rational distinction.

New York's reasons for recognizing and acting on this distinction—including prohibiting intentional killing and preserving life; preventing suicide; maintaining physicians' role as their patients' healers; protecting vulnerable people from indifference, prejudice, and psychological and financial pressure to end their lives; and avoiding a possible slide towards euthanasia—are discussed...in our opinion in Glucksberg. These valid and important public interests easily satisfy the constitutional requirement that a legislative classification bear a rational relation to some legitimate end.

The judgment of the Court of Appeals is reversed.

It is so ordered.

VIII Property Rights

VIII Property Rights

LYNDA BUTLER

The power of government to regulate property is now well accepted. The federal government derives its regulatory power from various provisions of the United States Constitution. State governments, on the other hand, base their regulatory authority on their inherent powers as sovereign and may delegate their powers to local governments. When state or local governments regulate persons and property, they often are said to be exercising their police power. Courts generally define the police power as the inherent power of government to achieve the reasons for its existence: promotion of the public health, welfare, safety, and morals. No provision in the United States Constitution expressly recognizes or defines the police power of state governments, though the Tenth Amendment confirms that powers not delegated to the federal government are reserved in the states.

When property owners challenge government action restricting their property rights, the basic dilemma and fundamental task faced by the reviewing court is to define the balance between the collective power of the majority, as reflected in the challenged government action, and the individual rights of citizens. Until 1792, the United States Constitution did not contain any provision explicitly protecting property rights from government action. Even those framers who regarded property rights as fundamental and inalienable apparently did not see the need to provide explicit protection for property in the Constitution of 1787. Then, in 1791, the states ratified the Fifth Amendment to the Constitution to provide protection against the deprivation of "life, liberty, or property, without due process of law" and to prohibit private property from being "taken for public use, without just compensation." The Due Process Clause of the Fifth Amendment generally protects property owners from government action that is arbitrary and unreasonable, and has no substantial relation to the public health, welfare, safety, or morals. Government generally has not experienced difficulty meeting this standard. But the Just Compensation or Takings Clause of the Fifth Amendment, which ensures that government will not confiscate or condemn private property for public use without payment of just compensation, has proved to be a more substantial hurdle.

Until the 1900s, the Supreme Court generally invoked the Takings Clause of the Fifth Amendment to protect property owners from outright condemnation or physical appropriation of their property without payment of just compensation. The Clause, in other words, had a narrow scope, generally only applying to physical takings. Then, in the 1922 decision *Pennsylvania Coal Company v. Mahon*, the Supreme Court recognized that regulation could be just as devastating to a property owner as physical appropriations of property. After introducing this concept of the regulatory taking, the Court then waited for more than fifty years to return to it. In the 1978 decision *Penn Central Transportation Company v. New York City*, the Supreme Court once again recognized the concept of a regulatory taking in evaluating the adverse economic impact of an historic preservation law on the property owner, but it then rejected a takings challenge to the law.

Several more recent decisions of the Supreme Court, contained in this section, have given renewed vitality to the concept of regulatory takings and arguably provide property owners with an important weapon against intensifying government regulation. In a 1987 decision, *Nollan v. California Coastal Commission*, the Court concluded that the California Coastal Commission could not condition the issuance of a building permit on the granting of public access across the landowners' beachfront property. In the 1992 decision *Lucas v. South Carolina Coastal Council*, the Court concluded that, as a general matter, a regulatory taking resulted when government totally deprived a property owner of economically viable use regardless of the importance of the public health, welfare, or safety interest being promoted by the government action. Finally, in the 1994 decision *Dolan v. City of Tigard*, the Supreme Court decided that a local government had to demonstrate a "rough proportionality" between a condition imposed on a development project and the projected impact of the proposed development. These three decisions have been interpreted by property rights advocates as signifying a new era in constitutional protection of property. Individually each case might not appear to be a significant victory for property owners. Collectively, however, the cases indicate a trend toward greater protection of property rights and against expansive views of the legitimate reach of government's regulatory powers.

Pennsylvania Coal Company v. Mahon   LYNDA BUTLER

In *Pennsylvania Coal Company v. Mahon*, landowners sued the Pennsylvania Coal Company to prevent the company from mining beneath the landowners' property in a way that caused subsidence—or sinking—of their surface land and homes. The coal company claimed the right to remove all the coal under plaintiffs' surface property based upon a deed transferring the surface property to plaintiffs' predecessors and reserving the defendant's right to mine beneath the property. Pennsylvania law recognized the right to remove minerals (mineral estate) and the right to control and use the strata of earth underlying the surface (support estate) as interests in land that are capable of being owned separately from the surface estate. Years after execution of the deed, however, the state had passed a statute that declared unlawful the mining of coal in a way that caused subsidence of certain structures on the land. This statute, known as the Kohler Act, apparently was necessitated by coal mining practices that had resulted in widespread subsidence of homes, churches, streets, railroad lines, and other structures. Before bringing the case, plaintiffs had received a letter informing them that in less than two weeks coal mining activities would cause their house and land to subside.

The majority of the Court concluded that the Kohler Act had gone too far, depriving the Coal Company of all commercially practical use of its interest in the coal in violation of the Takings Clause of the Constitution. Writing for the majority, Justice Holmes identified diminution in value as the key factor controlling the Court's decision. Because of the Act, the Coal Company no longer could mine the remaining coal and therefore had lost the value of that property interest. As you read Holmes's opinion, ask yourself how a court is to determine when the diminution in value is too great and has reached that "certain magnitude" referred to by Holmes.

One key difference between the majority and dissenting opinions involves the property benchmark that is used to measure the degree of loss. Justice Holmes disagreed with Justice Brandeis, author of the dissenting opinion, about the appropriate property benchmark to be used: Why does the choice matter so much? How does the choice affect the calculation of the degree of loss?

Another key difference between Holmes's majority opinion and Brandeis's dissenting opinion involves their treatment of the public interest being promoted by the Kohler Act. In his opinion, Holmes states: "No doubt there is a public interest even in this." He immediately, however, dismisses the public interest in a number of ways. How? Correspondence between Holmes and Chief Justice Taft indicates that Holmes initially drafted an opinion that did not even recognize the legitimacy of the public interest. The earlier opinion treated the dispute as a purely private one. Holmes apparently revised the opinion to include some recognition of a legitimate public interest to ensure that Taft voted with the majority. How legitimate is the public interest in preventing subsidence of surface property? Do you agree with Holmes that the owner of the surface property assumed the risk of subsidence by buying a surface estate that was separated from the right to mine? Is it fair to say the consequences of assuming that risk far exceeded the reasonable expectations of the parties to the original bargain? Significant changes in both coal mining technology and market conditions had occurred since the surface land had been sold separately from the mineral and support estates. Technology had increased the coal companies' ability to extract coal, including removal of the support pillars, while market changes had made the extraction financially feasible.

The two opinions in *Pennsylvania Coal* identify many of the key themes and fundamental issues shaping regulatory takings cases. Those themes and issues include the following matters:

▶ *Role of Diminution in Value.* What role should diminution in value play in resolving regulatory takings claims? Should a landowner have the right to conduct the use that could produce the highest yield or profit? If not, should a landowner have the right to conduct a use that could produce a reasonable return? When is a diminution in value too great?

▶ *The Appropriate Property Benchmark.* What property interests should a court consider in determining the degree of loss caused by government action? If only the regulated portion of the owner's property rights is considered, what incentives does this approach give property owners? If, instead, the property as a whole is considered, what factors are relevant to defining that benchmark? the coal already removed as well as the remaining coal? interdependencies between the regulated property interests (for example, the right to mine coal) and other property interests (for example, the surface estate)?

▶ *Role of the Public Interest.* What role should the public interest play in resolving regulatory takings challenges? Should the public interest just be part of the threshold inquiry into the basic rationality of the government action being challenged? Or should it also be part of the evaluation of the impact of the government action on private rights? In other words, should the public interest ever be weighed against the private interests in evaluating the impact on private property rights? Can the public interest ever be important enough to justify regulation that significantly or even totally diminishes the economic value of property? Would public safety concerns ever justify such regulation?

▶ *Regulation of Noxious Uses.* Should a landowner have the right to conduct a use that is noxious or harmful? Doesn't government have the power to regulate and even prohibit noxious or harmful uses without having to pay just compensation? Can't a legislature determine that conducting a land use in a certain way (for example, mining coal by removing the support pillars) has become harmful to the public because of its increasingly adverse effects (for example, subsidence of homes, churches, roads, utilities, and other structures)?

Pennsylvania Coal Company v. Mahon 260 U.S. 393 (1922)

Mr. Justice HOLMES delivered the opinion of the Court.

....Government hardly could go on if to some extent values incident to property could not be diminished without paying for every such change in the general law. As long recognized some values are enjoyed under an implied limitation and must yield to the police power. But obviously the implied limitation must have its limits or the contract and due process clauses are gone. One fact for consideration in determining such limits is the extent of the diminution. When it reaches a certain magnitude, in most if not in all cases there must be an exercise of eminent domain and compensation to sustain the act. So the question depends upon the particular facts. The greatest weight is given to the judgment of the legislature but it always is open to interested parties to contend that the legislature has gone beyond its constitutional power.

This is the case of a single private house. No doubt there is a public interest even in this, as there is in every purchase and sale and in all that happens within the commonwealth. Some existing rights may be modified even in such a case....But usually in ordinary private affairs the public interest does not warrant much of this kind of interference. A source of damage to such a house is not a public nuisance even if similar damage is inflicted on others in different places. The damage is not common or public....Furthermore, it is not justified as a protection of personal safety. That could be provided for by notice. Indeed the very foundation of this bill is that the defendant gave timely notice of its intent to mine under the house. On the other hand the extent of the taking is great. It purports to abolish what is recognized in Pennsylvania as an estate in land—a very valuable estate—and what is declared by the Court below to be a contract hitherto binding the plaintiffs. If we were called upon to deal with the plaintiffs' position alone we should think it clear that the statute does not disclose a public interest sufficient to warrant so extensive a destruction of the defendant's constitutionally protected rights....

It is our opinion that the act cannot be sustained as an exercise of the police power, so far as it affects the mining of coal under streets or cities in places where the right to mine such coal has been reserved....What makes the right to mine coal valuable is that it can be exercised with profit. To make it commercially impracticable to mine certain coal has very nearly the same effect for constitutional purposes as appropriating or destroying it. This we think that we are warranted in assuming that the statute does....

The rights of the public in a street purchased or laid out by eminent domain are those that it has paid for. If in any case its representatives have been so short sighted as to acquire only surface rights without the right of support we see no more authority for supplying the latter without compensation than there was for taking the right of way in the first place and refusing to pay for it because the public wanted it very much. The protection of private property in the Fifth Amendment presupposes that it is wanted for public use, but provides that it shall not be taken for such use without compensation....When this seemingly absolute protection is found to be qualified by the police power, the natural tendency of human nature is to extend the qualification more and more until at last private property disappears. But that cannot be accomplished in this way under the Constitution of the United States.

The general rule at least is that while property may be regulated to a certain extent, if regulation goes too far it will be recognized as a taking....We are in danger of forgetting that a strong public desire to improve the public condition is not enough to warrant achieving the desire by a shorter cut than the constitutional way of paying for the change. As we already have said this is a question of degree—and therefore cannot be disposed of by general propositions....

We assume, of course, that the statute was passed upon the conviction that an exigency existed that would warrant it, and we assume that an exigency exists that would warrant the exercise of eminent domain. But the question at bottom is upon whom the loss of the changes desired should fall. So far as private persons or communities have seen fit to take the risk of acquiring only surface rights, we cannot see that the fact that their risk has become a danger warrants the giving to them greater rights than they bought.

Decree reversed.

Mr. Justice BRANDEIS, dissenting.

...Coal in place is land, and the right of the owner to use his land is not absolute. He may not so use it as to create a public nuisance, and uses, once harmless, may, owing to changed conditions, seriously threaten the public welfare. Whenever they do, the Legislature has power to prohibit such uses without paying compensation; and the power to prohibit extends alike to the manner, the character and the purpose of the use. Are we justified in declaring that the Legislature of Pennsylvania has, in restricting the right to mine anthracite, exercised this power so arbitrarily as to violate the Fourteenth Amendment?

Every restriction upon the use of property imposed in the exercise of the police power deprives the owner of some right theretofore enjoyed, and is, in that sense, an abridgment by the state of rights in property without making compensation. But restriction imposed to protect the public health, safety or morals from dangers threatened is not a taking. The restriction here in question is merely the prohibition of a noxious use. The property so restricted remains in the possession of its owner. The state does not appropriate it or make any use of it. The state merely prevents the owner from making a use which interferes with paramount rights of the public. Whenever the use prohibited ceases to be noxious—as it may because of further change in local or social conditions—the restriction will have to be removed and the owner will again be free to enjoy his property as heretofore.

The restriction upon the use of this property cannot, of course, be lawfully imposed, unless its purpose is to protect the public. But the purpose of a restriction does not cease to be public, because incidentally some private persons may thereby receive gratuitously valuable special benefits. Thus, owners of low buildings may obtain, through statutory restrictions upon the height of neighboring structures, benefits equivalent to an easement of light and air....But to keep coal in place is surely an appropriate means of preventing subsidence of the surface; and ordinarily it is the only available means. Restriction upon use does not become inappropriate as a means, merely because it deprives the owner of the only use to which the property can then be profitably put....If by mining anthracite coal the owner would necessarily unloose poisonous gases, I suppose no one would doubt the power of the state to prevent the mining, without buying his coal fields. And why may not the state, likewise, without paying compensation, prohibit one from digging so deep or excavating so near the surface, as to expose the community to like dangers? In the latter case, as in the former, carrying on the business would be a public nuisance.

It is said that one fact for consideration in determining whether the limits of the police power have been exceeded is the extent of the resulting diminution in value, and that here the restriction destroys existing rights of property and contract. But values are relative. If we are to consider the value of the coal kept in place by the restriction, we should compare it with the value of all other parts of the land. That is, with the value not of the coal alone, but with the value of the whole property. The rights of an owner as against the public are not increased by dividing the interests in his property into surface and subsoil. The sum of the rights in the parts can not be greater than the rights in the whole....

A prohibition of mining which causes subsidence of such structures and facilities is obviously enacted for a public purpose; and it seems, likewise, clear that mere notice of intention to mine would not in this connection secure the public safety. Yet it is said that these provisions of the act cannot be sustained as an exercise of the police power where the right to mine such coal has been reserved. The conclusion seems to rest upon the assumption that in order to justify such exercise of the police power there must be 'an average reciprocity of advantage' as between the owner of the property restricted and the rest of the community; and that here such reciprocity is absent. Reciprocity of advantage is an important consideration, and may even be an essential, where the state's power is exercised for the purpose of conferring benefits upon the property of a neighborhood, as in drainage projects...or upon adjoining owners, as by party wall provisions....But where the police power is exercised, not to confer benefits upon property owners but to protect the public from detriment and danger, there is in my opinion, no room for considering reciprocity of advantage....

Penn Central Transportation Company v. City of New York   LYNDA BUTLER

In 1965 New York City enacted the Landmarks Preservation law to protect historic landmarks and neighborhoods from actions that destroy or fundamentally alter their character. Like many urban landmark laws, the New York City law achieved this goal by involving government in land use decisions affecting historic properties. Once a building was designated a landmark, the owner of the building had to maintain the exterior "in good repair" and secure approval of exterior alterations before they could be made. Owners of landmarks who had not developed their property to the full extent allowed under applicable zoning laws could, under certain circumstances, transfer development rights to other parcels. Under the law New York City designated Grand Central Terminal, owned by Penn Central Transportation Company, an historic landmark. Subsequent to that designation, Penn Central submitted a plan to construct a multistory office building over the Terminal. New York City rejected the plan because it would alter the Terminal's historic and aesthetic features. Penn Central then brought suit, claiming that the government decision had taken its property in violation of the Fifth Amendment.

The United States Supreme Court faced two key issues: 1) whether the restrictions imposed by the New York City law on Penn Central's Terminal site constituted a taking of its property for public use; and 2) if so, whether the transferable development rights given to Penn Central under the law constituted just compensation within the meaning of the Fifth Amendment. Because the Court concluded that a taking did not occur, it did not need to reach the second issue.

Factors that played an important role in the Court's decision included diminution in value, interference with investment-backed expectations, and the character of the government action. The Court did not clearly define any of these factors or their relationship with each other. This failure has caused considerable confusion about the Court's takings law principles. Some experts, for example, have interpreted the investment-backed expectations factor as nothing more than a restatement of the diminution in value factor. (See *Pennsylvania Coal Company v. Mahon*) Others have construed the investment-backed expectations factor as adding a further level of inquiry. Under that inquiry a court, in weighing the reasonableness of a use restriction, could consider whether the property owner reasonably relied on a particular government regulation in making investment decisions or whether the loss to the private party was basically self-imposed. How would ordinary citizens interpret the investment-backed expectations factor? Does either the majority opinion by Justice Brennan or the dissenting opinion by Justice Rehnquist suggest that Penn Central relied on government action in making its plans to develop the air space above the Terminal? When would such reliance exist?

In his dissenting opinion, Justice Rehnquist explains a key rationale for upholding land use restrictions under the Takings Clause even when they have an adverse economic impact on a property owner: average reciprocity of advantage—which refers to the partial offsetting of *decreases* in value that result from a government restriction by *increases* in value that result from imposing similar restrictions on neighboring properties. Why did Rehnquist believe that the New York City Landmarks Law failed to produce average reciprocity of advantage? Do you agree? Before responding, consider that under New York zoning law more than 90% of the legal development potential of the Grand Central Terminal site was unused, that the landmarks law prevented further development without approval, but that the landmarks law allowed Penn Central to receive a reasonable return on its property. Could an historic landmark or historic preservation law ever meet Rehnquist's definition of average reciprocity of advantage?

The majority opinion in *Penn Central Transportation Company v. New York City* clarifies some takings principles but then muddies others in explaining the Court's decision. Consider the following questions in evaluating the impact of the case.

▶ *Role of Diminution in Value.* Does diminution in value have the same significance in *Penn Central Transportation Company v. New York City* that it had in *Pennsylvania Coal Company v. Mahon*? Does the Court in *Penn Central Transportation Company v. New York City* recognize the right of a landowner to conduct a use that could give a reasonable return? the maximum return? Do courts only need to protect overall economic recoupment, or must they protect reasonable remaining economic use? Should the Court deduct the value added to private property by public projects and programs (for example, the costs of building surrounding infrastructure or the costs of providing police, rescue, and fire protection) in measuring diminution in value?

> ▶ *The Appropriate Property Benchmark.* How does the Court in *Penn Central Transportation Company v. New York City* define the appropriate property benchmark for measuring the degree of loss? What property interests should be considered in determining the severity of the impact on the property owner?
>
> ▶ *Role of the Public Interest.* Does the Court weigh the public interest in preserving historic landmarks against private interests in evaluating the impact of the law on Penn Central?
>
> ▶ *Regulation of Noxious Uses.* Does the Court include public harms in defining and applying its "factor test" for identifying takings?
>
> ▶ *Average Reciprocity of Advantage.* Why should average reciprocity of advantage matter? Will only laws with widespread effect produce average reciprocity of advantage?

Penn Central Transportation Company v. City of New York
438 U.S. 104 (1978)

Mr. Justice BRENNAN delivered the opinion of the Court.

The question presented is whether a city may, as part of a comprehensive program to preserve historic landmarks and historic districts, place restrictions on the development of individual historic landmarks–in addition to those imposed by applicable zoning ordinances—without effecting a "taking" requiring the payment of "just compensation." Specifically, we must decide whether the application of New York City's Landmarks Preservation Law to the parcel of land occupied by Grand Central Terminal has "taken" its owners' property in violation of the Fifth and Fourteenth Amendments....

Before considering appellants' specific contentions, it will be useful to review the factors that have shaped the jurisprudence of the Fifth Amendment injunction "nor shall private property be taken for public use, without just compensation." The question of what constitutes a "taking" for purposes of the Fifth Amendment has proved to be a problem of considerable difficulty. While this Court has recognized that the "Fifth Amendment's guarantee...[is] designed to bar Government from forcing some people alone to bear public burdens which, in all fairness and justice, should be borne by the public as a whole," *Armstrong v. United States*, 364 U.S. 40, 49 (1960), this Court, quite simply, has been unable to develop any "set formula" for determining when "justice and fairness" require that economic injuries caused by public action be compensated by the government, rather than remain disproportionately concentrated on a few persons. See *Goldblatt v. Hempstead*, 369 U.S. 590, 594 (1962). Indeed, we have frequently observed that whether a particular restriction will be rendered invalid by the government's failure to pay for any losses proximately caused by it depends largely "upon the particular circumstances [in that] case." *United States v. Central Eureka Mining Co.*, 357 U.S. 155, 168 (1958)....

In engaging in these essentially *ad hoc*, factual inquiries, the Court's decisions have identified several factors that have particular significance. The economic impact of the regulation on the claimant and, particularly, the extent to which the regulation has interfered with distinct investmentbacked expectations are, of course, relevant considerations....So, too, is the character of the governmental action. A "taking" may more readily be found when the interference with property can be characterized as a physical invasion by government...than when interference arises from some public program adjusting the benefits and burdens of economic life to promote the common good....

In contending that the New York City law has "taken" their property in violation of the Fifth and Fourteenth Amendments, appellants make a series of arguments, which, while tailored to the facts of this case, essentially urge that any substantial restriction imposed pursuant to a landmark law must be accompanied by just compensation if it is to be constitutional. Before considering these, we emphasize what is not in dispute. Because this Court has recognized, in a number of settings, that States and cities may enact landuse restrictions or controls to enhance the quality of life by preserving the character and desirable aesthetic features of a city,...appellants do not contest that New York City's objective of preserving structures and areas with special historic, architectural, or cultural significance is an entirely permissible governmental goal. They also do not dispute that the restrictions imposed on its parcel are appropriate means of securing the purposes of the New York City law. Finally, appellants do not challenge any of the specific factual premises of the decision below. They accept for present purposes both that the parcel of land occupied by Grand Central Terminal must, in its present state, be regarded as capable of earning a reasonable return,...and that the transferable development rights afforded appellants by virtue of the Terminal's designation as a landmark are valuable, even if not as valuable as the rights to construct above the Terminal. In appellants' view none of these factors derogate from their claim that New York City's law has effected a "taking."

They first observe that the airspace above the Terminal is a valuable property interest....They urge that the Landmarks Law has deprived them of any gainful use of their "air rights" above the Terminal and that, irrespective of the value of the remainder of their parcel, the city has "taken" their right to this superadjacent airspace, thus entitling them to "just compensation" measured by the fair market value of these air rights.

Apart from our own disagreement with appellants' characterization of the effect of the New York City law,...the submission that appellants may establish a "taking" simply by showing that they have been denied the ability to exploit a property interest that they heretofore had believed was available for development is quite simply untenable. Were this the rule, this Court would have erred not only in upholding laws restricting the development of air rights,...but also in approving those prohibiting both the subjacent...and the lateral...development of particular parcels. "Taking" jurisprudence does not divide a single parcel into discrete segments and attempt to determine whether rights in a particular segment have been entirely abrogated. In deciding whether a particular governmental action has effected a taking, this Court focuses rather both on the character of the action and on the nature and extent of the interference with rights in the parcel as a whole—here, the city tax block designated as the "landmark site."

Secondly, appellants, focusing on the character and impact of the New York City law, argue that it effects a "taking" because its operation has significantly diminished the value of the Terminal site. Appellants concede that the decisions sustaining other landuse regulations, which, like the New York City law, are reasonably related to the promotion of the general welfare, uniformly reject the proposition that diminution in property value, standing alone, can establish a "taking"....

Stated baldly, appellants' position appears to be that the only means of ensuring that selected owners are not singled out to endure financial hardship for no reason is to hold that any restriction imposed on individual landmarks pursuant to the New York City scheme is a "taking" requiring the payment of "just compensation." Agreement with this argument would, of course, invalidate not just New York City's law, but all comparable landmark legislation in the Nation. We find no merit in it.

It is true, as appellants emphasize, that both historicdistrict legislation and zoning laws regulate all properties within given physical communities whereas landmark laws apply only to selected parcels. But, contrary to appellants' suggestions, landmark laws are not like discriminatory, or "reverse spot," zoning: that is, a landuse decision which arbitrarily singles out a particular parcel for different, less favorable treatment than the neighboring ones....In contrast to discriminatory zoning, which is the antithesis of landuse control as part of some comprehensive plan, the New York City law embodies a comprehensive plan to preserve structures of historic or aesthetic interest wherever they might be found in the city, and as noted, over 400 landmarks and 31 historic districts have been designated pursuant to this plan....

Next, appellants observe that New York City's law differs from zoning laws and historicdistrict ordinances in that the Landmarks Law does not impose identical or similar restrictions on all structures located in particular physical communities. It follows, they argue, that New York City's law is inherently incapable of producing the fair and equitable distribution of benefits and burdens of governmental action which is characteristic of zoning laws and historicdistrict legislation and which they maintain is a constitutional requirement if "just compensation" is not to be afforded. It is, of course, true that the Landmarks Law has a more severe impact on some landowners than on others, but that in itself does not mean that the law effects a "taking." Legislation designed to promote the general welfare commonly burdens some more than others....Similarly, zoning laws often affect some property owners more severely than others but have not been held to be invalid on that account....

In any event, appellants' repeated suggestions that they are solely burdened and unbenefitted is factually inaccurate. This contention overlooks the fact that the New York City law applies to vast numbers of structures in the city in addition to the Terminal—all the structures contained in the 31 historic districts and over 400 individual landmarks, many of which are close to the Terminal. Unless we are to reject the judgment of the New York City Council that the preservation of landmarks benefits all New York citizens and all structures, both economically and by improving the quality of life in the city as a whole—which we are unwilling to do—we cannot conclude that the owners of the Terminal have in no sense been benefited by the Landmarks Law....

Rejection of appellants' broad arguments is not, however, the end of our inquiry, for all we thus far have established is that the New York City law is not rendered invalid by its failure to provide "just compensation" whenever a landmark owner is restricted in the exploitation of property interests, such as air rights, to a greater extent than provided for under applicable zoning laws. We now must consider whether the interference with appellants' property is of such a magnitude that "there must be an exercise of eminent domain and compensation to sustain [it]." *Pennsylvania Coal Co. v. Mahon.* That inquiry may be narrowed to the question of the severity of the impact of the law on appellants' parcel, and its resolution in turn requires a careful assessment of the impact of the regulation on the Terminal site.

...[T]he New York City law does not interfere in any way with the present uses of the Terminal. Its designation as a landmark not only permits but contemplates that appellants may continue to use the property precisely as it has been used for the past 65 years: as a railroad terminal containing office space and concessions. So the law does not interfere with what must be regarded as Penn Central's primary expectation concerning the use of the parcel. More importantly, on this record, we must regard the New York City law as permitting Penn Central not only to profit from the Terminal but also to obtain a "reasonable return" on its investment.

Appellants, moreover, exaggerate the effect of the law on their ability to make use of the air rights above the Terminal in two respects. First, it simply cannot be maintained, on this record, that appellants have been prohibited from occupying any portion of the airspace above the Terminal....Since appellants have not sought approval for the construction of a smaller structure, we do not know that appellants will be denied any use of any portion of the airspace above the Terminal.

Second, to the extent appellants have been denied the right to build above the Terminal, it is not literally accurate to say that they have been denied all use of even those preexisting air rights. Their ability to use these rights has not been abrogated; they are made transferable to at least eight parcels in the vicinity of the Terminal, one or two of which have been found suitable for the construction of new office buildings. Although appellants and others have argued that New York City's transferable developmentrights program is far from ideal, the New York courts here supportably found that, at least in the case of the Terminal, the rights afforded are valuable. While these rights may well not have constituted "just compensation" if a "taking" had occurred, the rights nevertheless undoubtedly mitigate whatever financial burdens the law has imposed on appellants and, for that reason, are to be taken into account in considering the impact of regulation....

On this record, we conclude that the application of New York City's Landmarks Law has not effected a "taking" of appellants' property. The restrictions imposed are substantially related to the promotion of the general welfare and not only permit reasonable beneficial use of the landmark site but also afford appellants opportunities further to enhance not only the Terminal site proper but also other properties.

Affirmed.

Mr. Justice REHNQUIST, with whom The CHIEF JUSTICE and Mr. Justice STEVENS join, dissenting.

Of the over one million buildings and structures in the city of New York, appellees have singled out 400 for designation as official landmarks. The owner of a building might initially be pleased that his property has been chosen by a distinguished committee of architects, historians, and city planners for such a singular distinction. But he may well discover, as appellant Penn Central Transportation Co. did here, that the landmark designation imposes upon him a substantial cost, with little or no offsetting benefit except for the honor of the designation. The question in this case is whether the cost associated with the city of New York's desire to preserve a limited number of "landmarks" within its borders must be borne by all of its taxpayers or whether it can instead be imposed entirely on the owners of the individual properties.

Only in the most superficial sense of the word can this case be said to involve "zoning." Typical zoning restrictions may, it is true, so limit the prospective uses of a piece of property as to diminish the value of that property in the abstract because it may not be used for the forbidden purposes. But any such abstract decrease in value will more than likely be at least partially offset by an increase in value which flows from similar restrictions as to use on neighboring properties. All property owners in a designated area are placed under the same restrictions, not only for the benefit of the municipality as a whole but also for the common benefit of one another. In the words of Mr. Justice Holmes, speaking for the Court in *Pennsylvania Coal Co. v. Mahon*, there is "an average reciprocity of advantage."

Where a relatively few individual buildings, all separated from one another, are singled out and treated differently from surrounding buildings, no such reciprocity exists. The cost to the property owner which results from the imposition of restrictions applicable only to his property and not that of his neighbors may be substantial—in this case, several million dollars—with no comparable reciprocal benefits. And the cost associated with landmark legislation is likely to be of a completely different order of magnitude than that which results from the imposition of normal zoning restrictions....Under the historiclandmark preservation scheme adopted by New York, the property owner is under an affirmative duty to *preserve* his property as a *landmark* at his own expense....

Here...a multimillion dollar loss has been imposed on appellants; it is uniquely felt and is not offset by any benefits flowing from the preservation of some 400 other "landmarks" in New York City. Appellees have imposed a substantial cost on less than one onetenth of one percent of the buildings in New York City for the general benefit of all its people. It is exactly this imposition of general costs on a few individuals at which the "taking" protection is directed....

Appellees contend that, even if they have "taken" appellants' property, TDR's [Transferrable Development Rights] constitute "just compensation." Appellants, of course, argue that TDR's are highly imperfect compensation. Because the lower courts held that there was no "taking," they did not have to reach the question of whether or not just compensation has already been awarded....Because the record on appeal is relatively slim, I would remand to the Court of Appeals for a determination of whether TDR's constitute a "full and perfect equivalent for the property taken."...

Nollan v. California Coastal Commission   LYNDA BUTLER

Nollan v. California Coastal Commission challenged the ability of a government agency (the Commission) to require public access to private beachfront property as a condition attached to a building permit. In its opinion the Supreme Court focused on two separate but critical factors: 1) government's permanent physical occupation of the Nollan's private property, and 2) the absence of an essential nexus between the permit condition imposed on the landowners (the means used) and the public interest purportedly promoted by the condition (the public end). The first factor, the permanent physical occupation, arose because the permit condition required the Nollans to grant to the public the right of lateral passage across their beachfront property. The presence of a physical occupation arguably limits the scope of the majority opinion in *Nollan*. As a general matter, the Court has found permanent physical invasions of private property to be takings regardless of the amount of the physical infringement, the degree of economic impact caused by the invasion, or the importance of the public interest. The second factor, the absence of an essential nexus between the means and the end, arguably supports a broader reading of the decision. Under that reading, the majority would be applying a more rigorous standard of judicial review to government action that adversely affects property rights. Which, if any, factor did dissenting Justice Brennan believe controlled the decision of the majority? Do you agree with him?

California law has long recognized public rights in the state's tidelands, including a right of access to navigable waters and tidelands. In California, owners of beachfront property generally hold title down to the high water mark, while the public generally has the right to use the tidal zone below the high water mark. Seaward expansion of private development, however, can threaten the exercise of the public rights, especially when, due to storms or significant erosion, the high tide mark suddenly is located above a seawall built to protect the private landowner's property. In *Nollan* that seawall consisted of concrete and was approximately eight feet high. Dissenting Justice Brennan argued that, given the constantly shifting boundary between public tidelands and privately owned beach, the permit condition was reasonably related to the threat to the public rights posed by the expansion of private development toward the high tide line. He accepted the Commission's explanation that it feared private landowners would intimidate members of the public and seek to prevent them from exercising their rights. If you saw private development located all along a beachfront area and extending close to (usually no more than 10 feet from) the high water mark, what would you expect as a member of the public?

The decision in *Nollan* invalidated a permit condition sometimes called an "exaction." Such a condition requires a landowner who is planning to develop property (usually a subdivision) to meet certain conditions (for example, improvement of public roads or extension of sewage and drainage systems) in exchange for permission to develop. Prior to *Nollan*, state courts generally had decided challenges to exactions. Although their standards varied, the state courts required an essential nexus between the condition and the need for the condition created by the proposed development. The Supreme Court in *Nollan* decided to require, as a matter of federal constitutional law, an essential nexus as well.

The majority opinion by Justice Scalia and the dissenting opinion by Justice Brennan offer conflicting judgements about the degree of nexus that should be required and about whether even a rational nexus existed. Scalia concluded that the lateral access condition was not even rationally related to the public interests of protecting the public's visual access to the beach, lowering psychological barriers to using public beaches created by a developed shoreline, and remedying additional congestion caused by the Nollans' new house. Justice Brennan, on the other hand, believed that the majority had taken too narrow an approach to evaluating the means/ends nexus. Brennan feared that the majority approach signaled the beginning of an era of unnecessarily aggressive judicial review of legislative acts and of state governments. Ever since the late 1930s, the Supreme Court has tended to defer to legislative findings about the nature of the public interest being promoted by government action. Does the majority opinion in Nollan undermine that tradition of deference, as Justice Brennan argues, or is the majority simply invalidating a condition that is not even rationally related to legitimate public interests, as Justice Scalia maintains? Keep Justice Brennan's arguments in mind as you read the Court's decision in *Dolan v. City of Tigard*.

The impact of the *Nollan* decision on takings law is far from clear. To help you evaluate some of the issues raised by the decision, consider the following questions.

▶ *Permanent Physical Occupation.* Should government's permanent physical occupation of private property always result in a taking, regardless of the degree of infringement, the amount of damage to the property owner, or the importance of the government interest? Is a permanent physical occupation that involves actual possession of private property different from a permanent physical occupation that involves persistent but often sporadic passage through private property? In other words, is a permanent physical occupation by government always so outrageous that it should require payment of just compensation regardless of the nature of the physical infringement or the degree of economic impact?

▶ *Essential Nexus.* Does the decision in *Nollan* impose a more demanding standard than rationality? Is the lateral access permit condition even rationally related to the public interest in access to the tidelands? Should the Supreme Court be more demanding in its review of legislative acts and of state governments?

Nollan v. California Coastal Commission 483 U.S. 825 (1987)

Justice SCALIA delivered the opinion of the Court.

James and Marilyn Nollan appeal from a decision of the California Court of Appeals ruling that the California Coastal Commission could condition its grant of permission to rebuild their house on their transfer to the public of an easement across their beachfront property. The California court rejected their claim that imposition of that condition violates the Takings Clause of the Fifth Amendment, as incorporated against the States by the Fourteenth Amendment....

The Nollans own a beachfront lot in Ventura County, California. A quarter mile north of their property is Faria County Park, an oceanside public park with a public beach and recreation area. Another public beach area, known locally as "the Cove," lies 1,800 feet south of their lot. A concrete seawall approximately eight feet high separates the beach portion of the Nollans' property from the rest of the lot. The historic mean high tide line determines the lot's oceanside boundary.

The Nollans originally leased their property with an option to buy. The building on the lot was a small bungalow, totaling 504 square feet, which for a time they rented to summer vacationers. After years of rental use, however, the building had fallen into disrepair, and could no longer be rented out.

The Nollans' option to purchase was conditioned on their promise to demolish the bungalow and replace it. In order to do so,...they were required to obtain a coastal development permit from the California Coastal Commission. On February 25, 1982, they submitted a permit application to the Commission in which they proposed to demolish the existing structure and replace it with a threebedroom house in keeping with the rest of the neighborhood.

The Nollans were informed that their application had been placed on the administrative calendar, and that the Commission staff had recommended that the permit be granted subject to the condition that they allow the public an easement to pass across a portion of their property bounded by the mean high tide line on one side, and their seawall on the other side. This would make it easier for the public to get to Faria County Park and the Cove. The Nollans protested imposition of the condition, but the Commission overruled their objections and granted the permit subject to their recordation of a deed restriction granting the easement....

Had California simply required the Nollans to make an easement across their beachfront available to the public on a permanent basis in order to increase public access to the beach, rather than conditioning their permit to rebuild their house on their agreeing to do so, we have no doubt there would have been a taking. To say that the appropriation of a public easement across a landowner's premises does not constitute the taking of a property interest but rather (as Justice Brennan contends) "a mere restriction on its use"...is to use words in a manner that deprives them of all their ordinary meaning. Indeed, one of the principal uses of the eminent domain power is to assure that the government be able to require conveyance of just such interests, so long as it pays for them....We have repeatedly held that, as to property reserved by its owner for private use, "the right to exclude [others is] 'one of the most essential sticks in the bundle of rights that are commonly characterized as property'"

....[W]here governmental action results in "[a] permanent physical occupation" of the property, by the government itself or by others ... "our cases uniformly have found a taking to the extent of the occupation, without regard to whether the action achieves an important public benefit or has only minimal economic impact on the owner." We think a "permanent physical occupation" has occurred, for purposes of that rule, where individuals are given a permanent and continuous right to pass to and fro, so that the real property may continuously be traversed, even though no particular individual is permitted to station himself permanently upon the premises.

Justice Brennan argues that while this might ordinarily be the case, the California Constitution's prohibition on any individual's "exclu[ding] the right of way to [any navigable] water whenever it is required for any public purpose," Art. X, Section 4, produces a different result here....There are a number of difficulties with that argument. Most obviously, the right of way sought here is not naturally described as one to navigable water (from the street to the sea) but along it; it is at least highly questionable whether the text of the California Constitution has any prima facie application to the situation before us....

Given, then, that requiring uncompensated conveyance of the easement outright would violate the Fourteenth Amendment, the question becomes whether requiring it to be conveyed as a condition for issuing a landuse permit alters the outcome. We have long recognized that landuse regulation does not effect a taking if it "substantially advance[s] legitimate state interests" and does not "den[y] an owner economically viable use of his land," *Agins v. Tiburon*....Our cases have not elaborated on the standards for determining what constitutes a "legitimate state interest" or what type of connection between the regulation and the state interest satisfies the requirement that the former "substantially advance" the latter. They have made clear, however, that a broad range of governmental purposes and regulations satisfies these requirements....The Commission argues that among these permissible purposes are protecting the public's ability to see the beach, assisting the public in overcoming the "psychological barrier" to using the beach created by a developed shorefront, and preventing congestion on the public beaches. We assume, without deciding, that this is so—in which case the Commission unquestionably would be able to deny the Nollans their permit outright if their new house (alone, or by reason of the cumulative impact produced in conjunction with other construction) would substantially impede these purposes, unless the denial would interfere so drastically with the Nollans' use of their property as to constitute a taking....

The Commission argues that a permit condition that serves the same legitimate policepower purpose as a refusal to issue the permit should not be found to be a taking if the refusal to issue the permit would not constitute a taking. We agree. Thus, if the Commission attached to the permit some condition that would have protected the public's ability to see the beach notwithstanding construction of the new house—for example, a height limitation, a width restriction, or a ban on fences—so long as the Commission could have exercised its police power (as we have assumed it could) to forbid construction of the house altogether, imposition of the condition would also be constitutional. Moreover (and here we come closer to the facts of the present case), the condition would be constitutional even if it consisted of the requirement that the Nollans provide a viewing spot on their property for passersby with whose sighting of the ocean their new house would interfere. Although such a requirement, constituting a permanent grant of continuous access to the property, would have to be considered a taking if it were not attached to a development permit, the Commission's assumed power to forbid construction of the house in order to protect the public's view of the beach must surely include the power to condition construction upon some concession by the owner, even a concession of property rights, that serves the same end. If a prohibition designed to accomplish that purpose would be a legitimate exercise of the police power rather than a taking, it would be strange to conclude that providing the owner an alternative to that prohibition which accomplishes the same purpose is not.

The evident constitutional propriety disappears, however, if the condition substituted for the prohibition utterly fails to further the end advanced as the justification for the prohibition. When that essential nexus is eliminated, the situation becomes the same as if California law forbade shouting fire in a crowded theater, but granted dispensations to those willing to contribute $100 to the state treasury. While a ban on shouting fire can be a core exercise of the State's police power to protect the public safety, and can thus meet even our stringent standards for regulation of speech, adding the unrelated condition alters the purpose to one which, while it may be legitimate, is inadequate to sustain the ban. Therefore, even though, in a sense, requiring a $100 tax contribution in order to shout fire is a lesser restriction on speech than an outright ban, it would not pass constitutional muster. Similarly here, the lack of nexus between the condition and the original purpose of the building restriction converts that purpose to something other than what it was. The purpose then becomes, quite simply, the obtaining of an easement to serve some valid governmental purpose, but without payment of compensation. Whatever may be the outer limits of "legitimate state interests" in the takings and landuse context, this is not one of them. In short, unless the permit condition serves the same governmental purpose as the development ban, the building restriction is not a valid regulation of land use but "an outandout plan of extortion." *J.E.D. Associates, Inc. v. Atkinson....*

The Commission claims that it concedes as much, and that we may sustain the condition at issue here by finding that it is reasonably related to the public need or burden that the Nollans' new house creates or to which it contributes. We can accept, for purposes of discussion, the Commission's proposed test as to how close a "fit" between the condition and the burden is required, because we find that this case does not meet even the most untailored standards....

...It is quite impossible to understand how a requirement that people already on the public beaches be able to walk across the Nollans' property reduces any obstacles to viewing the beach created by the new house. It is also impossible to understand how it lowers any "psychological barrier" to using the public beaches, or how it helps to remedy any additional congestion on them caused by construction of the Nollans' new house. We therefore find that the Commission's imposition of the permit condition cannot be treated as an exercise of its landuse power for any of these purposes. Our conclusion on this point is consistent with the approach taken by every other court that has considered the question, with the exception of the California state courts....

...As indicated earlier, our cases describe the condition for abridgement of property rights through the police power as a "substantial advanc[ing]" of a legitimate state interest.

We are inclined to be particularly careful about the adjective where the actual conveyance of property is made a condition to the lifting of a landuse restriction, since in that context there is heightened risk that the purpose is avoidance of the compensation requirement, rather than the stated policepower objective....

   Reversed.

Justice BRENNAN, with whom Justice MARSHALL joins, dissenting.

...The Court's conclusion that the permit condition imposed on appellants is unreasonable cannot withstand analysis. First, the Court demands a degree of exactitude that is inconsistent with our standard for reviewing the rationality of a State's exercise of its police power for the welfare of its citizens. Second, even if the nature of the publicaccess condition imposed must be identical to the precise burden on access created by appellants, this requirement is plainly satisfied.

   There can be no dispute that the police power of the States encompasses the authority to impose conditions on private development....The Coastal Commission, if it had so chosen, could have denied the Nollans' request for a development permit, since the property would have remained economically viable without the requested new development. Instead, the State sought to accommodate the Nollans' desire for new development, on the condition that the development not diminish the overall amount of public access to the coastline....

   The Court finds fault with this measure because it regards the condition as insufficiently tailored to address the precise type of reduction in access produced by the new development....Such a narrow conception of rationality, however, has long since been discredited as a judicial arrogation of legislative authority. "To make scientific precision a criterion of constitutional power would be to subject the State to an intolerable supervision hostile to the basic principles of our Government." *Sproles v. Binford*, 286 U.S. 374, 388 (1932)....

   Even if we accept the Court's unusual demand for a precise match between the condition imposed and the specific type of burden on access created by the appellants, the State's action easily satisfies this requirement. First, the lateral access condition serves to dissipate the impression that the beach that lies behind the wall of homes along the shore is for private use only. It requires no exceptional imaginative powers to find plausible the Commission's point that the average person passing along the road in front of a phalanx of imposing permanent residences, including the appellants' new home, is likely to conclude that this particular portion of the shore is not open to the public....The burden produced by the diminution in visual access—the impression that the beach is not open to the public—is thus directly alleviated by the provision for public access over the dry sand. The Court therefore has an unrealistically limited conception of what measures could reasonably be chosen to mitigate the burden produced by a diminution of visual access.

   The second flaw in the Court's analysis of the fit between burden and exaction is more fundamental. The Court assumes that the only burden with which the Coastal Commission was concerned was blockage of visual access to the beach. This is incorrect. The Commission specifically stated in its report in support of the permit condition that "[t]he Commission finds that the applicants' proposed development would present an increase in view blockage, *an increase in private use of the shorefront*, and that this impact would burden the public's ability to traverse to and along the shorefront." (emphasis added). It declared that the possibility that "the public may get the impression that the beachfront is no longer available for public use" would be "due to *the encroaching nature of private use immediately adjacent to the public use, as well as* the visual 'block' of increased residential buildout impacting the visual quality of the beachfront." (emphasis added)....

Finally, the character of the regulation in this case is not unilateral government action, but a condition on approval of a development request submitted by appellants. The State has not sought to interfere with any preexisting property interest, but has responded to appellants' proposal to intensify development on the coast....

Examination of the economic impact of the Commission's action reinforces the conclusion that no taking has occurred....Appellants have been allowed to replace a onestory, 521squarefoot beach home with a twostory, 1,674squarefoot residence and an attached twocar garage, resulting in development covering 2,464 square feet of the lot. Such development obviously significantly increases the value of appellants' property; appellants make no contention that this increase is offset by any diminution in value resulting from the deed restriction, much less that the restriction made the property less valuable than it would have been without the new construction. Furthermore, appellants gain an additional benefit from the Commission's permit condition program. They are able to walk along the beach beyond the confines of their own property only because the Commission has required deed restrictions as a condition of approving other new beach developments. Thus, appellants benefit both as private landowners and as members of the public from the fact that new development permit requests are conditioned on preservation of public access....

Lucas v. South Carolina Coastal Council LYNDA BUTLER

In *Lucas v. South Carolina Coastal Council*, the Supreme Court reviewed the efforts of the South Carolina legislature to protect its fragile coastal resources from intensifying development. Those efforts had effectively prohibited plaintiff Lucas from building any permanent habitable structure on his two beachfront lots even though permanent structures were located on neighboring lots. Writing for the majority, Justice Scalia concluded that a regulation prohibiting all economically beneficial use of land constituted a taking unless the prohibition "inhere[s] in the title itself, in the restrictions that background principles of the State's law of property and nuisance already place upon land ownership." A key aspect of the Court's holding was its assumption that Lucas's property was totally deprived of economically beneficial use. This assumption was based on the uncontested finding of the state trial court that the prohibition rendered Lucas's property valueless. But Lucas still owned the two beachfront lots. He could swim, picnic, camp, or live on the property in a movable trailer. The trial court accepted no evidence from the state regarding the property's value without a home, basing its finding on the landowner's valuation of the property in its best use as a luxury, single-family dwelling site.

A number of jurists and commentators have criticized Justice Scalia's inflexible rule that a total deprivation categorically results in a taking regardless of the importance of the public interest unless a pre-existing limitation inheres in the landowner's title. Justice Scalia justified his categorical approach by explaining that, from the property owner's perspective, the total deprivation was "the equivalent of a physical appropriation." He also noted that government action that leaves a property owner without economically viable use carries "a heightened risk that private property is being pressed into some form of public service under the guise of mitigating serious public harm." How does dissenting Justice Stevens counter Justice Scalia's arguments in support of his categorical rule?

Because the Supreme Court in *Lucas* assumed a total deprivation of value, it did not have to define the appropriate property benchmark for measuring diminution in value. In a footnote, however, Justice Scalia suggested that the answer "may lie in how the owner's reasonable expectations have been shaped by the State's law of property—i.e., whether and to what degree the State's law has accorded legal recognition and protection to the particular interest in land with respect to which the takings claimant alleges a diminution in value." What property benchmark is Scalia choosing? Suppose a regulation required a developer to leave 90% of a tract of land in its natural state. Using Justice Scalia's framework, would the proper inquiry be whether the owner has been deprived of all economically beneficial use of the burdened 90% or instead of the tract as a whole? Would the answer depend on whether the 10% of legally developable land can yield a reasonable return? Also consider Lucas's situation. Lucas paid almost $1 million for the two lots, which apparently was the highest amount ever paid for lots in the Beachwood subdivision of the Wild Dunes development. Yet Lucas was an "insider," having been associated with the subdivision development since 1979. He had served as a realtor, a contractor, and a planning assistant to the Wild Dunes board. Why would an insider wait so long to buy two lots for an unusually high price? Is this a pertinent question? Does it matter that nineteen months elapsed between the time Lucas purchased these lots and the time of passage of the South Carolina Beachfront Management Act—ample time, in other words, to submit a development plan prior to passage of the Act?

In recent years residential development on barrier islands and coastal beaches has far exceeded development in inland areas. The inevitable onslaught of hurricanes and other coastal storms and the fragile nature of coastal beaches, however, make coastal areas considerably less stable. What impact does *Lucas* have on government's ability to protect coastal and tidal resources from increasing development?

The *Lucas* decision is considered by many to be one of the most interesting and potentially significant takings cases to be decided in years. Consider the following questions in evaluating the implications of the decision.

▶ *Role of Diminution in Value.* Should a total diminution in value trump all other considerations except those reflected in pre-existing restrictions on the property owner's title? Could government, for example, totally destroy someone's home to prevent a fire from spreading without having to pay just compensation?

▶ *The Appropriate Property Benchmark.* If diminution in value is to be measured by focusing solely on the regulated portion, aren't property owners encouraged to manipulate the law by subdividing their property in a way that results in a total diminution in value? Won't a landowner who owns a ten-acre tract that includes three acres of wetlands try to develop the seven other acres first and then isolate the three acres to ensure that any prohibition on use of the three acres produces a total deprivation?

▶ *Role of the Public Interest.* To what extent does Lucas allow government to protect the environment by regulating private property? Does the Court in Lucas consider the public interest at all?

▶ *Regulation of Noxious Uses.* After the decision in Lucas, can government prohibit a harmful or noxious use without paying just compensation to the affected property owner?

Lucas v. South Carolina Coastal Council 505 U.S. 1003 (1992)

Justice SCALIA delivered the opinion of the Court.

In 1986, petitioner David H. Lucas paid $975,000 for two residential lots on the Isle of Palms in Charleston County, South Carolina, on which he intended to build singlefamily homes. In 1988, however, the South Carolina Legislature enacted the Beachfront Management Act, which had the direct effect of barring petitioner from erecting any permanent habitable structures on his two parcels. A state trial court found that this prohibition rendered Lucas's parcels "valueless." App. to Pet. for Cert. 37. This case requires us to decide whether the Act's dramatic effect on the economic value of Lucas's lots accomplished a taking of private property under the Fifth and Fourteenth Amendments requiring the payment of "just compensation." ...

...We have...described at least two discrete categories of regulatory action as compensable without casespecific inquiry into the public interest advanced in support of the restraint. The first encompasses regulations that compel the property owner to suffer a physical "invasion" of his property. In general (at least with regard to permanent invasions), no matter how minute the intrusion, and no matter how weighty the public purpose behind it, we have required compensation....

The second situation in which we have found categorical treatment appropriate is where regulation denies all economically beneficial or productive use of land....As we have said on numerous occasions, the Fifth Amendment is violated when landuse regulation "does not substantially advance legitimate state interests *or denies an owner economically viable use of his land.*" (emphasis added).

We have never set forth the justification for this rule. Perhaps it is simply, as Justice Brennan suggested, that total deprivation of beneficial use is, from the landowner's point of view, the equivalent of a physical appropriation....Surely, at least, in the extraordinary circumstance when no productive or economically beneficial use of land is permitted, it is less realistic to indulge our usual assumption that the legislature is simply "adjusting the benefits and burdens of economic life," *Penn Central Transportation Co.* in a manner that secures an "average reciprocity of advantage" to everyone concerned, *Pennsylvania Coal Co. v. Mahon....*

On the other side of the balance, affirmatively supporting a compensation requirement, is the fact that regulations that leave the owner of land without economically beneficial or productive options for its use—typically, as here, by requiring land to be left substantially in its natural state—carry with them a heightened risk that private property is being pressed into some form of public service under the guise of mitigating serious public harm....

...[Lucas] "concede[d] that the beach/dune area of South Carolina's shores is an extremely valuable public resource; that the erection of new construction, *inter alia*, contributes to the erosion and destruction of this public resource; and that discouraging new construction in close proximity to the beach/dune area is necessary to prevent a great public harm."...In the [State Supreme] court's view, these concessions brought petitioner's challenge within a long line of this Court's cases sustaining against Due Process and Takings Clause challenges the State's use of its "police powers" to enjoin a property owner from activities akin to public nuisances....

It is correct that many of our prior opinions have suggested that "harmful or noxious uses" of property may be proscribed by government regulation without the requirement of compensation. For a number of reasons, however, we think the South Carolina Supreme Court was too quick to conclude that that principle decides the present case. The "harmful or noxious uses" principle was the Court's early attempt to describe in theoretical terms why government may, consistent with the Takings Clause, affect property values by regulation without incurring an obligation to compensate—a reality we nowadays acknowledge explicitly with respect to the full scope of the State's police power....

The transition from our early focus on control of "noxious" uses to our contemporary understanding of the broad realm within which government may regulate without compensation was an easy one, since the distinction between "harmpreventing" and "benefitconferring" regulation is often in the eye of the beholder. It is quite possible, for example, to describe in *either* fashion the ecological, economic, and esthetic concerns that inspired the South Carolina Legislature in the present case. One could say that imposing a servitude on Lucas's land is necessary in order to prevent his use of it from "harming" South Carolina's ecological resources; or, instead, in order to achieve the "benefits" of an ecological preserve....Whether one or the other of the competing characterizations will come to one's lips in a particular case depends primarily upon one's evaluation of the worth of competing uses of real estate....A given restraint will be seen as mitigating "harm" to the adjacent parcels or securing a "benefit" for them, depending upon the observer's evaluation of the relative importance of the use that the restraint favors....

Where the State seeks to sustain regulation that deprives land of all economically beneficial use, we think it may resist compensation only if the logically antecedent inquiry into the nature of the owner's estate shows that the proscribed use interests were not part of his title to begin with. This accords, we think, with our "takings" jurisprudence, which has traditionally been guided by the understandings of our citizens regarding the content of, and the State's power over, the "bundle of rights" that they acquire when they obtain title to property. It seems to us that the property owner necessarily expects the uses of his property to be restricted, from time to time, by various measures newly enacted by the State in legitimate exercise of its police powers....And in the case of personal property, by reason of the State's traditionally high degree of control over commercial dealings, he ought to be aware of the possibility that new regulation might even render his property economically worthless (at least if the property's only economically productive use is sale or manufacture for sale)....In the case of land, however, we think the notion pressed by the Council that title is somehow held subject to the "implied limitation" that the State may subsequently eliminate all economically valuable use is inconsistent with the historical compact recorded in the Takings Clause that has become part of our constitutional culture.

Where "permanent physical occupation" of land is concerned, we have refused to allow the government to decree it anew (without compensation), no matter how weighty the asserted "public interests" involved ...—though we assuredly *would* permit the government to assert a permanent easement that was a preexisting limitation upon the landowner's title....We believe similar treatment must be accorded confiscatory regulations, i.e., regulations that prohibit all economically beneficial use of land. Any limitation so severe cannot be newly legislated or decreed (without compensation), but must inhere in the title itself, in the restrictions that background principles of the State's law of property and nuisance already place upon land ownership. A law or decree with such an effect must, in other words, do no more than duplicate the result that could have been achieved in the courts— by adjacent landowners (or other uniquely affected persons) under the State's law of private nuisance, or by the State under its complementary power to abate nuisances that affect the public generally, or otherwise.

It seems unlikely that commonlaw principles would have prevented the erection of any habitable or productive improvements on petitioner's land; they rarely support prohibition of the "essential use" of land....The question, however, is one of state law to be dealt with on remand. We emphasize that to win its case South Carolina must do more than proffer the legislature's declaration that the uses Lucas desires are inconsistent with the public interest....Instead, as it would be required to do if it sought to restrain Lucas in a commonlaw action for public nuisance, South Carolina must identify background principles of nuisance and property law that prohibit the uses he now intends in the circumstances in which the property is presently found. Only on this showing can the State fairly claim that, in proscribing all such beneficial uses, the Beachfront Management Act is taking nothing.

The judgment is reversed, and the case is remanded for proceedings not inconsistent with this opinion.

So ordered.

Justice BLACKMUN, dissenting.

Today the Court launches a missile to kill a mouse....

Petitioner Lucas is a contractor, manager, and part owner of the Wild Dune development on the Isle of Palms....The area is notoriously unstable...

The Beachfront Management Act includes a finding by the South Carolina General Assembly that the beach/dune system serves the purpose of "protect[ing] life and property by serving as a storm barrier which dissipates wave energy and contributes to shoreline stability in an economical and effective manner." The General Assembly also found that "development unwisely has been sited too close to the [beach/dune] system. This type of development has jeopardized the stability of the beach/dune system, accelerated erosion, and endangered adjacent property." ...

...[T]he State has full power to prohibit an owner's use of property if it is harmful to the public. "[S]ince no individual has a right to use his property so as to create a nuisance or otherwise harm others, the State has not 'taken' anything when it asserts its power to enjoin the nuisancelike activity." Keystone Bituminous Coal, 480 U.S., at 491, n. 20. It would make no sense under this theory to suggest that an owner has a constitutionally protected right to harm others, if only he makes the proper showing of economic loss....

Justice STEVENS, dissenting.

....In addition to lacking support in past decisions, the Court's new rule is wholly arbitrary. A landowner whose property is diminished in value 95% recovers nothing, while an owner whose property is diminished 100% recovers the land's full value....

Moreover, because of the elastic nature of property rights, the Court's new rule will also prove unsound in practice. In response to the rule, courts may define "property" broadly and only rarely find regulations to effect total takings. This is the approach the Court itself adopts in its revisionist reading of venerable precedents....

On the other hand, developers and investors may market specialized estates to take advantage of the Court's new rule. The smaller the estate, the more likely that a regulatory change will effect a total taking. Thus, an investor may, for example, purchase the right to build a multifamily home on a specific lot, with the result that a zoning regulation that allows only singlefamily homes would render the investor's property interest "valueless." In short, the categorical rule will likely have one of two effects: Either courts will alter the definition of the "denominator" in the takings "fraction," rendering the Court's categorical rule meaningless, or investors will manipulate the relevant property interests, giving the Court's rule sweeping effect. To my mind, neither of these results is desirable or appropriate, and both are distortions of our takings jurisprudence....

The Court's holding today effectively freezes the State's common law, denying the legislature much of its traditional power to revise the law governing the rights and uses of property. Until today, I had thought that we had long abandoned this approach to constitutional law. More than a century ago we recognized that "the great office of statutes is to remedy defects in the common law as they are developed, and to adapt it to the changes of time and circumstances." *Munn v. Illinois* (1877)....

Arresting the development of the common law is not only a departure from our prior decisions; it is also profoundly unwise. The human condition is one of constant learning and evolution—both moral and practical. Legislatures implement that new learning; in doing so they must often revise the definition of property and the rights of property owners. Thus, when the Nation came to understand that slavery was morally wrong and mandated the emancipation of all slaves, it, in effect, redefined "property." On a lesser scale, our ongoing selfeducation produces similar changes in the rights of property owners: New appreciation of the significance of endangered species,...the importance of wetlands,...and the vulnerability of coastal lands,...shapes our evolving understandings of property rights.

Of course, some legislative redefinitions of property will effect a taking and must be compensated—but it certainly cannot be the case that every movement away from common law does so. There is no reason, and less sense, in such an absolute rule. We live in a world in which changes in the economy and the environment occur with increasing frequency and importance. If it was wise a century ago to allow government "'the largest legislative discretion'" to deal with "'the special exigencies of the moment,'" *Mugler v. Kansas* (1887) it is imperative to do so today. The rule that should govern a decision in a case of this kind should focus on the future, not the past.

The Court's categorical approach rule will, I fear, greatly hamper the efforts of local officials and planners who must deal with increasingly complex problems in landuse and environmental regulation. As this case—in which the claims of an *individual* property owner exceed $1 million—well demonstrates, these officials face both substantial uncertainty because of the *ad hoc* nature of takings law and unacceptable penalties if they guess incorrectly about that law....

...[O]ne of the central concerns of our takings jurisprudence is "prevent[ing] the public from loading upon one individual more than his just share of the burdens of government." *Monongahela Navigation Co. v. United States* (1893). We have, therefore, in our takings law frequently looked to the *generality* of a regulation of property....

In considering Lucas' claim, the generality of the Beachfront Management Act is significant. The Act does not target particular landowners, but rather regulates the use of the coastline of the entire State....Indeed, South Carolina's Act is best understood as part of a national effort to protect the coastline, one initiated by the federal Coastal Zone Management Act of 1972....

The impact of the ban on developmental uses must also be viewed in light of the purposes of the Act....The State, with much science on its side, believes that the "beach/dune system [acts] as a buffer from high tides, storm surge, [and] hurricanes."...This is a traditional and important exercise of the State's police power, as demonstrated by Hurricane Hugo, which in 1989, caused 29 deaths and more than $6 billion in property damage in South Carolina alone.

In view of all of these factors, even assuming that petitioner's property was rendered valueless, the risk inherent in investments of the sort made by petitioner, the generality of the Act, and the compelling purpose motivating the South Carolina Legislature persuade me that the Act did not effect a taking of petitioner's property.

Accordingly, I respectfully dissent.

Dolan v. City of Tigard   LYNDA BUTLER

In recent years local and state governments have become increasingly concerned about development and growth and about their impact on important public interests. Those interests include such goals as protection of critical environmental areas, preservation of green space, promotion of aethestic and other quality-of-life values, flood prevention, reduction of traffic congestion, protection of air and water quality, and provision of adequate police, fire, education, and other public services. Among other strategies, local and state governments have imposed moratoria on development, prohibited development in critical environmental areas, and required provision of open space and greenway areas, reduction in the density of development projects, and improvement of roads, sewers, drainage systems, and other public utilities.

The decision in *Nollan* generated considerable uncertainty about the level of judicial scrutiny to be applied to government conditions imposed on landowners in exchange for permission to develop. Often called exactions, these conditions can promote important public interests by forcing landowners to internalize some of the social costs of private development. The conditions also can be a disguise for public acquisition of property without payment of just compensation. In *Dolan v. City of Tigard* the Supreme Court clarified that government is indeed subject to a heightened level of judicial review at least when it does not simply impose a restriction on use but rather requires the landowner to transfer some portion of the property to government. Under the heightened level of review, the condition first must meet the Nollan test and show an essential nexus between a legitimate state interest and the condition. If that standard is met, government then must show a rough proportionality between the condition and the projected impact of the development. Do you see a difference between the two levels of review? Do they really involve different nexus inquiries?

The *Dolan* nexus review imposes a difficult burden on government. Under *Dolan* government must "make some sort of individualized determination that the required...[condition] is related both in nature and extent to the impact of the proposed development." Although the Court states that "[n]o precise mathematical calculation is required," it then rejects the city's calculations as inadequate. The Court explains that the city did not show that the additional number of vehicles and bike trips generated by the proposed development was reasonably related to the condition. Given the Court's reaction to the calculations done by Tigard, how easy is it going to be for a local government to meet the *Dolan* test?

Both a narrow and a broad reading of the *Dolan* decision are plausible. To help you see both interpretations, consider the following questions.

▶ *Permanent Physical Occupation.* What impact does the city's condition of a forced conveyance have on the Court's decision? Did the city need to require a dedication of law to promote its legitimate public interests?

▶ *Appropriate Property Benchmark.* What property benchmark does the *Dolan* majority choose: only the property rights that the landowner has lost (the right to exclude the public and exclusively use the dedicated property) or the property as a whole (the entire development tract)?

▶ *Role of the Public Interest Determinations by Local Governments.* Like the Court in *Nollan,* the Court in *Dolan* imposes a burden on government that is contrary to the traditionally deferential approach to reviewing government decisions. Some jurists and commentators fear that the stricter judicial scrutiny required by the Court will result in micro-management of state decisions by federal courts. Do you agree?

▶ *Impact on Land Use Planning.* What impact will *Dolan* have on land use planning? Does *Dolan* give local governments greater incentive to deny permits outright rather than to make the calculations required by the Court? Has the Court been unrealistic in what it expects local governments to predict about the impact of proposed development?

Dolan v. City of Tigard 512 U.S. 374 (1994)

Chief Justice REHNQUIST delivered the opinion of the Court.

Petitioner challenges the decision of the Oregon Supreme Court which held that the city of Tigard could condition the approval of her building permit on the dedication of a portion of her property for flood control and traffic improvements....We granted *certiorari* to resolve a question left open by our decision in *Nollan v. California Coastal Commission* (1987), of what is the required degree of connection between the exactions imposed by the city and the projected impacts of the proposed development.

The State of Oregon enacted a comprehensive land use management program in 1973....Pursuant to the State's requirements, the city of Tigard, a community of some 30,000 residents on the southwest edge of Portland, developed a comprehensive plan and codified it in its Community Development Code (CDC)....

Petitioner Florence Dolan owns a plumbing and electric supply store located on Main Street in the Central Business District of the city. The store covers approximately 9,7 square feet on the eastern side of a 1.67acre parcel, which includes a gravel p Fanno Creek flows through the southwestern corner of the lot and along i ary. The yearround flow of the creek renders the area within the creek's 1 virtually unusable for commercial development. The city's comprehensive Fanno Creek floodplain as part of the city's greenway system.

Petitioner applied to the city for a permit to redevelop the site. Her proposed plans called for nearly doubling the size of the store to 17,600 square feet, and paving a 39space parking lot. The existing store, located on the opposite side of the parcel, would be razed in sections as construction progressed on the new building. In the second phase of the project, petitioner proposed to build an additional structure on the northeast side of the site for complementary businesses, and to provide more parking. The proposed expansion and intensified use are consistent with the city's zoning scheme in the Central Business District....

The City Planning Commission...granted petitioner's permit application subject to conditions...that petitioner dedicate the portion of her property lying within the 100-year floodplain for improvement of a storm drainage system along Fanno Creek and that she dedicate an additional 15-foot strip of land adjacent to the floodplain as a pedestrian/bicycle pathway....

...Without question, had the city simply required petitioner to dedicate a strip of land along Fanno Creek for public use, rather than conditioning the grant of her permit to redevelop her property on such a dedication, a taking would have occurred....Such public access would deprive petitioner of the right to exclude others, "one of the most essential sticks in the bundle of rights that are commonly characterized as property." *Kaiser Aetna v. United States*, 444 U.S. 164, 176 (1979)....

Petitioner contends that the city has forced her to choose between the building permit and her right under the Fifth Amendment to just compensation for the public easements. Petitioner does not quarrel with the city's authority to exact some forms of dedication as a condition for the grant of a building permit, but challenges the showing made by the city to justify these exactions. She argues that the city has identified "no special benefits" conferred on her, and has not identified any "special quantifiable burdens" created by her new store that would justify the particular dedications required from her which are not required from the public at large.

In evaluating petitioner's claim, we must first determine whether the "essential nexus" exists between the "legitimate state interest" and the permit condition exacted by the city. *Nollan*, 483 U.S., at 837. If we find that a nexus exists, we must then decide the required degree of connection between the exactions and the projected impact of the proposed development. We were not required to reach this question in Nollan, because we concluded that the connection did not meet even the loosest standard. Here, however, we must decide this question.

...Undoubtedly, the prevention of flooding along Fanno Creek and the reduction of traffic congestion in the Central Business District qualify as the type of legitimate public purposes we have upheld....It seems equally obvious that a nexus exists between preventing flooding along Fanno Creek and limiting development within the creek's 100year floodplain. Petitioner proposes to double the size of her retail store and to pave her nowgravel parking lot, thereby expanding the impervious surface on the property and increasing the amount of stormwater runoff into Fanno Creek.

The same may be said for the city's attempt to reduce traffic congestion by providing for alternative means of transportation. In theory, a pedestrian/bicycle pathway provides a useul alternative means of transportation for workers and shoppers....

The second part of our analysis requires us to determine whether the degree of the exactions demanded by the city's permit conditions bear the required relationship to the projected impact of petitioner's proposed development....

The city required that petitioner dedicate "to the city as Greenway all portions of the site that fall within the existing 100year floodplain [of Fanno Creek]...and all property 15 feet above [the floodplain] boundary." In addition, the city demanded that the retail store be designed so as not to intrude into the greenway area. The city relies on the Commission's rather tentative findings that increased stormwater flow from petitioner's property "can only add to the public need to manage the [floodplain] for drainage purposes" to support its conclusion that the "requirement of dedication of the floodplain area on the site is related to the applicant's plan to intensify development on the site."...

...We think a term such as "rough proportionality" best encapsulates what we hold to be the requirement of the Fifth Amendment. No precise mathematical calculation is required, but the city must make some sort of individualized determination that the required dedication is related both in nature and extent to the impact of the proposed development....

It is axiomatic that increasing the amount of impervious surface will increase the quantity and rate of stormwater flow from petitioner's property....Therefore, keeping the floodplain open and free from development would likely confine the pressures on Fanno Creek created by petitioner's development. In fact, because petitioner's property lies within the Central Business District, the Community Development Code already required that petitioner leave 15% of it as open space and the undeveloped floodplain would have nearly satisfied that requirement....But the city demanded more—it not only wanted petitioner not to build in the floodplain, but it also wanted petitioner's property along Fanno Creek for its Greenway system. The city has never said why a public greenway, as opposed to a private one, was required in the interest of flood control.

The difference to petitioner, of course, is the loss of her ability to exclude others....It is difficult to see why recreational visitors trampling along petitioner's floodplain easement are sufficiently related to the city's legitimate interest in reducing flooding problems along Fanno Creek, and the city has not attempted to make any individualized determination to support this part of its request....

If petitioner's proposed development had somehow encroached on existing greenway space in the city, it would have been reasonable to require petitioner to provide some alternative greenway space for the public either on her property or elsewhere....We conclude that the findings upon which the city relies do not show the required reasonable relationship between the floodplain easement and the petitioner's proposed new building.

With respect to the pedestrian/bicycle pathway, we have no doubt that the city was correct in finding that the larger retail sales facility proposed by petitioner will increase traffic on the streets of the Central Business District. The city estimates that the proposed development would generate roughly 435 additional trips per day. Dedications for streets, sidewalks, and other public ways are generally reasonable exactions to avoid excessive congestion from a proposed property use. But on the record before us, the city has not met its burden of demonstrating that the additional number of vehicle and bicycle trips generated by the petitioner's development reasonably relate to the city's requirement for a dedication of the pedestrian/bicycle pathway easement. The city simply found that the creation of the pathway "could offset some of the traffic demand...and lessen the increase in traffic congestion."

As Justice Peterson of the Supreme Court of Oregon explained in his dissenting opinion, however, "[t]he findings of fact that the bicycle pathway system 'could offset some of the traffic demand' is a far cry from a finding that the bicycle pathway system will, or is likely to, offset some of the traffic demand." (emphasis in original). No precise mathematical calculation is required, but the city must make some effort to quantify its findings in support of the dedication for the pedestrian/bicycle pathway beyond the conclusory statement that it could offset some of the traffic demand generated....

The judgment of the Supreme Court of Oregon is reversed, and the case is remanded for further proceedings consistent with this opinion.

Justice STEVENS, with whom Justice BLACKMUN and Justice GINSBURG join, dissenting.

...It is not merely state cases, but our own cases as well, that require the analysis to focus on the impact of the city's action on the entire parcel of private property. In *Penn Central Transportation Co. v. New York City* (1978), we stated that takings jurisprudence "does not divide a single parcel into discrete segments and attempt to determine whether rights in a particular segment have been entirely abrogated."...*Andrus v. Allard* (1979), reaffirmed the nondivisibility principle outlined in *Penn Central*, stating that "[a]t least where an owner possesses a full 'bundle' of property rights, the destruction of one 'strand' of the bundle is not a taking, because the aggregate must be viewed in its entirety." *Id.*, at 6566....Although limitation of the right to exclude others undoubtedly constitutes a significant infringement upon property ownership,...restrictions on that right do not alone constitute a taking, and do not do so in any event unless they "unreasonably impair the value or use" of the property. *PruneYard Shopping Center v. Robins* (1980)....

In our changing world one thing is certain: uncertainty will characterize predictions about the impact of new urban developments on the risks of floods, earthquakes, traffic congestion, or environmental harms. When there is doubt concerning the magnitude of those impacts, the public interest in averting them must outweigh the private interest of the commercial entrepreneur. If the government can demonstrate that the conditions it has imposed in a landuse permit are rational, impartial and conducive to fulfilling the aims of a valid landuse plan, a strong presumption of validity should attach to those conditions. The burden of demonstrating that those conditions have unreasonably impaired the economic value of the proposed improvement belongs squarely on the shoulders of the party challenging the state action's constitutionality. That allocation of burdens has served us well in the past. The Court has stumbled badly today by reversing it.

I respectfully dissent.

IX Federalism

IX Federalism

A. E. DICK HOWARD

After the War of the Revolution, the newly independent states were wary of centralized power. Many Americans held the view that republicanism flourished best in small units where popular control of government was most likely to take hold. Under the Articles of Confederation, each state retained its "sovereignty, freedom, and independence." The central government existed largely at the sufferance of the states.

Americans soon discovered, however, the problems of a loose confederacy. Commerce suffered because states treated each other as if they were foreign countries. On the foreign scene, the new nation found itself too weak to present a unified front to the established powers of the Old World. And domestic discontent, especially among hard-pressed debtors, raised fears of internal upheaval.

Thus delegates from the several states came to meet at Philadelphia in the summer of 1787. The Virginia Plan, largely the work of James Madison, called for Congress to have the power "to legislate in all cases in which the separate states are incompetent" and for Congress to have a veto over state laws. Most delegates agreed that the powers of the central government should be increased beyond those granted by the Articles of Confederation, but the smaller states feared their interests would be submerged under the Virginia Plan. Ultimately the competing proposals of large and small states were bridged in what history has recorded as the Connecticut Compromise—Congress to have a popularly elected house based on population, and an upper house elected by the state legislature and in which each state would have two members.

During the debate on the Constitution's ratification, Madison described the Constitution as a hybrid, "neither wholly national nor wholly federal." The Anti-Federalists, Patrick Henry among them, objected to the new Constitution both because it lacked a bill of rights and because it gave too much power to the federal government. When the Bill of Rights came into effect in 1791, it included not only protection for individual rights but also the Tenth Amendment, which provides, "The powers not delegated to the United States by the Constitution, nor prohibited by it to the States, are reserved to the States respectively, or to the people."

From the founders' time to our own, the nature and extent of federal power has been the subject of sharp, often divisive debate. Even the first words of the Constitution's preamble—"We the People"—are veiled in ambiguity. In a famous debate in 1830, Senator Robert Y. Hayne of South Carolina declared the Constitution to be a compact among sovereign states. In reply, Massachusetts' Daniel Webster declared the Constitution to be a compact of the sovereign people of the United States.

Civil War and Reconstruction settled the question of the Union's permanence. But those events have not stilled the debate over the relative scope of state and federal power. The American economy has been transformed in the two centuries since the founding era, giving rise to extensive national regulation. Wartime exigencies have enhanced central power. Social forces, notably the modern civil rights movement, have created yet further tendencies to national rules and standards.

In the midst of these social, economic, and political changes, the Supreme Court has had to decide what role it should play as an arbiter of the federal system. In John Marshall's day, the Court often spoke of "dual federalism," limiting federal actions thought to encroach on the domain of the states. After the so-called "constitutional revolution" of 1937, the Court seemed to abdicate its interest in the states' prerogatives; indeed, in 1942 the Court spoke of the Tenth Amendment as being merely a "truism"—in effect, an empty vessel.

In recent years, especially since the coming of age of the Rehnquist Court, we have seen a revived judicial concern for the values of federalism. No longer is federalism an arena left to historians and political theorists. As in the founding period, questions of federalism are once again a subject of intense constitutional scrutiny.

▶ What is the link between federalism and individual liberty?

▶ Are individual rights more likely to be protected by the federal government or by state and local governments?

▶ What is the connection between distributing powers among the branches of government (the separation of powers) and between the federal government and the states (federalism)?

▶ Should the states be seen as laboratories in which to undertake experiments in government, including the protection of rights? Should diversity among the states be seen as likely to lead to more liberty or less?

▶ What does historical record show? Have our rights, by and large, been better protected by the states and local governments? Or by the federal government?

▶ What role should the Supreme Court play as an arbiter of the federal system? Should it protect the states against federal power, just as it protects federal interests against state encroachments?

Garcia v. San Antonio Metropolitan Transit Authority   A. E. DICK HOWARD

In 1938 Congress enacted the Fair Labor Standards Act, requiring employers covered by the act to pay their employees a minimum hourly wage and to pay them at a rate of one and a half times their regular hourly pay for hours worked in excess of 40 hours a week. The original statute specifically excluded the states and their political subdivisions from coverage.

Over the years, however, Congress broadened the reach of the Act until, in 1974, its minimum wage and maximum hour provisions were extended to nearly all public employees of state and their political subdivisions. Various states and cities, as well as the National League of Cities and the National Governors' Conference, challenged this expansion of the statute as being unconstitutional.

In 1976, in *National League of Cities v. Usery*, the Supreme Court, by a vote of 5 to 4, held that the Constitution's grant (in Article I, Section 8) to Congress of the power to regulate commerce did not empower Congress to enforce provisions of the Fair Labor Standards Act against the states or their subdivisions "in areas of traditional governmental functions."

Usery's life proved to be a short one. In the years after 1976, the Supreme Court found ways to whittle away at the opinion's underlying effort to carve out a zone within which states and their subdivision would enjoy constitutional protection against congressional enactments. Finally, in 1985, *Usery* was overruled.

Like *Usery*, the Court's decision in *Garcia v. San Antonio Metropolitan Transit Authority* turned on a 5 to 4 vote. But this time the states lost; *Garcia* ruled the states must look to the political process, rather than to the courts, for protection of their interests. Thus, Congress was permitted, after all, to apply the wage and hours provisions of the Fair Labor Standards Act to the states and their political subdivisions.

▶ Should the states be treated like other political actors, that is, should they look to Congress and to the political process generally to protect their interests?

▶ In remitting the states to the political process, does the Court abdicate a judicial function which, under the Constitution, it should assume?

▶ Is the majority in *Garcia* correct in concluding that, as an empirical matter, the states do in fact have sufficient protection in the legislative and political process, for example, in Congress?

▶ Can you imagine a "failing" in the political process of such a kind that might satisfy Justice Blackmun that a state or states had been insufficiently protected by that process?

> ► Assuming *Garcia* were to be overruled (as Justice Rehnquist, in his dissent, clearly hopes it will be), what criteria might the Court fashion to define the zone within which the states and their subdivisions would be protected from federal legislation?

Garcia v. San Antonio Metropolitan Transit Authority
469 U.S. 528 (1985)

Justice BLACKMUN delivered the opinion of the Court.

We revisit in these cases an issue raised in *National League of Cities v. Usery*....In that litigation, this Court, by a sharply divided vote, ruled that the Commerce Clause does not empower Congress to enforce the minimum-wage and overtime provisions of the Fair Labor Standards Act (FLSA) against the States "in areas of traditional governmental functions."...Although *National League of Cities* supplied some examples of "traditional governmental functions," it did not offer a general explanation of how a "traditional" function is to be distinguished from a "nontraditional" one. Since then, federal and state courts have struggled with the task, thus imposed, of identifying a traditional function for purposes of state immunity under the Commerce Clause.

In the present case, a Federal District Court concluded that municipal ownership and operation of a mass-transit system is a traditional governmental function and thus, under *National League of Cities*, is exempt from the obligations imposed by the FLSA. Faced with the identical question, three Federal Courts of Appeals and one state appellate court have reached the opposite conclusion.

Our examination of this "function" standard applied in these and other cases over the last eight years now persuades us that the attempt to draw the boundaries of state regulatory immunity in terms of "traditional governmental function" is not only unworkable but is inconsistent with established principles of federalism and, indeed, with those very principles on which *National League of Cities* purported to rest. That case, accordingly, is overruled....

Appellees have not argued that SAMTA is immune from regulation under FLSA on the ground that it is a local transit system engaged in intrastate commercial activity. In a practical sense, SAMTA's operations might well be characterized as "local." Nonetheless, it long has been settled that Congress' authority under the Commerce Clause extends to intrastate economic activities that affect interstate commerce....Were SAMTA a privately owned and operated enterprise, it could not credibly argue that Congress exceeded the bounds of its Commerce Clause powers in prescribing minimum wages and overtime rates for SAMTA's employees. Any constitutional exemption from the requirements of the FLSA therefore must rest on SAMTA's status as a governmental entity rather than on the "local" nature of its operations....

The controversy in the present cases has focused on the [requirement of *Hodel v. Virginia Surface Mining & Reclamation Association* (1981)] that the challenged federal statute trench on "traditional governmental functions." The District Court voiced a common concern: "Despite the abundance of adjectives, identifying which particular state functions are immune remains difficult."...Just how troublesome the task has been is revealed by the results reached in other federal cases. Thus, courts have held that regulating ambulance services,...licensing automobile drivers, ...operating a municipal airport,...performing solid waste disposal,...and operating a highway authority...are functions protected under *National League of Cities*. At the same time, courts have held that issuance of industrial development bonds,...regulation of intrastate natural gas sales,...regulation of traffic on public roads,...regulation of air transportation,...operation of a telephone system,...leasing and sale of natural gas,...operation of a mental health facility,...and provision of in-house domestic services for the aged and handicapped...are not entitled to immunity. We find it difficult, if not impossible, to identify an organizing principle that places each of the cases in the first group on one side of a line and each of the cases in the second group on the other side. The constitutional distinction between licensing drivers and regulating traffic, for example, or between operating a highway authority and operating a mental health facility, is elusive at best....

We therefore now reject, as unsound in principle and unworkable in practice, a rule of state immunity from federal regulation that turns on a judicial appraisal of whether a particular governmental function is "integral" or "traditional." Any such rule leads to inconsistent results at the same time that it disserves principles of democratic self-governance, and it breeds inconsistency precisely because it is divorced from those principles. If there are to be limits on the Federal Government's power to interfere with state functions—as undoubtedly there are—we must look elsewhere to find them. We accordingly return to the underlying issue that confronted this Court in *National League of Cities*—the manner in which the Constitution insulates States from the reach of Congress' power under the Commerce Clause....

The states unquestionably do "retai[n] a significant measure of sovereign authority." ...They do so, however, only to the extent that the Constitution has not divested them of their original powers and transferred those powers to the Federal Government. In the words of James Madison to the Members of the First Congress: "Interference with the power of the States was no constitutional criterion of the power of Congress. If the power was not given, Congress could not exercise it; if given, they might exercise it, although it should interfere with the laws, or even the Constitution of the States."...

When we look for the States' "residuary and inviolable sovereignty," *The Federalist* No. 39...(J. Madison), in the shape of the constitutional scheme rather than in predetermined notions of sovereign power, a different measure of state sovereignty emerges. Apart from the limitation on federal authority inherent in the delegated nature of Congress' Article I powers, the principal means chosen by the Framers to ensure the role of the States in the federal system lies in the structure of the Federal Government itself. It is no novelty to observe that the composition of the Federal Government was designed in large part to protect the States from overreaching by Congress. The Framers thus gave the States a role in the selection both of the Executive and the Legislative Branches of the Federal Government. The States were vested with indirect influence over the House of Representatives and the Presidency by their control of electoral qualifications and their role in presidential elections. U.S. Const., Art. I, Section 2, and Art. II, Section 1. They were given more direct influence in the Senate, where each State received equal representation and each Senator was to be selected by the legislature of his State. Art. I, Section 3. The significance attached to the States' equal representation in the Senate is underscored by the prohibition of any constitutional amendment divesting a State of equal representation without the State's consent. Art. V.

...Madison placed particular reliance on the equal representation of the States in the Senate, which he saw as "at once a constitutional recognition of the portion of sovereignty remaining in the individual States, and an instrument for preserving that residuary sovereignty." *The Federalist* No. 62....He further noted that "the residuary sovereignty of the States [is] implied and *secured* by that principle of representation in one branch of the [federal] legislature" (emphasis added). *The Federalist* No. 43....In short, the Framers chose to rely on a federal system in which special restraints on federal power over the States inhered principally in the workings of the National Government itself, rather than in discrete limitations on the objects of federal authority. State sovereign interests, then, are more properly protected by procedural safeguards inherent in the structure of the federal system than by judicially created limitations on federal power.

The effectiveness of the federal political process in preserving the States' interests is apparent even today in the course of federal legislation. On the one hand, the States have been able to direct a substantial proportion of federal revenues into their own treasuries in the form of general and program-specific grants in aid. The federal role in assisting state and local governments is a longstanding one; Congress provided federal land grants to finance state governments from the beginning of the Republic, and direct cash grants were awarded as early as 1887 under the Hatch Act. In the past quarter-century alone, federal grants to States and localities have grown from $7 billion to $96 billion. As a result, federal grants now account for about one-fifth of state and local government expenditures. The States have obtained federal funding for such services as police and fire protection, education, public health and hospitals, parks and recreation, and sanitation. Moreover, at the same time that the States have exercised their influence to obtain federal support, they have been able to exempt themselves from a wide variety of obligations imposed by Congress under the Commerce Clause. For example, the Federal Power Act, the National Labor Relations Act, the Labor-Management Reporting and Disclosure Act, the Occupational Safety and Health Act, and the Sherman Act all contain express or implied exemptions for States and their subdivisions. The fact that some federal statutes such as the FLSA extend general obligations to the States cannot obscure the extent to which the political position of the States in the federal system has served to minimize the burdens that the States bear under the Commerce Clause.

We realize that changes in the structure of the Federal Government have taken place since 1789, not the least of which has been the substitution of popular election of Senators by the adoption of the Seventeenth Amendment in 1913, and that these changes may work to alter the influence of the States in the federal political process. Nonetheless, against this background, we are convinced that the fundamental limitation that the constitutional scheme imposes on the Commerce Clause to protect the "States as States" is one of process rather than one of result. Any substantive restraint on the exercise of Commerce Clause powers must find its justification in the procedural nature of this basic limitation, and it must be tailored to compensate for possible failings in the national political process rather than to dictate a "sacred province of state autonomy."...

Insofar as the present cases are concerned, then, we need go no further than to state that we perceive nothing in the overtime and minimum-wage requirements of the FLSA, as applied to SAMTA, that is destructive of state sovereignty or violative of any constitutional provision. SAMTA faces nothing more than the same minimum-wage and overtime obligations that hundreds of thousands of other employers, public as well as private, have to meet....

This analysis makes clear that Congress' action in affording SAMTA employees the protections of the wage and hour provisions of the FLSA contravened no affirmative limit on Congress' power under the Commerce Clause. The judgment of the District Court therefore must be reversed.

Of course, we continue to recognize that the States occupy a special and specific position in our constitutional system and that the scope of Congress' authority under the Commerce Clause must reflect that position. But the principal and basic limit on the federal commerce power is that inherent in all congressional action—the built-in restraints that our system provides through state participation in federal governmental action. The political process ensures that laws that unduly burden the States will not be promulgated. In the factual setting of these cases the internal safeguards of the political process have performed as intended.

These cases do not require us to identify or define what affirmative limits the constitutional structure might impose on federal action affecting the States under the Commerce Clause....

Justice POWELL, with whom The Chief Justice, Justice REHNQUIST, and Justice O'CONNOR join, dissenting....

A unique feature of the United States is the federal system of government guaranteed by the Constitution and implicit in the very name of our country. Despite some genuflecting in Court's opinion to the concept of federalism, today's decision effectively reduces the Tenth Amendment to meaningless rhetoric when Congress acts pursuant to the Commerce Clause....

In other words, the extent to which the States may exercise their authority, when Congress purports to act under the Commerce Clause, henceforth is to be determined from time to time by political decisions made by members of the federal government, decisions which the Court says will not be subject to judicial review. I note that it does not seem to have occurred to the Court that it—an unelected majority of five Justices—today rejects almost 200 years of the understanding of the constitutional status of federalism. In doing so, there is only a single passing reference to the Tenth Amendment. Nor is so much as a dictum of any court cited in support of the view that the role of the States in the federal system may depend upon the grace of elected federal officials, rather than on the Constitution as interpreted by this court....

Today's opinion does not explain how the States' role in the electoral process guarantees that particular exercises of the Commerce Clause power will not infringe on residual State sovereignty....

The fact that Congress generally does not transgress constitutional limits on its power to reach State activities does not make judicial review any less necessary to rectify the cases in which it does do so. The States' role in our system of government is a matter of constitutional law, not of legislative grace. "The powers not delegated to the United States by the Constitution, nor prohibited by it to the States, are reserved to the States, respectively, or to the people." U.S. Const., Amend. 10.

More troubling than the logical infirmities in the Court's reasoning is the result of its holding, i.e., that federal political officials, invoking the Commerce Clause, are the sole judges of the limits of their own power. This result is inconsistent with the fundamental principles of our constitutional system....At least since *Marbury v. Madison* it has been the settled province of the federal judiciary "to say what the law is" with respect to the constitutionality of acts of Congress....In rejecting the role of the judiciary in protecting the States from federal overreaching, the Court's opinion offers no explanation for ignoring the teaching of the most famous case in our history.

In our federal system, the States have a major role that cannot be preempted by the national government. As contemporaneous writings and the debates at the ratifying conventions make clear, the States' ratification of the Constitution was predicated on this understanding of federalism. Indeed, the Tenth Amendment was adopted specifically to ensure that the important role promised the States by the proponents of the Constitution was realized.

Much of the initial opposition to the Constitution was rooted in the fear that the national government would be too powerful and eventually would eliminate the States as viable political entities. This concern was voiced repeatedly until proponents of the Constitution made assurances that a bill of rights, including a provision explicitly reserving powers in the States, would be among the first business of the new Congress....

Far from being "unsound in principle,"...judicial enforcement of the Tenth Amendment is essential to maintaining the federal system so carefully designed by the Framers and adopted in the Constitution.

The Framers had definite ideas about the nature of the Constitution's division of authority between the federal and state governments. In *The Federalist* No. 39, for example, Madison explained this division by drawing a series of contrasts between the attributes of a "national" government and those of the government to be established by the Constitution. While a national form of government would possess an "indefinite supremacy" over all persons and things," the form of government contemplated by the Constitution instead consisted of "local or municipal authorities [which] form distinct and independent portions of the supremacy, no more subject within their respective spheres to the general authority than the general authority is subject to them, within its own sphere."...

Thus, the harm to the States that results from federal overreaching under the Commerce Clause is not simply a matter of dollars and cents....Nor is it a matter of the wisdom or folly of certain policy choices....Rather, by usurping functions traditionally performed by the

States, federal overreaching under the Commerce Clause undermines the constitutionally mandated balance of power between the States and the federal government, a balance designed to protect our fundamental liberties....

[The] Court today propounds a view of federalism that pays only lip service to the role of the States....[The Court's opinion] reflects the Court's unprecedented view that Congress is free under the Commerce Clause to assume a State's traditional sovereign power, and to do so without judicial review of its action. Indeed, the Court's view of federalism appears to relegate the States to precisely the trivial role that opponents of the Constitution feared they would occupy.

In *National League of Cities*, we spoke of fire prevention, police protection, sanitation, and public health as "typical of [the services] performed by state and local governments in discharging their dual functions of administering the public law and furnishing public services."...Not only are these activities remote from any normal concept of interstate commerce, they are also activities that epitomize the concerns of local, democratic self-government....In emphasizing the need to protect traditional governmental functions, we identified the kinds of activities engaged in by state and local governments that affect the everyday lives of citizens. These are services that people are in a position to understand and evaluate, and in a democracy, have the right to oversee. We recognized that "it is functions such as these which governments are created to provide... " and that the states and local governments are better able than the national government to perform them....

The financial impact on States and localities of displacing their control over wages, hours, overtime regulations, pensions, and labor relations with their employees could have serious, as well as unanticipated, effects on state and local planning, budgeting, and the levying of taxes....

The Court emphasizes that municipal operation of an intracity mass transit system is relatively new in the life of our country. It nevertheless is a classic example of the type of service traditionally provided by local government. It is local by definition. It is indistinguishable in principle from the traditional services of providing and maintaining streets, public lighting, traffic control, water, and sewerage systems. Services of this kind are precisely those "with which citizens are more 'familiarly and minutely conversant.'"...State and local officials of course must be intimately familiar with these services and sensitive to their quality as well as cost. Such officials also know that their constituents and the press respond to the inadequacy, fair distribution, and cost of these services. It is this kind of state and local control and accountability that the Framers understood would insure the vitality and preservation of the federal system that the Constitution explicitly requires....

Justice REHNQUIST, dissenting.

I join both Justice Powell's and Justice O'Connor's thoughtful dissents. Justice Powell's reference to the "balancing test" approved in *National League of Cities* is not identical with the language in that case, which recognized that Congress could not act under its commerce power to infringe on certain fundamental aspects of state sovereignty that are essential to "the States' separate and independent existence."...But [in any event] the judgment is this case should be affirmed, and I do not think it incumbent on those of us in dissent to spell out further the fine points of a principle that will, I am confident, in time again command the support of a majority of this Court.

Justice O'CONNOR, with whom Justice POWELL and Justice REHNQUIST join, dissenting....

The true "essence" of federalism is that the States *as States* have legitimate interests which the National Government is bound to respect even though its laws are supreme....If federalism so conceived and so carefully cultivated by the Framers of our Constitution is to remain meaningful, this Court cannot abdicate its constitutional responsibility to oversee the Federal Government's compliance with its duty to respect the legitimate interests of the States.

Due to the emergence of an integrated and industrialized national economy, this Court has been required to examine and review a breathtaking expansion of the powers of Congress. In doing so the Court correctly perceived that the Framers of our Constitution intended Congress to have sufficient power to address national problems. But the Framers were not single-minded. The Constitution is animated by an array of intentions....Just as surely as the Framers envisioned a National Government capable of solving national problems, they also envisioned a republic whose vitality was assured by the diffusion of power not only among the branches of the Federal Government, but also between the Federal Government and the States....In the 18th century these intentions did not conflict because technology had not yet converted every local problem into a national one. A conflict has now emerged, and the Court today retreats rather than reconcile the Constitution's dual concerns for federalism and an effective commerce power.

We would do well to recall the constitutional basis for federalism and the development of the commerce power which has come to displace it....The Framers' comments indicate that the sphere of state activity was to be a significant one, as Justice Powell's opinion clearly demonstrates....The States were to retain authority over those local concerns of greatest relevance and importance to the people....This division of authority, according to Madison, would produce efficient government and protect the rights of the people:

> In a single republic, all the power surrendered by the people, is submitted to
> the administration of a single government; and usurpations are guarded
> against by a division of the government into distinct and separate depart-
> ments. In the compound republic of America, the power surrendered by the
> people, is first divided between two distinct governments, and then the por-
> tion allotted to each, subdivided among distinct and separate departments.
> Hence a double security arises to the rights of the people. The different gov-
> ernments will be controuled by itself. *The Federalist* No. 51....

In the decades since ratification of the Constitution, interstate economic activity has steadily expanded. Industrialization, coupled with advances in transportation and communications, has created a national economy in which virtually every activity occurring within the borders of a State plays a part. The expansion and integration of the national economy brought with it a coordinate expansion in the scope of national problems. This Court has been increasingly generous in its interpretation of the commerce power of Congress, primarily to assure that the National Government would be able to deal with national economic problems....

It has been difficult for this Court to craft bright lines defining the scope of the state autonomy protected by *National League of Cities*. Such difficulty is to be expected whenever constitutional concerns as important as federalism and the effectiveness of the commerce power come into conflict. Regardless of the difficulty, it is and will remain the duty of this Court to reconcile these concerns in the final instance. That the Court shuns the task today by appealing to the "essence of federalism" can provide scant comfort to those who believe our federal system requires something more than a unitary, centralized government. I would not shirk the duty acknowledged by *National League of Cities* and its progeny, and I share Justice REHNQUIST'S belief that this Court will in time again assume its constitutional responsibility.

I respectfully dissent.

United States v. Lopez A. E. DICK HOWARD

Before the era of the New Deal, the Supreme Court had been willing to look to notions of "dual federalism"—a concern for the respective competence of the Federal Government and of the states—to place limits on Congress' exercise of its power, under the Constitution, to regulate "commerce." For example, in the early years of the twentieth century, the Court held that "production" of goods was a "purely local matter" and thus beyond the reach of the commerce power.

After the so-called "constitutional revolution" in the 1930s, the Court became far more deferential to Congress' judgment as to what constituted "commerce." As there is no federal "police power," Congress came increasingly to rely on a generous definition of commerce to achieve its regulatory purposes.

In 1990 Congress enacted the Gun-Free School Zones Act. That statute made it a federal criminal offense "for any individual knowingly to possess a firearm at a place that the individual knows, or has reasonable cause to believe, is a school zone." A twelfth-grade student in San Antonio came to school with a .38 caliber handgun and five bullets. He was arrested and charged under a Texas law forbidding the possession of firearms on school premises. The state charges were dismissed, however, when federal agents charged the defendant with violating the 1990 federal law.

Generations of law students had been taught that they would never see the day when the modern Supreme Court would find that Congress had exceeded its power under the commerce clause. That day came in *United States v. Lopez*. There, by a 5 to 4 vote, the Court found that the Gun Free School Zones Act "neither regulates a commercial activity nor contains a requirement that the possession be connected in any way to interstate commerce." Therefore, the Court concluded, the statute exceeded Congress' authority, under the Constitution, to regulate commerce.

▶ Do the constitutional principles of federalism require that the Supreme Court play a role in deciding at what point there are limits on Congress' commerce power?

▶ Without such limits, is there a danger that Congress will be able to exercise, in effect, a national police power?

▶ Are judges competent to review congressional determinations as to whether an activity (such as the possession of firearms in school zones) does in fact affect commerce?

▶ In defining "commerce," should the Court look to the "original understanding" as it might be gleaned in the era of the Constitution's framing? Or should the Court look to the conditions of a modern national economy and polity?

United States v. Lopez 514 U.S. 549 (1995)

Chief Justice REHNQUIST delivered the opinion of the Court.

...We start with first principles. The Constitution creates a Federal Government of enumerated powers....As James Madison wrote, "[t]he powers delegated by the proposed Constitution to the federal government are few and defined. Those which are to remain in the State governments are numerous and indefinite." *The Federalist* No. 45....This constitutionally mandated division of authority "was adopted by the Framers to ensure protection of our fundamental liberties."... "Just as the separation and independence of the coordinate branches of the Federal Government serves to prevent the accumulation of excessive power in any one branch, a healthy balance of power between the States and the Federal Government will reduce the risk of tyranny and abuse from either front."...

The Constitution delegates to Congress the power "[t]o regulate Commerce with foreign Nations, and among the several States, and with the Indian Tribes."...The Court, through Chief Justice Marshall, first defined the nature of Congress' commerce power in *Gibbons v. Ogden* (1824) ...

The *Gibbons* Court, however, acknowledged that limitations on the commerce power are inherent in the very language of the Commerce Clause.

> "It is not intended to say that these words comprehend that commerce, which
> is completely internal, which is carried on between man and man in a State,
> or between different parts of the same State, and which does not extend to or
> affect other States."...

For nearly a century thereafter, the Court's Commerce Clause decisions dealt but rarely with the extend of Congress' power, and almost entirely with the Commerce Clause as a limit on state legislation that discriminated against interstate commerce....

In 1887, Congress enacted the Interstate Commerce Act,...and in 1890, Congress enacted the Sherman Antitrust Act,...These laws ushered in a new era of federal regulation under the commerce power. When cases involving these laws first reached this Court, we imported from our negative Commerce Clause cases the approach that Congress could not regulate activities such as "production," "manufacturing," and "mining."...

[In cases decided during the era of the New Deal the Court] ushered in an era of Commerce Clause jurisprudence that greatly expanded the previously defined authority of Congress under that Clause. In part, this was a recognition of the great changes that had occurred in the way business was carried on in this country. Enterprises that had once been local or at most regional in nature had become national in scope. But the doctrinal change also reflected a view that earlier Commerce Clause cases artificially had constrained the authority of Congress to regulate interstate commerce.

But even these modern-era precedents which have expanded congressional power under the Commerce Clause confirm that this power is subject to outer limits....

Consistent with this structure, we have identified three broad categories of activity that Congress may regulate under its commerce power....First, Congress may regulate the use of the channels of interstate commerce....Second, Congress is empowered to regulate and protect the instrumentalities of interstate commerce, or persons or things in interstate commerce, even though the threat may come only from intrastate activities....Finally, Congress' commerce authority includes the power to regulate those activities having a substantial relation to interstate commerce,...i.e., those activities that substantially affect interstate commerce....

Within the final category, admittedly, our case law has not been clear whether an activity must "affect" or "substantially affect" interstate commerce in order to be within Congress' power to regulate it under the Commerce Clause....We conclude, consistent with the great weight of our case law, that the proper test requires an analysis of whether the regulated activity "substantially affects" interstate commerce.

We now turn to consider the power of Congress, in the light of this framework, to enact [the statute under review]. The first two categories of authority may be quickly disposed of: [the statute] is not a regulation of the use of the channels of interstate commerce, nor is it an attempt to prohibit the interstate transportation of a commodity through the channels of commerce; nor can [the statute] be justified as a regulation by which Congress has sought to protect an instrumentality of interstate commerce or a thing in interstate commerce. Thus, if [the statute] is to be sustained, it must be under the third category as a regulation of an activity that substantially affects interstate commerce.

First,...[the statute] is a criminal statute that by its terms has nothing to do with "commerce" or any sort of economic enterprise, however broadly one might define those terms....

Second, [the statute] contains no jurisdictional element which would ensure, through case-by-case inquiry, that the firearm possession in question affects interstate commerce....

...The Government argues that possession of a firearm in a school zone may result in violent crime and that violent crime can be expected to affect the functioning of the national economy in two ways. First, the costs of violent crime are substantial, and, through the mechanism of insurance, those costs are spread throughout the population....Second, violent crime reduces the willingness of individuals to travel to areas within the country that are perceived to be unsafe....The Government also argues that the presence of guns in schools poses a substantial threat to the educational process by threatening the learning environment. A handicapped educational process, in turn, will result in a less productive citizenry. That, in turn, would have an adverse effect on the Nation's economic well-being. As a result, the Government argues that Congress could rationally have concluded that [the statute] substantially affects interstate commerce.

We pause to consider the implications of the Government's arguments. The Government admits, under its "costs of crime" reasoning, that Congress could regulate not only all violent crime, but all activities that might lead to violent crime, regardless of how tenuously they relate to interstate commerce....Similarly, under the Government's "national productivity" reasoning, Congress could regulate any activity that it found was related to the economic productivity of individual citizens: family law (including marriage, divorce, and child custody), for example. Under the theories that the Government presents in support of [the statute], it is difficult to perceive any limitation on federal power, even in areas such as criminal law enforcement or education where States historically have been sovereign. Thus, if we were to accept the Government's arguments, we are hard-pressed to posit any activity by an individual that Congress is without power to regulate.

Although Justice Breyer argues that acceptance of the Government's rationales would not authorize a general federal police power, he is unable to identify any activity that the States may regulate but Congress may not....

For instance, if Congress can, pursuant to its Commerce Clause power, regulate activities that adversely affect the learning environment, then *a fortiori*, it also can regulate the educational process directly. Congress could determine that a school's curriculum has a "significant" effect on the extent of classroom learning. As a result, Congress could mandate a federal curriculum for local elementary and secondary schools because what is taught in local schools has a significant "effect on classroom learning, cf. *post*, at 9, and that, in turn has a substantial effect on interstate commerce....

Admittedly, a determination whether an intrastate activity is commercial or noncommercial may in some cases result in legal uncertainty....

...The possession of a gun in a local school zone is in no sense an economic activity that might, through repetition elsewhere, substantially affect any sort of interstate commerce. Respondent was a local student at a local school; there is no indication that he had recently moved in interstate commerce, and there is no requirement that his possession of the firearm have any concrete tie to interstate commerce.

To uphold the Government's contentions here, we would have to pile inference upon inference in a manner that would bid fair to convert congressional authority under the Commerce clause to a general police power of the sort retained by the States. Admittedly, some of our prior cases have taken long steps down that road, giving great deference to congressional action. See *supra*, at 8. The broad language in these opinions has suggested the possibility of additional expansion, but we decline here to proceed any further....

Affirmed.

Justice KENNEDY, with whom Justice O'CONNOR joins, concurring....

The history of our Commerce Clause decisions contains at least two lessons of relevance to this case. The first, as stated at the outset, is the imprecision of content-based boundaries used without more to define the limits of the Commerce Clause. The second, related to the first but of even greater consequence, is that the Court as an institution and the legal system as a whole have an immense stake in the stability of our Commerce Clause jurisprudence as it has evolved to this point. *Stare decisis* operates with great force in counseling us not to call in question the essential principles now in place respecting the congressional power to regulate transactions of a commercial nature....Congress can regulate in the commercial sphere on the assumption that we have a single market and an unified purpose to build a stable national economy.

...It does not follow, however, that in every instance the Court lacks the authority and responsibility to review congressional attempts to alter the federal balance....

Of the various structural elements in the Constitution, separation of powers, checks and balances, judicial review, and federalism, only concerning the last does there seem to be much uncertainty respecting the existence, and the content, of standards that allow the judiciary to play a significant role in maintaining the design contemplated by the Framers....

There is irony in this, because of the four structural elements in the Constitution just mentioned, federalism was the unique contribution of the Framers to political science and political theory....

...Were the Federal Government to take over the regulation of entire areas of traditional state concern, areas having nothing to do with the regulation of commercial activities, the boundaries between the spheres of federal and state authority would blur and political responsibility would become illusory....The resultant inability to hold either branch of the government answerable to the citizens is more dangerous even than devolving too much authority to the remote central power.

...Whatever the judicial role, it is axiomatic that Congress does have substantial discretion and control over the federal balance.

For these reasons, it would be mistaken and mischievous for the political branches to forget that the sworn obligation to preserve and protect the Constitution in maintaining the federal balance is their own in the first and primary instance....

At the same time, the absence of structural mechanisms to require those officials to undertake this principled task, and the momentary political convenience often attendant upon their failure to do so, argue against a complete renunciation of the judicial role. Although it is the obligation of all officers of the Government to respect the constitutional design,...the federal balance is too essential a part of our constitutional structure and plays too vital a role in securing freedom for us to admit inability to intervene when one or the other level of Government has tipped the scales too far.

...The substantial element of political judgment in Commerce Clause matters leaves our institutional capacity to intervene more in doubt than when we decide cases, for instance, under the Bill of Rights even though clear and bright lines are often absent in the latter class of disputes....But our cases do not teach that we have no role at all in determining the meaning of the Commerce Clause.

The statute before us upsets the federal balance to a degree that renders it an unconstitutional assertion of the commerce power, and our intervention is required. As the Chief Justice explains, unlike the earlier cases to come before the Court here neither the actors nor their conduct have a commercial character, and neither the purposes nor the design of the statute have an evident commercial nexus....[At] the least we must inquire whether the exercise of national power seeks to intrude upon an area of traditional state concern.

An interference of these dimensions occurs here, for it is well established that education is a traditional concern of the States....In these circumstances, we have a particular duty to insure that the federal-state balance is not destroyed....

While it is doubtful that any State, or indeed any reasonable person, would argue that it is wise policy to allow students to carry guns on school premises, considerable disagreement exists about how best to accomplish that goal. In this circumstance, the theory and utility of our federalism are revealed, for the States may perform their role as laboratories for experimentation to devise various solutions where the best solution is far from clear....

If a State or municipality determines that harsh criminal sanctions are necessary and wise to deter students from carrying guns on school premises, the reserved powers of the States are sufficient to enact those measures. Indeed, over 40 States already have criminal laws outlawing the possession of firearms on or near school grounds....

The statute now before us forecloses the States from experimenting and exercising their own judgment in an area to which States lay claim by right of history and expertise, and it does so by regulating an activity beyond the realm of commerce in the ordinary and usual sense of that term. The tendency of this statute to displace state regulation in areas of traditional state concern is evident from its territorial operation....

Justice THOMAS, concurring.

The Court today properly concludes that the Commerce Clause does not grant Congress the authority to prohibit gun possession within 1,000 feet of a school, as it attempted to do in the Gun-Free School Zones Act of 1990....Although I join the majority, I write separately to observe that our case law has drifted far from the original understanding of the Commerce Clause. In a future case, we ought to temper our Commerce Clause jurisprudence in a manner that both makes sense of our more recent case law and is more faithful to the original understanding of that Clause....

...[It] seems to me that the power to regulate "commerce" can by no means encompass authority over mere gun possession, any more than it empowers the Federal Government to regulate marriage, littering, or cruelty to animals, throughout the 50 States. Our Constitution quite properly leaves such matters to the individual States, notwithstanding these activities' effects on interstate commerce. Any interpretation of the Commerce Clause that even suggests that Congress could regulate such matters is in need of reexamination.

In an appropriate case, I believe that we must further reconsider our "substantial effects" test with an eye toward constructing a standard that reflects the text and history of the Commerce Clause without totally rejecting our more recent Commerce Clause jurisprudence....

The Constitution not only uses the word "commerce" in a narrower sense than our case law might suggest, it also does not support the proposition that Congress has authority over all activities that "substantially affect" interstate commerce....Clearly, the Framers could have drafted a Constitution that contained a "substantially affects interstate commerce" clause had that been their objective....

...Even though the boundary between commerce and other matters may ignore "economic reality" and thus seem arbitrary or artificial to some, we must nevertheless respect a constitutional line that does not grant Congress power over all that substantially affects interstate commerce....

These cases all establish a simple point: from the time of the ratification of the Constitution to the mid-1930's, it was widely understood that the Constitution granted Congress only limited powers, notwithstanding the Commerce Clause. Moreover, there was no question that activities wholly separated from business, such as gun possession, were beyond the reach of the commerce power. If anything, the "wrong turn" was the Court's dramatic departure in the 1930's from a century and a half of precedent.

Apart from its recent vintage and its corresponding lack of any grounding in the original understanding of the Constitution, the substantial effects test suffers from the further flaw that it appears to grant Congress a police power over the Nation. When asked at oral argument if there were *any* limits to the Commerce Clause, the Government was at a loss for words....Likewise, the principal dissent insists that there are limits, but it cannot muster even one example....Indeed, the dissent implicitly concedes that its reading has no limits when it criticizes the Court for "threaten[ing] legal uncertainty in an area of law that...seemed reasonably well settled."...The one advantage of the dissent's standard is certainty: it is certain that under its analysis everything may be regulated under the guise of the Commerce Clause.

The substantial effects test suffers from this flaw, in part, because of its "aggregation principle." Under so-called "class of activities" statutes, Congress can regulate whole categories of activities that are not themselves either "interstate" or "commerce." In applying the effects test, we ask whether the class or activities *as a whole* substantially affects interstate commerce, not whether any specific activity within the class has such effects when considered in isolation....

This extended discussion of the original understanding and our first century and a half of case law does not necessarily require a wholesale abandonment of our more recent opinions. It simply reveals that our substantial effects test is far removed from both the Constitution and from our early case law and that the Court's opinion should not be viewed as "radical" or another "wrong turn" that must be corrected in the future. The analysis also suggests that we ought to temper our Commerce Clause jurisprudence....

Justice SOUTER, dissenting.

In reviewing congressional legislation under the Commerce Clause, we defer to what is often a merely implicit congressional judgment that its regulation addresses a subject substantially affecting interstate commerce "if there is any rational basis for such a finding."...

The practice of deferring to rationally based legislative judgments "is a paradigm of judicial restraint."...In judicial review under the Commerce Clause, it reflects our respect for the institutional competence of the Congress on a subject expressly assigned to it by the

Constitution and our appreciation of the legitimacy that comes from Congress's political accountability in dealing with matters open to a wide range of possible choices....

...[Adoption] of rational basis review expressed the recognition that the Court had no sustainable basis for subjecting economic regulation as such to judicial policy judgments[.]

...Thus, it seems fair to ask whether the step taken by the Court today does anything but portend a return to the untenable jurisprudence from which the Court extricated itself almost 60 years ago. The answer is not reassuring....

Justice BREYER, with whom Justice STEVENS, Justice SOUTER, and Justice GINSBERG join, dissenting.

...In my view, the statute falls well within the scope of the commerce power as this Court has understood that power over the last half-century.

I

In reaching this conclusion, I apply three basic principles of Commerce Clause interpretation. First, the power to "regulate Commerce...among the several States"...encompasses the power to regulate local activities insofar as they significantly affect interstate commerce....

Second, in determining whether a local activity will likely have a significant effect upon interstate commerce, a court must consider, not the effect of any individual act (a single instance of gun possession), but rather the cumulative effect of all similar instances (*i.e.*, the effect of all guns possessed in or near schools)....

Third, the Constitution requires us to judge the connection between a regulated activity and interstate commerce, not directly, but at one remove. Courts must give Congress a degree of leeway in determining the existence of a significant factual connection between the regulated activity and interstate commerce—both because the Constitution delegates the commerce power directly to Congress and because the determination requires an empirical judgment of a kind that a legislature is more likely than a court to make with accuracy. The traditional words "rational basis" capture this leeway....Thus, the specific question before us, as the Court recognizes, is not whether the "regulated activity sufficiently affected interstate commerce," but, rather, whether Congress could have had "*a rational basis*" for so concluding. *Ante*, at 8 (emphasis added)....

Applying these principles to the case at hand, we must ask whether Congress could have had a *rational basis* for finding a significant (or substantial) connection between gun-related school violence and interstate commerce....Could Congress rationally have found that "violent crime in school zones," through its effect on the "quality of education," significantly (or substantially) affects "interstate" or "foreign commerce"?...[The] answer to this question must be yes. Numerous reports and studies—generated both inside and outside government—make clear that Congress could reasonably have found the empirical connection that its law, implicitly or explicitly, asserts....

For one thing, reports, hearings, and other readily available literature make clear that the problem of guns in and around schools is widespread and extremely serious....[T]his widespread violence in schools throughout the Nation significantly interferes with the quality of education in those schools....Congress obviously could have thought that guns and learning are mutually exclusive....And, Congress could therefore have found a substantial educational problem—teachers unable to teach, students unable to learn—and concluded that guns near schools contribute substantially to the size and scope of that problem.

Having found that guns in schools significantly undermine the quality of education in our Nation's classrooms, Congress could also have found, given the effect of education upon interstate and foreign commerce, that gun-related violence in and around schools is a commercial, as well as a human, problem. Education, although far more than a matter of economics, has long been inextricably intertwined with the Nation's economy....

In recent years the link between secondary education and business has strengthened, becoming both more direct and more important. Scholars on the subject report that technological changes and innovations in management techniques have altered the nature of the workplace so that more jobs now demand greater education skills....

Increasing global competition also has made primary and secondary education economically more important....

Finally, there is evidence that, today more than ever, many firms base their location decisions upon the presence, or absence, of a work force with a basic education....

The economic links I have just sketched seem fairly obvious. Why then is it not equally obvious, in light of those links, that a widespread, serious, and substantial physical threat to teaching and learning *also* substantially threatens the commerce to which that teaching and learning is inextricably tied? ...

...Upholding this legislation would no more than simply recognize that Congress had a "rational basis" for finding a significant connection between guns in or near schools and (through their effect on education) the interstate and foreign commerce they threaten. For these reasons, I would reverse the judgment of the Court of Appeals. Respectfully, I dissent.

U.S. Term Limits, Inc. v. Thornton   A. E. DICK HOWARD

From the republic's earliest days, theorists and political actors have debated the nature of the federal union. Is it an act of the states? Or is it an act of the people of the United States writ large?

A corollary question is: how should one regard the Congress? Does it represent the states? Or do its members represent the people of the United States?

This debate has taken on an intensely practical and immediate form during the movement to place limits on the terms which members of the United States Senate or the House of Representatives from a particular state may serve. Many states have sought to impose such limits. The Supreme Court has held that, insofar as the limits apply to state legislators, it is up to a state and its voters to decide whether or not to impose term limits.

Placing term limits on members of the federal Congress, however, raises much more difficult issues. The voters of Arkansas adopted an amendment to their state constitution imposing term limits on members of the state's executive and legislative branches and also on Arkansas's members of the United States House of Representatives and Senate. Any person having served three or more terms in the House of Representatives would not be eligible to have his or her name placed on the ballot for reelection; a similar bar was placed on any person who had served two or more terms in the United States Senate.

The Qualifications Clauses in Article I of the Constitution set forth certain requirements which must be met for one to serve in the United States Congress—qualifications regarding age, citizenship, and residence. In *U. S. Term Limits, Inc. v. Thornton*, the Supreme Court, by a vote of 5 to 4, held that the Constitution's enumeration of these qualifications precluded the states from imposing additional limitations, such as term limits. Otherwise, wrote Justice Stevens, the states could act inconsistently with "the Framers' vision of a uniform National Legislature representing the people of the United States."

> ▶ Should the states be free to add limitations beyond those of age, citizenship, and residence spelled out in the Constitution?
>
> ▶ In light of the Constitution's being silent on the specific question of term limits, should the Court presume that the states are free to impose such limits as are not expressly barred in the Constitution?
>
> ▶ Which is more consistent with a theory of democracy: allowing the voters of a state to reelect an incumbent as many times as they like, or allowing those voters to limit the number of terms an officeholder may serve?
>
> ▶ Does it matter that term limits in the Arkansas case were imposed on members of the U. S. House and Senate as opposed to members of the state legislature?

U.S. Term Limits, Inc. v. Thornton 514 U.S. 779 (1995)

Justice STEVENS delivered the opinion of the Court.

The Constitution sets forth qualifications for membership in the Congress of the United States. Article I, Section 2, cl. 2, which applies to the House of Representatives, provides:

> No Person shall be a Representative who shall not have attained to the Age of twenty five Years, and been seven Years a Citizen of the United States, and who shall not, when elected, be an Inhabitant of that State in which he shall be chosen.

Article I, Section 3, cl. 3, which applies to the Senate, similarly provides:

> No Person shall be a Senator who shall not have attained to the Age of thirty Years, and have been nine Years a Citizen of the United States, and who shall not, when elected, be an Inhabitant of that State for which he shall be chosen.

Today's cases present a challenge to an amendment to the Arkansas State Constitution that prohibits the name of an otherwise-eligible candidate for Congress from appearing on the general election ballot if that candidate has already served three terms in the House of Representatives or two terms in the Senate. The Arkansas Supreme Court held that the amendment violates the Federal Constitution. We agree with that holding. Such a state-imposed restriction is contrary to the "fundamental principle of our representative democracy," embodied in the Constitution, that "the people should choose whom they please to govern them."...Allowing individual States to adopt their own qualifications for congressional service would be inconsistent with the Framers' vision of a uniform National Legislature representing the people of the United States. If the qualifications set forth in the text of the Constitution are to be changed, that text must be amended....

[The] constitutionality of Amendment 73 depends critically on the resolution of two distinct issues. The first is whether the Constitution forbids States from adding to or altering the qualifications specifically enumerated in the Constitution. The second is, if the Constitution does so forbid, whether the fact that Amendment 73 is formulated as a ballot access restriction rather than as an outright disqualification is of constitutional significance. Our resolution of these issues draws upon our prior resolution of a related but distinct issue: whether Congress has the power to add to or alter the qualifications of its Members.

[In] *Powell v. McCormack*...(1969) we reviewed the history and text of the Qualifications Clauses in a case involving an attempted exclusion of a duly elected Member of Congress. The principal issue was whether the power granted to each House in Art. I, Section 5, to judge the "Qualifications of its own Members" includes the power to impose qualifications other than those set forth in the text of the Constitution. In an opinion by Chief Justice Warren for eight Members of the Court, we held that it does not....

Petitioners argue that the Constitution contains no express prohibition against state-added qualifications, and that Amendment 73 is therefore an appropriate exercise of a State's reserved power to place additional restrictions on the choices that its own voters may make. We disagree for two independent reasons. First, we conclude that the power to add qualifications is not within the "original powers" of the States, and thus is not reserved to the States by the Tenth Amendment. Second, even if States possessed some original power in this area, we conclude that the Framers intended the Constitution to be the exclusive source of qualifications for members of Congress, and that the Framers thereby "divested" States of any power to add qualifications....

Contrary to petitioners' assertions, the power to add qualifications is not part of the original powers of sovereignty that the Tenth Amendment reserved to the States. Petitioners' Tenth Amendment argument misconceives the nature of the right at issue because that Amendment could only "reserve" that which existed before. As Justice Story recognized, "the states can exercise no powers whatsoever, which exclusively spring out of the existence of the national government, which the constitution does not delegate to them....No state can say, that it has reserved, what it never possessed."...

With respect to setting qualifications for service in Congress, no such right existed before the Constitution was ratified. The contrary argument overlooks the revolutionary character of the government that the Framers conceived. Prior to the adoption of the Constitution, the States had joined together under the Articles of Confederation. In that system, "the States retained most of their sovereignty, like independent nations bound together only by treaties."...After the Constitutional Convention convened, the Framers were presented with, and eventually adopted a variation of, "a plan not merely to amend the Articles of Confederation but to create an entirely new National Government with a National Executive, National Judiciary, and a National Legislature."...In adopting that plan, the Framers envisioned a uniform national system, rejecting the notion that the Nation was a collection of States, and instead creating a direct link between the National Government and the people of the United States....In that National Government, representatives owe primary allegiance not to the people of a State, but to the people of the Nation....

Even if we believed that States possessed as part of their original powers some control over congressional qualifications, the text and structure of the Constitution, the relevant historical materials, and, most importantly, the "basic principles of our democratic system" all demonstrate that the Qualifications Clauses were intended to preclude the States from exercising any such power and to fix as exclusive the qualifications in the Constitution....

Our conclusion that States lack the power to impose qualifications vindicates the same "fundamental principle of our representative democracy" that we recognized in *Powell*, namely that "the people should choose whom they please to govern them."...

As we noted earlier, the *Powell* Court recognized that an egalitarian ideal—that election to the National Legislature should be open to all people of merit—provided a critical foundation for the Constitutional structure. This egalitarian theme echoes throughout the constitutional debates....

Similarly, we believe that state-imposed qualifications, as much as congressionally imposed qualifications, would undermine the second critical idea recognized in *Powell*: that an aspect of sovereignty is the right of the people to vote for whom they wish. Again, the source of the qualification is of little moment in assessing the qualification's restrictive impact.

Finally, state-imposed restrictions, unlike the congressionally imposed restrictions at issue in *Powell*, violate a third idea central to this basic principle: that the right to choose representatives belongs not to the States, but to the people....Thus the Framers, in perhaps their most important contribution, conceived of a Federal Government directly responsible to the people, possessed of direct power over the people, and chosen directly, not by States, but by the people. The Framers implemented this ideal most clearly in the provision, extant from the beginning of the Republic, that calls for the Members of the House of Representatives to be "chosen every second Year by the People of the several States."...

Consistent with these views, the constitutional structure provides for a uniform salary to be paid from the national treasury, allows the States but a limited role in federal elections, and maintains strict checks on state interference with the federal election process. The Constitution also provides that the qualifications of the representatives of each State will be judged by the representatives of the entire Nation. The Constitution thus creates a uniform national body representing the interests of a single people.

Permitting individual States to formulate diverse qualifications for their representatives would result in a patchwork of state qualifications, undermining the uniformity and the national character that the Framers envisioned and sought to ensure....

Petitioners attempt to overcome this formidable array of evidence against the States' power to impose qualifications by arguing that the practice of the States immediately after the adoption of the Constitution demonstrates their understanding that they possessed such power. One may properly question the extent to which the States' own practice is a reliable indicator of the contours of restrictions that the Constitution imposed on States, especially when no court has ever upheld a state-imposed qualification of any sort. See *supra*, at 18-19. But petitioners' argument is unpersuasive even on its own terms....

The contemporaneous state practice with respect to term limits is similar. At the time of the Convention, States widely supported term limits in at least some circumstances. The Articles of Confederation contained a provision for term limits. As we have noted, some members of the Convention had sought to impose term limits for Members of Congress. In addition, many States imposed term limits on state officers, four placed limits on delegates to the Continental Congress, and several States voiced support for term limits for Members of Congress. Despite this widespread support, no State sought to impose any term limits on its own federal representatives. Thus, a proper assessment of contemporaneous state practice provides further persuasive evidence of a general understanding that the qualifications in the Constitution were unalterable by the States....

Petitioners argue that, even if States may not add qualifications, Amendment 73 is constitutional because it is not such a qualification, and because Amendment 73 is a permissible exercise of state power to regulate the "Times, Places and Manner of Holding Elections." We reject these contentions....

In our view, Amendment 73 is an indirect attempt to accomplish what the Constitution prohibits Arkansas from accomplishing directly....

Petitioners do, however, contest the Arkansas Supreme Court's conclusion that the Amendment has the same practical effect as an absolute bar. They argue that the possibility of a write-in campaign creates a real possibility for victory, especially for an entrenched incumbent. One may reasonably question the merits of that contention....But even if petitioners are correct that incumbents may occasionally win reelection as write-in candidates, there is no denying that the ballot restrictions will make it significantly more difficult for the barred candidate to win the election. In our view, an amendment with the avowed purpose and obvious effect of evading the requirements of the Qualifications Clauses by handicapping a class of candidates cannot stand....

Justice KENNEDY, concurring.

A distinctive character of the National Government, the mark of its legitimacy, is that it owes its existence to the act of the whole people who created it. It must be remembered that the National Government too is republican in essence and in theory....Once the National Government was formed under our Constitution, the same republican principles continued to guide its operation and practice....

That the States may not invade the sphere of federal sovereignty is as incontestable, in my view, as the corollary proposition that the Federal Government must be held within the boundaries of its own power when it intrudes upon matters reserved to the States....

Justice THOMAS, with whom The CHIEF JUSTICE, Justice O'CONNOR, and Justice SCALIA join, dissenting.

It is ironic that the Court bases today's decision on the right of the people to "choose whom they please to govern them."...Under our Constitution, there is only one State whose people have the right to "choose whom they please" to represent Arkansas in Congress. The Court holds, however, that neither the elected legislature of that State nor the people themselves (acting by ballot initiative) may prescribe any qualifications for those representatives. The majority therefore defends the right of the people of Arkansas to "choose whom they please to govern them" by invalidating a provision that won nearly 60% of the votes cast in a direct election and that carried every congressional district in the State.

I dissent. Nothing in the Constitution deprives the people of each State of the power to prescribe eligibility requirements for the candidates who seek to represent them in Congress. The Constitution is simply silent on this question. And where the Constitution is silent, it raises no bar to action by the States or the people....

Our system of government rests on one overriding principle: all power stems from the consent of the people. To phrase the principle in this way, however, is to be imprecise about something important to the notion of "reserved" powers. The ultimate source of the Constitution's authority is the consent of the people of each individual State, not the consent of the undifferentiated people of the Nation as a whole....

As far as the Federal Constitution is concerned, then, the States can exercise all powers that the Constitution does not withhold from them. The Federal Government and the States thus face different default rules: where the Constitution is silent about the exercise of a particular power—that is, where the Constitution does not speak either expressly or by necessary implication—the Federal Government lacks that power and the States enjoy it.

These basic principles are enshrined in the Tenth Amendment, which declares that all powers neither delegated to the Federal Government not prohibited to the States "are reserved to the States respectively, or to the people." With this careful last phrase, the Amendment avoids taking any position on the division of power between the state governments and the people of the States: it is up to the people of each State to determine which "reserved" powers their state government may exercise. But the Amendment does make clear that powers reside at the state level except where the Constitution removes them from that level....

The majority begins by announcing an enormous and untenable limitation on the principle expressed by the Tenth Amendment. According to the majority, the States possess only those powers that the Constitution affirmatively grants to them or that they enjoyed before the Constitution was adopted; the Tenth Amendment "could only 'reserve' that which existed before."...

The majority is therefore quite wrong to conclude that the people of the States cannot authorize their state governments to exercise any powers that were unknown to the States when the Federal Constitution was drafted. Indeed, the majority's position frustrates the apparent purpose of the Amendment's final phrase....

The majority also sketches out what may be an alternative (and narrower) argument. Again citing Justice Story, the majority suggests that it would be inconsistent with the notion of "national sovereignty for the States or the people of the States to have any reserved powers over the selection of Members of Congress....The majority apparently reaches this conclusion in two steps. First, it asserts that because Congress as a whole is an institution of the National Government, the individual Members of Congress "owe primary allegiance not to the people of a State, but to the people of the Nation." See *ante*, at 23-24. Second, it concludes that because each Member of Congress has a nationwide constituency once he takes office, it would be inconsistent with the Framers' scheme to let a single State prescribe qualifications for him....

But the selection of representatives in Congress is indisputably an act of the people of each State, not some abstract people of the Nation as a whole....

When the people of Georgia pick their representatives in Congress, they are acting as the people of Georgia, not as the corporate agents for the undifferentiated people of the Nation as a whole. See *In re Green*, 134 U.S. 377, 379 (1890) ...

The Qualifications Clauses do prevent the individual States from abolishing all eligibility requirements for Congress....Because Congress wields power over all the States, the people of each State need some guarantee that the legislators elected by the people of other States will meet minimum standards of competence. The Qualifications Clauses provide that guarantee: they list the requirements that the Framers considered essential to protect the competence of the National Legislature.

If the people of a State decide that they would like their representatives to possess additional qualifications, however, they have done nothing to frustrate the policy behind the Qualifications Clauses....

Although the Qualifications Clauses neither state nor imply the prohibition that it finds in them, the majority infers from the Framers' "democratic principles" that the Clauses must have been generally understood to preclude the people of the States and their state legislatures from prescribing any additional qualifications for their representatives in Congress. But the majority's evidence on this point establishes only two more modest propositions: (1) the Framers did not want the Federal Constitution itself to impose a broad set of disqualifications for congressional office, and (2) the Framers did not want the Federal Congress to be able to supplement the few disqualifications that the Constitution does set forth....

In addition to its arguments about democratic principles, the majority asserts that more specific historical evidence supports its view that the Framers did not intend to permit supplementation of the Qualifications Clauses. But when one focuses on the distinction between congressional power to add qualifications for congressional office and the power of the people or their state legislatures to add such qualifications, one realizes that this assertion has little basis....

Here too, state practice immediately after the ratification of the Constitution refutes the majority's suggestion that the Qualifications Clauses were commonly understood as being exclusive. Five States supplemented the constitutional disqualifications in their very first election laws, and the surviving records suggest that the legislatures of these States considered and rejected the interpretation of the Constitution that the majority adopts today.

As the majority concedes, the first Virginia election law erected a property qualification for Virginia's contingent in the Federal House of Representatives....What is more, while the Constitution merely requires representatives to be inhabitants of their State, the legislatures of five of the seven States that divided themselves into districts for House elections added that representatives also had to be inhabitants of the district that elected them. Three of these States adopted durational residency requirements too, insisting that representatives have resided within their districts for at least a year (or, in one case, three years) before being elected....

No matter how narrowly construed,...today's decision reads the Qualifications Clauses to impose substantial implicit prohibitions on the States and the people of the States. I would not draw such an expansive negative inference from the fact that the Constitution requires Members of Congress to be a certain age, to be inhabitants of the States that they represent, and to have been United States citizens for a specified period. Rather, I would read the Qualifications Clauses to do no more than what they say. I respectfully dissent.

Printz v. United States A. E. DICK HOWARD

In a unitary system, national laws are administered either by officials of the national government or by local officials ultimately responsible to that government. In a federal system like that of the United States, federal officials typically execute federal laws, and state officials typically administer state laws.

It is not unusual, however, for state officials to cooperate with federal officers charged with enforcing federal law, for example, in the arena of law enforcement. State and local officials may furnish data helpful to federal law enforcement personnel. But may Congress, consistent with the Constitution, compel a state or local official to assist in the execution of federal law?

The Gun Control Act of 1968 establishes a detailed federal scheme governing the sale, distribution, and possession of firearms. Among other things, the law forbids transfer of a firearm to convicted felons, fugitives from justice, unlawful users of controlled substances, and persons adjudicated as mentally defective or committed to mental institutions.

In 1993, responding to what it described as an "epidemic of gun violence," Congress enacted the Brady Act. That statute required the Attorney General to establish a national instant background check system by 1998. In the meantime, interim provisions of the act imposed certain duties upon local "chief law enforcement officers" (CLEOs). When the CLEO received from a firearms dealer a notice of a proposed firearms transfer, the act required the CLEO to "make a reasonable effort to ascertain within 5 business days whether receipt or possession would be in violation of the law, including research in whatever State and local record keeping systems are available and in a national system designated by the Attorney General."

Two sheriffs, one in Montana, the other in Arizona, challenged the Brady Act's constitutionality. In *Printz v. United States*, decided by a 5 to 4 vote, the Supreme Court invalidated the Brady Act's requirement that CLEOs conduct background checks. That provision, Justice Scalia concluded, "commandeered" state executive officials into the administration of a federal program in violation of principles of state sovereignty.

▶ Should the principle of federalism be taken as barring federal laws which impose federal responsibilities on state or local officials?

▶ If there is to be such a limit on federal authority, should the limit be categorical, or should the Court "balance" the state and federal interests involved—tending to uphold the federal law where the national interest is an important one, and the burden on the state or local official a minor one?

▶ Does the decision in *Printz* make it more difficult to foster cooperative programs involving the federal and state governments?

▶ Might the *Printz* decision encourage federal legislation which, rather than calling upon state or local officials to undertake federal responsibilities, preempts the states altogether and creates a federal bureaucracy to administer the program?

▶ Does *Printz* have the virtue of making it easier for citizens to decide which officials, state or federal, should be held accountable for the enforcement and administration of government laws and programs?

Printz v. United States 521 U.S. 98 (1997)

Justice SCALIA delivered the opinion of the Court.

The question presented in these cases is whether certain interim provisions of the Brady Handgun Violence Prevention Act,...commanding state and local law enforcement officers to conduct background checks on prospective handgun purchases and to perform certain related tasks, violate the Constitution....

From the description set forth above, it is apparent that the Brady Act purports to direct state law enforcement officers to participate, albeit only temporarily, in the administration of a federally enacted regulatory scheme. Regulated firearms dealers are required to forward Brady Forms not to a federal officer or employee, but to the CLEOs, whose obligation to accept those forms is implicit in the duty imposed upon them to make "reasonable efforts" within five days to determine whether the sales reflected in the forms are lawful....

The petitioners here object to being pressed into federal service, and contend that congressional action compelling state officers to execute federal laws is unconstitutional. Because there is no constitutional text speaking to this precise question, the answer to the CLEO's challenge must be sought in historical understanding and practice, in the structure of the Constitution, and in the jurisprudence of this Court. We treat those three sources, in that order, in this and the next two sections of this opinion.

Petitioners contend that compelled enlistment of state executive officers for the administration of federal programs is, until very recent years at least, unprecedented. The Government contends, on the contrary, that "the earliest Congresses enacted statutes that required the participation of state officials in the implementation of federal laws."...

These early laws establish, at most, that the Constitution was originally understood to permit imposition of an obligation on state *judges* to enforce federal prescriptions, insofar as those prescriptions related to matters appropriate for the judicial power....

For these reasons, we do not think the early statutes imposing obligations on state courts imply a power of Congress to impress the state executive into its service....

In addition to early legislation, the Government also appeals to other sources we have usually regarded as indicative of the original understanding of the Constitution. It points to portions of *The Federalist*....But none of these statements necessarily implies—what is the critical point here—that Congress could impose these responsibilities *without the consent of the States*. They appear to rest on the natural assumption that the States would consent to allowing their officials to assist the Federal Government,...an assumption proved correct by the extensive mutual assistance the States and Federal Government voluntarily provided one another in the early days of the Republic...

To complete the historical record, we must note that there is not only an absence of executive-commandeering statutes in the early Congresses, but there is an absence of them in our later history as well, at least until very recent years....

The Government points to a number of federal statutes enacted within the past few decades that require the participation of state or local officials in implementing federal regulatory schemes. Some of these are connected to federal funding measures, and can perhaps be more accurately described as conditions upon the grant of federal funding than as mandates to the States; others, which require only the provision of information to the Federal Government, do not involve the precise issue before us here, which is the forced participation of the States' executive in the actual administration of a federal program. We of course do not address these or other currently operative enactments that are not before us; it will be time enough to do so if and when their validity is challenged in a proper case. For deciding the issue before us here, they are of little relevance. Even assuming they represent assertion of the very same congressional power challenged here, they are of such recent vintage that they are no more probative than the statute before us of a constitutional tradition that lends meaning to the text. Their persuasive force is far outweighed by almost two centuries of apparent congressional avoidance of the practice....

The constitutional practice we have examined above tends to negate the existence of the congressional power asserted here, but is not conclusive. We turn next to consideration of the structure of the Constitution, to see if we can discern among its "essential postulate[s]" ...a principle that controls the present cases.

It is incontestible that the Constitution established a system of "dual sovereignty."...Although the States surrendered many of their powers to the new Federal Government, they retained "a residuary and inviolable sovereignty," *The Federalist* No. 39 (J. Madison). This is reflected throughout the Constitution's text....Residual state sovereignty was also implicit, of course, in the Constitution's conferral upon Congress of not all governmental powers, but only discrete, enumerated ones, Art. I, Section 8, which implication was rendered express by the Tenth Amendment's assertion that "[t]he powers not delegated to the United States by the Constitution, nor prohibited by it to the States, are reserved to the States respectively, or to the people."

The Framers' experience under the Articles of Confederation had persuaded them that using the States as the instruments of federal governance was both ineffectual and provocative of federal-state conflict....Preservation of the States as independent political entities being the price of union, and "[t]he practicality of making laws, with coercive sanctions, for the States as political bodies" having been, in Madison's words, "exploded on all hands,"...the Framers rejected the concept of a central government that would act upon and through the States, and instead designed a system in which the state and federal governments would exercise concurrent authority over the people—who were, in Hamilton's words, "the only proper objects of government."... "The Framers explicitly chose a Constitution that confers upon Congress the power to regulate individuals, not States."...The great innovation of this design was that "our Citizens would have two political capacities, one state and one federal, each protected from incursion by the other" – "a legal system unprecedented in form and design, establishing two orders of government, each with its own direct relationship, its own privity, its own set of mutual rights and obligations to the people who sustain it and are governed by it."...The Constitution thus contemplates that a State's government will represent and remain accountable to its own citizens....

This separation of the two spheres is one of the Constitution's structural protections of liberty. "Just as the separation and independence of the coordinate branches of the Federal Government serve to prevent the accumulation of excessive power in any one branch, a healthy balance of power between the States and the Federal Government will reduce the risk of tyranny and abuse from either front."...To quote Madison once again:

> In the compound republic of America, the power surrendered by the people is first divided between two distinct governments, and then the portion allotted to each subdivided among distinct and separate departments. Hence a double security arises to the rights of the people. The different governments will control each other, at the same time that each will be controlled by itself. *The Federalist* No. 51....

The power of the Federal Government would be augmented immeasurably if it were able to impress into its service—and at no cost to itself—the police officers of the 50 States....

Finally, and most conclusively in the present litigation, we turn to the prior jurisprudence of this Court. Federal commandeering of state governments is such a novel phenomenon that this Court's first experience with it did not occur until the 1970's, when the Environmental Protection Agency promulgated regulations requiring States to prescribe auto emissions testing, monitoring and retrofit programs, and to designate preferential bus and carpool lanes....

Although we had no occasion to pass upon the subject in [the EPA Case], later opinions of ours have made clear that the Federal Government may not compel the States to implement, by legislation or executive action, federal regulatory programs....

When we were at last confronted squarely with a federal statute that unambiguously required the States to enact or administer a federal regulatory program, our decision should have come as no surprise. At issue in *New York v. United States*...(1992), were the so-called "take title" provisions of the Low-Level Radioactive Waste Policy Amendments Act of 1985, which required States either to enact legislation providing for the disposal of radioactive waste generated within their borders, or to take title to, and possession of the waste—

effectively requiring the States either to legislate pursuant to Congress's directions, or to implement an administrative solution....We concluded that Congress could constitutionally require the States to do neither.... "The Federal Government," we held, "may not compel the States to enact or administer a federal regulatory program."...

The Government contends that *New York* is distinguishable on the following ground: unlike the "take title" provisions invalidated there, the background-check provision of the Brady Act does not require state legislative or executive officials to make policy, but instead issues a final directive to state CLEOs. It is permissible, the Government asserts, for Congress to command state or local officials to assist in the implementation of federal law so long as "Congress itself devises a clear legislative solution that regulates private conduct" and requires state or local officers to provide only "limited, non-policymaking help in enforcing that law." "[T]he constitutional line is crossed only when Congress compels the States to make law in their sovereign capacities." Brief for United States....

Executive action that has utterly no policy-making component is rare, particularly at an executive level as high as a jurisdiction's chief law-enforcement officer....

Even assuming, moreover, that the Brady Act leaves no "policymaking" discretion with the States, we fail to see how that improves rather than worsens the intrusion upon state sovereignty. Preservation of the States as independent and autonomous political entities is arguably less undermined by requiring them to make policy in certain fields than (Judge Sneed aptly described it over two decades ago) by "reduc[ing] [them] to puppets of a ventriloquist Congress"...It is an essential attribute of the States' retained sovereignty that they remain independent and autonomous within their proper sphere of authority.... It is no more compatible with this independence and autonomy that their officers be "dragooned"...into administering federal law, than it would be compatible with the independence and autonomy of the United States that its officers be impressed into service for the execution of state laws....

By forcing state governments to absorb the financial burden of implementing a federal regulatory program, Members of Congress can take credit for "solving" problems without having to ask their constituents to pay for the solutions with higher federal taxes. And even when the States are not forced to absorb the costs of implementing a federal program, they are still put in the position of taking the blame for its burdensomeness and for its defects....Under the present law, for example, it will be the CLEO and not some federal official who stands between the gun purchaser and immediate possession of his gun. And it will likely be the CLEO, not some federal official, who will be blamed for any error (even one in the designated federal database) that causes a purchaser to be mistakenly rejected.

Finally, the Government puts forward a cluster of arguments that can be grouped under the heading: "The Brady Act serves very important purposes, is most efficiently administered by CLEOs during the interim period, and places a minimal and only temporary burden upon state officers."...But where, as here, it is the whole *object* of the law to direct the functioning of the state executive, and hence to compromise the structural framework of dual sovereignty, such a "balancing" analysis is inappropriate. It is the very *principle* of separate state sovereignty that such a law offends, and no comparative assessment of the various interests can overcome that fundamental defect....We adhere to that principle today, and conclude categorically, as we concluded categorically in *New York*. "The Federal Government may not compel the States to enact or administer a federal regulatory program."...The mandatory obligation imposed on CLEOs to perform background checks on prospective handgun purchasers plainly runs afoul of that rule....

Justice O'CONNOR, concurring.

Our precedent and our Nation's historical practices support the Court's holding today. The Brady Act violates the Tenth Amendment to the extent it forces States and local law enforcement officers to perform background checks on prospective handgun owners and to accept Brady Forms from firearms dealers....Our holding, of course, does not spell the end of the objectives of the Brady Act. States and chief law enforcement officers may voluntarily continue to participate in the federal program. Moreover, the directives to the States are merely interim provisions scheduled to terminate November 30, 1998....Congress is also free to amend the interim program to provide for its continuance on a contractual basis with the States if it wishes, as it does with a number of other federal programs. See, *e.g.*, [the federal law] conditioning States' receipt of federal funds for highway safety program on compliance with federal requirements.

In addition, the Court appropriately refrains from deciding whether other purely ministerial reporting requirements imposed by Congress on state and local authorities pursuant to its Commerce Clause powers are similarly invalid. See, *e.g.*, 42 U.S.C. Section 5779(a) (requiring state and local law enforcement agencies to report cases of missing children to the Department of Justice). The provisions invalidated here, however, which directly compel state officials to administer a federal regulatory program, utterly fail to adhere to the design and structure of our constitutional scheme....

Justice THOMAS, concurring.

The Court today properly holds that the Brady Act violates the Tenth Amendment in that it compels state law enforcement officers to "administer or enforce a federal regulatory program."...Although I join the Court's opinion in full, I write separately to emphasize that the Tenth Amendment affirms the undeniable notion that under our Constitution, the Federal Government is one of enumerated, hence limited, powers....

In my "revisionist" view,...the Federal Government's authority under the Commerce Clause, which merely allocates to Congress the power "to regulate Commerce...among the several states," does not extend to the regulation of wholly *intrastate*, point-of-sale transactions....Absent the underlying authority to regulate the intrastate transfer of firearms, Congress surely lacks the corollary power to impress state law enforcement officers into administering and enforcing such regulations. Although this Court has long interpreted the Constitution as ceding Congress extensive authority to regulate commerce (interstate or otherwise), I continue to believe that we must "temper our Commerce Clause jurisprudence" and return to an interpretation better rooted in the Clause's original understanding....

Justice STEVENS, with whom Justice SOUTER, Justice GINSBERG, and Justice BREYER join, dissenting.

When Congress exercises the powers delegated to it by the Constitution, it may impose affirmative obligations on executive and judicial officers of state and local governments as well as ordinary citizens. The conclusion is firmly supported by the text of the Constitution, and early history of the Nation, decisions of this Court, and a correct understanding of the basic structure of the Federal Government.

These cases do not implicate the more difficult questions associated with congressional coercion of state legislatures addressed in New York v. United States...(1992). Nor need we consider the wisdom of relying on local officials rather than federal agents to carry out aspects of a federal program, or even the question whether such officials may be required to perform a federal function on a permanent basis. The question is whether Congress, acting on behalf of the people of the entire Nation, may require local law enforcement officers to perform certain duties during the interim needed for the development of a federal gun control program....

Indeed, since the ultimate issue is one of power, we must consider its implications in times of national emergency. Matters such as the enlistment of air raid wardens, the administration of a military draft, the mass inoculation of children to forestall an epidemic, or perhaps the threat of an international terrorist, may require a national response before federal personnel can be made available to respond....

The text of the Constitution provides a sufficient basis for a correct disposition of this case.

Article I, Section 8, grants the Congress the power to regulate commerce among the States. Putting to one side the revisionist views expressed by Justice Thomas in his concurring opinion in *United States v. Lopez*...(1995), there can be no question that that provision adequately supports the regulation of commerce in handguns effected by the Brady Act. Moreover, the additional grant of authority in that section of the Constitution "[t]o make all Laws which shall be necessary and proper for carrying into Execution the foregoing Powers" is surely adequate to support the temporary enlistment of local police officers in the process of identifying persons who should not be entrusted with the possession of handguns. In short, the affirmative delegation of power in Article I provides ample authority for the congressional enactment.

Unlike the First Amendment, which prohibits the enactment of a category of laws that would otherwise be authorized by Article I, the Tenth Amendment imposes no restriction on the exercise of delegated powers....

There is not a clause, sentence, or paragraph in the entire text of the Constitution of the United States that supports the proposition that a local police officer can ignore a command contained in a statute enacted by Congress pursuant to an express delegation of power enumerated in Article I....

Indeed, the historical materials strongly suggest that the Founders intended to enhance the capacity of the federal government by empowering it—as a part of the new authority to make demands directly on individual citizens—to act through local officials. Hamilton made clear that the new Constitution, "by extending the authority of the federal head to the individual citizens of the several States, will enable the government to employ the ordinary magistracy of each, in the execution of its laws." *The Federalist* No. 27....Hamilton's meaning was unambiguous; the federal government was to have the power to demand that local officials implement national policy programs....

This point is made especially clear in Hamilton's statement that "the legislatures, courts, and magistrates, of the respective members, will be incorporated into the operations of the national government *as far as its just and constitutional authority extends; and will be rendered auxiliary to the enforcement of its laws.*" (emphasis added). It is hard to imagine a more unequivocal statement that state judicial and executive branch officials may be required to implement federal law where the National Government acts within the scope of its affirmative powers....

Bereft of support in the history of the founding, the Court rests its conclusion on the claim that there is little evidence the National Government actually exercised such a power in the early years of the Republic....This reasoning is misguided in principle and in fact....[We] have never suggested that the failure of the early Congresses to address the scope of federal power in a particular area or to exercise a particular authority was an argument against its existence. That position, if correct, would undermine most of our post-New Deal Commerce Clause jurisprudence....

More importantly, the fact that Congress did elect to rely on state judges and the clerks of state courts to perform a variety of executive functions is surely evidence of a contemporary understanding that their status as state officials did not immunize them from federal service. The majority's description of these early statutes is both incomplete and at times misleading....

[As to the] Court's "structural" arguments[, the]...fact that the Framers intended to preserve the sovereignty of the several States simply does not speak to the question whether individual state employees may be required federal obligations, such as registering young adults for the draft,...creating state emergency response commissions designed to manage the release of hazardous substances,...collecting and reporting data on underground storage tanks that may pose an environmental hazard,...and reporting traffic fatalities,...and missing children...to a federal agency.

Given the fact that the Members of Congress are elected by the people of the States, with each State receiving an equivalent number of Senators in order to ensure that even the smallest States have a powerful voice in the legislature, it is quite unrealistic to assume that they will ignore the sovereignty concerns of their constituents. It is far more reasonable to presume that their decisions to impose modest burdens on state officials from time to time reflect a considered judgment that the people in each of the States will benefit therefrom.

Indeed, the presumption of validity that supports all congressional enactments has added force with respect to policy judgments concerning the impact of a federal statute upon the respective States. The majority points to nothing suggesting that the political safeguards of federalism identified in *Garcia* need be supplemented by a rule, grounded in neither constitutional history nor text, flatly prohibiting the National Government from enlisting state and local officials in the implementation of federal law....

Perversely, the majority's rule seems more likely to damage than to preserve the safeguards against tyranny provided by the existence of vital state governments. By limiting the ability of the Federal Government to enlist state officials in the implementation of its programs, the Court creates incentives for the National Government to aggrandize itself. In the name of State's rights, the majority would have the Federal Government create vast national bureaucracies to implement its policies. This is exactly the sort of thing that the early Federalists promised would not occur, in part as a result of the National Government's ability to rely on the magistracy of the states....

Finally, the Court advises us that the "prior jurisprudence of this Court" is the most conclusive support for its position. Ante, at 26. That "prior jurisprudence" is *New York v. United States*....

Our statements, taken in context, clearly did not decide the question presented here, whether state executive officials—as opposed to state legislators—may in appropriate circumstances be enlisted to implement federal policy....

The provision of the Brady Act that crosses the Court's newly defined constitutional threshold is more comparable to a statute requiring local police officers to report the identity of missing children to the Crime Control Center of the Department of Justice than to an offensive federal command to a sovereign state. If Congress believes that such a statute will benefit the people of the Nation, and serve the interests of cooperative federalism better than an enlarged federal bureaucracy, we should respect both its policy judgment and its appraisal of its constitutional power.

Accordingly, I respectfully dissent.

Justice SOUTER, dissenting.

In deciding these cases, which I have found closer than I had anticipated, it is *The Federalist* that finally determines my position....The natural reading of [*Federalist* No. 27] is not merely that the officers of the various branches of state governments may be employed in the performance of national functions; Hamilton says that the state governmental machinery "will be incorporated" into the Nation's operation, and because the "auxiliary" status of the state officials will occur because they are "bound by the sanctity of an oath,"...I take him to mean that their auxiliary functions will be the products of their obligations thus undertaken to support federal law, not of their own, of the States', unfettered choices....

Madison in No. 44 supports this reading in his commentary on the oath requirement. He asks why state magistrates should have to swear to support the National Constitution when national officials will not be required to oblige themselves to support the state counterparts. His answer is that national officials "will have no agency in carrying the State Constitutions into effect. The members and officers of the State Governments, on the contrary, will have an essential agency in giving effect to the Federal Constitution."...

In the light of all these passages, I cannot persuade myself that the statements from No. 27 speak of anything less than the authority of the National Government, when exercising an otherwise legitimate power (the commerce power, say), to require state "auxiliaries" to take appropriate action. To be sure, it does not follow that any conceivable requirement may be imposed on any state official. I continue to agree, for example, that Congress may not require a state legislature to enact a regulatory scheme and that *New York v. United States*...was rightly decided (even though I now believe its dicta went too far toward immunizing state administration as well as state enactment of such a scheme from congressional mandate); after all, the essence of legislative power, within the limits of legislative jurisdiction, is a discretion not subject to command. But insofar as national law would require nothing from a state officer inconsistent with the power proper to his branch of tripartite state government (say, by obligating a state judge to exercise law enforcement powers), I suppose that the reach of federal law as Hamilton described it would not be exceeded....

Justice BREYER, with whom Justice STEVENS joins, dissenting.

I would add to the reasons Justice Stevens sets forth the fact that the United States is not the only nation that seeks to reconcile the practical need for a central authority with the democratic virtues of more local control. At least some other countries, facing the same basic problem, have found that local control is better maintained through application of a principle that is the direct opposite of the principle the majority derives from the silence of our Constitution. The federal systems of Switzerland, Germany,and the European Union, for example, all provide that constituent states, not federal bureaucracies, will themselves implement many of the laws, rules, regulations, or decrees enacted by the central "federal" body....

Of course, we are interpreting our own Constitution, not those of other nations, and there may be relevant political and structural differences between their systems and our own....But their experience may nonetheless cast an empirical light on the consequences of different solutions to a common legal problem—in this case the problem of reconciling central authority with the need to preserve the liberty-enhancing autonomy of a smaller constituent governmental entity....Thus, there is neither need nor reason to find in the Constitution an absolute principle, the inflexibility of which poses a surprising and technical obstacle to the enactment of a law that Congress believed necessary to solve an important national problem.

For these reasons and those set forth in Justice Stevens' opinion, I join his dissent.

X State Constitutions and State Bills of Rights

Virginia Bill of Rights

Pruneyard Shopping Center v. Robins (1980)

Robinson v. Cahill (1973)

San Antonio Independent School District v. Rodriguez (1973)

X State Constitutions and State Bills of Rights

A. E. DICK HOWARD

One of the richest veins in American constitutionalism—yet one sometimes over-looked—is that of the state constitutions and the state bills of rights. State courts must, of course, apply and enforce the provisions of the United States Constitution and of the federal Bill of Rights. But they interpret and enforce, as well, constitutional mandates laid down by the states' fundamental charters.

Much of the mid-20th century was a time of desuetude of interest in state consti-tutions and bills of rights. Too often the states had an unimpressive record in pro-tecting individual rights. Moreover, an activist Supreme Court, especially in the era of Chief Justice Earl Warren, made the federal Constitution and Bill of Rights an engine for social change, applying most of the commands of the Bill of Rights to the states.

Recent years, however, have brought a revival of interest in state constitutions and state bills of rights. Virginia's Commission on Constitutional Revision, reporting in 1969 to the Governor and General Assembly, caught the spirit of the times. The commissioners premised their report on a belief "that the people of Virginia want to shape their own destiny, that they do not want to abdicate decisions to others, such as the federal government, and that therefore they want a constitution which makes possible a viable, responsible state government."

Likewise, state courts have begun to make greater use of state constitutions and state bills of rights. A state judge cannot, of course, do less than the federal Constitution requires. A state court may, however, look to the state constitution and state bill of rights for imperatives quite beyond anything found in federal constitu-tional law. In other words, while the United States Constitution places a floor below which a state and its courts may not fall, it places no ceiling on what the states may do, acting through their own constitutions and bills of rights.

A few examples follow:

(1) Whereas the federal courts tend to avoid overseeing how states order their economic affairs, there are decisions in a number of states invalidating laws restrict-ing entry into particular trades or professions where it becomes evident that the purpose of the law is not to protect the public interest, but instead to give special advantage to some favored group.

(2) The United States Supreme Court has said that states may have juries of fewer than twelve jurors in criminal cases, but most state bills of rights expressly require a jury of twelve.

(3) Federal courts have refused to recognize a federal constitutional right to a decent environment. State constitutions often confer environmental rights, for example, by recognizing a "public trust" in states resources such as rivers and tidelands.

(4) The much debated Equal Rights Amendment to the United States Constitution failed of ratification. About a quarter of the states' bills of rights, however, have constitutional language expressly dealing with gender discrimination.

▶ Who stands to benefit from an expansive use of states' bills of rights?

▶ Assuming that the United States Supreme Court becomes more inclined (as some justices hope it will) to defer to legislatures and the political process, will litigants make greater use of state constitutions and state bills of rights?

▶ To what extent, in interpreting a state bill of rights, should a state court be influenced by the Supreme Court's mode of analyzing the federal Bill of Rights? For example, if the High Court decides, in religion cases, to relax the barriers between church and state, might a state court decide, relying on the state bill of rights, to insist on a high "wall of separation" between church and state?

▶ What restraints should operate on state judges deciding cases under state bills of rights? Does an activist use of state bills of rights by state courts raise questions about the proper place of judicial review in a democratic society?

▶ Should state courts' use of state bills of rights be seen as a way of bringing constitutional adjudication "back home," that is, placing more reliance on courts that are more in touch with local needs and attitudes?

▶ What limits does, or should, the amending process place on state courts' use of state bills of rights? If there is sufficient popular dislike of a state court's line of opinions, should the people simply amend the state constitution to overturn the court's decision (as the voters of California did when they amended that state's constitution to reinstate the death penalty after the Supreme Court of California had declared it invalid)?

▶ Should state bills of rights be viewed, not simply as legal norms, but as statements of a people's aspirations—the "frequent recurrence to fundamental principles" that George Mason spoke of in Virginia's 1776 Declaration of Rights?

Virginia Bill of Rights   A.E.DICK HOWARD

In May 1776 the Virginia convention, meeting at Williamsburg, instructed Virginia's delegates in the Continental Congress to introduce the resolution declaring the united colonies to be free and independent states. The Williamsburg convention then set to work on a frame of government and declaration of rights for Virginia.

George Mason, of Fairfax County, played a central role in drafting both documents. His Declaration of Rights was especially influential. It was a model for the bills of rights subsequently adopted in the other states, and it ultimately foreshadowed the Bill of Rights added to the United States Constitution in 1791.

Virginia's Constitution has been revised several times since 1776. New constitutions were adopted in 1830, 1851, 1870, 1902, and most, recently, in 1971. The body of the Constitution has been greatly changed over the years. Virginia's Bill of Rights has seen change, too, but much of its language still bears the stamp of George Mason and his colleagues, for example, the splendid passage (Section 15) about the qualities necessary to the preservation of free government.

Two other passages deserve special note. Section 16 incorporates into the Virginia Bill of Rights the language of Thomas Jefferson's Bill for Religious Freedom. The second paragraph of section 15, declaring education to be a fundamental value, was added to the Bill of Rights in 1971; its language is distilled from Jefferson's Bill for the More General Diffusion of Knowledge.

▶ What comparisons might one make between the Virginia Bill of Rights and the Bill of Rights of the United States Constitution? Where similar rights appear, are there instances when the Virginia language appears stronger than that of the federal document? Instances when it appears weaker?

▶ Does the Virginia Bill of Rights flow from natural law thinking, that is, from the belief that there are certain rights anterior to all government? If so, what is the implication of such a basis for a bill of rights?

▶ What do you make of the first four sections? Do they appear to lay down rules that could be enforced by a court?

▶ Are all of the provisions of Virginia's Bill of Rights *limitations* on government action? Might any of them be read to *require* government to act?

▶ Does Virginia's Bill of Rights specify what devices a court might use to *enforce* the Bill's provisions? What means of enforcement do you think a judge might devise?

▶ What changes would you make in the Virginia Bill of Rights? Would you add any new rights? Alter any existing statements?

Virginia Bill of Rights

A DECLARATION OF RIGHTS made by the good people of Virginia in the exercise of their sovereign powers, which rights do pertain to them and their posterity, as the basis and foundation of government.

SECTION 1. EQUALITY AND RIGHTS OF MEN.

That all men are by nature equally free and independent and have certain inherent rights, of which, when they enter into a state of society, they cannot, by any compact, deprive or divest their posterity; namely, the enjoyment of life and liberty, with the means of acquiring and possessing property, and pursuing and obtaining happiness and safety.

SECTION 2. PEOPLE THE SOURCE OF POWER.

That all power is vested in, and consequently derived from, the people, that magistrates are their trustees and servants, and at all times amenable to them.

SECTION 3. GOVERNMENT INSTITUTED FOR COMMON BENEFIT.

That government is, or ought to be, instituted for the common benefit, protection, and security of the people, nation, or community; of all the various modes and forms of government, that is best which is capable of producing the greatest degree of happiness and safety, and is most effectually secured against the danger of maladministration; and, whenever any government shall be found inadequate or contrary to these purposes, a majority of the community hath an indubitable, inalienable, and indefeasible right to reform, alter, or abolish it, in such manner as shall be judged most conductive to the public weal.

SECTION 4. NO EXCLUSIVE EMOLUMENTS OR PRIVILEGES; OFFICES NOT BE HEREDITARY.

That no man, or set of men, is entitled to exclusive or separate emoluments or privileges from the community, but in consideration of public services; which not being descendible, neither ought the offices of magistrate, legislator, or judge to be hereditary.

SECTION 5. SEPARATION OF LEGISLATIVE, EXECUTIVE, AND JUDICIAL DEPARTMENTS; PERIODICAL ELECTIONS.

That the legislative, executive and judicial departments of the Commonwealth should be separate and distinct; and that the members thereof may be restrained from oppression, by feeling and participating the burthens of the people, they should, at fixed periods, be reduced to a private station, return into that body from which they were originally taken, and the vacancies be supplied by regular elections, in which all or any part of the former members shall be again eligible, or ineligible, as the laws may direct.

SECTION 6. FREE ELECTIONS; CONSENT OF GOVERNED.

That all elections ought to be free; and that all men, having sufficient evidence of permanent common interest with, and attachment to, the community, have the right of suffrage, and cannot be taxed, or deprived of, or damaged in, their property for public uses, without their own consent, or that of their representatives duly elected, or bound by any law to which they have not, in like manner, assented for the public good.

SECTION 7. LAWS SHOULD NOT BE SUSPENDED.

That all power of suspending laws, or the execution of laws, by any authority, without consent of the representatives of the people, is injurious to their rights, and ought not to be exercised.

SECTION 8. CRIMINAL PROSECUTIONS.

That in criminal prosecutions a man hath a right to demand the cause and nature of his accusation, to be confronted with the accusers and witnesses, and to call for evidence in his favor, and he shall enjoy the right to a speedy and public trial, by an impartial jury of his vicinage, without whose unanimous consent he cannot be found guilty. He shall not be deprived of life or liberty, except by the law of the land or the judgement of his peers, not be compelled in any criminal proceeding to give evidence against himself, nor be put twice in jeopardy for the same offence.

Laws may be enacted providing for the trial of offenses not felonies by a court not of record without a jury, preserving the right of the accused to an appeal to and a trial by jury in some court of record having original criminal jurisdiction. Laws may also provide for juries consisting of less than twelve, but not less than five, for the trial of offenses not felonies, and may classify such cases, and prescribe the number of jurors for each class.

In criminal cases, the accused may plead guilty. If the accused plead not guilty, he may, with his consent and the concurrence of the Commonwealth's Attorney and of the court entered of record, be tried by a smaller number of jurors, or waive a jury. In case of such waiver or plea of guilty, the court shall try the case.

The provisions of this section shall be self-executing.

SECTION 9. PROHIBITION OF EXCESSIVE BAIL AND FINES, CRUEL AND UNUSUAL PUNISHMENT, SUSPENSION OF HABEAS CORPUS, BILLS OF ATTAINDER, AND EX POST FACTO LAWS.

That excessive bail ought not to be required, nor excessive fines imposed, nor cruel and unusual punishments inflicted; that the privilege of the writ of *habeas corpus* shall not be suspended unless when, in cases of invasion or rebellion, the public safety may require; and that the General Assembly shall not pass any bill of attainder, or any ex post facto law.

SECTION 10. GENERAL WARRANTS OF SEARCH OR SEIZURE PROHIBITED.

That general warrants, whereby an officer or messenger may be commanded to search suspected places without evidence of a fact committed, or to seize any person or persons not named, or whose offense is not particularly described and supported by evidence, are grievous and oppressive, and ought not to be granted.

SECTION 11. DUE PROCESS OF LAW; OBLIGATION OF CONTRACTS; TAKING OF PRIVATE PROPERTY; PROHIBITED DISCRIMINATION; JURY TRIAL IN CIVIL CASES.

That no person shall be deprived of his life, liberty, or property without due process of law; that the General Assembly shall not pass any law impairing the obligation of contracts, nor any law whereby private property shall be taken or damaged for public uses, without just compensation, the term "public uses" to be defined by the General Assembly; and that the right to be free from any governmental discrimination upon the basis of religious conviction, race, color, sex, or national origin shall not be abridged, except that the mere separation of the sexes shall not be considered discrimination.

That in controversies respecting property, and in suits between man and man, trial by jury is preferable to any other, and ought to be held sacred. The General Assembly may limit the number of jurors for civil cases in courts of record to not less than five.

SECTION 12. FREEDOM OF SPEECH AND OF THE PRESS; RIGHT PEACEABLY TO ASSEMBLE, AND TO PETITION.

That the freedoms of speech and of the press are among the great bulwarks of liberty, and can never be restrained except by despotic governments; that any citizen may freely speak, write, and publish his sentiments on all subjects, being responsible for the abuse of that right; that the General Assembly shall not pass any law abridging the freedom of speech or of the press, nor the right of the people peaceably to assemble, and to petition the government for the redress of grievances.

SECTION 13. MILITIA; STANDING ARMIES; MILITARY SUBORDINATE TO CIVIL POWER.

That a well regulated militia, composed of the body of the people, trained to arms, is the proper, natural, and safe defense of a free state, therefore, the right of the people to keep and bear arms shall not be infringed; that standing armies, in time of peace, should be avoided as dangerous to liberty; and that in all cases the military should be under strict subordination to, and governed by, the civil power.

SECTION 14. GOVERNMENT SHOULD BE UNIFORM.

That the people have a right to uniform government; and, therefore, that no government separate from, or independent of, the government of Virginia, ought to be erected or established within the limits thereof.

SECTION 15. QUALITIES NECESSARY TO PRESERVATION OF FREE GOVERNMENT.

That no free government, nor the blessings of liberty, can be preserved to any people, but by a firm adherence to justice, moderation, temperance, frugality, and virtue; by frequent recurrence to fundamental principles; and by the recognition by all citizens that they have duties as well as rights, and that such rights cannot be enjoyed save in a society where law is respected and due process is observed.

That free government rests, as does all progress, upon the broadest possible diffusion of knowledge, and that the Commonwealth should avail itself of those talents which nature has sown so liberally among its people by assuring the opportunity for their fullest development by an effective system of education throughout the Commonwealth.

SECTION 16. FREE EXERCISE OF RELIGION; NO ESTABLISHMENT OF RELIGION.

That religion or the duty which we owe to our Creator, and the manner of discharging it, can be directed only by reason and conviction, not by force or violence; and, therefore, all men are equally entitled to the free exercise of religion, according to the dictates of conscience; and that it is the mutual duty of all to practice Christian forbearance, love, and charity towards each other. No man shall be compelled to frequent or support any religious worship, place, or ministry whatsoever, nor shall be enforced, restrained, molested, or burthened in his body or goods, nor shall otherwise suffer on account of his religious opinions or belief; but all men shall be free to profess and by argument to maintain their opinions in matters of religion, and the same shall in nowise diminish, enlarge, or affect their civil capacities. And the General Assembly shall not prescribe any religious test whatever, or confer any peculiar privileges or advantages on any sect or denomination, or pass any law requiring or authorizing any religious society, or the people of any district within this Commonwealth, to levy on themselves or others, any tax for the erection or repair of any house of public worship, or for the support of any church or ministry; but it shall be left free to every person to select his religious instructor, and to make for his support such private contract as he shall please.

SECTION 17. CONSTRUCTION OF THE BILL OF RIGHTS.

The rights enumerated in this Bill of Rights shall not be construed to limit other rights of the people not therein expressed.

Pruneyard Shopping Center v. Robins   A. E. DICK HOWARD

Claims of a right to free speech and expression—claims based on the First Amendment—commonly involve obvious forms of government action. For example, demonstrators airing complaints against a government policy may seek to use a public park. Many First Amendment cases require that a court decide whether there is a "public forum," that is, a place where one is indeed entitled to exercise one's First Amendment rights.

Like the other provisions of the Bill of Rights, the First Amendment protects against *state action*, that is, against what government, its agents, or those acting in concert with the government does. Actions by private parties inhibiting another person's expression may violate some law (such as a civil rights statute), but typically such conduct would infringe no constitutional right.

What about efforts to use private property as a place for expression? In 1946, in *Marsh v. Alabama*, the Supreme Court held that a Jehovah's Witness could not be convicted of criminal trespass for distributing religious literature on the streets of a company-owned town. The property was privately owned, but in the Court's view it served a "public function."

Yesterday's company town is today's shopping center. Many have argued that shopping centers, even though privately owned, are natural meeting places and that, therefore, there should be a constitutional right to express one's views there (for example, to hand out leaflets or gather signatures on petitions).

In 1968, the Supreme Court relied on *Marsh* in holding that a state trespass law could not be used to enjoin peaceful picketing of a supermarket in a privately owned shopping center. In 1976, the Court reversed course, deciding that the First Amendment does not confer a right to expression at a private shopping center.

In 1980, California's Supreme Court interpreted its state constitution to guarantee access to a privately owned shopping center for high school students who sought to solicit signatures for a petition protesting a UN resolution against "Zionism." On review in the United States Supreme Court, Justice Rehnquist, for a unanimous Court, affirmed the California decision. He ruled that if a state wishes to confer rights of expression on those who enter such shopping centers, nothing in the federal Constitution stands in the way.

> ▶ Should the speech and expressions provisions of a state bill of rights be read as generously as possible, conferring rights beyond those flowing from the Supreme Court's reading of the First Amendment? Should a state bill of rights be read as giving a "preferred status" to speech and expression?
>
> ▶ How far may a state court, invoking a state bill of rights, go in allowing one person to use another's property for purposes of expression?
>
> ▶ To what other privately owned places might the principle of the *PruneYard* case apply? To private universities? To apartment houses? To retirement villages? Does the principle's application depend on the extent to which the place is open to the general public?

Pruneyard Shopping Center v. Robins 447 U.S. 74 (1980)

Mr. Justice REHNQUIST delivered the opinion of the Court.

Appellant PruneYard is a privately owned shopping center in the city of Campbell, Cal. It covers approximately 21 acres—5 devoted to parking and 16 occupied by walkways, plazas, side walks, and buildings that contain more than 65 specialty shops, 10 restaurants, and a movie theater. The PruneYard is open to the public for the purpose of encouraging the patronizing of its commercial establishments. It has a policy not to permit any visitor or tenant to engage in any publicly expressive activity, including the circulation of petitions, that is not directly related to its commercial purposes. This policy has been strictly enforced in a nondiscriminatory fashion. The PruneYard is owned by appellant Fred Sahadi.

Appellees are high school students who sought to solicit support for their opposition to a United Nations resolution against "Zionism." On a Saturday afternoon they set up a card table in a corner of PruneYard's central courtyard. They distributed pamphlets and asked passersby to sign petitions, which were to be sent to the President and Members of Congress. Their activity was peaceful and orderly and so far as the record indicates was not objected to by PruneYard's patrons.

Soon after appellees had begun soliciting signatures, a security guard informed them that they would have to leave because their activity violated PruneYard regulations. The guard suggested that they move to the public sidewalk at the PruneYard's perimeter. Appellees immediately left the premises and later filed this lawsuit in the California Superior Court of Santa Clara County. They sought to enjoin appellants from denying them access to the PruneYard for the purpose of circulating their petitions....

The California Supreme Court [held] that the California Constitution protects "speech and petitioning, reasonably exercised, in shopping centers even when the centers are privately owned." It concluded that appellees were entitled to conduct their activity on PruneYard property. [The court rejected] appellants' contention that such a result infringed property rights protected by the Federal Constitution....

Our reasoning [in holding that there is no First Amendment right to go on a privately owned shopping center] does not *ex proprio vigore* limit the authority of the State to exercise its police power or its sovereign right to adopt in its own Constitution individual liberties more expansive that those conferred by the Federal Constitution....

Appellants contend that a right to exclude others underlies the Fifth Amendment guarantee against the taking of property without just compensation and the Fourteenth Amendment guarantee against the deprivation of property without due process of law....

Here the requirement that appellants permit appellees to exercise state-protected rights of free expression and petition on shopping center property clearly does not amount to an unconstitutional infringement of appellants' property rights under the Taking Clause. There is nothing to suggest that preventing appellants from prohibiting this sort of activity will unreasonably impair the value or use of their property as a shopping center. The PruneYard is a large commercial complex that covers several city blocks, contains numerous separate business establishments, and is open to the public at large. The decision of the California Supreme Court makes it clear that the PruneYard may restrict expressive activity by adopting time, place, and manner regulations that will minimize any interference with its commercial functions. Appellees were orderly, and they limited their activity to the common areas of the shopping center. In these circumstances, the fact that they may have "physically invaded" appellants' property cannot be viewed as determinative....

Appellants finally contend that a private property owner has a First Amendment right not to be forced by the State to use his property as a forum for the speech of others....The shopping center by choice of its owner is not limited to the personal use of appellants. It is instead a business establishment that is open to the public to come and go as they please. The views expressed by members of the public in passing out pamphlets or seeking signatures for a petition thus will not likely be identified with those of the owner. Second, no specific message is dictated by the State to be displayed on appellant's property. There consequently is no danger of governmental discrimination for or against a particular message. Finally, as far as appears here appellants can expressly disavow any connection with the message by simply posting signs in the area where the speakers or handbillers stand. Such signs, for example, could disclaim any sponsorship of the message and could explain that the persons are communicating their own messages by virtue of state law....

We conclude that neither appellants' federally recognized property rights nor their First Amendment rights have been infringed by the California Supreme Court's decision recognizing a right of appellees to exercise state-protected rights of expression and petition on appellants' property. The judgment of the Supreme Court of California is therefore

Affirmed.

Robinson v. Cahill A. E. DICK HOWARD

What does it mean, in constitutional terms, to label a right or interest as being "fundamental"? During the 1960s, the Supreme Court, under Chief Justice Earl Warren, used the Fourteenth Amendment's equal protection clause to give heightened constitutional protection to those rights thought to be "fundamental." An example was the right to vote.

Commentators proposed that legislation impinging on life's "necessities," such as welfare and housing, be subject to heightened judicial scrutiny—"strict scrutiny," as the Court called it. The justices, however, refused this invitation to add "necessities" to the list of interests that would trigger special judicial concern.

What of education? One can make the case that, without an adequate education, the traditional rights—expression, voting, and others—have little meaning. Might the right to an education take its place alongside other previously recognized constitutional rights?

Nowhere does the United States Constitution mention education. This is not surprising, in light of the fact that public education as we know it did not exist at the time of the Constitution's drafting; indeed it began to develop only in the nineteenth century. Might a court nevertheless conclude that, in view of education's central place in democratic society, the Constitution ought to be interpreted to guarantee access to at least a basic education?

In *Brown v. Board of Education* (1954), the Supreme Court seemed to take such a position. Striking down the separation of the races in public schools, the Court declared that education

> is the very function of good citizenship. Today it is a principal instrument in awakening the child to cultural values, in preparing him for later professional training, and in helping him to adjust normally to his environment. In these days, it is doubtful that any child may reasonably be expected to succeed in life if he is denied the opportunity of an education. Such an opportunity, where the state has undertaken to provide it, is a right which must be made available to all on equal terms.

In 1973, however, the Supreme Court, in *San Antonio Independent School District v. Rodriguez*, refused to require that states equalize expenditures among wealthier and poorer school districts. Declining to employ "strict scrutiny" in reviewing Texas' system of financing public schools, the Court found sufficient basis to defer to the state's heavy reliance on local property taxes to fund schools.

State constitutions, however, offered an alternative avenue for those seeking greater equality in school funding. In contrast to the United States Constitution, state constitutions have detailed provisions on education. Typically those provisions address not only the powers of the state and its localities, but also their duties.

New Jersey's Constitution provides that the state legislature "shall provide for the maintenance and support of a thorough and efficient system of free public schools" for the instruction of the state's children. In *Robinson v. Cahill* (1973), the Supreme Court of New Jersey relied on that provision to invalidate the existing method of funding local schools.

Other state courts have looked to their state constitutions in ordering that school finances be equalized. In 1989, supreme courts in Texas, Kentucky, and Montana handed down such decisions.

> ▶ Should education be considered as a "fundamental" right, entitled to protection on the same plane as more traditional rights such as expression and free exercise of religion?
>
> ▶ How would a court go about deciding whether the right to an education has been infringed? Are judges competent to make judgments about educational policy?
>
> ▶ By what criteria would a court decide whether the state is giving a student an adequate education? By how much money is spent per student? By standardized test scores? By some other measure?
>
> ▶ How would a court go about enforcing a decree that a state's system of funding be reformed? Would the court require the legislature to act? What would the court do if the legislature refused or failed to act? Might the court cite the legislature for contempt? Would the court hire an expert to draw up a plan?
>
> ▶ What aspects of education, aside from funding, might be subject to judicial scrutiny if education is deemed to be a constitutional right? Curriculum? Placement of teachers? Discipline, such as suspensions and expulsions?

Robinson v. Cahill 62 N.J. 473, 303 A.2d 273 (1973)

This case involves the constitutionality of statutes providing for the financing of elementary and secondary schools. The funds are derived from three sources: local *ad valorem* taxation of real property, State aid, and federal aid. The trial court found that local taxes currently yielded 67% of the statewide total of operating expenses, State aid yielded 28% and federal aid the balance of 5%.

It is agreed there is a disparity in the number of dollars spent per pupil, depending upon the district of residence. As to the local property tax, the base is the taxable real property within the several districts, and of course the amount of taxable real property within a district is not related to the number of students within it. Although there is no statutory maximum upon the local tax for current educational expenses, there are practical limitations arising from the demands for other local services upon the same tax base. And it is clear also that State aid does not operate substantially to equalize the sums available per pupil.

There was testimony with respect to the correlation between dollar input per pupil and the end product of the educational process. Obviously equality of dollar input will not assure equality in educational results. There are individual and group disadvantages which play a part. Local conditions, too, are telling, for example, insofar as they attract or repel teachers who are free to choose one community rather than another. But it is nonetheless clear that there is a significant connection between the sums expended and the quality of the educational opportunity. And of course the Legislature has acted upon that premise in providing State aid on formulas designed to ameliorate in part the dollar disparities generated by a system of local taxation. Hence we accept the proposition that the quality of educational opportunity does depend in substantial measure upon the number of dollars invested, notwithstanding that the impact upon students may be unequal because of other factors, natural or environmental....

The provisions relating to public education were added to the Constitution of 1844 by amendments adopted in 1875. Art. IV, Section 7, Paragraph 6, was amended by adding this sentence:

> The Legislature shall provide for the maintenance and support of a thorough
> and efficient system of free public schools for the instruction of all the chil-
> dren in this State between the ages of five and eighteen year.

In the light of the foregoing, it cannot be said the 1875 amendments were intended to insure statewide equality among taxpayers. But we do not doubt that an equal educational opportunity for children was precisely in mind. The mandate that there be maintained and supported "a thorough and efficient system of free public schools for the instruction of all the children in the State between the ages of five and eighteen years" can have no other import. Whether the State acts directly or imposes the role upon local government, the end product must be what the Constitution commands. A system of instruction in any district of the State which is not thorough and efficient falls short of the constitutional command. Whatever the reason for the violation, the obligation is the State's to rectify it. If local government fails, the State government must compel it to act, and if the local government cannot carry the burden, the State must itself meet its continuing obligation....

The trial court found the constitutional demand had not been met and did so on the basis of discrepancies in dollar input per pupil. We agree. We deal with the problem in those terms because dollar input is plainly relevant and because we have been shown no other viable criterion for measuring compliance with the constitutional mandate. The constitutional mandate could not be said to be satisfied unless we were to suppose the unlikely proposition that the lowest level of dollar performance happens to coincide with the constitutional mandate and that all efforts beyond the lowest level are attributable to local decisions to do more than the State was obliged to do.

Surely the existing statutory system is not visibly geared to the mandate that there be "a thorough and efficient system of free public schools for the instruction of all the children in this state between the ages of five and eighteen years." Indeed the State has never spelled out the content of the educational opportunity the Constitution requires. Without some such prescription, it is even more difficult to understand how the tax burden can be left to local initiative with any hope that statewide equality of educational opportunity will emerge. The 1871 statute embraced a statewide tax because it was found that local taxation could not be expected to yield equal educational opportunity. Since then the State has returned the tax burden to local school districts to the point where at the time of the trial the State was meeting but 28% of the current operating expenses. There is no more evidence today than there was a hundred years ago that this approach will succeed....

We repeat that if the State chooses to assign its obligation under the 1875 amendment to local government, the State must do so by a plan which will fulfill the State's continuing obligation. To that end the State must define in some discernible way the educational obligation and must *compel* the local school districts to raise the money necessary to provide that opportunity. The State has never spelled out the content of the constitutionally mandated educational opportunity. Nor has the State *required* the school districts to raise moneys needed to achieve that unstated standard. Nor is the State aid program designed to compensate for local failures to reach that level. It must be evident that our present scheme is a patchy product reflecting provincial contests rather than a plan sensitive only to the constitutional mandate.

We have discussed the existing scene in terms of the current operating expenses. The State's obligation includes as well the capital expenditures without which the required educational opportunity could not be provided.

Upon the record before us, it may be doubted that the thorough and efficient system of schools required by the 1875 amendment can realistically be met by reliance upon local taxation. The discordant correlations between the educational needs of the school districts and their respective tax bases suggest any such effort would likely fail, and this wholly apart from the issues we left unresolved in Point I.

Although we have dealt with the constitutional problem in terms of dollar input per pupil, we should not be understood to mean that the State may not recognize differences in area costs, or a need for additional dollar input to equip classes of disadvantaged children for the educational opportunity. Nor do we say that if the State assumes the cost of providing the constitutionally mandated education, it may not authorize local government to go further and to tax to that further end, provided that such authorization does not become a device for diluting the State's mandated responsibility.

The present system being unconstitutional, we come to the subject of remedies. We agree with the trial court that relief must be prospective. The judiciary cannot unravel the fiscal skein. Obligations incurred must not be impaired. And since government must go on, and some period of time will be needed to establish another statutory system, obligations hereafter incurred pursuant to existing statutes will be valid in accordance with the terms of the statutes. In other respects we desire the further views of the parties as to the content of the judgment, including argument as to whether the judiciary may...order that moneys appropriated by the Legislature to implement the 1970 Act shall be distributed upon terms other than the legislated ones. A short date for argument will be fixed.

San Antonio Independent School District v. Rodriguez   MELVIN UROFSKY

Texas, like many states, finances its public education primarily through a combination of local property taxes and state funds. At the time this case was decided (1973), a Minimum Foundation School Program (MFSP) was used to reduce disparities among district tax bases, ans was funded by mandatory contributions from each district. In addition, Texas law allowed amd encouraged local districts to spend above the minimum level.

Poor areas, such as the Edgewood District in metropolitan San Antonio, lacked the tax base to make significant expenditures above the minimal level. In the 1967-68 school year (the year in which this suit arose), Edgewood had an assessed property value per pupil of $5,5960, and by taxing itself at a one percent rate—the highest in the metropolitan area—it raised, after the contribution to the MFSP, $26 for each student. That, together with state and federal support, brought the Edgewood expenditure up to $356 per pupil. In contrast, the affluent Alamo Heights district had a tax base of more than $49,000 per pupil; it taxed itself at only .85 percent, yet raised (after the MFSP allotment) $333 per pupil in local taxes, and had a total expenditure of $594 for each student. A group of parents from the predominantly Mexican - American Edgewood District sued on the grounds that the state plan discriminated against poor districts, and deprived students in those districts of a fundamental right—a quality education.

The Court has never defined poverty as a suspect classification, but it has ruled that lack of money can not be a reason to deny a person his or her fundamental rights. In *Griffin v. Illinois* (1956), the Court held that a state had to supply an indigent with a transcript in appeals; *Douglas v. California* (1963) extended the right of counsel to indigents in appeals cases; *Boddie v. Connecticut* (1971) struck down a state law requiring divorce applicants to file a fee while making no provision for those unable to pay. And in *Harper v. Virginia* (1966), the Court invalidated a state poll tax on grounds that it violated equal protection by denying voting rights to anyone who could not pay a fee.

It is clear that economic status cannot be used to deny a person the right to vote, to get married or secure a divorce, or to have a fair trial. It is also clear that more affluent persons do have access to better housing, better education for their children, better medical care and other goods and services that affect the quality of life. The Constitution, however, does not require economic equality.

> ▶ The Constitution, as Justice Powell points out, is not egalitarian; it does not promise that all persons must be treated equally. It merely forbids the states to impose unfair restrictions. He disagrees that education, important as it is, is constitutionally fundamental in the same way as voting. Justice Marshall makes a strong case for the recognition of education as a fundamental interest. Interestingly, both Powell and Marshall joined in support-

ing the majority in *Plyler v. Doe* (1982), in which the Court ruled that Texas could not deny access to public education to children of illegal aliens. Justice Brennan's opinion in that case came very close to categorizing education as a fundamental interest.

▶ Which opinion—Powell's or Marshall's—has a stronger constitutional basis?

▶ If a state permits economic inequality to affect the quality of education, is that the same as imposing a handicap on poor people?

▶ Is education a fundamental necessity in today's society? If so, should it be a right guaranteed under the Equal Protection Clause?

▶ Is Justice Powell's argument that it would be impossible to achieve an absolutely equal school system compelling? If he is right, what level of *inequality* should we tolerate?

▶ Justice Marshall's dissent is a clear statement of the "interpretationist" philosophy that the Constitution must be updated by judicial interpretation to bring it into conformity with contemporary standards. Do the courts— or do the legislatures—have primary responsibility to do this? Is his "sliding scale of values" an appropriate tool for analyzing constitutionality?

San Antonio Independent School District v. Rodriguez 411 U.S. 1 (1973)

Mr. Justice POWELL delivered the opinion of the Court.

We must decide, first whether the Texas system of financing public education operates to the disadvantage of some suspect class or impinges upon a fundamental right explicitly or implicitly protected by the Constitution, thereby requiring strict judicial scrutiny. If so, the judgment of the District Court should be affirmed. If not, the Texas scheme must still be examined to determine whether it rationally furthers some legitimate, articulated state purpose and therefore does not constitute an invidious discrimination in violation of the Equal Protection Clause of the Fourteenth Amendment.

We find neither the suspect-classification nor the fundamental interest analysis persuasive. The wealth discrimination discovered by the District Court, and by several other courts that have recently struck down school financing laws in other States, is quite unlike any of the forms of wealth discrimination heretofore reviewed by this Court. The individuals or groups of individuals who constituted the class discriminated against in our prior cases shared two distinguishing characteristics: because of their impecunity they were completely unable to pay for some desired benefit, and as a consequence, they sustained an absolute deprivation of a meaningful opportunity to enjoy that benefit....Even a cursory examination, however, demonstrates that neither of the two distinguishing characteristics of wealth classifications can be found here. First, there is reason to believe that the poorest families are not necessarily clustered in the poorest property districts. A recent Connecticut study found, not surprisingly, that the poor were clustered around commercial and industrial areas—those same areas that provide the most attractive sources of property tax income for school districts. There is no basis on the record in this case for assuming that the poorest people—defined by reference to any level of absolute impecunity—are concentrated in the poorest districts in Texas. Second, lack of personal resources has not occasioned an absolute deprivation of the desired benefit. The argument here is not that the children in districts having relatively low assessable property values are receiving no public education; rather, it is that they are receiving a poorer quality education than that available to children in districts having more assessable wealth. Apart from the unsettled and disputed question whether the quality of education may be determined by the amount of money expended for it, a sufficient answer to appellees' argument is that, at least where wealth is involved, the Equal Protection Clause does not require absolute equality or precisely equal advantages. Nor, indeed, in view of the infinite variables affecting the educational process, can any system assure equal quality of education except in the most relative sense. For these two reasons—the absence of any evidence that the financing system discriminates against any definable category of "poor" people or that it results in the absolute deprivation of education—the disadvantaged class is not susceptible of identification in traditional terms....

We thus conclude that the Texas system does not operate to the peculiar disadvantage of any suspect class. Recognizing that this Court has never heretofore held that wealth discrimination alone provides an adequate basis for invoking strict scrutiny, appellees also assert that the State's system impermissibly interferes with the exercise of a "fundamental" right requiring the strict standard of judicial review. It is this question—whether education is a fundamental right, in the sense that it is among the rights and liberties protected by the Constitution—which has so consumed the attention of courts and commentators in recent years.

In *Brown v. Board of Education* a unanimous Court recognized that "education is perhaps the most important function of state and local governments." Nothing this Court holds today in any way detracts from our historic dedication to public education. But the importance of a service performed by the State does not determine whether it must be regarded as fundamental for purposes of examination under the Equal Protection Clause....

It is not the province of this court to create substantive constitutional rights in the name of guaranteeing equal protection of the laws. Thus the key to discovering whether education is "fundamental" is not to be found in comparisons of the relative societal significance of education as opposed to subsistence or housing. Nor is it to be found by weighing whether education is as important as the right to travel. Rather, the answer lies in assessing whether there is a right to education explicitly or implicitly guaranteed by the Constitution.

Education, of course, is not among the rights afforded explicit protection under our Federal Constitution. Nor do we find any basis for saying it is implicitly so protected. As we have said, the undisputed importance of education will not alone cause this Court to depart from the usual standard for reviewing a State's social and economic legislation. It is appellees' contention, however, that education is distinguishable from other services and benefits provided by the State because it bears a peculiarly close relationship to other rights and liberties accorded protection under the Constitution. Specifically, they insist that education is itself a fundamental personal right because it is essential to the effective exercise of First Amendment freedoms and to intelligent utilization of the right to vote. In asserting a nexus between speech and education, appellees urge that the right to speak is meaningless unless the speaker is capable of articulating his thoughts intelligently and persuasively. The "marketplace of ideas" is an empty forum for those lacking basic communicative tools. A similar line of reasoning is pursued with respect to the right to vote. Exercise of the franchise, it is contended, cannot be divorced from the educational foundation of the voter. We need not dispute any of these propositions. The Court has long afforded zealous protection against unjustifiable governmental interference with the individual's rights to speak and to vote. Yet we have never presumed to possess either the ability or the authority to guarantee to the citizenry the most *effective* speech or the most *informed* electoral choice. That these may be desirable goals is not to be doubted. But they are not values to be implemented by judicial intrusion into otherwise legitimate state activities.

Even if it were conceded that some identifiable quantum of education is a constitutionally protected prerequisite to the meaningful exercise of either right, we have no indication that the present Texas financing system fails to provide each child with an opportunity to acquire the basic minimal skills necessary. Furthermore, the logical limitations on appellees' nexus theory are difficult to perceive. How, for instance, is education to be distinguished from the significant personal interests in the basics of decent food and shelter? Empirical examination might well buttress an assumption that the ill-fed, ill-clothed, and ill-housed are among the most ineffective participants in the political process and that they derive the least enjoyment from the benefits of the First Amendment....

The present case, in another basic sense, is significantly different from any of the cases in which we have applied strict scrutiny to legislation touching upon constitutionally protected rights....A critical distinction between those cases and the one now before us lies in what Texas is endeavoring to do with respect to education. Every step leading to the establishment of the system Texas utilizes today was implemented in an effort to *extend* public education and to improve its quality. Of course, every reform that benefits some more than others may be criticized for what it fails to accomplish. But we think it plain that, in substance, the thrust of the Texas system is affirmative and reformatory and, therefore, should be scrutinized under judicial principles sensitive to the nature of the State's efforts and to the rights reserved to the State's efforts and to the rights reserved to the States under the Constitution....

We continue to acknowledge that the Justices of this Court lack both the expertise and the familiarity with local problems so necessary to the making of wise decisions with respect to the raising and disposition of public revenues. Yet we are urged to direct the States either to alter drastically the present system or to throw out the property tax altogether in favor of some other form of taxation. No scheme of taxation, whether the tax is imposed on property, income, or purchases of goods and services, has yet been devised which is free of all discriminatory impact. In such a complex arena in which no perfect alternatives exist, the Court does well not to impose too rigorous a standard of scouting lest all local fiscal schemes become subjects of criticism under the Equal Protection Clause. In addition to matters of fiscal policy, this case also involves the most persistent and difficult questions of educational policy, another area in which this Court's lack of specialized knowledge and experience counsels against premature interference with the informed judgments made at the state and local levels....

The Texas system of school finance, while assuring a basic education for every child in the State, encourages a large measure of participation in and control of each district's schools at the local level. Appellees do not question the propriety of Texas' dedication to local control of education. To the contrary, they attack the school finance system precisely because, in their view, it does not provide the same level of local control and fiscal flexibility in all districts. Appellees suggest that local control could be preserved and promoted under other financing systems that resulted in more equality in educational expenditures. While it is no doubt true that reliance on local property taxation for school revenues provides less freedom of choice with respect to expenditures for some districts than for others, the existence of "some inequality" in the manner in which the State's rationale is achieved is not alone a sufficient basis for striking down the entire system. Nor must the financing system fail because, as appellees suggest, other methods of satisfying the State's interest, which occasion "less drastic" disparities in expenditures, might be conceived. Only where state action impinges on the exercise of fundamental constitutional rights or liberties must it be found to have chosen the least restrictive alternative. It is also well to remember that even those districts that have reduced ability to make free decisions with respect to how much they spend on education still retain under the present system a large measure of authority as to how available funds will be allocated. They further enjoy the power to make numerous other decisions with respect to the operation of the schools. The people of Texas may be justified in believing, that along with increased control of the purse strings at the State level will go increased control over local policies....

A cautionary postscript seems appropriate. Affirmance here would occasion in Texas and elsewhere an unprecedented upheaval in public education. Some commentators have concluded that, whatever the contours of the alternative financing programs that might be devised and approved, the result could not avoid being a beneficial one. But those who have devoted the most thoughtful attention to the practical ramifications of these cases have found no clear or dependable answers and their scholarship reflects no such unqualified confidence. The complexity of these problems is demonstrated by the lack of consensus with respect to whether it may be said with any assurance that the poor, the racial minorities, or the children in over-burdened core-city school districts would be benefitted by abrogation of traditional modes of financing education. These practical considerations, of course, play no role in the adjudication of the constitutional issues presented here. But they serve to highlight the wisdom of the traditional limitations on this Court's function. We hardly need add that this Court's action today is not to be viewed as placing its judicial imprimatur on the status quo. The need is apparent for reform in tax systems which may well have relied too long and too heavily on the local property tax. And certainly innovative new thinking as to public education, its methods and its funding, is necessary to assure both a higher level of quality and greater uniformity of opportunity. But the ultimate solutions must come from the lawmakers and from the democratic pressures of those who elect them.

Reversed.

Mr. Justice STEWART, concurring.

I join the opinion because I am convinced that any other course would mark an extraordinary departure from principled adjudication under the Equal Protection Clause of the 14th Amendment. The uncharted directions of such a departure are suggested, I think, by Justice Marshall's imaginative dissenting opinion. Unlike other provisions of the Constitution, the Equal Protection Clause confers no substantive rights and creates no substantive liberties. The function of the Equal Protection Clause, rather, is simply to measure the validity of *classifications* created by state laws....In refusing to invalidate the Texas system of financing its public schools, the Court today applies with thoughtfulness and understanding the basic principles [of equal protection].

Mr. Justice WHITE, with whom Mr. Justice DOUGLAS and Mr. Justice BRENNAN join, dissenting.

This case would be quite different if it were true that the Texas system, while insuring minimum educational expenditures in every district through state funding, extended a meaningful option to all local districts to increase their per-pupil expenditures. The system would then arguably provide a rational and sensible method of achieving the state aim of preserving an area for local initiative and decision. The difficulty with the Texas system, however, is that it provides a meaningful option to Alamo Heights and like school districts but almost none to Edgewood and those other districts with a low per-pupil real estate tax base. In these districts the Texas system utterly fails to extend a realistic choice to parents because the property tax, which is the only revenue-raising mechanism extended to school districts, is practically and legally unavailable. Requiring the State to establish only that unequal treatment is in furtherance of a permissible goal, without also requiring the State to show that the means chosen to effectuate that goal are rationally related to its achievement, makes equal protection analysis no more than an empty gesture....

Mr. Justice MARSHALL, with whom Mr. Justice DOUGLAS concurs, dissenting.

...I cannot accept the majority's labored efforts to demonstrate that fundamental interests, which call for strict scrutiny, encompass only established rights which we are somehow bound to recognize from the text of the Constitution itself. To be sure, some interests which the Court has deemed to be fundamental for purposes of equal protection analysis are themselves constitutionally protected rights. But it will not do to suggest that the "answer" to whether an interest is fundamental for purposes of equal protection analysis is *always* determined by whether that interest "is a right explicitly or implicitly guaranteed by the Constitution." I would like to know where the Constitution guarantees the right to procreate, or the right to vote in state elections, or the right to an appeal from a criminal conviction. These are instances in which, due to the importance of the interests at stake, the Court has displayed a strong concern with the existence of discriminatory state treatment. But the

Court has never said or indicated that these are interests which independently enjoy full-blown constitutional protection....

The majority is, of course, correct when it suggests that the process of determining which interests are fundamental is a difficult one. But I do not think the problem is insurmountable. And I certainly do not accept the view that the process need necessarily degenerate into an unprincipled, subjective "picking-and-choosing" between various interests or that it must involve this Court in creating "substantive constitutional rights in the name of guaranteeing equal protection of the laws." Although not all fundamental interests are constitutionally guaranteed, the determination of which interests are fundamental should be firmly rooted in the text of the Constitution. The task in every case should be to determine the extent to which constitutionally guaranteed rights are dependent on interests not mentioned in the Constitution. As the nexus between the specific constitutional guarantee and the nonconstitutional interest draws closer, the nonconstitutional interest becomes more fundamental and the degree of judicial scrutiny applied when the interest is infringed on a discriminatory basis must be adjusted accordingly. Thus, it cannot be denied that interests such as procreation, the exercise of the state franchise, and access to criminal appellate processes are not fully guaranteed to the citizen by our Constitution. But these interests have nonetheless been afforded special judicial consideration in the face of discrimination because they are, to some extent, interrelated with constitutional guarantees. Procreation is now understood to be important because of its interaction with the established constitutional right of privacy. The exercise of the state franchise is closely tied to basic civil and political rights inherent in the First Amendment. And access to criminal appellate processes enhances the integrity of the range of rights implicit in the 14th Amendment guarantee of due process of law. Only if we closely protect the related interests from state discrimination do we ultimately ensure the integrity of the constitutional guarantee itself. This is the real lesson that must be taken from our previous decisions involving interests deemed to be fundamental....

It seems to me inescapably clear that this Court has consistently adjusted the care with which it will review state discrimination in light of the constitutional significance of the interests affected and the invidiousness of the particular classification. In the context of economic interest, we find that discriminatory state action is almost always sustained, for such interests are generally far removed from constitutional guarantees. But the situation differs markedly when discrimination against important individual interests with constitutional implications and against particularly disadvantaged or powerless classes is involved. The majority suggests, however, that a variable standard of review would give this Court the appearance of a "super-legislature." I cannot agree. Such an approach seems to me a part of the guarantees of our Constitution and of the historic experiences with oppression of and discrimination against discrete, powerless minorities which underlie that document. In truth, the Court itself will be open to the criticism raised by the majority so long as it continues on its present course of effectively selecting in private which cases will be afforded special consideration without acknowledging the true basis of its action....

It is true that this Court has never deemed the provision of free public education to be required by the Constitution. Nevertheless, the fundamental importance of education is amply indicated by the prior decisions of this Court, by the unique status accorded public education by our society, and by the close relationship between education and some of our most basic constitutional values. Education directly affects the ability of a child to exercise his First Amendment interests both as a source and as a receiver of information and ideas. Of particular importance is the relationship between education and the political process. Of most immediate and direct concern must be the demonstrated effect of education on the exercise of the franchise by the electorate. It is this very sort of intimate relationship between a particular personal interest and specific constitutional guarantees that has heretofore caused the Court to attach special significance, for purposes of equal protection analysis, to individual interests such as procreation and the exercise of the state franchise. These factors compel us to recognize the fundamentality of education and to scrutinize with appropriate care the bases for state discrimination affecting equality of educational opportunity in Texas school districts—a conclusion which is only strengthened when we consider the character of the classification in this case....

The children of the disadvantaged Texas school districts are being discriminated against not necessarily because of their personal wealth or the wealth of their families, but because of the taxable property wealth of the residents of the district in which they happen to live. The appropriate question, then, is whether the same degree of judicial solicitude and scrutiny that has previously been afforded wealth classifications is warranted here.

That wealth classifications alone have not necessarily been considered to bear the same high degree of suspectness as have classifications based on, for instance, race or alienage may be explainable on a number of grounds. The "poor" may not be seen as politically powerless as certain discrete and insular minority groups. Personal poverty may entail much the same social stigma as historically attached to certain racial or ethnic groups but it is not a permanent disability; its shackles may be escaped. Perhaps, most importantly, though, personal wealth may not necessarily share the general irrelevance as a basis for legislative action that race or nationality is recognized to have. While the "poor" have frequently been a legally disadvantaged group, it cannot be ignored that social legislation must frequently take cognizance of the economic status of our citizens. Thus, we have generally gauged the invidiousness of wealth classifications with an awareness of the importance of the interests being affected and the relevance of personal wealth to those interests....

The disability of the disadvantaged class in this case extends as well into the political processes upon which we ordinarily rely as adequate for the protection and promotion of all interests. Nor can we ignore the extent to which, in contrast to our prior decisions, the State is responsible for the wealth discrimination in this instance. Prior cases have dealt with discrimination on the basis of indigency which was attributable to the operation of the private sector. But we have no such simple *de facto* wealth discrimination here. The means for financing public education in Texas are selected and specified by the State. At the same time, governmentally imposed land use controls have undoubtedly encouraged and rigidified natural trends in the allocation of particular areas for residential or commercial use, and thus determined each district's amount of taxable property wealth. In short, this case, in contrast to the Court's previous wealth discrimination decisions, can only be seen as "unusual in the extent to which governmental action is the cause of the wealth discriminations."

Here both the nature of the interest and the classification dictate close judicial scrutiny of the purposes which Texas seeks to serve with its present educational financing scheme and of the means it has selected to serve that purpose. I need not now decide how I might ultimately strike the balance were we confronted with a situation where the State's sincere concern for local control inevitably produced educational inequality. For on this record, it is apparent that the State's purported concern with local control is offered primarily as an excuse rather than as a justification for interdistrict inequality....

Contributors

LYNDA BUTLER is Professor of Law at the College of William and Mary's Marshall-Wythe School of Law, where her teaching and research have focused on the subjects of Property Rights, Land Use Regulation, and Environmental Law. She is a graduate of the University of Virginia School of Law; and prior to joining the William and Mary faculty in 1979, she was an attorney with the firm of Wilmer, Cutler & Pickering in Washington, D.C. She has also taught (as visiting professor) at Ohio State University and in the College of William and Mary Law School Summer Program in Exeter, England. Professor Butler is the author of *Virginia Tidal and Coastal Law* (Michie Co., 1988), and of numerous articles in law journals such as Brigham Young University Law Review, the University of Illinois Law Review, the University of Pittsburgh Law Review, the Virginia Environmental Law Journal, and the William and Mary Law Review. Her current work is focusing on the impact of property norms on ecosystem management.

A. E. DICK HOWARD is the White Burkett Miller Professor of Law and Public Affairs at the University of Virginia. After graduating from the University of Richmond, Oxford University (where he was a Rhodes Scholar), and the University of Virginia School of Law, Professor Howard began his career as a Law Clerk to Justice Hugo L. Black of the U.S. Supreme Court. He was the chief architect of Virginia's present constitution and chaired Virginia's Commission on the Bicentennial of the United States Constitution. Twice a Fellow of the Woodrow Wilson International Center for Scholars in Washington D.C., Professor Howard has argued before state and federal courts, and has been called upon to assist with the development of new constitutions in Brazil, Hong Kong, the Philippines, Hungary, Czechoslovakia, Poland, Bulgaria, Romania, Albania, Malawi, South Africa, and Swaziland. In 1994, *Washingtonian* magazine named him as "one of the most respected educators in the nation." In 1996, the Czech Republic, citing his "promotion of the idea of a civil society in Central Europe," awarded Professor Howard their Randa Medal—the first time this honor has been conferred upon anyone but a Czech citizen.

ROBERT M. O'NEIL is Professor of Law and University Professor at the University of Virginia, and is Founding Director of the Thomas Jefferson Center for the Protection of Free Expression, located in Charlottesville. A graduate of Harvard College and the Harvard Law School, Professor O'Neil served as a Law Clerk for Supreme Court Justice William Brennan. From 1980-85 he was President of the University of Wisconsin System, and from 1985-90 he served as President of the University of Virginia. He held previous administrative positions at the University of Cincinnati and Indiana University—Bloomington; and throughout, he taught courses on American constitutional law. He is the author of numerous books and articles, the most recent being *Free Speech in the College Community* (1997), and he currently teaches courses in the First Amendment field, including a new course entitled "Free Expression in Cyberspace." Professor O'Neil is a Trustee or Director of The Commonwealth Fund, the Fort James Corporation, TIAA-CREF, and WVPT Public Television. He also chairs the Committee on Academic Freedom and Tenure of the American Association of University Professors, and is President of the Virginia Coalition for Open Government.

BARBARA PERRY is Professor of Government and Chair of the Department of Government and International Affairs at Sweet Briar College. In 1995-96, she was a Research Fellow at the Virginia Foundation for the Humanities and Public Policy, where she wrote her forthcoming book *The Priestly Tribe: The Supreme Court's Image in the American Mind* (Praeger). Previously, she served as the 1994-95 judicial Fellow at the Supreme Court of the United States, and received the Tom C. Clark Award as the outstanding fellow. Her other books include *A "Representative" Supreme Court? The Impact of Race, Religion, and Gender on Appointments* (Greenwood) and a forthcoming collection of essays on the current members of the Supreme Court, entitled *"The Supremes"* (Peter Lang). In addition, she is co-author, with Henry J. Abraham, of the sixth and seventh editions of *Freedom and the Court: Civil Rights and Liberties in the United States* (Oxford University Press). Professor Perry has also published in the Journal of Church and State, the Journal of Law and Politics, and other law-related journals. She holds a Ph.D. in government from the University of Oxford.

RODNEY A. SMOLLA is the George E. Allen Professor of Law at the University of Richmond's T.C. Williams School of Law. He was previously the Arthur B. Hanson Professor of Law at the College of William and Mary's Marshall-Wythe School of Law where he served from 1988 to 1996 as Director of the Institute of Bill of Rights Law. Professor Smolla graduated from Yale and received his Law degree from Duke University, where he finished first in his class. He served as law clerk for Judge Charles Clark on the United States Court of Appeals for the Fifth Circuit, and after practicing law in Chicago, he taught at De Paul, the University of Illinois, and the University of Arkansas law schools before beginning at William and Mary. His books include *Free Speech in an Open Society* (Alfred A. Knopf, 1992), which won the William O. Douglas Award as the year's best monograph on freedom of expression; *A Year in the Life of the Supreme Court* [Editor] (Duke University Press, 1995), which won the American Bar Association's Silver Gavel Award Certificate of Merit; and *Jerry Falwell v. Larry Flynt: The First Amendment on Trial* (St. Martin's Press, 1988).

MELVIN UROFSKY is Director of the Doctoral Program in Public Policy and Professor of History at Virginia Commonwealth University. Prior to joining the V.C.U. faculty in 1974 (as Chair of the History Department) he taught at Ohio State and the State University of New York at Albany. He received his undergraduate and doctoral degrees from Columbia and his law degree from the University of Virginia School of Law. He has lectured at universities and law schools worldwide and is the author of more than 30 books and 100 articles, including a multi-volume edition of the Letters of Louis D. Brandeis (with David W. Levy); *American Zionism from Herzl to the Holocaust* (1975, 1995); *A March of Liberty: American Constitutional and Legal Development* (1987); *The Douglas Letters* (edited with his son Philip, 1987); *A Conflict of Rights: The Supreme Court and Affirmative Action* (1991, 1997); *Letting Go: Death, Dying, and The Law* (1993); and most recently *Division and Discord: The Supreme Court Under Stone and Vinson, 1941-1953* (1997). He is currently working on a study of American rights since World War II.

The Virginia Foundation for the Humanities and Public Policy

The Virginia Foundation for the Humanities and Public Policy (VFH) was established in September, 1974 as a not-for-profit organization dedicated to promoting the humanities and to using the humanities to address issues of broad public concern. In its first 25 years, the Foundation has supported more than 1,500 grant projects, including scores of seminars and related programs for teachers; awarded more than 200 individual and collaborative research fellowships; and sponsored a host of activities—major publications, exhibits, films, community discussion programs, conferences, and other events—many of them dealing with the subject of rights and responsibilities.

Throughout its history, the VFH has played a leading role in developing and supporting new programs on important issues and questions such as religious freedom; immigration and the challenge of diversity; violence and culture; globalization and community; the influence of technology and the media; and the role of science in society.

Currently, the Virginia Foundation includes active **Grant and Fellowship programs**; the **Virginia Folklife Program**; a network of **Regional Councils**; **Special Initiatives and Projects** including **The Institute on Violence, Culture and Survival** and **The Virginia Festival of the Book**; **Program Services** including access to the Foundation's **Media Center** and its **Film, Video, and Audio Editing Facilities**; and **Collaborative Projects** including support for the **Virginia Association of Museums**, administration of the **Southern Humanities Media Fund**, and production of the weekly radio series **"With Good Reason."**

In all its various programs, including *The Bill of Rights, The Courts, and The Law*, the Virginia Foundation works to make scholarship accessible; to promote thoughtful discussion of enduring and contemporary issues; and to broaden the range of educational opportunities available to all citizens, both in Virginia and nationwide. Central to our work is the belief that *"Ideas Matter"*: that—to paraphrase Jefferson—a broadly educated and informed citizenry is the bulwark of a sustainable democracy.

For further information, contact the **Virginia Foundation for the Humanities and Public Policy** at 145 Ednam Drive, Charlottesville, Virginia 22903. Phone (804) 924-3296. Website **www.virginia.edu/vfh**.